COMMANDER
STEVEN HAINES
ROYAL NAVY

THE LIMITS OF ETHICS IN INTERNATIONAL RELATIONS

The Limits of Ethics in International Relations

*Natural Law, Natural Rights, and
Human Rights in Transition*

DAVID BOUCHER

UNIVERSITY PRESS

Great Clarendon Street, Oxford OX2 6DP

Oxford University Press is a department of the University of Oxford.
It furthers the University's objective of excellence in research, scholarship,
and education by publishing worldwide in

Oxford New York

Auckland Cape Town Dar es Salaam Hong Kong Karachi
Kuala Lumpur Madrid Melbourne Mexico City Nairobi
New Delhi Shanghai Taipei Toronto

With offices in

Argentina Austria Brazil Chile Czech Republic France Greece
Guatemala Hungary Italy Japan Poland Portugal Singapore
South Korea Switzerland Thailand Turkey Ukraine Vietnam

Oxford is a registered trade mark of Oxford University Press
in the UK and in certain other countries

Published in the United States
by Oxford University Press Inc., New York

© David Boucher 2009

The moral rights of the author have been asserted
Database right Oxford University Press (maker)

First published 2009

All rights reserved. No part of this publication may be reproduced,
stored in a retrieval system, or transmitted, in any form or by any means,
without the prior permission in writing of Oxford University Press,
or as expressly permitted by law, or under terms agreed with the appropriate
reprographics rights organization. Enquiries concerning reproduction
outside the scope of the above should be sent to the Rights Department,
Oxford University Press, at the address above

You must not circulate this book in any other binding or cover
and you must impose the same condition on any acquirer

British Library Cataloguing in Publication Data
Data available

Library of Congress Cataloging in Publication Data
Library of Congress Control Number: 2008943415

Typeset by SPI Publisher Services, Pondicherry, India
Printed in Great Britain
on acid-free paper by
CPI Antony Rowe, Chippenham, Wiltshire

ISBN 978–0–19–920352–9

1 3 5 7 9 10 8 6 4 2

Acknowledgements

This book has taken eleven years to write and is the sequel to my *Political Theories of International Relations*, elevating one of its themes, a universal moral order, to further exploration and consideration, as it found expression in natural law, natural rights, and human rights. The principal contentions are that natural law and natural rights are constellations of ideas that are far more closely related than most thinkers want to admit, and that natural rights and human rights are far less closely related than is often contended. Natural rights, I contend, never strayed as far away from the religious foundationalism as commentators maintain. Conceptually the British Idealists play a crucial role in the transition from natural rights to human rights. While the British Idealists dispensed with the rationalist element in natural rights, they did not dispense with the religious. Rights develop over time, but within the context of a divine unfolding rationality. Human rights theories, for the most part, jettison the divine and offer foundationless universal constraints on the activities of individuals domestically and internationally, and within and between states. Furthermore, these so called universal rights and duties almost invariably turn out to be conditional, and upon close scrutiny end up being 'special' rights and privileges as my examples of multicultural encounters, slavery and racism, and women's rights demonstrate.

Over the last twenty-five years I have been working out these themes, at first with only a faint and hazy glimmer of light, gradually coming to see more clearly as the path to enlightenment was illuminated by luminaries in the specialist areas of this study, such as Knud Haakonssen, a former colleague in Canberra, Brian Tierney, Anthony Pagden, and Richard Tuck. While my own compass has taken me to places they would not want to go, I am nevertheless indebted to them for pointing the way. In the realm of the interface between international relations theory and political theory I have been influenced by the work of such writers as Chris Brown, Mervyn Frost, Andrew Linklater, Terry Nardin, Howard Williams, and many others too numerous to mention. I have been fortunate in being surrounded by many specialists in political philosophy who have provided inspiration and necessary conversation on the way. I am indebted to Andrew Vincent, Carole Pateman, Bruce Haddock, Peter Sutch, Peri Roberts, Rex Martin, and Graeme Garrard for their intellectual insights and stimulation. As always I cannot over-estimate the example and help of my teachers, in particular, the late W. H. Greenleaf, Joseph V. Femia, and Peter Nicholson. I owe a special debt to Peter for making British Idealism accessible to me, not an inconsiderable achievement, and for being so wonderfully generous in letting me have his copies of Pufendorf, Vattel, and Burlamaqui. He has always been tremendously supportive of my work, even to the extent of casting his discerning eye over the proofs. I am very grateful to him, with the usual proviso that the errors that remain are entirely my responsibility.

Over the years I have had the pleasure of supervising many gifted Ph.D. students, some in the area that this book covers. Two in particular have also acted as graduate assistants during periods when my administrative duties threatened to overwhelm me. I would like to thank Wendy Martineau who works in the area of cross-cultural understandings, and who has gone on to become an ESRC postdoctoral fellow at Bristol. Camilla Boisen has demonstrated the efficacy of postgraduate skills training. She has unfailingly tracked down and obtained numerous items, checked references, and read the chapters. Her own work on the emergence of ideas of humanitarian intervention overlaps to some extent with mine, and I have benefitted from being able to discuss some of the themes of this book with her over the last few years. I am also grateful for the help of the administrative staff in the School of European Studies who are always unfailingly supportive. In particular Gemma Broadhurst and Lisa Berni have done much to lighten the burden of producing endless drafts and versions of chapters.

Richard Mullender was very kind when, at the invitation of Thom Brookes, I presented a paper at Newcastle. Richard made some very useful suggestions for linking my ideas on international law with the common law tradition. Thomas Pink and Kees van der Pijl made useful suggestions when I presented my argument against the secularization of the natural rights tradition at the German Historical Institute in London. To some extent Julia Stapleton was the catalyst for this project in inviting me to give the inaugural Alan Milne memorial lecture at Durham. I have also benefitted from conversations with others who mine this field of the political theory of international relations, in particular, Beate Jahn, Nick Rengger, and Gabriella Slomp.

I have been very fortunate in obtaining support for my researches from the Arts and Humanities Research Council (or Board as it was then) and the Nuffield Foundation. Leverhulme offered me a one year fellowship which has enabled me to bring this project to completion. I am grateful to all three bodies, but especially to Leverhulme for its forebearance and generosity. I am also grateful to Mark Francis for inviting me to take up a fellowship at the department of politics and the Institute for the Study of Europe at Canterbury University, Christchurch, New Zealand. It was there that I had the time to put many of my ideas in order. I am also indebted to my long-time friend Ivan Molloy for inviting me to give a series of lectures at the University of the Sunshine Coast, Queensland, where I presented some of the arguments in this book for the first time as adjunct professor of international relations.

I am grateful to Oxford University Press for sticking with me all these years, and to Dominic Byatt who has been helpful, courteous, and patient in seeing this project through.

As usual the forbearance of my family is much appreciated. Once again I am grateful to Clare, Lucy, and Emma for their support and encouragement. Frasier and Niles, two black and white short-haired farm cats, took a feline interest in the project by sleeping on the desk or curling around the laptop and purring loudly.

I have published some of my conclusions in articles, and have drawn upon some of the arguments here: 'Tocqueville, Collingwood, history and extending the moral community', *British Journal of Politics and International Relations*, vol. 2 (2000), 326–51; 'British Idealism and the Human Rights Culture', *History of European Ideas*, vol. 27 (2001), pp. 61–78. 'Resurrecting Pufendorf and Capturing the Westphalian Moment'; *Review of International Studies*, vol. 27 (2002), pp. 557–77; 'Uniting What Right Permits with What Interest Prescribes: Rawls's Law of Peoples in Context' in Rex Martin and David A. Reidy (eds.), *Rawls's Law of Peoples: A Realistic Utopia* (Oxford, Blackwell, 2006), pp. 19–37; 'Thin Universalism and Distributive Justice' in Bruce Haddock, Peri Roberts, and Peter Sutch, eds., *Principles and Political Order* (London, Routledge, 2006), pp. 176–93.

Contents

Introduction	1
1. Classical Natural Law and the Law of Nations: The Greeks and the Romans	19
2. Christian Natural Law: A Universal Morality	43
3. Natural Law, the Law of Nations, and the Transition to Natural Rights	69
4. Natural Rights and Social Exclusion: Cultural Encounters	101
5. Natural Rights: Descriptive and Prescriptive	141
6. Natural Rights and Their Critics	167
7. Slavery and Racism in Natural Law and Natural Rights	187
8. Nonsense Upon Stilts? Tocqueville, Idealism, and the Expansion of the Moral Community	217
9. The Human Rights Culture and Its Discontents	245
10. Modern Constitutive Theories of Human Rights	285
11. Human Rights and the Juridical Revolution	311
12. Women and Human Rights	331
Conclusion	357
Bibliography	379
Index	409

Introduction

> Looking back today, what seems most surprising is the unity of purpose shown by the UN member states at the time in adopting the UDHR without a dissenting vote. Now, in the face of numerous, pressing human rights crises, there is no shared vision among world leaders to address contemporary challenges of human rights in a world that is increasingly endangered, unsafe and unequal (Amnesty International 2008: 5).
>
> In the market place of domestic politics and in international affairs, respect for rights is the new criterion of political legitimacy (Waldron 1987: 1).
>
> ...lack of agreement about what constitutes a human right breeds doubt about the very concept of human rights (Campbell 2001: 53).

Stephen D. Krasner has contended that of all the social environments in which human beings act, the international is one of the most complex and institutionally weak. It is characterized by a lack of authoritative hierarchies (Krasner 1999: 42). To compensate humankind has always attempted to mitigate the uncertainty and precariousness of the international human condition by invoking authorities that transcend individuals and political boundaries, and appeal to humanity as a whole. Universal principles have served as a standard by which to overcome the complexity, institutional weakness, and lack of authoritative hierarchy in the international sphere, and to curb the propensity towards arbitrary rule within the domestic. Foremost among them in the West, and exported to the rest of the world, are the grand conceptions of natural law, natural rights, and human rights. They are the ethical constraints in tempering man's inhumanity to man, and in constraining nations in their relations with each other within acceptable boundaries articulated in the Law of Nations. The overarching theme that holds this book together is the relationship between politics and morality. In particular, its primary focus is upon what in philosophy is known as moral realism. It takes many forms, but in broad brush strokes it may be characterized as that point of view that maintains that there are objective standards of truth and morality, independent of what we may wish or think, and from which rules of conduct may be derived, or to which individual actions should conform. An objective morality stands above the transitory unsettled surface of everyday politics and acts as a guide, and standard of moral appraisal. Politics, on this view, is subordinate to morality. It denotes a type of meta-ethical outlook, rather than a particular theory, and may take many forms ranging from naturalism, to moral rationalism or a full-blown version of religious foundationalism.

This, then, is the exact opposite of what is commonly understood as realism in politics and international relations. Here the relationship between politics and morality is inverted. There is not necessarily a rejection of morality, but instead a recognition that political order or stability is the primary principle, and the necessary prerequisite to a flourishing morality. The primacy of order over justice is what underlies the rationale of truth and reconciliation tribunals. Establishing and maintaining such order may require bracketing, or suspending, ordinary morality in the pursuit of politics. Machiavelli famously posited a parallel universe of ordinary morality and political expediency, whereas Hobbes conflated the two, making morality equivalent to expediency. The site in which morality is played out is typically the state or nation that provides the bounded community necessary for a shared moral life, and outside of which, and between one and another, expediency and reason of state prevails. For the moral realist, the objective standards of truth and morality transcend political communities, which have their place in, but which are not the arbiters of the moral universe in which they act.

Whatever synonyms there may be in non-Western cultures for this range of concepts related to moral realism, the constellation of ideas and values that emanated in the West were exported, and for the most part imposed, on the rest of the world. Born of European stock, when the Roman Empire and then Christendom were the primary reference points to one's ultimate identity, other cultures were understood through the conceptual and moral framework provided by natural law and natural rights. Contrary to much academic opinion, this tradition remained heavily underpinned by different readings of the Christian religion. The contemporary global human rights culture, imbued with the principles of self-determination and liberal democracy, is the latest manifestation of Western globalization. One may say with only a little exaggeration that Europe has released itself from considerations of geography. Just as Christendom before it, but much more successfully, Europe, and particularly European values, has insinuated itself way beyond its geographical confines. 'European', as Michael Oakeshott tells us, 'has become an adjective which refers to something which may be found in any part of the world' (Oakeshott 2004: 436). The exportation of the values, for example, the rule of law, human rights, and democracy are consciously imposed on prospective allies (if there is not some other strategic or economic consideration that may trump it) by both the European Union, and the offspring of European culture, the United States of America. John M. Headley, for example, subscribes to the idea of the Europeanization of the world. This consists in the idea of a common humanity and the principle of equality, manifest in the human rights culture; and the desirability of political dissent expressed through liberal democracy, with its emphasis upon political freedom (Headley 2008: 7). This tendency is welcomed, with varying allowances for sensitivity to cultural difference, by an unlikely array of scholars who inhabit radically different terrains on the political landscape, for example, Francis Fukuyama (1993), Will Kymlicka (2006), and Richard Rorty (1989). Kymlicka, for example, extolling the virtues of a tamed liberal nationalism praises European enlargement, arguing that 'Europeanization is morally progressive *because* it is consolidating and diffusing liberal nationhood' (Kymlicka 2006: 132). He goes on to suggest that, 'Far from transcending liberal nationhood, the EU is universalizing it, reordering Europe in its own image' (Kymlicka 2006: 135).

With the increasing number of books devoted to the study and explication of human rights the propensity for conceptual confusion has proliferated, despite the heroic efforts of some scholars to arrest the discord. There is a lack of clarity about what separates, and what unites, the natural law, natural rights, and human rights idioms of discourse within the field of international relations. My aim is to disentangle the different vocabularies that are so often indiscriminately intertwined in the contemporary human rights regime or culture in order to ultimately arrive at an answer to the question, 'what does it mean to have a human right in contemporary international relations', and what limits do such rights place on the actions of states in their relations with each other and with their own citizens.

I will argue that natural law, natural rights (both prescriptive and descriptive), and human rights are conceptually distinct, but are related to each other, not as answers to the same question, but as part of the same historical process by which one turns into the other. The purpose of achieving conceptual clarity is to clear up the confusions that surround modern day discussion of human rights in their legal, political, and philosophical forms.

The main contentions of this book are that natural law and natural rights, as constellations of ideas and presuppositions, are far more in harmony with each other than most commentators are prepared to admit, and that natural rights and human rights are far more conceptually distinct than is often maintained. Natural rights, despite arguments to the contrary, retained the foundation of a religious world view to sustain its moral claims. The most important natural rights thinkers (with the exception of Hobbes) continued to evoke God as the basis of obligation in their theories. Reason, for the most part, could not in itself create obligation. Reason is what enables us to come to know what our rights and duties are, while God provided the foundation for the enjoyment of the rights, and for fulfilling our obligations. The British Idealists are important in the story because they play an important role in the transition from natural rights to human rights. They jettison the rationalist element in natural rights, but retained the religious. Ideas of human rights, on the whole, abjure the divine and present us with foundationless universal principles that constrain the actions of individuals domestically and internationally, and within and between states. Furthermore, the universalism of natural law, natural rights, and human rights, almost without exception, turn out to be conditional, and in effect 'special' rights and privileges. This contention is demonstrable in the examples of, multicultural encounters, slavery and racism, and women's rights.

This project arises out of a previous study of the history of the political theory of international relations in which I tried to retrieve something of the classical traditions of thinking about issues of international relations (Boucher 1998). This current book is similarly inspired by the belief that present thinking about important issues such as human rights cannot be disengaged from the heritage out of which it emerges, and that the cursory historical allusion or sketch does a disservice to the complexity and sophistication of past thought, as well as impoverishes present thinking.

There can be no area of political thinking more demonstrative of the unity of political theory and international theory, and of the artificiality of rendering them asunder than the idea of a universal morality. There can be no better exemplification than to retrieve the vocabularies by which the ethical constraints on individuals and nations in relation to humanity as a whole were conceptualized. We need to take Leo Strauss seriously when he explains that, 'The problem of natural right is today a matter of recollection rather than of actual knowledge. We are therefore in need of historical studies in order to familiarize ourselves with the whole complexity of the issue. We have for some time to become students of what is called the "history of ideas"' (Strauss 1965: 7).

That aspect of political thought that concerns itself with international relations has in recent years become increasingly popular as an area of study. There has been a *rapprochement* between the history of political thought and the history of thought in international relations. There is a growing reluctance to take at face value Martin Wight's observation that there is no comparable canon of texts in international relations to rival those of political theory, or to accept the emblematic use of the figures of Hobbes, Grotius, and Kant to represent three distinct traditions, and to reify such concepts as the nation state, sovereignty, realism, and idealism (see Walker 1993 and Keene 2005).

The interface where the two disciplines meet is relatively amorphous and is yet to acquire a settled nomenclature, let alone a settled subject matter. This is largely because the term theory in international relations has been used to tolerate a wide variety of intellectual pursuits, including empirical and normative enquiries. Even in relation to empirical theory Kenneth N. Waltz complained that the term is used very loosely among specialists in international relations, often referring to any work that rises above mere description and which includes some analysis (Waltz 1979: 1).

NOMENCLATURE

A variety of labels have been attached to the area of study. Fred Parkinson, for example, perhaps wishing to get away from the pejorative connotation of the word theory in his discipline, called it the 'philosophy of international relations'. The use of the term philosophy is no more precise than the use of the term theory. It is not employed as a discriminating principle. His book encompasses levels of discourse ranging from philosophy to polemics (Parkinson 1977). Similarly, Martin Wight, an opponent of American empirical theories of international relations, uses the term 'International Theory' in as undiscriminating a way in the levels of discourse it encompasses (Wight 1991). The great political philosophers such as Hobbes, Rousseau, and Hegel rub shoulders with international jurists such as Grotius, Pufendorf, and Vattel, and polemicists such as Cobden, Bright, and Hobson, along with literary figures such as Tolstoy, Wells, and Huxley, and distinguished statesmen such as Lincoln, Bismarck, Gladstone, and Churchill. This intellectual egalitarianism, where the fact of theorizing is more important than the quality of the theory, is testimony to Raymond Aron's observation that theory has become a much over-used and abused word, particularly in the field of international relations where the most banal observations are dressed-up under the guise of theory (Aron 1967). Wight describes his version of international theory as 'an experiment in classification, in typology, and ... an exploration of continuity and recurrence, a study in the uniformity of political thought: and its leading premise is that political ideas do not change much, and the range of ideas is limited' (Wight 1991: 5). In essence, theory for Wight, in a much less sophisticated manner, is akin to Arthur Lovejoy's Unit Ideas whose components persist over vast periods of time.

With the wane of positivism in international relations, it has become relatively common to refer to the interface between political theory and international relations as international political theory (Donelan 1990; Linklater 1990; Williams 1992; Walker 1993; and Brown et al. 2002). Such terms as 'international thought' (Onuf 1998) and 'international political thought' (Keene 2005) are also gaining currency. What is encouraging about this literature is that far more stringent qualitative criteria of relevance and appropriateness are being applied. The fact that someone somewhere said something relating to international relations is no longer a qualification to be heard. One of the guiding principles of selection in the collection edited by Chris Brown, Terry Nardin, and Nicholas Rengger, for example, is that 'some thinkers clearly have produced more significant work than others' (Brown et al. 2002: 3).

In my own work I employ the term 'political theory of international relations' deliberately to be inclusive of only some levels of discourse. To use the term political philosophy of international relations would be too exclusive, especially if used in the Oakeshottian sense to refer to those reflections that seek to establish the connections in principle and in detail, mediately or directly, between politics and eternity, the masterpieces of which were produced by Plato, Hobbes, and Hegel (Oakeshott 1975a: 5). I wanted to include, what Oakeshott calls, the political theorist, such as Locke capable of producing the perfect abridgment of the British political tradition, and the theoretician, such as Jeremy Bentham, who having reflected upon an activity has recommendations for its better conduct.

One of the principal features of the political theory of international relations is what may be described as the 'historical turn'. I want to say something about what this is, and illustrate how it is of benefit for both political theory and the political theory of international relations. This whole book is an exemplification of the historical turn and how excavation of the rich resources of the past enables us to understand better where we are, and who we are, now.

THE HISTORICAL TURN

The historical turn in international relations is of missionary zeal and is characterized by an almost religious fervour to adopt the mantle of historian, to use Pocock's words, as guardian of the truth. Those who advocate the use of history as a weapon against prevailing orthodoxies see no incompatibility, as an Oakeshottian would, between a practical attitude towards the past and historical sensitivity. There is no suggestion that the past directly provides answers for present problems, but instead a belief that the role of history is to unmask, demystify, deconstruct, or expose the ossified and petrified prevailing paradigmatic icons of the discipline. The sources of this historical turn are various. R. B. J. Walker invokes Weber and Foucault (Walker 1992: 23–4), Andrew Linklater relies on Foucault and Collingwood (Linklater 1990: 212–21 and 227, n. 4), and Edward Keene (Keene 2005: 14–20) derives inspiration from Quentin Skinner, who in turn describes his approach as Collingwoodian (Skinner 2001: 175–88). The present study is inspired by both R. G. Collingwood and Michael Oakeshott who in their different ways established the integrity and autonomy of the historical mode of understanding in the English speaking world in the face of an increasingly shrill onslaught from positivism. Indeed, Collingwood's *An Essay on Metaphysics* (1938, revised edition, 1998) was a conscious rebuttal of logical positivism's contention that metaphysical statements are nonsense statements.

Constructivists, such as Nicholas Onuf, Alexander Wendt, and Beate Jahn, along with poststructuralists, such as R. B. J. Walker, William Connelly, and Jim George; constitutive theorists, such as Andrew Linklater, Mervyn Frost, and Chris Brown; and identity theorists, such as Edward Keene, although very different in their assumptions and analyses, have all taken the historical turn and have a number of things in common. First, they take the postulates and conclusions of 'conventional' international relations as social constructions, questioning their validity and efficacy. Second, they emphasize the contingency of the realities that we have constructed for ourselves, contending that far from universal principles, such as those that underpin realism in international relations, determining the structure of the world and how we are to respond to it, things could be, and have been, very different. Third, this has necessarily given rise to a plea for greater historical sensitivity in the unmasking of the emblematic moments in the world that international relations has created for itself. These include questioning the emblematic status of the Peace of Westphalia, the apparent immutability of state sovereignty, the efficacy of the Realism/Idealism dichotomy, and the usefulness of Wight's and Bull's three traditions, Hobbesian, Grotian, and Kantian in the theory and practice of international relations. Fourth, they have all contributed to the retrieval of the lost world of a canon of classic texts, in which thinkers in contributing their visions of the eternal in the transitory offer us the glimpse of alternatives, that do not directly solve our problems, but instead offer to the mind the potential for self-creation and transformation. And, fifth, what these writers have in common, along with a host of others coming at international relations from the directions of political theory (including modern analytic philosophers of distributive justice), and the history of political thought, is a refusal to acknowledge that international relations constitute a distinctive subject matter so different from other areas of social life that it demands its own methods, vocabularies, and patterns of thought appropriate to its uniqueness (Brown 2001: 14).

None of this may appear remarkable, but each constitutes a radical, fundamental and revolutionary, challenge to the self-identity of the discipline of international relations. The fifth may be the most radical challenge of all. Throughout all of its brief history the sub-discipline of international relations has self-consciously differentiated itself from politics. With the failure of liberal internationalism, the discipline of international relations severed its connection with the tradition of idealist 'miserable comforters', and refused to define itself in terms of a body of classic texts. This book is a contribution to retrieving what was set asunder, and an attempt to reintegrate some powerful thinkers into the mainstream of the political theory of international relations.

THE CHALLENGE TO TRADITIONS

Non-behaviouralist considerations of thinking about international relations, across the whole spectrum of thought, have been dominated by E. H. Carr's dualism of Idealism and Realism, and Martin Wight's and Hedley Bull's tripartite modification into the Machiavellian or Realist, the Grotian or Idealist, and the Kantian or Revolutionary (Bull 1991 and Wight 1991). Their dominance has been such as to distort much of what in other respects are excellent works of scholarship, obliged to enter into discussions about how a particular thinker or thinkers fit into one of the three traditions (see, for example, Welsh 1995: 6–9, 32, 35, and 58). The danger with these traditions is that their use often degenerates into exercises in classification, and sub-classification, for classification's sake. My own characterization of the history of political theories of international relations proposes an alternative in which Empirical Realism stands in antithesis to Universal Moral Order, which encompasses both the Grotian and Kantian traditions of Wight, and which results in the synthesis of the tradition of Historical Reason (Boucher 1998). The most important respect in which they differ from their alternatives is in the relation in which they stand to the individual thinkers discussed. Just as for Wilhelm Dilthey, the individual stands at the centre of systems of interaction, the political theorist of international relations is somehow attempting to resolve the tensions between all three in his or her own mind, and one, but not the same one, almost invariably dominates the other two. Even this is too constraining for some such as Knutsen (1992) and Keene (2005). Edward Keene, for example, rejects organizing his history of international political thought in terms of traditions because he believes that such an approach emphasizes the continuities at the expense of discontinuities, a unity rather than diversity, and assumes the perennial character of the issues. Keene appears to assume that placing thinkers and the concepts that they used in their appropriate historical contexts excludes an emphasis upon continuity. Any reader of F. H. Bradley (Bradley 1930), Michael Oakeshott (Oakeshott 1933), or R. G. Collingwood (Collingwood 1993) will know that starting and ending points in history are inevitably somewhat arbitrary, and that every identity is a unity in diversity, a continuity in change. Collingwood is famous, of course, for his denial of perennial problems in philosophy. He argued that when Plato talked about the Athenian state it is a completely different concept from that of Hobbes' seventeenth century state. Collingwood concedes there is a sense in which they are the same, but not as two different instances of a universal. 'The sameness', he argues, 'is the sameness of an historical process, and the difference is the difference between one thing which in the course of that process has turned into something else, and the other thing into which it has turned' (Collingwood 1970: 62).

What are the implications of this for political theory? I will take just a few examples to illustrate the mutual benefit that may accrue when the disciplines of political theory and the political theory of international relations converge and overlap (sometimes also with history and international law).

THE CHALLENGE TO SOVEREIGNTY

Much of the literature on international relations thought presupposes that the subject matter is defined by sovereign states in their relations with each other in a context of anarchy, or the anarchical society as Hedley Bull famously described it (Bull 1977; also see Wight 1991: 1). Chris Brown takes the concept of sovereignty to be a key feature among the differentiae of 'international political theory'. Such theorists share with political theorists concerns about rights and distributive justice, but are particularly focused upon how they are refracted through the medium of sovereignty, which he takes to be 'shorthand for a particular system of inclusion and exclusion' (Brown 2002: 11). The issue of sovereignty certainly frames many of the debates in the political theory of international relations. Issues of humanitarian intervention and of universal human rights are frustrated by the reified and entrenched, but often illusory, sanctity of sovereignty, which Stephen Krasner refers to as 'organised hypocrisy' (Krasner 1999). The dualism between the domestic and international is a postulate of political theory, whereas this division is increasingly interrogated in the political theory of international relations. Knutsen observes that a focus on sovereignty has a constraining influence on the scope of inquiries tending towards an inordinate preoccupation with Western events and European theorists (Knutsen 1992: 2). By shifting the focus off sovereignty ideas about imperialism, civilization, culture, and race come into prominence (Keene 2005: 13). Without the preoccupation with state sovereignty the received distinction between international and political theory (or to put it in Walker's terms, the inside/outside distinction) cannot be maintained (Walker 1992); without the sovereign individual, the traditional privileging of what Ashley calls the 'heroic' ideal of rational man is foundationless, and without the possibility of sovereign truth, the epistemological privileging of some forms of knowledge above others is unjustified. In short, without sovereignty, political space is endless and the borders between inside and outside dissolve.

This book explores a set of ideas that transcend sovereignty, or at least challenge it in significant ways. It is an exploration of that mode of thinking that I have called elsewhere the Universal Moral Order in which human beings are united with each other in a universal community whose sinews are moral ties. States or nations are contingent intrusions on this universal community, hence giving rise to the perpetual tension between the duties of a citizen and a person. The stronger the pull of the universal community the more corrosive it is to the barriers of sovereignty. Natural law, natural rights, and human rights all in their ways constitute standards or criteria by which the actions of ruling regimes may be measured, and brought to account before the international court of reason. There are times when the voice of universal morality may be little more than a faint whisper, and others when it is audible against no matter how much background noise events throw-up.

EUROPEAN ENCOUNTERS WITH THE NEW WORLD

Studies of the European relations with the Americas offer the opportunity to re-establish classic texts as central to the political theory of international relations, and expand on the canon of traditional texts in political theory. This is particularly the case in relation to Pufendorf who was the most widely read moral theorist of the seventeenth and eighteenth centuries until Kant's Copernican revolution, and whose theory of sovereignty may be read as a response to the theoretical issues posed by the Peace of Westphalia (Boucher 2006). There is a host of other issues that arose in relation to the Americas, including humanitarian intervention in relation to which important thinkers emerge, who hardly figure in the political theory canon, and who are beginning to appear more frequently in the political theory of international relations. They also appear in histories of international law, or the Law of Nations, because one of its sources is the writings of the classic jurists. Many of the classic thinkers in international relations, such as Gentili, Grotius, and Suarez, argued that acts which outraged humanity, such as human sacrifice and cannibalism, overrode the exclusiveness of domestic jurisdiction and gave grounds for just war, or what modern international lawyers would call humanitarian intervention (Meron 1998: 123–4).

Interest in European encounters with the Americas gives a sharper perspective on why discussions of property have such a prominent place in texts of political theory and the Law of Nations during the sixteenth and seventeenth centuries. While the issue of whether heathens and barbarians could legitimately be considered the owners of property was a lively issue during the Crusades, the question became even more pressing with the discovery of the Americas. The issues revolved around whether property was an institution established by civil society, or whether property rights are a matter of natural law. Vitoria, for example, argued that the Indians met the criteria for property ownership under natural law, while Sepúlveda maintained that property was a civil institution, a view that was attacked with some vehemence by Las Casas (Hanke 1974; Pagden 1993; and Jahn 2000). This context goes a long way to explain why both Grotius and Locke contended that property ownership in Europe was a matter of settled civil law, but prior to civil society there is a natural form of ownership regulated by natural law. This is reflected in Grotius' distinction between occupation and dominion. This move allowed them to argue that for the most part American Indians had not satisfied the criteria of appropriation and ownership.

The idea of *terra nullius*, vacant or waste land, provided the condition in which Grotius, Locke, and Vattel, for example, thought that the pre-social entitlement, or natural right, to property could be invoked. The doctrine of *terra nullius* denied both that native peoples were owners of lands, in Vattel's famous phrase they simply 'ranged through' rather than 'inhabited them,' (Vattel 1834: Bk. 1, chapt. 7, §81), and also it denied that native peoples possessed sovereignty, because they did not constitute political societies. Thus the land was there for the taking and title to it could be claimed by displaying the conventional signs of ownership, such as occupancy and possession. In a discipline obsessed with contemporary relevance and imbued with a utilitarian attitude to scholarship – that it must be useful or it cannot be any good – it may be wondered of what relevance such antiquated disputes about property may be? In the first place, at the macro level, they serve to explain how the world in which we live came to be what it is. The world's only superpower is a product of this European expansionism. In the second place, the doctrine of *terra nullius* and its denial of sovereignty to indigenous peoples has served permanently to exclude such nations within nations from the international sphere: they are diplomatically, in bilateral and multilateral relations among states, and by international organizations such as The League of Nations and the United Nations, denied direct representation, and are deemed to be virtually represented (to use Burke's phrase) by the dominant culture. The doctrine of *terra nullius* therefore needed to be supplemented with a theory of property that established a moral title to the ownership of the land. Possession was equated with cultivation. For Locke, the Indians, like everyone else, had a natural right to property, they had just not exercised it, and in addition were failing in their duty to God to cultivate the land and make the soil as productive as possible. Cultivation of the land was a solemn obligation, and those who were not discharging this obligation had no right in preventing those who do. Vattel contends that, 'The cultivation of the soil... [is] an obligation imposed by nature on mankind' (Vattel 1834: Bk. 1, chapt. 7, §81). Occupancy was not enough. Neither sovereignty nor property could be acknowledged in the Law of Nations over uninhabited countries, 'except those of which it has really taken actual possession, in which it has formed settlements, or of which it makes actual use' (Vattel 1834: §208).

This book will show how colonization was integrally related to the development of theories of property that legitimated occupation and possession of foreign lands. I use the example of cultural encounters to illustrate how universal moral standards may be used not as instruments of liberation, but of oppression. In this respect the book is about the globalization of values and how those values may become instruments of systematic injustice in the guise of the benevolent extension of the principle of universal rights to the whole of the world.

The application of natural law, and the Law of Nations, uniquely the product of the Western political experience, was conceived as universal, and from which local variations, at least in terms of fundamental beliefs, were regarded as violations. There was certainly a scale of civilization, which became gradually more refined, both explicit and implicit, that was used to determine to what extent those who did not belong to the higher civilized nations could exercise universal rights, for which certain qualifications had to be met.

What this study shows is that when natural law and its derivative rights are deemed to be universal, their application is often oppressive. They are the expression of the mind of a culture, the articulation of the values, and morality expected of its members. When applied to other cultures, their members are almost invariably likely to fall below those standards in crucial respects, which may be deemed a violation of the law of nature. Such violations provoke varying responses, but were often used in justification of exercising dominion over the person and property of the violators. Natural rights, positing some power, claim or capacity inherent in human beings, whether its source is God or nature, had like natural law, the capacity to be truly universal, but its social and political implications were so subversive and revolutionary that the issue became not so much the rights themselves, although these were contested by the likes of Burke, Rousseau, and Hume, but the question of who should possess them. It is here that the issue of race, and the disqualification of some, particularly blacks, on the grounds that they were not fully human, is of particular significance. Nor, indeed, did women fare well when discussed in this context.

The characteristics of being absolute, immutable, and inalienable when viewed through the application of universal moral principles to the issue of cultural encounters, of race and slavery, and of the condition of women, expose the extent to which these so-called universal rights turn out to be conditional, and only those who are deemed to meet the conditions, usually white adult males, can be said to possess and exercise them fully.

The language of human rights is now the lingua franca of the international order and invoked on a wide variety of issues ranging from religious toleration and economic development, to regime change and humanitarian intervention. Human rights are often indiscriminately linked with the natural law and natural rights traditions. Some contend that the three are basically the same and argue that the concept of human rights is incoherent and lacks moral force without the foundations that underpinned the natural law and natural rights traditions. Hersh Lauterpacht, for example, argued that natural law, natural rights, and human rights were almost indistinguishable, having a common ancestry (Lauterpacht 1945: 9).

Others want to distinguish natural law and natural rights by suggesting that the former emphasizes duties and obligations while the latter gives priority to claims and permissions (Mackinnon 1966). There is also a tendency to portray the shift from natural law to natural rights as a shift from a religiously based ethic to a more secular conception of rights (Pogge 2002). Discussions of human rights often assume that there is a continuity with the Rights of Man, and indeed, use the terms interchangeably. Theodor Meron, for example, refers to human rights when discussing Gentili on the common rights of mankind (Meron 1998: 128).

Others define the former in terms typical of the latter, namely that we have such rights by the mere fact that we are human, independently of governments. Peter Jones has argued that the modern doctrine of human rights is a direct descendant from liberal theories of natural rights. He argues that, 'The idea of a human right remains that of a right which is "natural" in that it is conceived as a moral entitlement which human beings possess in their natural capacity as humans, and not in virtue of any special arrangement into which they have entered or any particular system of law under whose jurisdiction they fall' (Jones 1991: 223). Brian Tierney uses the terms natural rights and human rights indifferently on the grounds that the two terms have pretty much the same meaning, 'Natural Rights or human rights are rights that inhere in persons by reason of their very humanity' (Tierney 2004: 1).

Many commentators wish to distinguish the natural rights from the natural law tradition by suggesting that natural rights represents the secularization of universal moral principles, grounding moral obligation in human reason. This, I contend, is a mistaken view. Such writers as Grotius and Pufendorf, it is true, tried to demonstrate the efficacy of natural law and natural rights by reasoning from indubitable data to logical conclusions. We have to distinguish, however, the issue of how we come to know the natural law, from our obligation to conform to it. Reason is the route to its discovery and declaration, but often reason in itself cannot create obligation. We are obliged to obey the natural law because it is God's law.

Nor can we distinguish natural law and natural rights by suggesting the rights associated with the former are derivative from natural law and therefore are objective rights, while natural rights are subjective, something that we possess by the mere fact of being human. Brian Tierney and Knud Haakonssen, for example, have shown how subjective rights were certainly a feature of much medieval thought, and that objective, or derivative rights were much more prevalent during the height of natural rights theories than were subjective rights (Haakonssen 1996 and Tierney 1997).

In this project I want to suggest that even though natural rights and human rights are often associated, in so far as it is claimed that we have them independently of governments and by the mere fact that we are human, they are in fact quite different. I want to argue that even though they differ, they are nevertheless related, not only in sharing similar objectives or policy goals, but also because they are part of the same historical process by which the one turns into the other.

It is also important to distinguish between 'descriptive' and 'prescriptive' natural rights, and both are often treated as if they are the same or have a common source. Let me illustrate the difference with an example. A tiger in the jungle needs meat to live, and in so far as animals and humans have a right to life, the tiger may be said to have a right to eat meat. The tiger will from time to time come across walking edible humans. The tiger has a right, but the human has no obligation to acknowledge that right. One could call them natural instincts, relating to our naturalistic selves. There is no duty correlative to the right. Hobbes is the exemplar here. They are really natural mights, or powers, which I enjoy in so far as I have the power to take what I want. The prescriptive version is quite different. Here the natural rights are normative and moral, and give rise to correlative obligations. This seems to me a very basic distinction that needs to be acknowledged. Hobbes is not talking about the same thing as Locke in using the idea of natural rights.

I suggest that there was not a sudden leap from the foundationalism of natural rights to the anti-foundationalism of human rights, and this transition finds its clearest articulation in little noticed work on natural rights done by the British Idealists who are often criticized for denying the rights of the individual by prioritizing the absolutism of the state. Despite the denial of natural rights in their traditional form, namely as resting upon some conception of human nature, universal principles, or as having some religious foundation, the Idealists suggested that the term was better used in the sense that there are certain rights that are absolutely imperative for the social relations of a community at any one time, and that these rights, despite the fact that they are conventional and justified on the principle of their contribution to the common good, could with justification be described as 'natural'. The Idealists, nevertheless, ultimately relied upon a metaphysic and a conception of the person that was difficult to reconcile with the conventionalism posited in their accounts of natural rights. Modern philosophers have retained the conventionalism, or communitarianism, sometimes called constitutive theory, and jettisoned the metaphysics. The Idealists, then, stand in an intermediary position between natural rights and the modern human rights culture, and have contributed significantly to modern ideas on the moral community and how conceptions of human rights have to be conceived in terms different from the natural rights tradition.

Am I making historical claims about the place of Idealism in this process, or am I making a normative point in relation to contemporary debates? I am doing both. I am trying to give a justification of how we may escape the traditional criticisms of natural rights, and conceive of them as nevertheless necessary and fundamental to any human society as we know it. I want to show how contemporary discussion of human rights in a variety of disciplines is moving in this direction, sometimes hampered by its lack of understanding of how its arguments are linked to an historical process by which natural rights have turned into human rights.

I want to suggest that there is a residue of the natural law and natural rights traditions in the modern human rights culture, regime or movement, as it is variously called, and that it serves to cloud and confuse the clarity with which human rights are understood. Apart from the residue, modern conceptions of human rights, legal, political, and philosophical, I suggest, rest on some version of conventionalism in ethics, or what is sometimes called constitutive theory. There is among the 'conventionalists' or 'consensus' theorists on human rights a tendency to think about what it means to have a human right, what human rights we may have, and what policy goals are implied in the assumption that we have them.

Throughout the book we will be dealing with the ambiguities of meanings, sometimes unintentional, and sometimes deliberately exploited in order to further arguments, or create confusion. The three terms that permeate the whole of this book are all open to exploitation and manipulation: natural, law, and rights in various permutations, and in normative or descriptive modes, generate ample opportunities for confusion.

In the case of a right, for example, we are familiar with a variety of uses. It is often used as the correlative of duty. Duty is generally accepted as something that one ought to do, and in this respect we are making a value judgement, suggesting that it is better to do something than not to do it. The standard employed is a moral standard, and one that we know to be generally accepted by our community. To have a duty in this sense is to have a duty towards some identifiable person, or a non-specified person who is the member of a group or class. To use the term duty means to specify a relation that holds between people, a moral relation that entails rights and duties. If someone has a duty, then someone has a right, even if the right holder is a member of a class, such as the poor, rather than a specific individual. Where the obligation correlates with a right held by a specific rightholder, it may be specified as a perfect right – the duty and the right are different sides of the same coin. Where the duty, say to reduce poverty in the world, is related to a class of people, rather than a specific person it may be said to be an imperfect obligation. No specified individual in that class has the right to demand of you that you fulfil your obligation to him or to her.

The term right is also used in a different sense where ideas of duty and ought are replaced by the notion of may; may, like ought, entails an evaluation. It means that to do something or not to do it are value neutral. In this sense we may have a right to do or not do something, but no duty is entailed. The permissiveness of the right to do or not to do denies that there exists an obligation in another to refrain. A right in this sense is the contradiction or denial of a duty, and is sometimes called a liberty, or in the plural liberties (see Radin 1949–50: 214).

PROPERTY, SLAVERY, AND THE SLAVE TRADE

A recurrent theme throughout the book is the relationship between property and slavery, and one which provided an insurmountable impediment to inclusivity during and immediately after the American Revolution. Aristotle's two justifications of slavery were the mainspring of such discussions for over two thousand years. First, his belief that some peoples are born for slavery because of their inferior natural intelligence, and therefore required the guidance of stronger intellects to compensate for their inadequacy was not universally accepted, although it surfaces from time to time, especially in relation to the American Indians and black Africans. It was possible to hold strong views about the inferiority of peoples in relation to each other without necessarily accepting that the implication was that Europeans had the right to enslave them, although the Christian hierarchical categorization of the three peoples generated by the sons of Noah, Japeth, Shem, and Ham, gave credence to the concept of natural slavery and subservience, and formed the basis for justifications of apartheid in both the United States and South Africa. It is important to distinguish between those, such as David Hume, who believed that non-whites, or just blacks, were congenitally inferior and therefore incapable of reaching the heights of civilization that Europeans had achieved, and those, such as Edmund Burke who believed in the educative duty of colonizers to raise peoples to the condition of self-government.

The second of Aristotle's justifications was the right of conquest. In exchange for their lives captives may subjugate themselves to their captors. This justification was almost universally accepted with, from time to time, certain provisos. The Church, for example, tended to frown upon the enslavement of fellow Christians. It was simply accepted that a life without freedom was better than no life at all. The practice of enslaving rather than slaughtering captives continued to be praised as a considerable step forward in civilization, even if the right of conquest to the enslavement of the conquered was no long acceptable. Even in the nineteenth century the French philosopher and sociologist Isadore Auguste Comte, and the British Idealist David Ritchie, could condemn contemporary slavery as unacceptable and incompatible with the ideals of freedom and self-realization, while praising its acceptance in Ancient Greece and Rome as a humane step in the civilizing process. Jean Jacques Rousseau, the champion of freedom as non-domination, was the first philosopher of significance to repudiate the justification of slavery by right of conquest, on the grounds that states, and not individuals, go to war, and that slavery, because of its illegitimacy and propensity to engender opportune resistance, prolonged rather than ameliorated the state of war.

The condition of slavery in relation to right was, then, extensively discussed, but the institution of slavery was rarely questioned, especially in its legally institutionalized form. Whereas Bodin clearly opposed slavery, the likes of Hobbes and Locke, in a modified form, were strong advocates of the classical justification. There were, of course, religious objections on the grounds of the equality of souls because Negro slaves were equally the children of God. Such arguments were not based on rights, but on our Christian duty to save souls. Even though Locke accepted that Negroes may share in religious liberty, that in no way exempted them from 'that civil dominion his master hath over him' (cited in Sypher 1939: 273).

It is ironic that the age of Enlightenment in Europe and America, championing reason and equality over religious superstition, was not itself renowned for its support of the abolition of slavery, or of emancipation, although there are many instances of condemnation of the Atlantic slave trade. Francis Hutcheson, a professor of Moral Philosophy at Glasgow and one of the leaders of the Scottish Enlightenment, however, did explicitly condemn classical justifications in substituting a reason based ethic by one of sentiment. Pity, for him, overrode all talk of just and unjust wars. Rousseau with his emphasis on pity repudiated classical justifications of slavery by condemning slavery *per se*; to renounce one's liberty was to renounce being a man, without specifically addressing the question of black slavery or the slave trade. For both Hutcheson and Rousseau the fact that slavery is tantamount to misery is enough to condemn it as an institution. Whereas Jefferson was ambivalent about how he might reconcile the equality of natural rights posited in his philosophy, with the practical issues of slavery, Hutcheson condemned it outright on the grounds that natural rights belong equally to all.

During the twentieth century there has been a juridical revolution in the idea of human rights. There has been a proliferation of documents in which human rights are specified, and a codification of customary law by the UN ad hoc criminal tribunals for the former Yugoslavia and Rwanda, as well as the treaty which established the International Criminal Court. Prospects of universal justice have been enhanced by such comprehensive lists of rights which act as standards by which the actions of governments and their agents may be held to account. In reality, however, the gap between aspiration and the effective possession, protection, and enforcement of human rights remains enormous. Women in most parts of the world remain subordinate to men within patriarchal societies, and their lives are valued much less than those of their male siblings. The cruel irony of the success of women in the professions in the West, while inequalities persist, is that those chores such as looking after the children, cleaning, and ironing have not on the whole been shared by male partners, but are done by imported cheap female labour from such countries as the Philippines. The abolition of slavery and the slave trade has not ended slavery, it has taken a different form, and women once again suffer disproportionately, especially as victims of the sex trade. The political will to ensure a successful and effective human rights regime is intermittent, and the principle of state sovereignty still strong and obstructive.

Multicultural encounters now take place in the West, not between it and territories it covets, but within established societies in which a dominant culture concedes, or affords, certain rights of protection for ethnic, or national communities, or at least concedes rights of inclusion. While the principle of multiculturalism was accepted, no one can deny the vast inequalities that remained and the silent condoning of practices that would be unacceptable within the dominant culture. With the advent of the war on terrorism that post-dates 9/11 the commitment to multiculturalism is far more tenuous than it was, and the freedoms and rights enjoyed by Muslims, in particular, far more precarious.

The story is not all pessimistic. While the enforcement and enjoyment of human rights over vast areas of the globe remain uncertain and unpredictable, the fact that the idea of human rights are acknowledged widely to be a standard to which states aspire, and which increasingly are among the conditions imposed for the enjoyment of benefits by one state from another, means that human rights are settled norms, accepted almost universally by the world community. No state openly boasts of human rights violations, and either tries to explain them away, as, for example, the United States has done by denying that producing the sensation of drowning by waterboarding prisoners is a form of torture. Alternatively, states that do engage in systematic violations of human rights try to do so clandestinely. In other words, human rights form a frame of reference that is not merely injunctive, but also acts as a constraint, however, tenuous. In addition, the legal apparatus that has been constructed to bring those to justice who commit gross violations of human rights, while at present ambiguous in its deterrent effect, will in time, as leaders see a growing political will within the international community to hold violators to account, and to endorse humanitarian intervention, not be able to hide behind the veil of sovereignty that protects them. The arrest of the former Bosnian Serb Leader, Radavan Karadzic, after thirteen years of impunity for crimes against humanity and war crimes, has given new inspiration to those who have faith in international justice. The conditions imposed on Serbia by the European Union for consideration of its future membership have led to his arrest for trial before the UN criminal Tribunal for the Former Yugoslavia at the Hague, but the ideas that he espoused still persist in Republicka Srpska. Perhaps the spectacle of Karadzic's arrest and impending trial, and the trials and sentencing of his right hand man, Momcilo Krajišnik and middle ranking colleagues, Dusko Tadic, Milomir Stakic, and Milan Kovacevic may not change deeply rooted prejudices, but they may in the long run deter those who hold them from putting them into action.

1

Classical Natural Law and the Law of Nations: The Greeks and the Romans

> Nor do I think that a decree of yours [Creon] –/ A man – could override the laws of Heaven/ Unwritten and unchanging. Not of today/ Or yesterday in their authority;/ They are eternal; no man saw their birth.
>
> (Sophocles 1994: 16 [450])

The concepts of natural law, natural rights, and human rights have in common a universal principle, that for some reason, and it may be different reasons, humanity inhabits a cosmopolis, superimposed upon which are political communities that do not necessarily override our loyalty to our fellow human beings. There must, then, be an idea of a universal community if universal obligations are to have a moral purchase. In Homer's *Odyssey*, for example, in which war and slaughter are taken for granted, the suppliant stranger who constitutes no, nor in good faith intends, harm may not be harassed or harmed, but instead requires protection and must be allowed to continue his journey with gifts of good will. By the mere fact that he is a man he has a claim on those Homeric Greeks who style themselves civilized (Radin 1949–50: 214). With reference to Odysseus, Alcinous remarks: 'To any man with the slightest claim to common sense, a guest and suppliant is as close as a brother' (Homer 2003: Book VIII, §540).

There may be times when obligations demanded of us by our political communities are inconsistent with those we have as human beings. How we resolve those tensions remains an intractable issue, but it is not the same issue perennially re-run, because it will differ in relation to the peculiar circumstances in which it arises. In this chapter, I want to explore the tension as it became manifest in the natural law thinking of the Greeks and Romans.

The idea of natural law has a long and intricate history, where the same terms often mean very different things, and where different terms may express the same idea or fundamental principle. Natural law, and the law of nature, may often coincide, but they may also express quite diverse ideas, and where their meanings converge, the relation in which they stand to the Law of Nations may differ. It is extremely important to be sensitive to the fact that in answer to the question, 'what is natural?', many different answers may and have been given. In the Greco-Roman and medieval periods the term 'natural' may refer to moral qualities, or it may merely be descriptive of physical capacities. The prescriptive and descriptive uses of the term must always in principle be separated in order to avoid the error of assuming that two thinkers have similar views of the world. Both Antiphon the Sophist, and Cicero the Stoic, for example, believed that we are united, transcending community boundaries, by having a common human nature, but for the former it is a naturalistic nature that overrides conventional morality, whereas for the latter it is a common rational nature that is reflected in common morality. Even when we find authors who suggest that morality is the artifice of human beings, rather than the product of nature, we may still discover that some authors believe it to be consistent with, and others opposed to nature.

We find in the writings of Homer glimmerings of the idea of law. There is no sense of a legislature or of a king who makes laws that citizens or subjects must obey, nor of the normative force of custom. Instead Homer talks of *themis*, a difficult concept to grasp, but at the centre of which lies the idea of decisions, directives, or findings inspired by the gods, that are morally appropriate for both gods and men. Every polis is divinely patronized, and in the first place *themis* is understood to be the voice or utterance of the gods, an expression of divine wisdom. Laws are not made, but a divine gift expressing divine wisdom. To apprehend *themistes* a Homeric king would hold the *spectron*, the staff of office, in his hand to extract them from Zeus. Kings were fallible and may mishear, or misinterpret the law, and in this respect even the early Greeks had a notion of a bad or unworkable law, which Homer called 'crooked' (Oakeshott 2006: 75–6). Unlike the Hebraic conception of Divine command, *themistes* is more like divine insight which has to be discovered, interpreted, and declared. Right conduct is that which conforms to divine insight, and to be in conformity with it, which is a matter of choice, is to be in accord with the nature of the world.

In conjunction with *themis* in the Homeric poems is the idea of *dike*, the meaning of which is much less precise than it later became. It did not mean abstract justice, or a lawsuit or even a judgement, but instead conveyed the sense of being the earthly law that imitates *themis*. It is therefore derivative and comes into being as a result of the sentencing of judges. *Themis*, then is venerable and revered and associated with supernatural beings and their inspiration of human rulers. *Dike* came to have a fully secular, and practical set of senses, but even in the Homeric epics gradually came to supplant *themis* (Kelly 1992: 7–8).

Themis had been a word evocative of the ancient customs and law of a tribe and sat uneasily in the context of the polis, and gradually came to be replaced by another word for law. This word was *thesmos*, at first a colloquial expression meaning 'custom' or 'use', but soon to acquire the more precise meaning of formal law. The change of vocabulary meant no fundamental alteration in the conception of law, it still retained the connection with divine wisdom. The manner of acquiring it, however, underwent a change. It was understood that a polis comprised many different tribes, each of which had brought with it its own *themistes*. The law of the polis was fundamentally a law common to the tribes that had to emerge out of the plurality of tribal *themistes*. The process by which this happened was understood as doing justice to the various tribal *themistes*, selecting the best and the most useful by which to regulate the polis (Oakeshott 2006: 78). The idea of *thesmos* has implied in it the suggestion that human beings establish their own laws by judicious reasoning from the customs of men.

Almost two centuries after the Homeric age the Greeks made a distinction between nature (*phusis*) and convention (*nomos*), and many believed that morality belonged to the realm of the conventional. *Nomos* was now the term that represented law and it became associated with *nous* (intelligence) and *logos* (reasoning). In this conception it is more clearly the case that law is made by a recognisable process, and that its maker had to be in possession of knowledge, that knowledge was to be of *phusis*, nature, which entailed not only knowledge of the general workings of the cosmos, but also of the particular circumstances of the polis such as the fertility of the soil. Oakeshott maintains that: 'when *nomos* replaced *themis* and *thesmos* as the ordinary word for "law" an essentially human, rational, almost secular idea of "law" had replaced an essentially religious idea' (Oakeshott 2006: 81).

There are thinkers in the classical world who have a claim to formulating nascent social contract theories, but they differ from the later theories that became associated with natural rights and the state of nature from which the contract delivered the contractees. Such thinkers as Antiphon, Hippias, Callicles, Democritus, Protagoras, Thrasymachus, and Glaucon contended that morality is a matter of convention and arises out of self-interest. For Antiphon, Callicles, and Thrasymachus (and to some extent Glaucon) morality is opposed to nature, and therefore unnatural. For Hippias, Democritus, and Protagoras, although conventional, morality is consistent with nature because it contributes to the realisation of human potential. Morality is necessary in order to constrain the destructiveness of pure self-interest. Both positions, however, believe that morality emerged in order to constrain the unmitigated pursuit of self interest. For Antiphon such constraints were contrary to nature. He maintained that appetites should be the guide to conduct. On the other hand, for Protagoras, the constraining influence of conventional morality was a positive force in society. It is against Protagoras that Plato is probably reacting when he declares that God is the measure of all things, much more so than man. The point he is making is that we cannot look to convention as the source or criterion of ethical principles (Keene 2005: 35). For Plato, nature, in its prescriptive, or normative, sense, was the source of law, and the criterion by which customs and rules should be judged. Plato, then, understands nature differently from the likes of Antiphon, Gorgias, or Callicles who used it in its descriptive sense.

Conventional morality on each of the accounts given by the Sophists does not transcend the state, unless the extension is effected by the interests of the polis or state itself. Morality may become universal by being extended over the whole world by conquest or by a policy of imperialism. This is what is known as particularism in ethics. The same values are exported from one community to another. Michael Walzer calls this covering law universalism (Walzer 1994). Particularist morality may also be extended by example or agreement inspired by rational self-interest. In addition, there is a third option. Conventional morality may be objured and replaced by a universal naturalistic ethic, such as a belief in the notion of the survival of the fittest derived from evolutionary theory, or such like.

Many moral conventionalists among the Greeks exhibit naturalistic tendencies leading them to question primary loyalties to the polis. They posit a natural equality which overrides conventional social hierarchies within and between states. Social distinctions and the division of the world into Greeks and barbarians was unnatural. These tendencies towards universalism of a naturalistic kind are evident in Democritus and Hippias (see Plato 1987: 71), but they are much more pronounced in Antiphon. Antiphon contends that men are naturally equal and subject to nature's laws which unite the whole of mankind. The laws of nature are opposed to conventional morality and instead dictate actions motivated by self-interest, even if they are damaging to the interests of others. The laws of nature, from the position of natural equality, license inequalities based on the natural relations of dominance and compliance (Plato 1934: 889–90).

A universal morality based on a prescriptive, or normative, natural law is not itself incompatible with living in a polis. For Plato and Aristotle the highest civil association is the polis, yet both subscribe to the idea of universal morality. Similarly, many of the Stoics saw no contradiction in loving one's *patria* while at the same time positing a common humanity, a world-wide moral community.

THE GREEKS

Greeks lived an intensely religious life that was integral to the idea of citizenship, its duties and obligations. The laws that regulated the polis could not be separated from religion. They were usually referred to as the sacred or unwritten laws, and were largely the application of religion to civic and social life. Breaches of the sacred law would incur the wrath of the gods who were its source, and they would therefore have to be appeased. Lycurgus the lawgiver of Sparta did not in his constitution make law, he declared the will of the real lawgiver Apollo (Phillipson 1911: 43). Such beliefs are not unusual in other cultures. Moses revealed to the Jews the word of God, and Numa transmitted to the Romans the law of the goddess.

Whereas invoking a higher law by which human laws may be judged is evident in the literature of Greece from time to time, and was a commonplace in early and late Christian thought, it was rather unusual in Greek thought, and almost unheard of in Greek philosophy, but Plato does rely upon some such idea (Kelly 1992: 20). Greek literature, and the philosophies of Plato and Aristotle are a counter to the claim of the Sophists that morality is a convenient conventionalism, no more than a contingent response to the inconveniences of mutual co-operation. Antigone goes against Creon's decree when she buried her brother. She proclaims that she is obeying a higher law which human law ought to reflect and cannot override (Sophocles 1994: 16 [450]). In Sophocles's *Oedipus the King*, the chorus sing of a law independent of human will: 'For there are laws enthroned above;/ Heaven Created them,/ Olympus was their father,/ And mortal men had no part in their birth' (Sophocles 1994: 77 [864]).

In Plato's *Republic* the transitory world of Becoming is contrasted with the world of Being. He posits a sphere of immutable, absolute, and eternal forms conforming to the rational law of the cosmos which stands outside the transitory world of experience. The comprehension of this rational law would assist us in overcoming the variable and uncertain world of Becoming, the world in which we live our everyday lives. The important point is that Law or Justice is discovered rather than made. In Aristotle's *Rhetoric* Sophocles is called upon to give added weight to his own distinction between *specific* and *common* laws. Laws are specific when defined by each people with reference to themselves, and common when they are based on nature. There is, Aristotle maintains, natural justice. We are all able to discern or divine what is just and unjust even if we have had no previous association or commerce with each other (Aristotle 1973).[1] Aristotle's view is refined in the distinction he makes between natural and conventional political justice. It is natural when it has universal validity and is unaffected by the view one may take of its justice. Conventional political justice has no fundamental reason why it should be what it is, rather than something else. The rule is a matter of agreement after which it holds good (Aristotle 1973: 157, Book 5, chapt. 7). Aristotle in the *Rhetoric* (1373b) demonstrates how the law of nature can be appealed to in the courts when positive law appears unfavourable (Watson 1971: 218). The ambiguity in the concept of nature, however, is often exploited. What Aristotle appears to mean is not natural laws in a moral sense, but in a physical sense, such as the fact that fire burns in Greece and in Persia.

For Plato and Aristotle, the polis is the natural association within which human potential may flourish. The individual is inexplicable in isolation from the whole (Aristotle 1988: 4). The citizen in relation to a state, not any particular state, is like an arm or a leg in relation to the body. The good of each part is dependent upon and inseparable from the good of the whole (Aristotle 1988: 185; also see Barnes 1991). Like Plato, Aristotle believes that the same virtues which individuals possess can be found in exactly the same form, and have the same nature, in the state (Aristotle 1988: 157).

Such views were perfectly compatible for them with the idea of a universal moral law. Although the state or polis is a natural organic unity of, and superior to, its parts, it is subject to a moral law independent of the rulers of each polis. This kind of law is not created, but instead discovered by reason. Aristotle argues that: 'he who bids the law rule may be deemed to bid God and Reason alone rule, but he who bids man rule adds an element of the beast; for desire is a wild beast, and

---

[1] Cf. his distinction between natural and conventional political justice: 'It is natural when it has the same validity everywhere and is unaffected by any view we may take about the justice of it. It is conventional when there is no original reason why it should take one form rather than another and the rule it imposes is reached by agreement, after which it holds good' (Aristotle 1973: 157, bk 5, chapt. 7).

passion perverts the minds of rulers, even when they are the best of men' (Aristotle 1988: 78, also see 80).

Within Greece itself Plato and Aristotle believed that each polis had attained its own degree of civilization, and that some were more civilized than others. The extent to which reason promoted the common good accounted for such differences of degree. Whatever their differences their relations among each other were naturally friendly because they shared a pan-Hellenic religion and civilisation. If disputes between them resulted in armed conflict they were to be considered 'internal and domestic', betraying a sickness in the social organism. Such tensions among friends were honourable, acceptable, and permissible if the intention was to restore peace. Greeks and non-Greeks, or barbarians, stood in a different relation, that of natural hostility. Conflicts between them were rightly to be called war, and were unconstrained by considerations of friendship. In war 'enslavement and destruction' are natural and permissible (Plato 1987: 258–9).

War between the Greeks and barbarians was considered natural for a number of reasons deeply rooted in Greek culture, and which revolved around the idea of slavery. Aristotle is the first among the Greeks to give a systematic account of the condition of slavery, but it was an institution so deeply embedded in Greek life that few acknowledged the need to justify it. The 'naturalness' of slavery for the Greeks after the heroic period is a concomitant of a growing pan-Hellenism contributing to a strong sense of Greek identity, culminating in a feeling of superiority after the Persian Wars, and a growing disdain for, and even hostility towards menial occupations (Schlaifer 1936: 167). In law slaves had no legal personality, and in Athens, for example, this was evident in the fact that the slave could not sue or be sued, and in this he or she was on a par with the foreigner or metic who had to transact business through agents. All three classes of people did not possess rights, and the state was not responsible for their protection. The murdering of a slave, though not illegal, nevertheless had a religious sanction in that the state was responsible for not angering the gods. Prohibitions against injuring slaves were not based upon any inherent right residing in the slave, but instead upon the right of the owner to protect his property (Schlaifer 1936: 181).

Non-Greeks, or barbarians, in their political submission to absolute monarchy, or despotism, were already enslaved, and the Greeks, being naturally suited for freedom, not only had a right but also a duty to enslave barbarians. Both Plato and Aristotle believed that this would provide the rational, or governing, element missing from, or underdeveloped in, their psyche. Such attitudes towards foreigners have been described as proto-racism in direct denial that racism is in fact a product of the nineteenth century, and particularly of the uses to which Darwinianism was put. It is also a denial of the view that the origins of racism do not precede Columbus and European expansionism (Isaac 2004).

Aristotle makes a distinction between natural free men and natural slaves. The origin of the idea of natural slavery rests upon a disdain for the physical appearance of slaves, and an abhorrence of the work slaves carried out which was both physically and morally demeaning. For Aristotle, natural slaves were the living property or instruments of naturally free men. They are compelled to live by the work of their bodies. They understand reason but do not possess it; follow orders, but are incapable of formulating them for themselves. Natural slaves require to be ruled in order to prevent passion dominating their lives (Aristotle 1988: 6–7). Aristotle contends that 'it is better for them as for all inferiors that they should be under the rule of a master' (Aristotle 1988: 7). A slave is not fully, or wholly, a man, and any virtues he may possess, he possesses only partially. In relation to natural slavery the implication is that natural slaves are not fully human, and are not capable of exercising reason in apprehending the natural law. In other words, Aristotle resorts to a familiar disclaimer in the history of thought in natural law, natural rights, and human rights. Human beings have certain qualities in common relevant to membership of a universal moral community, and those who do not possess those qualities are not eligible for entitlements of membership. Aristotle's argument was invoked as particularly important in justifying the enslavement of American Indians during European colonisation. The rediscovery of Aristotle in the late medieval period and the extent to which he became an epistemic authority, exploited to justify almost any political position, made him particularly useful as a weapon against those who argued that the American Indians are fully human in all relevant respects and could therefore possess rights, and property in their own account.

In contrast with natural slavery, there was conventional slavery usually resulting from capture in war. Aristotle acknowledges in the *Athenian Constitution* that there are compelling arguments for condemning the reduction of another rational human being to slavery by the exercise of force (Aristotle 1984: I, 6). In Aristotle's view the study of war should be to establish sufficient military strength to prevent enslavement, and ensure the safety of one's own citizens (Aristotle 1988: 178). The barbarians who understood reason but who did not possess it in the same degree as the Greeks deserved to be enslaved. But he did not sanction imperialistic adventurism, or self-interest as the motive for ruling over other peoples. If an empire is to be acquired, he insists, it should be 'for the good of the governed, and not for the sake of exercising a general despotism' (Aristotle 1988: 178).

This is not to say that there were not opponents of such a neat division of the world into the superior Greeks and inferior barbarians. As Hellenism became more associated with the spirit it had the potential to reach beyond nationality and race. The predominant focus of philosophy on ethical qualities, virtues, and knowledge led to an acknowledgement that barbarians may also share in them to a greater or lesser degree. These signs of a growing cosmopolitanism were exhibited, for example, in Euripides, Democritus, Hippias, and Antiphon (Schlaifer 1936: 170).

Alexander the Great, who was taught by Aristotle, attempted to overcome the divisions between Greeks and Persians in the idea of a universal concord and fellowship, underpinned by a natural equality, based on a religious conviction that God had entrusted him with the mission of harmonising and reconciling the world. Plutarch writes of Alexander that he: 'Did not overrun Asia in the spirit of a brigand, or as if it were a booty and the spoils of war...He wished to show that all things on earth were subject to one principle (*logos*) and included in one polity (*politeia*), and that all men were one people; and he demeaned himself accordingly' (Plutarch in Barker 1956: 8). The achievements of Alexander had some effect on the thinking of the Stoics, even if one does not subscribe to the view that he was the first to commit himself to the brotherhood of man (Watson 1971: 219). The shift of focus had already begun when such sophists as Antiphon found a fundamental unity of humanity in our common nature. Elsewhere Hellenism was beginning to be seen not as a natural attribute, but as a cultural attainment, shared with those whose intellectual, rather than racial, characteristics had been shaped by a similar education. Isocrates saw in the rise of Macedon the possibility of the realisation of a greater unity because the division between Greek and barbarian was not natural, and was, indeed, permeable. Conversion was a matter of individual intellectual effort (Linklater 1990: 21–2).

The ideals of Plato and Aristotle were abandoned by the Cynics who denied that the man of virtue and wisdom was subject to the law of any particular state. Wise men shared in a universal wisdom, and the law to which they were subject was that of virtue. The ties of the community were customary and conventional. The institutional constraints associated with them should be abandoned by the man of wisdom who transcends such encumbrances. The lot of the vast majority of humanity, however, was foolishness and ignorance. Cynicism was a negative doctrine in its rejection of the constraints of the city state and its conventional values, and not as such a celebration of cosmopolitanism.

What needs to be emphasized before discussing the Stoic notion of natural law, is that for the Ancient Greeks natural law was a deliberately ambiguous term because of the variety of meanings that both 'natural' and 'law' possessed, compounded when the terms were used together. Natural law implies a blurring or bringing together the distinction between *nomos* and *phusis*. The ambiguity was indeed often exploited by blurring the distinction between description and prescription (Watson 1971: 217, 221).

THE GREEK AND ROMAN STOICS

Epicureanism, as MacIntyre suggests, provided the rationale for withdrawal from public life, whereas Stoicism offers better reasons for participation in it (MacIntyre 1967: 108). Both doctrines were espoused in the fourth century BC, and famously find clear expression in two lectures on the principles of political order or justice delivered by Carneades, a citizen of Athens leading a diplomatic mission to Rome in 155 BC. On the first day he gave the Epicurean answer, and on the second the Stoic. The Epicureans provide an example, in addition to the Cynics, of turning away from the city state. The individual is viewed in the wider cosmic context, but it does not in itself succeed in providing a firm moral foundation. They posit a cosmic physical determinism, in the manner of Democritus, in which morality is a resident alien. The circumstances of ordinary mortals were a matter of indifference to the gods who did not therefore provide moral guidance (MacIntyre 1967: 107). Epicureans were not crude hedonists, but pleasure was their main goal, which was derived, not from indulgence in sensual pleasures but from an absence of pain and a lack of turmoil in the soul. Pleasure is not a matter of satisfying desires, but instead that of the mind at rest: 'For we do everything for the sake of being neither in pain nor in terror' (Epicurus in Inwood and Gerson, eds. 1988: 24 [10.28]). Situations that arouse emotions and cause perturbations should be avoided: 'The purest security is that which comes from a quiet life and withdrawal from the many' (Diogenes in Inwood and Gerson, eds. 1988: 27 [10 maxim, xiv]). Political life, except in extreme circumstances is to be avoided, in preference for a life spent in friendship with a small number of associates. Justice for Epicurus is that which is useful in human associations to prevent mutual harm. It is agreed proscriptions among individuals or nations. This is not to say that anything that is agreed must be just. Some agreements are naturally entailed in the development of society, and only those are just which benefit all of the members of a society that makes them (Sharples 1996: 116–7). Injustice is not intrinsically bad, but is to be avoided because after committing a crime the fear of being detected has an unsettling effect. No one can be confident of escaping detection (Diogenes in Inwood and Gerson, eds. 1988: 28 [10 maxims, xxxi–xxxv]). The inevitable anxiety of detection outweighs the appeal of committing crimes, and therefore acts as a deterrent.

Stoic philosophy was the dominant way of thinking in the late Roman republic, and the early empire. Almost all Roman jurists subscribed to Stoic principles, as did those Romans who were attracted to philosophical thinking, particularly Cicero who lived towards the end of the Republic; Seneca, a Roman of the first century AD; and Marcus Aurelius of the second (Kelly 1992: 48). While it is possible to find theories of natural justice in Greek thought, it was the Stoics who were primarily responsible for formulating a theory of natural law. Chrysippus develops the two crucial elements necessary for a theory of natural law. He emphasises the authority and control of law over both the divine and human, providing the criterion by which individuals can identify right and wrong, assisting them in living the good life by recommending what should be done and prohibiting those things that should not (Mitsis 1992: 4815). This is the basis of the Stoic theory that the rules of law are capable of being apprehended by reason and are naturally and universally valid. For the Stoics there is a natural concern among individuals for other human beings.

The writings of the Stoics provide firm foundations for a belief in a universal community subject to universal moral principles that transcend those of particularistic polities. From roughly 300 BC when Zeno (c. 336–264 BC), a native of Cyprus, ventured into Athens to about 200 AD Stoic philosophy was an integral part of the intellectual life of the ancients. The nature of the evidence for their beliefs, which have survived in fragments, has led to the charge of inconsistency between a materialism on the one hand and an intellectual, or rationalist, spiritualism on the other. Zeno believed that philosophical theory has three elements, those which concern nature (*phusis*), character (ethics), and rational discourse (logic), none of which is separate from the others (Diogenes, Inwood and Gerson, eds. 1988: 78–9 [7.38–41]).

For the Stoics only bodies exist, to which there are two related principles, activity and passivity: 'The passive is unqualified substance, i.e., matter, while the active is the rational principle [*logos*] in it, i.e., god. For he being eternal and [penetrating] all of matter, is the craftsman of all things' (Diogenes in Inwood and Gerson, eds. 1988: 96 [7.134]). Bodies are at once material and rational, a unity of *phusis*, or nature, and *logos*. There is no implication that everything in nature is rational. There is a rational order in nature governed by law, and it is therefore intelligible. It is this intelligibility that is the rational principle or *logos*. Plants and animals do not possess the guiding principle rationality, even though they are distinctive in nature and intelligible. Instead, they conform to the rational coherence and order of the universe (Creede 1992: 49).

The principle of rationality, however, guides men, in that it entails a free will. Some commentators have found this hard to reconcile with an apparent determinism, or fate, which implies that everything is as it should be and is the result of a chain of causes within a law-governed universe. (Inwood and Gerson, eds. 1988:127–35).

While Chrysippus subscribed to the idea of inexorable laws of nature, he also retained the notion of moral responsibility. He did this by distinguishing between basic and proximate causes. Basic causes refer to qualities that make a thing what it is. Men have the bodily parts they have, which constitute them as mortal men because of fate. On the other hand, proximate causes are contingent: things that may, or may not happen. A person may die in an aeroplane accident tomorrow, but it may not happen if he or she decides to travel by train. For Chrysippus fate is not that which is necessary in a deterministic sense. It is possible for us to change certain things which therefore render us morally responsible. Identical physical actions may be performed for different reasons. Avoiding a fight by walking away may be an act of cowardice if it is to save oneself from harm, or courageous if one backs down to avoid inflicting harm on another, despite the risk of losing one's reputation (MacIntyre 1967: 105). All causes would be basic if fate were derministic, and there would be no proximate causes. For Chrysippus things are true that have already happened in the past because they can no longer change. The same is true of present happenings. As far as the future is concerned what happens, happens; what will be will be, it is fate. This does not mean that by what will be will be, he meant *must* be (Rist 1977: 112–32).[2]

To live according to nature is the Stoic's most forceful injunction. This is not an injunction to pursue a primary impulse to seek pleasure. Nature is not being used in its descriptive sense. Self-preservation is the primary impulse that men share

---

[2] I have drawn upon the fine discussion of Fate and Necessity in J. M. Rist (1977: 112–32). St. Augustine's interpretation of the Stoics is similar. He contends that: 'Among those things which they wished not to be subject to necessity they placed our wills, knowing that they would not be free if subjected to necessity' (Augustine 1974: 184).

with animals, but nature is for the Stoics, as it was for Plato and Aristotle, more than a collection of brute instincts. Instead, nature is seen as a correlative with reason. Man's endowment of reason supervenes on the impulse to self-preservation, and as rational creatures right reason proscribes doing anything that is inconsistent with nature. For the Stoics God is not omnipotent nor absolute. The world necessarily includes moral and physical evil. Good includes its opposite evil as a punishment, as a by-product, or by negligence. Galen, for example, contrasts the Jewish God with that of the Stoics: 'To Moses it seems to be enough that God willed to create a cosmos and presently it was created...we, however...maintain on the contrary that certain things are impossible by nature, and these God would not even attempt to do' (cited in Edelstein 1966: 33).

Appropriate actions were for Zeno those constrained by right reason (Diogenes in Inwood and Gerson, eds. 1988: 139–41 [7.85–88, and 7.108]). To be guided by one's reason is to live according to nature. For the Stoics this results in a personal ethic, and not, as it was for Plato and Aristotle, an ethics of citizenship (Gough 1957: 15). Why, then, should the Stoic have concern for others? He may possess the virtues, but may have hardly any need of other persons. The Stoic may have knowledge of what is good or bad, the virtue of insight; have knowledge of what to fear and what not to fear, namely courage; knowledge of what to choose and what to avoid, that is the virtue of moderation. These virtues appear to be of use to himself and not to others (Edelstein 1966: 41). For the Stoics, reason as a guide to conduct is universal. Reason and nature, including human nature, because they are synonymous means that there are universal laws of nature to which we are all subject. To live according to reason is to live both socially and morally. Moral life requires a person capable of reasoning, and living morally entails living socially.

The Stoics maintain that the sage is endowed with a fourth virtue, in addition to insight, courage, and moderation, that of justice, knowledge of what one ought and ought not to give to others. Those who live according to reason have everything that is good in common. Doing good to others is necessarily to do good to oneself, and to harm others is to harm oneself. In contrast with the ideal of the Epicurean sage who longs to live secluded from the world, the Stoic way of life postulates living with others as its highest ideal. The Stoic sage is duty-bound never to think of himself as an isolated individual (Edelstein 1966: 72). For the Stoics the sage is born for others, not for the community in which he lives but for the community of mankind. We are all children of God, and those who follow reason come to have an awareness of this truth. It is only those who fail to follow their own reason who believe that their good is opposed to that of others. It is they who are condemned to live an isolated existence and are enemies of one another (Edelstein 1966: 42). In practical terms, this distinction between the wise man and the fool is the weakness that exposed Stoicism to the criticism of the Sceptics.

Reason and nature, for the Stoics, dispose us to practise the fundamental virtues of justice, courage, prudence, and temperance. Virtue is indivisible and it is therefore not possible to possess one to the exclusion of the others. One is either virtuous or not; there are no half measures. Virtue is intrinsically good and is pursued for its own sake, 'not because of some fear or hope or some extrinsic consideration' (Diogenes in Inwood and Gerson, eds. 1988: 137 [7.89]). Justice and morality are not for the Stoic conventional. They are natural because they follow from man's rationality (Diogenes in Inwood and Gerson, eds. 1988: 145 [7.128]). The cultivation of reason, peculiar to man, inevitably gives rise to a social life governed by morality and justice.

For the Stoic reason is exhibited in the law-governed universe, which betrays the existence of a rational lawgiver, God (Berki 1977: 57). The principles of natural law are ideal in that they become manifest only if men attain perfect rationality. For example, take the principle of equality. Zeno taught that we are naturally equal because we are rational creatures. The distinction between Greeks and barbarians, as it was for the Cynics, was merely conventional. The woman is equal to the man. They have the same virtue, and matrimony was much more than a unity of the body, it was also a unity of the soul. The husband finds his other self and his truest friend in his wife. Women were not deemed the property of men to do with as they pleased. The human qualities and the common life of both partners are enhanced in their union. In addition there is a natural equality of slave and master. Natural slavery is a misnomer, an impossibility contrary to nature; there are only enslaved individuals finding themselves in that condition through folly and wickedness.

Edelstein argues that in the Stoics we find the first steps in the acknowledgement of the dignity, rights, and humanity of other persons, including women and children. The choices of children to pursue their own way of life, and to educate themselves must be respected (Edelstein 1966: 74). Moreover, the Stoics also elevated the value of manual labour from the distain in which it was usually held by Greeks and Romans. Manual work is natural to humanity and in no way diminishes a person's capacity for a virtuous life. Manual labour is part of and is compatible with the moral order. The skills of an artisan are of no less value than the money of a businessman. They are equal with each other in wealth, the one in terms of skill or manual strength, the other in terms of capital. For both moral character must shine through their actions. Every workshop is a school of virtue.

Stoics and Cynics resemble each other in the distinction they make between the wise man and the fool. Wise men compose the world state, whereas only fools live in actual states. Chrysippus thought that the wise share a common citizenship of the city of the world (Sharples 1996: 125). Diogenes Laertius reports that Zeno denigrated general culture and believed that 'all those who are not virtuous are hostile and enemies and slaves and alien to each other, parents to children and brothers to brothers [and] relatives to relatives' (Diogenes, in Inwood and Gerson, eds. 1988: 74–5 [7.32]).

Stoicism's tendency to become divorced from the world as it was, positing a law to be emulated, but of no man's making, exposed it to criticism, especially from the Sceptics, among whom was Carneades who made it his vocation to expose the weaknesses of Stoic arguments (Diogenes in Inwood and Gerson, eds. 1988: 160. [4.62]).

In the first of his lectures in Rome Carneades gave the typically Stoic answer to the question of what are the principles of political order. He argued that there was order in the cosmos, governed by natural law, and that order in civil society was a reflection of the eternal natural order, discernible by human beings on account of their faculty of reason. Through the exercise of reason human beings were able to apprehend the natural law and construct societies whose social and legal structure replicated it. Even though humans had the capacity to construct arrangements that reflected this natural law, or order, they did not always succeed. Conformity to the rational order of the cosmos constituted just conduct in both the individual and society (Oakeshott 2006: 162–3).

On the second day Carneades gave the alternative Epicurean answer to the same question. He denied that the cosmos was a rational order exhibiting anything like a principle of justice with the authority to give each man his due. The cosmos was a fortuitous collection of atoms exhibiting no rational principle upon which human societies could be modelled. He argued that there is no certain criterion of truth (Sextus in Inwood and Gerson, eds. 1988: 166 [M. 7.159]) on the basis of which he subjected the major doctrines of Stoicism to sustained criticism. He argued that there is no such thing as natural law. The laws of states are simply conventional expressions of self-interest. Justice, or attending to the interests of others, is nothing but foolishness. War is the method by which all kingdoms and empires are acquired, and necessarily inflict injury on others and their gods. The Romans did not acquire their empire and riches by justice, and if they were required to return them, they would be obliged to revert back to dwelling in huts (Carneades view is expressed in Cicero 1986: 200–15).

The Stoics are not advocating a cosmopolis that would replace individual states. The universal law of nature is a guide to personal conduct, but we are unequivocally social creatures whose lived existence is within particular states, to whose laws we are subject. This means that to act appropriately, that is, according to reason, is to love one's fatherland, and among the goods external to oneself is a 'virtuous fatherland' (Diogenes in Inwood and Gerson, eds. 1988: 139 and 140 [7.95 and 7.108]). Ultimately, however, as rational creatures, we are united in a single cosmopolis, or city of God. All men, then, should consider themselves as fellow citizens subject to a common order (Barker 1934: xxxv). This vision of the world state is primarily religious and ethical, rather than political. It emphasises the point that a supreme law-giver regulates a rationally ordered cosmos in which we all have a common place. The vision is ethical because of its emphasis upon reason as the universal bond of mankind. It was these elements, rather than a conception of the state, or world state that gave the Stoics lasting significance.

In response to the scathing criticisms of the Sceptics, Panaetius of Rhodes, the then head of the Stoic school, in the second century BC, modified Stoicism which gave hope to those who had not yet attained virtue, but who were nevertheless striving towards it (Walbank 1992: 181). By means of services or duties regularly rendered, and not by the exercise of perfect virtue, man is making tentative progress towards attaining wisdom. Unlike traditional Stoics he rejected the claim that all human psychology can be traced back to the faculty of reason. Instead, Panaetius suggested that the psyche has both rational and irrational elements which have to be accommodated. *Pace* earlier Stoics he maintained that external things, such as property and health, are goods to be valued and pursued, not merely because they give content to virtue and a domain for its exercise, but also because they are valuable in themselves as long as they do not come into conflict with virtue (Arnold 1911: 100–3). For Panaetius, it was not possibile to live the life of perfect apathy. Instead of emphasising wisdom above all other virtues, as traditional Stoicism did, he privileged temperance, or soberness. Greater practical import was to be attained by acting with decorum. For Panaetius the natural law was a principle embodied in varying degrees in actual states, and not an ideal regulating the community of wise men. Political power is distinguishable from force, and justifiable as legitimate, with reference to the justness of its exercise and the rightness of its aims. Panaetius' form of Stoicism, accepting elements of Platonism, Aristotelianism, and the criticisms of Carneades, found sympathy among his Roman friends. One of them was Scipio Africanus minor (168–129 BC), the principal interlocutor in Cicero's *Commonwealth* (Sabine and Smith, 'Introduction' to Cicero, 1986: 32).

To a State that was gradually incorporating the peoples of the known world under its dominion, some of the Stoic doctrines, such as universal citizenship and the brotherhood of man, made it particularly attractive (McIlwain 1932: 106). The law of nature, or of reason, which found expression in Roman law was to have a profound influence on subsequent political thought. Towards the middle of the second century BC, soon after the Greeks had been subdued by the Romans, Stoicism, in the modified form represented by Panaetius, was adopted by Roman thinkers. The idea of a cosmic city, in contrast to the city in which one happens to be born, as Malcolm Schofield argues, 'mediates the transition from republicanism to natural law' (Schofield 1991: 103). The idea of the cosmic city attempts to retain the association between community and citizenship, while eliminating all contingency, such as geographic location and mutual acquaintance. Citizenship now becomes obedience to the dictates of right reason concerning the just treatment of other persons.

The most significant Roman Stoics were the eclectic consul Cicero (106–43 BC), Seneca (5 BC–65 AD) and the Emperor Marcus Aurelius Antoninus (121–180 AD), the author of the famous *Meditations*. On the whole they accepted the answers to the problems of logic and metaphysics offered by their Greek predecessors, enabling them to concentrate more fully on ethical and social problems.

CICERO (c. 106–43 BC)

It has been suggested by Gerard Watson that the name of the Stoics has been associated with natural law in later ages mainly because of Cicero (Watson 1971:

217–18). Cicero, the court advocate and politician, in dealing with the minutiae of ordinary law, rarely mentions the natural law, but as a philosopher Cicero attributed to human positive law a subordinate status to that of the law of nature (Kelly 1992: 59). Cicero rejects the view of Epicurus and Carneades that justice is simply convention devised by men to advance their own utility. For him, justice is a principle of the universal law of nature upon which the order of the universe rests. It is correlative with true or right reason, in conformity with nature, constant and eternal. This law compels us to fulfil our duties, and deters us from practising deceit (Carlyle 1970: vol. 1, 5–6). Both Cicero, and later Seneca, but not without a degree of inconsistency, reject Aristotle's argument that there is a natural inequality that befits some men to be slaves. Instead, Cicero and Seneca emphasize natural equality which is manifest in a universal capacity for learning. Nature has endowed all men with reason, namely right or true reason, revelatory of true law in commanding what is good and forbidding what is sinful or evil. Cicero is important not because he added anything new to ethics and political philosophy, but because he exemplifies the concerns of the later republic and the extent of Greek influence upon Roman thought. In order to advance his arguments he eclectically used whatever materials were to hand. Like the Stoics he believed in a universal fellowship of the human race, but he did not confine it to the wise, and in addition he allied it with the Roman idea of the Law of Nations (Sharples 1996:127). The fellowship is natural and based upon the unifying principles of reason, speech, and natural equality (Cicero 1991: I, 50, p. 21). There is no institutional expression in Cicero for this universal society, encompassing the whole of humanity. It is a fellowship established by the gods in which right reason, the 'royal power in the souls of men' (Cicero 1986: Book I, xxxviii, p. 144) accords with nature. Reason is what unites men with each other and with the gods. Cicero argues that the first thing that self-knowledge reveals to us is that we possess something of the divine, and that the reason that resides in us 'is a sort of consecrated image of the divine' (Cicero 1999: 126 [Book I, 59]).

Reason in harmony with nature exhibits a law that is unchanging and universal. This law is not thought up by human minds, nor is it legislation enacted by popular assemblies, 'but it is something eternal which rules the entire universe through the wisdom of its commands and prohibitions' (Cicero 1999: 132 [Book II, 9]). It acts as a constraint on wrongdoing for good men, but the wicked who have abandoned their better selves cannot be constrained. They may evade human punishment, but God nevertheless will visit the severest of consequences on them. Natural law cannot be annulled, and no act of human legislatures can absolve us from the duty of obedience to it (Cicero 1986: Book, III, xxii, p. 215–6). Cicero equates this natural law, or *ius naturale*, with the Law of Nations, *ius gentium*. He contends that it is ordained by nature and gives the substantive content of men's moral relations with each other, and the relations among the states in which they reside. *Ius civile*, or human positive law, is not wholly incorporated in *ius gentium*, but the whole of *ius gentium* should be incorporated in *ius civile* (Cicero 1991: Book III, 69, p. 126). The meaning and content of these terms is not always consistent among Roman writers, as we will see.

How does this natural law, or the Law of Nations, translate into prohibitions or injunctions to act? Cicero on the whole concentrates his efforts on the duties of citizens, and gives little attention to the duties of men to each other. The effects of his main prohibition, however, are wide-ranging. There is nothing so at variance with nature, and therefore nothing worse than benefiting at the expense of another. It is completely against our common fellowship of mankind to benefit by theft or violence. Respect for property is therefore a basic human duty, the disregard of which 'is more contrary to nature than death or pain or anything else of the type' (Cicero 1999: Book III, 24, p. 109) because it is destructive of human fellowship and community (Cicero 1999: Book III, 22, p. 108 and III, 28, p. 110).

Does this entail a positive duty at the general level of communal ties and obligations above that of desisting from profiting by violence? There appears to be no indication of a duty to make material sacrifices for the benefit of peoples of other nations who are in need: 'each should attend to what benefits him himself, so far as may be done without injustice to another' (Cicero 1999: Book III, 42, p. 115). Cicero explicitly says that we should not forego personal benefits by surrendering them to others if we ourselves are in need of them (Cicero 1999: III, 42, p. 115).

Human beings comprise a moral community united by reason and fellowship, but this community does not exhaust the extent of moral obligation. Although our obligations under the natural law, or Law of Nations, cannot be ignored, there are obligations which we owe to the state, to our relatives, and to our fellow citizens. They all may have a greater claim upon us when it comes to the active discharge of moral responsibilities. The world is one community, made up of many communities, each of which claims loyalty and affection from those individuals who belong to them.

While the early Stoics emphasized the virtue of wisdom and the community of the wise, Cicero favours the virtue of justice, in the absence of which the natural sociability of man would be undermined, and the nobility of spirit arising out of the love of learning would become little more than a form of savagery. Cicero argues that humans naturally and instinctively associate. It is not fear, nor want of necessities, that bring them together but their natural gregariousness (Cicero 1986: Book I, xxv, p. 129). The social duties that strengthen the social bond which unites us 'must be preferred to the duty that is limited to learning and knowledge' (Cicero 1991: I, 157, p. 61).

Fellowship is manifest in different degrees, ranging from the unlimited fellowship of the human species, to the more strictly limited fellowship of the family. The instinct of procreation gives rise to the fellowship of marriage, children, and the household that is communally shared. Fellowship extends outside of the household to the wider community of friends and relations, and intermarriage extends the bonds of fellowship to a wider circle of relatives, and eventually to the establishment of political communities (Cicero 1991: Book I, 54, p. 23). The Commonwealth, or 'the people's affair', is a specific type of association in which individuals are 'united by a common agreement about law and rights and by the desire to participate in mutual advantages' (Cicero 1986: Book I, xxv–xxvi, pp. 129–31). Furthermore, there are bonds of language, tribe, and race that are held together by love and good will, strengthened by common ancestral memories and religious rites.

Cicero makes it clear which among the levels of fellowship is the most precious. Of them all 'none is more serious, and none dearer, than that of each of us with the republic' (Cicero 1991: Book I, 57, p. 23. Cf. Book III, 95, p. 137). Sacrificing one's life for the benefit of the state is what is expected of all good men. The state is not a mere convenience for promoting individual interests, a refuge in a storm, or a sanctity for private learning and undisturbed leisure. To it we have a duty of public service. The state claims for itself the greater part of our physical and mental powers, and in return gives back for the benefit of private needs only that which is superfluous for its own (Cicero 1986: Book I, V, p. 110). The benefits that the state bestows upon us are so great that it is more venerable than a natural parent, and to it we owe a greater gratitude (Cicero 1986: Book I, fragment 2, p. 152). There is then a tension between the duties of men and those of citizens, and Cicero comes down on the side of the latter. For example, the bond of connection between all men implies the basic principle of generosity to strangers. The justification for this is that we all have a right to the things that nature has produced for us to enjoy in common. Such a right is, however, severely tempered by the injunction to respect private property as instituted in the civil laws of particular states (Keene 2005: 51).

It is only on moral grounds consistent with natural law that the exercise of political power may be justified. On this criterion he condoned the murder of Caesar on the grounds that fellowship between a people and a tyrant was impossible because tyrants are unjust and arbitrary rulers unconstrained by standards of civilized conduct and common decency. Tyrants in fact fall short of being human beings because of their wilful disregard of civilized conduct, and beastly demeanour (Cicero 1986: Book II, xxvi, p. 178–9). Tyrants are cancerous growths upon humanity that should be cut out with the surgeon's knife (Cicero 1986: Book III, 19, p. 107, and Book III, 32, p. 111).

Cicero argues that we are not born for ourselves. Our country and friends have claims upon us. Furthermore, we are born as humans to assist each other and have a duty to promote our common fellowship by exchanging goods, services and expertise. Injustice is not only caused by directly inflicting harm, but also by desisting from trying to prevent it being inflicted by others. He argues that: 'the man who does not defend someone, or obstructs injustice when he can, is at fault just as if he had abandoned his parents or his friends or his country' (Cicero 1991: I, 23, p. 10).

Cicero defends the method by which Rome acquired its empire by suggesting that its wars were just because they were in defence of Rome's allies and undertaken only as a last resort to secure peace and eliminate injustices. In this respect Rome, in relation to its empire, is best seen as a protectorate rather than a conqueror. Cicero was, of course, well aware that the allies Rome chose to protect were acquisitions.

Cicero contends that Rome now has power over the whole world, enjoying immense benefits as a consequence. Philus rhetorically asks in Cicero's *Commonwealth*, 'Was it by justice or by prudence that our nations rose from the least among states [to be the greatest of all]?' (Cicero 1986: Book III, xv, p. 211). In what remains of the text, however, we do not have his answer. In apparent disregard of his subscription to the principles of just war, and his view of Rome before Sulla as a protectorate, he appears in one passage of *On Duties* to condone whatever means are necessary to increase the power, land and revenues of Rome: 'Such are the deeds of men who are great; such deeds were achieved in our forefathers' day. Men who pursue these kinds of duties will win, along with the utmost benefit to the republic, both great gratitude and great glory for themselves' (Cicero 1991: Book II, 85, pp. 98–9). He nevertheless abhorred ruthless imperialism, holding it responsible for the decline of the state, and certainly would not subscribe to anything like the doctrine of reason of state.

Cicero developed his ideas on natural law in his treatise *On the Laws* (*De legibus*). In it he argues that people tend to think of law as that which is written down, but Cicero maintains that he will seek the root of justice in nature. When used in relation to man the term nature means reason. It is because of his reasoning abilities that man is naturally superior to animals, and better able than them to conceive of a wider community. This distinguishing feature of man entails wider obligations extensive with humanity in general. It is law that guides and enables man to discharge his wider obligations. The exemplar for all particularistic laws is the law of nature (Watson, 1971: 228). This law of nature has its origin in God, and is His Supreme Law in relation to which justice may be determined. The Supreme Law existed before any written laws and before any states were established (Cicero 1999: Book I, 19, p.111, Kelly 1991: 58). Cicero is at pains to show that just because a law is granted authority because it has been formulated by the acknowledged and legitimate procedure, does not mean that it is just. Cicero maintains that 'we are born for justice and that justice is established not by opinion but by nature' (Cicero 1999: Book I, 28, p.115). For that, it has to be based on right reason, and not on mere agreement in the edicts of the people or of princes, or in the decisions of judges. Although Cicero offers a strong moral condemnation of the injustice of positive laws that are at variance with natural law, he does not in fact declare them invalid.

SENECA (5 BC–65 AD) AND MARCUS AURELIUS (AD 121–180)

For Seneca and the Stoics of the early Empire, such as Musonius Rufus, Epictetus, and Marcus Aurelius the true city is a cosmic city. Seneca almost never refers to natural law, but the term nature appears to mean the same thing. To live in conformity with nature is to conform to the commands of reason. Nature is perpetual and constant, that which varies cannot be natural. Nature impresses upon us the true method of living one's life (Carlyle 1970: vol. I, 20). The quality of our lives depends upon the degree to which we actively use our rational capacities in future plans and bringing them to a conclusion. Nature has established norms for human life and we must use our powers of rationality to conform as close as we can to what nature prescribes. Such norms would include a healthy body and the absence of physical pain, material resources to maintain a commodious life, a settled and loving family life, and because of the social character of our natures, cooperation with and support of each member of humankind. It follows that we should avoid those things, or passions, that go against nature. This would include, for example, anger. Seneca maintains: 'Anger, I say, has this evil: it refuses to be governed. It rages at truth itself, if truth appears to conflict with its wishes' (Seneca 1995: Book I, 19, p. 37). Peace, or tranquillity is attained only in good conduct and the practice of wholesome precepts brought about by focusing upon and desiring virtue (Seneca 1995: Book III, 41, p. 114).

Seneca maintains that there are two commonwealths. The one great and truly Commonwealth in which gods and men reside. Zeus is the author of nature, its driving intelligence, and we are the only creatures that share in his rationality. The other commonwealth is the one that the particular circumstances of our birth have assigned us (Schofield 1991: 93). In conformity with and going beyond Cicero, Seneca contends that human nature is the same in the slave as it is in the master. Slaves are capable, as are free men, of conferring benefits by intent. Virtue is an attainment within the grasp of all, and knows no distinctions between wealth nor status. Slavery is not a natural condition, it is against nature, the product of fortune, and while it may subdue the body, it cannot subdue the mind. A truly virtuous and great man can come from a den of iniquity, or a palace. Nature turns no one away from her door. One looks not to the origins, but to the direction they lead (Timothy 1973: 40). Virtue is the highest good, and intrinsically valuable. The gain of having done something good is that you have done it, and it is reward enough in itself: 'We have to go to her with self-interest trampled underfoot; wherever she has summoned us, wherever she sends us, we must go, no matter what the cost, even to the cost of our very blood' (cited in Timothy 1973: 35). Happiness consists in goodness for goodness sake (Timothy 1973: 40). While such phrases are rhetorical, they nevertheless express the aspirations of human freedom and equality upon which the obligations and rights attributed to humans, as human, universally rest.

We should not assume that Seneca had an exalted view of human nature. He was well aware of human depravity, and like Augustine after him believed that man had, from an innocent and happy condition, descended into depravity. The state or government was both a consequence of this corruption, and the means of deliverance from it. The great institutions of society are a protection against vice: the institution of private property against the avarice of others; and a legal and governmental order a protection against tyranny. Government, then, is not a consequence of man's true nature, but instead a remedy for his corrupt nature (Carlyle 1970: vol. I, 25).

The Emperor Marcus Aurelius, and other Stoics writing in Greek, including Epictetus, ignored philosophers writing in Latin. Neither Aurelius nor Epictetus quotes from, nor discusses the ideas of Seneca (Seneca, introduction, 1995: xxxi). Aurelius argued that everything in the cosmos is implicated, and co-ordinated to constitute one ordered universe, pervaded by God who has provided one substance, law, reason and truth for all rational animals (Aurelius: no date: V, 16., VII, p. 9). It is not because we can have direct knowledge of the forms of his powers that we know God exists, but because we see his works all around us. We share in divinity because we have reason and intelligence like gods, despite having bodies like the animals. For Aurelius, everything is constituted for a purpose, and directed towards it because it is advantageous or good for it. Man, the possessor of reason, is made for society and in it finds his good (Aurelius, no date: V, p. 16). Rational animals are made to assist each other in society, and therefore injuries inflicted upon each other are acts of impiety against 'the highest divinity' (Aurelius, no date: IX, p. 1). Self-interested acts that have no immediate or remote social purpose are unnatural in that they go against reason (Aurelius, no date: IX, p. 23). Reason demands that we behave towards each other 'according to the natural law of fellowship with benevolence and justice' (Aurelius, no date: III, p. 11).

Marcus Aurelius sums up his philosophy in the following way:

If our intellectual part is common, the reason also in respect of which we are rational beings, is common: if this is so, common also is the reason which commands us what to do, and what not to do; if this is so, there is a common law also; if this is so, we are fellow-citizens; if this is so, we are members of some political community; if this is so, the world is in a manner a state. For of what other common political community will any one say that the whole human race are members? (Aurelius, no date: IV, p. 4).

He famously adds that, 'my nature is rational and social; and my city and country, so far as I am Antoninus, is Rome, but so far as I am a man, it is the world' (Aurelius, no date: VI, p. 43). The universal community in which every man is kin to every other man is not united by means of blood ties, but by something far more binding, intelligence, or reason (Aurelius, no date: XII, p. 26).

The Roman Stoics are important because they incorporated Greek philosophical ideas about a universal moral order into the traditional legal ideas of Rome, providing a unifying principle for the empire in the community of reason and reasonableness. It was within the context of the Roman tradition that the concept of a just war arose. In its formative years it was closely attached to religious rites and institutions. As in Greece, the sanction of the gods in matters of war and peace was an extremely important public ritual, and during the period of the kings (735–508 BC) the laws of war and peace were integral to the *jus sacrum*. One of the duties of the college of priest was the administering of the *jus sacrum*. The determination of whether Rome had been unjustly wronged or injured was a religious decision, deliberated by the college of priest. During the Republican period they would make the case for just cause before the Senate, and the Senate and the people of Rome decided whether to embark upon war. Such wars were both just and pious. Gradually the role of the priest diminished, and the justness of a war became associated with the infringement of law, that is, Rome had to be deemed legally wronged before a war could be pronounced just. War was therefore subject to both a moral and legal constraint. Cicero developed these ideas by associating the justness of a war with the Stoic idea of a universal moral, or natural law. The mature form of just war doctrine recognized four just causes. First, the violation of the frontiers of Rome; second, the insulting of Roman ambassadors or the violation of their persons; third, the breaking of treaties made with Rome; and, finally, the support of an enemy by a previously friendly nation (Draper 1990: 179).

THE ROMAN JURISTS

Pre-eminent among the values that constituted Roman political culture was that of legality. Michael Oakeshott contends that: 'The law of the Romans is by far the most comprehensive and elaborate system of law that any people, save in modern times, ever generated for themselves' (Oakeshott 2006: 235). A. P. D'Entréves suggests that the establishment of a universally valid system of laws was the greatest achievement in the development of natural law. This system found expression in the law books of the Roman emperor Justinian, who claimed universal validity for it (D'Entréves 1972: 24–5).

The idea of the law of nature (*lex naturalis*) was a concept that the Romans used to understand the relationship between law and justice. The legitimacy of a law may be determined because it came into being through the proper procedure, and therefore commands my obedience. Such a law may nevertheless still be considered to be unjust. Justice was the correspondence of an act, demand or duty with law. In order to determine the justice of law, that is *lex* or man made law, another law must be invoked that was not man-made, and not suspect itself of being unjust. Where *lex* was deemed unreasonable, appeal could be made to reason itself, expressed in natural law (Oakeshott 2006: 245).

The Carlyles sound a note of caution in understanding the theories of the lawyers on natural law and its relation to the Law of Nations, a difficulty compounded by the compilers of Justinian's *Institutes* which include incoherent and contradictory conceptions of it (Carlyle 1970: vol. I, 36). Gaius in the middle of the second century viewed the relation between natural law and the Law of Nations as essentially consistent and compatible, whereas by the end of the century Ulpian took the view that was to prevail among medieval thinkers. For him the two forms of law were to be sharply distinguished. Natural law for him is related to all God's creatures, and was in this sense naturalistic, whereas the Law of Nations is equated with reason. The compilers of Justinian's *Institutes* largely follow the lines of distinguishing the two forms of law, and on the whole think of natural law in a naturalistic or descriptive sense, but there are passages where it is intimated that this law has divine origin and is immutable in character (Carlyle 1970: vol. I, 72–4)

Gaius puts forward a number of propositions that makes his theory clear. First, the Law of Nations is universal, and embodies principles that are acknowledged by humanity. Second, these principles are taught to human beings from the earliest times by natural, or right reason. Property, for example, traditionally belongs to the Law of Nations, and is consistent with natural equity. In the *Institutes* of Gaius the law of nations is defined as that which natural reason, in its practical sense, has established among nations in their relations with each other (Kelly 1992: 61). Contrary to what is implied, the Roman jurists did not engage in comparative studies of legal systems in order to discern the *jus gentium*, instead they took elements of Roman law applicable to citizens that were general in principle and extended them to have application to disputes between foreigners on Roman territory or between a Roman and a foreigner.

The purpose of natural law, as the Romans understood it, was to temper and make more acceptable their archaic and harsh civil law, *jus civile*. Roman expansion required a transformation in its laws to accommodate its newly acquired supranational empire, and natural law proved to be the appropriate agent. In order to minimize the association of law with force Cicero was anxious to show the moral character of the *jus civile* and *jus gentium*. Justice on this reading did not result from law, but was prior to it (Parkinson, 1977: 12–13). In neither the Justinian *Institutes*, not without some equivocation, nor the Ulpian *Digest*, nor indeed in the *Institutes* of Gaius, is natural law posited as superior to human positive law, or *jus civile*. It is not claimed that the former acts as a judge of the latter, nor that it should take precedence in cases of conflict (Barker 1934: xxxvi–xxxvii, and Zuckert 1989: 76–7). Furthermore, it does not bestow upon human beings inalienable rights. Its importance was that it established the idea of the inherent value and worth of law, and of its equal applicability to everyone. It was a law based not on its power to compel, but instead upon its intrinsic worth (D'Entreves 1972: 35).

The Justinian code, for example, which was a compilation of existing codes, embodied many inconsistencies. The Roman Jurists used such terms as natural law (*ius naturale*) and natural reason (*naturalis ratio*) to refer to the natural characteristics of humans and the common sense that may be derived from such knowledge. It referred to the physical qualities of persons and things, and also to such things as business relations. It may also be invoked as a practical guide to what is consistent with human interests in a certain social context. Practical natural law is what offers itself as self-evident or 'natural', such as rules for dealing with property or for the treatment of children. This use of natural law was practical and mundane and did not have the aura of a transcendental natural law, the expression of God's reason. It is clear, however, in Gaius that generically law does not express the will of man. It is not created to serve utility, instead it is learned by rational apprehension. However, for Ulpian, the meaning of natural law takes on a more naturalistic character, reflecting a tension that has persisted to this day between descriptive and prescriptive conceptions of the natural law. The Carlyles are groping towards this distinction when they acknowledge that Ulpian appears to be talking about general instincts rather than anything that is rational or ethical (Carlyle 1970: vol. I, 40). For Ulpian the natural law is common to all animals. It is more like natural instincts, powers and inclination. The innate urge towards procreation and the caring for children is common to all animals, and not peculiar to man. The *jus gentium*, or Law of Nations, however, is that law which the nations observe in their relations. Unlike the natural law, it is a law peculiar to men (Carlyle 1970: vol. I, 39–40). The distinction between the two kinds of law is maintained by the compilers of Justinian's *Institutes* in the sixth century (Carlyle 1970: vol. I, 70).

As a practical legal ideal natural law was understood to be the universal element, as opposed to the parochial and particular elements, found in all legal codes. Natural law for the jurists is not a written code, it is an ideal which imbues the spirit of the application of law in the courts, and in this respect has some practical bearing upon it.

It is as a legal ideal that the *jus gentium* was often identified with natural law, or *jus naturale*, which according to Michael P. Zuckert is the law imposed on all creatures, it is 'that which nature has taught all animals' (Zuckert 1989: 76. Cf. Phillipson, 1911: 83). He suggests that much of the confusion about Roman Jurists' conceptions of natural law arises out of confusing them with those of Stoicism in which it is peculiar to humanity and discovered by right reason in conformity with nature, and the later Christian conception in which it stands above human law and acts as its judge. The *jus gentium* in the *Digest* is related to natural law, but is more strictly applicable to all of humanity, and in this respect it also can be deemed natural, but in a different sense from *jus naturale*. The natural law, *jus naturale*, for example, is sometimes different from the Law of Nations, *jus gentium*, and at other times identified with it. This reflects the equivocal meanings that they had from at least the time of Cicero. The *Digest* does not attribute to natural law the character that it was later to have. It does not override human positive law, but good law is that which is grounded on nature, reason, equity, and justice (Kretzmann et al. 1982: 705). In practical terms the *jus gentium* was a body of customs and agreements constituted into a body of commercial law, applicable to both citizens and foreigners in their commercial relations, and enforceable in the courts.

With respect to slavery the Roman Jurists do not on the whole sympathize with Aristotle. In so far as they give an explanation of their views, they are more inclined towards the positions of Cicero and Seneca. Gaius, and later Marcanianus, for example, although they say nothing of natural equality, suggest that the slave is legally *in postate*, and that the institution of slavery exists under *jus gentium*, and not natural law. The origin of slavery, they believe, is in capture during war. In addition, for Marcanianus, children born to slave women are also in a condition of slavery. Ulpian and Florentinus are more elucidating in that they clearly deny that slavery has any place under the *jus naturale* because under it men are free and equal. For the latter, a slave is so called because his life is preserved, which could have been taken away under the laws of war (Carlyle 1970: vol. I, 46–7). There was, then, a glimmering recognition of a common humanity, along with which came recognition that even slaves, who were equal in their capacity for reason and virtue with their masters, had certain protections. By the end of the second century, the theory of natural inequality no longer held court, and the natural equality and liberty of human nature was commonly recognized.

CONCLUSION

We see in Stoicism, then, the first glimmering of human equality, that of men, women, children, and slaves. There was an acknowledgement and respect for human dignity, and a belief in a universal moral community in which we have a duty to fulfil our social obligations. For them natural law governs all that is human and divine, and is the standard of what is right and wrong. To have knowledge of natural law, for the old Stoics, was a concomitant of the exercise of reason, the reason that informs men of their duties to their families, and of their economic obligations, as well as what it is to act fairly and justly. By the light of reason there is a natural equality of humankind. For the younger Stoics the voice of natural law was not only heard in reason, but also in one's conscience. For Seneca, conscience not only legislates before we act, but also judges afterwards. It is the expression of man's wish to be at peace with himself, to live in conformity with his nature and with the world (Edelstein 1966: 84). Conscience acts as the court before which we must answer for our actions. It is the divine voice that speaks within us.

It must be emphasized that reason and conscience do not prescribe inalienable, immutable and imprescriptible rights that were later to become the hallmark of natural rights theories. The natural law imposes obligations to desist from wrong, and to do what is right. It teaches that we must fulfil our obligations as cosmopolitans of the republic of men and as citizens of particular states. We must uphold both the Law of Nations and national laws because both are derived from the natural law.

Whereas the Old Stoa emphasized wisdom, moderation, and courage as the virtues of the individual, and justice as the sum of duties owed to others, the younger Stoics such as Seneca, Cicero, Epictetus, and Philo were more concerned with the altruistic virtue of philanthropy, or *humanitas*. We have a duty of benevolence to all of humanity without distinction because we comprise a brotherhood, a family (Edelstein 1966: 90). It is Cicero's account of natural law that the early Christians, such as Lactantius, Ambrose, and St. Augustine, take as indicative of the Stoic position. Although Cicero readily declares positive laws at variance with the natural as unjust, he is reluctant to declare them invalid. It is not difficult to see, however, how natural law in the hands of medieval Christianity came to acquire the character of an absolute standard against which the laws of princes and kings were to be judged.

2

Christian Natural Law: A Universal Morality

Natural law moral theories are deeply rooted in the culture of the West, emerging time and time again, albeit in slightly different forms. In times of social and political stability their appeal may not be so strong, but at times when man's inhumanity to man is apparent there are always those voices call our attention to our common humanity and the rights and duties that are correlative with it, and appeal to which transcends particularistic community based moralities, to distil the universal from the transitory (Nielsen 1959: 44). This has nonetheless been true of medieval times as it has been of the twentieth and twenty-first centuries. The early and late medieval conceptions of natural law were an amalgam of Greek and Roman Stoicism, overlaid with Christian conceptions of its derivation from and relation to Divine Law.

When the imperial seat was transferred to Constantinople, and the Empire constantly attacked by Barbarians, the ideal of unity rapidly eroded. With the adoption of Christianity, with its emphasis upon equality and universality, the process of disintegration was temporarily arrested (Parkinson 1977: 14).

Augustine (354–430), a sometime Manichaean and converted Christian, was to question some of the perfectibility theories of the ancients, and instead inclined towards the more sceptical elements of Cicero, especially the emphasis upon grace in the endowment of wisdom. Augustine believed that our ability to know ourselves, rationally to understand our impulses and desires, and those of others, had been severely impaired by the Fall. The impenetrable mystery of one's nature obscures the understanding of whether or not we as human beings are naturally inclined towards virtue. Our experience of the world is one in which we continuously encounter others who are irrational and inconsistent, and for whom the moral good does not appear an absolute priority. It was only through God's grace that a moral person, whose nature had been prepared and redeemed, could comprehend moral development as intelligible and believable. For fallen man, left to his own devices and experiences, the understanding of moral development could be nothing but unintelligible (Coleman 2000: 294–5).

This conception of human nature stood in contrast with that of Aristotle who was to exercise a profound influence on later medieval thought, including that of Aquinas. With the rediscovery of Aristotle, philosophers of the later middle ages tried to reconcile the Greek, Roman, and Christian elements of the moral authority of the natural law. One may without exaggeration identify St. Thomas Aquinas as the epitome of medieval natural law moral theory whose example has inspired moral universalists ever since, including those of the twentieth century, such as

Jaques Maritain, Frederick C. Copleston, James V. Schall, and Jose Manuel de Aguilar, reacting against the subversive and pernicious transformation of morality by totalitarian regimes. Just as St. Thomas has spawned a dual heritage in political philosophy, hailed as both a constitutionalist and absolutist (Greenleaf 1964: 747–60), his theory of natural law is hailed as paradigmatic, yet interpretations abound: on the one hand emphasising the centrality of God to the theory, and on the other the intellectualistic element in his thought that makes natural law independent of God (Lisska 1996).

In this chapter, I want to show how the notion of natural law in the West is inextricably connected to the constellation of ideas surrounding the Christian God and the law-governed nature of the universe. One of the main contentions of this book is that despite arguments to the contrary the natural rights tradition for the most part retained and relied upon these conceptions. During the medieval period the natural law became far more prescriptive and judgmental than it had been in the writings of the Roman Jurists. It now becomes the measure of positive law and of the actions of rulers, and the touchstone by which they may be pronounced illegitimate. This chapter also serves to contrast the pessimism of St. Augustine with the optimism of Aquinas who always held in view the positive possibility and power of redemption. We still find, however, the relationship between natural law and the Law of Nations is far from clear. Aquinas, for example, is equivocal on this issue. For him they are sometimes distinct, yet in other places he equates the secondary natural law, as many others after him, with the Law of Nations.

It is also my aim to introduce the importance of theories of property and their relation to just war theory as essential to understanding the relations among nations. This aspect of natural law thinking becomes crucial for the justification of European expansionism and the appropriation of foreign lands, even though they may be occupied by other peoples. Europeans, or Christians residing in Christendom, were accustomed to confronting beliefs alien from their own, and the cultural encounters of the Americas had their precursors close to home. Christians looked upon Muslims and Jews as distinctive communities of faith differentiated from their own by their own systems of laws. The crusades were a response not only to the enemy from without, the Saracens or anti-Christ Muslims, but also against the enemy within, the Jews who resided in Christendom. The conception of rights associated with the natural law was largely objective, that is, the former were derived from the latter, they were not powers or possessions. That is not to say that there were not strong intimations of subjective rights among medieval thinkers, as shown in Chapter Three.

THE CHURCH FATHERS AND NATURAL LAW

The Christian religion has given permanent character and shape to Europe, and its concept of natural law served as the criterion by which the whole world and its peoples were to be judged. Natural law lies at the heart of European morality and ethics and is widely acknowledged to be one of the fundamental pillars upon which European culture is built. In relation to the Christian community, Gerard Watson argues that Ambrose (c. 338–397) and Augustine 'took natural law from Cicero. Baptised it, and handed it on for preservation in the Church' (Watson 1971: 236). The identification of the natural law with God, which we find in Cicero, was a common tendency among Christian thinkers. Lactantius, for example, a harsh critic of the Greeks, nevertheless agreed with the likes of Zeno that nature, taken in its prescriptive sense, must be the guide of action because it embodies the teaching of God. If man is born to virtue, then it is a good principle that he should follow his nature. In general the Christian fathers believed that the natural law was written by God in men's hearts as an inner guide, or rule, to conduct. It was conferred upon the whole human race. Mosaic law was given to the Israelites because the natural law was being subverted, and was meant to reaffirm it as well as supplement it.

In the pre-Constantine Empire, persecuted Christians found a modified form of Stoicism, which preached equality before God and the hope of salvation, conducive to their condition. The natural law in their hands became far more prescriptive and judgmental than it had been in the hands of the Roman Jurists. Natural law embodied natural justice, taught the intrinsic dignity and worth of every human soul, and was the moral criterion against which human laws should be tested.

Natural law rarely surfaces explicitly in the New Testament, with the exception of a direct reference to it by St. Paul in his 'Letter to the Romans'. Even without knowledge of the Old Testament, he contends, without law, humans by nature do the things law prescribes. This, for him is evidence of a law written in their hearts, and confirmed by the testimony of conscience as if before a court of law (St. Paul, trans. Way, 1926: Romans, ii, 12–14). Natural law is consistent with the Decalogue (Luscombe 1982a: 705). St. Paul does make it clear that all authority derives from God: 'No authority exists save by God's sanction; such as do exist have been appointed by God' (St. Paul 1926: Romans, XIII, i).

The Church fathers were often not very meticulous or precise in the way that they used the term natural law. Often it was used as a way of approving of whatever idea they happened to want to recommend (Watson 1971: 235). Gratian and Rufinus, for example, were emphatic that natural law was superior to civil law, and indeed overrode those laws that were at variance with it. Rufinus maintained that: 'Whatever there may be in the laws of emperors, in the writings of authors, in the examples of saints, contrary to Natural Law, we hold to be null and void' (cited in Carlyle 1970: vol. II, 107).

Whereas the Church fathers preached natural equality, they nevertheless condoned slavery as a corollary of the institution of government, urging slave masters to remember their fundamental equality of souls, to desist from cruelty and forced prostitution. They also encouraged manumission as a virtue to be practiced by the slave-owner. Government and the institution of slavery are the consequence of sin. It is the Fall from Grace that necessitates government, and the sinfulness of man that justifies slavery, and the right of the master to expect respect and obedience from his slaves. For Augustine slavery is a Divine institution, sanctioned by God. It is at once a punishment for sin, and a remedy for the evil perpetrated on the world as a consequence of sin. It is part of the subjection of men by men sanctioned by God to mitigate the turmoil caused by sinfulness.

St. Augustine fuses Roman Stoicism with Christianity and lays the foundations for modern jurisprudence and political theory. He wrote *The City of God* almost a century after Constantine converted to Christianity, and about forty years after Theodosius I, Gratian, and Valentinian II issued the edict of Thessalonica (27 February 380), establishing Christianity as the official religion of the Roman Empire (Deane 1963: 124–5). Augustine concurs with traditional Christianity in believing that man is naturally social, and that this condition is to be distinguished from the government and legal order of the state. Sociability and friendship unite, or should unite, men into one universal community. It is on account of their endowment of reason that all men are related. Augustine continues the move made by Lactantius and Ambrose in contending that the eternal law is Divine reason, or God's will commanding the preservation of the natural order and forbidding its disturbance. While he saw much to admire in the Stoic ideas of the eternal and natural laws he rejected their Pantheistic and materialistic implications. He could not reconcile himself to the Stoic cosmic *logos* which identified God with the Eternal Law which permeates the physical universe (Chroust 1974: 2). He retained, however, the idea that the universe exhibits the characteristics of a sublime and perfect order. The Eternal Law is not itself God, but instead the creation of His deliberate act, the act of a personalist and theistic God, whose will and wisdom are equated with Eternal Law. It is the criterion in accordance with which the whole universe acts, defines and determines our relations with each other, to the universe and to God. It is the basis of morality and the most direct route to God. The will and intellect of God command us to conform to, and not to disturb the natural order. The Eternal Law, then, is a reflection, or is declaratory of God's sublime will and perfect intellect (Chroust 1974: 3). Because of his commitment to natural sociality, Augustine follows St. Paul and the Church fathers in acknowledging the existence of a law of nature, a fundamental moral law, engraved on men's hearts, and distinguishable from human and Divinely revealed law. Its basic premise is that one should not do unto others what you would not want done unto you. The relation in which the moral natural law stands to the Eternal Law is that in it rational man consciously participates, and natural law is the imprint of the Eternal Law written in the heart, soul and mind of man. Natural law is the personalized or subjective manifestation of the Eternal Law. Because natural law is innate it has existed since the creation of Adam, and is antecedent to the Fall and the intrusion of sin into the world. It is therefore knowable by all human beings with the capacity for right reasoning, irrespective of being a heathen, non-believer or depraved. It is the law that men use to judge whether a particular act is just or unjust, whether a particular deed is righteous or unrighteous (Deane 1963: 86–7). The moral natural law is incapable of being erased from the minds of men, but it may be obscured by depravity and vice. It is these vestiges of the Law of God imprinted in men that enable them to have some idea of justice that informs legal, economic, and political institutions.

Augustine wrote *The City of God* (Augustine 1998) when Rome was sacked by the Visigoths in 411. Hippo in North Africa, where he was Bishop, was under the protection of the Roman Army, and constantly threatened by invasion. The year after Augustine died Hippo fell to the Vandals in 431.

The inhabitants of the City of God, which has existed since the beginning of time, and the Earthly City, which came into being after the Fall, share the same earth, constitute a world community which transcends state and ethnic limits, are the descendants of Adam, and are afflicted with original sin. As a consequence of the Fall man has corrupted everything that is good. The state, although corrupt, is necessary to maintain peace and accommodate man's social, but imperfect nature. This reflects the common Stoic assumption that men were equal, free and self-sufficient in an original state of innocence which was lost with the appearance of human wickedness. Government is the necessary consequence of sin to restrain human wickedness (Luscombe 1982b: 756). The role of the state is to use force and coercion in order to minimize the harm that sinful and ignorant people may potentially inflict upon one another (Holmes 1989: 130). At the world level, Augustine argues, the multiplicity of languages divides men from one another, and when they are unable to communicate their thoughts to each other for want of a common language 'it is easier for dumb animals, even of different kinds, to associate together than these men, even though both are human beings' (Augustine 1998: XIX, 7).

When St. Augustine contended that government was necessary because of Man's Fall from Grace, and was the Divinely appointed remedy to sin, he was reiterating what had already become commonplace among the Church fathers such as St. Irenæus, St. Ambrose, and St. Gregory the Great. Ambrose, for example, had contended that government was imposed upon foolish people to compel them to obey the wise (Carlyle 1970: vol. I, 130). The activity of politics for Augustine is symptomatic of human frailty, the utilitarian manifestation of the unfulfilled needs of a fallen nature and not an achievement (Coleman 2000: 330). The notion of original sin was one of the issues over which Augustine relentlessly pursued the Pelagians who believed in the perfectibility of the soul. Augustine became obsessed with the issue of infant baptism to which many of the Pelagians were not opposed, but they sought debate and reform on issues of human redemption. Augustine's response was that God had fashioned human genitalia as instruments for the transmission of original sin (Johnson 1984: 120–1).

It is important for understanding Augustine to emphasize the distinction that he makes between true justice, found only in the kingdom of God, and the inferior temporal, earthly image of justice found in all well-ordered states whether they are *res publicae*, *civitates*, or *regna* (Deane 1963: 125). The fundamental principles of God's law are always the same and immutable because Christ, who is the manifestation of the Wisdom and Word of God, is ever present and eternal and unchanging. Justice does not vary, but the times in which it applies change, and therefore the customs and positive laws that govern human relations may change in response to circumstances, but they may, nevertheless, all be faithful to what is right and just. For St. Augustine civil government is both the consequence of and the mitigation of sin. Human activity is for him determined by two things: the inherited original sin of Adam that has corrupted human nature, and God's mitigation of the immediate consequences of sin by the institutions of the church and civil order.

Canon law, that is, church law was one of the main sources of law for medieval peoples. Like customary law it was a muddled amalgam of various sources, including the Old and New Testaments. Gratian's *Decretum* was an attempt to systematize this law. The canon lawyers were familiar with the texts of Roman law, but more importantly with the ideas that Roman lawyers used to invest law with authority, the principal one of which was the Stoic notion of natural law. It was a law common to all humanity, the law of the cosmopolis, and accessible to right reason. The commands of natural law were coincident with absolute justice, and could be used as the exemplar against which other laws could be judged. It was a law that embodied God's will for humanity. Embedded in this conception of law was the possibility of an inner conflict, which subsequently attained its potential. The problem was to reconcile the notion that just law conforms to natural law with the idea that just law is that which is approved by the community (Oakeshott 2006: 303).

In the *Decretum Gratiani* (c. 1140), the oldest collection of Church law, it is maintained, in conformity with the teaching of Isadore of Seville, that two laws rule mankind, natural and customary, the former being written in the Scriptures and the Gospel (Watson 1971: 236). The natural law commands man to do unto others what he would have done unto himself. Isadore's *Etymologies* exhibit a familiarity with the definitions of the Roman lawyers. Like many of them he describes natural law as that which is common to all nations and is the result of natural instinct, rather than legal convention. This law governs the union of males and females, procreation and education, the possession of all things in common, the acquisition of those things on land, the sea and in the sky, and universal liberty.

Before knowledge of the rediscovered Aristotle became widely known, twelfth-century philosophers, such as Peter Abelard (1079–1142) and William of Conches (c. 1100–1154), insisted on the equivalence between nature and reason. God's reason operates in man through Nature implanted in him. Personified, Nature is a goddess presiding over the universe and teaching natural law. For Abelard natural law is primitive law accessible to human reason before the formulation of Mosaic Law, which is largely a codification of natural law. What is important about Gratian's formulation of the natural law is its clear elevation to a criterion that nullifies human convention or law contrary to it (Luscombe 1982a: 706–7).

More than his predecessors such as Isadore of Seville (c. 560–636), St. Anselm (1033–1109), Abelard, Gratian (d. before 1159), and John of Salisbury (c. 1115–76), Rufinus (d. circa 1190), one of the most important interpreters of Gratian's *Decretum* among the Decretists, is more precise in his definition of natural law. He rejects what he takes to be the Roman definition of *jus naturale* – that which gives guidance to all living beings – and instead maintains that it is applicable only to man. It is 'a certain faculty of the human creature, implanted by nature, which tells him to do the good and avoid the opposite' (cited in Chroust 1974: 8). There are three elements to this law; commands that determine what is good or useful; prohibitions on what is harmful; and practical councils or instructions for what is appropriate behaviour. Because of sin our ability to know the natural law is diminished, and we have come to think almost everything is permissible or at least excusable. The Gospel performed the service of restoring original meaning to natural law. The commands and prohibitions cannot change, but instructions on appropriateness do because of changing circumstances. The Decretists were not unaware of the variety of senses of natural law and tried to systematize them. It was the teaching according to Scripture; or it is that which Divine command and prohibition left undetermined; the human capacity to know what is right and wrong; natural equity; and in its more naturalistic sense it is that natural instinct common to all animals, and the general law regulating all creation (Luscombe 1982a: 708).

For Aquinas everything in the world, including humans, has an inherent nature which is at once the cause of its activity and the end to which that activity is directed. At the basis of his conception of natural law is the principle of teleology. Everything has in its nature inclinations that direct it to the end appropriate to itself. The capacity of humanity to make rational choices designed to achieve the potential inherent in human nature is what constitutes its uniqueness. There will be impediments to rational choice, but original sin is not one that irredeemably impairs its exercise. This impairment can be transcended and human excellence attained through the exercise of rational choice. The moral virtues of justice, temperance, fortitude, and prudence were attainable without the intervention of Augustinian grace. These virtues, for Aquinas, have a value apart from the theological virtues of faith, hope, and charity. Salvation did nevertheless require Divine Grace.

From the time of Augustine to the time of Aquinas the understanding of society underwent a shift from voluntarism to rationalism. The Augustinian view was that people were united in society by common purpose and an agreement of will, rather than by a general conception of justice. For the rationalist, there is much greater emphasis on apprehending justice by the exercise of right reason in the natural law (Ramsey 1992: 19–20). The emphasis upon law and reason we find in Aquinas exemplifies this move towards rationalism. The political feasibility of a universal Christian Empire by the time of St. Thomas Aquinas had receded into the background, but it had not yet been replaced with the idea of the sovereign state. The most common political unit was the city-state with its own legislative authority. The universal element was the ideal of a rational natural law and the universal spiritual brotherhood of Christians in the church (Tooke 1965: 139).

It is this emphasis upon right reason that has led such commentators as Vernon J. Bourke to deny that Aquinas is a traditional natural law theorist in the sense that, for example, William of Ockham was. This view of law takes it to be Divinely implanted in men's minds by the legislative Will of God. Divine fiat determines what is good or bad, right or wrong for man. The alternative conception is to see it as the rational working-out of moral norms from the everyday experiences of humans, set against the context of a global environment consisting of many different things. Reason enables us to judge what is suitable or appropriate in the actions of men negotiating the lived experiences of moral life. Here natural law is not an imposition, but instead the rational appraisal of the appropriateness, or suitability of some actions, weighed empirically against the natural experiences of man. On such grounds bestiality may be deemed unsuitable to such a nature, but the union of a man and woman appropriate (Bourke 1974: 53).

Whereas Augustine had built a bridge between early Christian and Greek philosophy, especially that of Plato, Aquinas drew upon the content of the teaching of the Church while relying upon Aristotle for his method. For Aquinas the whole of the creation forms a linked hierarchy with everything in it having a purpose. That purpose is to strive towards the perfection that each creature, or species, has been created to attain. Every form of being has a value and a place, with associated duties. Aristotle says little about law, but Aquinas incorporates into his theory the Aristotelian emphasis that man is by nature a political social being. The common good takes priority over the good of the individual and society is itself teleological in nature.

For Aquinas, following Aristotle, humans are naturally social. Each has an endowment of reason, and each is able to create things to satisfy his needs, but no one is completely self-sufficient. Society is necessary both to sustain life, and also to live a full life. Political society promotes and encourages the development of the spiritual life of the community (Aquinas 1974: 191). The evidence for the sociability of men and for the belief that they are constituted to live in society is the fact that they have language and can express their ideas (Black 1992: 23). The individual is subordinate to the social organism of which he is part, and whose purpose is to pursue the common good. Society as a whole has a sphere of action which differs from its parts, just as, for example, the movement of a ship is not the result of any individual oarsman, but of the combined rowing of all the oarsmen (Aquinas 1974: 193). The unity of the whole, however, is conditional because the individuals who comprise it are also capable of acting independently of it.

The human association is purposive in assisting individuals better to fulfil their nature of being virtuous. Government is necessary in human society in order to attain this end. Within society there are two types of dominion: slavery and voluntary subjection of free men for their common benefit. Voluntary subjection, but not slavery, *pace* Augustine, was sanctioned by God in his original plan and existed before the Fall. The higher levels of personal virtue are, for Aquinas, associated with statesmanship, and in order to attain them there must be a government (Aquinas 1974: 3–9).

Aquinas's view of human nature emphasizes its potential for virtue, he is under no illusion about its actual depravity and sinfulness. Aquinas, in contrast with Augustine, maintained that the Fall from Grace impaired human virtue, and led to a loss of privilege, but did not irredeemably corrupt or destroy it (Tooke 1965: 96). All people have the capacity for, and are capable of, virtuous action, conditional on the exercise of self-discipline. To cultivate our natural aptitude for good most of us, with a few exceptions, require mutual aid and support. Generally, the necessary discipline has to be imposed by force and fear in the hope of instilling the habit of doing voluntarily what was once compelled by fear, and to prevent harm being done to the rest of the community.

Individual good and the good of the whole, or common good, are not the same. The common good unites a community whereas individual interests differ. The pursuit of individual self-interest leads to fragmentation. Individuals are able only through the community and political association to attain their potential. It is impossible to conceive of an individual apart from the community. Each community needs to be guided by a body promoting the common good, which constitutes the unifying principle of society (Aquinas 1988: 264).

John Finnis maintains that general justice has as its object the common good, and that general justice can be distinguished into forms of particular justice, principally a fair distribution of advantages and disadvantages of social life, and due respect for others when our conduct affects them. Particular justice has as its object the other person's rights. Respect for and promotion of the common good is necessarily the respect for and promotion of rights. Finnis argues that, 'When Aquinas says that *ius* is the object of justice, he means: what justice is about, and what doing justice secures, is the *right* of some other person or persons – what is due them, what they are entitled to, what is rightfully theirs' (Finnis 1998: 133).

The term *ius* or *iura* also means law, or laws, and Aquinas often uses it in this sense interchangeably with *lex*. Rights and laws have a rational connection in Aquinas's thought. To assert that someone has a right is to make a claim regarding what practical reasonableness demands of each or every person. Practical reasonableness is moulded by principles and norms, at first by the principles of natural law or reason, and then by the rules that give natural law a specific determination for a community. I have a natural right, then, by virtue of natural law, and a legal right by virtue of civil law (Finnis 1998: 135). Finnis does not himself distinguish between natural rights and human rights, and contends that although Aquinas does not use anything equivalent to the latter term, he may be credited with having the concept of human rights. He concludes this from the fact that Aquinas attributes the precepts of justice to everyone universally, and not to specific individuals for reasons particular to them. As members of God's great republic each has a right not to be killed, or physically harmed by another private person, falsely defamed or accused, cuckolded nor subjected to loss or damage of one's property. Finnis sums up by contending that, 'Such a list of *iniure* – violations of right(s) – is implicitly a list precisely of rights to which one is entitled simply by virtue of being a person' (Finnis 1998: 136). The dignity of each and every person is not something conferred or which can be taken away. It is a reality to be acknowledged (Finnis 1998: 176). While this is a fair description of natural rights, one of the purposes of this book is to show that they are not correlative with human rights other than in confused and superficial ways.

The state, for Aquinas, has a moral purpose in maintaining justice and promoting the virtuous life. Governments formulate laws for the community that guide individuals towards perfection. The purpose of the civil law is to make the moral code explicit, thus enabling citizens to become more virtuous: 'the true object of law is to induce those subject to it to seek their own virtue...[and] the proper effect of law is the welfare of those for whom it is promulgated' (Aquinas 1988: 117).

What is the source of human law? In his conception of law Aquinas looks to the Old Testament, Roman Law, and the philosophy of the Stoics, bringing to bear his impressive powers of synthesis and systematization. The premise of such thinking was that God exhibits perfect rationality and is capable of producing a coherently designed and ordered universe in which everything has its place. The whole universe is law-governed. God is the orchestrator. Law is the expression and embodiment of reason, excepting of the law of sin. Law is the means by which God instructs us, to achieve Grace. Aquinas distinguishes four types of rational law, each of which exhibits a different type of reason. The Eternal Law is the Divine Wisdom of God manifest in the whole of creation. It embodies all the purposes for which God's creatures were created and exemplifies God's reason in a rationally ordered universe (Aquinas 1988: 121). It is in fact God's mind reflected in the universe (Oakeshott 2006: 352). Humans are not able to comprehend the mystery of the overall scheme of things embodied in this law. Humans are able to have some degree of knowledge of it because things and actions have reflected in them the unchanging truth of the Eternal Law. The Eternal Law, like that of Plato's Good, is immutable, absolute, transcendental, and rational, with its appearances manifest in the world.

The Eternal Law is likened to a plan which directs things to an end. The master plan is designed by a prime mover, and the implementation of aspects of it is possible by devising subordinate plans which are derived from the first. What is the relationship between Eternal Law and other types of law? God's Eternal Law is the plan of government for the universe, and the 'plans of government' implemented by subordinate governors are therefore 'derived from the eternal law' (Aquinas 1988: 121). Aquinas' understanding of law is closely related to his view that human beings are naturally social and disposed to live in political communities. Thus inferior magistrates derive their plans for governance from 'the king's command'.

The different types of law for Aquinas, then, are derivations from the Eternal Law. This law provides the plan or model towards which all forms of law must look for guidance. Like Pufendorf after him, Aquinas believes that all law emanates from the will and reason of a sovereign or law-giver, 'the divine and natural laws from the reasonable will of God, the human law from the will of man regulated by reason' (Aquinas 1988: 80).

The second kind of law is the natural law. This law is the reflection of Divine reason in all the things which God has created. It refers to those things which make up our natures. The world is inhabited by two types of beings, intelligent and those less endowed with reason. For the latter, the law of nature directs them to the attainment of their inherent excellences. Obedience to the law is not a matter of choice. For intelligent creatures, such as angels and men, natural law is no less a guide to the achievement of their inherent excellences, a plan to be apprehended and consciously followed, but also capable of being disobeyed at the cost of committing a sin.

We share with other forms of existence the instinct to preserve ourselves according to our own nature. This includes, for humans, a natural inclination to be good. Self-preservation and an inclination to goodness are, then, laws of nature. Natural inclinations, such as those towards the rearing of children, and sexual desire we share with animals. Because human beings are rational by nature there are certain instincts in the natural law that apply only to us, such as our natural inclination to strive to know God's truth, and to live with other human beings in a society. All actions related to these inclinations fall under the natural law, 'namely, that a man should avoid ignorance, that he must not give offence to others with whom he must associate and all actions of the like' (Aquinas 1988: 123).

By being subject to the Eternal Law we may be said to participate in it, 'all things partake somewhat of the eternal law insofar as, namely from being imprinted on them, they derive their respective inclinations to their proper acts and ends' (Aquinas 1988: 20). Rational creatures participate in the Eternal Law in a more exalted way. It is through the natural law that humans are said to participate in God's Eternal Law: it is because of this participation that we are able to distinguish good from evil 'which pertains to the natural law' (Aquinas 1988: 20). Both humans and angels, in some degree, have been endowed with reason which we use to learn what is good and evil. Knowledge of what is good and bad and the possession of a conscience is evidence of the Divine light shining in us.

The law of nature signifies the rational choices to be made to attain the excellences of the nature endowed upon us by God. It stands as the criterion by which the actions of men may be judged. It contains two kinds of precepts, primary and secondary. The law of nature in its general first principles is the standard of right conduct for us all. The truth of abstract or speculative reason and the principles and conclusions derived from them are the same for everyone. The truth that all God's creatures need nourishment for preservation is the same for everyone. Just as in matters of practical reason, the general principles of the law of nature are universal.

It is self-evident, according to Aquinas, that it is a general principle of the natural law that we should act according to reason. From this principle we conclude that there is a general rule that we should repay our debts. There may, of course, be exceptions in its application, as when repayment may cause an injury or serious harm. To repay the debt in such circumstances would be to reject reason and act irrationally. It would not be reasonable, for example, to repay money if that money were to be used to fund a terrorist attack on one's own community. The general principle, however, is always right, that is, that we must act according to reason, but the conclusion we derive from the general principle in its application may not hold in all practical circumstances.

Natural law may be subject to other variations. General principles always hold good, but because of differing abilities the conclusions drawn from them may be inconsistent. Reason, which is our capacity to know the conclusions to be drawn from the general principles may, for example, be depraved or subverted by passion, or by some 'evil habit of nature'. Murder is contrary to the natural law, but if reason is corrupted, as it is in some societies, murder may be an acceptable practice.

In summary, then, human beings are rational and through the exercise of reason know the difference between right and wrong, which constitutes participation in God's Eternal Law. We have in common with the animals a natural inclination to self-preservation and procreation, but are distinguished from them in possessing a desire, and in our natural inclination, to know God and his truths. Humans are not self-sufficient and are therefore naturally social, requiring to be governed by an authority whose purpose is to promote the common good. Because we possess the capacity to pursue good in differing degrees we need mutual assistance, the constraint of force and fear.

The natural law is general in its precepts and may lack directives for specific guidance, and therefore requires supplementary rules pertaining to particularist conditions. Both God and human beings have the capacity to make these additional laws, which are 'positive laws' (*lex positivus*). Positive law signified that it was not something inherent, but is made or imposed. Human society, Aquinas contends, could not exist without human laws. Human laws are in effect the application, but not the deduction, and particularization of the principles of natural law to specific conditions. It is not something that can be deduced from Divine and human nature, but is instead contingent and related to the mutable. There are three types of positive law. First, with which God himself has supplemented the inherent natural law Divine Law such as that to be found in the Bible, and the Ten Commandments. It is a gracious gift from God to humankind. Second, there is canon law, made by the pope and church councils to cover the conduct of ecclesiastic personnel, and on occasions that of the lay person. Although it is human law it is made under Divine authority, and is contingent.

Third, human positive law, in addition, is distinguished into civil law and the Law of Nations. Just as individuals draw conclusions from the general principles of the natural law in making their own moral judgement, the state declares its laws derived from the same source in response to local and contingent circumstances. The laws of states, in being conclusions drawn from the principles of natural law, may differ from one state to another. For example, murder and theft are condemned by the principles of natural law, but the criteria and definition of what constitutes murder and theft and the penalties for such crimes may differ from state to state. The variation in detail makes them no less legitimate proving that they are consistent with the natural law. The relation between civil law and natural law is nicely encapsulated by Oakeshott: 'It is, perhaps, the relationship of a tactical move to a strategic plan: the one cannot be deduced from the other, but elaborates and extends it' (Oakeshott 2006: 355).

Human law is subject to change for two reasons: either because circumstances change, or because there has been an improvement in reason resulting in better solutions to problems. Proposed new legislation must promise a substantive improvement if change is to be justified (McGrade 1982: 753). Human laws require a great deal of ingenuity and skill in their formulation and offer a good deal of scope for change and improvement over time (Black 1992: 39). Civil law, although contingent, is not arbitrary. It must exhibit the following four characteristics. It must exhibit reasonableness and not be in conflict with the necessary conditions for a good life. In other words it must neither conflict with nor override natural law. It must be for the common good and in the public interest. It must also be authoritative, and therefore made by a legitimate body or ruler. Civil law must be promulgated so that those subject to it are aware of their obligations, just as God's supplementary law is promulgated in the Scriptures. The purpose of civil law is to promote the common good. Aquinas maintains that 'the end of law is the common good.... [and] law should take account of many things, as to persons, as to occupations, and as to times' (Aquinas 1988: 65). Individual rights and interests are subordinate to the common good. Social or public interests must always be promoted even at the expense of the rights of the individual.

In Michel Tilley's view, Aquinas follows Aristotle's understanding of *'dikaion'* or in Latin, *ius*. It has two senses, neither of which corresponds to the modern idea of a subjective right. On the one hand justice is understood as a moral virtue, and on the other as an objectively right condition in a particular context which is inherent in the situation, denoting what is fair. The second is for Tilley the foundation of the philosophy of law. What is right or fair may be discerned, *pace* Hume and Kant, from observing external conditions. We observe, for example, that the offspring of humans require a long period of nurture and education, from which we conclude that a stable parental family relationship is required (see Tierney 1988: 9). This explains why both Aristotle and Aquinas did not emphasize the rights and powers of individuals, but instead emphasized the common good and harmonious relationships.

Aquinas also acknowledges and elaborates upon the authority of customary law. Human reason and will, a prerequisite for the making of positive law, are not only manifest in speech, but may also be evident in deeds. The repetition of actions is evidence of the thought patterns of human reason: 'by repeated actions, the inward movement of the will and concepts of reason are most effectually declared; for when a thing is done again and again, it seems to proceed from a deliberate judgment of reason. Accordingly, custom has the force of law, abolished law, and is the interpreter of law' (Aquinas 1988: 80). Law would usually prevail over custom, except in circumstances when law is rendered obsolete, or ineffective, and opposed to deeply engrained customs of a country. Customs are declaratory of the genius of a certain people and expressive of its particular way of life, and should therefore never be ignored (Chroust 1974: 33).

During the medieval period it was common among the Church fathers, theologians, and glossators to discuss matters relating to the Law of Nations. They appropriated the Roman vocabulary of *ius civile*, *ius naturale*, *ius gentium*, and also of *ius divinum* and *ius humanum*, adapting and elaborating it to conform to the significantly transformed international system (Phillipson in Gentili 1933: 9a).

Such matters as relations among civil rulers within Christendom, the swearing of treaties in church, the sanctioning of war, and the safe conduct of ambassadors were claimed by many popes, particularly Innocent III, to be in the jurisdiction of ecclesiastic authorities. For Aquinas such relations were subject not to canon law but to *jus gentium*, the Law of Nations, the law devised by the Romans to pertain between individuals of different nations. Aquinas is not consistent in his use of the term. At times he separates natural law and the Law of Nations, and at others identifies the two. At the very least he identifies the law of nations with what he calls the secondary law of nature.

In addressing the question of their relation directly, at first Aquinas differs from Cicero in that he does not identify the *jus gentium* and *jus naturale*, but instead approvingly cites Justinian's *Digest* in distinguishing them, 'the latter is common to all animals while the former is common to men only' (Aquinas 1988: 141). Elsewhere, however, he adheres more firmly to the Roman idea of a *jus gentium* that is commonly made use of by all peoples. Gaius and Ulpian divide law into *ius naturale* and *ius gentium*. *Jus natural* is, taught to all creatures by nature. In this respect it is more like animal instinct rather than rational apprehension or judgment (Carlyle 1970: vol. II, 29). *Ius gentium* is the law which reason has established, or which men make use of (Chroust 1974: 35). In this respect it is allied to Aquinas's secondary natural law (Chroust 1942: 27). Similarly his discussions on the source of *jus gentium* exhibit this equivocation. Consistent with its positivist character it has its source in historical contingencies, and mutual agreements, and in the consent of men, or it may be determined by common necessity, or by considerations of a common good or utility (Chroust 1942: 27). On the other hand Aquinas says that the laws of nations are the immediate conclusion from the natural law, the logical conclusions from first principles (see Schall 1991–2: 1021). By this Aquinas means that those things we share with animals, such as our natural propensity to procreate and nourish children, are absolute and universal. The law or right of nations is common to human beings only, and results from the application of natural law. The determination of the Law of Nations is a matter of deriving conclusions from first principles (Schall 1991–2: 998). In this respect Aquinas concurs with the definition of *jus gentium* offered by Gaius in the *Institutes*, 'Whatever natural reason decrees among all men is observed by all equally and is called right common among nations' (Aquinas 1988: 141). Natural law does not tell us in the abstract to whom a piece of land ought to belong, but in practical terms relating to its propensity for cultivation, reason may demonstrate that one man has a better claim than another to call it his property (Aquinas 1988: 140–1). For Aquinas this law was predominantly pertinent between realms and their rulers. Without the laws of nations no community could exist.

The spiritual unity was re-enforced by the humanist Desiderius Erasmus of Rotterdam (1466–1536). All of the divisions between and among peoples of Europe, both social and political, were of little significance in comparison with their fundamental unity. It is Christendom and not Europe that constitutes the focus of unity for Erasmus (den Boer 1995: 37).

At this point I want to introduce the Christian notions of property, just war, and the crusades because as shown in Chapter Four, when natural law and natural rights are observed in action, as they were applied to particular problems and for particular justifications, they form the basis for the European appropriation and exploitation of the American Indians.

PROPERTY AND JUST WAR

The New Testament has very little to say about property, the institution is merely assumed throughout, and the duty of charity impressed upon all good Christian souls. It is clear from the writings of 'Barnabus' and 'The Teaching of the Twelve Apostles' that Christians were deemed to have a claim upon their fellow brethren for that which was necessary for sustenance. The idea of a state of nature and the institution of civil society became a commonplace in Christian thought and among the early Christian fathers can be detected the view that private property was not in fact natural, but instead the invention of human society. This does not mean that private property is usurpation, but that it is conventional and therefore a restricted right. For St. Ambrose nature gives us a common use right to the things of the earth, but it is continuous use and habit that produces private right. Amplifying Seneca's position, Ambrose contends that private property is the consequence of avarice, it is therefore only a matter of justice that the man of property should share with others what God gave to all humankind, a sentiment expressed more strongly by Ambrosiaster in the fourth century who maintained that such a duty was not to be limited even by the obligations one had to provide for one's own family (Carlyle 1970: vol. I, 136–7). The theory of property of the Christian fathers which acknowledges a use right in the pre-civil condition, and the establishment of private property rights in civil society, is in effect understood as a constraint on man's wicked and depraved nature following the Fall. Given the avaricious and covetous tendencies in man the regulation of the use of property by human society was both useful and desirable.

We see here the intimations of the much more clearly expressed and thoroughly worked-out theory of property formulated by St. Thomas Aquinas, which was however never entirely coherent because of the ambiguous relation in which natural law and the Law of Nations stand to each other in his theory. At first he insists upon a universal community of property and possession, and the complete freedom of all men. Private property and slavery for him are not institutions of nature, but instead human inventions observed in the general customs among nations. He makes a distinction between property as a right to personal use and property as a right to distribution. This right, he argues, extends only so far to the acquisition and distribution of things. In using such things we are obliged to consider them as things open to all. A person may use what he needs, but holds the rest for common use. Both private property and slavery form part of the secondary natural law in that they are beneficial to the human race and result from necessity and utility in pursuit of the common good. Once introduced these secondary natural laws must be obeyed with the same consistency as primary precepts of natural law (Chroust 1942: 28).

Exploiting the ambiguity of the New Testament on the permitted use of war the Church appropriated and refined the Roman tradition of justified war (*justum bellum*) in order to permit, and even require, Christians to participate in the prosecution of just wars. From 380, when the Edict of Thessalonica established Christianity as the official religion of the Empire, until the middle ages, the Church became one of the most powerful institutions in the West, employing methods of violence against the infidels and heretics that had been used against itself in its infancy (Holmes 1989: 318).

Eusebius (*c*. 260; d. before 341), Athanasius (*c*. 296–373), St. Ambrose (*c*. 340–397), and St. Augustine (354–430), for example, justify Christian involvement in war in order to secure the boundaries of the Empire under Constantine against the barbarian military threat. St. Ambrose gives emphasis to the Platonic and Stoic virtues of prudence, justice, courage, and temperance, maintaining that living a life in accordance with them is a prerequisite to salvation. This entails the promotion of justice, and on occasion, its enforcement. St. Ambrose followed Cicero in believing that desisting from preventing harm being done by another to a friend makes one as guilty as the perpetrator.

Not only must there be a just cause for war, but its conduct must also be just, *jus in bello*. Even enemy soldiers must be treated as moral equals, and dealt with in accordance with their good or bad conduct, and a distinction must be made between innocent and guilty parties on the enemy side when justice is applied to the vanquished (Christopher 1994: 23–29). By the time of Augustine, Lactantius' 'pacificism' was largely rejected and the legitimacy of waging war accepted (Markus 1983:12).

Augustine believes that social hierarchies are motivated by self love and the desire for power, and are therefore always more or less unjust. The passions drive individuals in politics to gain material advantage at the expense of others. The unrestrained pursuit of private goals results in warfare. Agents of the state, or agents of authority, such as soldiers and public hangmen, are necessary for the attainment of peace and order, and are not personally liable for the orders of their superiors. Central to Augustine's thinking is the view that war is both a consequence of and a remedy for sin. The end towards which wars must always aim is peace of some kind. Even in this earthly life, St. Augustine tells us, there is nothing 'desired with greater longing', nor anything better to be enjoyed than peace (Augustine 1998: XIX, 11, pp. 932–4).

Whether or not wars are just depends upon whether they are to avenge a wrong done, for example, by a nation in failing to return something unjustly acquired, that is, unjust aggression, or to punish its own citizens for wrongs against one's own state. In addition, just war could only be waged by a legitimate authority, acting not out of revenge or malice. War was not evil in itself, but instead the usual accompaniment of the evils of greed, the lust for power, and the love of cruelty (Russell 1975: 16). To punish a wicked ruler in order to prevent further wickedness, as long as there is no motive of revenge or for the pleasure of inflicting suffering, is, for Augustine, an act of love. Unjust wrongs had to be resisted for the sake of upholding Christian values, and he therefore exhorted Christians, for example, to protect the Roman Empire against marauding Sahara tribesmen (Chadwick 1986: 104).

An additional just cause, not acknowledged by the Romans, was the kind of war which God Himself ordains (Christopher 1994: 40). Here we have the question not only of the justness of a war, but also its righteousness. As the agent of God the ruler's subjective judgement sanctifies any war he initiates in an attempt to rectify wrongs against the moral order, and could be perpetrated for the good of the vanquished in order to extirpate lust and vice from its community. Wicked rulers can therefore serve God's purpose, punishing other peoples who have sinned. Augustine's just war theory goes beyond that of Cicero and the Romans. Just war for reparation, or to protect a friendly ally, sought to reestablish the status quo, but Augustine's principles could be used to justify much more than this. War could be waged in order to inflict punishment for unlawful crimes, but also to avenge the moral degradation of sin. War was to uphold righteousness as well as legality (Russell 1975:19). Augustine argues that the injustices of the opposing side places on the wise man the duty of waging wars.

Augustine acknowledges traditional Christian pacifism in denying to individuals the right to wage war. Individuals who harm others for wrongs received cannot avoid being intent on perpetrating revenge. Augustine even prohibits private self-defence on the grounds that it would be devoid of love and accompanied by hatred. Russell sums up Augustine's position when he argues that 'Private pacifism was thus joined to a justification of public warfare that underscored the later medieval emphasis on the legitimate authority necessary to wage just wars' (Russell 1975: 18). In Augustine's theory the ruler or God decides upon the merits of, and authorizes, a just war. Only soldiers may legitimately act under such authority. Private citizens and the clergy are not sanctioned to kill (Augustine 1998: I, 26, p. 39).

Augustine, like Thucydides, believes that civil wars are much more pernicious in their consequences than foreign wars. The expansion of the Empire, he believed, had increased the possibility and occasion of civil war, the consequences and miseries of which were far worse than in foreign wars (Augustine 1998: XIX, 7, p. 928–9). Factious civil wars in Rome, Augustine argues, under the auspices of pagan Gods, were far more brutal and devastating than anything ever known in foreign combat, and far worse than any calamity that befell Rome in the Christian era. The avenging of Marisa's savagery by Sulla, for example, prosecuted under the pretext of peace, resulted in the slaughter of innocent and defenceless people. The law of war should have spared them because they bore no arms, and offered no resistance. The murders, Augustine argues, were 'so numerous that they could not be counted', and did not stop 'until it was suggested to Sulla that a few ought to be allowed to live so that there might be some people for the victors to rule over!' (Augustine 1998: III, 28, p. 129).

The justness of foreign war in Augustine's theory, however, loses the objective criterion which the Romans and Stoics tried to supply. Augustine's theory licenses the holy war which was pursued with such righteous zeal during the crusades. Almost any war sanctioned by a ruler and believed to have the blessing of God could be deemed a holy war. Citizens do not have the right to resist the ruler's orders on grounds of conscience. They are absolved from culpable blame when acting in an official capacity even if they believe that the orders to kill an enemy are unjust. Augustine argues that 'he who is commanded to perform this ministry does not himself slay. Rather, he is like a sword which is the instrument of its user'(Augustine 1998: I, 21, p. 32). The soldier who kills on authority, then, is not legally culpable. It is not clear, however, and on this point he is not consistent, whether Augustine thinks that this person has sinned against a higher law, for which punishment will be inflicted by God (Holmes 1989: 329).

There is little in St. Augustine to suggest that his doctrine of just war erects safeguards for the innocent. Killing the innocent is not permissible for private gain or in self-defence if acting as a private person, but if God orders the killing of the innocent, as he did Abraham sacrifice his son Isaac, then we have no choice but to do so. It is also the case that as agents or officials of the state we are obliged to carry out the orders of our superiors (Markus 1983: 4). Furthermore, torture, for Augustine, was a legitimate means of extracting information, even though there was a risk of the guilty and innocent dying in the process. In such circumstances one does not knowingly kill the innocent, but there are no safeguards to prevent it from happening.

The scattered remarks of Augustine and his successors were collected and put into order by twelfth-century canon lawyers, and best represented by Gratian's *Decretum* (Barnes 1982: 772). Between Augustine and Aquinas there are two main modifications to the idea of just war. The first, as we have seen, is the shift from voluntarism to rationalism in comprehending the nature of the political community, and secondly as a consequence more emphasis was given to the natural law concept of justice in discerning the causes that justify war (Ramsey 1961: 32).

Aquinas' discussion of just war draws very heavily upon St. Augustine. For Aquinas, a just war must satisfy three conditions. First, war must be declared by a proper authority, and not by private individuals. Private individuals were in a position to seek redress of grievances through the courts. Private individuals during the middle ages did claim a right to declare war and many of the more powerful maintained armies, and had diplomatic representation at the major courts. They entered into agreements and treaties independently of the sovereign ruler. Aquinas was here reflecting the emergence of more centralized political communities with the legitimate authority entrusted with both external and internal security. The legitimate authority, then, acts in accordance with the common good. We should not lose sight of the fact, however, that the legitimate authority was not always as clearly identifiable as it was later to become.

The second condition that Aquinas specifies for a just war is a just cause. In other words the state against which war is waged must deserve to be attacked, or to have arms taken up against it in self-defence. That state must have done something demonstratively wrong. Aquinas' conception of just war is far more limiting than that of Augustine. Imperialistic expansionism, or the mere fear of a neighbouring state, would not constitute just cause.

Thirdly, even though war is declared by a legitimate authority for a just cause, it may still be unjust if there is a wicked intention. Aquinas argues that 'it is necessary that the belligerents should have a rightful intention, so that they intend the advancement of good or the avoidance of evil' (Aquinas 1988: 221). In practical terms this can mean inflicting injury on an enemy in order to promote the good of justice, or in order to avoid greater harm. The punishment of evil doers in order to restore moral harmony and concord has, in Aquinas's view, Divine authorization (Russell 1975: 260–1). As long as the intention is honourable it would not be an injustice in a just war to take the spoils of war as one's own. If the individual's intention for fighting in a just war is for profit by booty, rather than to promote justice, then the spoils of war are robbery, that is, the taking from someone something that is his due. Similarly in an unjust war those who profit from the spoils are committing robbery and are bound to restore what they have taken (Aquinas 1988: 188).

To what extent are wars against the infidel, or unbelievers, justifiable? In other words, did Thomas Aquinas approve of, and justify, crusades instituted by the church. The question of crusades was, by the time Aquinas wrote, less pressing than it had been, and the enthusiasm for upholding their ideals was on the wane. Aquinas does not give a systematic treatment to the issue of the Christian response to the infidel, but he does make some scattered remarks. Unbelief for Aquinas was one of the greatest sins, but he did not think that unbelievers could be forced to accept the Christian faith. This had to be a matter of will. Where there is a danger, however, of the blasphemous and evil practices of unbelievers 'hindering the faith of Christ' then war may be waged against unbelievers (Aquinas 1988: 250). Although he disapproved of the extension of infidel rule over believers and thought that the church was justified in preventing it because of the effect that it would have upon the morale of the weaker members of the faith, the mere fact of being an infidel did not constitute justification for a holy crusade of conquest. On prudential grounds in order to prevent greater harms ensuing, or on account of some positive good, it may be necessary for the occasional toleration of the rites of infidels, and although Aquinas is here talking of lands over which one has jurisdiction it could also be extended to external relations, or wars. Lapsed believers, however, who renege on an obligation to uphold the faith may justifiably be persecuted.

Aquinas does address the question of whether a ruler is justified in taxing his subjects. The levying of tribute for private gain or aggrandizement is prohibited because 'rulers of countries are appointed by God, not that they may seek their own gain, but that they may prosper the common welfare' (Aquinas 1974: 91).

It is just, however, that wealth, when required for maintaining the public good, be contributed by citizens, in order to facilitate the ruler's discharge of his obligations (Aquinas 1974: 93). It would not be unjust in circumstances relating to 'safeguarding the common good' to exact levies by force (Aquinas 1988: 188). Aquinas simply assumes that military service is obligatory as part of our general obligation to pledge obedience to the legitimate ruler. He contends that 'even a good king, without being a tyrant, may take away the sons and make them tribunes and centurions and may take many things from his subjects in order to secure the common weal' (Aquinas 1988: 119).

Following Aquinas, Thomist theologians gave their imprimatur to the idea of a justified war waged for the benefit of the common good, while continuing to condemn those wars motivated by vice. The political practices of the newly emerging territorial units, along with military service and warfare, received conditional theological sanction. War was no longer merely a consequence of sinfulness, but a necessary concomitant of human communities consistent with human nature (Russell 1975: 267).

With the coming of the crusades the Church's eagerness to support armed conflict is in marked contrast with the pacifist implications of much of Christ's teaching. Pacifism became associated with the heretical fringes of Christianity, such as the Waldensians, or *Vaudois*, who were followers of Peter Waldo of Lyons, and hence known as the poor men of Lyons. The movement began in about 1170 and sought to follow the teachings of the Gospels. In contrast, the Church gave greater emphasis to the development of principles relating to the justice of resorting to war (*jus ad bellum*), and the right or just conduct of war (*ius in bellum*).

MEDIEVAL ENCOUNTERS WITH THE OTHER: CHRISTIANS, MUSLIMS, AND JEWS AS FAITH COMMUNITIES

Christianity made the transition from victim to persecutor with some ease. From being the oppressed, enacting the role of oppressor in protecting the purity of the faith was of paramount importance. The protection of religion took precedence over the upholding of civil law. For St. Ambrose, for example, the Jews were a problem in that they were a significant minority within the Empire who would not accept Christian norms, and who assisted the Emperor Julian in his policy of pagan revival. Attacks on Jews and synagogues became increasingly popular even though it was against public policy. The Bishop of Callinicum, for example, instigated the burning of the local synagogue, to which the Emperor Theodosius responded by ordering its reconstruction at Christian expense. St. Ambrose vehemently opposed the move and forced him to back down on the grounds that publicly humiliating the Bishop would damage Christianity, asking what is more important, religious interest or the enforcement of civil law? This was an important step in the construction of a community in which only Christians enjoyed and exercised full rights.

Augustine was the champion of enforced conformism. Heretics were to be forced to accept orthodoxy, renounce their heresy, or be condemned to death. The church was to be much more active in its persecution, investigating potential or incipient heresy in order to expose it and force its expositors to recant, or face the prospect of being declared a heretic (Johnson 1984: 105, 116–7).

For medieval people law was fundamental. What distinguished communities was not their governments, but their laws. By the seventh century Christians had a heightened awareness of other religious communities than themselves, the Jews and the Muslims, and what distinguished them was that the former was governed by the laws of Moses, and the latter of Muhammad. They constitute three legally distinct communities, who by the later middle ages were perceived as a threat to each other. During the crusades, the Muslims were the enemy without, and the Jews, the enemy within.

Europe was a word that was used, but it had little emotional or empirical content. Christendom was the dominant category in terms of the universal community to which individuals thought of themselves as belonging rather than Europe. In answer to the question, 'who am I?' Christians did not answer 'I am a European'. Even though the term Europe was found in scholarly characterizations of the *orbis*, along with Asia and Africa, these geographical entities were not the mode of identity in terms of which people viewed themselves. To be a Christian, a Jew or a Muslim was the important distinction.[1] The territorial consciousness of Christendom was accelerated by the Muslim threat from the seventh to the tenth century, during which Christian territories, including Jerusalem, and parts of Europe, such as Spain and Sicily, were lost to Islam. The Muslim 'menace' served to mobilize Latin Christendom and produced a sharp construction of an ideologically and politically distinct and hostile enemy intent on the destruction of Christendom. From the eleventh to the thirteenth century holy war in defence of the boundaries of Christendom constituted an almost permanent crusade. Pope Urban II, for example in 1095, sought to prohibit knights fighting against fellow Christians, and exhorted them to wage wars against the infidel. Wars against the enemies of the faith were both authorized and sanctified by the papacy, completely destroying the vestiges of early Christian pacifism (Russell 1975: 35–6). It is during Urban's pontificate that the concept of Christendom becomes more clearly defined as encompassing Greek and Latin Christians, united in a global mission, the spread of the word of Jesus. The brotherhood of the community of Christians

---

[1] Since 11 September, 2001 George Bush Junior has been continuously criticized for conceiving the war against terrorism in terms of the Christian West and the Islamic East. The universal community of Christians is now a vague and barely articulated concept, whereas Islam is the primary mode of unity among Muslims, and the state to which one belongs is merely an artificial administrative convenience, loyalty to which is secondary to one's obligation to Islam. For Muslims everyone is born a Muslim, even Christians, and in this sense there can be no conversion to Islam, merely a return to it.

came to be more than an abstraction, and became identified territorially as well as spiritually.

The medieval Church worshipped a jealous God intolerant of those standing outside of the faith. Such theologians as Bartolus, Baldus, Joannes da Lignano, and John Wycliffe thought it perfectly justified that Christendom should take a hostile stance to Jews, Saracens, infidels, heretics, and barbarians. With the Ottoman threat to Europe, the xenophobia intensified, and differences of religion were deemed adequate grounds for waging just war (Phillipson in Gentili 1933: 34a). The first crusade following the Council of Claremont in November 1095 was a combination of the continuation of holy war and a pilgrimage, in which Urban II succeeded in invoking familiar religious values and making them resonate with the everyday lives of thousands of individuals. Crusaders were largely penitential pilgrims who were called upon to fight, unless they were exempted on grounds of gender, age, or category of ordination (Housley 2006: 16). What distinguished the first crusade from holy war was not the Church's readiness to sanctify violence, that had its roots preceding the reform Papacies of Leo IX, Alexander II, and most importantly Gregory VII, but the special status afforded Jerusalem and its holy places (Housley 2006: 35). It was not until Innocent III (1198–1216) that crusading found coherent ideological expression as the foreign policy of *Christianitas*, the Christian community, which in more juridical and political terms was the *respublica Christiana*. As a result the role of the Roman *curia* in the initiation and management of Christendom's crusading policy was enhanced. It was at this time that Innocent developed the doctrine that the pope was Christ's representative on earth, his vicar or lieutenant (Housley 2006: 55).

Hatred of the enemy was fuelled by crusade preaching, and the anti-Islamic rhetoric is likely to have precipitated the 1099 massacres in Palestine. There are examples of unusual cruelty perpetrated against Muslims, the by-product of the veneration in which Christ and the holy places were held (Housley 2006: 88). The struggle to regain the lands of Christ was at once an expression of love for the Saviour and an act of charity towards Christians persecuted by the enemies of Christ.

The counterpart was vengeance, especially against the Muslims whose very presence in the holy land amounted to pollution. From just before 1100 the prevailing image of Islam preached by Catholic Christendom found expression in crusading songs, poetry, and stories. Muslims were often referred to as Saracens, a term that sometimes covered all those peoples who were not Christian or Jewish. Muhammad was particularly detested by crusade preachers and apologists, and Muslims in general were caricatured as sub-human, irrational, polytheistic, worshippers of the devil, and slaves to sex (Tolan 2002: 105–69). They were identified with the antichrist. Whereas Satan is the abstract representation of evil, the antichrist is the manifestation of Satan in actual circumstances or events. The Muslims, therefore, were one of a long line of antichrists.

Part of the characterization of the motivation for the crusades right from the start, and which was to be an increasingly dominant theme in the Christianity of the twelfth and thirteenth centuries was the love for Christ the Saviour, and the charity owed to fellow Christians in rescuing and safeguarding them against enemies of the faith, the antichrist (Riley-Smith 1980). One may say that this was a nascent expression of the principle of humanitarian intervention, and was to be invoked quite frequently by those advocates of 'just war' against the American Indians.

For Islam, both Christianity and Judaism constituted the enemy. They both had their prophets, from whose revelation Arabs had been excluded. With the coming of Muhammad, Arabs too had their prophet. Muhammad saw himself as the successor to the Christian Judaic tradition. In the process of destroying Zoroastrianism – the ancient Persian religion that taught Ormunzd the creator and Angel of good will overcome and triumph over Ahriman, the evil spirit – Islam retained some of its elements. This battle between good and evil was retained by Islam, and was common to both Christianity and Judaism. The idea of the *jihad* in Islam should not be understood in purely militaristic terms, nor should the common translation of 'holy war' be taken literally. In classical Islamic doctrine nothing associated with humanity, and especially not war, could be understood as holy or sacred. If Islam inspired people to make war on the enemies of their God, representing the forces of good against evil, that is a different matter. *Jihad* has two meanings in Islam. The Great *Jihad* refers to religious striving, and may operate in all spheres of life, representing the striving of the individual for goodness and righteousness. The small *jihad*, which can be offensive or defensive, is the duty of Muslims to defend Islam against religious enemies from without, or against those who have abandoned Islam. The equivalent of *ius in bellum* comes into play in conflicts between Islamic countries (*harb*), and the enemy is not deemed to represent evil. Alternatively, wars with non-believers (*razzia*) bring no ethical limits into play in defeating the forces of evil. The distinction represents two world views, that of the believer being *umma*, which when geographically represented is *Dar al-Islam* (the world of Islam), in opposition to *Dar el-Harb* (the world of war). It is the religious duty of the believer to expand the former at the expense of the latter. The missionary element is in practice secondary to the pragmatic motivation for war, the acquisition of wealth, and the expansion of the tax paying community (Harle 2000: 75–6). While there can be no permanent peace among believers and non-believers, the antagonism is reduced by a blurring of the rigorous division of *Dar al-Islam* and *Dar el-Harb* by 'the world of reconciliation and mutual understanding (*Dar al-Sulh*)' (Harle 2000: 77).

The external enemy to Christianity was Islam, but there was also a perceived internal threat, namely Judaism. Anti-Semitism as well as anti-Muslim sentiments served to give unity and cohesiveness to the idea of Christendom and Europe. Anti-Judaism was not uncommon in the ancient world, and when Christianity became the state religion of Rome, the Emperor Constantine gave legal legitimacy to equating in name the synagogue with a brothel, and generally speaking put Jews on a par with Christian heretics, subjecting them to similar legal disabilities. The period between 430 and the first crusade in 1096 is generally considered to have been less anti-Semitic than the period before or after.

The crusades were not merely for the purpose of driving back the Muslim hordes, but were also directed vehemently against the Jews. Jews became demonized and portrayed as progeny of the devil, in Satan's employ expressly to perpetrate harm to Christians. The first crusade of 1096 resulted in unprecedented massacres of Jews by Christians. In the twelfth century they were accused of murdering children and of organising a secret government comprising rabbis, and located in Spain, orchestrating clandestine war against Christendom and using sorcery as the main weapon in its armoury (Harle 2000: 63).

Jews were accused of harbouring the intention of destroying Christianity and of taking over the world, of the ritual killing of children, and of being poisoners. In Bohemia in 1161, for example, eighty six Jews were executed for being implicated in a conspiracy of physicians to poison the population. Martin Luther was particularly obsessed with the prospect of being poisoned by Jews. The Jews were labelled Christ-killers and enemies of the faith. An estimated 10,000 Jews were massacred in the first six months of 1096, roughly twenty to twenty-five per cent of the Jewish population of Germany and northern France.

The crusaders were recruited from the lower echelons of society in Northern Europe and on their way to the Holy Land decimated the Jewish quarters in French and German towns, claiming that they were acts of vengeance against the enemies of Christianity in their own back yard. Riley-Smith has shown that the first wave of anti-Semitic attacks was not, as previously believed, the responsibility of out of control *pauperers* (the crusades of the poor), who sometimes were not officially sponsored, and often lacked organization, but such sentiments did from the start thoroughly permeate the crusading ideology at all social levels (Riley-Smith 1984). It was among the *pauperes*, however, that the belief in crusaders being the elect of God made the deepest impression, and it was with great enthusiasm that they discharged their responsibilities of recovering the holy shrine.

Crusades were not confined to the Latin East and Jerusalem, but were also directed against the pagans of northern Europe starting in the spring of 1147, and were sometimes waged against Christians who were not accused of heresy, but of opposing the pope, as for example the crusade proclaimed by Innocent III in 1199 against Markward of Anweiler. He was lieutenant to the emperor Henry VI who opposed the pope's claim to rule the south as regent for the minor Frederick II (Housley 2006: 116).

Calls for crusading in the north had, however, come much earlier than 1147. Arguments were used for the enforced conversion of the enemies of Christ, and for denying their rights of dominion, arguments that were later to gain prominence during the conquest of the Americas. In 1108 there was a call to conquer the new Canaan of the north, dispossessing wicked gentiles of land overflowing with honey, meat, corn, and birds. Pagans were derelict in their duty to God in failing to cultivate the land effectively. To seize it from the pagans would be an act of salvation (reproduced in Riley-Smith 1987: 74–7). Hostiensis, the thirteenth-century canonist, for example, contended that pagans did not enjoy God's grace and therefore had no rights of lordship under the natural law and could not legitimately defend the lands they occupied against Christian crusaders.

CONCLUSION

Even though human reason plays a significant role in the philosophy of the middle ages in relation to natural law, it would be a mistake to separate it from the spiritual concerns that permeate it (McGrade 1982). In general, then, the references to a higher law discussed in this and the previous chapter give rise to the idea that rights are derivative from it. The notion of rights in this sense is objective. We do not find in the Greeks, the Roman Jurists, or the Stoics, in the Church fathers or Aquinas, the conception of rights as a power or possession, giving us autonomy within a limited moral sphere to do or not to do, to claim or not to claim, certain things in relation to another or others. Although we find in some thinkers, for example, St. Paul that natural law is innate, written on men's hearts by their Creator, there is no suggestion that they have been endowed with inalienable rights. As Tierney contends, 'In Aristotle or Gaius or Aquinas we can find a vague notion of rights, though the concept remains peripheral and unelucidated in their thought. The main point for us is that they have no idea' of subjective rights as human or natural, rights inherent in the human person' (Tierney 1989: 618 fn 11). Chapters Three and Five show how subjective rights were intimated in the writings of some medieval thinkers, and came to play a much more significant role in natural rights theories. Even in those theories, however, the idea that rights were derived from objective laws was still the predominant conception of rights.

This chapter has served to show how natural law becomes much better defined in the medieval period and how tensions between descriptive and prescriptive conceptions of it persisted. It is also clear that the relationship between natural law and the law of nations provided intractable problems in discussing the role of the former in relation to the latter. Chapter Three shows that these problems were no less intractable for writers of the early modern period, and why such writers as Rachel were frustrated by the ambiguous way in which some theorists characterized the relationship.

This chapter has also served to show how theories of property were integral to the idea of just war, and how for Christians the system of laws that differentiated them from other faith communities was seen to be superior. Chapter Five shows how the application of these laws as the standards by which to judge the known world, far from endowing non-Europeans with rights and protections, more often than not was invoked to deny that peoples from far away places did not fully possess the necessary qualifications for full possession and exercise of these rights. In other words, the universal laws and rights were applied and exercised in ways that were far from universal, and turned out instead to be special rights and privileges, the preserve of those who followed God's law.

3

Natural Law, the Law of Nations, and the Transition to Natural Rights

> For the civil law governs those matters which pertain to the association of a single people, while the law of nations regulates those which look to the common association of the human race (Grotius 2004: 107).

> Not only has Nature provided its own Law for men, whereby, as if by a world-wide chain, they are bound to one another in virtue of being men, but mankind has itself also laid down various positive laws for its own guidance, not merely those by which in every State the government binds its subjects to itself or by which these bind themselves to one another, but also those which the human race, divided up as it is into independent peoples and different States, employs as a common bond of obligation; and peoples of different forms of government and of different size lie under the control of these rules, which depend for their efficacy upon 'mutual good faith' (Rachel 1916: Diss. II, §i).

INTRODUCTION

The emergence of the modern European state represents a significant change in thinking about law. Whereas Aquinas recognized the activity of making law, principally the civil law, as a supplement to natural law, law making became the single most distinguishing feature of the modern European state in contrast with medieval government. In the modern European state governing became a sovereign activity, backed-up by large concentrations of power. To be sovereign was to acknowledge no superior legal authority unless expressly choosing to do so. To be sovereign was to be independent of and not subordinate to other authorities, but it also denoted a legal relationship with its own subjects and the law. The sovereign authority was the sole law making body with the powers to amend or abolish law (Oakeshott 2006: 386–7).

It was fear of the arbitrary exercise of this power that gave rise both to the attempts to put at least some rights outside of the purview of the sovereign glance, and to recommend arrangements for constitutional constraints on the activities of governments to determine what was and what was not *ultra vires*. With the emergence of the modern European state came the age of discovery and exploration. Whereas Christians were used to encounters with the other in the form of Muslims and Jews, as we saw in the previous chapter, and even with what they regarded as the more savage peoples of Africa, all could be accommodated in the biblical world-view. The Christian West, however, was ill prepared for what it found in the Americas.

The discovery of the New World was at once an exhilarating and disconcerting experience. At first sight it was as if all the fantastical and fantastic imagery of enchanted woods, giants, mystical, and mythical creatures such as the Griffin and the Unicorn, mountains of gold and Eldorado had all materialized in the New World to delight the senses of travellers and explorers alike. Once the veneer of fantasia became tarnished by what appeared unmitigated savagery, inhumanity, and repulsion at practices completely alien to the Christian mind, perpetrated by creatures who appeared human, but which did not resemble any race known to man, attitudes changed. They were either not human at all, in which case the Christian myth of Noah dividing the world among his three sons, Japeth, Shem, and Ham, giving rise to the progeny of Europe, Asia, and Africa, respectively, remained intact. If they were human, then an explanation had to be found. Were they, for example, the lost tribe of Israel? Or were they a hybrid people, the result of an encounter between races, unknown and unrecorded? If both the Ancients and the Christian Church were ignorant of the existence of another continent, and indeed, more problematically, wrong about the nature and composition of the world, what else might they be mistaken about.

In this chapter, I want to explore early modern conceptions of natural law and its relation to the Law of Nations and to natural rights. It was in the context of the emergence of the modern state and the discovery of the Americas that these ideas were refined by philosophers, jurists, and theologians alike. In the next chapter, I will consider the practical implications of these ideas.

NATURAL LAW: ABSOLUTE AND IMPRESCRIPTIBLE

The natural law is almost invariably regarded as immutable. Human positive law may be derived from it, which may vary in different circumstances, but the principles from which they are concluded are sacrosanct. The natural law is absolute and imprescriptible. Suarez defends this view by distinguishing between intrinsic and extrinsic change, and positive and negative precepts. What is invariable about natural law is its intrinsic precepts, but they cannot anticipate all possible circumstances, such as killing in self-defence, and it is the extrinsic precepts of natural law that must be adapted to respond to changing circumstances.

Private property falls negatively under the natural law. The emergence of private property when God gave the earth in common is not itself a sign that natural law can be changed or overridden by man. A use right is permitted, but private ownership is not proscribed. Natural law forbids only excessive taking of property that may hinder the reasonable use by others. Not even God can alter the precepts of natural law because they pertain to intrinsic goodness and wrongfulness. It is, for example, impossible for God to command man to hate him (Luscombe 1982*a*: 718). As the author of the rationally ordered universe it would be a contradiction, and create discord, if He were to go against it. Ayala(*c*.1548–84), for example, contends that 'the law of nature is immutable and the *jus gentium* cannot derogate from it' (Ayala 1912: Book II, chapt. V, [16], p. 40). In relation to the freedom of the seas, for example, Grotius contends that it is the right of all men and nations to navigate the oceans in pursuance of their natural right to trade. No king, nor even the pope, has authority to take these rights away. The pope, Grotius contends, has no authority to derogate the 'perpetual law of nature and nations' (Grotius 2004: 38 and 52).

The prince exercises dominion and is responsible for making laws not only for human affairs, but also in relation to matters Divine, 'but he cannot order what has been forbidden by God or forbid what has been ordered by God. The supreme power has the judgement over civil laws and guardianship and protection over divine law, natural law and the law of nations' (Grotius 2004: 130). In this both Samuel Rachel (1628–91) and Samuel von Pufendorf (1632–94) agree. Natural law, for them, derives directly from Divine Providence. Natural law is invariable and has the same force the world over, independently of the will of any lawgiver (Rachel 1916: Diss. I, §ix). While it is legitimate for a ruler to change arbitrary law, 'so it is alike futile and unlawful to attempt the same in regard of Natural Law' (Rachel 1916: Diss. I, §xiv). No pact among individuals, for example, can have obligatory force if it in any way infringes the natural law (Rachel 1916: Diss. I, §lxi).

Rachel goes to some pains to define the law of nature because of its prescriptive injunctive force. He contends that the natural law 'is a law moving from Divine Providence in harmony with the idea of Eternal Law, and adapted to the rational and social nature of man, which, being promulgated in man's mind by means of Right Reason, binds him to conform his conduct to the standard of this Law and so to attain happiness' (Rachel 1916: Diss. I, §xxxiii).

Natural law is not only inviolable in relation to human will, but also in relation to God Himself: 'For God never will nor can use this power so as to allow or approve sins and go counter to Himself and His own Justice, a thing absurd and impious to say' (Rachel 1916: Diss. I, §lvi). For Pufendorf, the term that we have for natural law has been given to it by custom, but we may with equal justification call it the law *Universal* and *Perpetual* in that it binds the whole body of humanity, and is unchangeable (Pufendorf 1717: Book II, chapt. iii, §I).

Johann Wolfgang Textor (1638–1701), whose family according to the fashion of the time Latinized their surname of Weber, was professor of jurisprudence at Heidelberg and assistant judge of the Court and of the Matrimonial Tribunal. He published his *Synopsis juris gentium* (1680) two years after Rachel published his treatise, but makes no mention of it. Textor, in fact, steers a course closer to Roman law and to the writing of Grotius. Textor makes a distinction between those rules that are the conclusion of natural reason alone, that is 'Naked' or simple natural reason, and those rules that have arisen as a consequence of the imperative needs of humanity, the result of compound natural reason (Textor 1916: II, 3). The former are immutable, while the latter are subject to changes as circumstances vary (Textor 1916: v and II, 13).

Even though Christian Wolff (1679–1754) is considered among others to be the father of modern international law, there are still respects in which he is firmly tied to his predecessors. Like them, he unhesitatingly contends that the natural law is immutable, but further than this he contends that the voluntary Law of Nations which is deduced from the law of nature is equally immutable. He contends that 'the immutability of the necessary law of nations arises from the very immutability of the Natural Law' (Wolff 1934: Prolegomena, §5). The obligations that arise from both are therefore absolutely binding and no nation has the right to abrogate them, nor to release other nations from them (Wolff 1934: Prolegomena, §6). Wolff was careful, however, to distinguish clearly between perceptive natural law which commands actions, prohibitive which forbids them, and permissive which confers a right to act (see Tierney 2004: 8).

Francisco Suarez (1548–1617), along with Dominic de Soto (1494–1560), Robert Bellarmine (1542–1621), Gabriel Vásquez (1549 or 1551–1604), and Richard Hooker (1554–1600), represents a distinct revival of natural law and of the teachings of Aquinas in the sixteenth century. Suarez's importance is that he addresses the various versions of natural law, finds them wanting, and develops his own in relation to them. For him natural law truly is law. He wants to be much stricter in his definition than Aquinas. He wants to contend that things that lack reason are not susceptible to law because the concept of obedience and disobedience is not comprehended by them. Law is for him a rule, and not the working out of, or effect of a rule. He defines natural law as 'a certain measure of moral acts in the sense that such acts are characterized by moral rectitude through their conformity to law, and by perversity, if they are out of harmony with law'. It 'dwells within the human mind in order that right may be distinguished from wrong' (cited in Luscombe 1982a: 716). Reason is the foundation of natural law and provides the criterion of objective right and wrong, it is not itself law. He maintains that law requires a lawmaker, it is a command. Against those, such as Gregory of Rimini (d. 1358) and Gabriel Biel (c. 1425–95), who *pace* William of Ockham (1287–1347) suggest that natural law does not come from the will of God the lawmaker because as dictates of right reason they have the character of indicative law even if God did not exist, Suarez maintained that only perceptive law that commands and prohibits is genuine law because law requires a legislator to impose it. Suarez maintains that 'since the law in question is true law and God is its Author, it cannot be other than righteous; and therefore, it cannot prescribe anything save that which is righteous, neither can it prohibit anything which is not opposed to righteousness' (Suarez 1944: 208). He departs from Ockham, however, in not wanting to equate the whole of law with the will of what is permitted and prohibited by God. This is simply to resolve it into God's Eternal Law of Divine commands and prohibition. For Ockham, the role of natural reason is to reveal to man God's will for him (Luscombe 1982a: 717).

Suarez's theory of natural law may be summed up in three propositions. Natural law is genuinely law in a perceptive and prescriptive sense. It is not merely knowledge of self-evident principles because to transgress is to violate God's will and mandate. Second, in addition to being percepts and prohibitions natural law is also the will of God prescribing acts that are good or bad for human nature. Human reason apprehends this law for humanity demonstrating that acts contrary to natural law are also contrary to Divine Law. Thirdly, because God is its legislator natural law is truly Divine Law (Luscombe 1982*a*: 717).

NATURAL LAW AND THE SOURCE OF OBLIGATION

The source of moral obligation in the writings of Suarez is, then, God. For Suarez there would be no moral obligations without Divine will or command. A. S. McGrade is typical in contending that from the time of John of Salisbury to Richard Hooker and Francisco Suarez the theory of natural rights arose out of the religious view of society. After this time, McGrade suggests, the politics of rights more or less dispensed with religion (McGrade 1982: 739). It is my contention that even natural rights theorists who are said to have secularized the tradition, such as Hugo Grotius, Samuel von Pufendorf, John Locke and Johann Wolfgang Textor retain such a heavy residue of theological absolute presuppositions that their arguments would collapse at crucial points without the religious worldview. In a world so thoroughly permeated with religious imagery and explanation, there could be nothing more powerful than to invoke God as the reason for living the moral life. Even those philosophers who were less than convincing in their religious genuflections nevertheless accepted the utility of a ruler invoking His authority to demand allegiance. This relates to what Charles Taylor calls the 'conditions of belief'. The difference between then and now is that those conditions have changed. The lived experience of being a believer or an unbeliever has become transformed. Belief in God was almost unchallenged, and any alternative almost inconceivable. Now it is no longer axiomatic to believe in God because there are alternatives, and in such circumstances it may be difficult to sustain one's faith (see Taylor 2007). If a philosopher did not rely at some stage in his argument on God as the ultimate foundation of obligation, sometimes alongside other compelling reasons, we would need to seek an explanation for the omission. Nowadays, we seek an explanation for the inclusion of such grounds.

Arthur Nussbaum is a firm believer that both Grotius and Pufendorf justifiably lay claim to the secularization of natural law (Nussbaum 1953). James Griffin, for example, suggests that using reason as the means by which to discover natural law and as the ground of our obligation is the hallmark of modern natural rights theory. He wrongly identifies Grotius, Pufendorf, and Locke as modern in the relevant sense (Griffin 2008: 10–12). Griffin confidently tells us that Pufendorf, like Grotius, believed that the 'power of reason' alone is all that is necessary both to discover and prove the efficacy of natural law (Griffin 2008: 10).

It is important in the classic writers, however, to distinguish between the method or means by which we come to know natural law, and the grounds for our obligation to obey it. Later thinkers want to say that reason provides both. My view is that for many of the most important earlier thinkers who we associate with the development of constraints on international relations reason enables us to know the law; God obliges us to obey it. In fact, the likes of Gentili, Suarez, Grotius, and Pufendorf and most of the early modern natural law theorists, although giving great emphasis to reason, nevertheless ground the obligation to conform with the precepts of natural law firmly in the fact that God is its author. Reason alone cannot create or sustain the obligation (although some argue that Grotius contends exactly this). Vattel is an exception here. He is cognisant of the importance of the distinction between the way we come to know natural law and grounds of obligation. He rejects both God and Reason as the grounds and posits instead human interest (Vattel 2008: 747–71).

We will return to the issue of the secularization of the tradition in Chapter Five, but it is necessary at this point to establish the point that God, and not reason only, is the source of the obligation for so many so called modern thinkers, just as He is the source of the natural law. It is difficult to see what would give moral and intellectual force to their arguments, and the obligations and rights that individuals and nations have under the natural law had not God willed it so. It is common during the later medieval period explicitly to invoke God as the ground for obedience to the natural law. In the *Decretum Gratiani* (*c*. 1140), for example, Gratian maintains that any principle that can be determined as a pre-conventional natural right must be regarded to be a reflection of Divine wisdom and will. Such right stands in the same authoritative relation to human law as do the Holy Scriptures. Anything contrary to the Divine will or canonical scriptures is contrary to natural right itself. Gratian contends that 'nothing is commanded by natural right except that which God wishes to be done, and nothing forbidden except that which God forbids to be done' (cited in Porter 2007: 89).

Commentators are much less inclined to accept that God remains the source of obligation in many of the early modern writers on natural law and natural rights. However, for Gentili, those who have no religion, that is those who worship no God, stand outside the natural law and have no place in its protection (Gentili 1933: Book I, chapt. ix, 65). Implicit in the arguments of Balthazar Ayala is a firm commitment to the idea of the Divine right of kings. Both good kings and bad kings are sent by God to reward or punish their respective peoples. Peoples oppressed by a bad king have no right to depose him, 'however unjust or cruel his conduct may be' unless, in certain circumstances, he is a tyrant who has illegally usurped power (Ayala 1912: Book I, chapt. ii, [23], p. 17). Ayala argues that, 'by the ordinance of God, all sovereignty and power has been conferred on the prince as against the people, the people can not pass judgment on him, for the inferior can not bind the superior in judgment' (Ayala 1912: Book I, chapt. ii, [26], p. 18). This is because it is contrary to natural law.

I am not suggesting, of course, that all natural law thinkers ultimately rely on God as the ground of obligation (see Pink 2004 and 2005). Merely that those thinkers who have been most strongly associated with secularising the natural law and natural rights have tended on the whole *not* to have abandoned God as the ultimate source of obligation. Why, indeed, would they want to, given the contemporary conditions of belief? This is not to say that individuals do not obligate themselves through promises and agreements. Private property in Grotius and Pufendorf, for example, arises from agreement. Pufendorf distinguishes between congenital obligations which are not self-imposed, and adventitious obligations which are. Ultimately, however, we keep our promises because the natural law demands it of us. The reason why we are obliged to follow it is because it is God's 'Will and Command we should act according to that Law' (Pufendorf 1717: Book II, chapt. iii, §XIII). It is true that Pufendorf did not believe that the natural law was inscribed in men's hearts by God. He believed himself to be in conformity with orthodoxy when he said 'most are agreed, that the Law of Nature is to be drawn from Man's Reason; flowing from the true Current of that Faculty, when unperverted' (Pufendorf 1717: Book II, chapt. iii, §XIII). However, not only does God endow us with the reason we use for coming to know the natural law, the reason why we are obliged to follow it is because it is His 'Will and Command we should act according to that Law' (Pufendorf 1717: Book II, chapt. iii, §XIII).

Grotius, Pufendorf, and Rachel are clear that the law of nature pertains only to humans, and is obligatory in its force. They are quite emphatic that the natural law does not extend to non-human creatures. Law presupposes reasons, and freedom of choice. Pufendorf maintains that it is impossible to conceive how a creature could at once be capable of law and incapable of reason. Beasts are therefore excluded from the natural law. Pufendorf is without doubt separating the prescriptive law of nature from anything that may be conceived as the law of nature in naturalistic terms. Men and brutes may appear to perform the same actions, but in reality they are very different. Beasts act out of simple inclination of nature and men out of obligation (Pufendorf 1717: Book II, chapt. iii, §II). For Rachel, it is not reason, however, that gives natural law its obligatory force. The source of natural law is Divine Providence, and its obligatory force derives from the same source, 'For if the obligation of every law derives its authority in paramount fashion from God, Natural Law receives its authority in the highest possible degree from that same source ...' (Rachel 1916: Diss. I, §xlv).

An indubitable and immutable human nature provides the basis for natural law. Starting from the basis of our natural sociableness Grotius suggests that proofs of the natural law are almost as self-evident as the data we receive through the senses. Our moral reasoning, however, is not as certain as mathematical demonstrations because circumstantial factors often cloud the issues (Grotius 2005: Book II, chapt. xxiii, I). Nevertheless, natural law is so inextricably tied to human nature that even if God did not exist, and He had no interest in the welfare of humanity, the law would remain valid (Grotius 2005: Book I, Preliminary Discourse, §11). This has often been taken to be Grotius' secularization of the natural law. Such a view is anachronistic.

When one examines Grotius' argument closely, it is evident that his statement is partially rhetorical, and that what drives and gives substance to our obligations is God, and as Jean Barbeyrac comments in his notes to Grotius' text, 'the Duty and Obligation, or the indispensable Necessity of conforming to these Ideas, and Maxims, necessarily supposes a superior Power, a supreme Master of Mankind, who can be no other than the Creator, or supreme Divinity' (Grotius 2005: Preliminary Discourse, fn 1 to §XI). Grotius contends that there are compelling reasons for ascribing the principles of the natural law to God. He has made them so evident and clear even to those 'less capable of strict Reasoning' that He forbids us to give in to impetuous passions that are contrary to our own and others' interests and which divert us from conforming to the rules of reason (Grotius 2005: Preliminary Discourse, §13). In the *Mare Liberum* (*The Free Sea*) Grotius goes further and suggests that God directly insinuates certain precepts into men's minds, which are 'sufficient to induce obligation even if no reason is apparent' (Grotius 2004: 105).

Pufendorf is certainly an immensely important figure in the history of natural law, whose place in the history of philosophy in general was eclipsed by Kant's revolution in ethics. Pufendorf thought Grotius the first to make an accurate distinction between natural law and human law and to place them in their proper relation. He acknowledged that the New Testament included much that was of importance to natural law, but that it could not be used as a guide to it because there was much that was unacceptable to non-Christians contained within it, and which would undermine its credibility of being truly universal (Tuck 1987: 103).

Despite the fact that Pufendorf is acknowledged to derive the natural law from God, and explicitly rejected the tentative Grotian suggestion that the natural law would retain its force even if God did not exist, Nussbaum argues that in practical terms Pufendorf is so little influenced by theological and religious sentiments that he became 'considered the true founder of a secular law of nature' (Nussbaum 1953: 148). I find this quite a remarkable suppression of the evidence. Pufendorf explicitly states that the dictates of reason do not alone achieve the power and dignity of laws. For that a higher principle must be invoked in order to instil an immutable obligation. There can be no law without a sovereign, and as sovereign of the universe God is the creator and enforcer of natural law. It is in virtue of God's sovereignty that He has obliged us to observe the natural law (Pufendorf 1717: Book II, chapt. iii, §xx). Pufendorf believed that Grotius was wrong in thinking that the laws of nature were equivalent to the laws of logic comparable to such analytic propositions as a triangle has three sides. While denying the foundation, he could agree with much of the superstructure, in particular, the belief that the laws of nature comprised a body of rules for the preservation of individuals. They both believed that what is right is also profitable or useful. Hence he could speak of Hobbes with approval. Pufendorf, however, went further in arguing that to demonstrate that something was profitable was not in itself sufficient to generate a belief in an agent that the action was morally obligatory. To endow the dictates of reason with the power and dignity of laws it was necessary to invoke a higher principle, and that is the will of God (Tuck 1987: 106).

Pufendorf denies Hobbes' contention that justice and injustice are the product of the will of the sovereign. He argues that they are defined by natural law and bind the consciences of men (Pufendorf 1717: Book VIII, chapt. i, §5). States, Pufendorf contended, could not have been created by compact without some notion of justice and injustice existing prior to the institution of the state. There could be no binding force to a pact without the knowledge that it is just to uphold it and unjust to break it.

For him it is absolutely presupposed that every law has an author, and, in addition, to qualify properly as law it must also be enforceable. Both natural law and human positive law satisfy these criteria. Natural law, from which our natural rights derive, is the creation of God, who, should we transgress against it, punishes our actions. Pufendorf argues that 'the obligation of Natural Law proceeds from God himself, the great Creator and supreme Governor of Mankind; who by Virtue of his Sovereignty hath bound Men to the observation of it' (Pufendorf 1717: Book II, chapt. iii, §20). Because of our limited intelligence and reason, and because punishments may not immediately follow the crime, we often fail to make the connection between our actions and the punishment that God delivers. Rights and duties in the state of nature are 'imperfect' because they are not enforceable against each other, whereas legal rights and duties are 'perfect' because they are enforceable. It is often the case that what was once compelled by conscience became codified and enforceable in positive law. The important point is that Pufendorf thinks that both are equally morally obligatory (Pufendorf 1991: Book I, chap. 9, §4).

The idea of a prescriptive natural law, as Rachel attests, invoking the authority of Grotius, rests upon certain unquestionable postulates which are the ultimate source of obligation. The first or primary such postulate is the existence of God; the second is the Existence of Divine Providence, that is the idea that God watches over us with goodness and justice; and third, the immortality of the soul, or at least its survival after death. These truths are so self-evident for Rachel that they stand as the basis of all explanation. Following Aristotle, he contends that only those doubts are permitted that are a consequence of our weakness in reasoning. We cannot doubt those things that are so gross as to demand punishment, and which arise as a result of obtuse perception or reasoning. For Rachel, denial of the existence of God falls into this category, and therefore deserves punishment (Rachel 1916: Diss. I, §§cxiv–cxv).

Johann Wolfgang Textor perhaps has one of the strongest claims to secularising the natural law. He follows and modifies the theories of Grotius and Hobbes. Textor thinks it self-evident that we share some aspects of natural law with the animals. He excludes what he regards as instincts such as eating and drinking, standing and running, but includes such activities as self-defence against violence, union between males and females, procreation and the nurturing of offspring, because 'there is an element of right and wrong, of honest and base' in them and they are subject to the dictates of right reason.

Other aspects of the natural law are peculiar to humans, including 'dutifulness to God, respect to parents, ownership and its varieties, original acquisition, and obligations arising from human contracts and agreements' (Textor 1916: II, 15). The law of nature for him issues direct from natural reason. This Reason, however, is implanted in men by God, and one of the self-evident laws of nature is that we must fulfil our obligations to God. Without God, whose existence Textor goes to some pains to prove, there is no basis for obligation and civil society would collapse (Textor 1916: VI, 1–28).

Even in the mid eighteenth century natural law was still being inextricably linked to God's authority. Jean Jacques Burlamaqui (1694–1748), an influential Swiss jurist whose chief works are *Principles of Natural Law* (1747) and *Principles of Political Law* (1751) set out to demonstrate the efficacy of natural law by relating it to its original source in God's rule, and to human reason and moral instinct. International and domestic laws were, for him, based on natural law. Burlamaqui firmly believes that the natural law may be apprehended by the pure light of reason in the discovery of principles from which our duties are to be deduced. Such is the power of reason that there is no need to ask whether God has sufficiently promulgated these laws to us (Burlamaqui 1819: Part II, chapt. V, §i). Against those, including Pufendorf, who convict Grotius of presenting us with a vicious circle of reasoning, Burlamaqui maintains the religious foundation of his thought. Referring to book 1, chapter I, §10 of Grotius' *Rights of War and Peace*, Burlamaqui aligns himself with the contention that the law of nature consists in certain principles of right reason which teaches us what is right and wrong, according to the extent to which it agrees or disagrees with man's rational and sociable nature. Accordingly God, the author of nature, commands or forbids those actions. The obligation to obey the natural law, then, is ultimately a duty to God (Burlamaqui 1819. Part II, chapt. VII, §§ xii–xvi).

> As soon as we have acknowledged a Creator, it is evident that he has a supreme right to lay His commands on man, to prescribe rules of conduct to him, and to subject him to laws; and it is no less evident that man on his side finds himself, by his natural constitution, under an obligation of subjecting his actions to the will of this supreme being (Burlamaqui 1819: Part II, chapt. I, xi).

NATURAL LAW AND THE LAW OF NATIONS

The relationship between customary law, natural law, and the Law of Nations is often poorly articulated, and imprecisely delineated among jurists and theologians from the twelfth century onwards. To look to classical Rome for guidance was merely further to compound the confusion. Peter Stein has argued that Roman Jurists often used the terms indifferently and without distinction (Stein 1988: 44). Whereas the natural law lacked any real legal force for classical jurists because it was a philosophical concept aspirational in its high ideals, for medieval canonists and theologians it came to have the function that we commonly associate with it, namely the criterion by which other laws were to be judged, and from which no civil law could derogate. Should the two conflict, natural law overrode civil law (Tierney 2007: 104). We saw in Chapter Two how the *Decretals* of Gratian and the writings of Aquinas gave priority to natural law when it came into conflict with human law. We have also seen how in addition to issuing commands and prohibitions, the natural law came to have a permissive sense which recommended as desirable and good certain kinds of actions or institutions, but did not require them. It is at this point, that of the permissive natural law, where we see much intersection with the Law of Nations, but the exact relation between the two was often laboured, and deliberately vague. Was it, for example, a logical extension of natural law, or something entirely separate, and if separate were there circumstances when it could derogate the natural law?

Unlike Sepúlveda who had used the Roman term *ius gentium* in its original sense as regulating the relations between individuals, Vitoria applied this term in the course of the debate concerning the Indies to the relations between political communities (Parry 1990: 146). It is in this sense that Vitoria can be considered the founder of modern international law, for in his discussion of the American question he had clearly established rights and obligations of political communities irrespective of religion (Parry 1981: 307 and Jahn 2000: 67). The relationship between natural law and the Law of Nations is not one that he systematically addresses, and when each passage in which he considers it is compared no consistent principles are discerned to provide a coherent manifold.

Vitoria suggests that within 'perfect communities', such as kingdoms, commonwealths or principalities, we are related to each other as citizens, but because of the interdependence of such communities there is a wider universal moral community to which we belong. The natural law takes first place in constraining both relations among citizens, and between individuals and states in the wider world community. Beyond natural law, however, special rules established by custom and usage supplement what natural reason has discovered. The Law of Nations for Vitoria is what natural reason has established as common among all nations, often identical with the natural law, or more often arising out of it (Tierney 1991: 307). The *jus gentium* is for him natural law *inter gentes*, or a necessary customary supplement to it, but he is clear that such customary rules are both special and few (Nussbaum 1953: 87–88). He does not elaborate upon the mutual dependence of states, and the basis of the limited rules that emanate from the *jus gentium* is mutual love and charity, applied later by Suarez not to states, but to individual strangers from any nation.

At times Vitoria implies that the Law of Nations and customary law are to be equated with human positive law, and not with the natural law. He takes his lead from Roman jurisprudence but extends the meaning of *ius gentium*. For him international law is the body of rules established by natural reason as applicable to all nations. Vitoria made the significant move, sometimes attributed to Zouche, from the definition of the *Institutes* (I, 2.i) which refers to the law between nations (*ius inter gentes*) to the Law of Nations (*ius gentium*). As Coleman Phillipson contends, 'It implies a recognition at once of the independence and of the interdependence of States, and of their reciprocal rights and obligations. It points to the existence of a juridical tie between nations, which constitute therefore an international society' (Phillipson 1915: 180).

The relation between natural law and the Law of Nations is nevertheless intimate. The Law of Nations, Vitoria contends, 'either is or derives from Natural Law' (Vitoria 1991: 278). If natural law as a dictate of reason prohibits the killing of the innocent, the Law of Nations as a deduction from this determines who are to be regarded as innocent (Hartigan 1973: 83). James Turner Johnson suggests that for Vitoria the '*jus gentium* is a conscious, though culturally relative, expression of the law of nature' (Johnson 1981:97).

There are some things in the Law of Nations, Vitoria suggests, which manifestly derive from the law of nature. There are others, however, whose title rests 'on the consent of the greater part of the world' (Vitoria 1991: 281). Gentili is as ambiguous about the relation between natural law and the Law of Nations. He appears to equate the two but in fact wishes to separate them. At first he maintains that 'questions of war ought to be settled in accordance with the law of nations, which is the law of nature' (Gentili 1933: Book I, chapt. i, 5). The law of nature and the Law of Nations do exist, he suggests, but they are extremely difficult to come to know. The Law of Nations is discernible, however, by recourse to a variety of sources. Light is shed upon it by recourse to authors and founders of laws who maintain that the Law of Nations is that law to which all nations commonly adhere, and which is the result of native reason. It is 'that which has successively seemed acceptable to all men' and is therefore regarded as the law of nature (Gentili 1933: Book I, chapt. i, 10–11).

It may be inferred from Ayala's method of argument that the exercise of right reason dictates certain precepts that are so evident that no man could deny them. The law of nature, for example, dictates that it is just to defend oneself, whether acting in the capacity of the state, or as a private person. It is lawful, therefore, to defend one's empire, person, friends, allies, or property (Ayala 1912, Book I, chapt. ii, [11]). For such conclusions, reason itself is the measure against which they are tested. Matters relating to the declaration, conduct, and etiquette of war are often the result of usage, custom, and agreement, and which are embodied in the Law of Nations. The evidence is to be found in Scripture, the writings of the Greeks and Romans, as well as in theologians, and the actual practice of states.

Francisco Suarez does not doubt the existence of *ius gentium* because it 'is assumed by all authorities as an established fact' (Suarez 1944: Book II, chapt. XVII, §1, p. 325). What troubles him is that it is insufficiently distinguished from the natural law, which for many writers either comprises the Law of Nations, or forms part of it. For Suarez the Law of Nations has a close affinity, but should not be confused with natural law. For him, it was a form of customary law that pertained to relations among nations, and in that respect was to be distinguished from civil law that held within nations. Although it was definitely a form of human law it came between natural law and civil law.

He points to an ambiguity in the use of the terms Law of Nations, and convicted the Roman law of sometimes conflating it with natural law (Tierney 2007: 115), that was to be taken up by later writers. He maintained that the term was used in two senses. First, it is the law that all peoples must observe in their relations with other peoples. Second, it is the law that citizens obey within states, and which is replicated widely throughout the world, especially by civilized peoples. This communality of law is also called *jus gentium*, or the Law of Nations (Nussbaum 1953: 85–6). *Jus gentium* for him was distinguished by its customary character, as opposed to civil law which is largely written and backed by a sovereign (Haakonssen 1996: 19). What is important, however, is that *jus gentium* in the two senses that he identifies nowhere near exhausts the code regulating relations among *populos* or *gentes*. These, like all human relations, are primarily regulated by natural law which is of Divine origin, and the *jus gentium* is a mere supplement standing somewhere between natural law and civil law. They are alike, however, in that although different, they pertain only to humans (Suarez 1944: Book II, chapt. XVII, §9, p. 333). Their subject matter is also applicable only to humans, but the Law of Nations may on occasion formulate some precepts that relate to brutes, for example, in the area of animal husbandry.

The Law of Nations is not concerned with primary moral principles and does not prescribe any mode of conduct as being necessary for righteous conduct, nor does it forbid anything on the grounds that it is intrinsically evil. Such matters are the subject of the natural law (Suarez 1944, Book II, chapt. XVII, §9, p. 333). The Law of Nations does not prohibit acts because they are evil, in prohibiting acts it creates the evil. In other words, 'the *ius gentium* is not so much indicative of what is [inherently] evil, as it is constitutive of evil' (Suarez 1944, Book II, chapt. XIX, §2, p. 342). They differ also in that the natural law is immutable and based upon nature, and the Law of Nations is customary. It is its customary character that distinguishes it from civil laws. He argues that such laws are not 'established in written form; they are established through the customs not of one or two states or provinces, but nearly all nations... Furthermore, unwritten law is made up of customs, and if it has been introduced by the custom of one particular nation and is binding upon the conduct of that nation only, it is called civil law; if on the other hand, it has been introduced by the customs of all nations and thus is binding upon all, we believe it to be the *ius gentium* properly so called' (Suarez 1944: Book II, chapt. XIX, §6, p. 345).

Gentili, who is yet another who has been called the father of the modern Law of Nations (Gentili 1933: 18a), rejected the *a priori* methods of philosophers in favour of the historical approach. He favoured the examination of existing practices, and by a process of induction inferred the general rules regulating the Law of Nations, with reference to both ancient and contemporary authorities (Gentili 1933: 19a–21a). The Law of Nations is those rules and standards which all, or the major part of, nations agree upon, explicitly or in their habitual conduct, to regulate their relations. It is not capricious or fortuitous, however, because the laws derive from natural reason which dictates justice and right. Like his predecessors he subjected the Law of Nations to the test of natural law, but did not elaborate its content, and instead often divested it of its metaphysical mysticism, anchoring it to the common sense, justice, and humanity of mankind. His discussions of the

Law of Nations are not consistent. Sometimes he identifies it with natural law, at others it is a derivation from it, relating not to states as such, but to the universal community of mankind (Nussbaum 1953: 98).

For Gentili, nations comprised a '*societas gentium*' which was in his formulation quite remarkable because it included non-Catholic and non-Christian nations, including those of the infidel, idolator, and heretic, whose sovereigns were vested with the right of dominium. In a radical departure from most of his predecessors, Gentili did not designate these deviations from Christianity just causes of war, and therefore grounds for rejecting claims to dominium. Instead they were to be afforded the usual courtesies under the Law of Nations, including diplomatic immunity and treaty making powers. Atheists, or those with no religion, however, could not be trusted and had to be treated as pirates or brigands, outside of the protection of the Law of Nations.

From traders who have experience of many lands, knowledge of the commonly accepted laws and customs controlling commerce and trade indicates the content of the Law of Nations by which such matters are regulated. Furthermore, reason itself and the arguments and authority of philosophers, 'approved by the judgement of every age' (Gentili 1933: Book I, chapt. i, 17), along with the Holy Scriptures shed light upon the law of nature and nations. In Gentili, we have an emphasis upon the positive aspect of the Law of Nations, as that which is generally agreed or well established by custom, having its basis in natural reason and natural law. Gentili's position is further complicated by the fact that he thinks both the law of nature and the Law of Nations are expressions of the Divine Will. This to a large extent detracts from the view that he secularizes the natural law and the Law of Nations (Gentili 1933: Book I, chapt. xii, 92).[1]

Gentili, too, maintains the distinction between the law of nature and the Law of Nations. He contends that the civil law is an agreement and bond between all citizens, 'the same is true of the Law of Nations as regards nations, and the Law of Nature as regards mankind' (Gentili 1933: Book I, chapt. xxv, 202–3).

I have suggested that in Vitoria and Gentili the relationship between natural law and the Law of Nations is not always clear. Suarez was much more consistent and explicit. Grotius, too, consistent with his principle not to conflate those things that should be distinguished, makes a more pronounced differentiation between the two. Grotius was one of the most significant political thinkers of the seventeenth century and was extensively cited as an authority. His natural law theory differed from that of the discredited scholastics, and at the same time offered an alternative to the scepticism of Montaigne and Pierre Charron (Tuck 1993: 499).

In Grotius' view natural law may not be abrogated or overridden by custom or prescription, but there are circumstances where there are commonly accepted precepts which are not self-evidently derived from natural law, nor do they appear at variance with the law of nature. The obligation in such cases arises out of tacit

---

[1] 'Let the Theologians keep silent about a matter which is outside of their province' (Gentili 1933: Book I, chapt. xii, 92). He did think that jurists and theologians had different areas of competence, but this does not imply that he rejected the religious foundations of law and society.

consent, evidenced by usage and custom. The Law of Nations, then, may contain precepts created by nations themselves, and whether they arise from Divine instinct or mutual consent 'are testified to both by the most ancient usage of civilised nations and by the authority of the wisest men' (Grotius 2004: 106). Much of the Law of Nations, he contends, arises out of custom. Neither prescription, time out of mind, nor custom can override the precepts of natural law. Grotius argues that custom is a kind of positive law which cannot derogate or override the perpetual law of nature (Grotius 2004: 43 and 53).

Both Hobbes and Pufendorf denied the existence, or efficacy, of Law of Nations separate from natural law. For Hobbes, as we will see, the natural law is simply descriptive, and for Pufendorf it is prescriptive, or provides us with moral injunctions. We saw how Aquinas attributed the Law of Nations to that part of the natural law that pertains only to humans. He does in effect, then, equate the Law of Nations and the natural law. Hobbes equates the two in a different way. The laws of nature are universally applicable to individual humans, but equally there are laws that apply to the relations between and among cities, and these he calls the Law of Nations. In his view, there is little difference between the two because cities acquire the personal properties of men, and are subject to the same laws under the guise of a different name, the right of nations (Hobbes 1841: chapter 14, §4).

Pufendorf, approving of Hobbes' analysis, had made it clear in his *Elements of Universal Jurisprudence in Three Books* (1660), and in *The Law of Nature and Nations* (1672), that states were bound by the universal law of nature. In the latter, for example, he explicitly addresses the relationship between natural law and Law of Nations concurring completely with the view of Hobbes. The Law of Nations is simply the law of nature applied to states (Pufendorf 1717: Book II, chapt. iii, §XXIV). There are also agreements among nations that confer rights based on treaties, and customs in conformity with which civilized nations behave. The treaty rights, he contends, are valid only between those signatories to the treaty, and as to customs, states may renounce them at their pleasure (Pufendorf 1931: Book I, definition 13, §§24–26 and Pufendorf 1717: Book II, chapt. iii, §23). In other words, Pufendorf denied the efficacy of customary international law, or the Law of Nations. The Law of Nations was nothing more than the precepts derived from natural law discovered by *a priori* reasoning.

In opposition to the failure to distinguish the law of nature and the Law of Nations from each other, Samuel Rachel, a native of Lunden, Holstein, and professor of the law of nature and nations at the University of Kiel, set out to refute the position adhered to by Grotius, Hobbes, and Pufendorf. He argued that Aristotle had correctly distinguished between natural and arbitrary law in his *Nichomachean Ethics*. For Rachel, natural law and the Law of Nations were distinct, and the latter was part of the *jus arbitrarium*, having its basis in agreement, or in custom. Custom is an implied agreement, and because states are independent of each other obligations between them are created only by agreement. Customary law need not be the result of all nations implicitly agreeing, it may be sufficient when several, especially of the civilized nations, agree to establish a binding rule. Both individuals and nations, in Rachel's view, are bound by natural law and the

Law of Nations. He does not underestimate the complexity of distinguishing the natural law from positive law, but claims that the better a student has been in his study of natural law the better he will be able to distinguish it from Positive Law (Rachel 1916: Diss. I, §cxxxv). Rachel contends that 'the Law of Nations is founded on the agreement of Nations. For no one State has authority over another...' (Rachel 1916: Diss. II, §ii).

Rachel wanted clearly to distinguish between natural law and the Law of Nations, and conceived the former in traditional terms. He denies that knowledge of the natural law is innate. We are born with the capacities, or faculties, to acquire such knowledge, but not with the knowledge itself. For him, natural law has four important features. First, its authority and origin are derived from Divine Providence. Second, its rules and precepts are in conformity with the rational and social nature of human beings. Third, coming to know natural law entails 'that which can be perceived and recognized by the light of Natural Reason' (Rachel 1916: Diss. I, §xx). And, fourth, natural law is consistent with nature in what he calls the active sense, 'that is, with God Himself, from Whose Justice these rays of light issue' (Rachel 1916: Diss. I, §xx).

Textor's *Synopsis Juris Gentium*, published in 1680, is more faithful to how the relationship between natural law and the Law of Nations was understood in practice, and in fact goes into more detail in codifying the Law of Nations than Rachel. The law of nature in its application to the relations among states is for Textor identical with the primitive Law of Nations. He argues that 'the same Law that, by reference to its basis in principles of Natural Reason, is called Natural Law is, by reference to world-wide reception, called the Law of Nations' (Textor 1916: iv). The Law of Nations therefore has two elements, primordial and secondary, the natural law and customary international law, or that law which derives its binding force from customs (*exercitium*) (Textor 1916: II, 1–7). Textor does not raise the difficult question of which of these two components has priority, or lays claim to real law, in a dispute between nations if customary law is contrary to natural law. Grotius, for example, had attempted to address this issue by making a distinction between the Law of Nations that is compelling in conscience, '*internum*', and one that merely binds external actions. Textor does not want to restrict the secondary Law of Nations only to that which is customary, and acknowledges that explicit agreements among sovereigns may add to such law, lamenting, nevertheless, that 'The world, however, has not yet beheld such common Law of Nations affirmed by express assent, and perhaps never will behold it, so great is the preference shown for settling the affairs of Kings and peoples by the sword and arms, rather than by equity and justice' (Textor 1916: I, 24).

Vattel reflects the extent to which the state had by the middle of the eighteenth century become the central actor in international relations. Both Christian Wolff and Emerich Vattel distinguish between the Necessary Law of Nations and the Voluntary Law of Nations (Ruddy 1975: 97). For Wolff, beginning with the legal fiction of a *civitas maxima*, the Voluntary Law of Nations is equivalent to the civil law within states, and both must be derived from the natural law. Vattel thought natural law was the basis of the Law of Nations, but he did not identify the two (Vattel 1834: 3a and 4). Individuals, the subjects of natural law, have rights and obligations in relation to each other. States differ from individuals. States are related to each other in a condition analogous to the state of nature, but in order to accommodate them the laws of nature had to be transformed into the Law of Nations. Christian Wolff, Vattel's mentor, and following Pufendorf, contends that states are themselves corporate moral persons with rights and duties different from those of individual persons and as the creation of the individuals who comprise them they exercise on behalf of their citizens the duties that those individuals have to mankind as whole (Wolff 1934: Prolegomena, §3). The state differs from an ordinary individual in that its decisions are not often the result of the whims of one man or of the rashness of the moment, but based instead upon consultation and deliberation. Vattel contends that the state is a 'moral person, who possesses an understanding and a will peculiar to herself, and it is susceptible of obligations and rights' (Vattel 1834: Preliminaries, §2).

Christian Wolff is much less concerned with evidentially based customary and treaty law in the content of his Law of Nations, than with the philosophical deduction of principles from the law of nature. This is, in fact, unsurprising since he had little or no experience of affairs of state, nor of the practice of law. Like Hobbes he begins his enquiry with a hypothetical state of nature. The natural law that governs this state of nature for him is prescriptive, and not as in Hobbes' case descriptive and prudential.[2] Wolff posits a strong connection between natural law and ethics. He maintains that rights are based on duties, and because there are innate duties, there are also innate rights. We have natural rights to anything that enables us to fulfil our natural obligations. These rights are universal, the same the world over. He posits a natural equality, from which our liberties flow, and contends that no one has the right to dominion over any other. Differences in rights, then, arise only for acquired rights, and not for those that are congenital (Wolff 1934: Introduction, p. xxxi).

God has initially placed all humans in a universal society, regulated by natural laws. Civil societies are the result of contract, and the constitutional laws agreed upon by the sovereign people, even when they establish an absolute monarch, are the fundamental laws derived or deduced from the natural law. Peoples can resist rulers whose commands contravene the natural law, and who have no right to require anything that is at variance with the fundamental laws. The universal society of individuals continues as a universal society of nations. If this were not the case, the establishment of civil societies would be contrary to the Will of God (Wolff 1934: Prolegomena, §7).

What is important about Wolff is that he addresses the question of the relation between the natural law and the Law of Nations. He does not entirely separate the two, but goes some way to indicate what aspects of the Law of Nations derive from what sources. The first source is the Natural, or necessary, Law of Nations which derives directly from the rights and duties individuals have in a state of

---

[2] The distinction between the prescriptive and descriptive laws of nature will be explored more fully in Chapter Five.

nature, adapted to acknowledge that nations are not like physical persons. These rights and duties are universal. In this respect all nations are equal, having the same rights, duties and liberties. None may impede the freedoms of others, nor has any a right over the actions of another state. Nations have the right to self-preservation, and the right to resort to war if necessary in pursuance of that right. Nations may also enter into agreements that bind other nations, and thus may acquire rights. This aspect of the Law of Nations, that is the Natural or necessary, is immutable in that modifications made to adapt to nations must not undermine or contradict the natural law, and therefore no nation may abrogate it.

Wolff's *Jus gentium voluntarium*, or volitional Law of Nations, proved to be controversial because it is so strongly connected to the natural law. It goes under various names, such as the necessary Law of Nations, or the natural law of Nations, and even the 'internal Law of Nations' by Grotius and his successors, because it binds nations in conscience (Wolff 1934: Prolegomena, §4). He acknowledges that he uses the term voluntary Law of Nations in a much more restricted sense than Grotius. Wolff contends that, 'far be it from you to imagine that this voluntary law of nations is developed from the will of nations in such a way that their will is free to establish it and that freewill alone takes the place of reason, without any regard to Natural Law' (Wolff 1934: Preface, 6). The voluntary Law of Nations, because it is derived from natural law and is a dictate of reason, rests upon the presumed consent of nations (Wolff 1934: Prolegomena, §25). In a situation where war, or difficulties between nations, may be resolved, and ought to come to an end, such a result should be sought, even if this means changing the conclusions, within reason, of the law of nature in order to achieve the end (Wolff 1934: chap. VII, §887).

This leads to an idea closely connected with it, and which obliges nations to agree to the voluntary law, namely the *civitas maxima*. Nature has fashioned nations into a supreme state, and prescribed the method by which the voluntary Law of Nations may be deduced from the laws of nature, 'so that nations are bound to agree to that law, and is not left to their caprice as to whether they should prefer to agree or not' (Wolff 1934: Preface, 6). Nations, like individuals, have an obligation for self-improvement by individual and collective effort. This also entails the right of nations to act collectively against a nation that undermines or endangers the *civitas maxima* (Wolff 1934: Prolegomena, §13). The law that regulates this society of nations is deduced from the natural law, and Wolff calls it *jus gentium voluntarium*, and rests it upon the implied consent of nations. To these two forms of law which comprise the Law of Nations he adds treaty law, which he calls 'stipulative' or 'particular' because in his view it binds only those states which conclude the treaties. This law rests upon the explicit consent of nations (Wolff 1934: Prolegomena, §23). Finally, the Law of Nations includes customary law which Wolff defines as that law which 'has been brought in by long usage and observed as law' (Wolff 1934: Prolegomena, §24). This rests on the tacit consent of nations, and like the stipulative law is particular in its scope. All three together – the voluntary, stipulative, and customary – comprise the positive Law of Nations.

Cornelius Van Bynkershoek (1673–1743) and his successors, such as Johann Jakob Moser (1701–1785) and Georg Friedrich von Martens (1756–1821), represent a methodological move that gradually betrays distinctly positivist leanings, both implicitly and explicitly, rejecting natural law and natural right as the moral basis of the Law of Nations. They were indeed religious men, and did not explicitly deny the natural law, but were cognizant that its very abstractness lent itself to quite varied interpretations. Moser, for example, suggested that even the greatest scholars disagree on its fundamentals, and whatever one contends, another repays in kind (Nussbaum 1953: 177). The Law of Nations, or international law, was explicitly equated with customary law, the practice of states, and the pronouncements of the most significant authorities, who in Bynkershoek's case were Grotius and Pufendorf. For Cornelius Van Bynkershoek both individuals and states are the subjects of this Law of Nations. He emphasizes the role of reason in determining the content of the Law of Nations, but the confirmation of reason demands the authority that accompanies usage and practice. This is a clear move away from the scholastic remnants found in Wolff. For Wolff it would be wrong to assign to custom what reason itself compels us to believe should be law among all nations (Wolff 1934: Prolegomena, §25). Bynkershoek contends that while reason is universal, it is often ambiguous and frequently errs. In such cases it is continuous custom with reference to precedent, that decides. Unlike Wolff, Bynkershoek was essentially a jurist, and not much interested in the philosophical foundations of the origins of obedience to law, or of the acquisition of property. Justice for him is inextricably related to law, and is something completely separate and distinguishable from humanity. He makes reference to natural law, but it does not have an important place in his thought, and he equates the Law of Nations with international law.

Despite this positivist move throughout the eighteenth century, it was nevertheless towards its latter part that the famous declarations of the rights of man and of citizens were produced. Their truths, their authors suggested, were self-evident. We will see how natural rights nevertheless dominated debates in the eighteenth century, and how even their most radical exponents still retained a heavy residue of religious foundationalism. What is interesting about von Martens is that he moves away from the emphasis on the obligations of states, by extending what was nascent in both Wolff and Vattel. Martens contends that states have certain absolute, primitive, or natural rights that are derived from the law of nature, and which differ from acquired rights. Among these natural rights of states are territorial sovereignty, independence, equality of treatment, and even aggrandizement (Nussbaum 1953: 183).

THE NECESSARY AND VOLUNTARY LAW OF NATIONS

We have already encountered distinctions within the Law of Nations which allow for a degree of overlap with the natural law. I want now to explore this mutual relation a little further. For Gentili the Law of Nations is that law which all, or the majority of, nations agree upon. It is the law that regulates the *societas gentium*, or community of states, comprising members who are at once independent and interdependent. The laws for him have both a customary character, *usus gentium*, but are also the product of natural reason which reveals the fundamental precepts of justice and right universally impressed upon the minds of all men.

Primary, or first, laws of nations are for the most part correlative with natural law. Grotius, for example, clearly correlates the two when he contends that by the first Law of Nations, 'which sometimes is also called natural', there was no property and everything was held in common (Grotius 2004: 21). For Grotius one of the primary laws of nations is that which allows any nation to trade with any other, and thus entails freedom of passage (Grotius 2004: 10). Grotius sometimes refers to those precepts to which all nations conform, not through habit, or imitation, but because they are truly universal, as 'the law of nations properly so called' or the 'real law of nations' (Grotius 2004: 125–6).

Richard Zouche (1590–1661), the Regius professor of Civil Law at Oxford University, and the next but one successor to Gentili, was a great admirer of his illustrious predecessor and of the distinguished work of Hugo Grotius. Zouche was the first to move towards the modern nomenclature for the Law of Nations adopted by Jeremy Bentham, the celebrated critic of natural rights. Zouche uses the term 'Law between Nations', which Bentham modified to 'international law'. Zouche makes the tentative move that was to characterize modern international law, designating states as its principal appropriate subjects, but he did not exclude private relations between peoples of different nations entirely. In addition, he still wants to retain a link between natural law and the Law between Nations. He argues that many people from different times and places lay down the same principles which are to be deemed right conclusions derived from 'the first principles of nature, or some general agreement, of which the former points to the Law of Nature, the latter to the Law of Nations' (Zouche 1911: part I, §1). Here the implication is that there is a primary or compulsory Law of Nations that corresponds to the natural law, and a secondary, or permissive Law of Nations that also includes the law between nations.

There is, he argues, the Law of Nations, and this is the common element found in the laws that each state employs among its own subjects, relating for example, to the status of freemen and slaves, the holding of private property, and the binding of individuals to contracts. The Law between Nations, however, is of a different character. By it nations are separated, new kingdoms or principalities founded, international commerce instituted, and wars initiated (Zouche 1911: Book I, §1). Zouche is certainly not theoretically inclined, and offers little by way of philosophical elaboration. Nevertheless, he does distinguish between natural law, the Law of Nations and the Law between Nations – *jus inter gentes*, the last of which is unequivocally based on custom, on condition that it is reasonable, and on bilateral and multilateral treaties (Nussbaum 1953: 167).

Rachel, because he distinguished clearly between the law of nature and the Law of Nations, consistently denies the frequently asserted categorization of the primary and secondary Law of Nations. He contends that the Law of Nations in the proper sense is a species of the genus Arbitrary Law, and should not be confounded with the natural law (Rachel 1916: Diss. II, §iv). 'The Law of Nations', Rachel maintains, 'is a law developed by the consent or agreement, either expressly or tacitly given, of many free nations, whereby for the sake of utility they are mutually bound to one another' (Rachel 1916: Diss. II, §xvi). He did nevertheless follow Grotius in distinguishing between the *jus gentium externum* and a *jus gentium internum*. In this respect there is a Law of Nations that is in harmony with the law of nature (*jus gentium verum*), and one that is contrary to the law of nature, and consequently unjust (*jus gentium putativum*).

Inspired by Christian Wolff, Vattel contended that the Law of Nations is in fact a modification of natural law, which took into account the different composition of the character of the moral person of the state and that of the individual. He distinguished the Law of Nations into the *necessary* which binds the conscience of sovereigns, and the *voluntary*, or positive, which rests on the will of the sovereign and accommodates the practical and prudential considerations which have to be acknowledged in order to mitigate the effects of war.

Vattel is concerned to establish the point that the Law of Nations does not rest upon the consent of individual nations in order to impress upon sovereign states that the origin of their rights and duties is more fundamental and morally obligatory. In this respect Vattel wishes to dispel any confusion over those practices which are good and obligatory in themselves, and those which of necessity are merely tolerated. The Law of Nations, he argues, is in fact the application of the law of nature to the moral persons of states in their mutual relations. Like Wolff, Vattel distinguishes the Law of Nations into the *necessary* and *voluntary*. The necessary law, derived immediately from nature, binds the consciences of individuals and nations alike and must be observed in their personal conduct. It is *necessary* because its obligations are absolutely binding upon one's conscience. This law is not subject to change or alteration by human design, nor can individuals and states release themselves from its obligations (Vattel 1834: Preliminaries, §§6–9).

Whereas one state may have a perfect right in conscience the obligation to which it gives rise in another state is imperfect because that state has the right to judge for itself what its obligations are, and whether it can discharge them without detriment to itself. It is only by means of the consent of states that imperfect obligations can be transformed into perfect enforceable obligations (Linklater 1990: 85). The *necessary* law 'recommends the observance' of the *voluntary* Law of Nations in that the voluntary law's obligatory precepts are conducive to the common good and welfare of nations in their mutual relations (Vattel 1916: Preface, 11a). The Voluntary Law of Nations does result from the will of sovereigns and is effectively positive international law. The source of both the *necessary* and *voluntary* Law of Nations is in the law of nature. Nations by will or consent may also give rise to the *arbitrary* Law of Nations. Agreements, treaties, and promises establish the *conventional* Law of Nations, which is binding upon the contracting parties, whereas the tacit consent implied in the subscription to common practices establishes *custom* which must be observed by those nations which have accepted the principles by 'long usage'. The obligatory nature of the arbitrary Law of Nations is nevertheless grounded in the binding force that the law of nature gives to the honouring of express and tacit promises. The *necessary* Law of Nations acts as a criterion in terms of which treatises and conventions may be judged lawful or unlawful, and customs just or unjust.

At the root of Vattel's necessary Law of Nations stands the crucial idea that nature has established a universal society among all mankind, and that the individual's limited attributes are convincing proof that nature intended that we render each other mutual assistance. Agreements to establish communities or nations are consistent with our natural interdependence, and therefore nature established the great society of nations, which similarly requires mutual assistance (Butler 1978: 50–1). Like Pufendorf, Vattel denies that nations are as vulnerable as individuals, and are therefore more self-sufficient. For this reason nations do not need to constitute themselves into an international civil society (Linklater 1990: 81). Human society depends upon justice without which the mutual assistance and respect afforded each other would become nothing more than 'a vast scene of robbery' (Vattel 1834: II, v, §63). Because of the horrific consequences of war it is even more imperative that justice be observed among nations.

Vattel praises Cicero for acknowledging that the duties of the individual do not cease at state boundaries, and that the duties of nations are prescribed by the law of nature (Vattel 1834: II, 1, §1). The human race, Vattel contends, comprises a universal society whose interests and duties all men are bound to advance. Our common humanity obliges us to render mutual assistance to those in need. Our obligations are based upon a common human nature and therefore cannot be denied on grounds of religious differences. Vattel believes that we are naturally social because by nature we are not self-sufficient and depend upon others for protection and welfare. Agreements made among a limited number of individuals do not override these obligations to humanity, the difference being that they are now to be discharged by the state to which they have submitted their wills and given up their rights in order to advance the common good (Vattel 1834: Preliminaries, §11).

It is unrealistic to think that in a great society of equal sovereigns each nation in dispute, having the right to judge their own moral obligations by their own consciences, would not claim justice on their side. No nation can be released, as a matter of conscience, from observing the Necessary Law of Nations. The attempted enforcement of the Necessary Law of Nations by neutral nations during the conduct of war, however, is likely to exacerbate the conflict. A reliance on individual conscience is, however, not sufficiently robust, and something more palpable and of more certain application must be invoked. The Voluntary Law of Nations fulfils this function.

A sovereign's conscience should always be guided by the Necessary Law of Nations, but not to the exclusion of the Voluntary Law of Nations, the precepts of which are to formulate what can be demanded from other sovereigns, and which are meant to secure the safety and welfare of the great society of nations. For practical reasons, if law is to constrain the methods used in warfare, it must be presumed with regard to the effects of war, that justice resides on both sides. We must be careful to distinguish such issues as the effects of war and the validity of claims to acquisitions made in war. These are issues of the legality of the conduct of war, and are separate from judgements about whether the cause is just.

Vattel maintains that the Voluntary Law of Nations is ill equipped to make pronouncements about the justice of the causes of war. The Voluntary Law of Nations cannot therefore be invoked to accuse any side of engaging in illegitimate methods on the ground of an unjust cause. As a practical expedient, if war is to be regulated by law, it must be presumed that each side has equal justification. Because of the presumption of equal justification each side is permitted to do as the other does. The Voluntary Law of Nations condones no more in the conduct of war than the law of nature permits. The Voluntary Law of Nations does not make what is wrong right. It does not confer true rights upon those who wage war unjustly. In conscience the acts are and remain unjust. Through necessity and because of the determination to constrain the conduct of war, the Voluntary Law of Nations legalizes such acts and lifts the threat of punishment (Vattel 1834: III, xii, §192).

Acquisition during war is illustrative of what Vattel means. Under the Necessary Law of Nations a just title can only be conferred on a combatant if his cause is just. A right cannot be conferred by unjust action. There is no right to conquered property if the war is not just under the Necessary Law of Nations. In order to avoid protracted disputes which exacerbate conflicts between nations, however, the Voluntary Law of Nations allows simple conquest as the basis of title without questioning the justice of the cause (Vattel 1834: III, xiii, §§195–6).

Burlamaqui too wishes to associate the Law of Nations with the natural law. Just as men form a universal society, states which arose in order best to protect those individuals form something of a society. He contends that:

The law of nations properly so called, and considered as law proceeding from a superior, is nothing else, but the law of nature itself, not applied to men considered simply as such but to nations, states, or their chiefs, in the relations they have together, and the several interests they have to manage between each other (Burlamaqui 1819: book II, VI, v).

He does acknowledge, nevertheless, a fundamental Law of Nations that no sovereign may change, and which is absolute and immutable, and one that is 'arbitrary and free' and rests on the tacit and explicit consent of nations. The obligatory force of the latter, however, rests on the law of nature, 'which commands us to be true to our engagements' (Burlamaqui 1819: book II, VI, ix).

COMING TO KNOW NATURAL LAW, NATURAL RIGHTS, AND THE LAW OF NATIONS

Following Aquinas, Vitoria contended that natural law was knowable independently of revelation. It could be discovered by the exercise of right reason. Natural law is not innately planted in the souls of men. For Vitoria it is natural because we have the capacity to judge what is right 'by natural inclination' (Vitoria

1991: 169). The test of what is contrary to the natural law is 'when it is universally held by all [civilised people] to be unnatural' (Vitoria 1991: 209). Balthazar Ayala thought that apprehending and comprehending the natural law was a matter of wise men exercising 'right reason', implanted in them by nature (Ayala 1912: Preface, viii).

For Gentili the natural law and the Law of Nations are discoverable with reference to what is agreed or practiced by the greater part of mankind. Such agreement is for him the manifestation of natural or right reason. From widespread practice and agreement one may infer from parts of the world one knows that adherence will be evident elsewhere. Gentili does not purport to offer 'demonstrations' of the natural law, after the fashion of a mathematician. Such demonstrations, in his view, are not possible. Gentili argues that some things are so well known, such as one should worship God, 'that if you should try to prove them, you would render them obscure' (Gentili 1933: Book I, chapt. i, 14). Gentili's method of coming to know the natural law, and the Law of Nations, is what may be termed historical or *a posteriori*, rather than *a priori*. It is then, an evidentially based method, in which the actions, rules, and customs common to nations are taken to be proof of the existence of the laws of nature and nations. In addition, it is not sufficient to observe such practices, but one's own conclusions need to be confirmed, or validated, by 'authorities' because it is the 'habit of philosophers and of other wise men to speak according to the promptings of nature' (Gentili 1933: Book I, chapt. i, 15). Philosophers are more likely to possess natural reason, a quality that varies considerably depending upon the level of an individual's intelligence. The rules of philosophers have to be confirmed by 'the judgement of every age [which will] undoubtedly possess natural reason, as the wise Alciato declares' (Gentili 1933: Book I, chapt. i, 16). Gentili suggests that he employs the method of 'reasoning', as he has observed its use elsewhere, because that too is an 'imitation of nature' (Gentili 1933: Book I, chapt. i, 16). In addition, special weight is given to God's words as revealed in Holy Scripture which are universally applicable.

Suarez, as we saw, at times makes a clear division between natural law and the Law of Nations, and they are also distinguished in the manner in which we come to know them. Suarez contends that primary moral principles and all precepts that may clearly be inferred by reason from them are written in the hearts of men by God. The Law of Nations, however, is of human design and arises from the free will and agreement of mankind, relating either to the whole of the human community, or to a major portion of it. It is not therefore written on the hearts of mankind, and may be observed *a posteriori* in the customary practices of men and nations.

It was Grotius' contention that the laws of nature are the product of the Divine Will and that they can be universally apprehended and comprehended by the exercise of right reason, that is, natural reason:

That law by whose prescript form we are to judge is not hard to be found out, being the same with all and easy to be understood, which being bred with everyone is engrafted in the minds of all. But the right which we desire is such that the king himself ought not to deny unto his subjects, nor a Christian to infidels, for it hath its original from nature, which is an indifferent and equal parent to all, bountiful towards all, whose royal authority extendeth itself over those who rule the nations and is most sacred amongst them who have profited most in piety (Grotius 2004: 8).

Rights over those things in common have been granted to the human race by nature, or by God its author (Grotius 2004: 116).

Developing this Grotius maintained that the natural law can be discovered *a priori* through the exercise of reason, and *a posteriori* by observing the customs, tradition, and rules that humanity appears to agree upon. This convergence is for him evidence of God's natural law. Natural law may be known by, and must be in conformity with right reason. It is a natural law, for example, that the sea has always been for the common use of mankind, and that no one by nature can claim a property right in it. For Grotius, this is a pronouncement of right reason, and the test of its veracity is that nowhere in Holy Writ is it contradicted, and it is in complete harmony with the 'surest witnesses', nature and Scripture (Grotius 2004: 83). The content of natural law can be determined in two ways. First it may be known *a priori* as a dictate of right reason compatible with our rational and social natures. Second, we may come to know it *a posteriori* with a high degree of probability by identifying what all civilized nations agree upon. The latter must be deemed to have the same cause in all nations, that is, nothing other than 'Common Sense' (Grotius 2005: Book I, chapt. i, XII). Stephen Buckle contends that in this respect Grotius' conception of natural law is both innate or rationalist, as well as historical (Buckle 1991: 6). It is important to note, however, that our coming to know it may have an historical dimension, but its timelessness is attested by the fact, as we have seen, that it is unalterable by God Himself. In other words, its discovery and applicability is embedded in time, whereas its existence is not. The test of natural law must be that it logically derives from nature, or can 'be deduced from certain principles by just consequences' (Grotius 2005: Preliminary Discourse, §41). The usefulness of History is that it can confirm that some judgements are universally held, and that they testify to the existence of the law of nature. The law of nature, then, does not rest on the will of individuals. It is an objective criterion of human action, not of man's making. It is its self-evidence as a rational precept of the human condition, rather than any naturalistic quality, that makes it a law of nature.

There are for Grotius natural laws, as we have seen, by which we are obliged that have been insinuated into the minds of men by God for which there is no apparent reason. In the case of the prohibition of the marriage of those with close blood ties we cannot ignore the Roman Jurists who pronounced that such unions would constitute incest by the Law of Nations. It is not easy to give a reason for this precept that would go uncontested. We simply have to accept that God in his judgement has willed it. Such precepts are evidence of the disclosure by nations of the law written in their hearts and to which their conscience bears witness (Grotius 2004: 105, referring to Romans 2: 15). An indubitable and immutable human nature provides the basis for natural law. Starting from the basis of our natural sociableness Grotius suggests that proofs of the natural law are almost as self-evident as the data we receive through the senses (Grotius 2005: Preliminary Discourse, §40).

Grotius distinguishes law, or right, into natural and volitional. Natural law is a dictate of right reason determining what is consistent with human nature as by necessity morally right, and what is repugnant to it, morally wrong (Grotius 2005: Book I, chapt. 1, x and Book I, chapt. 2, i). As the author of nature God is the author of these logically deducible natural laws or rights. Given our nature such a law would be binding irrespective of its author. This has to be distinguished from volitional laws which are either human or Divine. God's volitional Divine Law is that which it has pleased him to reveal, and which is binding either for a single people, or universally (Grotius 2005: Book I, chapt. 1, xv). Human volitional laws are contingently related to the circumstances to which they are a response, and are either civil laws or the volitional Law of Nations, which must themselves be derived from, or at least not subvert the natural law.

To ascertain the Law of Nations, however, there is no other means but the historical and empirical (Grotius 2005: Preliminary Discourse, §xlvii). The Law of Nations does not have an objective existence, and does not logically follow self-evidently from the indubitable data of human nature, but instead emanates from the will, 'for that which cannot be deduced from certain principles by just consequences, and yet appears to be everywhere observed, must owe its rise to free and arbitrary will' (Grotius 2005: Preliminary Discourse, xli; cf. Wight 2005: 41). Grotius is suggesting, then, that the Law of Nations relates to what nations agree ought to be the case.

Ius gentium is that law consented to by nations and which supplements natural law, both of which together regulate international relations in their entirety (Remec 1960: 28). Because the Law of Nations is the product of human agreement, it is in certain respects liable to change. Typically *ius gentium* refers to treaties establishing law between states. It may also refer to the conventions which have grown up around the practices of states in their relations with each other. Just as the civil law is designed to benefit the state, by mutual consent the Law of Nations benefits 'all in general' (Grotius 2005: Preliminary Discourse, §17). It is that law for the benefit of the society of humanity which is clearly observed by all nations, or the more civilized among them, but which cannot clearly be deduced from first principles (Remec 1960: 28).[3]

For Pufendorf the law of nature is apprehended by means of the exercise of reason. He does not think it necessary that natural laws are innate or imprinted in men's minds. Natural law is the dictate of Right Reason, by which he means that man is endowed with the power of discovering this law by contemplating the human condition. This artificial way of knowing the law of nature is not open

---

[3] Remec argues that, 'The law of nations as such only supplements the law of nature in certain specific aspects, where the nations agree to such a regulation. Where no firm supplementary rule has been established by the consent of nations, one must find out what is permissible according to the law of nature and then direct his actions in consonance with these principles' (Remec 1960: 81).

to all men. Indeed, most people come to know its precepts by custom, or in the course of their everyday business, just as, for example, someone who practices a trade may do so by imitation or the use of instruments, in ignorance of and without prejudice to the principles that underpin their practice (Pufendorf 1717: Book II, chapt. iii, §XIII). Pufendorf suggests that it is not a complicated matter to come to know the foundations of natural law. Human beings are foremost desirous of self-preservation, and are unable to do so without the aid of fellow human beings. At the same time they are easily provoked, capable of mischief, cheating, and being insolent. Men are motivated to enter into society in order to enjoy the protection of others, and are united with them in benevolence, peace, and charity. It is the duty of all humanity to promote and practise sociableness because it is the condition of our safety and flourishing. It follows that anything conducive to it is commanded by the law of nature, and anything that detracts from it is forbidden (Pufendorf 1717: Book II, chapt. iii, §XV).

Natural Law and Natural Rights

What change of circumstances gave rise to the shift of emphasis from natural law to natural rights, and what necessitated the change of emphasis from objective to subjective rights? It is important to note that there are no paradigmatic shifts that entail radical disjuncture. Natural law in many of its iterations was perfectly compatible with natural rights, and did not imply, as Michel Villey and Leo Strauss and some of his followers suggest, a basic incompatibility. Brian Tierney argues, for example, that the precepts and prohibitions of natural law imply natural rights. The precept of natural law commanding that 'Thou shalt not steal' logically entails others having natural rights to appropriate property (Tierney 1988: 20). Natural law and natural rights are integrally related in the medieval period, and natural law is understood to confer rights upon individuals, and indeed natural duties. The issue is essentially this, if a right can for all intents and purposes be re-described as a duty owed by someone else, derived from a higher law, or fundamental moral principles, then why is it necessary to have a separate language of rights at all? Wouldn't we be better off just sticking with the vocabulary of natural law?

This whole natural law discourse is, however, a constellation of questions and answers and if obligations in many cases have clearly implied rights, there is no reason, in the appropriate circumstances, why we should not talk of both rights and duties in the objective sense, that is, as somehow being derived from a higher law. In addition to these rights relating to what we may be owed, that is, what is one's due, such commentators as Michel Villey, Brian Tierney, Richard Tuck, and Knud Haakonssen emphasize a sphere of rights that may be called subjective. They are rights to do something, which confer on the individual a degree of autonomy to do or not to do certain things within the appropriate spheres of his or her moral world, and in this sense they may be said to be permissive.

It is important, however, not to exaggerate the extent to which individual subjective rights came to replace the objective idea of right. Haakonssen reminds us that natural law theory on the whole was not heavily individualistic and obsessed with subjective rights. Much of the rights talk in early modern Europe was not about the idea of moral agency entailing claims to be asserted against others without guidance from any other source but one's inner light. Nor was it a widespread belief that the construction of a social world had to be achieved by accommodating in some way competing claims. Most natural lawyers of the seventeenth and eighteenth centuries adhered to the objective view of rights. The moral agent was subject to natural law and obliged to discharge its duties. Rights were understood to be derivative in the sense that they were the means by which duties could be fulfilled (Haakonssen 1996: 5–6).

In the Aristotelian/Thomist tradition the idea of right – *dikaion, ius* – is primarily objective, meaning giving someone his or her just due, what is just, or the just thing to do. The issue is, to what extent this Aristotelian/Thomist conception of natural right lays claim to be the precursor of the modern version of natural rights. The modern version, however, has moved towards the subjective understanding of a right being something that the individual possesses, or which inheres in the person giving rise to the natural rights or rights of man we encounter in the eighteenth century. We should not, however, assume that the one replaces the other. The language of objective rights persisted during the eighteenth century.

In the subjective version we find the linking of right (*ius*) with power (*potestas*) (Tierney 1991: 298–9). Michel Villey, for example, accredits Ockham with this identification and suggests that he inaugurates the modern conception of a subjective right. Ockham contended that all rights and liberties are endowed upon individuals by God, and his concern was to ensure that they were not trampled upon by ecclesiastical or secular institutions. He was particularly concerned to argue that the Pope exercised only limited secular power, and could not do anything he liked to the faithful as long as it did not transgress Divine and natural law. Ockham contended that it was absurd to think that anyone could be deprived of a right without fault or reasonable cause (Ockham 1992: 23). This is a conception of right that is not a permission or grace, and constitutes a subjective rather than an objective right.

This alternative view of a natural right to that associated with the Aristotelian and Thomist tradition was never fully articulated in any treatise devoted to natural rights, nor was it extensively developed in the context of discussions of rights, but a vocabulary arose which clearly differentiated the subjective and objective meanings of natural rights. Brian Tierney has done a great deal to bring to prominence the importance of this vocabulary. He argues that rights to do something, or rights understood as claims to be enforced against others are commonly encountered in twelfth-century juridical works (Tierney 1984: 435). It is the contention that *ius naturale*, or natural right, could at once denote an area of human liberty as well as a body of constraining law that was crucial in the development of the modern language of rights (Tierney 1989: 616).

As Tuck contends, 'by describing a *ius* as a *potestas*, Ockham was merely signalling that he too was using *ius* in an active sense' (Tuck 1979: 23). For Tuck, the crucial move was made by Jean Gerson who defined *ius* as a faculty, an ability or power pertaining to anyone according to 'divine right reason'. His notion of right was not restricted to human beings. According to his understanding, the sky has the right to rain, or the sun to shine. Gerson brought together what the Romans had always kept apart, *ius* and *libertas*. He contended that, '*Ius* is a *facultas* or power appropriate to someone and in accordance with the dictates of right reason. *Libertas* is a *facultas* of the reason and will towards whatever possibility is selected...*Lex* is a practical and right reason according to which the movements and workings of things are directed towards their ordained ends' (cited in Tuck 1979: 26–27). His distinction here between right and law became a hallmark of some seventeenth-century theories of natural rights.

Intimations of the subjective view, however, may be found in abundance during the medieval period, especially in the commentaries on the Gregorian *Decretals*. The Decretists, such as Rufinus, Ricardus, Huguccio, and Alanus, contributed to the development of a vocabulary which saw *ius naturale* not only as natural law and cosmic harmony, but also as a faculty, ability or power related to individual right reason and moral judgement in which the liberty to act is permissive. As we saw natural law was not exclusively a body of restraints on power, commands and prohibitions, but was also capable of circumscribing an area of right activity that was permitted, but not required or commanded. It was permissive, in that a person or group of persons may choose to do or not to do it (Tierney 2004: 8). The canonists around 1200 developed a vocabulary, Tierney maintains, that clearly distinguished between claim rights and active rights, *ius ad rem* and *ius in re* (Tierney 1989: 625–29). Neither Ockham nor Gerson needed to precipitate a semantic revolution because the subjective sense of rights associated with *potestas* was already being articulated within a rich vocabulary of rights (Tierney 1988: 17 and 31). Within the triad of perceptive, prohibitive, and permissive natural law, it was the last that gave grounds for a conception of natural rights based upon natural law, and which was not therefore opposed to subjective rights as Hobbes came to conceive them. Indeed, many jurists and philosophers attempted to justify private property with reference to permissive natural law. Initially God gave the world to humanity in common, but at the same time the inconveniences that arose through a combination of increased population, the propensity to human depravity, and simply the practicalities of calling something one's own gave rise to the permissive natural law of taking possession of something, and by doing so placing others under an obligation to respect the property right that one has created (Tierney 2001: 384). How such first possession gave rise to an obligation on the part of others without their explicit consent was a problem that bedevilled most thinkers, including Kant. Hobbes simply confronted the issue straight on by positing a right to take anything we want in a state of nature, but no correlative obligation on the part of others followed. Other writers, such as Huguccio (d. 1210), reverted to more accommodating strategies which did not refer to God's gift of the world in common as a precept, but instead a permission which allowed some property to be held in common and some to be private.

The idea of a right, or *ius*, in Roman law and Aquinas is that which is in conformity with law. It is the judgement of what is right or just, for example, in the making or conduct of war (Grotius 2005: Book I, chapt. i, III). Grotius more clearly than Vitoria or Gentili transforms this conception of right into something that we possess: it is a moral quality. Vitoria had used the term *ius* to refer to a faculty or power to do or not to do something within a sphere of human autonomy (Tierney 1989: 638).

Subjective Right

Suarez had a clear distinction in his own mind between law and right. He acknowledges that as well as rights that are derivative from natural law, there are also rights that relate to the powers and claims of individuals. He contends that, 'According to its strict signification *ius* is called a kind of moral power (*facultas*) which everyone has concerning his own property or something due to him. So the owner of a thing is said to have a right in the thing and a workman is said to have a right to his wages' (cited in Tierney 1989: 621). The subjective rights about which Suarez speaks are the means to accomplish the goals set by natural law. They include powers, *dominia* that we have over ourselves, or liberties, over the world, that is property, and over others. Subjective rights are also seen as concessions; in that natural reason dictates what is necessary and what is permitted (Haakonssen 1996: 23). In Suarez's view private property and individual possessions are part of the permissive law of nature.

Both Grotius and Pufendorf acknowledge a subjective sense to the concept of natural rights. In discussing the right of war, for example, Grotius attributes three meanings to *ius*. First, he says that the concept signifies what is just. A right of war therefore means that which may be done without injustice to the enemy. Secondly, *ius* may mean a kind of law in which *ius naturale* is a dictate of reason. He nevertheless gives emphasis to a third meaning at the centre of which is the individual. In this sense *ius* is '*a moral Quality* annexed to the person, *enabling him to have, or do, something justly*' (Grotius 2005: Book I, chapt. IV, iii–iv). He goes on to suggest that in this third sense a moral quality may be deemed a faculty that each person has signifying a power over oneself, namely liberty, or a claim on or power over other persons or things.

In addition to being what is just, Grotius, more explicitly than Vitoria, argues that a 'RIGHT is a moral quality annexed to the person, justly entitling him to possess some particular privilege, or to perform some particular act' (Grotius 2005: Book I, chapt. i, IV). A right is something that we have (see Tierney 1997: 324–6 for the meanings of *ius* in Grotius). For Grotius there is a natural moral order in which the individual's rights are sustained by law. Law sustains, rather than creates morality (Haakonssen 1985: 240). The law of nature becomes the assertion of the principle of having respect for one another's rights, that is, having rights implies a certain duty on the part of others to respect them (Vincent 1986: 25).

From our indubitable natural sociableness four fundamental rights of nature follow. First there is the right to have people abstain from what is mine. Second, to have that restored to me which is mine along with any profit. Third, promises must be honoured. And, fourth, there is the right to punish wrongdoing, which differs from the other rights in that it is not strictly speaking a moral power, and therefore has a somewhat ambiguous status (Grotius 2005: 8; cf. Haakonssen, 1985: 242). Without such fundamental axioms human society could not exist, let alone flourish. In this respect the natural law stands as the foundation of all law.

Similarly, Pufendorf recognizes this subjective use of the term *ius*. Pufendorf points out the ambiguity of the Latin term *ius*, suggesting that it may mean law, a system of municipal laws or constitutions, or the sentence passed by a judge. The senses in which Pufendorf prefers to use it, nevertheless, are subjective, 'Right is that Moral Quality by which we justly obtain either the Government of Persons, or the Possession of Things, or by the Force of Which we may claim somewhat as due to us' (Pufendorf 1717: Book I, chapt. i, §XX). Pufendorf uses the term *ius* to refer to four types of deontic powers. The first is *libertas*, or power over one's actions. The second is *imperium* which relates to power over other persons actions. Third, there is *dominium*, meaning power over one's own things. And fourth, there is *servitas* meaning power over another person's property (Haakonssen 1996: 40).

Christian Wolff, however, provides the best example among eighteenth-century enlightenment thinkers of a fully worked out theory of the relationship between subjective natural rights and the natural law. For Wolff laws are rules to which we are obligated, and the natural law, which is innately associated with the rational nature of man, puts him under an obligation to strive towards perfection. Moral action, that is, the ability to discharge one's moral obligations requires free will, or a degree of freedom of choice. The moral power or faculty to choose or act in this way is for Wolff a right. The relationship between natural law and rights is clear. What natural law obliges us to do, rights provide the means to fulfil the obligation. The natural law puts us under an obligation of self-preservation, and we have a right to food in order to fulfil it. In addition to being a series of commands and prohibitions, the natural law may also be permissive in that it indicates what is permitted, lawful or allowable, but which is not obligatory. Natural rights operate in this area of permissiveness (see Tierney 1989: 622).

In essence, subjective natural rights for Suarez, Grotius, Pufendorf, and Wolff are moral powers or qualities, and not as they were for Hobbes, as we shall see, liberties to do whatever one liked in a state of nature, or within civil society to do that which the law does not proscribe.[4]

---

[4] I will return to the distinction between prescriptive and prescriptive natural rights in Chapter 5.

CONCLUSION

The relationship between natural law and the Law of Nations, and the law between nations was by no means uncontentious. Evidence of the existence of the Law of Nations, in addition to its direct derivation from the law of nature, was a customary practice that was prescriptive in character. However, the matter was complicated by the fact that the customary basis of the Law of Nations was taken to be unrelated to the often rationalist basis of the law of nature, apprehended through the exercise of right reason. The customary character of knowledge of the Law of Nations, the fact that certain practices had been subscribed to since time immemorial, was evidence for some that the Law of Nations was rooted in natural law. In addition, the voluntary Law of Nations, that is, those rules of conduct upon which the civilized nations agree, were not necessarily sanctioned by or derived from natural law. While Rachel was not the first to make a conceptual distinction between natural law and the Law of Nations, he was the most emphatic in maintaining that distinction.

In addition, this chapter has explored the relation between objective and subjective rights, pointing out that the latter is not exclusively related to modern natural rights, and that the former, that is, a right derived from natural law persisted and remained dominant.

4

Natural Rights and Social Exclusion: Cultural Encounters

INTRODUCTION

In March 2007, amid considerable protest from indigenous peoples, Her Majesty Queen Elizabeth II visited Virginia to commemorate European settlement in North America. Some weeks later, on 13 May 2007 Pope Benedict XVI, formerly Cardinal Ratzinger the leading voice in the *Congregatio pro Doctrina Fidei*, once known as the Holy Office of the Inquistion, responsible under Pope John Paul II for counteracting the dangerous tendencies in Liberation Theology, addressed the Bishops of Latin America in Brazil. In this address he makes concessions to Liberation Theology, acknowledging the injustices of autocratic governments, and unbridled capitalism in Latin America. Marxist governments, however, he warned, have been equally destructive, both economically and ecologically. For the regeneration of Christianity in Latin America, and the spiritual values that counteract the iniquities of capitalism and Marxism, we must look to the family. In offering his support to feminism, he says that among those tendencies that serve to undermine the family is the persistence of a chauvinist mentality that fails to acknowledge the equal dignity and responsibility of women and men.

In his address he pointed to the dangers and benefits of globalization. Globalization, he maintained, has generated a vast network of relationships that is to some extent an expression of humanity's 'profound aspiration to unity' (Benedict XVI 2007: 3). He warned that such a world-wide phenomenon is in danger of generating vast monopolies, and elevating profit to the status of a supreme value. Globalization, he proclaimed, must be led by ethics, 'placing everything at the service of the human person, created in the image of God' (Benedict XVI 2007: 3).

What caught the attention of the world, however, and of indigenous peoples, was his apparent insensitivity to the suffering that the introduction of Christianity into the continent of America had brought in its wake. He first thanked God for the great gift of the Christian faith that He had bestowed upon the people, and which had animated the continent for five centuries. What Christianity meant for the indigenous peoples was the welcoming of a God that their ancestors had been seeking, unknowingly, in their religious traditions. To add insult to injury, Pope Benedict XVI added:

In effect, the proclamation of Jesus and of his Gospel did not at any point involve an alienation of the pre-Columbian cultures, nor was it the imposition of a foreign culture. Authentic cultures are not closed in upon themselves, nor are they set in stone at a particular point in history, but they are open, or better still, they are seeking an encounter with other cultures, hoping to reach universality through encounter and dialogue with other ways of life... (Benedict XVI 2007: 1–2).

A similar sentiment was expressed by Pope Paul III almost five centuries earlier. In 1537 he declared that 'We... consider, however, that the Indians are truly men and that they are not only capable of understanding the Catholic faith, but, according to our information, they desire exceedingly to receive it' (cited in Hanke 1949: 73).

I want in this chapter to explore the practical implications of the ideas of natural law and natural rights. The cases of the European encounters with the American Indians and Australian Aborigines provide no better illustration of how such abstract doctrines, with their universal standards and applicability, when translated into concrete social and political contexts, requiring practical prescriptions and imperative injunctions, led to widely differing conclusions, but ultimately, even among apologists for the Indians, could provide justifications for occupation. Even the more humanitarian of Europeans of the seventeenth through to the twentieth century believed that Indians were primitive, but that with proper training in the Christian religion, European agricultural methods, and literacy they could become civilized. Furthermore, I want to illustrate what is a general proposition. Discussions of universal rights have almost invariably included significant disqualifications of their enjoyment by peoples deemed incapable of possessing the necessary attributes for their exercise, or who simply haven't taken advantage of the rights they have, even though they are unlikely to have known about them. Such people were nevertheless deemed to have the same duties as Europeans, and failure to fulfill them had serious consequences, affording others further opportunities to exercise their rights to dominate or oppress.

Various strategies were adopted to effect such opportunities. Charles Mills argues that white settlers joined in expropriation contracts, creating societies, with the clear implication that no society had previously existed (Mills 1997: 13, 24, and 49–50). Tully has argued that European theories of property since settlement have served to misrecognize the systems of property and the political organizations of the Aboriginal peoples they encountered (Tully 1999: 158). Carole Pateman extends these ideas to talk about a specific form of Charles Mill's expropriation contract. This she calls the 'settler contract' which has among it principal components the right to husbandry, and the establishment of sovereignty where the natives were deemed insufficiently organized and civilized to conceive of it, let alone exercise it. On the strict logic of the settler contract natives are excluded, as in Australia, and on the modified logic they are afforded certain concessionary rights and partially accommodated, as in America under English settlement.

The application of natural law, and the Law of Nations, uniquely the product of the Western political experience, were conceived as universal, and local variations, at least in terms of fundamental beliefs, were regarded as violations. There was certainly a scale of civilization, which became gradually more refined, both explicit and implicit, that was used to determine to what extent those who did not belong to the higher civilized nations could exercise universal rights, for which certain qualifications had to be met.

The early dealings of Europeans with non-Europeans were characterized by this attitude, and manifest in the myth of the three sons of Noah and the continents they inherited, the hierarchy of which was extended to the New Worlds of America and Australia, with the former being placed above, and the latter below, Africa on the continuum of civilization. Even during the late nineteenth century the Law of Nations was deemed formally to embrace a scale of civilization, comprising savagery, barbarism, and civilization with rights that inhere in the higher, inaccessible to the lower because of some impediment correlative with the stage of human development people had so far attained, or that may even congenitally prevent such enjoyment of rights.

Miguel Leon-Portilla suggests that the conquest of America by Hernán Cortés and his army of Spaniards constituted probably the most historic and consequential of meetings ever experienced between cultures (Leon-Portilla 1992: xi). The European encounter with the American Indians required a vast readjustment of traditionally held views, and conceptualizing peoples and practices from an alien world initially entailed trying to understand them in terms of familiar categories, such as property; the propriety of their manner of behaviour and dress; and their conformity to natural law. As Anthony Pagden contends, following the discovery of the New World Europeans did their best to transform it and its native peoples into something resembling the Old. For three centuries the continent was dominated by intellectual cultures that were certain of their conviction that the world was an exemplification of preordained laws of nature, in terms of which everything was explicable (Pagden 1993: 10).

For peoples, such as the Aztecs, they interpreted the encounter in terms of their familiar categories, myths, and legends. Both the Spanish and the Aztecs were expansionist nations, and both had become the most powerful on their respective continents. By 1519, when Cortéz arrived on the continent of America, the Aztecs ruled over more than 3 million people who spoke several languages. Their empire extended from the Pacific Ocean to the Gulf coast, and from central Mexico to what is now Guatemala. Both peoples inhabited a world-view coloured by religious imagery, and structured by philosophies of history with spiritual significance, through which they interpreted the 'other'. Central to the religion of the Aztecs was the god Huitzilopochtli-the-Sun, the source of all life, and they saw themselves as the people of the Sun, attributing a mystical and primary significance to warfare as a cultural institution.

The conquest of other peoples in practical terms provided a continuous source of sacrificial victims. The sun as the source of life must be fed the most sacred of all foods, human blood, in order to sustain its creative force. The entry of Cortés, accompanied by 600 Spaniards, into the great city of Mexico (Tenochtitlan), the lake island capital of the Aztecs, signified for Montecuhzoma, not a source of sacrifice, but the prophesized return of Quetzalcoatl and other gods from across the Gulf of Mexico. On hearing of the arrival of Cortés and his men, Montecuhzoma sent a deputation bearing gifts worthy of the returning God. He dispatched with them captives who were sacrificed in the presence of the strangers so that their blood may be drunk. The Spaniards were shocked, and some physically sickened by the abhorrent sight. They refused to eat the food sprinkled with blood, and were repulsed by the people who greeted them (Sahagun's informants in Leon-Portilla 1992: 33).

At first the Spaniards tended to look at America through medieval eyes, transferring myths and legends about fantastical creatures and magical enchantments to the lost continent. It was the land of unicorns, giants, griffins, trumpet blowing monkeys, and strange creatures resembling people in appearance, but not in habit. These first impressions were succeeded by perceptions of a dangerous, hostile, and savage continent that had to be tamed and brought under the tutelage of the rulers of Spain and the Christian religion (Hanke 1959: 5–8).

The significance of the encounter for Europeans is that it forced philosophers, jurists, theologians, and politicians to interrogate the foundations of their convictions, and to ask questions that stretched traditional natural law and natural rights theories to the boundaries of their conceptual limits. Questions of who or what were these creatures resembling humans; about the capacity of Indians to qualify fully as members of humanity; how should they be treated, and whether they had the ability to comprehend and receive the word of God. If so, how was it to be instilled in them, through education or by force? Given the depths of their depravity whether they possessed sufficient rationality to own property, or indeed, whether they themselves were eligible on Aristotelian grounds to be classified as natural slaves, able to understand rational commands but not able to formulate and execute them for themselves. For the conquistadors the issue boiled down to that of when just war was permissible to force the Indians to submit to God, the king, and the conquerors. For the ecclesiastics the issue was how could the natives be changed from what they are into what they ought to be (Hanke 1959: 8). For Vitoria, the prime professor of Theology in the University of Salamanca, the issue was not about the jurisdiction of the Pope or the Emperor, nor of Roman Law. Instead, the Indian question was one of natural law and the issue of rights was consequently not one of juridic, but of natural rights (Pagden 1987: 80).

Natural law and natural rights were the universal standards employed by Europeans to judge what they encountered, and to arrive at answers to the most fundamental of questions. There could be no exceptions to these rational universal standards, but there may be mitigating circumstances, such as invincible ignorance, that made some initial judgments less severe. Few Europeans would deny that there were natural rights, and that all humans had them by the mere fact of being human: what was at issue was whether the American Indians met the qualifications, or fell short in some way, of being fully human. If they qualify then like every human they possess natural rights, and participate in the universal community of humankind. This, however, was a doubled-edged sword. Far from offering the American Indians unqualified protections against violations by Europeans, it presented a set of criteria from which deviation constituted a just cause for war, during which time many of these human rights were in abeyance. There were disputes as to the circumstances that gave rise to just cause, or about practices that invited what we would now call humanitarian intervention, but few would argue that there were no conditions that could not give rise to the justifiable acquisition of territories, and dominion in the Americas, on the principle of the natural right of *terra nullius*, or *res nullius*, or on grounds of violations of natural rights by the Indians themselves against their own peoples or against Europeans.

The appearance of the universalism of natural rights is undermined in practice by what amounts to an imposition of European Christian standards of conduct and rationality. Fundamentally, Francisco Vitoria's arguments, for example, rest upon universal rights which take priority over those of specific communities, the contravention of which justifiably legitimates intervention by a foreign state to restore the rights and punish the perpetrators of the wrong. Indeed, Vitoria believed in a universal community which was not merely confined to Christians. Each state has a right and a legal obligation to compel rogue states to conform to international law and to the customary law of the '*societa gentium*'.

Vitoria (1480–1546) was a voice of some significance in the sixteenth century. His opinion was sought on most of the controversies of the day. Henry VIII referred to him the divorce controversy, the pope consulted him on difficult matters of conscience and Charles V solicited his views on disputes which arose out of the conquest of America (Phillipson 1915: 177). Vitoria assumed that not only Christians, but also the American Indians could discover natural law by the exercise of right reason, and that just as the Spanish had to act in a manner appropriate to it, they had the right to expect the Indians to do likewise. The laudable intention to constrain heavily armed Spanish soldiers in their relations with native Indians by reference to the natural law broke down ultimately when the Indians, as Vitoria conceived it, acted in a manner at variance with that law (Johnson 1981: 77).

In addition, despite the variations in the definition of the Law of Nations and its relation to the law of nature, an aspect of that law, at least, was based upon the usage or custom of 'civilized' states, to which all other nations were subject irrespective of exhibiting signs of consent. As late as 1680, Textor, invoking the example of the American Indians and Africans of the Cape of Good Hope, argued that, 'if there be a people so wild and inhumane as to live without Law, The Law of Nations, which Reason dictates and Usage affirms, is not on that account any the less the Law of Nations' (Textor 1916: I, 3).

The Spanish conquest of the Americas gave prominence to questions that had hitherto not been at the forefront of the minds of theologians, jurists, and philosophers. The discovery of new territories raised the question by what right a foreign power could occupy and take possession of lands inhabited by other peoples.

To legitimate such acquisition familiar terms of reference had to be invoked. A theory of property needed to be developed in order to justify the occupation of the lands of 'primitive peoples', subject these people as slaves, and even massacre them. The question of the justice of acquisition was immensely important. At the heart of the issue was the question of property and the terms of its appropriation and ownership. Here the American Indians were often excluded on the grounds of insufficient rationality, falling foul of a restricted conception of labour, or for not constituting a nation.

JUST WAR, PROPERTY, AND HUMANITARIAN INTERVENTION

Vitoria's and Gentili's attempts to apply just war theory to the case of the American Indians constitute genuine attempts to make the precepts of the natural law truly universal, and offer the prospects of protection against unlawful aggression and usurpation. Vitoria was not himself as strong an advocate of humanitarian intervention as Gentili, who was much more disposed to favour it. Vitoria was far less willing to allow the sinful practices of the Indians, such as sodomy, bestiality, and incest, even though they were unnatural, to act as a pretext for Spanish intervention (Vitoria 1991: 218–9, 224, and 272–5). For Vitoria the only legitimate justification for war (excepting God's command) is the violation of right, and the occupation by the Spaniards of some tracts of land, in the Indies, and the exercise of dominion over their inhabitants was because the Indians had in some way violated the rights of the Spaniards.

There were, however, circumstances under which one people may intervene on behalf of another, and they relate to the unconditional right to protect the lives of innocent human beings. Having established that the American Indians have rights, the violation of those rights may give occasion for what we would now call humanitarian intervention. Cannibalism and human sacrifice were of a different order from bestiality, incest, and sodomy because they entailed the taking of innocent lives (Vitoria 1991: 207–30). Those whose lives are threatened by such practices should be rescued from their predicament, by individuals or agents of the state. Such intervention may even go as far as regime change, and the potential victims of cannibalism and human sacrifice have no right to renounce their right to life by declining the help of a third party. Furthermore, intervention may be justified to save a people from a cruel tyrant, irrespective of whether the invasion is welcome, and the invaders hailed as liberators. The grounds he gives are that the victims are our neighbours and we have a duty to deliver them from mortal danger, even without the authority of the pope.

The gospels (Mark 16: 15) command Christians to spread the word throughout the world, and if the Indians obstruct them, or punish the converted, the Spaniards 'may take up arms and declare war on them, in so far as this provides the safety and opportunity needed to preach the Gospel' (Vitoria 1991: Q 3, Article 2, §§9–11, pp. 284–5). Vitoria recognized a number of just claims to dominion which even if not applicable in the Spanish case could provide strong pretexts for the justification of colonization. The Law of Nations (*jus gentium*) which is, or is derived from, the natural law allows unimpeded travel and communication on condition that harm is not perpetrated by the traveller. The traveller has a *right* under natural law and the Law of Nations to trade and enjoy those things that the indigenous peoples hold in common. Denial of these rights constitutes a just cause of war. Furthermore, Vitoria grants a right to spread the gospel, but not forcibly to impose it, as a result of which converts secure rights of protection which if violated constitute just causes of war. A just cause, of course, gives the injured party claims to dominion that he would not previously have been able to press (Vitoria 1991: 231–92).

On the other hand there are those who wish to uphold the right of intervention for reasons beyond saving lives. In 1516 More maintained that his Utopians having pity for a people oppressed by a tyrant may for humanitarian reasons liberate them from the tyrant's yoke and bondage (Barnes 1982: 778). Gentili argues, for example, that love of our neighbour and the desire to live in peace confer a right to wage war against those who violate the 'common law of humanity' and wrong mankind (Gentili 1933: Book I, chapt. xxv, 202). He maintains that there is a natural impulse towards self-protection and that if our rights are infringed we have a right to avenge ourselves. It is a law common to all mortals that they have a right to punish those who seize their property (Gentili 1933: Book I, chapt. xviii, 134). As we have seen, however, those who claim such a right must first be deemed to own the property and not themselves to have infringed the natural law and thus give just cause and forfeit those rights. As Gentili contends, 'One who attempts what is unlawful loses his lawful rights' (Gentili 1933: Book I, chapt. xix, 140). When hostilities cease buildings and places remain in the power of those who hold them, unless otherwise stated in the peace treaty (Gentili 1933: Book II, chapt. xvii, 623). In terms of moveable property, Gentili argues that it does belong to the enemy who seizes it until it is taken 'clear through' to a point within its own fortified lines (Gentili 1921: Book I, chapt. ii, 5). For Cornelius van Bynkershoek, writing in 1737, title to property by capture is as strong a claim as that of inheritance or contract. He contends that 'It is evident that the enemies' goods, whether moveable or not, may be taken by the laws of war' (Bynkershoek 1930: Book I, chapt. iv, 26). The issue for him was at what point may ownership be deemed to have changed hands (Bynkershoek 1930: Book I, chapts. iv–vii). In relation to immoveables Bynkershoek regards every occupation as a valid title to property, until such time the occupier is expelled, or vacates the territory.

For all their protestations of universality, however, the medieval just war theorists were concerned with Christian belligerents and the justness of their causes, and not with the rights of non-Christian peoples (Johnson 1981: 75). The idea of natural rights, far from protecting the Indians against the brutality of the Spaniards, was used to justify their subjugation. The natural rights of the Spaniards, it was claimed, were being violated by the American Indians who had a duty to respect them.

By applying the universal standards of natural law, natural rights, and the Law of Nations, even though the Indians may be protected from some of the precepts on grounds of invincible ignorance, justifications could be given for waging war against them. If certain of their internal societal arrangements, such as human sacrifice and cannibalism, were an affront to humanity, intervention to save innocent victims may be justified. Even where such affronts were not acknowledged, transgressing the Law of Nations provided ample excuse. Impediments to the rights of passage, attempts to prevent the appropriation of 'vacant land', or acquire gold from the ground that the world held in common gave just cause for war. Juan Ginés de Sepúlveda went as far as to argue that if natural slaves, such as the Indians, resisted the natural dominion of their superiors they gave grounds for just war against them with no more injustice than one would hunt down a wild and savage beast (Hanke 1959: 45). Sepúlveda and Las Casas represented opposite ends of the spectrum at the famous inquiry into the conduct of the Spaniards held at Valladolid in 1550, to which we will return in Chapter Seven.

With copious reference to the Scriptures Sepúlveda argued that the American Indians were barbarians by habit and by nature, and were contaminated by their barbarous vices. By right of nature, he claims, races of this sort must obey the more civilized and prudent. If they refuse to do so they may 'be forced with arms and that war would be justified by right of nature according to the authority of Aristotle and Aquinas' (Sepúlveda 1973: 9). This was a view with which Ayala could concur. It is self-evident, as far as Ayala is concerned, that human depravity may be constrained by war, captivity, and slavery (Ayala 1912: Preface, viii).

Sepúlveda went further and advanced an argument that later characterized Locke's attitude towards the Indians, and indeed, that of the eighteenth-century natural law theorist M. de Wattell (cf. Pagden 1987: 92). Since God had given a use right to the American Indians, they had abused that right by not making nature as productive as possible, and in particular, by violating use rights in the person by practicing human sacrifice and cannibalism. Private property was for him a legal construct, and the product of civil society. American Indians not only abused their use rights, their excuses for societies were no more than could be found among certain kinds of beast. They had no right in resisting more industrious peoples from appropriating the land.

The sixteenth-century Italian jurist Pierino Belli (1502–1575), writing in 1558, shortly after the inquiry at Valladolid, contended that 'things captured in war belong to the captors is maintained by the laws, and that too not only things moveable or self-moving, but also immovable' (Belli 1936: Part II, chapt. xii, p. 85). Even the protestant Gentili, who was more sympathetic than most, thought that the Spaniards had just cause for waging war against the Indians on the grounds that they had interfered with the universal natural rights afforded by nature. These include the right of passage, safe harbour, provisions, and to trade, thus denying the right of lawful commerce (Gentili 1933: Book I, chapt. xix, 138). Gentili does suggest that, because the New World is now joined to our own, warfare against the Indians 'seems to be justified' because of the denial of commerce to the Spaniards.

The intentions of the Spaniards were, however, dominion rather than trade, as if to take possession of land previously unknown to us was the same as land previously possessed by no one. Gentili does not follow through the implications. Instead he says that hence there arose a dispute between the kings of Spain and Portugal which was resolved by the pope who set out what lands in the New World may lawfully be possessed (Gentili 1933: Book I, chapt. xix, 144).

Suarez questioned the legitimacy of the punishment of injuries by third parties, which was something that Grotius condoned, over the world, 'what some assert, that sovereign kings have power to punish injuries over the whole world, is altogether false, and confounds all order and distinction of jurisdictions' (cited in Barnes 1982: 779).

HUMANITARIAN INTERVENTION

One of the traditional doctrines of the Church was the obligation to aid innocent people in danger of being killed unjustly. Gentili, for example, refers to Constantine's remark that those who live according to the precepts of God will regard an injury to another as one done to themselves. We have an obligation to save the injured from the hands of the injurer, as long as we do not put our own lives at risk (Gentili 1933: Book I, chapt. xv, 113–4). The practices of the American Indians, usually referred to as barbarians even by their defenders, such as Vitoria and Las Casas, were so abhorrent to many Europeans that they in themselves constituted a just cause of war. Even opponents in the debate concerning the appropriate treatment of the native Americans could agree that there are certain conditions that necessitate and justify the duty to intervene in the cultural life of the Indians. Vitoria, Gentili, Sepúlveda, Suarez, and Grotius, for example, consider one such just cause to be intervention on behalf of the innocent against certain categories of crime in breach of the natural law. Gentili argued that intervention was justifiable on a wide variety of grounds including the defence of subjects of another state against their ruler, if he is grossly unjust and cruel to them (Gentili 1933: Book I, chapt. xviii and Book I, chapt. xix).

Tyrannical oppression of the innocent, human sacrifice, euthanasia, and cannibalism, for Vitoria, provide just causes for intervention in 'defence of our neighbours' (Vitoria 1991: 347; cf. 287–8). For those sins against nature that did not threaten lives, as we have seen, he was more circumspect.

Sepúlveda, however, was far more interventionist for humanitarian reasons. He argues that all men are commanded by Divine and natural law to save innocent victims from slaughter, if it can be done without significant disadvantage to themselves. The Indians, in his view, engaged in such widespread human sacrifice that to subject them to the government of Spain which abhors such practices is to do them a great service. Waging war against the Indians was to protect the weak among them from the barbaric practices they were forced to endure (Hanke 1959: 41). Furthermore, Divine and natural law impels us to draw back to salvation even those whose errors lead them to destruction, whether knowingly or unwittingly. It is a duty of all sound men to drag them to salvation even against their will. Sepúlveda contends that, 'the barbarians are rightfully compelled to justice for the sake of their salvation' (Sepúlveda 1973: 18). We have a duty to intervene, then, not only to save lives, but also to save souls.

For Gentili the Spaniards were justified in waging war against the Indians who 'practised abominable lewdness even with beasts, and who ate human flesh, slaying men for that purpose' (Gentili 1933: Book I, chapt. xxv, 198–9). He maintained that those peoples who have broken the natural bonds of union between all men by violating natural and Divine laws forfeit their natural rights. For Sepúlveda, their devil worship, cannibalism, the burial alive of important persons, and other crimes in breach of the natural law, whose description is extremely offensive to the ears of, and horrifies, civilized peoples, justify intervention by the Spanish in order to save innocent people. On these grounds alone, God and nature confer the right 'to wage war against these barbarians to submit them to Spanish rule' (cited in Hanke 1974: 86). Armed intervention is necessary in order to prevent gross violations of the natural law to which all are subject. Towards the end of his life Sepúlveda was less severe in his judgment of the American Indians, but he still maintained that the Spaniards comply 'with the duty of mankind' in eradicating customs contrary to the natural law. The Indians should be forced to 'change their lives and adopt the obligations of Natural Law' (cited in Hanke 1974: 118).

For Gentili there was an obligation on the part of civilized nations to act on behalf of the *societas gentium* in general in intervening where sodomy and bestiality were commonly practiced, and to come to the aid of victims of cannibalism and immolation, ridding the world of such abhorrent regimes that perpetrated or condoned the crimes. To justify intervention the grounds had to be sufficiently serious, and the violation of rights had to be by sovereigns or peoples, and not the random acts of individuals (Gentili 1933: Book I, chapt. xxv).

Francisco Suarez was more attuned to Gentili and less inclined than Las Casas to make allowances for barbaric practices, but he was not as ready as Sepúlveda to intervene on the grounds of converting heathens. Suarez argued that, 'in order to defend the innocent, it is allowable to use violence against the infidels in question, that they may be prevented from sacrificing infants to their gods; inasmuch as such a war is permissible in the order of charity and is, indeed, a positive duty if it can be conveniently waged' (Suarez 1944: disp. XVIII, §iv, p. 770). Suarez did not limit intervention to the rescuing of children. In the case of adults, even if they consent to being sacrificed to idols, they must be deemed insane, incapable of controlling their lives, and it is therefore permissible to rescue them from sacrifice. If, however, infidels sacrifice only those found guilty of serious crimes and sentenced to death, then the excuse of defending the innocent no longer applies (Suarez 1944: disp. XVIII, §iv, p. 771).

Suarez nevertheless elsewhere sounded a note of caution, maintaining that God was capable of inflicting punishments for himself, and that if this power had been granted to the whole human race it would have led to widespread disorder, and 'it would always be permissible to declare such a war on the ground of protecting innocent little children' (Suarez 1944: disp. XII, §v, p. 824, also cited in Green and Dickason 1993: 210).

In the course of discussing the principles of just war, Grotius extends this principle found in Suarez. In disagreement with Vitoria he argued that states have a natural right to punish excessive violations of nature, such as inhumanity to one's parents, and cannibalism, whether the injuries are perpetrated against themselves or against others with whom they have no direct involvement. Following Isocrates, Grotius maintains that the most just of wars is against 'wild rapacious beasts', and the next is against those men who act like beasts (Grotius 2005: Book II, chap. xx, §XL, 3–4, p. 1022–4). The cannibals of the East Indies and the Americas, who for Grotius were little better than beasts, could justifiably be punished by Europeans.

Vitoria and Gentili recognized a number of just claims to dominion which could provide strong pretexts for the justification of colonization. The Law of Nations accommodates both individuals and states in its provisions. In relation to individuals the Law of Nations allows unimpeded travel and communication on condition that harm is not perpetrated by the traveller. The traveller has a right to trade and enjoy those things that the indigenous peoples hold in common. This includes digging for gold or diving for pearls in the seas and rivers. Under the Law of Nations things that have not already been appropriated become the property of the 'first taker' (Vitoria 1991: 280). Denial of these rights, or what Gentili called the privileges of nature, constitutes a just cause of war. A just cause, of course, gives the injured party claims to dominion that he would not previously have been able to press, and under the Law of Nations everything captured in war becomes the property of the victor (Vitoria 1991: 231–92).

Like Vitoria before him, and Grotius, Gentili subscribed to the commonly held view that the Law of Nations prescribed rights of passage for travellers, and it was therefore unlawful to exclude people from entering harbours, obtaining provisions, engaging in commerce, or conducting trade (Gentili 1933: I, xix, 138). The Spanish war with the Indians could be justified on the ground that the Indians refused to enter into commerce with the Spaniards.

Gentili suggests, however, that the Spanish are not there to conduct commerce, but instead to exercise dominion in the belief that they have the right to appropriate lands that have recently been discovered, 'just as if to be known to none of us were the same thing as to be possessed by no one' (Gentili 1933: I, xix, 144). Coleman Phillipson has misunderstood this passage in suggesting that Gentili thinks that the Spaniards justly waged war on the American Indians (see his introduction to Gentili 1933: 28a and Phillipson 1968: 123). It is perfectly just, Gentili argues, to oppose the Spaniards 'who are planning and plotting universal dominion' (Gentili 1933: I, xiv, 103). Those who seek to extend their dominion are not short of pretexts for resorting to war. Furthermore Gentili suggests that the Spaniards have unjustly committed terrible acts of cruelty against the Indians (Gentili 1933: III, viii, 529).

Gentili thought, nevertheless, that the Spaniards did have a just claim to wage war on the Indians. Vitoria and Gentili consider a just cause of war to be intervention on behalf of the innocent against certain categories of crime in breach of the natural law. Tyrannical oppression of the innocent, human sacrifice, euthanasia, and cannibalism, for Vitoria, provide just causes for intervention in 'defence of our neighbours' (Vitoria 1991: 347 and 287–8). Gentili contends that he agrees with those who believe that the Spaniards have a just cause for war in punishing the Indians 'who practised abominable lewdness even with beasts, and who ate human flesh, slaying men for that purpose' (Gentili 1933: I, xxv, 198). Such practices violate the common sentiments of mankind and the law of nature.

Grotius agrees with Vitoria and Gentili that intervention on behalf of the violated innocents is lawful. Grotius' third criterion of just war is an extension of this principle. States have a right to punish excessive violations of the natural law, whether the injuries are perpetrated against themselves or others with whom they have no direct involvement. Grotius contends that:

kings and those who are invested with a Power equal to that of Kings, have a Right to exact punishments, not only for injuries committed against themselves, or their Subjects, but likewise, for those which do not peculiarly concern them, but which are, in any Persons whatsoever, grievous Violations of the Law of Nature or Nations (Grotius 2005: Book II, chapt. xx, §XL, p. 1021).

Grotius agrees with Ayala that just war cannot be waged against the infidel simply because they are infidels, not even on the authority of the papacy. The obstruction of those who seek to teach Christianity, which is not subversive to civil society, is however an entirely different matter (Grotius 2005: Book I, chapt. xx, §§XLIV–XLIX, pp. 1027–52). Ayala suggests that just war may be waged against infidels when they 'hinder by their blasphemies and false arguments the Christian faith' which Christians have a right to teach 'over the whole world' (Ayala 1912: Book I, chapt. ii, [29], p. 21).

Grotius is also convinced that war can be justly waged against those who persecute upholders of the Christian faith, or who deny the fundamental principles upon which society is based, namely the existence of a Divinity which has an active interest in human affairs (Grotius 2005: Book II, chapt. xx, §XLVI and §XLVIII). The cannibals of the East Indies and the Americas, and not all were cannibals, who for Grotius were little better than beasts, could justifiably be punished for transgressing the natural law by Europeans (Grotius 2005: Book II, chapt. xx, §XL).

Pufendorf is much more on the side of the Indians. They are under no unconditional obligation to admit foreigners, and to restrict access would not in itself constitute a just cause of war. In addition, the practices that Vitoria and Grotius found so abhorrent were not for Pufendorf grounds to subdue and punish their practitioners. Eating the flesh of members of their own religion is permissible. Eating that of strangers constitutes insufficient injury in itself. The question must be asked whether 'those strangers come as enemies and robbers; as innocent guests and travellers; or as forced by the stress of weather? For this last case only, not of any of the others, can give a prince a '*Right of War*' against them; and this to those princes only, whose subjects have been used with that inhumanity by them' (Pufendorf 1717: Book VIII, chapt. vi, §5).

For Locke, Americans are deemed to have no right to defend their traditional ways of life against European encroachment, after all their way of life is inherently inferior to that of Europeans, and the natives were deficient in discharging their obligations to God. We have a natural right to punish Indians (Locke 1988: §9), and to gather together one's kith and kin to gain reparations from the Indians for injuries caused (Locke 1988: §130). Locke simply takes for granted the injustice of native resistance to the appropriation of waste lands, and the justice of developers to counter such aggression (Glausser 1990: 209).

Whereas the language of Christian Wolff is less belligerent in tone, his conclusions imply similar outcomes. He makes a distinction between barbarous and civilized nations, maintaining that the latter have a duty under natural law to assist the former in areas where clear deficiencies and impediments are evident to the perfection and cultivation of a civilized way of life. Each nation owes to itself self-preservation and the perfection of its government, and owes as much to other nations. A nation that fails to do this is failing in its duty to itself and to humanity. He contends that, 'one nation is bound to contribute whatever it can to the preservation and perfection of another in that in which the other is not self-sufficient' (Wolff 1934*b*: chapt. II, §166, p. 88). There is, then, a duty to assist, and by implication where a country lacks the resources, a duty to accept assistance, otherwise it is denying the right of the assisting nation to fulfill its duty to itself and humankind (Wolff 1934*b*: chapt. II, §180, p. 94). The implication is that the refusal of such assistance constitutes grounds for the waging of just war against them (Green and Dickason 1993: 68). For those peoples who conformed to his definition of a nation, and therefore met the conditions of civility, and civilized learning, the principle of sovereignty is sacrosanct.

Like Hobbes, and indeed Pufendorf, Wolff extends his analysis of the State of Nature to the relations among nations. Nations are moral persons whose rights and duties arise from natural law as a result only of the social contract. Nations differ in nature and essence from individual physical persons, so the laws of nature must be adapted to fit the moral persons of nations in their relations. From his initial premises certain logical deductions follow. The law of nature for him relates to self-preservation and self-improvement or perfection. These are obligations that both individuals and nations owe primarily to themselves. Towards others both individuals and nations owe assistance to help achieve preservation and perfection (Wolff 1934*b*: chapt. II, §156). Using their combined powers nations are obliged to promote the common good (Wolff 1934*b*: Prolegomena, §8). This latter obligation is imperfect because the person of whom, or nation of which, assistance is requested is the sole judge of whether the extension of such assistance would harm or endanger its preservation or improvement. To refuse assistance when one is in a position to offer it is unfair, but it is not wrong because failure to perform an imperfect obligation does not violate a perfect right (Wolff 1934*b*: chapt. II, §159).

Vattel proposes a theory that may in its implications be called, as with Christian Wolff, a duty to assist. Men, he argues, are duty bound to work together to improve their condition. This entails first and foremost labouring for oneself, but in addition, labouring for others. He maintains that nations in their way owe every duty to other states that individuals owe to each other. The duty to assist obliges nations to give assistance in so far as such actions are not harmful to themselves. What this means in practice is that when a neighbouring state is attacked by a more powerful nation which threatens to oppress it, it is your duty to defend it as long as you do not expose yourself to great danger. Similarly, 'if a nation is afflicted with famine all those who have provisions to spare ought to relieve her distress, without, however, exposing themselves to want' (Vattel 1834: book II, chap. I, §5). In addition, Vattel strongly defended the rights of the Incas against the Spanish who accused their ruler Athualpa of killing his subjects and taking several wives. Vattel contended that a ruler who violated the fundamental laws of his state and of nature gives his subjects a legal right to resist him. In such circumstances, 'every foreign power has a right to succour an oppressed people who implore their assistance' (Vattel 1834: book II, chap. IV, §56, p. 155).

The Case against Intervention

As we saw, for Vitoria, only when innocent lives were endangered in human sacrifice, cannibalism or through tyranny could humanitarian intervention be condoned. Sodomy, and incest and other unnatural pratices were not sufficient grounds to provide justification for intervention. Because American Indians were not Christians they did not fall under the jurisdiction of the pope, and because they had not had the gospel preached to them, they were 'invincibly' ignorant. War against Christians committing such acts was not permissible, and yet the sin is clearly greater, so why should the Indians who are ignorant of the sinful nature of their acts give just cause for war? (Vitoria 1991: Q3, Article 5, §§39–40, pp. 272–5). Nevertheless, he almost immediately retracts this constraint when discussing just titles for the Spanish occupation. The Spanish may force the barbarians from the '*practising of nefarious custom or rite*', and if they refuse 'war may be declared upon them, and the laws of war enforced upon them' (Vitoria 1992: Q3, Article 5, §15, pp. 285–6). In order to prevent the persecution of Christians, and to stamp out nefarious and abhorrent practices, the Spaniards may be justified in intervening to bring about regime change.

Gentili did not think that the Spaniards had a just cause for war in the refusal of the Indians to hear the word of the Gospels. Such claims, he thought, are a pretext (Gentili 1933: Book I, chapt. xxv, 200). Las Casas agreed with Sepúlveda and Vitoria on the important point of doctrine, that there is an obligation to aid the innocent against unjust killing. Did it, however, apply to the Indians? Sepúlveda was in no doubt about it, while Vitoria was less sure. Las Casas argued that if the doctrine was to be applied it must be on the grounds of the lesser evil. One must desist from war, and even tolerate the deaths of a few innocent women and children, sacrificed or cannibalized, if intervention against a multitude of people, including the innocent, destroys their governments, and implants in them an immense hatred of the Christian religion. Even if a wicked person avoids punishment, this would be the lesser of the evils.

Las Casas was not wholly opposed to human sacrifice; sacrifice to the true God, or the one imagined to be God, is in accordance with natural law. The things to be sacrificed to God are a matter of human law. He concluded that it cannot be wholly abhorrent to sacrifice human beings to God, because God himself ordered Abraham to sacrifice his only son (Hanke 1974: 95). Las Casas, however, condemned the Spaniards for the devastation and inhumanity of their conduct. They had in their wanton disregard for the lives of the Indians, and in their greed for possessions and land, relinquished any rights they may have had under the natural law. In describing the conduct of the Spanish in New Spain (Mexico), he contentiously asserts that, 'the only rights these perfidious crusaders have earned which can be upheld in human, Divine, or Natural Law are the right to eternal damnation...' (Las Casas 2004: 53–4). No violation against natural law could be so horrible as to justify unmitigated conquest and wholesale enslavement of a people (Green and Dickason 1993: 209). While Las Casas often refers to rights in the objective sense, as doing what is just, or giving one one's just deserts, or what is prescribed by law, he also talks of the rights of Indians in a subjective sense. As Brian Tierney argues, Las Casas, when talking about the powers and jurisdictions of Indians, referred to them as rights (*iura*) conferred by natural law, and which are immutable beyond the reach of civil laws to extinguish them (Tierney 1991: 300–1).

Both Wolff and his protégé Vattel strongly disagree with Grotius' grounds for humanitarian intervention. Wolff allows no right of conversion; allows for the expulsion of unwanted missionaries; and denies the right of any prince to interfere in the affairs of another on the grounds of failing to uphold the basic rights of humanity to his subjects (Wolff 1934: chap. II, §§258–62, pp. 132–5). Vattel maintains that Grotius was mistaken in thinking that all nations have a right and duty to punish other nations for gross infringements of the natural law. It is only when direct harm is incurred or is likely as a consequence. For Vattel, because men have the right to provide for their safety the right to punish is its corollary. In consequence, it exists only against those who have injured them.

Vattel in conformity with Vitoria, Grotius, and Pufendorf did not accept that conquest, usurpation of property (Vattel 1834: book II, chap. i, §5), or religious differences were a just cause of war. European Nations who subjected the American Indians to avaricious rule on the pretext of teaching the true religion and civilizing them based their claim upon unjust and ridiculous grounds. Vattel thought, however, that allowing a right of intervention, as Vitoria, Grotius, and Pufendorf did to punish inhumane crimes against the natural law, provided too readily a pretext for zealots and brigands of all sorts to subject peoples of foreign lands. Only when the issue of safety arises and when injury is done or threatened does an individual in the state of nature, or a nation among other nations, have a right to punish. When no injury is received no right of punishment exists in matters that are not the concern of an outside state (Vattel 1834: book II, chap. i, §7 and book III, chap. iii, §41). A nation has a humanitarian duty to provide assistance to those nations in need, but the prospective host nation has to be judge of the need and whether it wishes to accept the assistance. In general a nation has no right to intervene in the affairs of another sovereign nation because each is deemed an autonomous and independent moral person.

TERRA NULLIUS, OCCUPATION AND OWNERSHIP

The idea that vacant land may be occupied through necessity was well established among the Greeks and Romans. In order to alleviate overpopulation in the polis or city, establishing a colony elsewhere provided a practical solution to a pressing problem. Vitoria, for example, did not as such disagree with the doctrine, but denied that mere discovery, '*ius inventionis*' was a legitimate claim to ownership. Occupation of land for him is a manner of appropriating territory that has no owner, that is, '*illa quae sunt deserta, quod in nullius bonis est*' (Phillipson 1915: 184). For him, under natural law, originally all men had a right to everything. Because of God's premonition of Man's sinfulness He made provision for private property in permissive natural law in so far as men could come together and agree that, 'You take this and you this and I will have this' (cited in Tierney 2001: 389). Vitoria was in no doubt that the American Indians did have ownership rights and that their land was not *res nullius*. *Res nullius* is not an exact equivalent for *terra nullius*. The former refers to items in general without an owner, such as buffalo roaming the ranges which are common to everyone, or to things that cannot be owned, such as the air we breathe or the oceans we sail.

Balthazar Ayala contends that under natural law, in primitive times, all things were in common, and no individual owned anything. Community of goods, however, did not suit man's debased nature. Natural reason informed the Law of Nations that a system of private property was required to mitigate the sinfulness of mortals (Ayala 1912: Book II, chapt. v, [16], p. 41). Suarez, using Isidore's *Etymologies* (Bk. V, chapt. vi), contends that *ius gentium*, or the natural law, confers upon individuals the right to occupy places not previously occupied by others (Suarez 1944: 837). Alberico Gentili, starting from the premise that humanity comprises a universal society, claiming Tacitus as an authority, and developing an idea from Thomas More's *Utopia*, concluded that exiles from their own countries, out of necessity, were entitled to wage offensive wars in their quest for habitable territory, and that vacant lands may be colonized by people who need them for their own use. Unoccupied land belongs to no one and those who take it have a right to do so. Nature abhors a vacuum. Under the rule of Spain, he argues, almost all of the New World remains unoccupied. The implication is that the right to occupy it by means of possession still stood (Gentili 1933: Book I, chapt. xvii, p. 81 [131–2]).

This justification of appropriation, on the grounds of what John Winthrop, Governor of Massachusetts, called *vacuum domicilium* (Green and Dickason 1993: 235), rarely found expression in French or Spanish writers, but was to become increasingly important for Dutch and English apologists for colonizing the New World (Tuck 1999: 47–50). America was a vast continent, with a variety of social structures and religions, parts of which were recognized to have sophisticated political and cultural orders, while others conformed to no recognizable system of authority, whose life styles appeared nomadic, and whose economies entailed no recognizable system of cultivation. Such peoples enjoyed the rights of the earth in common, use rights, and what they picked, killed, or gathered became their own. In Grotius' view, for example, God had given the world to man in common, but also made provision for the acquisition of property through individual labour and industry, as long as it conformed to two primary conditions, or natural laws. These were, first, that everyone may use common things without causing harm to others, and second, that everyman be content with his portion, and abstain from coveting another's (Grotius 2004: 6).

For Grotius there is a difference between 'occupation' (*occupatio*) and 'ownership' (*dominium*). Occupation is a natural right which pertains to self-preservation. There is a rudimentary form of private property in owning one's body, for example, and that extends to the appropriation of things, such as fruit and animals for preserving that body. 'Ownership' (*dominium*) is an institution created by civil society, and is the result of agreement.

Various legal cases in the United States retrospectively and anachronistically served to reinforce the distinction between occupation and ownership. *Johnson v. M'Intosh* (1823) reaffirmed the belief that when John Cabbot discovered and symbolically occupied North America in 1497 he delivered full proprietary title to Henry VII and natives either became trespassers or attained some other title. They, and other Aboriginals, were deemed licensees of the Crown, allowed rights of occupancy on sufferance, but not of ownership unless explicitly given such title by the Crown (Lester 1984: 3). The implication is an affirmation of Grotius' point. If land rights are conferred by the Crown or government then they qualify for protection by the legal system just like the rights of any other American, Canadian, or Australian who derived their titles from the government or Crown. In other words land rights are a legal construct and prior occupation is no ground for title. *Johnson v. M'Intosh* has remained at the heart of land rights issues for two centuries despite the fact that it was historically inaccurate in claiming that the Crown never recognized the property rights of Indians, and that the Indian rights of occupancy had been an aspect of English law since colonization first began.

Grotius distinguished between property and jurisdiction. Jurisdiction, for him, amounted to its exercise over people rather than over things, and may be territorially defined in the right to exercise jurisdiction over all people entering a certain territory. Everyone had a natural right to inhabit and possess waste uncultivated land, on condition that due acknowledgement is given to the relevant political authority that is obliged to allow one to settle. If the indigenous authorities refuse to recognize the right of settlement then it has violated the natural law and given just cause for war.

What the idea of vacant land effectively meant for Grotius was that proprietary or ownership rights were deemed to have validity only within the context of a system of law. In arguing that the Portuguese had no right of possession in the East Indies, for example, Grotius contended that the Portuguese could not claim a right of first possession, because the East Indies was not vacant land. They were in the possession of their native rulers, who even though they were partly idolators and Muslims did not debar them from the rights of dominion (Grotius 2004: 14). The islands of Java, Sumatra, and large parts of the Moluccas 'always had their kings, their commonwealth, their laws and liberties' (Grotius 2004: 13). Vattel, writing in 1758, is categorical in his condemnation of the 'notorious usurpation' constituted by the conquest of the 'civilised Empires of Peru and Mexico' because these lands could not be deemed unoccupied (Vattel 1834: book I, chap. vii, §81, p. 35). Furthermore, the Spanish were guilty of violating the inviolable principle of sovereignty. In convicting the Inca Athualpa under Spanish law they were guilty of 'extravagant injustice'. Athualpa had done nothing under the Law of Nations to violate Spanish rights. They accused him of putting several of his subjects to death, and of having several wives. It was the Spaniards, however, who were in violation of the Law of Nations in disregarding the sovereign rights of Peru (Vattel 1834: book II, chap. IV, §55).

Where there was a recognizable social structure and system of authority – and this, of course, never went uncontested irrespective of religion, the peoples were deemed to have the same rights and duties under the natural law as Europeans. From this point of view the universality of the natural law and of natural rights appear to work for the benefit of indigenous peoples who conformed to universal, that is European, standards of social and political relations.

There was a distinction to be made, then, between the use of the land by American Indians and ownership, between occupation and possession. Thomas Hobbes (1588–1679), although less fulsome in his discussion, subscribed to the view of More, Gentili, and Grotius that the lands of the Americas were plentiful enough to accommodate a people that was still increasing in population and needed to expand into extra territories. This did not give settlers a right to massacre the natives, but they could constrain them to live closer together (Hobbes 1991: 239).

The idea of waste land was to figure prominently in Locke's justification of acquisition, without Gentili's requirement of necessity. The fact that the land was deemed empty was justification for occupancy, but occupancy in itself did not in the eyes of many apologists give sufficient grounds for title, or ownership. As with Grotius, occupancy, for Locke, had to be equated with possession. The principle of appropriating waste territories therefore needed to be supplemented with a theory of property that established a moral title to the ownership of the land. Possession was equated with cultivation. For Locke the Indians certainly had a natural right to property, just like everyone else, they just hadn't exercised it, and what is more they were in dereliction of their duty to God to make the soil as productive as possible by cultivating the land. Vattel, too, was quite clear that occupancy was not enough, 'The law of nations will, therefore, not acknowledge the property and sovereignty of a nation over any uninhabited countries, except those of which it has really taken actual possession, in which it has formed settlements, or of which it makes actual use' (Vattel 1834: book I, chap. xviii, §208, p. 99).

For Grotius, first sighting was not in itself a legitimate ground for title to ownership. Occupancy was an important criterion to undermine possible claims to ownership on first sighting. Property claims had to be public. No property rights could be generated by subjective thought because no one could guess at what someone else intended to appropriate. Richard Tuck suggests that by putting forward this theory of property, 'Grotius had provided a useful ideology for competition over material resources in the non-European world...' (Tuck 1979: 62).

By the time that James Cook claimed New South Wales, then, on the grounds of first sighting, it was already well established that this was not a valid mode of taking possession. Furthermore in 1770 the British established no settlements and could not therefore legitimately claim ownership of Australia.

European monarchs held great tracts of land in the Americas on behalf of the whole community of their subjects. Such land was a legitimate possession if there was a demonstrable intention to divide it into private sections for cultivation. This justified what in fact both the English and Dutch were practicing in the Americas, and demanded that their 'legitimate' claims be respected by other European monarchs (Arneil 1992: 589 and 593).

Locke follows Hobbes and Pufendorf, rather than Grotius in identifying the natural law with the Law of Nations (Locke 1988: II, 276, §14). Locke believed that the human condition was naturally social, and that God gave the earth to men in common. Unlike Grotius and Pufendorf, for Locke agreement, or consent, was not necessary to create private property. If it were, Locke argued, private property would be contrary to God's intention. Private property existed in the state of nature from the outset in that every person had a property in himself over which no one, because of the principle of natural equality, could exercise dominion without consent. Vattel, Wolff's protégé, was much more permissive in allowing for appropriation, but he was nevertheless much more circumspect than he is commonly portrayed by those who claim that he is an advocate of the doctrine of *terra nullius*.

A great deal has been made of this idea of vacant or empty lands, especially in relation to Australia, but it is also invoked in discussions of European appropriation of New Zealand, and of continental America, including Canada. What needs to be noted is that European policies towards Aboriginal peoples change, and what is true of one period may not be true of another, with the added complication that landmark legal decisions that define the relationship between Aboriginals and settlers, have served retrospectively to attribute policies and doctrines that had current credence to the past in which they did not. The most famous legal reinterpretation of history that became definitive for the United States, and was cited extensively as case law elsewhere, for example in Canada and Australia, was the *Johnson v. M'Intosh* ruling, and to a lesser extent the Mabo ruling in Australia. In the first instance, Justice Marshall anachronistically ruled that it was Crown policy that while the American Indians occupied the land they had no ownership rights over it, and in the second, Justice Brennan ruled that the British colonization of Australia was based on the illegitimate assumption that the land was unoccupied.

The doctrine of vacant or unoccupied lands, available for others to acquire and appropriate, was a central pillar in conceptualizing relations between European and non-European nations, that is, between civilized, barbarous, and savage societies. It was an important issue because unoccupied did not literally merely mean uninhabited, it also came to mean under-used, or uncultivated or under-cultivated land available for appropriation, and in this respect it was an important consideration in the partition of Africa.

The term *terra nullius* itself has come to be emblematic of some of the more pernicious acts of Europeans perpetrated upon Australian Aboriginals subsequent to taking possession. Stuart Banner, for example, contends that, '*terra nullius* is so self-evidently a fact of Australian history, and so "firmly part of the law" that it is easy to lose sight of the fact that it was anomalous in relation to the broader context of British colonization' (Banner 2005*a*: 1).

The Settler Contract

The settler contract, as I suggested earlier, is a sub-species of what Charles Mills calls the expropriation contract. Integral to the settler contract is a group of ideas that have retrospectively been termed the idea of *terra nullius*. The Latin *terra* means land, earth, or ground, and *nullius* means no one's, hence vacant or empty land, or at least unoccupied by anyone who qualifies as capable of ownership.

There are two aspects of Carole Pateman's 'Settler Contract' that deserve further exploration: the right to husbandry with the associated issues of property rights and the issue of sovereignty. In relation to the first, there is no doubt that such a right has strong support in the Law of Nations, which comprises elements of natural law, the customary practice of states, the opinions of philosophers and jurists, and case law. There were various ways to invoke this right, not all of which were consistently nor universally accepted. First, by 'discovery' or 'first sighting', the grounds which James Cook gave for taking possession of Eastern Australia in 1770 in the name of the Crown, and which was consolidated with more permanent settlement in 1778. This was also often the ground upon which sovereignty was frequently claimed, and is different from claiming a property right. To claim sovereignty is to assert the right to rule.

Second, by secession when a limited native title is acknowledged and the natives are conceded to be capable of alienating it, as was the case in many parts of North America.

Third, to be denied the right to husbandry in cases of necessity, or where vacant land lies idle, is to give just cause for war, and the right to husbandry would then be exercised by conquest, as was the case in Mexico and Peru, and some parts of North America. For a short period after the American war of independence, for example, American Indians, apart from two tribes, were treated as defeated and conquered nations because they fought on the side of the English. The Spanish in their foray into North America had explicit intentions of conquest. The instructions of the ill-fated fleet of Pánfilo de Narváez that left Spain on 27th June 1527 was 'to conquer and govern the provinces that extend from the River of the Palms [in Mexico] to the Cape of Florida...' (De Vaca 2007: 1).

Finally, a fourth way of invoking the right to husbandry was to assume the duty of trusteeship, that is, of becoming the guardians of natives whose rational capacities are judged to fall far short of those required for responsible cultivation, and who needed to be governed for their own good and guided towards civilized standards, as was the case with the Europeans in Africa, who viewed the population as childlike and incapable of entering into social contracts.

To focus upon husbandry as a right, however, is to imply that the natives had a duty to allow settlement (from the point of view of the settlers), and to give up lands that were vacant, or not fully used. This correlation is certainly to be found in commentaries on the Law of Nations and Nature. Locke's influential argument is emphatic, if American Indians attempt to subject Europeans to their system of rules, or deny them the right to husbandry, it is they who have violated natural law and given just cause for war in which case the injured parties may punish the transgressors and seek reparations. In conditions of war the injured may justifiably 'destroy' the violators as 'dangerous and noxious Creatures' bent on their destruction (Locke 1988: II, §§10–11 and §16).

The emphasis upon the right of husbandry, or of cultivation, that both Tully and Pateman give, does, nevertheless, hide from view, or at the very least obscure, the more fundamental moral justification for appropriating native lands. It is the application of a universal principle, against which savages and barbarians are found wanting. It is a principle derived from the natural law, and deeply ingrained in the Christian religion. It is the duty imposed by God upon humanity of self-preservation which requires making the earth productive and bountiful. The more efficiently this is done the better. To optimize productivity of the soil and fulfill one's duty to God require the development of techniques of cultivation, and just as importantly the establishment of civil society, or sovereignty, to ensure good governance and security in order to protect oneself from harm and to cultivate in safety.

To judge indigenous peoples against the universal obligation to cultivate or exploit the land to its optimum meant that they fell short of their moral duty in a number of respects.

Hunters and gatherers were deemed to be merely parasitic of the land, while rudimentary agriculture that exhausted the nutrients in the soil and required abandoning one location for another, while fulfilling the obligation to a greater degree, still fell far short of efficient exploitation. In this respect cultivation becomes the only recognized form of labour that fulfils the religious obligation. It is the fact that land is not cultivated that makes it no man's land, not the fact that there are no people on it. In other words, a certain type of labour was deemed synonymous with civilization. This deeply held conviction was expressed without any compunction by Thomas Arnold (1795–1842), the headmaster of

Rugby School, 'so much does the right of property go along with labour that civilized nations have never scrupled to take possession of countries inhabited only by tribes of savages – countries which have been *hunted over* but never *subdued* or cultivated' (Arnold 1831*b*: 157). The hunting grounds of the American Indians belonged to no one, and in taking them Englishmen were simply exercising 'a right which God has inseparably united with industry and knowledge' (Arnold 1831*b*: 157).

These ideas were entwined with an increasingly more formalized conception of stages of civilization, each having a distinctive form of subsistence and relationship with the land attached to it. Such ideas were not unfamiliar to classical scholars who needed only to look in the pages of Cicero and Virgil to find notions of property associated with the cultivation of land. The likes of Grotius, Pufendorf, and Locke concurred with the association, but this stadial theory of modes of subsistence was articulated most fully by the thinkers of the Scottish Enlightenment such as Dugald Stewart, Adam Ferguson, and Adam Smith, and became a presupposition of discussions about land rights that also referred extensively to the Law of Nations, and to American case law. In essence, it became common to view human progress in terms of the Ages of Hunters, Shepherds, Farmers, and Commercial Society, each entailing different and more sophisticated, or civilized, property relations.

Hunters and gatherers, such as many of the American Indian Tribes, and paradigmatically the Australian Aboriginals, fell far short of fulfilling their obligation to cultivate the land and make it plentiful. Indeed, they could not effectively fulfil the minimum requirements of a society very well, that is, to protect its members from attack. Adam Smith, for example, contends that 'Among nations of hunters, the lowest and rudest state of society, such as we find among the native tribes of North America, every man is a warrior as well as a hunter' (Smith 1982: vol. 2, 689–90). But even those peoples who practiced agriculture such as the New Zealand Māori, and some American Indians, could be accused of inefficient production because of their crude farming implements and tendency to exhaust the soil and move on to new areas of cultivation. Ferguson, for example, while recognizing variations in the primitiveness of different American tribes, nevertheless characterized their relation to the soil as that of sharing things in common. Hunters and gatherers, he contends, conceive of property rights only in the weapons, utensils, and furs they carry, whereas their catch accrues to the community. He acknowledges that in most parts of America 'savage nations' mix hunting and gathering with 'some species of rude agriculture', but nevertheless still conform to the same principle of enjoying the 'fruits of the harvest in common' (Ferguson 1966: 82).

For most of the eminent writers on the natural law and Law of Nations native peoples, then, were morally derelict in failing to fulfil their obligation to God in making the earth bountiful, and in failing to establish civil societies to ensure efficient exploitation of the soil. Locke, for example, admonishes hunter gatherers in comparison with civilized communities for producing one hundredth or even one thousandth of the products for commodious living that their European counterparts produce. Europeans use one tenth, or even one hundredth, less land than American Indians to produce the same or equivalent products (Locke 1988: II, §§40–42).

Vattel was not so specific in quantifying the extent to which native peoples fell short of their obligation, but he was equally as critical: 'Those who still pursue this idle mode of life, usurp more extensive territories than, with a reasonable share of labour, they would have occasion for, and have, therefore, no reason to complain, if other nations, more industrious and too closely confined, come to take possession of part of those lands' (Vattel 1834: book I, chap. vii, §81, p. 35).

Strategies were pragmatic, of course, and the use of the idea of waste land, *terra nullius*, was one such strategy to take possession of lands that were not under cultivation. Even Māori who were deemed to occupy a higher level of civilization than the Australian Aboriginal, and were designated agriculturalists and acknowledged to own the land they cultivated, and, unlike the Australian Aboriginals, were credited with a capacity to alienate it, nevertheless failed to meet the conditions necessary for the full exercise of the universal rights enjoyed by civilized nations. The Māori, and American Indian farmers, were thought rudimentary agriculturalists who had not developed plough technology. They moved on to new lands when the soil was exhausted. The fact that they were not hunters was used by many to the opposite effect to what one would expect, in order to argue that they did not need as much land as hunter gatherers over which to roam in search of game, and that their proprietary rights should be restricted to that land which they actually cultivated, and not extended to that which they claimed (Hickford 2006: 123). In Connecticut, for example, the minister John Bulkley contended that the law of nature 'makes the Land a *Man Tills and Subdues* to be his *Peculiar Property*' (cited in Banner 2005b: 34). In so far as they had failed to leave the state of nature and develop institutions capable of sustaining property rights in uncultivated land, their property rights extended only to that which they had cultivated. By the 1800s there was a widespread, but mistaken belief that the American Indians had not engaged in cultivation prior to settlement, and that their mode of existence was hunter gatherers. In Boston in 1804, pastor John Lathrop reiterated the obligation that Jehovah imposed on mankind, that is to subdue the earth and replenish it. Lathrop emphasized the duty of whites to inculcate this obligation in the American savage (Banner 2005b: 154). This made it easier for post revolutionary Americans to believe what became formalized by the American Supreme Court in the *Johnson v. M'Intosh* ruling, that the Indians had a right of occupancy rather than ownership over the lands of America.

In New Zealand the Crown was to exercise Eminent Domain and assume sovereign responsibility, which it claimed in relation to the North Island of New Zealand in the wake of the Treaty of Waitangi of 1840, on the ground of cession, and over the South Island on the grounds of Cook's 'discovery' or 'first sighting' of 1769–70.

Further evidence that the central idea to focus upon is the failure to exploit the potential productive capacity of the land is the fact that the argument is used to justify European Trusteeship in Africa in the latter part of the nineteenth century. The Dual Mandate was based on the principle that the exploitation of African resources was to be for the mutual benefit of the industrial classes of Europe and the peoples of Africa. It entailed an obligation of trusteeship which was enshrined in international law by the Berlin Conference 1884–1885. Lord Lugard best exemplifies the understanding of this relationship. It is one based on the familiar assumption that God gave the world to men in common and that it is by natural right the inheritance of mankind. Africans, unable to appreciate the value of the resources under their feet, have no right to prevent others from exploiting them. Lugard asks, 'Who can deny the right of the hungry people of Europe to utilize the wasted bounties of nature, or the task of developing these resources... a "trust for civilisation" and for the benefit of mankind' (Lugard 1928: 615, cited in Bain 2003: 62).

The obligation assumed by European powers at the Berlin Conference entailed taking charge of the internal affairs of African territories thus effectively collapsing the distinction between a colony and a protectorate, with the express intention of more efficiently eradicating slavery from the continent. These self-imposed duties of the higher civilizations to nurture the lower towards maturity gave them the self-endowed right to acquire jurisdiction without having to pretend that it was ceded by treaty with peoples who did not understand, and to whose way of thinking the idea was alien (Bain 2003: 67).

Consent was not necessary because Africans, like the Aboriginals, were not deemed to have fully developed rational faculties because of their child-like nature. In relation to Africans, but not in relation to Aboriginals, Europeans assumed an obligation to act as guardians and trustees until they matured. For many the Aboriginals of Australia hardly figured on the scale of civilization at all. As late as 1930 it was still deemed necessary to give a defence of why Aboriginals are human beings (Bennett 1930).

There was clearly a perception that Australia was sparsely populated, but whether this constitutes evidence that it should be treated as if it were waste, empty, uncultivated, uninhabited land is the issue under contention in what has been called the 'history wars' in Australia. Indeed, the assumption that Aboriginals did not own land, or have a sense of being bounded by territory was doubted by many during the early years of occupation and after. Aboriginal tribes certainly associated themselves with territories and took their names from them, but more surprisingly they parcelled some of the land to individuals who were able to pass it on by heredity, and who 'punished those who trespassed on it' (Banner 2005*a*: 14).

Many jurists and philosophers in the natural law and natural rights traditions simply would not accept such a concept of ownership qualifying for the protection of universal rights, because the obligation to make the land as productive as possible was not being fulfilled. In other words Aboriginals were not farmers.

Complicit in the use of universal standards to dispossess peoples of their lands, to oppress them, deny them sovereignty, and condemn them to permanent exclusion from the international society of nations, were most of the great early modern and enlightenment philosophers hailed as the champions of reason and liberalism. I want to counter two dismissals of their importance, and therefore indirectly deflect what would potentially undermine Carole Pateman's contention that the doctrine of *terra nullius* and its concomitant ideas were central to the 'Settler Contract' (Pateman and Mills 2007: 38).

Michael Connor simply dismisses this body of international and juristic and philosophical opinion as of no legal substance and irrelevant to his claim that the term itself was not used by government officers and settlers in the eighteenth century (Connor 2005: 4). To say that it has no legal substance is, however, to overstate the case. Michael Connor accuses Henry Reynolds (1992), a leading proponent of the *terra nullius* thesis, of fabricating the doctrine on the grounds that it had no basis in British nor European law, and that his use of Vattel to substantiate his case was illegitimate in that Vattel was 'not making up rules of law for men to follow, he was a writer, a publicist, a theorist' (Connor 2005: 23, 25). Connor's criticism assumes an excessively positivistic conception of international law. The Law of Nations, or *ius gentium*, was not a law enacted by an international legislature, nor was it enforced in international courts, it was legal in the sense that it was inferred from the accepted practice of 'civilized' states as either directly derivative from the natural law, or from international custom, but also from the opinions of learned theologians, philosophers, and jurists. It was a law that comprised a curious amalgam of moral, political, and legal arguments in the justification of state and individual practice.

There was no doubting its existence, as Suarez suggests, because it 'is assumed by all authorities to be an established fact, or so we gather from their very frequent use of the term' (Suarez 1944: Book II, chapt. XVII, §1, p. 325). One of its distinguishing features is that its precepts 'are not established in written form' and 'it consequently differs in this respect from all written civil law, even from that imperial law which is applicable to all' (Suarez 1944: Book II, chapt. XIX, §6, p. 345). Furthermore the Law of Nations differs from natural law in that the latter is truly universal, common to all peoples, and accepted by everyone. Only in error can it fail to be observed. The former, however, may not always be observed by all nations, and what is considered by some to be the Law of Nations, may not be considered so by others, and therefore 'without fault fail to be observed' (Suarez 1944: Book II, chapt. XIX, §2, p. 342). As we saw, Rachel too maintains that the Law of Nations acts as a common bond of obligation binding peoples of differing population and under different forms of government; depending for its veracity upon 'mutual good faith' (Rachel 1916: Diss. II, §I, p. 157).

Merete Borch has suggested that, 'it is difficult to see that any of the frequently quoted international jurists provided arguments for seeing indigenous land as *terra nullius* either during the eighteenth century or before it' (Borch 2001: 232). This view is, I think, mistaken. It is incontrovertible that the authorities on the Law of Nations generally acknowledged a right to the occupation of unoccupied lands, and in some instances even if they were under the eminent domain of a recognizable sovereign. The basic premise among jurists and philosophers in the early modern period regarding property rights was that God gave the whole world in common to mankind, and those portions that remained unoccupied, or uncultivated, which did not necessarily mean upon which no people resided, were available for legitimate occupation.

Locke, Wolff, and Vattel, for example, contend that people have an obligation to cultivate the land, and if they did not they had no right to prevent those who would. Wolff, for example, confirms that uninhabited lands may be colonized and appropriated because they are the property of no one. The nation appropriating the vacant land acquires property rights in it and sovereignty over it. Unlike Locke, for example, he acknowledges ownership and sovereignty by nations over the lands they occupy, even if those lands are waste and barren. Nevertheless, since every nation should perfect its condition, such land that lies vacant should be given to foreigners (Wolff 1934: chap. III, §§275–92, pp. 140–152).

Vattel suggests that, 'Every nation is obliged by the law of nature to cultivate the land that has fallen to its share', and that 'The cultivation of the soil...is...an obligation imposed upon man by nature' (Vattel 1834: book I, chap. vii, §81, p. 35). The land would simply not feed its inhabitants if it were allowed to lie vacant. It may have been all right in primitive times to live the life of hunting and gathering, but now that the population has greatly increased each nation 'is obliged by the law of nature to cultivate the land that has fallen to its share' (Vattel 1834: book I, chap. vii, §81, p. 35).

Vattel was quite clear that occupancy was not enough, 'The law of nations will, therefore, not acknowledge the property and sovereignty of a nation over any uninhabited countries, except those of which it has really taken actual possession, in which it has formed settlements, or of which it makes actual use' (Vattel 1834: book I, chap. xviii, §208, p. 99). It was lands considered to be in common, over which everyone in the world still exercised use rights, that were designated unoccupied or uncultivated, that is, vacant or waste land, not because there were no inhabitants, but because, in Vattel's famous phrase, they roamed over them. He claimed that 'erratic nations' who have 'unsettled habitation' in vast regions cannot really be deemed to have taken 'true and legal' possession (Vattel 1834: book I, chap. xviii, §209, pp. 100–101). There was a distinction to be made, then, between the use of the land by American Indians and ownership, between occupation and possession. Even though this was not the widespread practice in America, it nevertheless informed the famous *Johnson v. M'Intosh* decision, which was itself evidentially supported with reference to the authorities on the Law of Nations. Prior to this decision, however, perception had already deviated from the fact. It came to be a widespread belief that Indians were hunter gatherers, and for centuries the Law of Nations did not acknowledge that the land over which they hunted was owned by them. Indeed, if agriculturalists settled on the same land it was they who were deemed to own it (Banner 2005*b*: 168).

Private property existed in the state of nature from the outset in that every person had a property in himself over which no one, because of the principle of natural equality, could exercise dominion without consent. God wills that we sustain and protect this property in ourselves by cultivating and appropriating the things of nature (Locke 1988: II, §26 and §86, pp. 286–7, and 323). The use of the gifts of nature requires that we first take possession of those things. We do so by means of an instrument inherent in the person, labour. It is labour, and not consent, which creates property in things, 'The *labour* that was mine, removing them out of that common state they were in, hath *fixed* my Property in them' (Locke 1988: II, §28). God has granted us life, a property in the person, and we have an obligation to preserve it, and as far as we can, to preserve the life of others. Preservation of property in the person is enhanced by the efficient use of the resources of the Earth. We are also, therefore, under an obligation to God to make the land and all that lives and grows on it as productive as possible.

Locke's theory of private property in the state of nature does not require the context of civil society. In addition to Grotius' primitive form of property in which each has the right to the fruit he or she picks, of the animals hunted and killed, Locke wants to go further and establish ownership in land. The problem was how to do this without conceding that the American Indians already owned the land. The device he used was to employ a very restricted definition of labour.

It is important to see how subtle Locke's theory the shift from ownership of things to ownership of land is. The labour expended by hunter-gatherers, deep-sea fishermen, bakers or craftsmen entitles them in the state of nature to what they have killed, gathered or made. When it comes to land, however, there is a change of emphasis. In the *First Treatise* Locke excludes certain types of 'labour' from affording a property title. Referring to the Bible, Locke recalls the curse placed upon Adam requiring men to labour because of their impoverished and destitute condition (Locke 1988: I, §6, pp. 144–5). The earth requires long and sustained labour in order to yield its fruits and make it productive. Mere occupancy or appropriation, that is taking possession, does not qualify.

Ownership and labour is now clearly associated with cultivation. Locke contends that, '*As much Land* as a man Tills, Plants, Improves, Cultivates, and can use the Product of, so much is his *Property*' (Locke 1988: II, §32, pp. 290–1; cf. Waldron 2002: 164–70). The crucial point is this, Locke excludes such activities as roaming over the uncultivated land, hunting and gathering, or grazing one's sheep on it, from securing a title to property. What is of more significance is that not only does labour provide a title for the ownership of property in the state of nature, but Locke also wanted to establish the moral obligation to engage in labour. It is not enough to mix one's labour in the land, say by enclosing it and planting trees, but we are obliged to develop it to its greatest productive capacity as industrious and rational creatures. God did, after all, give men the world 'for their benefit. And the greatest Conveniences of Life they were capable to draw from it' (Locke 1988: II, §34, p. 291, cf. Lebovics 1986, 577).

By implication, the American Indians, and later when Australia was discovered, the Aborigines, in failing to cultivate the land to its full productive capacity, were rather less than industrious and rational and had no grounds for preventing those who are from fulfilling God's destiny for men. Locke's argument, whether the settlers realized it or not, gave the philosophical foundation to the contention frequently made that the British had just as much right to settle the land in Australia as the Aboriginals. In landing in Australia the British simply exercised a right that they held in common with Aboriginals, and of which the Aboriginals singularly failed to avail themselves (see Banner 2005b: 20).

Locke's view of the Indians was that they were wretched creatures, barely achieving subsistence levels, and whose kings were worse off than English day labourers. They were ignorant and barely able to raise themselves above the level of the brutes. In his journal entry for 1677 he says that their 'minds are as ill clad as their bodies' (cited in Cox 1960: 98–9). It is difficult to know to what extent Locke exaggerated the brutish condition of the American Indians for personal gain and self-justification, given that he himself profited from lands and slaves in Carolina. It was a considerable exaggeration to suggest that the American Indians did not engage in agriculture. Colonists frequently reported agricultural activity throughout eastern North America, and it was well known that parts of what is now North Carolina had extensive cultivated fields, as is evidenced by a late sixteenth-century drawing by John White of Indians, permanent structures, and cultivated plots of land. It was the growing acknowledgement that Indians farmed the land that contributed to the recognition of their right in property (Banner 2005b: 38).

The obligations to God of self-preservation and of cultivating the earth in order to make it more productive and conducive to self-preservation are better discharged within a political society. The inconveniences of the state of nature, regulated by a law that is not written down, willful and innocent misinterpretation of the law with no common superior to arbitrate, and no power to enforce it, make it imperative to set up by agreement political society and government.

The implication of Locke's discussions of the American Indians is that they fall short of adequately discharging their obligations to God. They still live outside political society in a state of nature and they fail to add to the common stock of mankind by improving the productivity of the land. In so doing they have no claim on vast territories in the Americas that '*lie waste*'. By this Locke means more than land that is simply left barren. Land that was not efficiently utilized and whose produce was allowed to rot, regardless of its being enclosed, 'was still to be looked on as Waste, and might be the Possession of any other' (Locke 1988: II, 295, §38).

There were, of course, alternative views to those of Locke, in which irrespective of the cultivation of the land, communities exercised eminent domain over it. Grotius before him distinguished between property and jurisdiction, the latter remaining with the 'ancient nation' even when strangers justifiably claim waste land. Christian Wolff after him, however, ostensibly endorses Pufendorf's position, claiming that nations exercise eminent domain, or sovereignty, even over those tracts of land that appear to lie waste. The seizure of such lands is therefore contrary to the laws of nature and nations (Wolff 1934: chap. VII, §866). Wolff acknowledged that originally all land was in common, but such ownership became modified by families or communities jointly holding territory as a proprietary right. Whether they used all the land or not made no difference to ownership. Land belonging to such families or communities cannot be taken or occupied by others coming into the territory (also see Borch 2001: 234).

More important, I think, are the issues that relate to sovereignty. Irrespective of whether native Aboriginals were deemed to own the land, and if they did it could be 'purchased' from them, the question arose, could they be deemed to constitute civil societies, sufficiently recognizable to possess sovereignty? The important issues are these, first, do the native inhabitants have some sort of private property title in the land? They as communities may have what was called eminent domain, that is, have jurisdiction over the land, but that would not prevent individuals from elsewhere claiming specific tracts of it, without undermining eminent domain.

Indeed, five years before the voyage of Captain James Cook it was British Imperial Government official policy that land in America not already in the possession of settlers belonged to the native Americans, from whom it may be purchased, but not seized. Indeed, the assumption among government officials was that in establishing new colonies the land would have to be purchased from the inhabitants (Banner 2005*a*: 3).

It is a widespread misperception that Europeans refused to acknowledge Indian land rights, a myth perpetuated by the classic *Johnson v. M'Intosh* (1823) ruling by Chief Justice John Marshall that because the English had not recognized the Indians as property owners nor should the United States (Banner 2005*b*: 11). In fact, there was widespread acknowledgement of Indian property rights, often for the benefit of the settlers who ruthlessly exploited them, rather than from any altruistic motives or moral conscience. Even when land rights were granted to indigenous peoples, governments had little compunction in seizing them if their value became reassessed.

Like the idea of sovereignty in relation to the Peace of Westphalia, however, there is little evidence of a conscious doctrine of *terra nullius* being to the fore of the minds of governments or settlers. To focus on the issue of *terra nullius* is, I think to give emphasis to ideas that were related to a much more important belief, namely, the religious obligation imposed by God on man to cultivate the earth and make it bountiful. That is not to say that such ideas were not often invoked in argument. Even William Penn who readily acknowledged the property rights of Indians and scrupulously purchased their lands, maintained that they had no claim to 'Waste, or uncultivated Country' (cited in Banner 2005*b*: 31).

Contemporary Relevance

To maintain that the idea of *terra nullius* is the basis of the acquisition of land in foreign parts is not of merely antiquarian interest. It has contemporary political importance because there are serious legal and practical implications. If Australia was settled on the grounds that it was desert and uncultivated, then the settlers take with them such English law as is their birthright applicable to the new surroundings by right of occupancy (Blackstone 1765: bk 1, pp. 104–5). If, however, the land is already owned or cultivated, possession of it can be gained only by conquest or ceded by treaty. These methods of acquisition were the only three proposed by Sir William Blackstone, claiming that they are founded on the law of nature, 'or at least on the Law of Nations' (Blackstone 1765: bk 1, pp. 104–5). Blackstone's *Commentaries* were written before Captain James Cook 'discovered' Australia in 1770. If it could be shown that grounds for believing that Australia was unoccupied were spurious, and that Aboriginals certainly never ceded their territory, then the only other ground, on Blackstone's authority, was conquest. If conquest, the laws of Aboriginals antecedent to conquest remain intact until such time as they are expressly superseded by the new sovereign. Discovery or peaceful settlement differs in a numbers of important ways from conquest. English common law and statutes enacted prior to settlement apply automatically to the new territory. Secondly, English law is literally imported into the new territory, and is not something that stands outside it, and therefore any inhabitants of newly settled territories become subjects of the Crown (Lester 1984: 15).

Hence the importance of the issue of whether Australia was conquered or peacefully settled. Because no termination of Aboriginal rights was ever enacted, it could be, and was contended by Paul Coe in 1977, that Australia was not *terra nullius*, and that the method of occupation was conquest. The dispossession of Aboriginals since 1788 was therefore unlawful (Maddock 1983: 15). Coe was unsuccessful both in his High Court case and the appeal in 1979. The subsequent seizure of the concept by historians and land rights activists invested the term with the meaning of vacant and uninhabited lands, and imputed to it a far more concrete legal foundation than it actually had in British and Australian law (for example, see Frost, 1980–81; Reynolds 1992, 1999, and 2004; Broome 2002: 238; and Pateman and Mills 2007: 37).

The basic premise among jurists and philosophers in the early modern period regarding property rights was that God gave the whole world in common to mankind, and those portions that remained unoccupied, or uncultivated, which did not necessarily mean upon which no people resided, were available for legitimate occupation. The group of ideas that had currency among writers on the Law of Nations came to be encapsulated in the twentieth century in the doctrine of *terra nullius*. Its fully formulated and systematic form is an invention of recent origin, often imputed to governments and settlers as consciously informing their actions, when in fact they felt little need for the subtleties of such justification, when others sufficed perfectly well. The term itself was not used by government officers and settlers in the eighteenth century (Connor 2005: 4). It gained notoriety in the famous *Mabo* case (1992) in Australia which claimed that *terra nullius* was part of the English common law which gave claim to settlers over vacant land. Justice Brennan ruled that Australia was not *terra nullius* at the time of occupation. The ruling allowed Aboriginals to claim title to land that was in the ownership of the State, but not that privately owned. It became commonplace to refer to *terra nullius* as if it was an official doctrine consciously employed by settlers and government officials. Geoffrey Robertson, for example, refers to the 'pernicious common law theory of *terra nullius*' which allowed the dispossession of 'native inhabitants as if they were part of the flora and fauna' (Robertson 2000: 149).

It was instead part of the customary Law of Nations which while not universally observed gave grounds for laying claim to territory under the sovereignty of no one, or in exceptional circumstances of extreme necessity to territory already under a sovereign.

After 1670, that is long after the first European acquisition of the Americas, and before the 'discovery' of Australia, territorial acquisition by 'plantation' begins to be used as a justification in legal cases (Lester 1984: 17). Discovery, or first sighting, however, was one ground that was not widely accepted amongst jurists and theologians, who believed, despite Captain Cook's appropriation of Australia on grounds of first sighting, that more permanent signs of settlement and occupation were required for title. From about the 1660s discovery and symbolic acts of possession were no longer regarded as constituting *plenum dominium* for the discovering sovereign, but instead a pre-emptive or preference right to acquire the title. In this respect, then, the settlements of 1778 secured the *dominium* for the British Crown and established title (Lester 1984: 28)

Nevertheless, Chief Justice Marshall's ruling in *Johnson v. M'Intosh* (1823) is premised on the belief that the plenary proprietary title to territory in the New World derives from discovery and the symbolic act of taking possession (Lester 1984: 7). This American case law was deemed relevant in the *Milirrpum v. Nabalco* (1971) decision in Australia when Justice Blackburn contended that what we call *terra nullius* always included territory in which primitive and uncivilized people lived (Connor 2005: 276). The plaintiffs lost the case on the grounds that they could not point to the act of recognition or grant from the sovereign (Lester 1984: 12).

It is clear that Captain James Cook was under the impression that first sighting established some sort of claim to sovereignty. His instructions, dated 30 July, 1768, relating to his first voyage of 1769–70 were clear. His main object was to find the Southern Continent, in the course of which he was to chart the location of islands that had not previously been sighted by Europeans and take possession of them in the name of His Majesty.[1] These instructions are consistent with those given to John Cabot in 1495, and according to Chief Justice Marshall informed, at least partially, the subsequent claims of most European states. In relying heavily on Marshall the constitutional lawyer, Supreme Court Justice, Joseph Story summarized the position in 1833:

The principle, then, that discovery gave title to the government, by whose subjects or by whose authority it was made, against all other European governments, being once established, it followed almost as a matter of course, that every government within the limits of its discoveries excluded all other persons from any right to acquire the soil by any grant whatsoever from the natives. No nation would suffer either its own subjects or those

---

[1] http://www.foundingdocs.gov.au/item.asp?sdID=67. Accessed 19 August, 2007.

of any other nation to set up or vindicate any such title. It was deemed a right exclusively belonging to the government in its sovereign capacity to extinguish the Indian title, and to perfect its own dominion over the soil, and dispose of it according to its own good pleasure (Story 1833: bk 1, chapt. 1, §6).[2]

James Cook's instructions were, 'with the Consent of the Natives to take Possession of Convenient Situations in the Country in the Name of the King of Great Britain. Or: if you find the Country uninhabited take possession for His Majesty by setting up Proper Marks and Inscriptions, as first discoverors and Possessors'.[3] In 1770 Cook operated on the basis of first discovery and his journal shows that although he was aware that the lands of which he took possession for His Majesty were inhabited, he did not seek the consent of the natives. Cook clearly took possession of territories on the basis of discovery and first sighting, and acknowledges that the Dutch have title to those territories they first sighted.

The issues, but not the term 'first sighting', were still being discussed in 1885 at the Berlin Conference on the partition of Africa, and the responsibilities of Europeans with respect to new occupations. The conference rejected the idea of first arrival giving grounds for the declaration of a sphere of influence, without political responsibility. Instead it opted for the principle of 'effective occupation' and by implication rejected first sighting as a justification of title.[4]

Had the colonizers of Australia wished to disregard the fact that Australia was inhabited, or extended the meaning of what uninhabited meant, and taken possession of it on the grounds that it was vacant land they could have found ample justification, as we have seen, in the writings of jurists and philosophers. The fact Aboriginals were believed to be hunter gatherers, with no recognizable system of private property rights, and no serious cultivation of the land, placed the land technically in the category of waste or unoccupied as understood by most reputable jurists and philosophers of the natural law and Law of Nations.

TERRA NULLIUS AND SOVEREIGNTY

Sovereignty is a related but different issue which does not relate to property rights as such, but to who, or what body, has the authority to govern. The assertion of sovereignty was similarly based on the assumption of European superiority, and stages of civilization. To claim sovereignty, or the right to govern, was generally accepted by Europeans irrespective of whether one believed that the Indians or Aboriginals owned the land.

---

[2] Story refuses to enter into the natural justice of such claims suggesting that they lay outside of the scope of lectures on the law of a single nation, and belong more to a treatise on natural law. See Story 1833, bk. 1, chap. 1, §4.

[3] http://www.foundingdocs.gov.au/item.asp?sdID=67

[4] I am grateful to William Bain for alerting me to this point. Also see chapter three of Bain (2003).

The crucial issue amounts to this, private ownership of land was for most government officials, philosophers, and jurists, such as Grotius, Pufendorf, and Wolff, regarded as separate from the issue of sovereignty, or eminent domain. For example, for Grotius land used only by hunters and gatherers was to be deemed vacant because it was uncultivated, and remained common and available for appropriation. Grotius maintains that 'waste or barren Land' must be given to strangers at their request, or it may be 'lawfully possessed' by them 'because whatever remains uncultivated, is not to be esteemed Property, only so far as concerns Jurisdiction, which always continues the Right of the antient People' (Grotius 2005: Book II, chapt. ii, §17, p. 448). The English in North America did not merely claim *imperium*, or territorial sovereignty, but also claimed *dominium*, that is, private property rights. Indeed, when claims were first advanced against the New World there was no conception of territorial sovereignty or legislative power distinct from ownership of the land. Jurisdictional rights and legislative power were derived from ownership of the land, or lordship, and the king was at once *rex* and *dominus* (Lester 1984: 27).

In practice even when it was acknowledged that native peoples exercised ownership rights, the colonizing country retained for itself the rights of eminent domain, and denied sovereignty to native peoples by conquest or cession. The early settlers acquired Indian land by contract, even though many of the transactions included dubious and fraudulent practice, including purchases from those who had no authority to sell tribal lands. After the war with France in the 1750s, in which Indians tended to side with the French because of their distrust of the English, the method of acquisition moved from contract to treaty. In other words, where the natural right of individuals to property was acknowledged, community rights under the Law of Nations were withheld because they were not deemed fully sovereign nations. Indeed, although treaties paid lip service to Indian sovereignty, there was no suggestion of equality.

During the eighteenth century in America it became common practice among British officials to acknowledge the land rights of the Indians, while emphasizing that sovereignty had been ceded. A 1761 report of the Board of Trade on the settlements on the Mohawk River, for instance, complained of the cruelty and injustice perpetrated against the Indians by depriving them of their hunting grounds in violation of the compacts in which they had ceded their 'Dominion' but not the property of those lands. A Royal Proclamation of 1763 indicates that the British believed that they had acquired the sovereignty of territory between the colonies and the Mississippi in establishing an Indian territory under British 'Sovereignty, Protection and Dominion' (see Borch 2001: 229). Joseph Story encapsulates the principle when he contended that, 'As infidels, heathens, and savages, they were not allowed to possess the prerogatives belonging to absolute, sovereign and independent nations' (Story 1833: bk. 1, chapt. 136, §152).

Similar understandings were expressed in Australia. In 1836, for example, in deciding the issue of whether Aboriginals were subject to English law, the Supreme Court of New South Wales granted that the Aboriginals of New Holland should be regarded as civilized nations, free and independent, entitled to the enjoyments of the rights that are important to them. However, 'the various tribes had not attained at the first settlement of the English people amongst them to such a position in point of numbers and civilization, and to such a form of Government and laws, as to be entitled to be recognized as so many *sovereign states governed by laws of their own*'(cited in Connor 2005: 288). Whereas the treaty of Waitangi has attained emblematic status, and separates the Australian from the New Zealand Aboriginal experience, in that the latter were judged to be in the process of appropriating land and developing civil government, and therefore capable of concluding a treaty, they were not, however, deemed capable of enforcing it. It was an ambivalent judgment which at once asserted both capacity and incapacity (Pocock 2001: 84).

In case law throughout the Commonwealth and the United States, until the mid-1950s, in relation to the claim for property rights, the preponderance of decisions affirmed the 'Doctrine of Recognition'. A licence of occupancy is assumed, unless there is evidence of the granting of property rights. In 1954, for example, the American Supreme Court ruled that without the sovereign first having recognized their rights the Tee-Hit-Ton Indians had no property right compensable under the Constitution (Lester 1984: 4).

Social Contract theory, in its classic form, which included the idea of a state of nature, was central to theories of sovereignty. The Aboriginal peoples who roamed over but did not occupy or possess territories were deemed not to have made such contracts and therefore did not possess sovereignty. Indeed, both America and Australia were used as testimony that a state of nature exists. Whether indigenous peoples were deemed to own the land over which they 'roamed', or whether they merely had a use right in common, they were not deemed to have entered into a social contract among themselves, and therefore they were not deemed to have instituted sovereign political societies. In the case of the Australian Aboriginals, they were believed to be so primitive that they lived in a 'genuine state of nature' such that all men must have lived in prior to constituting civil society (cited in Banner 2005a: 10). If on Locke's criteria they lived in a state of nature they had use rights in the land over which they roamed, but they did not have property rights, nor sovereignty. The legacy has been the permanent exclusion from the international realm of minority nations within nations, on the grounds that they do not constitute sovereign political communities.

Christian Wolff, for example, confirms that uninhabited lands may be colonized and appropriated because they are the property of no one. The nation appropriating the vacant land acquires property rights in it and sovereignty over it. He acknowledges ownership and sovereignty by nations over the lands they occupy, even if those lands are waste and barren. Nevertheless, since every nation should perfect its condition, such land that lays vacant should be given to foreigners (Wolff 1934: chap. III, §§275–92, pp. 140–52).

Those who occupy the sovereignty of a territory also exercise eminent domain over property and persons (Wolff 1934: chap. VII, §866). This would seem to imply that native Americans own and have sovereignty over the lands they occupy.

However, just as earlier theorists tried to disqualify them on grounds of lacking fully human attributes, or because of their sinfulness, or because they engage in the wrong sort of labour, Wolff applies stringent criteria for what constitutes a nation. He argues that, 'it denotes a number of men who have united into a civil society, so that therefore no nation can be conceived of without a civil sovereignty. For groups of men dwelling together in certain limits but without civil sovereignty are not nations' (Wolff 1934: chap. III, §309, pp. 156–67). For Adam Smith, 'nations of hunter gatherers whose society could not sustain or maintain an army for self defence could neither properly be considered a commonwealth nor sovereign' (Smith 1976: vol. 2, 690).

Ostensibly, the Westphalian model of the relation between rulers and ruled legitimizes the autonomy of the state to deal with its minorities as it sees fit. In practice, however, the international 'community' always took an interest in such matters. As we have seen, many of the international jurists and philosophers supported in some measure a principle of humanitarian intervention. As Stephen Krasner has argued, intervention by rulers in the relationship between rulers and ruled in other countries, by means of coercion or imposition, especially by powerful states, has been commonplace, and usually motivated not by a concern for rights, but for international stability. Every major treaty between Westphalia and Vienna included provision for religious toleration in one guise or another, with the latter including for the first time provision for respecting the rights of Poles to preserve their nationality where they constituted minorities in Prussia, Russia, and Austria (Krasner 1999: 83). A concern for minority rights was characteristic of the international community from the nineteenth century to the Second World War, most explicitly exemplified by the provisions of the Treaty of Versailles in 1919. Many rulers have tried to constrain their successors by entering into conventions which protect minorities, but such conventions had little effect unless there was domestic support for them (Krasner 1999: 75). Such provisions for minority rights, however, were rarely successful in practice, and almost completely abandoned in the post World War II era in favour of human rights, and when they were the explicit conditions of recognition of states, for example, in the former Yugoslavia, respect for ethic diversity was far from evident in practice.

RECOURSE TO LAW

In 1831 the Supreme Court of the United States of America provided its first extensive deliberation on the issue of sovereignty. Once again it was Chief Justice Marshall who wrote the opinion that was to become definitive in modern law. The court ruled that Indian tribes are not foreign states, and that therefore they lack the authority to bring suits directly to the Supreme Court. Nor were they American states. Instead, they were to be understood as 'denominated domestic dependent nations' (Banner 2005*b*: 220). In 1871 Congress enacted a statute that ceased recognizing Indian tribes as nations or powers with which the United States could enter into treaties.

As far as international law is concerned it never required that every acre of 'acquired' territory be inhabited or settled. What was important was that the ruler claiming sovereignty was able to establish a solid enough claim to prevent any other ruler from contesting the title. International law did not recognize Aboriginal peoples holding any rights against the colonizers or 'discoverers' of their territories. Under international law Aboriginal peoples became the subjects of the sovereign power. Such rights as they held against their national government were not recognized in international law.

Given that sovereignty subsequently became the membership card for entry into the international club, this constituted permanent exclusion for minority nations. The legality of such exclusion was put to the test on many occasions, for example, soon after the establishment of the League of Nations when the Six Nations Iroquois Confederacy attempted to gain recognition of their independence, and to resolve their on-going dispute with Canada. Between 1922 and 1924 they petitioned the League of Nations to accept them as a member and to intervene to prevent further encroachment by the Canadian government on their independence. They argued that the six nations had long been a highly organized self-governing people, whose confederacy of self-governing states had been acknowledged in treaties, and through diplomatic activity with the Dutch, French, Americans, and British since at least 1613. The Canadian Government responded to the petition by claiming that there was no provision in the Covenant of the League for discussion of the internal matters of a sovereign state in its dealings with individuals who owe the state allegiance. In other words the answer presumed what was in dispute. The League did not accept the petition (Nichols 2005: 42–3).

In 1926 the Cayuga Indian nation, one of the Six Nations, disputed the nature of the treaty between itself and the State of New York. In the course of the opinion delivered by the Anglo-United States Arbitral Tribunal the question of the international status of the Cayuga nation was addressed. The ruling contended that, 'So far as the Indian tribe exists as a legal unit, it is by virtue of the domestic law of the sovereign nation within whose territory the tribe occupies land, and so far only as the law recognizes it'. It was emphatic in pronouncing that the tribe was 'not a legal unit of international law' (cited in Green and Dickason 1993: 84). The fact that the rights Canadian Indians have are against Canada and are to be interpreted by Canadian courts was affirmed in 1982 by the English Court of Appeal. It was declared that 'treaties' between the Indians and the Crown do not have the same sense as they have in international law because they are not made between sovereign states (Green and Dickason 1993: 124).

The status of American Indians as separate nations, and exhibiting the features of statehood, has, however, on occasion, been affirmed by domestic courts in the United States. In 1831, for example, the chief architect of federal Indian law, Chief Justice Marshall, conceded that the Indians were originally self-governing tribes. He argued that the Cherokees were a state, 'a distinct political society, separated from others, capable of managing its own affairs and governing itself' (cited in Clinebell and Thomson 1977–8: 675). More recently in *United States v. Consolidated Wounded Knee Cases*, federal district judge Warren K. Urbom contended that the Sioux and many other tribes had well developed governmental systems, religions that respected the sacredness of nature and like, and dispositions towards peacefulness at least as effective as the white intruders' (Clinebell and Thomson 1977–8: 675).

The landmark case in Australia was *Mabo* (1992). The *Mabo* judgment assumes that Australian land rights and the legal system were based upon the foundation of *terra nullius*, and relied to some extent on the 1975 International Court of Justice *Advisory Opinion on Western Sahara*. The Mabo case was concerned with land rights on the Murray Islands in the Torres Straights annexed by Queensland in 1878. The findings of the High Court judges were, however, applicable to the whole of Australia. The main opinions were that Australian occupation was based on *terra nullius* as the mode of acquisition, and that Australia was not in fact *terra nullius* at the time of occupation. On the basis of its wrong assumption that Australia's claim to sovereignty rested on such a doctrine, the logical implication was that white Australian sovereignty is illegitimate, and the Court itself would therefore be deprived of authority to pronounce on the case. The Court, of course, did not go so far as to declare itself illegitimate. It nevertheless recognized native title, not in land already in private hands, but to government-owned lands (see the relevant documents in Bartlett 1993). The decision followed the 1991 Year of Indigenous Peoples, inaugurated by Prime Minister John Keating, declaring that, 'It was we who did the dispossessing. We committed the murders. We took the children from their mothers. We practised discrimination and exclusion' (cited in Lindquist 2007: 205).

Although Land Rights were recognized, Aboriginals are nevertheless still subject to Australian sovereignty, and indeed the Mabo decision was considerably diluted by amendments to the Native Title Act made by the new Liberal/National Government of 1996, under the leadership of John Howard. Claims were prevented over large areas of pastoral and mining land, and in order to make claims to territories Aboriginals have to demonstrate a continuing connection with the land over which they lay claim. Many, because their ancestors were dispossessed, or because they were abducted from their parents, or because they left their native area because of poverty, are not able to meet such a criterion.

CONCLUSION

The use of universal rights as instruments of oppressions is not a phenomenon of the past consigned to ruder times when white Europeans were ignorant of, or oblivious to, the wrongs they inflicted in the name of humanity. The very idea of universal rights, the same for everyone everywhere, while laudable in the abstract, is often in practice discriminatory against, or oppressive to, those who belong to minorities different from the dominant culture. Where white settlers comprise the dominant culture in such societies as the United States, New Zealand, Canada, and Australia the indigenous people's prior claims to rights over extensive territories have often been ignored or silenced, on the grounds that such peoples had no concept of right, or notion of private property, before European arrival. Australian Aboriginals, for example, were ruthlessly exploited by both the owners of, and white workers on, cattle and sheep stations, forced to work for less than subsistence, and paid in kind by allowing them to choose trinkets and clothes from the wagons of traveling packmen during their infrequent visits, while additionally, the women were serially sexually abused by white drovers and shearers, and by Aboriginal males themselves.

As late as 1969 in the United States, for example, a small group of Indians reclaimed Alcatraz Island in the name of the 'Indians of all Tribes'. This rare gesture of inter-tribal cooperation was meant to highlight the injustices of white occupation of American lands. To highlight the derisory nature of what recognition native land ownership meant they parodied the 1626 purchase of Manhattan Island by offering to purchase Alcatraz from the federal government for $24 in beads, trading goods, and coloured cloth. Alcatraz was chosen as symbolic of Indian reservations in being isolated from modern facilities; having poor terrain and unproductive soil, and being unable to support game. The occupation lasted for nineteen months.

While a great deal has been done to improve the condition of such minority nations, it has been on condition that there would not be any significant violation of the rights of members of the dominant culture. The condition of Canadian Indians, of Indians of the United States of America, and of the blacks who were forced to work there as slaves, of Australian Aborigines, and of New Zealand Māoris, while an improvement on the disdain in which they were held from settlement to the late 1960s, is, nevertheless, as minority groups in each country, comparatively disadvantaged, in terms of life expectancy, socially and economically. Such groups may indeed be damaged by the exercise of universal rights by members of the dominant culture, and calls for special protection rights, which provide barriers against exploitation in the name of freedom and universal rights, are common to all of them.

A more limited criticism of human rights accepts that they are a valuable achievement, but contends that they do not go far enough to protect minority cultures against a wide range of injustices. In essence, this criticism accepts the liberal contention that human rights empower people to resist persecution and injustice, but also accepts the view that human rights can be used as instruments of oppression by exclusionary tactics, imposing universal norms and denying legitimacy to minority cultures. The list of human rights needs to be supplemented with an additional list of cultural or collective rights (Kymlicka 1998: 3). Kymlicka argues, for example, that it is a mistake to think of human rights as individualistic, and cultural or collective rights as communal. Many human rights, such as the freedom of conscience and worship, facilitate group activity. Without such freedom many religions may have died out. The liberal tends to believe that where such fundamental human rights as freedom of speech, conscience, and association exist there is no need for special minority rights because these individual rights are sufficient to ensure a diversity of communities within society. Kymlicka argues, however, that particularly in states with national minorities which developed their own institutions, territories, culture, and language prior to incorporation into larger states, universal human rights are insufficient to ensure ethno-cultural justice. Justice may be undermined in a number of ways, among them through adverse migration and language policies. First, immigration policies used to place national minorities at a disadvantage may be exacerbated or even justified by human rights doctrines. The right to freedom of movement may be claimed as universal in order to redress the imbalance between a national minority and the dominant culture in a particular territory. Special rights, such as land rights, may be asserted or claimed by a national minority such as the Australian Aboriginals to prevent their culture and resources being undermined. This is not really an issue between group rights and individual rights because the dominant culture reserves the right to restrict immigration into the state, and those who are allowed in are expected to assimilate. All that a national minority within such a state is claiming is that same right to preserve its integrity by restricting immigration into its territory.

Kymlicka contends that, 'Unless supplemented by minority rights, majoritarian democracy and individual mobility rights may simply lead to minority oppression...human rights and minority rights must be treated together, as equally important components of a just society' (Kymlicka 1998: 16). In this respect the minority has to be held responsible for respecting the individual rights of its members, but likewise the majority has to be held responsible for respecting minority rights. These minority rights are unlikely to be able to be expressed in universal terms, and many must of necessity be specific to the peculiarities of particular circumstances. There should nevertheless be some 'impartial enforcement mechanism' by which both universal and particular rights are seen to be respected.

The concern for minority rights by the international community during the inter-war years and which was deemed a failure did not, however, extend to Aboriginal communities in the New World, and this was principally because no security issue was involved. Globalization, and its concomitant liberal universalism, has brought in its wake a growing sensitivity to the compatibility of minority rights and universal rights. In 1989 (convention 169), for example, the International Labour Organization effectively renounced its previous paternalistic assimilationist policy towards indigenous peoples, and instead recognized the aspirations of these peoples to take control of their institutions, including land, language, and their customary law.

The predominant focus of this chapter has been upon minority nations, and how European dominated universalism led to oppressions and gross injustice, often despite the highest of motives such as saving souls. Contemporary discussions about minority nations predominantly focus upon rectifying the historic injustices. Minority nations, for Kymlicka, have a greater claim for protective rights than ethnic minorities which have emigrated to a country. While he does not wish to suppress difference, he thinks that the special rights that they ought to have are inclusion rights, and that the barriers to their equally participating in the society to which they have emigrated be dismantled.

Modern multiculturalism, however, is largely confronted with a different set of considerations, namely, post colonial immigration and the mutual accommodation of a diversity of ethnic groupings which are often viewed as homogeneous on essentialist criteria, such as being of the Muslim faith, or emanating from broadly the same geographic origin, but who are nevertheless extremely diverse.

The desire to accommodate ethno-cultural diversity does not, however, extend to ethno-religious diversity. Modern multiculturalism tends to be secularist, and to a large extent mirrors the belief that state and religion should be separated, with the latter being a matter of belief and choice, that is, a private matter (Modood 2007: 70). The cultural encounters that have dominated the pages of this chapter were largely religious, where the practice of a religion different from Christianity automatically rendered a people inferior, and where the ostensible aim was, along with many others, to save their souls and assist them, through education, or by brute force, on the path to God. The distinctiveness of modern multiculturalism, as Tariq Modood points out, is that it introduces into western nation-states an ethno-religious amalgam on a scale previously unknown, and brings to bear questions of democratic citizenship and individual rights on the issues of the co-presence of ethnic and religious communities. Modood, quite rightly, wants to bring religion back in because it cannot be divorced from questions of ethnicity and culture, and is not merely a question of personal preference and choice (Modood 2007). It is also important to avoid fruitless arguments about culture, and cultural belonging, which reify cultures to the extent which they do not reify themselves. We should take the multi in multiculturalism more seriously, and acknowledge that individuals are moral agents, not culturally determined, but imbued with situationally varied cultural values (Phillips 2007).

For almost two decades an international process of diffusion has been underway which disseminates ideals and standards of good practice with respect to multicultural values and minority rights to which all states should aspire. Coupled with this process has been the increasing codification of norms below which no state should fall (Kymlicka 2007: 5). The UN culminated the process by declaring the International Decade of Indigenous Peoples (1995–2004). In September 2007, 143 of the UN General Assembly's member states, against the opposition of some of the most powerful states, adopted the 'Declaration of the Rights of Indigenous Peoples'. The Liberal Australian government voted against, but only two months later the newly elected Labour premier, Kevin Rudd, made a public apology to the Australian Aboriginals for the grief, suffering and loss caused them (Amnesty International 2008: 4)

5

Natural Rights: Descriptive and Prescriptive

> Hobbes claims that I have the right to do whatever I conceive necessary for my own preservation – in this sense, certainly, I have the natural right to live. But no one therefore has the duty to allow me to do whatever I consider necessary to my preservation. You, having the right to do what you consider necessary to your preservation, may judge my demise advantageous, and so may with right kill me. You deprive me of my life, and prevent my exercise of my right of nature, but you do not violate my right of nature (Gauthier 1969: 31).

In this chapter, I want to suggest that natural rights need to be distinguished into descriptive and prescriptive traditions, and if either has a claim to secularizing subjective rights it is the former. The descriptive strand is, however, something of an aberration, finding its finest exponent in Thomas Hobbes. The prescriptive tradition associated with such thinkers as Locke, Price, Priestley, Paine, and Wollstonecraft, as well as with the great charters of rights, still retains a significant element of rights derivative from natural law, as well as elements of subjective rights, or powers. It is still the product of a heavily religious society, in relation to which God predominantly stands as the reason for obedience to natural law, and respect of the rights of individuals.

The modern obsession with rights has led to a revival of interest in the natural rights tradition, and a preoccupation among theorists with the importance of human rights attaching to the individual independently of society. Robert Nozick gives one of the strongest reiterations of this individualist conception of rights: 'Individuals have rights, and there are things no person or group may do to them (without violating their rights)' (Nozick 1974: 5).

There are some writers who suggest that human rights and natural rights are basically the same. Immediately after the Second World War the highly respected international lawyer Hersch Lauterpacht argued that natural law, natural rights, and human rights were almost indistinguishable, having a common ancestry, and that any attempt to sever an international bill of rights from its religiously grounded ancestors would rob it of its moral force (Lauterpacht 1945: 9). More recently, Peter Jones, as we saw in the 'Introduction', believes that human rights are the direct descendants of liberal theories of natural rights, and share with them the same features. We have them by the mere fact of being human as a moral entitlement quite independently of governments and any particular systems of law in which we may find ourselves (Jones 1991: 223). In criticism of Rawls's he suggests that 'human rights have generally been conceived as rights possessed by human beings as such and as rights that must therefore be respected in all the various contexts and circumstances in which human beings find themselves' (Jones 1996: 189). H. L. A. Hart also suggests that people are conceived to have human rights 'by virtue of their humanity and not by virtue of human fiat, law or convention'(Hart 1999: 405). What I want to suggest is that contrary to these views, there is more of a gap than writers want to acknowledge between the modern human rights culture and the natural rights tradition that is often assumed to underpin it.

There is a tendency to portray the shift from natural law to natural rights as a shift from a religiously based ethic to a more secular conception of rights. John M. Headley, for instance, claims that the move to natural rights constitutes the 'shedding of natural law's specifically religious framework' (Headley 2008: 103). In addition, Thomas Pogge has recently claimed that 'the shift from natural-law to natural rights language constitutes a secularisation which facilitates the presentation of a select set of moral demands as broadly sharable in a world that has become much larger and more heterogeneous' (Pogge 2002: 55).

The emphasis upon the secularization of natural rights considerably distorts the extent to which the conclusions of thinkers such as Grotius, Pufendorf, Locke, Priestley, Price, Paine, Hamilton, and Wollstonecraft, who are claimed as part of the heritage of the contemporary human rights culture, depend upon a Christian world view and a shared belief in God, the Creator of the moral world and of the human beings who inhabit it. This belief is sometimes a full-blown Christian theology or merely contains lingering remnants of deism lacking the elements of Divine intent, command, and purpose, or in the case of Paine he places natural religion at the foundation of natural rights. Any element of Christianity or deism, of course, is in contemporary discussion of human rights an embarrassment, especially when one wants to emphasize their universality.

Those who emphasize the secularization of natural rights often fail to make the crucial distinction between descriptive and prescriptive, or naturalistic and moral natural rights. The former certainly does constitute a secularization of natural law and natural rights, but the latter does not.

THE DESCRIPTIVE VERSION OF NATURAL RIGHTS

Descriptive theories of natural rights have no intrinsic moral content. Their objectivity derives from the so-called 'facts' of human nature, without having to rely upon the authority of religion for their efficacy (Huxley 2001: 338). We saw that many of the Roman Jurists tended to think of natural law in naturalistic terms, and not in the way that the Greek and Roman Stoics conceived it. For the jurists, something that was unnatural was contrary to law or common sense. The idea of a right was only nascent in their thought, and was not foremost in their considerations. Often the term *jus*, or *ius* was used in an objective sense, meaning the right thing to do in a particular situation, and this is the way that St. Thomas Aquinas predominantly used it. Rarely was right (*jus*) equated with property (*dominium*) (Tuck 1979: 10–11).

As we saw, the ambiguity of the terms law and nature were often exploited by the Greeks and Romans, and Thomas Hobbes, the translator of Thucydides' *History of the Peloponnesian War*, was well aware of its rhetorical potential. He remarks, for example, that: 'All authors agree not concerning the definition of the *natural law*, who not withstanding do very often make use of this term in their writings...' (Hobbes 1841: 14). Hobbes employs the idea of a law of nature, but he is at pains to distinguish law from right. Right for him is permissive, 'to do, or to forebeare', and therefore subjective. Law, on the other hand, determines what one should do or desist from (Hobbes 1991: I, xiv [64]). In Hobbes's state of nature, law is prudential and not moral. A right is simply the liberty that each person has to exercise his or her own power for self-preservation, where liberty is understood as the absence of external impediments that hinder the power a person has 'to do what hee would' (Hobbes 1991: I, xiv [64]). Both Nussbaum and Tierney quite rightly observed that the moral element is missing from Hobbes's definitions. Hobbes' definition of *ius* was completely subjective and devoid of the idea of 'moral rightness' (Tierney 1989: 622), and 'his law of nature is not a law properly so called; it denotes conclusions on how to act for self-preservation and defence' (Nussbaum 1953: 145).

In Hobbes we have natural rights, but more strictly speaking they are not rights at all because no one has any obligation to acknowledge or respect them. They are in fact powers and capacities, or natural inclinations. The fact that we have certain powers or liberties in nature is justification for their use. To have a faculty and the right to use it are one and the same thing. To say that lions are carnivores and therefore have a right to eat flesh does not place an obligation on their prey to respect this right: 'it were a hard condition of mankind, that a fierce and savage beast should with more right kill a man, than the man a beast' (Hobbes 1994: Part II, chapt. xxii, p. 129). It is really a misuse of language to call it a law or a right and all that is being said is that lions have a primary instinct that is involuntary and which motivates their behaviour, and no moral blame can be attached to them for that. Hobbes expressly argues that the law of nature precedes Divine positive law, the manifestation of God's will in the Scriptures. In the state of nature men may kill and subdue others for their safety, and may do the same to animals, for safety, use, and food by the law of nature.

The law of nature operates in the state of nature, or pre-civil condition, and when states are instituted it is the will of the sovereign that determines what is right and wrong. The justification of a law need be only the determination of its authoritative source, namely the Leviathan. Relations among citizens are regulated by the laws of their state. Relations among states, however, are analogous to the pre-civil state of nature, and the law that governs them is the Law of Nations, which he equates directly with the law of nature, not in the prescriptive, but in its descriptive sense.

Nature was often invoked in discussions of rights independently of their relation to Divine origin. In this respect, they are a continuation of certain Greek and Roman uses of the term natural, and to think of certain rights as alienable would be to think of the act as contrary to nature, or simply unnatural. Richard Overton, for example, argued that: 'They which contract to obey their own ruine, or having so contracted, they which esteeeme such a contract before their owne preservation are felonious to themselves and rebellious to nature' (cited in Waldron 1987: 14–15).

The ambiguity, and the exploitation of the ambiguity, of the term nature, and of designating what is natural led Herbert Spencer in the nineteenth century into all sorts of difficulties. First he denied the natural right of private property, and then asserted. Despite the criticisms of natural right from the likes of Hume, Burke, and Bentham, to which I will return in the next chapter, the doctrine retained its rhetorical appeal for many in the political debates of the latter half of the nineteenth century where it was used both to resist and to support the extension of the role of the state.

Spencer formulated two versions of the principle of justice. The first is related to his Law of Conduct and Consequence. This is often described as a desert theory of justice (Taylor 1992: 234), but it is much more subtle than that. In fact, it is better described as an entitlement theory because whatever the consequences of one's actions the individual was entitled not only to the benefits, but also the evils that may accrue (Spencer 1978: 17). The evils should only be mitigated, that is some form of charitable assistance offered, if they are an unanticipated consequence, not of effort, but of fortuitous invention such as the near obsolescence of candles as a consequence of the invention of gas lighting. These were the deserving poor, as opposed to the undeserving poor who should be left to suffer the full consequences of their desultory lives. His entitlement theory is premised on the fact that the market is the most adequate mechanism to determine the value of individual effort. He did not extend his principles to the receipt of unearned dividends which were the result of fortuitous fluctuations in the stock market, nor to inheritance unrelated to effort. For him complete ownership of something incorporates the principle of being able to transfer it to someone else.

Spencer's views on entitlement were related to his evolutionary theory and the doctrine of the survival of the fittest in which state interference was not only unnatural, but potentially catastrophic. Redistributive justice, the taking of earned benefits and giving them to those who have not earned them, renders a society weak. He argued that a society 'will be unable to hold its own in the struggle with other societies, if it disadvantages its superior units that it may advantage its inferior units' (Spencer 1982: 105). On the same basis eradicating illness by investing in better sanitation would lead to the perpetuation of weaker elements in society prone to succumb to disease.

Spencer's Law of Conduct and Consequence was the positive formulation of his theory of justice, that is the entitlement to the fruits of one's labour. This was complemented by his negative formulation in the Law of Equal Freedom. If men lived solitary existences then the Law of Conduct and Consequence would for Spencer have provided an adequate formulation of justice. The social environment, however, in which humans interact requires a further principle which guarantees men the capacity to pursue their own designs, and this is the Law of Equal Freedom. Weinstein contends that it is the key to Spencer's utilitarianism and the conceptual centre to which all else is related (Weinstein 1990: 120). It is premised on two assumptions. First, that individuals are more capable of providing for their own welfare than governments, and, second, that individuals intelligently promoting their own interests best achieve the common welfare (see Taylor 1992: 222). The whole range of natural rights was encompassed by, and the equality at which justice aims was manifest in, the Law of Equal Freedom. Although he sought to demonstrate that evidence for the natural right to Liberty could be derived from many sources, including the customs of ancient societies in which property rights existed prior to governments, his principal argument was to claim that 'the laws of life' gave force to his conclusions (Spencer 1982: 149). He argued that in order to sustain life, the essence of which is the utilitarian principle of a surplus of pleasure over pain (Spencer 1978: 80), we value certain activities and the exercise of the faculties to engage in them which are essential to the attainment of human happiness and self-preservation (Weinstein 1990: 120–1):

Those who hold that life is valuable, hold by implication, that men ought not to be prevented from carrying on life-sustaining activities. In other words, if it is said to be "right" that they should carry them on, then, by permutation, we get the assertion that they "have a right" to carry them on. Clearly the conception of "natural rights" originates in recognition of the truth that life is justifiable, there must be a justification for the performance of acts essential to its preservation; and, therefore, a justification for those liberties and claims which make such acts possible (Spencer 1982: 150).

Spencer's formulation of natural right is unlike that of Hobbes because it has an ethical dimension. Without adequately explaining the reasons, except to appeal *a priori* to the 'mutual limitation of spheres of action', and *a posteriori* to anthropological evidence to demonstrate the recognition of 'mutual restraints', Spencer believes that in humans this right that also pertains to animals is mitigated by a sense of limitation on what actions are permissible for sustaining life (Spencer 1982: 150–1). Like Rousseau, Spencer believes that it is the sentiment of sympathy that leads to the development of restraints. Sympathy is what transforms our egoistic sentiments into altruistic sentiments (Weinstein 1990: 123). Whereas Hobbes's conception of Liberty entailed no duties towards respecting the liberty of others, for Spencer the Law of Equal Freedom, to do whatever a man desires to sustain life, gives rise to obligations of a negative kind, that is, not to interfere with the freedom of others. In this way his argument combines both the Law of Conduct and Consequence and the Law of Equal Freedom. The former is positive in that if each person is to be the recipient of both the good and bad consequences of his or her actions then each person must be free to act. The latter is negative in that actions must be subject to some restraints in a social context where others also have similar claims.

Spencer's natural rights, which include the right to life, personal liberty, the use of the earth, private property, and exchange are all corollaries of the Law of Equal Freedom. Spencer wants to deny Bentham's contention that rights are conferred upon people by governments, and he also wants to deny the Hobbesian claim that government is in some way the product of a social contract. Spencer nevertheless wants to maintain that the doctrine of natural rights is fully warranted. How, then do we know what human rights there are? In his most extended discussion of rights the implication is that we may discover them *a posteriori* by engaging in a sort of comparative anthropology. Prior to government, which often codifies pre-existing rights, natural rights find expression in human customs. 'The fact is,' he argues, 'that property was well recognized before law existed' (Spencer 1982: 142). Although details may differ, at the level of fundamentals the laws of governments are largely the same forbidding homicide, theft, and adultery, indicating universal acceptance that individuals may not be violated in certain ways. This is no coincidence, Spencer declares, because the creation of rights is nothing less than formally sanctioning and giving greater precision 'to those assertions of claims which naturally originate from the individual desires of men who have to live in presence of each other' (Spencer 1982: 144). Natural rights, for Spencer, are 'essential pre-requisites for individual welfare' (Spencer 1982: 146), and their independent recognition in the codes of law of different nations 'imply, not an artificial source for individual rights, but a natural source' (Spencer 1982: 159).

In the twentieth century Robert Nozick and David Gauthier represent the revival of natural rights in their descriptive form. What is descriptively 'true' of human beings somehow has 'moral' force in determining what rights they possess by the mere fact that they are human. Whereas his project resembles that of Locke's, Nozick lacks the same foundational motivation that Locke builds into his theory in order to generate rights. The main features of his theory of rights are that they are negative, requiring non-interference; they are significant barriers or constraints and cannot be ignored or overridden even on the grounds of the greater good; while there are other values, the only political considerations relate to enforceable obligations attached to rights; and these rights are absolute in character (see Wolff 1991: 16–35).

Nozick wants to take seriously the separateness of persons, and rejects utilitarian justifications for trading-off one person's rights against another's, measured against a standard of the greatest happiness of the greatness number. Such a measure may be used to justify depriving a small group of individuals of some good, so that the rest may enjoy a greater benefit. Taxation, on this view, is enforced labour, the taking away of what is someone's by right, and the giving of it in terms of general benefits to others. Tom Campbell describes Nozick as a rampant individualist (Campbell 2001: 57) because justice is not about agreeing fair principles of redistribution, but instead respecting the right of individuals to self-ownership (Swift 2001: 30). Nozick's position is that prior to the establishment of social and political systems individuals have rights. Taking as his starting point the separateness of individuals Nozick claims that there are certain things that they have an absolute right to control, and which cannot be overridden by considerations of social welfare or general benefit. These rights include life and liberty, as well the general right to establish specific property rights, including self-ownership. These rights are entitlements with which no one may interfere. The extreme example he uses to illustrate his case is that however beneficial it may be to others, the forcible redistribution of body parts is a gross violation of rights (Nozick 1974: 206).

Like Spencer, he has an entitlement theory of justice and rights. He is not arguing, for example, that the famous basketball player Wilt Chamberlain deserved the extra money that people were prepared to pay him, only that he is entitled to it. Even if he was a far worse player, and people just liked his looks and were prepared to pay extra, Chamberlain would have been entitled to it, whether he deserved it or not. Campbell has skilfully broken down the entitlement theory of rights to its component parts. First, such rights are not dependent on recognition by any institution or culture, they are natural or moral. Second, they are absolute in that the right is not dependent upon the desert, needs or usefulness of the rights holder. Third, they are inviolable in that they cannot be overridden by any consideration of the general welfare or the benefit of others. Fourth, they are negative in that they are correlative with the duty others have not to interfere with the exercise of the rights. Fifth, the rights are alienable, in that the right-holder may waive them. Finally, the rights are not substantive goals to be pursued, but instead constraints that limit the conduct of others (Campbell 2001: 59).

Despite the confusion that surrounds, and the unsatisfactory nature of, the distinction between negative and positive liberty (MacCallum 1967: and Connolly 1983: 143–73), it serves to clarify Nozick's position. Rights for him are like the powers and liberties in Hobbes, namely negative rights, with the difference that we are expected to respect them. Why? Nozick is notoriously evasive on this issue. It certainly has to do with certain features that human beings possess. Rationality, free will and moral agency are all features that Nozick recognizes as important, but none has the ability to justify, for example, if I have free will, why I should be allowed to act freely. Nozick tries to complete the picture by maintaining that it is because of the human ability to formulate an overall purpose or conception of one's life, and to make choices that conform to it. It is something that gives meaning to life. But Nozick's theory is as susceptible to criticism for idealization as that of Hobbes. Idealization is what Onora O'Neill suggests is the taking and privileging of certain characteristics, at the expense of others, from which to generate moral principles. Nozick privileges the separateness of persons at the expense of the value they give to and benefit they derive from their relationships with others.

What sorts of rights does Nozick want to protect? A positive right to something, entails a correlative obligation on the part of some or all individuals. If my right to self-preservation is a positive right, then everyone, including you, has a duty to assist me if I am in danger of starving to death. The negative right to self-preservation only requires that others desist from interfering with my ability to exercise my right of self-preservation. Positive rights, for Nozick, are by and large self-imposed, by means, for example, of a contract. Nozick's negative natural rights are 'side constraints', or barriers that cannot be crossed even if a 'common good' justification is offered. He does not subscribe to consequentialism. Individual rights must be honoured whatever the consequences. While society may concern itself with all sorts of values, aesthetic, moral, or historic, political philosophy concerns itself with enforceable obligations exhausted by rights (Wolff 1996: 23). For Nozick, natural rights are absolute and inviolable.

Nozick's Libertarianism may imply that he wishes to protect the status quo, but in fact his theory has quite radical implications for international relations and the protection of natural rights. Property may be acquired in three ways: First, by initial acquisition; second, by voluntary transfer; and, third, by rectification or recompense. It is clear on these principles that in the case of the European settlement of America, and Australia, for example, land and possession changed hands through involuntary transfer. Nozick's third principle, that of rectification, bestows an entitlement upon those unjustly deprived of property, to be recompensed. He recognizes the difficulty of implementing this principle, and suggests that one way around it may be to start by giving everyone equal quantities of property (see Swift 2001: 33–4 and Knowles 2001: 177–88).

The theory of David Gauthier is even more radically individualistic, as the title of his book betrays, *Morals By Agreement*. Gauthier believes that morality faces a foundational crisis, and that the only plausible way out of it is offered by contractarianism. What he seeks to provide is a rational basis for morality (Gauthier 1986: 2). By morals he does not mean absolute standards, but instead agreed constraints on our behaviour, a rational limiting of our natural rights. He wants to show how morality, understood as rational constraints, can be generated from the non-moral premises of rational choice (Gauthier 1986: 4). In his hypothetical state of nature we already possess natural rights, but these rights are not moral rights. Morality comes about by agreement. Gauthier's influences include both Hobbes and David Hume. Hobbes, in showing how agreements to give up certain liberties give rise to actual constraints, albeit through the efficacy of the political sovereign, is the 'true ancestor' of Gauthier's theory (Gauthier 1986: 10).

Hume rejected many strands of contractarianism, mainly because they were historically incredible, but Gauthier takes him to be a contractarian of a different type. In agreement with Hume and Nozick, Gauthier rejects utilitarianism because it does not take adequate account of the distinction between individuals. It can justify social arrangements which are prejudicial to minorities as long as the utility of the whole is increased. Like the utilitarian, Gauthier contends that no constraints on human behaviour can be justified unless they benefit society as a whole, but in addition, he adds the proviso that no one should be worse off than he or she would otherwise be independently of co-operative social relations. He acknowledges that the traditional foundations for underpinning morality have been discredited. Alternatively, rational behaviour, independent of moral premises, can generate mutually agreed constraints which comprise a moral code. Why should anyone agree to self-imposed constraints? Or to put it another way, why should anyone be moral? In contradiction of those Ancient Greeks such as Antiphon, Callicles,

Thrasymachus, and Glaucon, who believed that morality was conventional, and against the interests of the stronger, Gauthier answers that it is rational to be moral, because it is in everyone's interest to be so. Gauthier gives a strongly individualist account of rationality (Gauthier and Sugden 1993: 187). Society is 'a co-operative venture for mutual advantage' and the purpose of justice, or morality, is to strike a 'justifiable balance between the principle of the separateness of persons on the one hand and the ideal of a social union on the other' (Gauthier and Sugden 1993: 78 and 176). His starting point is a hypothetical state of nature in which each bargainer is aware of his or her talents and advantages, unlike those clothed under a veil of ignorance in Rawls's original position, in order to ensure that inequalities are transmitted into society (Gauthier and Sugden 1993: 181). The individuals have natural rights, as Hobbes's individuals do. What is subject to agreement is not the establishment of a sovereign Leviathan to impose constraints, but the constraints themselves. No individual would give up the benefits which he or she has achieved, or may yet attain, independent of co-operation. What is subject to negotiation is the co-operative surplus, because no one would rationally give up what he or she already has. The surplus is to be divided unequally according to what each brings to the table in unequal abilities and talents.

Gauthier stipulates that the initial position must be free from coercion and assumes that no individual would make concessions that he or she did not expect others, similarly situated, to make. In addition, no one can benefit from the bargain at the expense of others. Gauthier here adapts Nozick's modification of Locke's proviso that individuals may acquire property as long as they allow 'enough, and as good left in common for others' (Gauthier and Sugden 1993: 87). Gauthier contends that the weakness of traditional contractarian theory is its failure to convince us of the rationality of compliance. He introduces the conception of 'constrained maximizers' who are willing to co-operate as long as others also comply. Constrained maximizers enjoy more opportunities for co-operation and mutual advantage than 'straight maximizers'. The theory is based upon a conception of instrumental rationality motivated by utility maximization. On such assumptions each person is concerned to give the minimum relative concession for the maximum relative benefit (that is the principle of minimax relative concession). Gauthier argues that:

The just person is disposed to comply with the requirements of the principle of minimax relative concession in interacting with those of his fellows whom he believes to be similarly disposed. The just person is fit for society because he has internalised the idea of mutual benefit, so that in choosing his course of action he gives primary consideration to the prospect of realising the co-operative outcome (Gauthier 1986: 157).

Gauthier contends that the initial bargaining position is devoid of moral values and that it is the 'bargaining outcome' that has 'moral significance' (Gauthier and Sugden 1993: 126). Why, one may ask, do we have natural rights in this hypothetical state of nature, and why is their content not subject to rational agreement? This would then make the process a two-stage bargaining contract. That consideration aside, Gauthier offers the prospect of agreed universal principles of morality, that is constrained behaviour, that Hobbes's theory cannot.

THE PRESCRIPTIVE VERSION OF NATURAL RIGHTS

Rachel, writing in 1676, denied the efficacy and logic of using the concept of natural law or the law of nature in a naturalistic sense. Law necessarily implies reason, and animals cannot be deemed to share in this rationality peculiar to man. In his view, men and animals are not bound by the same law. His argument is thus: 'For Law, properly so called, curtails or determines in a definite manner freedom of action; but freedom of action necessarily implies reason, and as brutes are not endowed with this they also lack capacity for any Law whatever, and especially for natural law' (Rachel 1916: Diss. I, §xxxix).

Rachel accuses Hobbes of being both foolish and foul in postulating a state of nature which is more like the state of the Devil, and for promulgating utility as the measure of natural law. Utility is the measure of positive law, and may in part also pertain to natural law, but principally its measure is Righteousness, that is, the conformity of the human will to the Divine will which results from obedience to 'the eternally and intrinsically good laws of nature' (Rachel 1916: §cvii).

In general natural law theories had the function of acting as guides to conduct and as standards by which to judge the laws of governments. The emphasis was distinctly upon the common good of the community and the obligations, or duties, it owed to God, or to upholding God's laws. During the later medieval period talk of religious obligations gradually became transformed into talk of rights. Individual human beings were understood to be related to each other in a world moral community in which rights were held and duties owed by the mere fact of being human. The predominant manner of thinking about such rights was the objective tradition in which rights are derived from objective moral laws.

During the sixteenth century within the natural law tradition, ideas of individual possessing inalienable and inviolable natural rights became more prevalent. MacKinnon argues that this shift towards natural rights was characterized by changing concerns. Whereas natural law emphasized 'constraints and limitations', natural rights theories were concerned with 'demands and permissions' (MacKinnon 1966: 79). The typical features of a natural rights theory are characterized in the following way. First, they were not created by human artifice, or convention. They were derived from nature and have validity even if they were not posited by human beings. Second, natural rights are inalienable and imprescriptible. Human beings have no authority to alter them or deny them. They are not the product of the human mind and cannot therefore be interfered with by humanity, although for some many of the rights may be transferred. Third, the rights are innate. We have them simply by the fact that we are human.

They are possessed by human beings prior to the existence of the state. Fourth, the rights are regarded as immutable, that is, universal, timeless, and unchanging. Contingent rights may be inferred from them in order to respond to changing circumstances. And, fifth, natural rights are self-evident, and fundamental, that is the rights are rational and discoverable by the exercise of reason. Anthony Flew argues that prescriptive natural rights entail a belief that certain entitlements are in some way objective, and that the establishment of this objectivity is usually made with reference to the Creator (Flew 1982: 278).

We have seen that there were intimations of subjective rights theories in medieval writers such as the Decretists and Ockham who conceived as moral powers or capacities, injecting a much more individualist element into the vocabulary. Further steps towards establishing a natural rights theory were taken during the Reformation when gradually the religious duties to resist tyrants became transformed into the rights of resistance. The Huguenots, after the Massacre of Saint Bartholomew, developed powerful theories which asserted the political rights of the subject against the ruling sovereign. Mornay, for example, argues that people create governments for their mutual benefit, and in doing so do not give up their sovereignty, but merely delegate to the king the right to exercise it. Magistrates are therefore responsible to the people who create them and not to the king. Kings are the agents of the people who supervise and execute the laws. They are equally subject to the laws as are ordinary citizens. Because the king is instituted by the body of people collectively, no individual has the right to resist the king. The right of resistance is that of the collectivity. The king, however, makes his promises to the magistrates to whom the people 'have given their sword' (Skinner 1978: vol. 2, 334). It is the magistrates, therefore, who possess the right of resistance.

The importance of the Huguenot theories of resistance was that they did not rest purely on religious grounds. They formulated genuine political theories which viewed civil society as the creation of a contract which in turn creates a moral right, and not just a religious duty, to resist rulers who do not fulfil their obligation to promote the common good. This, in essence, was a theory of representative rather than popular sovereignty. The Calvinist Buchanan and the Jesuit Marianna went on to develop an even more radical doctrine which vested the right to resist in every individual citizen.

Let me take a few obvious and not so obvious examples to suggest that the prescriptive version of natural rights derived from natural law did not necessarily constitute secularization. The point, I think, can easily be illustrated not only in the work of philosophers, but also in the most famous documents that articulate and embody natural rights.

Most of the natural law thinkers, as I contended in Chapter Three, thought it inconceivable that there could be obligation without God. Scholastics from at least Gregory of Rimini maintain that human beings without invoking God have the capacity to discriminate what is good and bad. They have no obligation, however, to conform to what is good without God's command (Haakonssen 1996: 21 and 29). The supposed secularization of the religious conception of natural law and its corollary natural rights, as we have seen, is usually attributed to Hugo Grotius who is said to have succeeded, to a large extent, in severing the connection between natural and Divine law. D'Entrève, in his book, *Natural Law*, testifies to the importance of Grotius in this respect, by claiming that: 'Thus Grotius' famous proposition, that natural law would retain its validity even if God did not exist, once again appears as a turning point in the history of thought' (D'Entrèves 1972: 71; Cf. Griffin 2008: 10). This view as contested in chapter Three.

Developing upon the work of Suárez, the Spanish Jesuit, Grotius was concerned to come to terms with the realities of the world in which he lived; a world in which there stood Catholic and Protestant States. His conclusions were not radically different from those of his predecessors, but his method of treating law scientifically was significant. Law, the Dutchman claimed, must be considered in terms of definitions and logical deduction. The science of the principles of the law of nature must leave aside all that is subject to change, or variation from place to place. The laws of nature, he claims, are fundamental and nearly as evident to those who pay due heed as that which we perceive by means of the senses. In the theories of Grotius the law of nature becomes the assertion of the principle of having respect for one another's rights, that is, having rights implies a certain duty on the part of others to respect them (Vincent 1986: 25). The Law of Nations is restrained by the rights and duties embodied in the natural law. It is a distinctly ethical doctrine which views moral action in terms of obedience to law.

It is John Locke's conception of natural rights that is usually taken more forcefully to underpin the tradition. For Locke the state of nature is a moral condition regulated by natural law. We are all naturally equal, by which he means all heads of families, exercising the right to execute the natural law – punishing those who transgress our rights. We are each our own authorities, and no one has the right to exercise authority over us without our own consent. The right of property plays an important role in Locke's theory because it includes not only a right of property in things, but also a property in the self. Ultimately because we are created by God we are all God's property and have a duty to preserve it, that is, a duty of self-preservation and in so far as we can, to preserve the lives of others. This of course entails the right not to be harmed by others. The inconveniences of the state of nature, even though a social condition, bring people into conflict and puts lives at risk. Establishing governments best fulfils our duty to God of self-preservation. The purpose of government in Locke's theory is the preservation of property which includes the person. Its role is to protect our natural rights. If it fails to do so, it ceases to have executive authority, and no longer has a claim to political obligation. In Locke, then, the theory of natural rights includes the right to resist, the famous appeal to heaven. Locke, in essence, develops the Huguenot theory of resistance to its logical conclusion. He establishes the right to resist a ruler entirely in terms of the language of rights and natural rights, allowing the people as a body, and even individuals, to exercise this right.

Locke summarizes what he takes to be the purpose and function of the natural law, and its relation to human action. He states that: 'Thus the Law of Nature stands as an Eternal Rule to all Men, *Legislators* as well as others. The *Rules* that they make for other Men's Actions, be conformable to the Law of Nature, i.e. to the Will of God, of which that is a Declaration, and the *fundamental Law of Nature* being *the preservation of Mankind*, no Humane Sanction can be good, or valid against it' (Locke 1988: II, 135, §§26–32).

In Locke's view the state of nature is one vast community of mankind subject to one common law (Locke 1988: II, 128, §§3–6), that is, the law of nature which governs it, and to which everyone is obligated. Locke's view of the law of nature was not significantly different from the conventional views of his time. The law of nature was not for him a human artefact. It gave prescriptions for human conduct which are independent of human convention. Irrespective of what individuals may do or think the natural law is valid because its source is outside of humanity. It is therefore separate from human positive law. Although human law *ought* to comply with natural law it may not always do so. Locke closely allies the natural law with reason. The law of nature can be known by the exercise of reason, and to obey it is to act rationally. To disobey it is to be irrational. To obey the law of nature is a duty to God whose revelations in the bible correspond to the conclusions of reason. In addition, the law of nature is a universal law applicable to all men at all times and in all places (Thomas 1995: 15–6).

The law of nature obliges us not to do harm to each other because we are all servants of the Creator whose property we remain and whose duration on this earth is at His, and not each other's pleasure. We are bound to act in ways conducive to self-preservation, and as far as possible contribute to the preservation of the rest of mankind. Every person has the executive authority to punish those who transgress the natural law and put themselves at variance with the peace and preservation of mankind.

The obligation we have to preserve mankind in general, and of self-preservation in particular, would seem difficult to discharge in the state of nature, where our property is not as secure against encroachment as the law of nature dictates. Political Society is meant to remedy the defects that the want of a supreme executive authority precipitates, and comes into existence when the executive power of each in the state of nature is given up to society as a whole and a legislature is empowered to make certain the law of nature and an executive is empowered to enforce it.

Even though the law of nature is equated with reason in Locke it is not self-evidently rational that the end of human existence is self-preservation and the preservation of others. Ultimately Locke's argument rests on theological assumptions. It is our obligation of self-preservation, which appears to be a right against other people, but which is in fact an obligation to God who having made us, owns us, which is the rational basis for being obliged to a government which enhances our prospects of self-preservation.

Consent, in fact, identifies the occasion on which such obligations are incurred and is an acknowledgement of the legitimacy of the political power to which we are subjected, and not as such our ground for obeying it. The distinction here needs to be spelt out. What I am claiming is that *generically* our obligation to obey government ultimately rests upon the obligation we owe to God of self-preservation as the products of His workmanship (Locke 1988: II, p. 270, §6). The obligation we have to obey a *specific* government rests on consent. The ground for obeying government whose purpose is to protect the person and property of its citizen is the obligation we owe to God of self-preservation. The reason why we obey the particular government we obey is because we have consented to it.

How can the obligation of self-preservation be the ground of political obligation when Locke explicitly says in a number of places that the purpose of government is the protection of property? For example, 'The preservation of Property being the end of Government, and that for which Men enter into Society' (Locke 1988: II, 138, §§2–4). But property, for Locke, is broadly conceived and sometimes refers to the 'Lives, Liberties and Estates' of the people (Locke 1988: II, p. 123, §§17). In this respect Locke says that 'Government being for the Preservation of every Man's Right and Property, by preserving him from the Violence or Injury of others, is for the good of the Governed' (Locke 1988: II, p. 92, §§5–8; cf. II, p. 129, §§1–6).

In summary, Locke's whole theory of rights and obligations ultimately rests upon our duty to God of self-preservation, and in so far as others are the property of God, the preservation of those others. This is because we are the products of His workmanship and political obligation derives from this generic obligation to God (Locke, 1988: II, p. 270–1, 56). The obligation we have to obey a *specific* government rests on consent. Locke says: 'If he finds that God has made him and other men in a state wherein they cannot subsist without society, can he but conclude that he is obliged and that God requires him to follow those rules which conduce to the preservation of society?' (Dunn 1984: 31). Jeremy Waldron has recently explored the theological basis of Locke's arguments and concludes that he gives the strongest grounding for natural equality possible by making it an axiom of Christian New Testament theology (Waldron 2002: 6 and Dunn 1969: 99).

THE RIGHTS OF MAN

The idea of natural rights, as we know, reached its high watermark in the American and French Revolutions. As John Vincent contends, there appear to be three characteristic features to mature natural rights doctrine. First, the language of natural rights is individualistic in tone, giving the individual priority over the community or society. Second, the doctrine is excessively rationalist: by the exercise of reason, independent of experience, these rights can be discovered. Third, the characteristic of natural rights theory was its radicalism. The rights of individuals were asserted against any authority which appeared to be subverting them. The declaration of rights of the French National Assembly in 1791 proclaimed: 'People, behold your rights! If a single article of them be violated, insurrection is not your right only, but the most sacred of your duties'.[1] Because of these obvious features there is a tendency to emphasize the features that appear to anticipate what came later in time rather than the quite traditional religious assumptions which give them their moral force.

The religious and theological assumptions found in the philosophers are also manifest in the great charters of natural rights. Take 'The Rights of Man and of Citizens' (1789). The National Assembly made a 'solemn declaration' of rights which it claimed were 'sacred', 'natural, imprescriptible, and inalienable'. The early declarations assume a relation between the rights declared and a Creator. They are in fact declarations of rights and duties. The Virginia Declaration of Rights, 12 June 1776 begins in what appear secular terms: 'That all men are by nature equally free and independent, and have certain inherent rights, of which, when they enter into a state of society, they cannot by any compact deprive or divest their posterity...' It concludes with article XVI which includes the statement 'that it is the duty of all to practice Christian forbearance, love and charity towards each other.' The Declaration of Independence of the United States of America, 4 July 1776 includes the famous assertion: 'We hold these truths to be self-evident, that all men are created equal, that they are endowed by their Creator with certain inalienable Rights, that among these are Life, Liberty, and the Pursuit of Happiness.' One of the great architects of the American Constitution Alexander Hamilton, maintained that: 'The sacred rights of mankind are not to be rummaged for amongst old parchments or musty records. They are written, as with a sunbeam, in the whole volume of human nature by the hands of divinity itself, and can never be erased or obscured' (cited in Joyce 1978: 7). James Hutson maintains that: 'Rights, then, for the founding generation were grounded in religion, if not the religion of the New Testament, as some insisted, at least in Judea-Christian morality' (Hutson 1992: 74). Indeed the notion of creating rights was anathema to most Americans. What they believed themselves to be doing was declaring preexisting rights, that were bestowed on men by 'God' or the 'Creator', and which were derivative from natural law, the most fundamental of which were life, liberty and property. Natural law continued to be considered the bedrock of natural rights at least until 1820, despite the inherent ambiguity of the concept, and was still of considerable, but declining juridical importance up to the Civil War (Hutson 1992: 97).

The French Declaration of 1789, and prefixed to the 1791 Constitution, gives sanctity to its pronouncement by stating that the National Assembly recognizes, which implies that they pre-exist, and declares the rights of man and citizens in the presence of the 'Supreme Being'. Indeed, the intention of prefixing the Declaration of the Rights of Man and of the Citizen to the 1791 Constitution was to bestow upon the former an authority to which the Constitution itself was subordinate.

---

[1] This declaration became the preamble to the Constitution of 1791, but that Constitution was superseded in 1792. It wasn't until 1946 that the Declaration found its place in French Constitutional Law.

Thouret, the *rapporteur*, at the framing of the new constitution explained that the Declaration remained intact because it 'had acquired, in a sense, a sacred and religious character' (cited in Lauterpacht 1945: 28).

These declarations ground human rights both in the idea of a supreme law giver and in human reason, they follow logically and rationally from the notion of being human – they are claimed to be self-evident. Those defenders of the rights of man of which both the American and French Revolutions are declaratory do not rely upon naturalistic, or descriptive principles. For all the principal defenders the moral obligations to which natural rights give rise are ultimately derivable from God. The Rational Dissenters, for example, among whom were Richard Price and Joseph Priestley, who in turn influenced Mary Wollstonecraft, at this time subscribed to two principles: the central significance of scripture and the sufficiency of reason. The main thrust of their protestant dissent was a right to private judgement (Priestley 1993: xxii). While Paine rejected the authority of scripture, or revelation, unless it conformed to reason, he nevertheless espoused a form of natural religion in which the word of God, expressed in the creation, was central. Paine too emphasized the sufficiency of reason, and based moral obligation on the presupposition of God as the first cause.

The radical whigs of Paine's time focused upon the idea of political corruption and the revival of civic virtue. They looked back to the golden age of the Commonwealth men of the revolutions of the seventeenth century. The leading exponents of Commonwealth men ideas in the eighteenth century were the natural rights theorists Richard Price and Joseph Priestley, best known for his discovery of dephlogisticated air, or oxygen. Because Dissenters did not subscribe to the orthodox Trinitarianism they were not protected by the Toleration Act of 1689. They suffered severe penalties because they did not conform to the ritual of the sacrament prescribed by the Anglican Church. They were excluded from holding Crown and municipal offices and could not study at Oxford, and were not allowed to take a degree at Cambridge (Thomas in Price 1991: ix). They were at the forefront in calling for Parliamentary reform, which included redistribution of seats and the extension of the franchise to universal manhood suffrage. The Dissenters argued that in order to be virtuous one must be free. Price, who Thomas Paine described as 'one of the best hearted men that exists' (Paine 1989: 53), for example, wanted to establish the objectivity of moral judgement by equating it with reason. It is the exercise of reason which enables us to apprehend the necessary truths of morality. In this respect he was a rationalist moral philosopher. He argued for the independence of the religious consciousness free from government interference, and identified independence with the free exercise of reason. This is why Price and his associates were known as Rational Dissenters. In *A Discourse on the Love of One's Country*, the sermon which Burke attacks in the *Reflections*, Price asserts the existence of natural and inalienable rights. The universal enjoyment of natural rights would, he believed, lead to an improvement in individual virtue, and the promotion of peace between nations. The *Discourse* ends with the rousing cry:

Tremble all ye oppressors of the world! Take warning all ye supporters of slavish governments and slavish hierarchies! Call no more (absurdly and wickedly) reformation, innovation. You cannot now hold the world in darkness. Struggle no longer against increasing light and liberality. Restore to mankind their rights and consent to the correction of abuses, before they and you are destroyed together (Price 1991: 196).

Priestley believed in the humanity of Jesus which lay at the heart of his conviction that investigation of the natural world was the key to understanding. He was not as radical as Price who believed in natural equality, and thought that all social status arose out of consensual agreements. Priestley argues that the power an individual surrenders when entering society is limited to that which is necessary for securing his safety and happiness. He surrenders his powers only in relation to those things that are better provided collectively (Priestley 1993: 141). The power to elect officials and to have one's opinion become part of the public provision he calls political liberty. In contrast, but dependent upon political liberty for its protection is civil liberty. Civil liberty essentially comprises those natural rights that we retain on entering society. They are the rights which relate to making personal provision for those things that the state is less able to provide.

Mary Wollstonecraft's *A Vindication of the Rights of Women,* to take another example, extends the arguments made by the Rational Dissenters Richard Price and Joseph Priestley. They argue that all men have equal rights, but fail to incorporate women as right holders. Wollstonecraft extends their arguments to encompass women on the grounds that all human beings have rational capacities. Access to education would allow them to develop. Her work also drew on the tradition of devotional literature associated with Richard Allestree and Mary Astell, emphasizing one's duties to God.

Wollstonecraft's analysis of rational equality, the tendency of bodily passions to corrupt rationality, the need to restrain the passions within marriage, and the necessity for knowledge to aid the development of virtue, are all themes that she would have found in the writers of devotional literature (McCrystal 1992: 4). The importance she gave to rights, however, can be traced directly to the writings of the Rational Dissenters. Wollstonecraft, like Price and Priestley, is deeply devoted to fundamental Christian beliefs. In other words, our natural rights come from God, and all human beings should have them because we are all in principle capable of exercising reason, subject to a rational education. Both men and women, she maintains, have strayed from the rational path that God deemed we follow.

Most surprisingly, perhaps, we also find this religious foundation in Thomas Paine. Mark Philp, for example, contends that: 'It is not difficult to see that Paine's deism helps to explain both our natural tendency towards society and how our natural sympathies and affections lead us to recognize our moral duties to others' (Philp 1989: 110). Paine's *Rights of Man* is, like Wollstonecraft's *Vindication of the Rights of Man,* a reply to Edmund Burke's *Reflections,* and is prefixed with a translation of the 'Declaration of the Rights of Man and of Citizens' (1789). Paine certainly had little time for orthodox religion of any persuasion or denomination, but he was a firm believer in God. In 1776, for instance, he contended that: 'I am as confident as I am that God governs the world as I am that America will never be happy till she gets clear of foreign dominion' (Paine 1989: 45). In 1794 the abolition of the national order of priesthood and all compulsory systems of religion and articles of faith in France prompted Paine's own declaration of faith, *Age of Reason*. Although there are many scattered remarks about God and religion throughout Paine's writings, they do not amount to anything like a doctrine or coherent theory. In *Age of Reason*, however, we have his full profession of faith. He maintained that he believed in one God, and that justice, mercy, and contributing to the happiness of our fellow creatures are religious duties (Paine 1989: 207). We know the word of God, he argued, not from the Scriptures, but from the Creation which we behold. He maintains that: 'It is an ever existing original which every man can read. It cannot be forged; it cannot be counterfeited; it cannot be lost; it cannot be altered; it cannot be suppressed...' (Paine 1989: 227).

What does he mean by this? Paine believes that natural rights are both universal and equally accessible to everyone. The foundation upon which this contention rests is two-fold. First, the word of God is imprescriptible, the same always and everywhere, and it is expressed in a language for all to understand. No one may claim privileged access, or a special relationship with its author. That which is required of all to believe must be based on evidence that is universally available to all: 'The creation speaketh a universal language...(Paine 1989: 227).

The second aspect to the foundation is the contention that true belief is based on reason and the laws of probability. For example, Paine contends that the only idea that man can associate with God is that of first cause. Disbelieving this is ten times more difficult than believing it (Paine 1989: 228). By a process of reasoning we deduce from the certainty that we have not made ourselves, and that no other thing could make itself save the first cause which is superior to all other things (Paine 1989: 230, also see Philp 1989: 100).

He rejected the commonly held beliefs of Protestant Christianity such as the virgin birth, the Holy Trinity, and the resurrection of Christ on the grounds that they did not bear rational scrutiny, and that the evidence of the Bible was contradictory (Paine 1989: x). God conveys his word through Creation to the faculty of reason, making his design accessible to all, and their duties to him evident. Revelation is only relevant to religious belief when it conforms with reason. Reason and common sense are the criteria of what in conscience we believe. No higher authority exists than one's own mind to which God's creation speaks. There is no need for the mediation of religious sects of any kind.

Paine's doctrine is then a natural religion. We know God through his creation which speaks to the rational faculty of the mind. Religion is not a matter of faith. It is a branch of science because it is based on reason, and therefore there can be only one true religion: 'there can be but ONE that is true; and that one necessarily must, as it ever will, be in all things consistent with the ever-existing word of God that we behold in his works' (Paine 1989: 249).

MARY WOLLSTONECRAFT'S AND THOMAS PAINE'S DEFENCE OF NATURAL RIGHTS

René Descartes' rationalism was of considerable importance to the refinement of natural rights doctrines, including their extension to feminist arguments, and to the establishment of reason as the criterion of their efficacy. Descartes argued that all knowledge came from experience and self-reflection. True principles could be formulated by the exercise of reason independently of authority or tradition. Knowledge did not require painstaking study of the classics, but instead could be attained by the exercise of right reason reflecting upon first principles. All humans possess reason and all are therefore in principle capable of attaining true knowledge. He was widely acclaimed by women in the eighteenth century as a liberating force. The French salons from the middle of the seventeenth century were the main disseminators of his thought. Descartes' books were mainly read by women and it was they who were responsible for organizing drawing room lectures where the new scientific truths of experimental philosophy could be discussed. Others, in addition to Descartes, such as Bernard le Bovier de Fontenelle, encouraged women to assert themselves as rational creatures. Joseph Addison's (1672–1719) translation of Fontenelle's *Conversations on the Philosophy of World's* included an introductory poem by the translator with an injunction to: 'Assert your claim to sense, and show mankind/That reason is not to themselves confined' (see Caton 1988: 85–6).

The Rational Dissenters, including Wollstonecraft, were able to combine a Cartesian emphasis on rationalism with a belief in the Deity, evidence for which was to be found in God's rational creation of the universe itself. Paine, as we saw, went a step further in advocating a natural religion with God as the First Cause, conveying His wisdom to us through nature. The truth of which was conformity to right reason and common sense.

Both Paine and Wollstonecraft were outraged by Edmund Burke's response to the French Revolution, all the more so because he was a friend of the oppressed in Ireland and defended the American colonists' stance against the British on the grounds that they were being deprived of their rights as Englishmen. Burke rejected abstract or metaphysical rights, and defended socially constituted rights manifest in the civil social person. His argument for such rights which were the traditional inheritance of the nation and the product of prejudice, prescription and presumption precipitated the most vehement personal attacks upon him. Prescription, for example, for Burke, was the greatest of all titles because it had the effect of legitimizing over a long period of time that which had no, or even a dubious, original title. He maintains that: 'prescription...through long usage, mellows into legality governments that were violent in their commencement' (cited in Fennessy 1963: 131).

Wollstonecraft and Paine were expeditious in their replies in a language that is at once shocking, vicious and insulting, exhibiting the same exaggerated rhetorical flourishes and personal attacks to which Burke himself was no stranger.

In her lesser known book *A Vindication of the Rights of Man (1790)* Wollstonecraft sought to assert the claim of individual reason and the rights of man against Burke's prescriptive principle. She sought to undermine his character, his arguments and his characterization of the British constitution, and in doing so she asserted the equality of reason in men and women. The first course of action was to denounce Burke's character by casting doubt upon his motives and sincerity. She contended that Burke's popularity had so considerably waned that he would adopt any position, employ any rhetorical device, and sacrifice any principles to regain his reputation. So insincere was Burke, she claimed, that had he been a Frenchman he would have supported the Revolution with equal passion and enthusiasm (Wollstonecarft 1988: 43).

Wollstonecraft's second line of argument was to re-establish the centrality of individual reason in the development of virtue. She argued that every person has an innate right to such a degree of liberty as is consistent with the exercise of the same degree of liberty as those with whom we are associated in a social contract. Without the liberty to exercise reason moral progress is impossible. Virtue, for Wollstonecraft, has little to do with the instincts and everything to do with reason. Progress in civilization is achieved only through the refinement of reason. It is reason that distinguishes humans from animals and which provides the continuity in our social relations. It is clear that she would not wish to sanction the idea of prescriptive right because it would legitimize those social practices that she deplored. Morality must have as its test something higher than prescription: 'the more man discovers of the nature of his mind and body, the more clearly he is convinced, that to act according to the dictates of reason is to conform to the law of God' (Wollstonecraft 1989: 51).

Burke's arguments, Wollstonecraft contends, could not undermine the grand designs of the National Assembly in France, who in instituting a constitution for the happiness of millions know better than to use as their model the 'imagined virtues of their forefathers' (Wollstonecraft 1989: 41). She does not deny that the past must have an important bearing on our present deliberations, not as an exemplar but as a warning against roads that we should not travel down.

She accused Burke of idealizing the British Constitution and of revering ignorant prejudices which have emerged from the 'rust of antiquity' (Wollstonecraft 1989: 10). The Constitution, she argued, 'was settled in the dark days of ignorance, when the minds of men were shackled by the grossest prejudices and most immoral superstition' (Wollstonecraft 1989: 13). Our ignorant ancestors lacked an adequate understanding of the dignity of man, and if we were to revere their heritage, as Burke says we must, such abominable practices as slavery would last in perpetuity (Wollstonecraft 1989: 14).

Mary Wollstonecraft's second vindication, *Vindication of the Rights of Woman with Strictures on Political and Moral Subjects* (1792) amplifies the themes that she had begun in the first. Essentially the argument of the book is that humans are distinguished from animals by their capacity to reason, and that they are distinguished from each other in their attainment of knowledge and virtue. The differences in male and female character she largely attributes to nurture rather than nature. A variety of impediments that particularly affect women, but which are not without their effects on soldiers and the rich, conspire to undermine the development of reason and allow the senses and passions to rule. Unbridled passions have a propensity to lead to corruption and vice, producing a degeneration in morals and family life. Her remedy was to admit women into full citizenship of society, enjoying full political and property rights, and the right to work. She attributes to the laws of property and primogeniture the impediments to the development of both male and female virtue.

Fundamentally, women must enjoy the right to be educated. Knowledge is a prerequisite to the cultivation of virtue. Without virtue, women cannot become the worthy companions of men. They design to excite men emotionally, but not intellectually. They have the affection of men but not their friendship. Friendship is the solid foundation upon which a sound marriage can be built, and this can be achieved only by severe regulation and suppression of our animal passions. If men and women allow their passions to run riot, children are neglected, and when the heat of passion runs cold, husband and wife seek emotional gratification in adulterous relationships. It is man's lack of chastity and the encouragement of a false feminine character that caused the degradation of women in society (Wollstonecraft 1988: 150).

Anna Wilson has criticized Wollstonecraft for denying to women a special language of knowing and moving about in the world. Wollstonecraft characterizes feminine language as subversive to the soul, and the rejection of sensibility is in fact the rejection of female otherness. In other words, Wollstonecraft is accused of denying the special value of women's emotions in order to claim the right to the male conception of sense and reason. In essence, Wilson wants to contend that there are different ways of men and women knowing (Wilson 1989). If Wollstonecraft were to accept such a view, however, her case against Rousseau and James Fordyce would be considerably weakened. They both argued that women have different natures from men, and that their educations should be designed to cultivate those natures. Had Wollstonecraft admitted of such a difference then she would have given ammunition to those who wanted to perpetuate female subordination.

It seems to me that Wollstonecraft was far from exalting male reason and prescribing that women emulate it. She was equally as scathing about male and female modes of understanding in her contemporary society. The organization of society was such that liberty of reason was constrained at every turn by excessive attention to frivolities and the seeking of pleasure. The mind, whose quality is reason, was for Wollstonecraft sexless. The attainment of virtue through reason required a thorough re-examination and reformation of both male and female understandings and the relation in which they stood to each other.

In order to establish her case she needed to show that the idea of a sexual character was not a product of nature but the design of artifice. She tried to show that women were conditioned by upbringing to fulfil gender roles. Women do not, Wollstonecraft argued against Rousseau, have a natural inclination for dolls, dressing prettily and idly chatting. Having been compelled to keep the company of nursemaids whose conversation leaves a lot to be desired, and hours in the company of their mothers who constantly attend to their own appearances in order to attract flattery, young girls are bound to imitate that which they see. It is part of a perverse social system in which women come to see their daughters as rivals for the attention of men, rather than as friends (Wollstonecraft 1988: 49). In other words, Wollstonecraft is saying that human nature can be blown off its true course by the intervention of societal conditioning. Even men of genius, she argues, fail to rise entirely above their social circumstances, as their theories testify all too often (Wollstonecraft 1988: 42). How can one expect women, forced to see the world through a false medium, rise above the example they are given and all the legal and social impediments which stultify their understandings? The contention that the innocence of girls and women needs to be preserved is simply a euphemism for ignorance which justifies starving women of the truth. Women are forced 'to assume an artificial character before their faculties have acquired any strength' (Wollstonecraft 1988: 44).

In order further to establish that women's character is the product of nurture she needed to show that similar circumstances would produce similar results in certain sectors of the male population. She argues that among the upper classes that it is rare to find men of superior or even of common rational abilities. They are born into an unnatural condition in which the want of necessity retards the development of their faculties (Wollstonecraft 1988: 45). 'May it not be fairly inferred', Wollstonecraft contends, 'that their local situation swallowed up the man, and produced a character similar to that of women, who are *localised*, if I may be allowed the word, by their rank they are placed in, by courtesy?' (Wollstonecraft 1988: 58).

Perhaps a more striking comparison and one with considerable rhetorical force was the identification of the character of soldiers, by which she meant the officer classes, with the female character. Soldiers, she argued, are seldom strong in their passion or intellect. Depth of understanding is as rare in the army as among women, and she attributes this to a common cause. Army officers are taught to please. Their manners are acquired before their morals, and their view of life formed from experience without the benefit of reflection. Soldiers accept common assumptions and prejudices, taking their opinions from others and submitting unquestioningly to authority. Like women, they delight in the art of ridicule, dancing, adventures, and rooms full of people. Their whole lives, like those of women, are obsessed with gallantry. Furthermore, soldiers and women exhibit the trivial virtues with scrupulous politeness (Wollstonecraft 1988: 24). In consequence, Wollstonecraft asks: 'Where is the sexual difference, when the education has been the same? All the difference that I can discern, arises from the superior advantage of liberty, which enables the former to see more of life' (Wollstonecraft 1988: 32).

Having established that sexual character is a human artifice she can go on to maintain that there can be only one standard of what is right and virtuous, and even if women possess virtue to a lesser degree it must be of the same kind and quality, and not different from the virtue of men. As a result there can be only one path to knowledge and virtue, and both sexes must take it (Wollstonecraft 1988: 19, 26, and 36).

Paine's personal contribution to the furtherance of the rights of man has resonated down the centuries from the first appearance of his infamous book in 1791. *The Rights of Man* is not philosophically rigorous, indeed Foot and Kramnick describe his style as 'uncomplicated, unscholarly, and unsophisticated' (in Paine 1987: 14), yet he eclipsed all of those who fought for the same cause, including Price, Priestley, Godwin, and Wollstonecraft whose theories were much more systematic. He appealed not only to intellectual radicals such as the novelist and playwright Thomas Holcroft (1745–1809) and the poet William Blake (1757–1827), but also to hundreds and thousands of journeymen and artisans who read it and were inspired by its simple message, namely that the burden of tradition had no prescriptive hold on present or future generations, and that unjustifiable hereditary impositions and privileges should be replaced with a set of arrangements at the heart of which should be the principles of talent and merit. His ideas so inflamed those who hated democracy, republicanism and the very ideas of equality, fraternity and liberty that Paine fled to France in fear of his life following charges of seditious libel. Paine was found guilty of seditious libel in absentia at the end of December 1792 and prohibited from entering Britain ever again.

Paine, like Wollstonecraft, launched a personal attack on Edmund Burke impugning his character and motives. Paine accused Burke of flagrantly misrepresenting the events and principles of the French Revolution. Burke's *Reflections* is, Paine maintained, 'an outrageous abuse on the French Revolution and the principles of Liberty, it is an imposition on the rest of the world' (Paine 1989: 51). It is an unprovoked exemplar of the incivilities by which nations and individuals taunt and irritate each other (Paine 1989: 53). Paine ridicules Burke for denying that people have natural rights to choose those who govern them, and to hold them to account for misconduct, as well as to frame their own government. With an element of delight, Paine points out how ridiculous Burke's claim is that the people of England disclaim any such rights, and will defend with their lives and fortunes any attempt to assert them. Paine adds sarcastically: 'That men will take up arms, and spend their lives and fortunes *not* to maintain their rights, but to maintain that they have *not* rights, is an entire new species of discovery, and suited to the paradoxical genius of Mr. Burke' (Paine 1989: 54). Furthermore, Burke's attempt to instruct the French Revolutionaries is contemptuously dismissed as 'darkness attempting to illuminate light' (Paine 1987: 58). In contrast with Burke's 'dry, barren, and obscure' attribution of the source of rights, Paine approvingly quotes M. de la Fayette: 'Call to mind the sentiments which nature has engraved in the heart of every citizen, and which take a new force when they are solemnly recognized by all: – for a nation to love liberty, it is sufficient that she knows it; and to be free it is sufficient that she wills it' (Paine 1989: 59).

Paine argued that the rights of man had been usurped in a former age, and that the contemporary generation should cast off the oppression of the relics of feudalism. The rights of man were not to be found by rummaging about in history because we are quite as likely to find that those original rights have been usurped or perverted. To discover what these rights are, he argued in *The Rights of Man*, we must go back to their origin. Disputes over what these rights are must be referred back to the source of their authority, namely, 'the divine origin of the rights of man at the creation' (Paine 1989: 76).

Natural rights, then, are possessed by individuals outside of society and were endowed upon man at the creation in perpetuity. Men do not enter society to become worse off than they were before, nor to have fewer rights as a consequence, but instead to secure those rights better. Society is for Paine distinct from government, a position he maintained consistently from the time he wrote *Common Sense* (Paine 1989: 3). The principles of society pertain even in the absence of government, which even at its best is a necessary evil. The reciprocity of interests, and mutual inter-dependence that each individual feels with others, and upon all parts of civilized communities, establishes a 'great chain of connection' (Paine 1989: 155) which binds and pulls people together 'into society as naturally as gravitation acts to the centre' (Paine 1989: 155). Society, in Paine's view, does almost everything that may be ascribed to governments. Indeed, governments often impair or subvert the operations of the natural law by which society is regulated. Governments may act in their own right promoting, instead of preventing, privilege and favour. Individuals, Paine contends, inhabit a civilization based on universal principles, and it is governments who prevent them from operating effectively. Governments stand in relation to each other in a perpetual condition of war, just as we imagine savage uncivilized life to be. Governments put themselves beyond the laws of nature and of God, 'and are, with respect to reciprocal conduct, like so many individuals in a state of nature' (Paine 1989: 195). The fundamental questions we have to address are whether, given the perversity of governments, men will inherit their natural rights, and enjoy universal civilization, receiving the full fruits of their labours.

Paine makes a distinction between natural rights which we have by the mere fact of being human, and civil rights that we hold in society and which are themselves derived from natural rights. Civil rights are those, such as to security and protection, which the individual may not in all cases be competent to discharge. The rights that the individual retains on entering society are those which he has the power to exercise. This is for him a perfect right, and this class of rights include intellectual rights and rights of the mind, including freedom of worship. Those natural rights that are given up to the common stock, even though he possesses them perfectly as far as the rights of the mind are concerned, are those that he does not have the power to execute, such as juridical powers that are better administered by society. Paine asserts that: 'Society *grants* him nothing. Every man is a proprietor in society, and draws on the capital as a matter of right' (Paine 1989: 79). He contends that from these premises three certain conclusions can be deduced:

1st That every civil right grows out of a natural right; or, in other words, is a natural right exchanged.

2nd That the civil power, properly considered as such, is made up of the aggregate of that class of the natural rights of man which becomes defective in the individual in the point of power, and answers not his purpose, but when collected to focus, becomes competent to the purpose of everyone.

3nd That the power produced by the aggregate of natural rights, imperfect in power in the individual, cannot be applied to invade the natural rights which are retained in the individual, and in which the power to execute is as perfect as the right itself (Paine 1989: 79).

Any declaration of rights, such as that of the National Assembly of France is also a declaration of duties. Whatever right as a man I may have, the same right is that of every other. In addition to possessing such rights it is also my duty to guarantee them (Paine 1989: 117). Our civil rights, derived as they are from natural rights, are indivisible, non-transferable, and incapable of being destroyed. Whatever one generation may foolishly do to impair or undermine rights, it cannot bind future generations. (Paine 1989: 125).

Paine's radicalism is of the liberal persuasion, and his emphasis upon equality of merit was to remove obstacles to opportunities, and not to promote equality of outcomes. He was a proponent of small government and believed that the more the government retreated from the social and commercial realms, the better able people would be to exercise their natural rights. The enemy of individual freedom was not industry and free enterprise, but instead governments who by their regulation of corporations undermine the freedom of those citizens who comprise them. He was not strictly speaking a rationalist, in Michael Oakeshott's terms (Oakeshott 1991: 6–42). Paine, like the rationalist, believed that by the exercise of reason, and with the aid of common sense, you can arrive at first principles on the basis of which the perfectibility of man was possible. Unlike the rationalist he had no great faith in the powers of government to assist this process. Governments put hindrances, such as taxation, on the road to perfectibility. However, it must be emphasized that rationalism is a manner of government, and the issue of how little or how much is not relevant to its style.

CONCLUSION

We have seen that much of the discussion of human rights can be resolved into the question of what is their source. This is sometimes avoided or left deliberately ambiguous, as in Nozick and Gauthier. The constraints upon natural rights are self-imposed, with the exception in Nozick's case, for example, of the negative rights of non-interference. Positive rights and obligations are subject to agreement.

The natural powers, or rights, in Hobbes's state of nature and Gauthier's original position are not moral constraints. Moral constraints are introduced in order to mitigate the effects of natural rights. In Hobbes the contractees establish the Leviathan which decides what is right and wrong. For Gauthier the contractees formulate the constraints themselves (hence morals by agreement). The analogy may be drawn between T. H. Huxley's cosmic evolution, nature red in tooth and claw, and ethical evolution that constrains or militates against the effects of cosmic evolution. Nozick's position is slightly different. The pre-social natural rights are negative rights and require others to desist from placing impediments in the way of your choices. Hobbes and Gauthier are more or less assuming a distinction between natural and conventional. They do not, *pace* Thrasymachus, Glaucon, Antiphon, and Callicles see convention opposed to nature because morality in Hobbes and Gauthier constrains natural rights for the purpose of mutual benefit. We are motivated to act morally because it is in our interests.

The prescriptive version of natural rights, I have suggested, still retained a considerable element of believing that rights were derivative from natural law. There was, nevertheless, a greater emphasis upon permissive subjective rights and protecting the individual from the arbitrary power of the state. The worldview of the Rational Dissenters, among them, Mary Wollstonecraft, continued be religiously inspired. Such an inspiration was reflected in the great declarations of rights of the eighteenth century. Even Paine's natural religion could hardly claim to have secularized the tradition.

6

Natural Rights and Their Critics

> Indeed in the gross and complicated mass of human passions and concerns, the primitive rights of men undergo such a variety of refractions and reflections, that it becomes absurd to talk of them as if they continued in the simplicity of their original direction (Burke 1999*a*: vol. 2, 153).

INTRODUCTION

The doctrine of natural rights was criticized from many different political and philosophical perspectives. The prescriptive versions were dismissed by David Hume who maintained that it was impossible to derive statements of value from statements of fact, that is, the famous is/ought question (Hume 1992: book, III, pt. III, §I, p. 469). How from a statement of fact can normatively loaded principles be derived? It was just as legitimate to characterize nature red in tooth and claw as it was to think of it as a harmonious whole conducive to order. Hume maintained that nature had no more regard for good in preference to evil than for heat in preference to cold (Waldron 1987: 15). Furthermore he criticized the idea of a social contract as the foundation of society, maintaining that it was an historical absurdity, a pernicious fiction. Most famously the prescriptive and descriptive versions were criticized by Rousseau, Edmund Burke, Hegel, Jeremy Bentham, and Karl Marx, and the British Idealists. They all argue, for example, that it was quite ridiculous to postulate rights which exist prior to society.

It is not that any of the thinkers deny the importance of rights (unless in Marx's case they happen to be bourgeois rights), it is the mode of analysis, including the idea that there is a pre-social state of nature, and that political obligation rests upon consent to confer authority in a social contract, that is being contested. All of these critics have in common a critique, although they are different critiques, of the relation between the individual and society that natural rights theories posit. In this chapter, I will explore the ideas of the eighteenth century critics of natural rights.

THE NATURAL RIGHTS FALLACY

The relationship of Hume (1711–76), Rousseau (1712–78), and Burke (1729–97) to the natural law and natural rights traditions is complex and ambivalent. None endorsed the foundations laid by the objectivism of natural law which saw rights as derivative from it, nor did they endorse either the descriptive, nor prescriptive, versions of natural rights which relied very heavily upon the role of reason in their discovery and formulation. They all came to the conclusion, in their different ways, that even though the sources of morality may be in the passions and sentiments, there were fundamental rules of morality or justice that are of human invention and integral to sustaining and promoting social relations, the formulation of and adherence to which relied very heavily upon convention and custom.

Hume, Rousseau, and Burke were contemporaries. Hume died in the year of the American Declaration of Independence and Rousseau two years later, Burke lived on to witness the French Revolution and became one of the most infamous critics of it and the doctrine of natural rights that lay at the core of its belief system. They were familiar with each others' works. Rousseau and Hume were well acquainted. When they met in Paris in 1765, Rousseau had gained for himself a certain notoriety, and Hume had already been feted by the *philosophes*, among whom he counted the *Encyclopédistes* Diderot and d'Alembert his friends (Ayer 1992: 197). In fear of arrest Rousseau was persuaded to stay with Hume in London during 1766. Hume was at first sympathetic to Rousseau, but was nevertheless aware of a dark side to his character, which manifest itself in 'Frequent and long Fits of Spleen' (Letter Rev. Hugh Blair, 25 March, 1766, Rousseau 1988: 197), during which times Rousseau avoided company. Their relationship was increasingly uneasy and Rousseau accused Hume of conspiring with Voltaire and others to dishonour him. Hume's crime seems to have been that he secured a pension for Rousseau which the Frenchman took pleasure in declining because he objected to charity and did not want to be indebted to someone he perceived as his enemy (O'Hagan 2003: 6–7). By July of 1766 Hume had lost patience with Rousseau and was deeply hurt by his irrational behaviour. In a letter to Richard Davenport, sixth July, he went as far as to say: 'I repent heartily, that I ever had any Connexions with so pernicious and dangerous a Man' (Rousseau, 1988: 198).

Rousseau and Hume to some extent endorse a naturalistic, or descriptive, conception of natural rights, while Burke sometimes appeals to natural law in his more rhetorical moments, but all reject the rationalism that accompanied these doctrines. There are natural sentiments which form the basis of some elements of morality which may be said to correspond with Pufendorf's congenital obligations, and an artificial morality essential for social co-operation, which corresponds to his adventitious obligations. Nevertheless, but to a lesser extent in Burke, they jettison the predominantly religious element of rights talk prevalent during the eighteenth century in which rights are derivative from the natural law of God, who is conceived to be the foundation of obligation.

Hume, Rousseau, and Burke are critics of conventional understandings of the role of reason in the apprehension of natural law and natural rights. Hume and Rousseau both maintain that morality, in some of its fundamentals, derives from natural instincts or passions, which act upon reason. Hume's moral theory was partly intended to steer a course between those who subscribed to a system of morals based on reason, and those who based it on sentiment (Castiglione 1994: 97). Rousseau is happy to employ the typical device of natural rights theorists, that is, the idea of a social contract, on the understanding that it is merely a convenient fiction, and the purpose for which he uses it is not to show how pre-existing natural rights are protected by government, but how instead inequalities that are a perversion of nature are consolidated in society by the more powerful who formulate in their own interests the terms of the contract and force them upon everyone else.

Hume

Hume famously exposes as a fiction the idea of a social contract as the foundation of political obligation, but does not deny that there may have been something like a contract among people in primitive society. Whereas there may have been agreements of sorts in the dim and distant past, with the intervention of time and the modification of circumstance they cannot now form the basis of obedience to government. It is almost invariable that present governments were founded on conquest and violence and were obeyed out of necessity. People did not imagine that their consent gave the prince authority, but they give their consent because longevity of possession has conferred the title, independent of choice or preference (Hume 1994: 186–201; cf. Hume 1992: book III, pt. II, §x, p. 556). Hume asserts that: 'Present possession has considerable authority in these cases' (Hume 1994: 200). The important point is that political obligation stands apart from the obligation of fidelity to promises and contracts, because it is the government which uphold contracts and ensures that promises are performed (Forbes 1975: 66). Political obligation, then, rests on habit and convention (Hume 1992: book II, pt. II, §iii, pp. 508–9, and §viii, p. 546). It does not matter much how a government came into being. What is important is that it has the capacity to fulfil its main functions, namely, to uphold peace and tranquillity (Castiglione 1994: 104).

Hume is fundamentally an empiricist in philosophy. His aim was to place morality on a firm foundation of experience and observation, that is, a science of man (Forbes 1975: 59). In doing so he tried to assimilate natural and moral philosophy (Ayer 1992: 202). He objected to the tendency within the natural law tradition empirically to identify certain facts about human nature, such as self-preservation, sociality, and the sexual instinct, and then to suggest that they are natural laws that constitute a rational system of laws, duties, and imperatives which are the commands of God. For him, the religious hypothesis had no place in the experimental method of natural philosophy (Forbes 1975: 60–61). In A. J. Ayer's view, one of Hume's principal aims was to discredit all forms of religious belief (Ayer 1992: 206). Unhindered by religious scruples Hume was able to take empiricism to its logical conclusion, scepticism (Werner 1972: 440).

He makes a distinction between impressions and ideas. The former are what he calls 'stronger perceptions', which are sensations, impressions, and sentiments, and the latter he suggests are 'fainter perceptions', which are reproductions of the stronger perceptions in memory and imagination (Advertisement to book III). Hume maintains that '...every idea, with which the imagination is furnish'd, first makes its appearance in a correspondent impression' (Hume 1992: book I, §III, p. 33). The senses receive impressions, and the ideas associated with these impressions are connected on the principle of causation. There is no underlying reality beneath the impressions. Impressions are, for Hume, innate in that they are not copied from any previous perception and they arise immediately from nature. He seems chiefly to have in mind the passions, such as resentment of injuries, self-love, and sexual excitement because they are inherent in human nature (Ayer 1992: 208). Reality is for us a constantly changing aggregate of feelings contiguously related and bound by the psychological or social force of custom (Werner 1972: 440).

The question he poses is whether the distinction we make between vice and virtue, and the pronouncement whether an action deserves praise or blame can be attributed to the stronger or fainter perceptions (Hume 1992: book III, pt. I, §I, p. 456). Hume wants to determine the efficacy of the contentions of natural law and natural rights thinkers that there are immutable standards of right and wrong that impose obligations, and maintain that morality, like truth, may be apprehended by reason. Is it possible, Hume asks, to distinguish between good and evil by reason alone? He maintains that the passions can never be the slave of reason, but on the contrary, reason is the slave of the passions. It is a common fallacy, he maintains, that we subdue our passions by reason. Morality influences action, but the rules of morality are not the conclusions of reason. Reason alone, he argues, can never 'be a motive to any action of the will' (Hume 1992: book II, pt. III, §III, p. 413).

Understanding is achieved by two different means, either by abstractly relating ideas, or by relating objects about which experience provides information. The first form of reasoning can never be the cause of an action because it operates in the realm of ideas, whereas the will firmly places us in the realm of realities in which the demonstration of abstract relations and volition are quite separate from each other. The second form of reasoning attempts to establish causes and effects. It needs to be noted that Hume used the term cause in a much wider sense than in current currency. For him it meant any law-like connection between matters of fact (Ayer 1992: 236). Objects produce in us the emotion of aversion or attraction, and the emotion leads us to cast about to the wider context in order to discern the causal relations of the original object to others. The impulse itself to make connections between objects is not initiated by reason. Hume argues that: 'Where objects themselves do not affect us, their connexion can never give them any influence; and 'tis plain, that as reason is nothing but the discovery of this connexion, it cannot be by its means that the objects are able to affect us' (Hume 1992: book II, pt. III, §III, p. 414). Reason, then, serves and obeys the passions. Passions cannot in themselves be contrary to reason, and can only be unreasonable if they are accompanied by some judgement. For example, if judgements of hope or fear, or grief and joy are based on the presumption of the existence of objects that really do not exist, they may be said to be unreasonable. Alternatively, when passionately performing an action reason may be deceived in its assessment of causes and effects and choose insufficient means to bring about the desired end. In order for a passion to be considered unreasonable it must be accompanied by a false judgement, and strictly speaking it is the judgement and not the passion that is unreasonable. Hume famously concludes that: "'Tis not contrary to reason to prefer the destruction of the whole world to the scratching of my finger' (Hume 1992: book II, pt. III, §III, p. 416).

Hume argues that morality does not consist in any relations that are the objects of science, no, in any matter of fact discoverable by the understanding. In relation to the first, he asks why if incest is criminal among human beings it is not also criminal among animals. It is not good enough to maintain that animals lack reason capable of discovering morality because this is merely a circular argument, because the immorality would have to have a prior existence in order for reason to discover it, and therefore, irrespective of reason the same act would be immoral in animals as it is in humans, and they must be subject to the same virtues and vices to which we attribute praise and blame (Hume 1992: book III, pt. I, §I, p. 467–8). Likewise, morality does not consist '*in any matter of fact*, which can be discovered by the understanding' (Hume 1992: book III, pt. I, §I, p. 468). It is impossible, he argues, when you examine any matter of fact, to see anything that we call vice. When considering the object all you will find are passions, motives, volitions, and thoughts, until you turn to self-reflection. It is then that you find a strong moral disapproval that emanates from you towards the action. It is a matter of fact that lies in the self rather than in the object, and is a matter of feeling rather than reason. In judging an action or character to be vicious, it means nothing other than in contemplating it, given the nature of your constitution, you feel that it is blameworthy.

He argues that moral duties are capable of being divided into two kinds. The first are those that arise from natural instincts which act on men independently of reason such as beneficence, clemency, and moderation. They include love of children, gratitude to those from whom we benefit, and pity of the unfortunate, all of which are 'entirely natural, and have no dependence on the artifice and contrivance of men' (Hume 1992: book III, pt. III, §I, p. 578). These are what are called the social virtues because when we reflect on such humane instincts and the benefits they confer on society we justly attribute moral approval. The person motivated by such instincts feels them prior to any such reflection. The second category of moral duties is not excited by natural instincts. They are performed as a result of consideration of what duties are required to sustain civil society, they are social practices (Haakonssen 1996: 106). 'It is thus', Hume contends, '*justice* or a regard to the property of others, *fidelity* or the observance of promises, become obligatory, and acquire an authority over mankind' (Hume 1994: 196).[1] Although justice is artificial it is not arbitrary. Hume is well aware of the ambiguity of the

---

[1] David Gauthier contends that Hume's later work sustains his theory of property and justice, that is a system of rules defining property and its exclusive use, and the adherence to those rules, as resting

term nature, and uses it in this context simply in contrast to artifice. Using the term in another sense, no principle of the human mind could be more natural than that of virtue, and no virtue more natural than that of justice (Hume 1992: book III, pt. II, §I, p. 484). It is the invention of men in society, the spontaneous product of social life, which may even be described as a requirement of it. Justice arises because of human selfishness and limited generosity in conditions of scarcity. If men were benevolent there would be no need for such rules to arise. Justice is not discovered by the exercise of right reason. Its principles are not 'eternal, immutable, and universally obligatory' (Hume 1992: book III, pt. II, §ii, p. 496).

It is concern for our own and for the public interest that make us establish the rules of justice. It is impressions and sentiments, without which everything in nature is a matter of indifference to us, that give rise to our concern for justice. It is therefore not natural to the minds of men but is the product of convention and artifice. Without the rules of justice, security of property, its transference by agreement, and the keeping of promises, human society as we know it would be impossible (Hume 1992: book III, pt. II, §viii, pp. 541–2). The rules of justice, in this respect, may be termed 'natural laws' because 'they are as old and as universal as society and the human species, but prior to government and positive law' (Forbes 1975: 70). The important point, as Annette Baier has emphasized, is that concepts such as justice, promise, and contracts are cultural achievements dependent upon cultural invention and human artifice (Baier 1988: 762).

Hume, although a conservative in temperament, was, like Burke, sympathetic to the American cause. From as early as 1768, Hume advocated unconditional independence (Livingstone 1989: 1). They both, however, rejected the conception of natural rights upon which American Independence was premised. Hume avoided rights talk as far as he could, except to place them within a framework of the rule of law, because he had fundamental problems with both of the principal traditions. He rejected those who maintained that rights are the result of qualities inherent in the person as primary features of the moral personality, and which gave rise to claims on the world and on each other. The emphasis upon will, consent and contract as the basis of obligation, as we have seen, does not fit well with his empiricism, which bases obligation on prescription, custom, and habit. The purpose of natural rights is to sever human thought from custom and prejudice by formulating first principles independent of experience. Hume also rejected the view that far from being inherent in the moral personality of the individual, rights are derived from natural law which attributes rights and duties to individuals. This form of argument rested very firmly on religious presuppositions for its justification (Haakonssen 1996: 117–20).

The principles of justice which Hume refers to as natural laws are also applicable to nations in their relations. In keeping with the prevalent views of his age Hume

on contractarian grounds, without contradicting the anti-contractarian arguments of the theory of moral sentiments proposed in *A Treatise of Human Nature* (Gauthier, 1998: 17–44).

believed that the body politic was equivalent to a single person, and in its relations with other bodies politic had need of rules to assist and promote commerce, and they are the same rules that individuals need to subsist within a society. There must be stability in possessions, or there would be constant conflict and friction providing occasions for war. There also must be recognized methods of transfering property by consent, otherwise no commerce is possible. In addition, princes must be held to promises just as individuals are. Fidelity to the obligation of promises is a prerequisite of entering into leagues and alliances. Bodies politic, however, are to a lesser degree than individuals dependent upon the reciprocal assistance of others, and may, without serious moral censure, renege on agreements for causes that would not justify an individual doing the same. Hume wants to emphasize that it is the same morality that governs individuals and nations, but that its force is diminished in relations among princes whom we indulge to a much greater extent when they deceive each other than if a private individual breaks his word of honour (Hume 1992: book III, pt. II, §xi, pp. 567–9).

Rousseau

Rousseau, although critical of the idea of a state of nature if it is claimed ever to have had an historical identity, nevertheless finds it useful as a heuristic device (also see Boucher 2003*a*: 235–52). His characterization of the state of nature has certain distinctive features. He is distinguished from Locke and Pufendorf in believing that the state of nature is neither a moral nor a social condition. He agrees with Locke, Pufendorf, and Hobbes that nature confers no authority on us to rule over others. Following Hobbes, rather than Locke and Pufendorf, Rousseau maintains that in their natural condition men are strangers to the ideas of justice and injustice. Individuals in a state of nature are solitary and self-sufficient. Rousseau's point of departure from both the descriptive and prescriptive versions of the state of nature is in positing that it is not a rational condition. In the state of nature humans are only nascently and rudimentarily rational. Humans in a state of nature have not fully developed reason. Instead of reason people have certain sentiments or instincts; those of self-preservation and pity.

Self-preservation, of course, is generally accepted among natural law and natural rights theorists as a fundamental feature of human nature. Humans pursue their own interests, and have a capacity for self-preservation. In Grotius we saw how each must respect the rights of others, and in both Locke and Pufendorf there is the additional positive obligation of promoting the good of others if we can do so without harming ourselves. Like Hobbes, Rousseau does not characterize his individuals with such positive obligations, yet the sentiment of pity, as we shall see, for Rousseau's noble savages would incline them towards assisting those in distress. In contrast with Hobbes, there is no natural right to everything merely because we have certain needs. Rousseau does claim, however, for different reasons, that man in the state of nature has 'an unlimited right to everything that tempts him and that he can acquire' (Rousseau 1987: 151). Rousseau complains, as Hegel was later to do, that Hobbes and other exponents of a state of nature, is guilty of projecting human characteristics that are developed only in society onto the state of nature. Hobbes's natural man pursuing self-interest and self-preservation is a positive danger to the survival of others. Whereas Hobbes was right to reject the conceptions of natural rights of his predecessors, the conclusion he reached from his own conception indicates that it is no less erroneous (Rousseau 1987: 53).

Rousseau argues that what motivates self-preservation is not egoism, but instead self-respect. In the state of nature egoism and adversarial feelings do not feature. Without denying Hobbes's genius Rousseau believes him to be somewhat perverse in characterizing the human predicament in which the survival and welfare of each depends on the destruction of others. In his desire to establish absolute rule and absolute obedience to authority Hobbes was forced to portray man in a perpetual war with his fellow men (Rousseau 1991: 45).

Rousseau pejoratively credits Hobbes with the view that in the absence of goodness in the state of nature man is naturally evil, and that having no obligation nothing motivates people to help each other. The condition for Hobbes is, of course, amoral, and if self-interest is served, such as securing protection, individuals may band together in a state of nature to provide mutual assistance against, for example, marauding gangs. This aside, in maintaining that by nature man is good Rousseau rejected the fundamental Christian notion of original sin. In *Emile* Rousseau contended that: 'There is no original perversity in the human heart. There is not a single vice to be found in it of which it cannot be said how and whence it entered' (cited in O'Hagan 2003: 61–2). If sin is not original, human abasement needs to be explained in terms of human actions. The point of this is to attribute to humanity responsibility for its own corruption, and to indicate that by their own efforts redemption is possible. In this, then, Rousseau sides with the Pelagians against Augustine.

Rousseau further reproaches Hobbes for ignoring the importance of the human sentiment of pity prior to the development of reason. For Rousseau it is the 'only natural virtue' (Rousseau 1987: 53). Pity is a natural virtue or capacity, prior to all reflection, which tempers the brutality of self-preservation. Our natural adversity to the suffering of others is the source of all human virtues. Rousseau maintained that: 'Pity is what takes us without reflection to the aid of those we see suffering. Pity is what, in the state of nature, takes the place of laws, mores, and virtue, with the advantage that no one is tempted to disobey its sweet voice' (Rousseau 1987: 55). The implication is that knowledge of a transcendental natural law is impossible in the state of nature, because we do not have the facility to apprehend it. It is the natural sentiments and not reason that make us averse to certain kinds of action.

Rousseau's pre-social humans are compassionate but not naturally social. Despite the fact that they have not yet developed reason, they understand the principles of self-preservation and pity (Chapman 1956: 3–4). Rousseau's state of nature is populated by individuals who have little need or inclination to associate, other than to procreate. Peace and tranquillity are the desires of the savage man.

Men are relatively equal in the state of nature, and each is innocent and good. Those inequalities that are evident among men are due to their natural limitations (Rousseau 1991: 37).

Humans are distinguished from animals in the state of nature in not being completely governed by impulse. Although not being rationally developed, humans have the potential to be free and are conscious of alternatives and to a certain degree free to choose between them. Animals, on the other hand, are dominated by the impulses of nature. Nevertheless, the potential in man for self-determination is merely latent in the state of nature and manifests itself in immediate self-survival. The necessity to adapt to changing conditions provides the impetus for natural man to enter into social relations. The pressures of an increased population, climate change, and a scarcity of resources alter the delicate balance between man and nature. As the satisfaction of desires becomes more difficult during times of comparative scarcity, humans are impelled to ponder their predicament and deliberate with others, even occasionally to co-operate to achieve mutual benefits.

The process from an isolated noble savage to social cooperation is irreversible because more sophisticated wants emerge once desires are stimulated by intelligence, and cannot be achieved in isolation. A nature capable of development has inherent in it the potential for human improvement or perfectibility. Rousseau indicates that this development is self-directional unless our choices divert or pervert its course. As humans acquire reason, they begin to discern an idea of what this potential perfectibility intimates, and what obligations and values are implied by it. Individuals may choose to follow this course, or deviate from it. The facility we possess for self-improvement when acted upon by circumstances precipitates the development of the rest of our faculties. Fully developed human potential entails finding the greatest contentment in values and courses of action deemed right by conscience and reason.

As we saw Rousseau does not attribute evil to original sin, nor is it the consequence of anything inherent in human nature. Rousseau's noble savage is not an ideal to which humanity can or ought to return. The noble savage is merely a stage in the development of human consciousness, and at that stage humans are isolated, relatively content, innocent, and sympathetic to each others' suffering. The individual in the state of nature is characterized by *amour de soi*, or self-love, and it is not until entering into society that he or she exhibits *amour propre*, vanity or selfish love. It is selfish love, argues Ernst Cassirer, the famous interpreter of Rousseau, that 'contains the cause of all future depravity and fosters man's vanity and thirst for power'. In suggesting that *amour propre*, or vanity is absent from the state of nature in its non-social condition Rousseau denies the dominant paradigm of attributing to the selfish passions the motivation for our propensity to set up society (Cassirer 1989: 58).

Whereas in the state of nature there are natural inequalities, the invention of property is the source of inequalities of power and reputation which give rise to most of the depravities manifest in the human race. The only conceivable source of a claim on property is the mixing of one's labour with the land, which in turn suggests an entitlement to the produce. The wheat I cultivate in the field is mine. Cultivation of the field over successive years must have given rise to the claim that it is one's own. However, the powerful among the inhabitants of the state of nature realized their strength and described their own needs as 'a sort of right' to the property of others, which gave rise to a vicious conflict between 'the right of the strongest and the right of the first occupant'. Thus Rousseau argued: 'Emerging society gave way to the most horrible state of war... [and] brought itself to the brink of ruin' (Rousseau 1987: 68). Man's self-interestedness (*amour propre*), or pride, is the wrong foundation for society and can lead only to disputes. Egoistic individualism led to the breakdown of emerging society into a Hobbesian war of all against all. To resolve the conflict by basing the social contract on similar principles, as Hobbes does, is extreme folly.

Those accustomed to society are not content with living within themselves and live only for the attention and recognition of others. It is in the judgement of others that they are aware of their own existence. The disputes which arose as a consequence of property led those advantaged by them to propose the establishment of society in order to protect themselves and their property. In the state of nature there are, of course, natural inequalities of age, strength, ability, and health. People are unsuspectingly duped into consenting to those very institutions, based on egoistic individualism or self-love, that compound artificial inequalities that are social in origin: honour, prestige, power, and privilege. The establishment of society immediately destroyed natural liberty and legitimized the acts of usurpation by which property had been acquired and inequality instituted, condemning the whole of the human race to 'labour, servitude and misery' (Rousseau 1987: 70). What Rousseau wanted to emphasize was that the passions that incline us to violence, aggression, and war are not pre-societal, but actually acquired in society itself. In this context men and women, motivated by pride, acquire their characteristics and values from their associates, and are unable to acknowledge their propensity for virtue and morality. Reason and conscience is unable to influence the formation of their characters because they have fallen victim to reciprocal egoism.

It is important to emphasize that Rousseau's *Social Contract* is an attempt to overcome the immorality and degradation consequent upon establishing a society based on a multiplicity of particular wills. A society based on the principle of the general will, at the heart of which is the idea of the common good, would eradicate the ills of modern society. He is committed to civil equality and the full responsibility of all citizens to participate in the legislative process.

The state of war is for Hobbes a consequence of human nature. Without a Leviathan to keep states in awe they will always adopt the posture of war in relation to each other. States sustain a way of life and make life more commodious for their citizens, so that the posture of war against other states is never as unmitigated as it is in the state of nature. For Rousseau, war is the result of a corruption of human nature. It is a condition that prevails among states and not among individuals, and its consequences are far more destructive. Instead of alleviating violence, states accentuate it. Rousseau maintains that the weak consider themselves bound to the strong by informal agreements, alliances, and treaties. The strong, on the other hand, feel no similar obligation to the weak. There is no claim here that the strong have a right in nature to dominate the weak.

Rousseau uses the vocabulary of the natural law school, but not in the way that he found it in the writings of Grotius, Pufendorf, and Burlamaqui. He does not deny that God is the source of all justice. Indeed, he suggests that independently of conventions that which conforms with order is good. Rousseau qualifies his position, however, by suggesting that we are unable to receive justice from such an abstract source. It is therefore necessary for us to establish governments (Rousseau 1987: 160). Natural law in the state of nature is related to natural sentiments which make us turn away from acts of cruelty. It is not a law of nature discoverable by, nor consistent with, reason. Natural man has not yet developed rational capacities that would enable him to know this law. This must await the institution of civil society.

Rousseau argued that modern exponents of natural law restrict its scope to moral relations among rational men, whose reason enables them to apprehend it. They are all agreed, despite variety in definition, that it is impossible to come to know the precepts of natural law and to obey them without being a 'great reasoner and profound metaphysician' (Rousseau 1987: 34). The state of nature is a condition in which individuals acknowledge no duties or other moral relations (Moore 1991: 74). They possess rights in the sense that Hobbes used the term, that is, as capacities or powers, but they possess no such developed faculty of reasoning that Hobbes attributes to his natural men. Paradoxically, in order to establish society men must already require what only a select few acquire within it: a highly developed rational faculty. In order to make just laws, men should already be what they will become as a result of the laws (Rousseau 1987: 164). Natural right for Rousseau means the ability of individuals to use their capacities in conformity with their instincts of self-love and pity, or compassion.

Rousseau denied one of the most typical claims of natural law theorists and contended that it is fallacious to assume a general society of mankind united under a universal moral law. The common feeling necessary to constitute humanity as one is not evident, nor is there any sense that in acting as an individual an end relative and general to the whole is being pursued. Ideas of God and natural law could not, in Rousseau's view, be innate in men's hearts. If they were, it would not be necessary to teach them. Far from the moral community of humanity being manifest in society—the universal giving rise to the particular—it is actually constituted societies that engender ideas of an imagined universal society on humankind. In order to conceive ourselves as men, we must first become citizens. The facts confirm what reason teaches. The laudable ideas of natural right and the brotherhood of man emerge relatively late in human development, and they do not become widely accepted until the advent of Christianity, and even then such beliefs are unsettled and intermittently held. Even under the laws of Justinian the humanity of the Romans extended only as far as the boundaries of the empire (Rousseau 1991: 104–9). Rousseau denied, then, that men in a state of nature have natural rights that they carry over into political society, and hold against the state. The only sense in which he has a conception of natural rights is in maintaining a general right or perhaps potential would be a better word, to self-realization.

Whatever other qualities men in the state of nature may have possessed when looked at retrospectively, they were nevertheless still brutes and savages. They were not self-conscious of being free and knew nothing of human relationships. Within the state of nature principles of natural law would simply be inapplicable because its inhabitants have no recognizable moral relations with, nor obligations to, each other. They simply lack the capacity of following its precepts. The inequalities found among men in society are not sanctioned by the moral natural law in a state of nature; they are in Rousseau's view most certainly the consequence of human law.

Exponents of natural law begin by identifying rules that it would be appropriate for men to agree upon as socially useful and give to them the name of natural law on no other grounds than the supposed good that would result from their universal observance. Such explanations of the nature of things are based on more or less arbitrary notions of what seems right. Rousseau's main contention against natural law jurists was that they assume what they seek to prove. They consistently fail to strip away those characteristics of man acquired in society. They take what men have socially acquired and project it back into a state of nature. In other words, natural law jurists fail to go back far enough or deep enough into the origins of man.

We saw that the only legitimate title for property is the mixing of one's labour, and in this respect Rousseau agrees with Locke in viewing cultivation as the paradigm of labour. It is, in the absence of legal title 'the only sign of property' that ought to be respected by others. Locke had subscribed to the idea of *terra nullius* and denied that American Indians had any greater claim to the land they roamed over than Europeans who enjoyed the same use rights as them. Rousseau, however, was vehemently opposed to colonialism and in the Geneva manuscript of the *Social Contract* he addresses the question of the legitimacy of appropriating vast tracts of land. Surely, he contends, if the whole of the world is given to men in common, it must be a punishable offence to deprive the rest of the world of territory, dwellings and food. If we accept that man has to labour to satisfy his needs, then we can accept a right of first occupation, but not without limitation. Having sufficient force to chase away the inhabitants and prevent them from returning, to what extent does possession establish a property right? Force cannot create right. It is not enough to set foot on a common piece of ground to claim exclusive ownership. In a footnote, Rousseau alludes to a French propaganda tract, *L'Observateur Hollandois*, in which the author Jacob N. Moreau contends that we may 'consider as vacant lands all those that are only inhabited by savages' (editor's note in Rousseau 1994: vol. IV, 238, fn 20). Rousseau dismisses with incredulity the claim that by a matter of right individuals may occupy the 'vacant' lands inhabited by Indians 'without doing them any wrong according to natural right' (Rousseau 1991: 115, fn 2). Elsewhere, in defending his view that the advancement of the arts and sciences has contributed to a decline in morals, his tone is sarcastic. He asks rhetorically, can it really be a sign of valour to conquer America, with canons, maritime maps, and compasses. All it indicates, he argues, is that an adroit and subtle person may obtain by effort that which a brave man may expect only by valour. He contends bitterly: 'Whom shall we judge to be more courageous: odious Cortez subjugating Mexico by means of gunpowder, perfidy, and betrayals, or unfortunate Guatimozin stretched out on burning coals by decent Europeans for his treasures, scolding one of his Officers from whom the same treatment evoked some moans, and saying to him proudly: and I, am I on roses?' (Rousseau 1994: vol. II, 125). In addition to cultivating the land the right of first occupant must conform to two further rules: that the land may not already be occupied, and that no one is entitled to occupy more than is needed for subsistence (Rousseau 1987: 152). In sum, Rousseau's objection to colonial possession rests on three grounds. In the first place, it employs the illegitimate use of force to disperse those who already live on the land—might cannot create right. Second, it assumes a spurious title to first occupancy, and third, it violates the sufficiency criterion in that more is being unjustifiably withdrawn from common usage than is needed.

Although the right of first occupancy is stronger than that based on force, which is no right at all, it does not strictly speaking become a right until the institution of property and property rights are established in civil society, at which time the right consists in not so much respecting what belongs to others, but respecting what does not belong to you (Rousseau 1987: 151–2). Rousseau, then, differs from Locke, in maintaining that there is no natural right to property. The whole tenor of Rousseau's political philosophy is collectivist rather than individualist. On entering civil society each is required to give up the rights of nature, and the property each has acquired, and has it returned by the community, or sovereign body, to each more equitably and legally protected. Each comes to identify his or her personal interest with that of the whole. There is certainly a significant change brought about in the individual as a consequence. Prior to constituting themselves into a sovereign body in which the general will is the expression of the real will of the whole, agreements may have been entered into and kept out for purely self-interested motives. It is not therefore a moral relationship, but instead a prudential one, similar to that of the slave in exchanging his freedom for servitude, which the individual deviates from if his or her interests are not being promoted.

The transformation is quite remarkable, from natural liberty limited only by force, to civil liberty limited by the general will, and from possession which is the result of force or the right of first occupant, to proprietary ownership regulated by law. It is the exchange of one type of freedom for another, from natural to moral liberty. Natural liberty, driven by appetite, is a form of slavery, whereas 'obedience to the law one has prescribed for oneself is liberty' (Rousseau 1987: 151; cf. Jennings, 1994: 117–8). Rousseau throughout his life abhorred slavery of any kind. It also entails a substitution of rational justice for natural goodness. In the civil condition individuals acquire rights in the ordinary sense of the word, that is, as claims on others which are the counterpart of obligations (Moore 1991: 78–9).

Martin Hollis has suggested that the transformation that individuals undergo as a result of subjecting themselves to the general will is that from acting in accordance with instrumental rationality, to expressive rationality (Hollis 1996: 128 and 263–81). This is the sort of rationality that Hegel was to develop in his *Elements of the Philosophy of Right*, and which is represented by Hegel in the transition from 'civil society' to the 'State'. The individual comes to identify with a greater whole and sees the laws not as other, and externally imposed, but instead as the reflection and expression of one's real will which constitutes his or her identity.

Burke

It is well known that Burke was one of the most severe critics of natural rights, exemplified by their manifestation in the thinking of the French Revolutionaries and their supporters. What he criticized was the abstract metaphysical method of arriving at knowledge of their content. We have already seen that the tendency among thinkers in the natural law and natural rights traditions was to have great faith in the power of individual reason to discover the abstract principles that comprised a transcendental and transhistorical code of conduct. We have seen also that this code, may be revealed, by comparative anthropology. The *a posteriori* identification of that which is common among nations, is for some thinkers evidence of natural law itself, or of derivations from it, and also, in its descriptive version, by attributing moral conclusions to natural 'facts'. The natural law tradition with the idea of derivative rights remained the paradigm of moral philosophy during the eighteenth century (Haakonssen 1996: 312).

Whereas for modern international relations theorists the Peace of Westphalia (1648) is emblematic of the emergence of the modern states system, it was the Peace of Utrecht (comprising the Treaties of Utrecht 1713, Rastatt and Baden 1714) that was of more significance for eighteenth century thinkers and political actors. It was the treaty that brought to an end the Spanish War of Succession, and brought about the partition of the Spanish Empire. The guarantee of the successions in Britain and France represented an important crystallization of the idea of collective security (Shennan 1995). Pufendorf, in coming to terms with the implications of the difficult conceptual issues surrounding the idea of sovereignty after 1648, gave impetus to a greater acknowledgment of the person of the state having rights and duties, equivalent to those of the individual under natural law (Boucher 1998: 223–54). Vattel consolidates the tendency to place the nation or the person of the state as the central subject of the Law of Nations. His *Law of Nations, or Principles of the Law of Nature applied to the Conduct and Affairs of Nations and Sovereigns (1758)* very quickly became one of the most authoritative sources of international law, and was translated into English and published in two volumes in 1759–60. In the book, Vattel predominantly focuses upon the state's duties to God and to itself, and to other states. He argues for a right of intervention especially to fulfil one's duty to assist (Vattel 1834: book II, chapt. I, §5).

Burke's relation to the natural law tradition is ambivalent, and there is no doubt that he occasionally appeals to its universal authority, especially, for example, in making his case against Warren Hastings, who as Governor of the East India Company had exercised arbitrary rule and systematically violated the universal laws to which all humanity is subject (Boucher 1991: 128–48). Those who wish to claim him as a natural law thinker seize upon Burke's use of Vattel in arguing for intervention in the internal affairs of another state, contending that in doing so he invokes the authority of natural law without being committed to the modern doctrine of natural rights. Stanlis places Burke firmly in the natural law tradition, and contends that in relation to the derivation of the Law of Nations from natural law he 'is certainly in the tradition of Suarez and Grotius' (Stanlis 1953: 400, 2003: 88, also see Welsh 1995: 39–43). David Armitage suggests that those elements of *raison d'etat* detectable in Burke are not inconsistent with the Stoic and natural law tradition. Armitage contends that Burke 'was in fact a classic early modern theorist of reason of state within the natural-law tradition revived by Grotius and revised by Vattel' (Armitage 2000: 633).

It is well to note at this point that right reason was not the only way in which the natural law could to discovered. We saw, for example, that Grotius contended that there are two ways of coming to know natural law. The first by means of the exercise of right reason *a priori* and the second by the *a posteriori* method, that is, that which is believed by all civilized nations to be the case must be assumed to be derived from the same source, namely God. Burke's occasional appeals to natural law are clearly of this second order, and the fact that he rejected abstract reasoning cannot therefore be taken as unequivocal evidence that he rejected a universal moral order. Welsh, for example, maintains that Burke's method of coming to know the principles of natural law and the Law of Nations is through 'human custom and precedent' (Welsh 1995: 41, cf. 44)

What differentiates Burke in this respect from Grotius is that Burke does not contend that the confirmation of natural law, as may be observed in customary practice, is its deduction from indubitable principles through logically certain reasoning. Burke argued that on all possible grounds Hastings' resort to arbitrary rule could not be justified. What, however, were the grounds of Burke's objections? Hastings' claim to have been delegated, or to have inherited arbitrary power could not rest upon prescription. The British constitution was, for Burke, prescriptive. By this Burke meant, 'it is a constitution whose sole authority is, that it has existed time out of mind' (Burke 1907: vol. iii, 354). Arbitrary power was never any part of this constitution, and therefore could not have been delegated to Hastings. '*He* have arbitrary power! My lords, the East-India Company have not arbitrary power to give him; the king has no arbitrary power to give him; your lordships have not; nor the Commons; nor the whole legislature' (Burke 1987: vol. I, 99). Furthermore, it was never any part of the Mohamedan constitution, sanctioned by law and the Koran, nor the Institutes of Genghis Khan or Tamerlane (Burke 1987: vol. I, 104–14 and vol. II, 4). In other words, Hastings could derive no prescriptive right from the constitutions of Asia to rule by arbitrary will.

What is interesting is that Burke is not satisfied to rest his case on prescription. It is unlikely that Burke thought that he could win a legal victory against Hastings, but he was determined to take the moral prize. In enunciating the principle of trusteeship for the governance of India, Burke frequently appeals to God's universal and immutable laws of morality as a standard against which Hastings should be judged. Is there a case, then, for suggesting that Burke rightly belongs to the tradition of natural law when he articulates a criterion of state conduct? It is certainly the case that Burke wished to refute Hastings' appeal to moral relativism in justification of his conduct. In defiance of the principle of 'geographical morality' Burke contends that:

the laws of morality are the same everywhere; and that there is no action, which would pass for an act of extortion, of peculation, of bribery, and of oppression in England, that is not an act of extortion, of peculation, of bribery, and of oppression in Europe, Asia, Africa, and all the world over (Burke 1987: vol. I, 94).

He maintains that God is the source of all authority, and those in whom it is invested are subject to 'the eternal laws of Him that gave it, with which no human authority can dispense' (Burke 1987: vol. I, 99). The eternal laws of justice, humanity, and equity are primeval, and the human positive laws which share their character are declaratory of them (Burke 1987: vol. I, 14, 99, 101, 231, and 504: II, 410 and 439). These laws of justice are our birthright placed in our breasts as guides to conduct. They are immutable, independent of human design, pre-exist society and are destined to survive its destruction (Burke 1987: I, 14, 99: II, 410). It is appeals such as these which have enabled commentators to enlist Burke in the service of a common humanity against the totalitarian excesses of Hitler and Stalin (Kirk 1987; O'Brien 1969; Pocock 1987; and Stanlis 2003).

Burke's resort to natural law is, however, somewhat perplexing. In fact, his attitude to religion in general, although there is no cause to doubt a genuine belief, is in one crucial respect very like that of Thucydides, Machiavelli, and Hobbes. Burke tended when talking about religion to praise it in terms of its social and political utility, rather than its truth or theological virtues. Religion stands at the foundation of society and is a source of energy in the people (Burke 1907: vol. ii, 187; vol. vi, 404 and vol. iv, 98). It is, he tells us, 'our boast and comfort, and one great source of civilization amongst us, and among other nations' (Burke 1907: vol. iv, 99–100). Religion is a source of happiness and consolation. It is an opiate in that it pacifies the victims of injustice with the promise of salvation. The importance of religion to the stability of society required freedom of conscience and thus religious toleration (Freeman 1980: 142). We have received our natures from God who for the virtuous perfection of His people has willed the existence of the state (Burke 1907: vol. iv, 107). The state and religion are therefore inseparable. Toleration is a matter of political expedience, whereas atheism must be suppressed with the full weight of the law because it strikes at the very foundation of the state

(Burke 1907: vol. iv, 99). This is not to say that Burke was unaware of the dangers of religious fanaticism, both dissenting and established, to the political stability of the state.

In essence, Burke's view of Christianity is instrumental; it serves a politically and socially useful purpose, and this he was at pains to demonstrate, irrespective of what he thought of its theological truth. Similarly Burke uses natural law for political ends. He frequently invokes it for rhetorical impact in sustaining principles which in different circumstances he supports with reference to prescription. He is quite prepared to let the authority of the British Constitution rest on prescription when advocating extreme caution in parliamentary reform, but the same ground could with difficulty be extended to India and the conduct of Warren Hastings. In this instance prescription is reinforced with the rhetorical weight of natural law (for a fuller discussion of these issues see Boucher 2003*b*: 363–82).

There is no doubt that for Burke, God is the prime mover in human affairs who has set us out on a journey, but its destination is of our own choosing. Man is, then, 'in a great degree a creature of his own making' (Burke 1907: vol. iv, 101). God, in Burke's writings, is shrouded in mystery. He is the 'Governor of the Universe', 'the mysterious Governor', and 'Great Disposer' to whom Burke often refers, in the way that Machiavelli invoked *Fortuna*, to explain that which is inexplicable (Burke 1987: vol. I, 94; 1907: vol. iv, 87 and 182). It may well be the case that God's interventions and dispensations mysteriously rescue a nation from ruin, but it would be reckless to put one's trust 'in an unknown order of dispensations, in defiance of the rules of prudence' (Burke 1907: vol. vi, 182).

Iain Hampsher-Monk has argued that whereas Burke did rely upon Vattel, and hence upon the authority of natural law, in the early years of the French Revolution, it soon became evident to him that the jurist's principles did not in fact fit the circumstances that prevailed in France and could not therefore be invoked to support intervention in the circumstances after the regicide. It was then that Burke accentuated a tendency already evident in his work and relied upon concepts in Roman law to maintain that Europe constituted one commonwealth with a common heritage, and that its members had a right under the principle of vicinage to prevent the erection of a monstrosity, that is, the French State, that constituted a danger to others (Hampsher-Monk 2005: 65–100). In order to make this move Burke 'completely abandoned Vattel's presupposition of states as individuals in a state of nature, and postulated a European juridical community within which intervention was a domestic, not an international act' (Hampsher-Monk 2005: 66).

What I want to suggest is that it would have been very unusual for Burke, a trained lawyer and upholder of the principle of the rule of law, not to have invoked the authority of one of the most respected jurists in advocating the intervention of one state in the affairs of another (see Fenwick 1913: 395–410, 1914: 375–92). In other words, he sought a legal foundation and initially found the best that he could in Vattel. It is misleading, however, to suggest that although nascent in his earlier thought, he came to rely upon the authority of the principles of Roman law in advocating replacing the government of the French state. Whatever the original source of the principles to which he appealed, the authority by which European states could act was not because of their status in Roman law, but because they had acquired the same authority upon which he based his case for political obligation within the state, prescription, presumption, and prejudice. The commonwealth of Europe shared a customary common law, common heritage, and common manners, lending authority to those actions undertaken in conformity with them.

The confidence of Enlightenment thinkers in the ability of right reason to discover the true principles upon which to base our laws and institutions without regard for historical precedent, or established practices, was an extension of the rationalism of the natural law theorists. David Cameron suggests that the essence of the Enlightenment's conception of natural law is 'its belief in the individual's rational capacity to discern the rights of nature' (Cameron 1973: 58–9). Burke, however, summarily dismissed such reliance upon individual reason, and unceremoniously rejected the applicability of abstract principles like the so-called rights of man to concrete political situations. Burke contends that: 'The individual is foolish, the multitude, for the moment, is foolish when they act without deliberation; but the species is wise, and when time is given to it, as a species, it almost always acts right' (Burke 1907: vol. iii, 355).

Burke relentlessly maintains that it is potentially dangerous, and always foolish to deduce from abstract principles practical policies for the conduct of affairs. Metaphysicians and abstract speculative philosophers, with whom he is little impressed, derive their theories from experience, it is therefore fallacious to think that experience conforms to the principles deduced, and to criticize governments for not corresponding to them (Burke 1907: vol. ii, 357). No rational person, he contends, could presume to direct his or her affairs by 'abstractions and universals' (Burke 1907: vol. iii, 316). Their 'abstract perfection' is in fact 'their practical defect' (Burke 1907: vol. iv, 65). Politics is an eminently practical activity requiring an enormous amount of experience, more than one man can acquire in a lifetime, it is therefore extremely reckless to dismantle an established constitution or replace it on the basis of the metaphysical rights of man. These 'pretended rights', Burke tells us, 'are all extremes: and in proportion as they are metaphysically true, they are morally and politically false' (Burke 1907: vol. iv, 66–7).

Burke was aware that the multiplicity of discrete actions required a manifold of principle, otherwise there 'would be only a confused jumble of particular facts and details, without the means of drawing out any sort of theoretical or practical conclusions' (Burke 1907: vol. iv, 317). On the other hand it is madness to be guided solely by principles. Abstractly speaking liberty is good, but abstract liberty is nowhere to be found (Burke 1902: vol. ii, 185). Burke does not deny the efficacy of rights, but such rights are acquired in civil society. Civil society, he contends, is the product of convention, and that convention is its laws. Burke argues that:

> ... how can any man claim, under the conventions of civil society, rights which do not so much as suppose its existence? Rights which are absolutely repugnant to it?... Men cannot enjoy the rights of an uncivil and of a civil state together. That he may obtain justice he

gives up his right of determining what it is in points the most essential to him. That he may secure some liberty, he makes a surrender in trust of the whole of it (Waldron 1987: 105).

'The circumstances,' Burke tells us, 'are what render every civil and political scheme beneficial or noxious to mankind' (Burke 1907: vol. iv, 7–8). These circumstances give rise to infinite variations, and nothing can be settled among them by the application of 'any abstract rule' (Burke 1907: vol. iv, 65). He argues that: 'A statesman, never losing sight of principles, is to be guided by circumstances' (Burke 1907: vol. iii, 317). The rights of man are not to be found in a pre-societal state of nature, or the abstract speculations of metaphysicians, but 'in a sort of *middle*, incapable of definition but not impossible to be discerned' (Burke 1907: vol. iv, 67).The implication is that principles and rules which guide conduct are immanent in the historical process itself, in which our individual and national characters are formed.

Only in its most basic features is there a universal human nature, in a descriptive rather than prescriptive sense. Burke does have a conception of a universal human nature, particularly in relation to experience of the sublime and the beautiful, but his political insights are almost exclusively directed at the accommodation of our second natures (White 1994: 35). Because of his emphasis upon history and circumstance Burke saw human nature, that is, our socially produced second natures, as at once historically and geographically variable.

The 'civil social man' (Burke 1907: vol. iv, 64), in Burke's view, is at once the product of our own making and of circumstance. Human beings are interdependent within the context of specific societies, and their actions invariably have a bearing upon the lives of others. The social relationships into which we enter have implicated in them certain degrees of responsibility for one's conduct. The conventions and constraints which modify our behaviour arise out of our social relations. Burke argues that 'the *situations* in which men relatively stand produce the rules and principles of that responsibility, and afford directions to prudence in exacting it' (Burke 1907: vol. vi, 158). This is why Burke prefers to talk, not of the rights of man, but the rights of Englishmen who enjoy them as an inheritance from their forefathers to which they are entitled 'without any reference whatever to any other more general or prior right' (Burke 1907: vol. iv, 35). In respect of the most suitable government there is no ideal form of government to which all states should conform, 'the circumstances and habits of every country, which it is always perilous and productive of the greatest calamities to force are to decide upon the form of its government' (Burke 1907: vol. vi, 155).

It is our common sympathies that give rise to the moral constraints under which we live, and afford us the rights of civil society:

Men are not tied to one another by papers and seals. They are led to associate by resemblances, by conformities, by sympathies. It is with nations as with individuals. Nothing is so strong a tie of amity between nation and nation as correspondence in laws, customs, manners, and habits of life. They have more than the force of treaties in themselves. They are obligations written in the heart. They approximate men to men, without their knowledge, and sometimes against their intentions. The secret, unseen, but irrefragable bond of habitual intercourse holds them together, even when their perverse and litigious nature sets them to equivocate, scuffle, and fight about the terms of their written obligations (Burke 1907: vol. vi, 155–6).

The title to authority is neither power, nor divine sanction, nor indeed consent arising from the social contract, but prescription. The reason why we obey the authority is presumption, and not to protect our primordial natural rights. We prefer the certainty of a time honoured and settled form of government, or set of arrangements, to the uncertainty of untried projects. The constitution of a country or the relations in which nations stand to each other are not the result of the choice of one day, or one generation of people, but are 'made by the peculiar circumstances, occasions, tempers, dispositions, and moral, civil, and social habitudes of the people, which disclose themselves only in a long space of time' (Burke 1907: vol. iii, 355). Prescription, and not abstract philosophizing, establishes our rights, the authority of government, and our political obligations.

CONCLUSION

At a time, then, when the doctrine of natural rights was at its height and the political manifestations most evident, criticisms were at their most shrill. In their relentless questioning of the postulates upon which natural law and natural rights built their edifice, Rousseau, Hume, and Burke brought it tumbling down. Rousseau's and Burke's relationship to natural law is ambivalent, but irrespective of their apparently unorthodox attachments to natural law, both constitute significant subversive and corrosive critics of its traditional formulations. We will return to criticisms of natural rights in Chapter Eight, but first I want to turn to the practical implication of the ideas of both adherents and critics of natural law and natural rights in relation to their views on race and slavery.

7

Slavery and Racism in Natural Law and Natural Rights

> But since humanity bids us never to forget that a slave is in any case a man, we should by no means treat him like other property, which we may use, abuse and destroy at our pleasure. And when one decides to transfer to another a slave of this kind, one should take even greater pains that the slave deserves to ensure that he is not sent somewhere where he will be treated inhumanely (Pufendorf 1991: 131).

2007 marked the bicentenary of the abolition of the slave trade in Great Britain. There were both moral and economic factors that played their part on the pro and anti-slavery side. It was not uncommon for men of the cloth to denounce slavery. The erstwhile ships' surgeon, turned pastor, James Ramsey, on the basis of his experience in St. Kitts, could argue more authoritatively than most philosophers, 'That there is any essential difference between European and African mental powers, as far as my experience has gone, I positively deny' (cited in Schama 2005: 204). Chattel slavery was widespread, and the demand for slaves outstripped the supply. The capture, acquisition, and transport of slaves added a huge premium to their cost. They were considered an investment and their liberation was not something easily contemplated by their owners. The abolition of the slave trade in the nineteenth century is an exemplar of humanitarian considerations triumphing over interest. It demonstrates that moral issues may rise to the top of the international agenda, and that the international community of states is capable of setting standards and acting upon them. Unlike the human rights regime of the twentieth century (with the exception of economic sanctions against South Africa), it was not associated with conventions and voluntary agreements, but in great part the outcome of coercion by Great Britain (Krasner 1999: 105–6). Through a series of treaty initiatives, coercion and the seizure of slave cargo from Portuguese and Brazilian ships, 'Britain's commitment to ending international commerce in human beings triumphed over non-intervention' (Krasner 1999: 108). The slave trade was abolished by the Brussels Convention of 1892, and slavery itself was formally proscribed by the Slave Convention of 1926 (Brown et al. 2002: 119).

NATURAL LAW, NATURAL RIGHTS, AND SLAVERY

The moral philosophy of the School of Salamanca, which included Vitoria and his followers down to the Jesuits Luis de Molina (1535–1600) and Suárez (1548–1617), was based on an Aristotelian and Thomist interpretation of natural law. The idea of property, or *dominium*, is at the heart of their moral theory. The transition from the uncertain condition of the state of nature to an understanding of morality and the security of civil society entailed renouncing certain rights that made the human condition precarious while retaining those for which protection was sought. These were their natural and inalienable rights. Principal among them was *dominium*. For the scholastics this meant not only in relation to private property, as it later became restricted by Grotius and Pufendorf, but over goods, actions, and to some extent over their bodies. *Dominium* was the manifold holding together the tripartite division of the natural world by the Roman Jurist Gaius into persons, things, and actions (Pagden 1987: 80–81). *Dominium* amounted to more than possession, it entailed more than a mere right to make use of something, but also to be able to do with it as one wishes, including giving it away, or alienating it.

As we saw in Chapter One, Aristotle's conception of natural slavery was not widely held among the Church Fathers, and the general view seemed to be that like government slavery was the consequence of sin, and because of the natural equality of souls, slave holders had certain duties of care towards their slaves, and they in turn had obligations not to attempt escape. Aristotle's view did resurface from time to time, as, for example, in the ninth century with Hrabanus Maurus (*c*. 780–856), who recognized the legal condition of slavery as a consequence of having one's life spared, but also as the natural and justifiable right of the superior in reason to rule over those of less intelligence. To believe in natural equality did not necessarily exclude inequalities of capacity and intelligence (Carlyle 1970: vol. 1, 204).

Slavery was an extremely important issue in disputes over the rights of the American Indians. The issue was whether the American Indians could be legitimately enslaved, and if so upon what grounds. In other words, how could slavery be justified in the Americas? The Spaniards were, of course, used to owning Negro slaves, but they appeared less at ease with the idea of Indian slavery. It is not surprising given Aristotle's epistemic authority that 'the philosopher' should be invoked for his arguments establishing the concept of natural slaves.

The issue was fundamental: whether a certain part of humanity was born by nature for servitude to another who live the life of virtue, released from considerations of manual labour (Hanke 1959: 13). Aristotle had indicated that certain groups of people, perhaps whole races, did not fully partake of reason in that they had the capacity to understand but not to deliberate. They lacked what Aristotle called practical reason, which would have enabled them to issue commands in addition to understanding them. Understanding requires only judgement (Aristotle, *Politics*, 1254^b 20–2, and *Nichomachean Ethics* $1143^a 8$–9). This was not, however, the view of St. Paul. Although he was clearly not condemning the institution of slavery, he thought it a mere external condition of no significance in the eyes of God, before Whom all men have the capacity for the religious life, possess reason, and are capable of virtue (Carlyle 1970: vol. 2, 85–6). There were a number of positions that could be taken on this issue. First, to reject Aristotle's distinction outright and to argue that he simply wrongly identified a legal condition with a psychological disposition, as some of Vitoria's followers accused him. Second, one could accept Aristotle's distinction and claim that, for example, the American Indians met the criteria proposed, as Sepúlveda did. Thirdly, without explicitly denying the authority of Aristotle, one could apply his criteria and contend, as Las Casas did, that the American Indians possessed the requisite attributes for describing them as free men, indeed, free subjects of the Spanish Crown. The Spanish had no claim to *dominium rerum* in the Indies, and if they were to have any claim at all it must be on the grounds that the Indians themselves had chosen to be vassals of Charles V, and thus he exercised, as Vitoria had suggested, *dominium iurisdictionis* (Pagden 1987: 95).

In conditions of a just war property relations become transformed, and even slavery, irrespective of whether one believed in natural slavery, was justifiable. Even Vitoria acknowledged that enslavement was permissible in a just war, but not on the grounds that some humans were born natural slaves. He condoned the Portuguese slave trade in Africans on the grounds that if they were humanely treated it was preferable for them to be slaves among Christians, receiving the word, than to be free men in their own lands (Pagden 1982: 32–3).

The different attitudes towards enslaving blacks, or even whites, from the Balkans, and American Indians were not based on race or colour. The enslavement of blacks and whites who were sold in the markets of Seville was not the responsibility of the Spanish Crown. The Crown did not claim suzerainty over the territories from which they came, and did not need to pronounce on the justness of the wars in which the captives became slaves. In America, however, Spain did claim political responsibility, and needed to assure itself that its treatment of the natives was legitimate.

Sepúlveda's defence of the treatment of American Indians by Spanish officials and conquistadors was based upon the justness of the wars as a necessary pre-requisite to their Christianization. Even without the Aristotelian argument, Sepúlveda could justify the enslavement of the American Indians and the confiscation of their property. Indians who gave just cause for war, for example, because of the gravity of their sin and idolatry, or because of their resistance to the faith, could with impunity be killed, or spared by enslavement and the confiscation of their property (Hanke 1959: 68).

While Ayala repudiates Aristotle's idea that there are natural slaves because all men are born free and equal, he nevertheless defends the institution of slavery as a human institution necessary for constraining the wickedness of man (Ayala 1912: Book II, chapt. v, [17], p. 42). Captives in war are 'no longer persons but things subject to ownership' (Ayala 1912: Book II, chapt. v, [15], p. 40). Slaves were, of course, the living property of their masters. Alberico Gentili (1552–1608) says that the same laws apply to slaves as to other things, 'because slaves are things' (Gentili 1921: 54 [§ 50]). In slavery, Gentili contends, 'one is deprived of one's nature and becomes a chattel instead of a person', reducing the person to 'the condition of a beast' (Gentili 1933: III, ix, p. 328 [535]). Among Christians by the sixteenth century the practice of enslaving fellow Christians had by custom become abjured, preferring instead to detain captives until the price of ransom had been paid (Zouche 1911: part I, §8, i).

Different considerations came into operation in relations between Christians and non Christians. In the thirteenth century Pope Innocent IV maintained that all rational creatures, whether Christian or Pagan, had the right under natural law to self-government and property ownership (Green and Dickason 1993: x). What was at issue in the Americas was a question of rationality. As early as 1510 the Scottish philosopher and Dominican John Major applied the Aristotelian argument to the Americans, giving grounds to the belief of some that the American Indians did not have *dominium* prior to the arrival of the Spanish. In being capable of understanding, but not of practical wisdom (*phronesis*), they lacked the capacity for having a subject right to *dominium* (Pagden 1987: 85). This gave rise to the rebuttal of Matías de Paz, *Concerning the Rule of the Kings of Spain over the Indians* (Hanke 1959: 15 and Pagden 1990: 20). Francisco Vitoria argued strongly against the right of the Spaniards to enslave the American Indians, discounting the usual justificatory arguments; that they are like children; that they are irrational; and that they are unbelievers. His argument rests on a number of claims, which in the end come back to the capacity of American Indians to possess property rights, and therefore, if deprived of their property, to be able to suffer an injustice.

Given Aristotle's 'authority' he could not merely be dismissed. First, Vitoria shows that the American Indians do possess reason in the requisite sense. There is order in their affairs; they are subject to magistrates and overlords, within a framework of recognizable laws; and have regulated marriages, commerce, and industry. They even have a kind of religion and have a common understanding. There were, then, sufficient grounds to infer that the Indians exhibited signs of practical reason. Deficiencies may be attributed to socialization, or what Vitoria called 'their evil and barbarous education' (Vitoria 1991: 250). Vitoria contended that it would be harsh to deny the Indians, who had done the Spaniards no harm, the natural rights to property that are conceded to Saracens and Jews, who are enemies to the Christian religion.

Vitoria's second line of defence was to suggest that even if the Indians were insufficiently rational to govern themselves, Aristotle could not have meant that by nature they belong to others and therefore have no rights of ownership in their bodies or possessions. Vitoria argues that slavery is a legal and civil condition. Nature knows of no such station. What Aristotle meant to say was that those of less intelligence are naturally deficient, and need others to govern them, not that it was legal to seize their goods, lands, and enslave them. His intention is clear, Vitoria contends, when one looks at the obverse, that some men are natural masters. What this means is not that their natural intelligence gives them a legal right to arrogate power to themselves over others, 'but merely that they are fitted by nature to be princes and guides' (Vitoria 1991: 251). This did not, however, amount to a ringing endorsement of the capacities of the Indians. They were 'many years outside the state of salvation' for want of the use of reason to prompt them to baptism and the other things necessary for salvation (Vitoria 1991: 250). Even though they were not natural slaves in the Aristotelian sense, nor were they yet capable of the life of contemplation, their civil condition met only the minimum standards because they were ignorant of the liberal arts, almost devoid of agriculture, and had few skilled artisans. Without a true *nobilitas* (in Aristotelian and Thomist sense) they could not enjoy the life of true contemplation (Pagden 1987: 85).

The most famous exchange regarding the enslavement of the American Indians, on the grounds of their religious and intellectual capacities, culminated after the death of Vitoria (1546), between Juan Ginés de Sepúlveda and Bartolomé de Las Casas. Sepúlveda was a prominent humanist who had studied in Italy for more than twenty years and was a leading figure in the recovery of the 'true' Aristotle. He published a Latin translation of Aristotle's *Politics* in 1548, just prior to the confrontation between himself and Las Casas at Valladolid in 1550. Sepúlveda had no first hand experience of the American aboriginals, and relied upon those such as Gonzalo Fernández de Oviedo y Valdes, the author of the earliest account of the flora, fauna, and native peoples, *Historia general y natural de las Indias*. His experience of the natives led him to believe that they were something less than human with heads not like those of other men, but more like helmets, so hard that swords broke on striking them. He concluded that 'their understanding was bestial and evilly inclined' (cited in Pagden 1993: 57).

Such was the furore surrounding the conquest of America, and the treatment of the natives by the Spaniards that the Holy Roman Emperor, Charles V, ordered that new conquests be suspended until the outcome of the inquiry by the Council of the Indies at Valladolid (Hanke 1959: 36).

All of Las Casas's vast, if erratic learning, was levelled against those, such as Sepúlveda, and his source of 'information' Oviedo, who maintained that the conquest of America gave rights to the Crown of Castille over the goods and labour of the natives (Las Casas 2004: xiv–xv). Las Casas had long fought for changes to the legal status of American aboriginals, and in 1542 the efforts of himself and his fellow supporters of Indian rights won a victory with the promulgation of the 'New Laws'. They proscribed ill-treatment of the natives, but more importantly made provision for the abolition of the *encomienda* system.

The *encomienda* system was not technically slavery, but Indians assigned to *encomienderos* for personal profit served their masters in a serf-like capacity. They were not free to come and go as they pleased, and although legally different from slaves they were paid very low wages and treated like slaves (Pagden 1982: 36). Unlike the *encomienda* grants in medieval Spain, in America the *encomienderos* were expected to provide religious instruction to their charges. Such was the power of the *encomienderos* and the tenuousness of the power exercised from Spain, that open revolt looked imminent. The provision was suspended in 1545, and the *encomienderos* agitated for the grants of *encomienda* to become perpetual.

Sepúlveda supported this economic system for those Indians who voluntarily gave up their religion, agreed to become Christians, and submitted to Spanish rule. These were likely to be a small minority who may benefit from peaceful example and education. The rest would need to be beaten into submission, before being forced to accept Christianity. The central issue at Valladolid was not itself the abolition of the *encomienda* system, that had already to some extent been resolved by Charles V in 1545 when he revoked the relevant provision of the 'New Laws'. Instead, what was at stake was the justice of waging war against the Indians, and to this question Sepúlveda gave the answer that the Indians were natural slaves in the Aristotelian sense, and therefore the Spaniards had every right, and indeed a duty, to wage war against them as a prerequisite to converting them to Christianity.

Robert Quirk has defended Sepúlveda in suggesting that when he described the Indians as exemplars of Aristotle's natural slaves what he really meant was that they resembled the condition of medieval Spanish serfs (Quirk 1954: 358). Given that Sepúlveda was an Aristotelian scholar of some note, it is unlikely that he took Aristotle's natural slave to be indicative of mediaeval Spanish serfdom. His Latin translation of the *Politics* of Arsitotle, while not without its faults, was regarded for over a century and a half after its publication in 1548 as the best available (Green 1940: 339–42).

Las Casas defended the American Indians at Valladolid in 1550 against the contention of Sepúlveda that they should be considered the natural slaves of the Spanish. At the basis of his defence of the American Indians was his belief that, 'They are our brothers, and Christ died for them' (cited in Tierney 2004: 11). Las Casas defended the Indians against the four main justifications given by Sepúlveda for waging war against the Indians. First, that they were idolators and committed gross sins against nature. Second, that they possessed little by way of reason, and were of rude nature and naturally inferior, making them fitted to serve those with more refined natures, such as the Spanish. Third, the natives needed to be subjugated before it was possible to spread the faith. Finally, the natives needed protection from themselves (Hanke 1959: 41). The title of the book Las Casas later wrote on the basis of his defence indicates the thrust of his argument: *Defence Against the Persecutors and Slanderers of the Peoples of the New World Discovered Across the Seas*.

After 1498 two broad camps emerged, with of course positions in between, on the question of the capacity of the American Indians to receive the gospel. On the one hand they were deemed malicious savages who lacked the natural reason or judgement, and needed to be subjected to those who did possess such capacities for their own benefit. On the other hand there were those who viewed the Indians as noble savages.

Among those who thought the Indians malicious savages was Antonio de Villasante, expressing a view widely held by colonists, that the Indians were incapable of government, and if left to their own devices would revert to their repugnant habits of eating spiders and snakes, believing in witch doctors, and engaging in drunkenness, greed, and improvidence (Hanke 1974: 10). It was justifiable, according to Sepúlveda, to wage just war upon the Indians in order to convert them to the gospels. On the other hand, in 1549 Las Casas, in a letter to an unknown correspondent, probably Domingo de Soto, the Confessor of Charles V, asked, 'where in the world have rational men in happy and populous lands been subjugated by such cruel and unjust wars called conquests, and then been divided up by the same cruel butchers and tyrannical robbers as though they were inanimate things... enslaved in an infernal way, worse than in Pharaoh's day, treated like cattle being weighed in the meatmarket' (cited in Hanke 1974: 67).

There was no consensus among jurists, ecclesiastics, colonists, nor royal officials on the capacity of the Indians, and upon the question of educating them to receive the faith. It is not surprising that the Crown and the Crown's officials turned to a commission of experts to hear both sides at Valladolid in 1550. The question to be addressed was on the legality of the war against the Indians, before preaching the faith to them, in order to subject them to the rule of the king of Spain, rendering it easier to instruct them in the faith (Hanke 1974: 67).

Sepúlveda contended that the Indians were barbarians and wild men because of their savage behaviour; they had no written language; they conformed to the Aristotelian category of barbarism, rendering them natural slaves. They were, he argued, evil and wicked, lacking in reason, and having no recognizable way of life fitting human beings. They were not in awe of laws, and led the life of brute animals. His judgement of the Indians is severe: 'In prudence, talent, virtue, and humanity they are inferior to the Spaniards as children to adults, women to men, as the wild and cruel to the meek, as the prodigiously intemperate to the continent and temperate, that I have almost said, as monkeys to men' (cited in Hanke 1974: 84).

Las Casas does not directly try to discredit Aristotle's theory of natural slavery. Instead he contested its applicability to the condition of the American Indians. While he does not deny that some men are so far lacking in reason and intelligence as to need guidance in their everyday affairs, no whole race could be condemned to such a station. In other words, while he does not deny that there may be natural slaves, he does not think that the category is widely applicable or particularly helpful (Hanke 1959: 58–9). Las Casas contested the view that the Indians were ignorant, unintelligent, and incapable of self-government. He argued in his *Defence* that they were immensely talented and skilful, more so than any nation in the world in the mechanical arts. In their works they demonstrate a refinement and skill inferior to none. When they have been taught grammar and logic, he continues, they are remarkably adept. If there are such people as natural slaves, the Indians are not among them. They have laws, kingdoms, and legitimate governments, which provide settled lives for large numbers of people in societies. They engage in commercial activities, buying, selling, lending, and other contractual relations in accordance with the Law of Nations. In his summation at the close of the *Defence*, Las Casas maintained that, 'The Indians are our brothers, and Christ has given his life for them. Why, then, do we persecute them with such inhuman savagery when they do not deserve such treatment?'(cited in Hanke 1974: 76). Later he went as far as to suggest that Indians themselves had just cause for war for the treatment they had suffered under the Spanish. The Spaniards, he claimed, descended on these gentle lambs 'like ravening wolves upon the fold, or like tigers and savage lions who have not eaten meat for days' (Las Casas 2004: 11).

The lasting consequence of the dispute, however, was that the great jurists of the eighteenth century could no longer assert the right of Europeans to appropriate the person and property of the American Indians, but on the whole still justified slavery and the appropriation of property on the grounds of just war.

The dispute at Valladolid did not end arguments about the legitimacy of enslaving Native Americans. In 1558 the Italian jurist Pierino Belli (1502–75) wrote his *De re militari et de bello tractatus*, published in Venice in 1563. In it he contends that if a people has no bonds of friendship or hospitality with others who come among them, then seizure and enslavement are justified irrespective of whether a condition of war prevails, 'With good right, therefore, the Spaniards enslaved those Indians of the West, who live far away from our world, and were unknown to the Greeks and Romans' (Belli 1936a: II, xii, 5, p. 85). Belli did not think it necessary for Europeans to make peace with the aboriginal natives.

Their mere existence and the fact that they were not allied to any European countries were grounds enough for subjugating them into slavery. What is implied here, then, is that no automatic universal community among men is assumed, but that nevertheless the same Law of Nations derived from the application of natural law applies to everyone. Christians do, however, form a moral community. Like the Romans, as the Scriptures show, they are brothers and fellow citizens, and not enemies. Warfare among them does not confer the right on captors to enslave fellow Christians, as the Israelites discovered when they seized a large number of captives in Jerusalem. They were ordered by a prophet to release the prisoners, or incur the wrath of God (Belli referring to Chronicles, xxviii 9ff. Belli 1936a: Part IV, chapt. I, p. 116)

Belli's fellow countryman and contemporary, Balthazar Ayala, was a firm believer that, just as in peace, matters of war were regulated by law. Following Augustine he contends that the wickedness of the enemy is evidence enough for the wise that not only is just war right, it is also a necessity. Indeed, God Himself ordered the Israelites to wage war against many people, including the Amorites (Ayala 1912: Preface, vii). It is just, he argues, to use force against those who refuse to accede to fair demands, or refuse to be restrained by reason. Slavery, in his view, on the grounds of state expediency, is perfectly justifiable against those who wage an unjust war. For slaves it is a blessing because they are deprived of further opportunities of wrong-doing, and they behave better under someone else's direction than under their own (Ayala 1912: Preface, viii).

The natural law predates the *jus gentium*, and by it all men were born free and equal. The *jus gentium* is rooted in natural reason, and as human wickedness increased that reason dictated that it ought to be 'restrained by war and captivity and slavery' (Ayala 1912: Book II, chapt. v, [16], p. 41). It was the *jus gentium* that introduced war and slavery in order to punish wickedness and constrain those who would wage unjust wars. Slavery, then, is not natural, *pace* Aristotle, it is 'an institution of *jus gentium*' (Ayala 1912: Book II, chapt. v, [17], p. 42).

Like Belli the Protestant Gentili argued that there could be no slavery among Christians because they were all brothers in Christ, and constituted one Christendom. Wars among Christians, as among ancient Greeks, was to be deemed civil. That there is no true condition of slavery among Christians has been established, he contends, by 'invariable custom' (Gentili 1933: III, ix, p. 329 [537]). In order to give weight to his own view, Gentili refers to 'the philosopher' who thought that Greeks were part of the same fatherland and shared religious rites.

For Gentili slavery is not contrary to natural reason, which is at the basis of the Law of Nations. He denies, however, that there is a condition of natural slavery. Gentili, argued, for example, that we are by nature related (Gentili 1933: I, ix, p. 54 [87]). He concurs with St. Thomas Aquinas that slavery is not in accordance with nature's first intent, which is the condition of natural equality, but is in accordance with the second intent, that sinners should be punished. Gentili contends that Aristotle's argument of the natural origin of slavery is apposite because even though he is referring to those with servile natures, his arguments have force in relation to those who have 'become slaves because of their wickedness and sins' (Gentili 1933: III, ix, p. 330 [538]). This does not, however, in accordance with the law of God, permit the ill-treatment of slaves.

For Vattel, the issue of slavery is hardly worth considering because 'that disgrace to humanity has happily been banished from Europe' because it is a condition 'contrary to the nature of man' (Vattel 1834: III, viii, §152, p. 356). For him, the right of individuals not to be enslaved is upheld, except in exceptional circumstances. A prisoner of war may be enslaved only if he has 'committed a crime deserving of death'. In such circumstances if he considers it a favour to be spared his life, cast in chains, and forced to do the bidding of someone else, so be it (Vattel 1834: III, viii, §152, p. 356).

In general, slavery was considered by natural law and natural rights thinkers of the sixteenth and seventeenth centuries as a human institution, sanctioned by natural law and the Law of Nations, an acceptable alternative to death in conditions of conquest, but also for sins committed that may otherwise lead to death or indefinite incarceration. During such time slaves became pieces of property who could be bought and sold as other possessions. While it was acknowledged that many peoples outside of Europe, as indeed some within, were uncivilized and barbaric in comparison with Europeans, it was not generally the case that such inferiority was deemed congenital or racial. Uncivilized peoples could with education, religion, and discipline be elevated to a higher status.

THE TRANSATLANTIC SLAVE TRADE

Despite Las Casas' spirited defence of the American Indians he nevertheless supported his case by arguing that American native slaves could be replaced by

Africans. He did come to regret his suggestion, and denounced the slave trade. It is true to say, however, he never opposed African slavery with the same passion as he opposed American Indian enslavement (Talbot 2005: 80).

The transatlantic slave trade exploited tribal conflicts in Africa, often supplying weapons to encourage the waging of war in which captives could justifiably be considered slaves. As the property of their black captors, they could dispose of them as they wished to the white slavers along the African Coast. While slaves were appallingly treated it was not in the interests of the slave owner to neglect their health completely. The financial loss to slave owners of abolition was a significant factor in slowing down the process of liberating slaves. Compensation was often the only course that made it politically acceptable. In Puerto Rico, for example, when slavery was finally abolished by the Spanish National Assembly on March 22, 1873, slave owners were compensated with 35 million pesetas per slave.

No simple distinction could be made between idealist religious dreamers and hard headed businessmen. Quakers were opposed to the exploitation of fellow humans by slavery, but many nevertheless were successful businessmen. It was not a matter then, of morality versus economics, the issues were much more complex drawing upon pseudo-biological evidence, self-interest, pure ignorance and prejudice, and fear. Modern chattel slavery was almost invariably justified on the grounds of the inferiority of the blacks to the whites.

If one turned to the cool white light of philosophical reason was there anything to guide one there as to the rights and wrongs of slavery, and as to whether humanity is one, or comprised separate, and perhaps related, races? The issues of race and slavery were connected with the wider philosophical debate about human nature. Women, for example, were generally regarded as human, but intrinsically different from, and inferior to men. Non-whites were considered barely human, and some considered more so than others, but their humanity continued to be an issue of debate. The relationship of animals, especially the 'orangutans', by which they meant the higher primates, who were clearly not human, but who may nevertheless possess souls, was of crucial importance. If humans are continuous with animals, and animals possess souls, then it has a considerable bearing on how humans may treat them (Garrett 2006: 161, 169 and 177–83).

Natural rights in relation to animals were usually discussed in terms of the rights of humans in relation to animals. William Paley, for example, when discussing the general rights of mankind, was reluctant to base our right to eat animals on the ground that animals prey on other animals. He argued that, 'Some excuse seems necessary for the pain and loss which we occasion to brutes, by restraining them of their liberty, mutilating their bodies, and, at last, putting an end to their lives (which we suppose to be the whole of their existence), for our pleasure or conveniency' (Paley 1799: 95). The crucial difference between us and animals of prey is that carnivores cannot live without meat, whereas humans can, and therefore the eating of meat cannot be wholly grounded in human reason. We have to look to Scripture for our justification to eat meat and to God granting permission, not to Adam, but to Noah and his progeny after the Flood. When God gave the animals as meat to men it was by divine dispensation, that is, special permission, and not of natural right. Animals are therefore protected from capricious and systematic cruelty by men (Paley 1799: 97).

Derogatory attitudes towards non-Europeans have been common enough among philosophers, and even those with the most creditable liberal credentials have not failed to expose their prejudices in language that would simply be unacceptable by today's standards. Where among the works of our great philosophers are the spirited defences of blacks, passionate denunciations of slavery, or denunciations of the conquest of the Indies (Mills 1997: 94)? Kant, for example, is notorious for the extremity of his racist views in his anthropological writings. Kant believed, for example, taking his lead from Hume, that 'the Negroes of Africa have by nature no feeling that rises above the trifling' (cited in Morton 2002: 11), and the fact that a Negro is black all over is a clear sign that what he says is 'stupid' (Popkin 1977: 218). Kant did not claim that there are different species of humans, believing instead that they were all derived from the same stock, but constituting different races that maintained themselves in different areas of the world, and breeding between which produced hybrids, mulattoes (Kant 1997a: 40). The different races, he contended, have their origin in the same 'stem genus', and all deviate from it in having adapted to different climatic conditions. Of the four races, northern European, American Indian, Black, and Asian Indians, whites between 31st and 52nd parallel are the most authentic, having deviated least from the original.

He has an admiration for the American Indians who display sublime mental characters reminiscent of the Ancients and who treat women with a respect that not even Europeans can emulate. Should a Lawgiver like Lycurgus arise among the six Nations in the Indies 'one would see a Spartan Republic arise in the New World' (Kant 1997b: 56). They nevertheless lack sensitivity, having very little capacity for the finer feelings. The blacks, however, are almost beneath his contempt. In comparing blacks and whites Kant contends that 'So fundamental is the difference between these two races of man, and it appears to be as great in regard to mental capacities as in colour. The religion of fetishes so widespread among them is perhaps a sort of idolatry that sinks as deeply into the trifling as appears to be possible to human nature' (Kant 1997b: 55–6).

Discussions of race during the eighteenth century were by no means clear cut. The term took on a variety of meanings ranging from a methodological classificatory category for sub-dividing species, to differentiating humanity according to skin colour. Exemplifying the former is Buffon's contention that species usually have two races, the masculine and the feminine. Kant exemplifies the latter equation of race with skin colour (Garrett 2006: 182). Both Kant and Hume, by giving weight to the thesis that there are human races that are differentiated both culturally and physically by heredity, without being refuted by philosophers considered of equal rank, were widely cited as authorities by defenders of slavery. Hume and Kant were considered serious obstacles to success by abolitionists (Zack 1999: 302). Even Jefferson the champion of natural rights and equality believed that the development of the 'Indians' was retarded by environmental factors, but believed, not without equivocation, that blacks were congenitally inferior, evidence of which was their rapacious sexual appetites (Diggins 1976: 212).

Racism did not necessarily entail a commitment to the efficacy of slavery. Some of the most extreme exponents of racial differentiation and gradation, such as Edward Long and Charles White, were opponents of slavery (Garrett 2004: 131).

The authority of philosophers who expressed racist attitudes, however, was certainly invoked to support the arguments of those who did advocate and defend slavery. We have already seen how the issue of slavery was not one commonly associated with race, but it very much became so as the need for cheap labour in labour intensive industries increased in colonial territories. Spirited defences of slavery were mounted to justify the continuing subjugation of the American Indians by their Spanish masters. Those who defended the Indians against such claims often did so on the grounds that they exhibited all of the necessary features of humanity including organized society and government, as well as significant cultural achievements. Such defenders usually either remained silent about the condition of blacks, or were extremely equivocal or deliberately excluded them altogether.

There were occasional objections to black slavery before the eighteenth century, but they were directed towards refuting the claim that blacks were not children of God. Such objections were primarily concerned with saving their souls, a consideration that also figured prominently for Las Casas in his discussion of the American Indians. The most vilified among blacks were the Aboriginals of Australia after its 'discovery' in 1778. Accounts of travellers and explorers, which came to inform much of the later anthropological literature of the nineteenth century, portrayed them as non-human, and, if human, as occupying such a low point on the scale of civilization that they could barely be treated as such. They were largely considered to be vermin, so primitive that they were completely incommensurable with humanity, and better eradicated rather than enslaved. Their land in particular was considered *terra nullius* or *res nullius* because of their nomadic lifestyles and no apparent signs of civilization.

Representatives of both the descriptive and prescriptive traditions of natural rights who justify the institution of slavery are not difficult to find. For the most part up until the eighteenth century Aristotle's two main arguments lay at the basis of support for slavery. If it did not rest on the belief in congenital inferiority, then the institution was justified by conquest. In the case of both Hobbes and Locke, representatives of the descriptive and prescriptive version of natural rights, their intimate familiarity with American colonization does not lead them to discuss slavery in terms of compassion or pity, nor to formulate an ethical justification of the institution of slavery. Both believe that slavery is a relationship of force, the stronger exercising power over the weaker, and this they distinguish from being a servant, a condition that arises by agreement. A slave who as a captive agrees to serve without compulsion becomes a servant. The point, to some extent, is semantic because Hobbes, for example, wants to show that by means of agreement an obligation has been incurred. In exchange for one's life the captive enters a condition of servitude, 'The Master of the Servant, is Master also of all he hath; and may exact the use thereof; that is to say, of his goods, of his labour, of his servants, and of his children, as often as he shall think fit' (Hobbes 1991: book II, chapt. XX, p. 142 [104]).

Elsewhere, Hobbes is emphatic that the master has the same right over servants as he has over slaves, having 'absolute dominion over both' (Hobbes 1994: Pt. II, chapt. xxii, p. 127). This he calls the right of 'property or dominion', acquired by conquest in the case of slavery, and by compact, irrespective of if it is under duress, in the case of the servant. Both are the property of the master. While Hobbes does not directly comment on the morality of the slave trade, and his theory is not racially grounded, he does nevertheless provide a theoretical justification of it. Slaves, nor servants, have any rights against the master, except perhaps the right of self-preservation, which none of us can rationally relinquish (with the possible exception of volunteering to join the army). There is a difference however: defeat and capture do not create an obligation to the master. It is the covenant between the two that establishes the right to obedience. Until then the slave may justly escape from prison, kill or hold captive his master. Upon making a covenant the slave becomes a servant obligated to the master, and as the property of a master a servant may be disposed of in anyway the master sees fit, that is, sold, bequeathed, or manumitted (Hobbes 1994: Pt. II, chapt. xxii, p. 128).

On Hobbes' justification of slavery all men and women are equally eligible for servitude, in that he, like Aristotle, believed in the right of conquest. Unlike Aristotle, however, he did not believe in natural slavery. Each person in the state of nature is more or less the equal of others in body and in mind. He was a supporter of both plantation and colonization, but he did urge his fellow countrymen not to exterminate the people they found on arrival because they too had a degree of morality, skills of husbandry, and experience of contract (Hannaford 1996: 193).

Among those who subscribe to the prescriptive strand of natural rights, Grotius notably endorses the right of captors to enslave their captives. In his discussion of supreme power, or sovereignty, Grotius remarks that just as it is lawful for an individual to enslave himself to whom so ever he so pleases, why should it not be lawful for a whole people to subject themselves to one or more people transferring the right of governance without retaining any for themselves? In this context he even goes as far as to endorse Aristotle's contention that some men are born to be slaves, extending it to whole nations. Grotius contends that, 'And some Nations also are of such a Temper, that they know better how to obey than command' (Grotius 2005: I, chapt. III, §viii; cf. Keane, 2002: 44–5 and Tierney 1997: 337). However, elsewhere in his *The Rights of War and Peace* Grotius denied that there are natural slaves, on the grounds that all men are born equal. He did not, however, attribute a right to human beings against being enslaved (Grotius 2005: II, chapt. XII, §xi). Slavery had its origin in human acts, but this did not make it inconsistent with natural justice. Men may become slaves by agreement, or as a consequence of committing a crime, or according to the Law of Nations by capture in war (Grotius 2005: III, chapt. VII, §I). Even children born to bondswomen are slaves.

Slaves are for Grotius just like property, and a slave owner has the power to transfer the right (Grotius 2005: III, chapt. VII, §v). He also asserts that anyone is permitted to enslave himself into the private ownership of another by means of agreement or contract, but that the slave owner does not have the power of life and death over him. This may take the form of complete slavery which is a life-long commitment to service in return for the necessities of subsistence. Alternatively, one may commit oneself to a more limited or incomplete form of slavery which may entail the hire of one's labour for pay (see Pateman 1988: 68–9).

Pufendorf directly addresses Aristotle's contention that some men are born natural slaves, and that the Greeks have a right to enslave the barbarians on the grounds that they are intellectually and culturally inferior. The idea of natural slavery is at once absurd and repugnant, and flies in the face of the principle of the natural equality of men. Hardly anyone, argues Pufendorf, is so feeble of mind as to think that to be subjected to the will of another is preferable to living according to his own liberty. He does not deny that some men are wiser than others, and may exercise better judgement than someone intellectually inferior, but who may nevertheless have greater bodily strength. Both may benefit from the wiser directing the affairs of the 'extremely stupid and heavy' (Pufendorf 1717: bk. III, chapt. II, §viii). To admit of such benefits is not to suggest that nature has invested the wise with sovereignty over the foolish, nor with a right to force them to obey against their wills. All men enjoy the same degree and measure of natural liberty, and no one has a right to deprive him of it without his consent. Pufendorf contends that, 'this must be fixted as a most undoubted Principle, that the bare force of such a *Natural Aptitude*, does neither give the one the right of imposing a condition of servitude, nor oblige the other to receive it' (Pufendorf 1717: bk. III, chapt. II, §viii). The distinction between bondage and freedom arises out of civil laws, and is a consequence of the distinction between soldiery and country, whereby humane pacts following capture of enemy troops permit of slavery.

Pufendorf is equally contemptuous of Aristotle's implication that barbarians are to be equated with natural slaves. It is both arrogant and unreasonable to think that those who differ from us in manners and customs, and who are on that account deemed barbarians, are to be equated with natural slaves and lawfully subjected.

When Locke begins the *First Treatise* with a castigation of Sir Robert Filmer for advocating slavery, 'so vile and miserable Estate of man', against the 'Temper and Courage of our Nation' (Locke 1988: I, §1, p. 141), one may be forgiven for believing that this was an outright condemnation of the institution because the power he is condemning being exercised by one over fellow human beings is 'so that he may take or alienate their Estates, sell, castrate, or use their Persons as he pleases, they being all his Slaves' (Locke 1988: I, §9, p. 148).

Far from it, Locke too worked within the parameters that Aristotle had set. Whereas he does not talk of natural slaves, it is clear that he thinks the American Indians have been morally negligent in falling down on their duty to God to make the land as productive as possible. In so far as they did not cultivate the land, the only form of labour that Locke was prepared to acknowledge in a state of nature, they did not own, but simply held it in common with the rest of mankind for use. It is primarily for the 'Industrious and Rational' to cultivate it by means of labour in order to lay title to it (Locke 1988: II, §34, p. 291). By implication the American Indians were neither industrious nor rational, because they did not avail themselves of the opportunity and discharge their obligation to God.

Like the rest of the whole world the American Indians were subject to natural law. Property for Locke is intrinsic to one's political *personae*, and without it individuals had few rights. Slaves are devoid of political rights because they have no property. Those who violate the natural law put themselves in a state of war with others. A condition of slavery arises in a just war when conquest subjects the vanquished to the victors, subjecting them to despotic power. If violation of the natural law is such to merit the forfeiture of his life, 'he to whom he has forfeited it, may (when he has him in his Power) delay to take it, and make use of him to his own Service, and he does him no injury by it' (Locke 1988: II, §24, p. 284). Slavery is, in effect, as Hobbes also believed, a continuation of war. This state of war ceases if the slave is given a choice to preserve his life by entering into a compact (Locke 1988: II, §24, p. 284 and §172, p. 382). He is thus transformed from being a slave into a servant. He suggests that the authority exercised by a Lord over a slave is different from that exercised by a master over a servant (Locke 1988: II, §2, p. 268). Locke defines this form of power over slaves as despotic and it is exercised over those 'such as have no property at all' (Locke 1988: II, §172–3, p. 382–4). To be Lord of a slave is to have absolute power of life and death over him, and one cannot give away that which one does not have, that is the power over one's life. A compact of servitude vests a limited power in the master which is not 'Absolute, Arbitrary, Despotical Power'. Where we find men selling themselves, as among Jews and other nations, it is into drudgery rather than slavery (Locke 1988: II, §28, p. 285). The servant on Locke's definition receives wages, and the power exercised over him is limited by contract (Locke 1988: II, §85, p. 322).

Wylie Sypher suggests that both Hobbes and Locke fail to consider the institution of slavery by purchase (Sypher 1939: 269). We have already seen that Hobbes' theory by implication condones it. What about Locke? While he does not enter into the morality of slavery by purchase he certainly implies that it is perfectly legitimate. In arguing against Filmer, Locke wanted to show that paternal power was quite distinct from political power, which rests on consent. He is willing to agree with Filmer that the Patriarchs of the bible exercised patriarchal power, but argued that they did not exercise the political power of sovereigns. He uses the analogy of a planter in the West Indies to illustrate his case. Such a person may gather around him sons, servants born in his house, as well as 'bought with his Money' to seek reparations from Indians who have caused him some injury, but he would not on that account be a sovereign and exercise political power. In relation to slaves it is perfectly legitimate to gain dominion over them, as one would over horses, 'by Bargain and Purchase' (Locke 1988: I, §130, p. 237). The Patriarchs, like the plantation owners, 'bought Men and Maid Servants, and by their increase as well as purchasing new, came to have large and numerous Families' (Locke 1988: I, §130, p. 237).

Locke, then, does differ from Hobbes in his theory of slavery. Whereas in Hobbes the master has the same rights over the slave and servant, the servant has greater obligations to the master by having entered into a compact, and therefore is entrusted with a certain degree of liberty. For Locke, the compact between master and servant sets distinct parameters that serve to define and constrain the master's rights. Neither Hobbes nor Locke explicitly argues for the concept of natural slavery, and both defend the Aristotelian notion of the rights of conquest. Furthermore, neither explicitly defends the 'slave trade', but both condone the sale and purchase of slaves, or servants, by simply taking it for granted that such transactions are part and parcel of the rights of the master or slave owner.

Do critics of the traditions of natural law and natural rights fare any better in their attitudes towards other races, and indeed towards the issue of slavery? It is important to distinguish a number of aspects to this question. Europeans generally believed that they occupied a higher level of civilization than other races. Often this amounted to seeing something of themselves in other peoples who were contemporaneous in time, but distant in the place they occupied in the civilizing process. To believe that other peoples stood at different points on the road to civilization, or as it became in the nineteenth century, in the evolutionary process, did not have any necessary implications for one's attitude towards slavery. It was not unusual to find spirited vilifications of blacks as barely human, combined with passionate attacks on the slave trade as inhumane, as for example, in Benjamin Franklin (1706–1790), Thomas Jefferson (1743–1826), David Hume (1711–1776), and François-Marie Arouet (1694–1778), better known by his pen name of Voltaire, and for his extreme anti-semitism. Few philosophers were active in the practical movement for abolition, except for a few notable exceptions such as Marquis de Condorcet (1743–1794), William Paley (1743–1805), and James Beattie (1735–1803), a great admirer of Wilberforce.

Slavery, as we have seen, was commonly justified with reference to conquest, yet such views were not generally acceptable without severe qualification among jurists of the eighteenth century. Yet slavery was a fact upon which the prosperity of colonial enterprises depended. The acceleration in the slave trade required to be justified against those who thought that it was fundamentally immoral.

Rousseau, although not kind to women in his educational views, against which much of Wollstonecraft's *Vindication of the Rights of Women* is directed, was nevertheless a strong opponent of slavery and argued directly against its natural law and natural right exponents. Rousseau takes as his target specific arguments advanced by natural law thinkers, such as those relating to the legitimacy of slavery in relation to conquest, and colonialism in relation to property and the idea of *terra nullius*, or vacant land. Rousseau is opposed to the idea of slavery as a natural condition, and of enslavement as a right of conquest in war. In addressing the issue of 'the alleged right of slavery' (Rousseau 1987: 145) Rousseau contends that Aristotle before all others had argued that some men are 'born for slavery and others for domination' (Rousseau 1987: 142). Aristotle was not wrong in his observation; the mistake he made was to take the effect for the cause. To be born into slavery is to be born for slavery. Chained and devoid of the desire to escape, slaves love the security of their servitude. Rousseau maintains that 'If there are slaves by nature, it is because there have been slaves against nature. Force has produced the first slaves; their cowardice has perpetuated them' (Rousseau 1987: 143). In effect, then, Rousseau is suggesting that man, and not nature, is responsible for his predicament. Slavery is a human institution in which slaves themselves are complicit, and from which slaves may, with difficulty, liberate themselves.

Although Rousseau acknowledges that it is a general tendency, he specifically names Grotius as one of those who derive a right to slavery from victory in battle. The victors have the right to kill the vanquished, and therefore if the vanquished exchange their lives for servitude, each of the parties gains. Rousseau disputes the derivation. In a state of nature, he argues, relationships are so infrequent and intermittent that they are not sufficiently constant to bring about either a state of war or peace. Men are not, as they are in Hobbes's state of nature, natural enemies. Rousseau maintains that, 'war is not therefore a relationship between one man and another, but a relationship between one state and another. In war private individuals are enemies only incidentally: not as men or even as citizens, but as soldiers; not as members of the homeland but as defenders' (Rousseau 1987:145). In his view, each state can have as enemies only other states, because there can be no real relationship between things of unalike natures. The so-called right of conquest is merely based on force and therefore is no right at all. The right to enslave the vanquished on the basis of the right to massacre captives is an absurdity.

Rousseau does equivocate. He implies that there is a right to slavery, albeit not a real right, when he suggests that victors only have the right to kill if the enemy cannot be enslaved, and that therefore, the right to slavery cannot be based on the right to kill. The point that Rousseau is making is that it is nonsense to talk of the spurious purchase of one's life in exchange for liberty from someone who has no right over that life in the first place. Where such a relationship is established by force those enslaved are under no moral obligation to serve, except on prudential grounds until such time they can escape and exact revenge. Far from a war coming to an end by vanquishing and enslaving the enemy, it is merely perpetuated (Rousseau 1987: 146). This abhorrence of slavery was not based on race, as the opening lines of the *Social Contract* shows: men are born free but everywhere they are in chains. Nevertheless, his general argument against the illegitimacy of enslavement served to bolster the case against black slavery. It is not surprising that Robespierre and other revolutionary leaders who were indebted to Rousseau were adamant that Negroes be among those who enjoyed the newly acquired Liberty, Equality, and Fraternity (Cook 1936: 301).[1]

---

[1] Rousseau had given an idyllic description of the noble savage in his *Discourse on the Origins of Inequality*, and he was curious to explore the relationship between the higher primates and man

During the latter part of the eighteenth century there were two main sets of beliefs associated with racism. The first may be termed the 'degeneracy theory'. It acknowledges that all races comprise humanity, but that the non-white races had somehow regressed (Popkin 1993: 83 and Immerwahr 1992: 482). A variation of such beliefs is that different races have progressed at different rates up the scale of savagery, barbarism, and civilization. Factors such as harshness of climate, divine punishment, or perverse education were invoked to account for both varieties. It was a condition that was, generally speaking, redeemable by means of exposure to the right manners, religion, and education.

Both Montesquieu's and Burke's views on race and colonialism were of this type. Montesquieu, more explicitly than Burke, subscribed to the degeneracy theory attributing differences in race to variations in climate. Burke's attribution of differences had more to do with customs, manners, and cultural practices. While both subscribed to the view that different races stood at different points on the scale of civilization, neither supported, nor implicitly condoned the institution of slavery. It was for both an abhorrence and an affront to humanity and humaneness. Like Burke after him, Montesquieu had to acknowledge the existence, and persistence, of slavery, and realized that its abolition was unlikely if merely advocated on first principles and metaphysical theory. They both wanted first to regulate the immoral trade, leading to its eventual abolition.

As an observer of variations in attributes, according to climatic change, the subtlety and irony of some of Montesquieu's observations are often lost, and even taken as a defence of the institution (Fletcher 1933: 416). Since its first publication in 1748 interpreters have been puzzled by the apparent lack of coherence and consistency of *The Spirit of the Laws*. Montesquieu himself throughout the work gives credence to the classic statement of the style of philosophizing embodying what Leo Strauss in his *Persecution and the Art of Writing* described as exoteric and esoteric doctrines. The exoteric doctrine is for the uninitiated, uncritical, and unquestioning reader, upon which every society depends blindly to adhere to its traditions and *mores*. The exoteric plan or doctrine is for philosophers prepared to make the effort of deciphering the hidden plan (Strauss 1952: and Boucher 1985: 89–90). Montesquieu gives three reasons for presenting his philosophy in this way. The first is to avoid the danger of censorship and persecution for presenting unorthodox doctrines. The second is, he believed that all philosophy is to some extent subversive of the foundations of decent societies in so far as it raises fundamental questions. It must therefore be done in a manner that is not immediately discernible. The most important reason, however, was educative. The philosopher

---

in footnote 10 of the essay. Because travellers to exotic places have tended not to be philosophically minded, Rousseau suspects that they may have been blinded by their prejudices, and failed to have recognized primitive or savage man. Had the likes of Montesquieu, Buffon, Diderot, Duclos, d'Alembert, and Condillac travelled to exotic places with the intention of describing and observing what they saw, as only they knew how, 'I say that when such observers will affirm of an animal that it is a man and of another that it is a beast, we will have to believe them' (Rousseau 1978: 100). The criterion that Rousseau offers to distinguish the human from the non-human is the ability to perfect itself (Rousseau 1978: 98).

should not preach a message, but instead try to stimulate the reader into retracing the steps of the philosopher and rethinking for himself the problems and puzzles that first stimulated the discussion (Pangle 1991: 345). Montesquieu claims to derive his principles, not from prejudices, but from the nature of things themselves (Montesquieu 1989: author's Preface). His relationship to natural law and natural rights theories is ambivalent. I take him here as a critic because, like Rousseau after him, he denies some of the fundamental tenets of both. He believes that survival, security, and procreation are basic natural laws that circumscribe the parameters of human activity and morality. However, instead of relying on instinct, as animals do, man is guided by a fragile, fallible, and often misguided intelligence. The natural laws of which he speaks are prior to such notions as justice and equity, because both presuppose society and intelligence. Even Hobbes' state of nature is too social a description of the pre-social condition for Montesquieu. It is, for him, a terrifying and miserable existence, and even our deliverance from it plunges us into continuous war because our inhibitions and fear of others are eroded.

The immediacy of danger and the imminence of death quickly lead to the development of reason which indicates to us certain precepts consistent with security. The laws of reason, however, speak to us in very soft tones, and what is audible above the noise and confusion are some minimal principles that appear almost universal, principally that despotic government is against nature. They do not tell us what forms of government are universally consistent with it, nor do the laws of reason supply a criterion by which we can judge the legitimacy of government, such as we find in Locke, for example, in the social contract, or the principle of consent.

As with Burke, there is a substratum of human nature dictating certain needs, layered on top of which is the civil social person who responds to these needs differently and who is the product of the society, government, and the spirit of the laws, which are all themselves influenced by the natural and historical environments. Hence the considerable variation that his work demonstrates in cultures, governments, and social practices.

Montesquieu begins book 15 of *The Spirit of the Laws* with a condemnation of slavery, 'It is not good by its nature; it is useful neither to the master nor to the slave' (Montesquieu 1989: book 15, chapt. I, p. 246). Montesquieu can find no justification for slavery on any of the three main grounds that its supporters offer, the Law of Nations, civil law, and natural right.

Against Aristotle's second justification of slavery, that is the exchange of one's life for enslavement, Montesquieu argues that the Law of Nations condones the right of killing the enemy only in cases of absolute necessity. If the enemy is taken alive it is testimony to the fact that killing was not an absolute necessity. Without such necessity the Law of Nations confers no right to kill. Montesquieu contends that 'Murdering in cold blood by soldiers after the heat of the action is condemned by all the nations of the world' (Montesquieu 1989: book 15, chapt. 2, p. 247). The life of the captive, then, does not become the property of the captor to dispose of as he sees fit.

Slavery under civil law is simply an absurdity. The amount of money a free man receives for selling himself into slavery, immediately becomes the property along with himself of the person who purchased him. In other words, the seller receives nothing, and the purchaser gives nothing, and hence there can be no contract. If slavery by right of conquest cannot be sustained, and the sale of a free man into slavery is an absurdity, the grounds for the offspring of those subjected to such injustices being forced or sold into the same condition cannot be upheld by natural law.

The slavery of one nation by another is not based on knowledge and reason, which tends to make men gentle and more humane, but upon prejudice occasioned by the scorn felt from differing customs. Montesquieu ironically maintains that it was differing customs, principally in eating different food, that was abhorrent, and in the smoking tobacco and wearing beards of a different cut, that gave the Spaniards the right to enslave the Americans. Montesquieu goes on to say that if he had to defend the right to enslave Negroes he would do so by pointing out that having exterminated the peoples of America, Europeans have to enslave Negroes who are black from head to toe, have flat noses, and probably have no souls, in order to clear the land to grow sugar at economical rates (Montesquieu 1989: book15, chapt. 5, p. 250).

Montesquieu welcomes the abolition of slavery in Europe, but acknowledges that under political despotism, or as he calls it political slavery, it is understandable how civil slavery came about, and in some places where political slavery is accompanied by a hot climate, which makes people lazy, slavery may even be a necessity. On balance, however, he thinks that it is probably the laws that made men lazy, and he finds it hard to imagine a climate on earth where freemen could not be engaged to work. Nevertheless, however it is justified, 'civil laws must seek to remove, on the one hand, its abuses, and on the other, its dangers' (Montesquieu 1989: book 15, chapt. 11, p. 254). The laws should regulate the feeding, clothing, and well being of slaves to protect them from abuse (Montesquieu 1989: book 15, chapt. 17, p. 259).

Among the abusers of slavery are Muslim states, in which the majority of the nation exists 'in order to serve the voluptuousness of the other' (Montesquieu 1989: book 15, chapt. 12, p. 255). It is against reason, he argues, that the virtue and honour of female slaves should be violated by their masters. The laws of modesty, he claims, are a natural right that ought to be observed by all nations of the world, because even where slavery does exist it should be for its utility and not for sexual indulgence.

Following Grotius and Montesquieu, Burke believed that the colonization of a country, by conquest or consent, did not confer a right to impose arbitrary rule. Colonies were under the tutelage of the mother country, and should be encouraged to grow and mature into the best that its traditions intimate. He acknowledged that each nation has a character peculiar to itself, and that it should be respected in all of England's dealings with it. Even in the governance of colonies every effort should be made to adhere to the time-honoured traditions either of the colonizers, as was the case in America, who could justifiably claim the rights of Englishmen, or of both the colonizers and the indigenous peoples, as in the case of India. In both cases there is the additional consideration of universal principles, arrived at through experience rather than abstract reasoning.

There could be no question in Burke's mind of trying to impose a uniform system of government over an empire. Government is a practical matter designed to further the happiness of humanity. It is not meant to gratify the visionary schemes of politicians in their symmetry and uniformity. 'I never was,' Burke argued, 'wild enough to conceive, that one method would serve for the whole' of the empire (Burke 1907: vol ii. 272). Even though Burke valued the dignity and spirit of nations, he was, then, not averse to empire as long as the ruling country took due heed of the spirit of the people over whom it ruled and was faithful to their traditions and mindful of allowing them a degree of relative autonomy.

In its relationship with India, Great Britain had entered into a virtual Act of Union and was bound to promote the common good of the Indian people by preserving the rights, laws, and liberties which their natural original sovereign would have supported. In practice, India was subject to the tyranny of the East India Company, which 'in Asia is a state in the disguise of a merchant. Its whole service is a system of public offices in the disguise of a counting-house' (Burke 1987: vol. ii. 23). As early as 1783 Burke highlighted the gross injustices perpetrated in India in the name of the British state (Burke 1999*a*: vol. iv. 124).

Burke was a firm believer in a benevolent form of colonialism in which the colonizer had a duty to assist those peoples in its charge to attain political and social maturation. It was a duty that extended to the emancipation of slaves. As in everything, including his definition of beauty, there should be no sharp sudden change in direction. It was not something that could be brought about by the application of abstract principles. It was to be a gradual process in which the welfare of the slave as well as the interests of the owners and traders, both black and white, were to be accommodated. Burke wrote his 'Sketch of the Negro Code' in 1780 (Burke 1999*b*), some seven years before the foundation of the Abolition Society in England by William Wilberforce and Thomas Clarkson. Matters in America, however, distracted both him and his Parliamentary colleagues for almost a decade. He returned to the question in 1788 when he argued strongly that the trade should be totally abolished. He recognized, nevertheless, that this was unlikely and advocated regulation.

In a letter dated April 9, 1792, to Henry Dundas, the Home Secretary to William Pitt the Younger's government, in response to a request for a copy of his 'Negro Code', Burke made it clear that he thought the trade evil, but that its complete and sudden abolition would simply drive the trade under ground. It was instead to be regulated with a view to abolition. He advocated the reduction of a great evil into a smaller one with the eventual achievement of good. The process was to be an integrated one that aimed at the abolition of slavery in the West Indies 'with regard to its supply from the Coast of Africa' (Burke 1999*b*: 257). What

Burke presents in his 'Negro Code' is a system of duties, obligations, rights, and protections designed to improve the condition of blacks. The rights are not based on abstract universal principles, but clearly derived from those of an Englishman. This entailed regulation by authorized inspection of the quality of ships used in the trade; the manner, place, and conditions of the trade; the treatment of blacks *en route* to the West Indies; and, the proper government protection of them in the colonies and plantations of the West Indies. There were to be designated marts on the Coast of Africa with officials unconnected with the slave trade who were to ensure the welfare and safety of the blacks destined for slavery, and alternative occupations for the black traders that 'may tend to civilizing them', many of whom were to be apprenticed into trades 'more advantageous and honourable to all parties' (Burke 1999*b*: 263). There were to be strict criteria of sale enforced by government inspectors, such as the prohibition on the sale of those who are 'able to read in the Arabian or any other book' (Burke 1999*b*: 267). Signs of civilization, then, exempted those who exhibited them. There was also to be basic health care provision, both on land and on board ship, and protections for women against both officers and sailors in the form of monetary deterrents for would-be abusers. The passage was to be made more congenial by the receipt of a small gift, and the provision of musical instruments native to their homelands. Individuals and families were to have legally enforceable rights. No woman, for example, should be obliged to do any heavy work for one month before and six weeks after the delivery of her baby. Owners had the duty to provide, and slaves the right to receive, instruction in the Christian religion. Furthermore, work would cease at 11.00 a.m. on a Saturday until the normal working hour on a Monday.

The fact that the slave trade and slave ownership had long been practiced did not, on that account, give prescriptive rights to the practitioners. To deny blacks any rights or freedoms was to deny them the possibility of being inducted into the civilizing process, and to integrate them into aspects of English society, wherever that society may geographically be located. Colonialism entailed for Burke the imposition of obligations and the enjoyment of rights for mutual benefit.

His friend, the liberal Whig Charles Fox, could not condone what he took to be complicity in the crime. You cannot, he believed, regulate robbery and murder. The last motion that Fox successfully introduced in the House of Commons on 10th June, 1806, passed by an overwhelming majority of 114 to 15, was to abolish slavery (Fletcher 1933: 422 and 424).

A much more pernicious form of racism than the ideas associated with degeneracy related to a set of beliefs known as 'polygenesis'. This theory was often associated with atheism because it denied the 'monogenism' of all races being descended from the same genesis of Adam and Eve (Garrett 2004: 132–3). This denies that man has a common ancestry and contends that each race constitutes a different species. Thomas Jefferson, an advocate of natural rights, and David Hume, an opponent, both epitomizing the rationalism of the Enlightenment, entertained the belief in polygenesis. If the inferiority of the blacks was congenital, then it was difficult to determine what factors may be responsible for it other than distinct and separate heredity. Neither conclusively threw his weight behind this doctrine, nor did either offer an outright denial of it. In 1781 Thomas Jefferson wrote his *Notes on the State of Virginia*, which he revised in 1782. In it he put forward the tentative hypothesis 'that blacks, whether originally a distinct race, or made distinct by time and circumstances, are inferior to whites in the endowments both of body and mind' (Jefferson 1964: [132–8]).

About a century before Lincoln sought to abolish slavery in the United States Paine had tried to insert a clause for abolition in the Constitution. As a member of the first anti-slavery society established in America Paine wrote 'African Slavery in America' in 1775, in which he called upon his new compatriots to repudiate and condemn the evil practice in the name of 'justice and humanity' (Paine 1987: 56). Appealing to reason and innate sympathy Paine condemns the traders of slaves for turning their backs on these principles, sacrificing conscience and integrity of character to 'that golden idol' (Paine 1987: 52). In full rhetorical flourish Paine asserts, 'Most shocking of all is alleging the sacred scriptures to favour wicked practices. One would have thought none but infidel cavillers would endeavour to make them appear contrary to the plain dictates of natural light, and conscience, in a matter of common justice and humanity; which they cannot be' (Paine 1987: 53). Africans cannot be accused of forfeiting their freedom, 'they still have natural perfect right to it' (Paine 1987: 54).

After being partially responsible for persuading Jefferson to purchase Louisiana, and suggesting to him that it was the ideal opportunity to redeem America's sins by outlawing slavery there and granting freed slaves parcels of land, Paine was bitterly disappointed that Jefferson gave in to the sugar interests, in the same way that he had supported tobacco interests in his native Virginia. Both industries were labour intensive and relied upon a cheap underclass. Jefferson, a champion of natural rights, and America's third President, although opposed to slavery in principle, was himself an owner of human property. Despite doing much to outlaw the slave trade, including sending the American fleet to the Mediterranean to suppress the slave trade conducted by the Islamic regimes of North Africa, he was opposed to emancipation. He supported manumission, which meant that slaves who were freed would not be allowed to settle in America, but instead were to be sent back to Africa, or to colonies in the Caribbean. Part of the reason for this was that Jefferson feared slave revenge against their enslavers (Hitchens 2007). He was probably aware of the numerous slave revolts and uprisings between 1711 and 1777 in such places as Brazil, Suriname, Haiti, St. John, Tobago, St. Kitts, Montserrat, and Jamaica (Morton 2002: 3).

The Founding Fathers did not advocate immediate emancipation for a variety of reasons. The first was their primary commitment to create and sustain a republic. Second, they viewed slavery as a form of property which was therefore protected by the Constitution. It was this failure in natural rights doctrines to distinguish between human and property rights that constituted an insurmountable barrier. And, third, they were prejudiced by their undeniable belief in racial superiority (Diggins 1976: 216 and 222). Jefferson, while believing that blacks possess a moral sense, was of the opinion that they were inferior in both body and mind. Enslavement, he repeatedly acknowledged, violated their natural rights. While reciprocity of recognition is absent, might replaces right as the basis of justice. Like many other Europeans he was inherently uncomfortable about treating American Indians as they would blacks. While vehemently opposed to intermarriage between blacks and whites, because blacks were congenitally ugly, and would bring down the average intelligence, he thought the offspring of whites and Indians perhaps enhanced the looks of both, and did not detract from the overall level of intelligence because Indians were equal in both body and mind (Griswold 1992: 198).

Jefferson owned hundreds of slaves on his estate, and came up with all sorts of excuses why they should not be freed. He thought emancipation neither in the interests of the slave-owners, nor the slaves, because of the continuing prejudices of the whites, seething resentment by the blacks of the whites, and numerous other conditions that would lead to the extermination of one race by the other. Because he believed in repatriation, the abolition of slavery was not an immediate prospect (Griswold 1992: 180, 190, and 196).

Some years earlier, in 1753 and five years after its original publication, Hume added a footnote to his 'Of National Character' for which he has been accused of subscribing to the theory of polygenesis, and for providing ammunition for defenders of slavery (Immerwahr 1992: 482). This is surprising, of course, given that his view of a universal human nature implies no such difference. He maintains that, 'It is universally acknowledged that there is a great uniformity among the actions of men, in all nations and ages, and that human nature remains still the same, in its principles and operations' (Hume 2004: Section VIII, part I, 65).

Hume's attitude towards blacks is evidence of how pernicious and endemic racism was becoming in the eighteenth century. He is, as Richard Popkin has suggested, the least likely you would expect to hold such views, given that Hume is regarded with some justification 'one of the gentlest and most benign critics of superstition and prejudice during the Enlightenment' (Popkin 1977: 211). Hume contended that, 'I am apt to suspect the negroes and in general all other species of men (for there are four or five different kinds) to be naturally inferior to the whites. There never was a civilized nation of any other complexion than white, nor even any individual eminent in action or speculation' (Hume 1964: vol. III, 253).

James Beattie, a contemporary critic, friend of William Wilberforce and follower of Montesquieu, took Hume to task on the grounds that he seemed to be perilously close to arguing something like Aristotle's case for natural slavery. Beattie, while not disagreeing with the general view that non-white savages are lower on the scale of civilization than whites, contended that two thousand years ago the inhabitants of Britain and France were just as savage. Civilization, he contended, is a thing of time, not of race. Furthermore, Beattie contested Hume's assertion that 'there *never was*' (Beattie's italics, Beattie 1770: 479) a civilization other than white, who scaled the heights of higher learning.

Like Las Casas against Sepulvéda, Beattie protests the sophistication of the American Indians, particularly Peruvians and Mexicans. Unlike Las Casas, he also indicates that, despite their condition of slavery, 'negroes have often discovered symptoms of ingenuity' (Beattie 1770: 481). He maintains that it is unreasonable, given the deprivation to which Negroes are subject, to expect signs of genius in those who live among us. Furthermore, he warns against using European standards to judge those of other civilizations. An account of our notorious practitioners of duelling, gambling and adultery, to name but a few, 'would exhibit specimens of brutish barbarity and sottish infatuation, such as might vie with any that ever appeared in Kamschatka, California, or the land of the Hottentots' (Beattie 1770: 484).

It may have been in response to these criticisms that Hume revised the footnote for the edition of his *Essays* that was to be published posthumously in 1777 (Immerwahr 1992: 484). Popkin is unaware of this change, when he accuses Hume of ignoring the empirical evidence that was readily available to him and of never having revised his views (Popkin 1992: 64–75). In the last edition to appear in Hume's lifetime he already appears to take on board some of the criticism that was becoming widespread. Instead of suggesting that there *never* was an example of significant achievement, that is of a non-white civilization, he contends that there is *scarcely* an example of a civilization or an individual of black complexion who achieved anything of practical or intellectual significance (Hume 1994: 86 fn. f), thus acknowledging that there may be isolated incidents, without retracting the polygenetic implications of his remarks.

Hume asks the question whether the differences between blacks and whites may be attributed to such things as climate, a view to which Montesquieu subscribed, or whether there is something more fundamental that prevents them from advancing, as Europeans have done, from barbarism to civilization. Hume contends that the character of a nation very much depends on moral causes. These he says are the circumstances that stimulate motives and reasons in men's minds, such as the government under which they live, their economic condition, and the condition of the nation in relation to its neighbours. It is these factors, rather than climatic and geographical variation which characterizes much of Montequieu's explanation, that facilitate progress of human beings from a condition of barbarity to civility (see Popkin 1977: 217).

Blacks – in the first version it was all non-whites – have not been provided by nature with the necessary mental and spiritual capacities to develop in the same way as Europeans. Indeed, so lacking in these capacities are they that they are easily corruptible and will sell their parents, wives or mistresses in exchange for strong drink (Hume 1994: 91). Hume contended that 'Such a uniform and constant difference could not happen, in so many countries and ages, if nature had not made an original distinction between these breeds of men' (Hume 1994: 86 fn. f; cf. Morton 2002: 9).

The changes Hume made to the footnote that appears in the posthumously published edition of 1777 concede much more. He eliminates any suspicion that he might subscribe to the doctrine of polygenesis.

I am apt to suspect the negroes to be naturally inferior to the whites. There scarcely ever was a civilized nation of that complexion, nor even any individual eminent either in action or speculation. No ingenious manufactures amongst them, no arts, no sciences. On the other hand, the most rude and barbarous of the whites, such as the ancient GERMANS, the present TARTARS, have still something eminent about them, in their valour, form of government, or some other particular. Such a uniform and constant difference could not happen, in so many countries and ages, if nature had not made an original distinction between these breeds of men. Not to mention our colonies, there are NEGROE slaves dispersed all over EUROPE, of whom none ever discovered any symptoms of ingenuity; though low people, without education, will start up amongst us, and distinguish themselves in every profession. In JAMAICA, indeed, they talk of one negroe as a man of parts and learning; but it is likely he is admired for slender accomplishments, like a parrot, who speaks a few words plainly. (Hume 1987: 629 fn. 10)

Hume appears, implicitly, to accept the widely held view that American Indians were redeemable, and therefore he partially concedes the empirical evidence offered by Beattie and others. While previously casting aspersions on all non-white peoples, he now singles-out only the blacks as 'naturally inferior', while holding out the possibility of rare examples of achievement among them.

Hume's epistemological principles do not support the views expressed in his infamous footnote (Popkin 1992: 64), but the views expressed in it cannot be dismissed as a careless indiscretion. While there is no evidence to suggest that he was an advocate for slavery or the slave trade, Hume was the principal living philosopher invoked by pro-slavery supporters to prove that blacks were naturally inferior (Jordan 1968: 305–307), and when he did revise his footnote to take account of some of the empirical evidence that refuted his general contention, he still perpetuated the racial inferiority claim in relation to blacks. One has to conclude that he took a considered stance on the issue, and in doing so he was one of the first to link inferiority with colour.

Hume died in 1776, thirteen years before the French Revolution which produced the second of the great declarations of rights. The French National Assembly in 1789 'set forth in a solemn declaration...natural, imprescriptible, and inalienable rights' among which were the right to liberty, property, security, and resistance of oppression (Melden 1970: 140). The French Revolutionaries were as equivocal and ambivalent on the issues of slaves, and the rights of free blacks as were the Americans. The majority of deputies were apprehensive about the economic consequences for France and its colonies of the abolition of the slave trade, or of slavery. In the face of such strong slave-owning and ship-owning interests the issue of the abolition of slavery was only tentatively proposed. It was not only whites, but also freed blacks and mulattoes, who owned slaves and did not wish to be deprived of their property. The most prosperous of French colonies, Saint Dominique, modern Haiti, had 465, 000 slaves, 30,000 whites, and 27,000 freed blacks and mulattoes, whose rights were greater than the slaves', but less than the whites'. They owned a third of plantation property and a quarter of the slaves on Saint Dominique. Both white and mulatto planters despatched delegates to France to plead for representation in the Assembly, and to protect their slave-owning interests. The Revolution itself set a precedent, or provided an exemplar of the overthrow of oppression and the attainment of freedom, which blacks in the colonies applauded.

We have three sets of interests, then, in tension with each other. The whites who wanted to withhold full rights from freed slaves and mulattoes; the freed blacks and mulattoes who wanted the same rights as whites, but opposed emancipation; and black slaves, who demanded their freedom. The colonial committee of the National Assembly agreed in March 1790 to exempt the colonies from the Constitution, failing to extend rights to freed slaves, and remaining silent on the issue of emancipation. The mulattoes of Saint Dominique rebelled and were defeated. Its leaders, among them Vincent Ogé a free mulatto, who was among the delegation in Paris in 1789, were executed (Schama 2005: 305–6). The pressure intensified on the National Assembly and it made a concession to grant political rights to blacks and mulattoes born of free parents, which amounted to no more than 350 out of the 27,000 on Saint Dominique. Despite the small numbers involved the whites threatened to resist the implementation of the law, and successfully pressed for rescinding the rights in September 1791. Meanwhile the blacks began an uprising against their masters, and the mulattoes took up arms against the whites. The Legislative Assembly which replaced the National Assembly considered the issue again in 1792. Armand Guy Kersaint, himself a former slave-owner and with interests still in the colonies, proposed a transition that would lead to emancipation (Hunt 1996: 112–5). The Assembly decided to reinstate the rights, but remained silent on the issue of slavery.

French agents were sent to Saint Dominique to quell the black rebellion that was gaining ground, and amid fears that the rebels would assist Britain and Spain in an invasion of the colony, the agents abolished slavery in the colony. In opposition to protests from some white and mulatto slave owners, the National Convention, at first angry at the sudden emancipation of slaves, decided on the representations of a free black, a white, and a mulatto who explained the situation in Saint Dominique, to abolish slavery in all the French colonies on 4 February, 1794. All men residing in the colonies without distinction of colour were to enjoy the rights of French citizenship (Hunt 1996: 116). Practically, however, the reality was very different. In some colonies the decree was disregarded, while in others slavery was simply converted into forced labour. In 1802 Bonaparte reinstituted slavery and the slave trade, and rescinded the rights of free blacks. The former slaves of San Dominique resumed their struggle, and in 1804 established the independent republic of Haiti (Hunt 1996: 26).

Slavery still persists, even though it is now legally outlawed throughout the world. The League of Nations 'Slavery Convention' that came into force on 9th March, 1927, amended by the United Nations protocol which came into force on 7th December, 1953, obliged the signatories to take the necessary steps to abolish and outlaw both the slave trade and slavery. The 1957 'Supplementary Convention on the Abolition of Slavery, the Slave Trade, and Institutions and Practices Similar to Slavery' acknowledged that progress had been made since the 1927 Convention, but that the practice, and slave-like practices still persisted.

Signatories were charged with bringing about the end of enforced child labour, debt bondage, servitude, and practices of forced marriage, the transfer of a wife to another for payment, and the inheritance of a woman by another person on the death of her husband. On 25 July 1951, the 'Convention for the Suppression of the Traffic in Persons and of the Exploitation of the Prostitution of Others' sought to consolidate the array of agreements already in existence in order to reinforce its determination to eradicate the trafficking of people for slavery or sexual exploitation.

New slavery flourishes, but differs in many respects from that which prevailed prior to 'abolition'. Slaves in the eighteenth and nineteenth centuries were expensive. It was difficult to capture a slave and then transport him or her to the US. An average slave in the American South in 1850 would cost the equivalent of £20,000 on today's prices. Modern slavery revolves around economic and social vulnerability, rather than race or ethnic background. Millions of people around the world find themselves vulnerable and potential victims of slavery or enforced labour. The 'supply' of potential slaves makes them cheaper today than they have ever been. A slave in modern society costs an average of £50. Slaves are no longer a relatively major investment and the economic incentive for maintaining their health and strength is no longer at a premium. Sickness, injury, ageing, or simply becoming a nuisance to the slave owner are motivations for dumping or killing them. Ownership itself can be an inconvenience for most slave-holders. They already control the individual's labour and profits. Profits are of more significance than whether the holder and slave are of different ethnic backgrounds. In modern slavery skin colour is trumped by profit. It has been estimated that between 800,000 and 900,000 people a year are trafficked in what has been called 'The New Global Slave Trade', many of them women and young girls sold into prostitution in what is a multi-billion dollar criminally organized systematic disregard for human rights (Koh 2006: 235–6).

CONCLUSION

Advocates and critics of universal rights could not be lined-up uniformly into the pro- and anti-slavery camps, respectively. Indeed, many champions of universal rights, made them conditional. Indians, and especially blacks, were deemed by many not to meet these conditions. While subscription to Aristotle's belief in natural slavery surfaces from time to time, it was in general rejected. A commitment to the inferiority of non-whites on the grounds that they occupied a low level of civilization, or were even congenitally inferior, did not necessarily mean that the exponents of such ideas subscribed to slavery. It was quite common, however, to accept the second of Aristotle's justifications for slavery, that is, through conquest and the sparing of one's life in return for servitude. During the seventeenth and eighteenth centuries this was not on the whole regarded as an appropriate practice, among the civilized nations of Europe, but because of the occupation of different levels of civilization between Europeans and non-whites, enslavement of American Indians, and especially blacks was perfectly justifiable to many, with the exception of more enlightened philosophers such as Beattie, Montesquieu, Rousseau, and Burke. Even the authors of the two great documents of natural rights, the American and the French, were extremely reluctant to abolish slavery and the slave trade, and recognize Negroes as equal in their right holding capacity.

8

Nonsense Upon Stilts? Tocqueville, Idealism, and the Expansion of the Moral Community

> ... it is almost an axiom of popular Ethics that there is at least a potential duty of every man to every man – a duty which becomes actual as soon as one comes to have any dealing with the other (Green 1899: §206, p. 245).

In this chapter, I want to show how the natural law and natural rights traditions ceased to be compelling, and how philosophically they were bankrupt by the latter part of the nineteenth century. Among political polemicists, however, an appeal to natural rights remained rhetorically effective on all sides of the political spectrum. Tocqueville had emphasized, following in the footsteps of Burke, that fundamental rights had to emerge from and be embedded in a moral community in order to take root and flourish. For Burke, Bentham, and Marx it was the rights of man declared in the French revolution that provided the occasion and the focus of their attacks.

They did not subscribe to the idea of an original contract that established governments to protect pre-existing rights. The social contract was a fiction, and even if there was an agreement among individuals in a state of nature it could have no obligatory force. As Bentham maintained, contract is the creation of law, and not law of contract (Bentham 1988: chapter I, 'The Formation of Governments'). Natural rights are criticized for being abstractions. Without governments there could be no rights; no property because there would be no legal security to protect it. In what is now a famous dismissal of the doctrine Bentham says: 'Natural Rights is simply nonsense – nonsense upon stilts' (Bentham in Melden 1970: 32). The Marxist critique of natural rights maintains that the language is individualist, and that it defends the position of particular interests. It had its historical role in the eighteenth century in freeing individuals from the residue of feudal society, but the purpose it served in the nineteenth century, according to Marx, was to consolidate and make acceptable an unequal distribution of property within society. More recently, Michael Oakeshott, taking his inspiration from both Burke and the British Idealists maintains that natural rights are the product of 'rationalist' thinking, which is ill-conceived and logically flawed. The British Idealists, taking their inspiration from Hegel, were critical of traditional conceptions of natural rights, but nevertheless argued that there were some rights so fundamental to particular societies that they functioned as, or may just as well be called, natural rights.

BENTHAM AND MARX

Bentham and Marx offer what may be described as cosmopolitan critiques of the universalist doctrine of natural rights, while Hegel enters the fray from a communitarian or particularist perspective (Brown 1992: 23–81). To some extent these categories are misleading. Both Hegel and Marx exhibit both universal and cosmopolitan tendencies. Hegel's constitutive theory of the self is posited in the context of a universal reason manifesting itself in time as the gradual revelation of freedom. Marx's universalism in which capitalism is transformed into communism and man's species being ceases to be alienated and is freely able to express itself, is tempered by his constitutive theory of the self. Like Hegel, he believes that every man is a child of his times, a reflection of the mode of production within which he toils. Human nature develops over time, and becomes free only under communism which dissolves the artificial boundaries that divide humanity, including the institutions of the state (Boucher 2000a: 217–39). For our purposes here, the categories of particularism and universalism are useful because they identify a scale of forms in which the variable, humanity, is identical with the generic essence. Particularism is a certain way of conceptualizing humanity, and universalism another. There are issues, of course, about at what point the scale starts, as we saw in our discussion of cultural encounters and in racism and slavery, that is, such questions as: are certain things that resemble humans, humans at all. When something is identified as embodying the generic essence of humanity, to whatever degree, it appears on the scale. Particularism and universalism differ in the kind of way they conceptualize humanity, and also in the degree to which they see humanity as one, but they are not absolute opposites. Each specification is at once a difference in degree and in kind of the idea of humanity. There is no point on the scale at which humanity is completely absent, that is, absolute zero, nor at which it is completely manifest, absolute infinity. So in other words, there is no absolute opposition between particularism and universalism. And there is no point on the scale at which the absolute opposite of humanity, that is, the denial of elements of universalism, is absent. However, within the scale, because each specification is distinct, it is relatively opposed to the others beyond it. The scale starts, then, not at zero, but at unity in which a minimal degree of the idea of humanity is present (Collingwood 2005b: 55–91).

The point is this: what is important is not the question of particularism versus universalism, but from where on the scale does a thinker begin, and to what extent does he or she envisage the idea of humanity already manifest, or in the process of being manifest. Here we need to differentiate between the view that a thinker takes of things as they currently stand, and things as they may yet become. The British Idealists have frequently been criticized for being 'Realists' in international relations. They are accused of making rights community-dependent and of privileging the state above the individual. Such a view misunderstands the extent to which qualification as a state entails embracing certain principles and values which maintain a system of rights conducive to the promotion of the common good. Rights, then, are dependent upon a moral community. None of the British Idealists imagined that the moral community was bounded completely by the state. They differ in the degree to which they thought that the wider moral community was already manifest, but not in the belief that it had the potential to encompass wider and wider domains, until such time as everyone is considered to be one's neighbour. To this extent they could, as indeed Leonard Hobhouse and John Hobson did, despite misunderstandings to the contrary, advocate the right sort of imperialism, that is, the sort that respected local traditions, but which nevertheless promoted the civilizing and self-realization processes.

Bentham's *Anarchical Fallacies* is a systematic critique of the various declarations and proposals for bills of rights produced by the French National Assembly between 1789 and 1795. Bentham's tone and manner is typical of the genre of 'candour', to which both Burke and Wollstonecraft subscribed. With reference to Article I of the Declaration of Rights, Bentham retorts, with a vehemence characteristic of this 'candour': 'All men born free? Absurd and miserable nonsense' (Waldron ed., 1987: 50). With reference to the constitution, he fulminates: 'what execrable trash the choicest talents of the French nation have produced' (Waldron ed., 1987: 66).

Bentham's criticisms of natural rights doctrines do not take issue with the method of some of its most able exponents. Political theory could still proceed along the same structural lines. It had to start from first principles. From the starting point of the basic characteristics of humankind political principles could be deduced. For Bentham, however, the initial postulates are not the possession of inalienable natural rights, but the identification of indubitable inclinations – the propensity to pursue pleasure and avoid pain. Bentham argues that the greatest happiness of the greatest number is the standard by which to judge right and wrong (Bentham 1988: 3). He was not concerned with what current law is, but with what it ought to be.

Natural rights theories entailed abstractions, discovered by introspection, and universalized as essential features of humanity. To substitute empirical springs of action, the desire for pleasure and aversion to pain, was the basis of utilitarianism and grounded morality and politics in the actual wants of individuals, and not on their abstract natural rights. Both doctrines are universal in that they postulate universal characteristics, the one claims to be based on empirical reality, the other upon metaphysical inalienable attributes.

Bentham's starting point is the contention that nature has put men under the sovereign directive of pain and pleasure, and that any ethical theory has to have these as its primary reference points. The measure of pleasure and pain is utility, and law can be evaluated on the basis of its contribution to the greatest happiness of the greatest number. The public good could be reduced to the experiences of pleasure and pain of each individual. Rights, for Bentham, are not 'natural', they are the creation of law. Rights and law are correlative. Natural rights stand opposed to law, they are invoked to resist law and to undermine it. Just as scissors were designed to cut cloth, natural rights were designed to 'cut up law, and legal rights' (Waldron ed., 1987: 73). Natural rights and natural law were dangerous doctrines when invoked to be the standard by which human positive law was to be judged. Such ideas were an incitement to rebellion. Bentham objects to their radicalness and subversiveness, and denies that governments were ever instituted to protect them. They are, for him, as they were for Burke, 'mischievous nonsense' (Waldron ed., 1987: 53). Bentham argues that:

... there be scarce any law whatever but what those who have not liked it have found, on some account or another, to be repugnant to some text of scripture; I see no remedy but that the natural tendency of such doctrines is to impel a man, by the force of conscience, to rise up in arms against any law whatever that he happens not to like. What sort of government it is that can consist with such a disposition (Bentham 1988: 95–6).

Rights and duties, for Bentham, were not tangible, their use in argument was merely rhetorical, and dangerously so at that. Concepts had to be experienced and be verifiable. Law, sovereignty, and punishment (or sanction) were part of our lived experience and could readily be equated with commands, commanders and the purposive administering of pain. The vocabulary of rights and duties, in order to make any sense, had to be translated into the language of laws, sovereign authority, and sanctions. Natural rights and natural duties were complete nonsense unless they made reference to the commands of a divine sovereign. Grotius and Pufendorf, as I contended, did, of course, attribute the efficacy of natural law to God the law-maker, but Bentham contends, wrongly on my view, that these 'quiet' and 'dull' men (Waldron ed., 1987: 75), as well as the Enlightenment revolutionaries were reticent to make such an association, and denied the divinity of natural rights. Although, as we have seen, this is not an altogether accurate view, the main thrust of Bentham's criticism is directed against the descriptive strand of natural rights, and he has in mind the architects of the French, and to a lesser extent the American declarations of Rights. It is perfectly intelligible, Bentham argues in 'Supply Without Burthen or Escheat *Vice* Taxation', to talk of divine law giving rise to a divine right, just as human political laws generate political human rights. Because such a law cannot be proved, however, it is nothing less than useless (Waldron ed., 1987: 73). He claims that the revolutionaries deny a divine law giver, the sovereign authority that could give meaning and sanction to such notions of natural rights. Where do these rights come from, he asks, 'made by what? Not by God – they allow of none, but by their Goddess, Nature' (Waldron ed., 1987: 55). To write the law giver out of the picture, is to erase the law. Rights and duties without law and without a sovereign to enforce them are nonsensical. This is what Bentham means when he contends that '*Natural Rights* is simple nonsense: natural and imprescriptible rights, rhetorical nonsense, – nonsense upon stilts' (Waldron ed., 1987: 53).

There is a standard Marxian critique of natural rights based on the individualist assumptions that underpin them, and upon which capitalist society depends. Natural rights are bourgeois in both form and content. Natural rights, such as those to property, liberty, and personal security reflect the interests of the bourgeoisie. Their form is individualistic. They are the negative rights which allow capitalists to pursue their interests free of social constraints, free of considerations of social welfare or of social justice (Waldron 1987: 126). Natural rights are, in effect, special rights, reflecting the interests of one class of people, masquerading as universal. They are rights which are justified by and necessary to a certain phase in history, namely the capitalist mode of production, and were required to emancipate individuals from the bonds of feudalism. As Waldron suggests, these rights are constitutive of the mentality required for a capitalist economy driven by the profit motive.

The rights of man, Marx contends, are an invention of the eighteenth century, discovered by the North Americans and the French. Among them is the freedom of conscience, the natural right to worship the deity of one's choice (Marx 1978: 41). The so-called rights of man, Marx contends are not differentiated from those of the citizen. Those to life, liberty, and security, posit an egoistic man as a member of civil society, 'an individual separated from the community, withdrawn into himself, wholly preoccupied with his private interest and acting in accordance with his private caprice' (Marx 1978: 43). Marx argues that the rights of man are based upon a limited conception of human nature and of the relations of one man to another. They emphasize the egoistic person, natural necessity, private interests and desires, and the protection of property. The right to security, for example, does not raise civil society above egoism, but instead is the guarantee of egoism.

The person is not being considered as a species being fulfilled in society. Society is viewed as alien to the individual, a constraint and limitation on the original independence of the person. The rights of man posit a perverted self. The citizen is degraded to the status of a partial being, the servant of his ego. Bourgeois man is portrayed as 'the *true* and *authentic* man' (Marx 1978: 43).

THE I IN THE THOU

Burke in rejecting natural rights as metaphysical nonsense, pointed the way, as Rousseau also did, to a way of thinking about rights as immanent in society's social life and practices, and which emerge or arise in contexts of growing familiarization and sympathy, requiring constraints that are not merely abstract and divorced from the reality to which they are meant to apply, but also not completely subjective and harnessed to capricious self-interested whims. The justification of rights must be the contribution they make to the common good, or civility of the community in which they emerge.

In discussing the influence of democracy upon manners Alexis de Tocqueville (1805–1859) gives an account of this very process in which mutual rights and obligations, what he calls a mildness of manners, emerge not by civilization and education but are the result of 'equality of conditions' (Tocqueville 1976: 166). Equality of conditions was for him a general conception, or generative fact, that had considerable explanatory value (Wolin 2001: 143–5). Indeed, as far as he was concerned there was scarce a significant event of the previous seven hundred years that had not contributed in some way to the attainment of such equality (see Zunz and Kahan 2002: 66).

Before we can feel sympathy and empathy for others we must recognize something of ourselves in them. Authors are able powerfully to capture the imagination and sympathy of a reader by anthropomorphically portraying the predicament of animals. Tocqueville argues that the same is true of stimulating our understanding and sympathies for others. The more we see them like us, the less we are inclined to disregard their humanity. In an Aristocratic society each class or caste, has its own modes of living, with associated feelings, rights, customs, and opinions. There is little in common between the aristocracy and the mass of people who inhabit the same society, but who think and feel differently from them. The aristocracy look upon the common people with incomprehension, unable to judge their feelings and scarcely able to believe that they belong to the same race. They are nevertheless in close proximity and extend to each other mutual assistance. Even though people of the same society are radically differentiated they were bound to each other through mutual and close political ties. Serfs had an interest in serving the nobles, and nobles reciprocated by feeling honour bound to defend those who resided on their lands. Tocqueville makes it clear that 'It is evident that these mutual obligations did not originate in the law of nature, but in the law of society; and that the claim of social duty was more stringent than that of mere humanity' (Tocqueville 1976, 163; cf. Boucher 2000*b*: 326–7).

The feudal relationship did not, however, foster a common sympathy, nor did it lessen the harshness of manners and customs, despite giving rise to a greater generosity. The aristocracy acknowledged no one as being like themselves save their own kind. They were in their chronicles able to express genuine, abundant, and evident grief on the death of a fellow nobleman, but in relating the massacre of common people, because they were uninterested in their fate, were unable to express the merest hint of sadness at the sufferings of the poor classes.

Tocqueville suggests that insensitivity between the classes was mutual. There were, of course, many cases of self-devotion by a vassal to a lord, but there were also abundant instances of brutal atrocities. Even though public order and education improved, as long as society remained aristocratic mutual insensibility remained undiminished. As evidence for his contention Tocqueville refers to the punishments, including hanging, drawing, and quartering following a revolt by the lower orders in Brittany against the imposition of a tax in 1675. He cites a letter from Madame de Sévigné which comments with jocularity and complete detachment on the severity of the punishments. She casually remarks that an example has been set that will teach others elsewhere to have respect for authority. Tocqueville remarks that Madame de Sévigné was not an insensitive, cruel, or unkind woman. She was the model of kindness to her servants and family, but was nevertheless completely incapable of comprehending the suffering of 'anyone who was not a person of quality' (Tocqueville 1976: 165). In his own day, Tocqueville observed, circumstances are different, not because men had become more sensitive than their predecessors, but instead because their sensibility had extended to a wider frame of reference. The reason, he claims, is evidently because of a greater degree of equality among the different ranks in society. He contends that:

When all ranks of a community are nearly equal, as all men think and feel in nearly the same manner, each of them may judge in a moment of the sensations of all the others; he casts a rapid glance upon himself, and that is enough. There is no wretchedness into which he cannot readily enter, and a secret instinct reveals to him its extent. It signifies not that strangers or foes are sufferers; imagination puts him in their place; something like a personal feeling is mingled with his pity and makes himself suffer while the body of his fellow creature is in torture (Tocqueville 1976: 166).

This is nowhere more evident, Tocqueville argues, than in America. Even there, however, the inequality between blacks and whites, slaves and freemen, confirms his theory. Slaves are denied the recognition of equal status and continue to be treated inhumanely despite advances in civilization and education. The conclusion that one has to draw, Tocqueville maintains, is that it is 'equality of conditions' that give rise to milder manners, and 'in proportion as nations become more like each other, they become reciprocally more compassionate, and the Law of Nations is mitigated' (Tocqueville 1976: 166).

In addressing the issues concerning reciprocal respect and compassion among peoples of a nation, and between peoples of different nations, Tocqueville does not base his conclusions on universal principles rooted in human nature or natural law. He suggests instead that civility is first practiced among one's own kind, and is extended to others within one's own polity only in so far as we incorporate the excluded classes into our own moral communities. It is not a question of the denial of human rights, but one of who is to be counted as a human, or at least fully human in the relevant respects, and deserving of inclusion and recognition. Tocqueville holds out the hope that from the exemplar of particular instances of civility, or mildness of manners, gradually nations will come to respect each other and inhabit the same universal moral community.

HEGEL AND THE BRITISH IDEALISTS

The British Idealists were among the severest critics of natural rights traditionally conceived, yet they were prepared to acknowledge that there are fundamental rights to which we may usefully give this label. Before discussing their ideas it is necessary to examine briefly the philosophical source of their general outlook and attitude to natural law and natural rights in their traditional forms.

G. W. F. Hegel (1770–1831) was a critic of a variety of social contract theories, including that integral to the idea of natural rights. The state is not a voluntary association, and it is a mistake to conceive of it as the product of an agreement for mutual advantage, based upon the presuppositions of the sphere of private property (Haddock 1994: 149). Hegel divides natural law theorizing into empirical or naturalistic, and formal or universalistic methods of enquiry. The empirical type, exemplified by Hobbes, takes natural instincts, passions, and desires as the basis of rights. Nature, or man in a pre-political condition, is understood to be the foundation of rights. These so called rights are more prudential imperatives. The formalistic methods of enquiry, exemplified by Kant, derive rights from abstract principles, which turn out to be incapable of generating moral content. In Hegel's view, both methods are deficient.

In distinguishing the accidental from the necessary features of existence the empirical, or naturalistic, method lacks a criterion. From the multiplicity of factors that compose a complex social situation, fundamental principles are arbitrarily abstracted, and projected back into the chaotic world of an original condition or position. This original position is stripped of its social complexity, and those features arbitrarily abstracted are designated the true causes of human behaviour. The guiding principle of such a method must be to retain just so much as is necessary to be able to account for certain features of modern society. What we want to justify in a contemporaneous institution simply requires the intrusion of an abstracted appropriate quality or capacity into the original condition, which can then be used to generate and justify what we set out to demonstrate in the first place. What is absent, however, is a unifying principle. All of the elements that co-exist, and which are deemed superfluous in relation to the arbitrarily designated fundamental principles, can with equal veracity present themselves as viable alternatives to the designated idealized crucial or essential elements (Hegel 1975: 58–65).

The empirical method was employed, for example, by Thucydides, Machiavelli, and Hobbes. They all selected and elevated aspects of experience to the status of fundamental principles to explain or justify an existing condition. Hegel is not, however, completely dismissive of the method. In its emphasis upon experience, empiricism contains much that is positive. Like philosophy proper, it is concerned with what is, and not with what ought to be. Empiricism contains within itself, in Hegel's view, the crucial principle of freedom; 'namely, that what ought to count in our human knowing, we ought to see *for ourselves*, and to know *ourselves* as *present* in it.' (Hegel 1991a: §38). One of the great merits of Hobbes was that he 'tried to trace the social union, the nature of state power, back to principles which lie in ourselves, which we recognise as our own' (cited in Riedel 1971: 98). Like Burke, Hegel appreciated the value of a method which obstinately opposed any 'artificial framework of principles' (Hegel 1975: 69). Empiricism could justifiably reproach abstract philosophising for corrupting and perverting a content which the former has given.

Where empiricism falls down and contradicts itself is in its attempts to become more than a negative force against philosophy and present a philosophy of its own. Empiricism rarely remains pure because what is alleged to be an empirical method is merely more deficient that the formal or universalist method in abstraction. It is less capable of distinguishing and fixing its limited range of concepts, which it does not itself select, but which are instead entwined with concepts that are embedded in the culture of the day, and because they are taken as given in common sense appear to be drawn 'directly from experience' (Hegel 1975: 65–70). The implication is that empiricism is itself theory laden, but much less self-consciously than abstract philosophy.

On the other hand Hegel also rejects one-sided universalism, and the claims of all doctrines that posit higher laws. Formalism was, for Hegel, typically exemplified by Kant's moral criterion of universalizability (Smith 1989: 70), and by the fact that it did not purport to derive from experience, but instead imposed itself on it (Norman 1976: 69).

This does not constitute a denial of the universalizability of rational activity. Hegel is rejecting that which has become formal, abstract, and hypothetical. Genuine universality must be actual and manifest in the laws and customs of the state, and it is therefore inadequate to put forward as a moral criterion the principles of universalizability and non-contradiction because they are merely formal criteria with no content. Non-contradiction in itself is, for Hegel, a formal principle that annihilates itself. If we adopt the universal maxim that we must help the poor, eventually there would be no poor and the maxim would be cancelled. If in order to fulfil our duty of helping the poor we adopt measures to ensure that poverty persists we in fact prevent the duty being discharged (Hegel 1975: 80). The point that Hegel wants to make is this: contradiction has to contradict something, and it is that something which has to be presupposed. If the principle of theft is universalized it is not contradictory in itself. Only if property is presupposed to be of value and of importance to society can the universal principle of theft be convicted of contradiction. In other words the content of Kant's moral principles is in fact derived from an existent social condition and is not the product of his formalism. As Hegel pertinently says: 'It is not, therefore, because I find something is not self-contradictory that it is right; on the contrary, it is right because it is what is right' (Hegel 1977: §437).

Formalism is an advance on empiricism in that it releases itself from the paralysis of finite empiricism and exhibits a 'loftiness of outlook' (Hegel 1991*a*: §133A). Formalism does, however, have a down side. It is a universalism severed from experience. It offers a criterion of conduct so abstract that it fails to connect with the will and interests of the individual. Take, for example, Kant's idea of perpetual peace. It is divorced from experience in that it fails to take account of the individuality of states, and presupposes agreement between the states, which dependent as it is upon the 'particular sovereign wills', irrespective of the grounds of agreement 'would therefore continue to be tainted with contingency' (Hegel 1991*b*: §333; cf. §324 and Hegel 1964: 208). Hegel's theory rejects universal morality and is an assertion of the 'moral primacy of the community' (Thompson 1992: 112).

What is curious, given that the idea of natural rights had been subjected to such devastating criticism, is that the British Idealists addressed the question of natural rights at all. The first problem that I want to explore is why they resurrected this discredited philosophical vocabulary at all, given that they rejected almost everything associated with it? Secondly, I want to explore their alternative theory of 'Natural Rights' which I suggest is the bridge between natural rights and modern conceptions of human rights.

Philosophically natural rights may have been discredited, but politically they enjoyed something of a renaissance during the latter part of the nineteenth century. Henry George, for example, drew upon ideas of natural right and natural law in order to argue for the redistribution of land. George's *Progress and Poverty* (George 1884) put the case for socialism against Malthusian competition and private property. The proliferation of such ideas worried many moderates, including James Knowles, the founding editor of the *Nineteenth Century*, who thought that the book had had an immense impact. The concern was that exposure to such ideas might encourage the discontented working man to revolt against his superiors.

The radical heritage of natural rights doctrines was no impediment to their adoption by extreme right wing radicals vehemently opposed to the extension of state 'interference'. Some Libertarians adopted the language of natural rights in order to champion individual responsibility against the state erosion of liberties. For some individualists, such as Herbert Spencer, Auberon Herbert, and M. D. O'Brien, the vocabulary of natural rights was part of the Individualism versus Socialism, or Libertarianism versus Collectivism, debate.

The British Idealists proved themselves to be politically astute. They were political commentators, well aware that they needed to strike a chord with the view of the common person. They had a remarkable facility for taking views which captured the public imagination, but with which they profoundly disagreed. They were able to take popular ideas and transform them into something more consistent with the Idealist world view. They very effectively appropriated the language of their opponents, while transforming its meaning in the process.

The British Idealists were not hostile to natural rights, they took issue over their source. They could, indeed, be a useful fiction (Ritchie 1998*a*: 440), but the main problem with natural rights from the Idealist perspective was their very abstractness which allowed for divergent and contradictory applications. David Ritchie complained that: 'the theory of Natural Rights is used by Anarchists to condemn the existing inequalities of social conditions, and by Conservatives to check attempts on the part of government to remedy these inequalities' (Ritchie 1903*b*: 14–15).

While the idealists rejected natural rights in the traditional understanding of the term, that is, associated with a state of nature, they nevertheless retained the vocabulary and pronounced themselves happy to use the term for those rights which were basic or fundamental to a society, without which social life would be intolerable or impossible. In so far as there are fundamental rights necessary for the life of a community and which could be justified as contributing to the common good, they could legitimately be termed 'natural rights' providing they were not attributed to an abstract individual independent of communities. Green expressed the Idealist position concisely: 'without society, no persons' (Green 1899: §288). We must recognize, Ritchie argues, that 'personality is a conception meaningless apart from society' (Ritchie 1894: 102). Bosanquet's *Philosophical Theory of the State*, for example, was intended to be an extended critique of social atomism and an affirmation of the view that self-realization was only possible within society. If any theory or practice was to be taken seriously, Bosanquet argued, it had to be based on the faith that the common or moral self has greater reality than the so-called individual (Bosanquet 1923: 144). Green's objection against natural rights theorists such as Spinoza, Hobbes, and Locke was that they fail to appreciate the development of a person through the development of society. They mistakenly believe that the higher essence of the person is somehow separable from society and its norms (Tyler 1997: 174).

I will begin by discussing Green, and broaden the discussion to explore the implications of his theory in the writings of the British Idealists in general. Green's *Lectures on the Principles of Political Obligation* have, with some justice, been described as 'perhaps the finest book in the philosophy of rights written to date' (Martin 1986: 104). Green wanted to maintain that rights exist not independently of society, but independently of political society, in, for example, the family or even among a group of slaves in their relations with each other, and with the wider community in which they live. For Green, rights are those powers of an individual that are recognized by others as being necessary for the attainment or achievement of a good in which they all share. There are three elements to this claim: (*a*) that a right is a power; (*b*) that it is recognized by society, or by other persons, and (*c*) it contributes to a common good (Gaus 2006: 209). Rights are, for Green, made by recognition. This is not, of course a sufficient condition, because rights must also be powers, and contribute to the common good. The possession of such powers, or capabilities, guaranteed by society, and those that society exercises over the individual, are justifiable only on the grounds that they are a necessary prerequisite to fulfilling 'man's vocation as a moral being' (Green 1917: §21, p. 41). This social conception of rights entails, for Green, correlative obligations. What is pernicious about the idea of pre-social natural rights is the idea that they are not derived from society and that the state is created to protect them. It encourages irreverence to the state on the assumption that the individual has rights against society irrespective of fulfilling any duties that he or she may have towards it. Powers exercised by the state are conceived as restraints upon individual freedom that may rightly be defied as far as is safely possible (Green 1917: §32; also see Richter 1996: 232).

The justification for any particular right is that it tends to promote the true or common good. This differs from the utilitarian justification for respecting civil rights. The utilitarian thinks that rights are useful in that they assist in the attainment of pleasure or the avoidance of pain. We ought to respect them because 'the ultimate sanction is fear of what the consequences would be if we did not' (Green 1917: §23, p. 43). What both theories have in common, Green maintains, is that neither grounds actual rights in prior natural rights. Instead, they are grounded in the conception of an end, the greatest happiness of the greatest number, or of moral self-realization, to which the maintenance of a system of rights contributes. The point that Green wants to make is that even if civil and political rights could be shown to derive from natural rights, we are still left with the question why certain powers are recognized by people in their relations with others as powers that ought to be exercised, or secured for possible exercise. In other words, it is no justification of a right to maintain that it is natural. A right presupposes that the right holder is a member of a society, in which some common good is recognized by its members as their ideal which is pertinent to each of them. The powers or rights that are recognized, and indeed regulated by that recognition, are deemed necessary for, or contributory to, the common good (Green 1917: §26, p. 45). The foundation of rights, then, is not that they are natural, but that the individual has a capacity to conceive of a good that is common, the same for himself, or herself, as for others, and of being moved to act by that conception. Rights are what enable that capacity to be realized (Green 1917: §29, p. 47).

It is this capacity to conceive of a good that is the same as that of others and to act upon it that for Green defines the moral person. The rights or powers necessary to the fulfilment of such a conception of the moral person are innate or natural in a different sense from that associated with the natural law and natural rights traditions. People are not born with them. They do not have them outside of society, and they do not inhere in individual persons. Furthermore they are not the creation of law or custom. They are 'natural' because 'they arise out of, and are necessary for the fulfilment of, a moral capacity without which a man would not be a man' (Green 1917: 47).

As Henry Jones argued, certain rights are 'natural' in that 'They are innate, and they are inalienable, and their ground is in the man himself. They are intrinsic. But they are in him as a social being. They belong to him in virtue of the recognition of a common good by the community in which and by which he lives a more or less rational life' (Jones 1919: 148). Ritchie argues that 'We can only allow natural rights to be talked about in the sense in which natural rights mean those legal or customary rights which we have come to think or may come to think it most advantageous to recognise' (Ritchie 1894: 270). They are an appeal to what is socially useful, not merely for the present generation, but also for future generations and as far as possible for humanity as a whole (Ritchie 1894: 103). John Watson maintains that we may call rights 'natural' as long as we do not imply that they belong to people in isolation. He contends that humans have rights not by any fictitious right of nature but because without the liberty to conduct his or her life under recognized external conditions his or her personal contribution to the common good would not be possible. These rights are not made by legislation, *pace* Bentham, but recognized as essential to the development of the common good (Watson 1919: 222–3).

Even in Michael Oakeshott's famous inaugural lecture, 'Political Education', he is not criticizing natural rights as such, but merely our manner of conceiving them as premeditated principles determining the end to be pursued in politics. They are, he argues, abstracted from political activity, and not independently acquired prior to it (Oakeshott 1991: 51). The Declaration of the Rights of Man on 4 August 1789 replaced the complex and bankrupt French system, not with new principles but with 'the common law rights of Englishmen, the gift not of independent premeditation or divine munificence, but of centuries of the day-to-day attending to the arrangements of an historic society' (Oakeshott 1991: 53).

Spencer was one of the principal targets of the Idealists not only because of his immensely influential evolutionary defence of the idea of the survival of the fittest, but also because he defended it from the position of natural rights. The Idealists thought that Spencer was a second rate biologist and a third rate philosopher, but they knew that they could not ignore him, nor merely ridicule him. If evolution and natural rights were to be put centre stage in politics, then Idealism would capitalize on their popularity and appropriate the concepts for themselves endowing them with different meanings, and using them to support different conclusions.

Idealism had to combat two types of contemporary Individualism. The first based its conclusions on *a priori* assumptions, or first principles, and deduced the limits of state activity from them. These were the Spencerite individualists.[1] On the other hand there were utilitarian individualists associated with Benthamism and the Manchester School. It was the Spencerite individualists who largely, but not without exceptions, such as Wordsworth Donisthorpe, based their conclusions on natural rights.

Both T. H. Huxley, the evolutionary biologist, and the Idealist David Ritchie felt it necessary to lay the ghost to rest once again. In answer to the charge that he was tilting at windmills in resurrecting the dead, Huxley retorted, with his usual impatience, that there was 'abundant evidence that the vicious method of *a priori* political speculation ... is not only in full vigour, but that it is exerting an influence upon the political action of our contemporaries, which is extremely serious' (Huxley 1890*b*: 174). Despite the fact that Ritchie himself said 'It becomes tiresome to kill the dead too often' (Ritchie 1998*b*: 575), he, along with many of his fellow British Idealists, felt it necessary to respond to natural rights arguments. Ritchie wryly comments that Tom Paine would get perverse pleasure out of hearing that natural rights had been commandeered by the Knights and Dames of the Primrose League and were espoused by a Tory Lord Chancellor (Taylor 1993: 260).[2] This was because the abstractness of natural rights made them particularly

---

[1] Spencer argued that state inference was wrong on two grounds, morally and practically. In order to demonstrate his deductive conclusions he produced evidence to show that state inference almost always led to unintended unfavourable consequences. In other words there were elements of utilitarian consequentialism in his writings, as there were also in one of his foremost opponents among the Idealists, D. G. Ritchie.

[2] The Primrose League was founded in 1883 by Lord Randolph Churchill and John Gorst. Its purpose was to facilitate a smooth adaptation to democracy by Conservative Party members. The League combined a variety of activities ranging from political propaganda to social events, such as music hall shows, cycling clubs, dances, and train excursions. Its membership grew from 200,000 in 1886 to over a million by 1891. Over half were women. The Tory Lord Chancellor to whom Ritchie refers was Hardinge Stanley Giffard (1886–1892 and 1895–1905), 1st Earl of Halsbury.

amenable to diverse and conflicting applications from the Anarchist's use in order to condemn current inequalities in society, to the Conservative attempts to maintain the status quo by opposing state interference (Ritchie 1894: 14–15). This, in Ritchie's view, is a fault of abstract theorizing in general: 'it is the characteristic of an abstract theory to admit of quite opposite applications' (Ritchie 1891a: 87). Ritchie complained of the appropriation of abstract ideas of natural right to reach very different conclusions: 'the theory of natural rights is used by Anarchists to condemn the existing inequalities of social conditions, and by Conservatives to check attempts on the part of government to remedy these inequalities' (Ritchie 1894: 15).

Herbert Spencer's version of natural rights is not traditional in its formulation, but his ideas, nevertheless, carried considerable weight in late nineteenth-century Britain. He maintained that every person has the freedom to do what he pleases provided that it does not impinge upon the equal freedom of others to do what they please. The Law of Equal Freedom was for Spencer a natural right from which other rights flowed. Auberon Herbert was an admirer of Spencer and drew even more extreme individualistic conclusions from the Spencerian starting point of the equal liberty of all. In 1877, he was involved in the organization of the Personal Rights and Self-Help Association, and finding the liberalism of even Spencer a little tame he established his own Party of Individual Liberty in 1885. Herbert espoused a form of Lockean self-ownership which entitled every person to the fruits of his or her own labour. Men have an inalienable right over their possessions, which follows from their right over themselves (Herbert 1978: 161 and 176).

The demand for freedom in all human transactions entailed a call for taxation to be voluntary, and the condemnation not only of socialists, but also tax compelling individualists who differed from socialists only in degree rather than kind. In his statement of the basic principles of his party he contends that self government through majority rule is no more justification for restricting liberty than the bayonet: 'The freedom of a man to use either his faculties or his possessions, as he himself wills, is the great moral fact that exists in independence of every form of government' (Herbert 1978: 129).

The Idealists were conceptually clear in distinguishing descriptive and prescriptive natural rights. Hence, in criticism of Hobbes and Spinoza, for example, Green denies that what they call rights are rights at all because they have no second-party duties attached to them. Green wants to distinguish between what Hobbes and Spinoza call rights in a state of nature, and rights proper. The former are mere natural powers or liberties, whereas the latter imply or are correlated with duties (Martin 1986: 108 and 110). Ritchie complains that students of natural science in talking of 'natural laws' are not only affecting conceptions of economics, but also, because they study human society in the same way that they would examine vegetable or animal life, have introduced causality into ethics and natural rights. Their 'laws of nature' have no connection with the 'Law of Nature' (*jus naturale*) of the Roman jurist, medieval theologians and intuitional moralists. The difference, Ritchie argues, is plain. Whereas 'natural laws' in the causal sense are incapable of being broken, natural law in the ethical sense is a statement of what men and women ought to do, and are therefore capable of being ignored. Spencer, Ritchie maintains, plays on the ambiguity of language when he claims that acts of parliament violate natural laws. Mr Spencer need have no fear about the folly of members of parliament if they attempt to do what is impossible. What Spencer does, argues Ritchie, is to draw his own practical conclusions from his study of nature, and some acts of parliament are at odds with them, nothing more:

> Natural rights have been explained as "biological rights," by which, I understand, is meant that there are certain *natural instincts* or tendencies in human nature which must be respected by legislation. This is obviously very much less than is meant by "rights" under the law of nature in its old sense. It is simply an appeal to fact; and I do not see that it settles for us which instincts deserve our respect and which do not, and that is just the important matter in practice (Ritchie 1903: 46–7).

Criticisms of both left-wing and right-wing natural rights radicalism appeared in the popular journals to combat the *a priori* arguments of their proponents. The evolutionary biologist T. H. Huxley attacked the arguments of Henry George (1889) in two controversial articles in *The Nineteenth Century*, the first thinly disguised by taking Rousseau as the target (Huxley 1890a), and the second a direct and savage dissection (Huxley 1890b). These articles were also, by implication, an attack on Huxley's evolutionary ally Alfred Russel Wallace, a long time socialist and supporter of George's ideas. Huxley's target was *a priori* ideas, the deductions from which supported conclusions which he found absurd. He argued against Rousseau that there never was, nor would there ever be a natural equality of humankind. Errors in the *a priori* reasoning of thinkers come when they confound moral and natural rights (which is not, as we have seen, something of which Rousseau could be accused). Huxley argues that there is a tendency to confuse the meanings of the two types of natural right.

The first he equates with the idea that might is right, in which existence in nature and its justification are co-extensive. In other words the possession of a faculty is justification for its use. Tigers are by nature carnivorous and in order to preserve their existence have a natural right to kill and eat their prey, including the flesh of humans. Humans, on the other hand, also have a natural right to preserve their existence, and have no obligation to submit to the tiger's natural right. The natural rights of humans and of tigers are likewise founded on the law of nature, but they are nevertheless diametrically opposed. To impede or prevent their exercise does not constitute a wrong. The law of nature is not a command to do or desist from anything, but nothing more than a statement of what a given creature tends to do for the preservation of its existence in given circumstances (Huxley 1890b: 179). Moral and civil rights arise in a social context because of a desire for peace and co-operation, and they act as constraints on natural rights, and give rise to correlative obligations: 'there is not the least connection between the natural rights of the solitary individual and the moral or civil rights of the man who has entered into association with others' (Huxley

1890*b*: 186–7). This argument is consistent with his famous Romanes lecture in which he distinguishes between cosmic evolution and ethical evolution. Natural rights are related to the former while moral rights pertain to the latter (Huxley 1989).

Huxley was perceived as a defender of the status quo, but this defence entailed denying the arguments of Spencer who favoured the minimal state. Huxley was a proponent of state education, public libraries, government funding of science, and a modern State Secretariat. Radical individualists, such as Wordsworth Donisthorpe in defence of individualism against Huxley, were also disturbed by the resurrection of natural rights because of their abstractness. Abstract natural rights, in his view, could hardly generate practical working doctrines (Donisthorpe 1981: 133). There could be no *a priori* limits to state action, only those to be discerned through the study of history. His objections to state interference were largely pragmatic on the grounds that the reasons for certain types of regulation no longer exist, or that regulation has exacerbated rather than alleviated problems it had tried to solve.

Idealism and Natural Rights

There are a number of aspects common to all of the accounts of 'Natural Rights' found in the works of British Idealists. They reject arguments for natural rights which equate might with right, as for instance in Hobbes's conception of a pre-social state of nature in which rights have no correlate obligations. They also reject accounts based on intuitionism and the idea of an external law standing above and outside of social existence, a reference point to which we must make our actions conform, as for example in the state of nature conceived by Locke. They all agree that as part of their definition social recognition, whether by society or the state, or both, is essential to the idea of natural right, or indeed any right. Without recognition, we have no right. Such rights are justified with reference to their contribution to the common good. In other words, they must link up with the real interests of individuals, what Bosanquet calls the general will, and partly, at least, have demonstrable benefits or utility. Both aspects of what they mean by 'Natural Right' are meant to counter the charge that they are abstract and incapable of being translated into moral injunctions, and that they are capricious and arbitrary based on individual self-interest and human desires.

What then determines rights? The British Idealists basically follow the same pattern. The idea of recognition is crucial to their arguments. This aspect of their theory was criticized by W. D. Ross who argued that in order for something to be recognized, it must already exist (Ross 1930: 51). Gaus maintains, however, that by recognition Green means it in the sense that it is used when the chair of a committee recognizes the floor, or a speaker, that is, gives the person recognized a certain status (Gaus 2006: 211). But even in this meaning of the term, that is rights creation, something has to be recognized to give it the status of a right. What this something is, is a moral claim, that becomes a right in being recognized and acknowledged as a power that ought to be accepted as necessary to the promotion of the common good (Martin 1993: 75–77).

Ritchie and Watson closely follow Green in distinguishing between legal and moral rights (Green 1919: §9). Rights require social recognition, without which they are something less than rights. In other words, recognition is itself part of the concept of a right. Ritchie loosely defines a legal right as 'the claim of an individual upon others, recognised by the State. The correlative obligations are, then, enforceable. A legal right need not necessarily have been created by the State (e.g., by statute); but it must be such that the law courts will recognise it, and in all orderly communities, the force of the State is at the back of all legal decisions.' (Ritchie 1903: 78).

A moral right, in Ritchie's view, is 'the claim of an individual upon others recognised by society, irrespective of its recognition by the State' (Ritchie 1903: 78–9; cf. Watson 1919: 229). Moral rights are less precisely formulated than legal rights, and much more difficult to determine because of changing public opinion, and the diversity of opinion among communities within the State. It is in these circumstances that an appeal to the law of nature, from which natural rights are said to derive, is often made. Bosanquet goes much further than Ritchie in wanting to make a logical connection between moral and legal rights. Rights, properly understood, are morally imperative claims which ought to be and are recognized by the state. The state has a moral end which is the rational life of its members, understood in terms of the collective or social, rather than individual, perfection of human personality. Rights constitute a system, and are the conditions for achieving the goal of perfection. For Bosanquet, a right implies a moral end and is therefore necessarily a moral right and moral imperative (Bosanquet 1923: 188–9, and Sweet 1997).

That is not to say that Idealists endorse relativism. They certainly see some rights as more fundamental than others, and these they are prepared to call 'Natural Rights', not because they exist independently of the power of society to enforce them, but 'because they are necessary to the end which it is the vocation of human society to realise' (Green 1919: §9; cf. Ritchie 1894: 87). This denial of relativism is further reinforced by a developmental view of human reason and morality. What Onora O'Neill says of Hegel is equally true of the British Idealists. She contends that Hegel embeds his particularistic theory of the stages of development in 'a more inclusive universal reason' (O'Neill 1996: 29). While jettisoning the metaphysics and foundationalism of traditional theories of natural law and natural rights, the Idealists do not reject foundationalism *per se*. This particularist account of the emergence of rights is set in an inclusive context of universal reason. In other words, a metaphysics of the person relating to self-realization and freedom of choice underlies what rights would necessarily get recognized as contributory to the common good (Dimova-Cookson 2000).

The Idealist theory of rights consciously attempts to overcome the deficiencies in the individualism of both social contract and utilitarian theories. Idealists explored not individuals as such, but the relations of individuals which they saw as essential to, or even constitutive of, individuality (Jones 1997: 3 and 25). Rights belong to individuals as members of a community. They are justifiable claims recognized as rational and necessary for the common good of society. The self that is to be realized through moral activity is 'determined, characterised, made what it is by relation to others' (Bradley 1927: 116; cf. Green 1899: §184).

The justification of rights in terms of social ends is for Green teleological. Here he acknowledges that utilitarianism is able to avoid the defects of social contract by offering a justification of rights in terms of the ends which they sustain, but it ultimately fails because of its hedonism in refusing to acknowledge that there can be any other object of desire than pleasure (Green 1899: §373, 1919: §23). It fails to account for moral actions which cannot be reduced to the pursuit of pleasure or happiness.

Ritchie's approach to natural rights follows a well established idealist formula (see Boucher and Vincent 2000: 127–56). He identifies two antithetical and one-sided views of the idea and arrives at a synthesis by acknowledging what is best in each theory and transforming those elements. What was valuable and 'true' about the theory of natural rights, what gave it its practical import, was the belief in Nature as an ideal embodying a divine purpose which was discoverable through the exercise of reason, and which human beings should attempt to emulate. Its defect was that the ideals were conceived in abstract terms antithetical to the actual historical circumstances to which they were meant to be a guide. He abhorred intuitionism which proclaimed *a priori* natural rights in the name of liberalism. Henry Jones is even more dismissive of natural rights in their traditional formulation. He argues that the theories are so rife with contradictions that they fail to achieve their objective in limiting the power of the state because they annihilate it, without at the same time affording any rights to the individual because they fail to be recognized (Jones 1919: 148).

Ritchie, like Bosanquet and the rest of the British Idealists, was concerned to advance our understanding of rights beyond the negative conception of liberty. The individual in natural rights theories, and indeed in utilitarian criticisms of them, was nothing but an abstraction (Otter 1996: 160–66). Even though Spencer advanced a form of natural rights theory, he nevertheless adhered to the negative conception of liberty held by Jeremy Bentham and J. S. Mill (Sweet 1997: 11–16).

With advances of our understanding of society in terms of evolutionary theory, and by use of the historical method in exploring institutions and problems, it was now possible to think of the ideal associated with natural rights theories, not as something fully formed and definitive, but as something whose revelation is gradual in the education of the human race. Following Hegel, Ritchie maintained that any satisfactory theory of rights or of the state must rest upon a philosophy of history (Ritchie 1903: 286). For him philosophical reasoning went hand in hand with historical studies.

To claim natural rights, Ritchie argued, is to claim something fundamental from which other rights may be derived, but the question exactly what rights every society *ought* to guarantee its citizens has been answered from different perspectives. This, then, is a different question from definition and moves us on to justification. This may be with reference to an 'Authority' external to the mind of individuals; to 'Nature' in the sense of something known to an inner voice; and 'Utility' which derives from experience and reason. Firstly, when based on external authority natural rights may appear to rest on an obvious contradiction. If the end of government is to preserve our natural rights, then we cannot allow governments to determine what our natural rights are, because the very legitimacy of government is supposed to be judged by reference to them. Ritchie maintains, however, that those rights which people think that they ought to have, are exactly those rights which they have been accustomed to have, and are claimed because they have been sanctioned by the 'authority of social recognition'. When such traditional custom or constituted authority proves to be unsatisfactory and a disjunction appears between law and conscience in the minds of reformers, appeal may be made, not to external authority, but to the feelings that Nature has implanted in our breasts. The difficulty is that conscience differs from individual to individual, and when scrutinized more closely the individual's conscience tends to mirror the society in which he or she has grown up, even to the extent that a revolt against its institutions betrays its unavoidable influence (Ritchie 1903: 85). In the conflicting impulses, desires, and interest of individuals it is impossible to discern a settled standard of conduct, we must therefore go to something more fundamental and look at nature in its essentials. What is being appealed to, however, is human society and the mutual claims that it is necessary to recognize if that society is to avoid disintegration. Nature in this respect is not an appeal to feelings but to reason, and in principle the competing claims can be adjudicated impartially with reference to the criterion of the general welfare. The result is that 'the details of a professedly Intuitionalist ethical code are filled up on Utilitarian principles' (Ritchie 1903: 87). In this respect Nature may just as well be dispensed with and utilitarian considerations brought in from the outset.

The difficulty is that people are just as inclined to disagree on what is useful as they are to disagree on what is right or just with reference to the natural law. What is useful is as ambiguous as the just, but it is capable of further specification because what is useful has always to be in relation to something. It is in answering the question useful for what that utilitarianism stands in need of reformulation. Although Benthamism rejects the rhetoric of natural rights it retains the abstract individualism that is an important part of that doctrine.

Traditional utilitarianism treats individuals as more or less homogeneous moral atoms with similar feelings which can be quantified, and among whom a quantity of pleasures can be distributed. It demands of institutions that they justify themselves in terms of their conduciveness to the general happiness. Ritchie maintains that Benthamist utilitarianism is itself open to many of the criticisms of the theory of natural rights. The appeal to nature tries to reconcile the abstract individualism of the multiplicity of isolated instincts with the abstract universalism of the consent of humanity. Like the appeal to nature, utilitarianism assumes a uniformity of human nature over time and place. It combines the abstract individualism of treating every person as a discrete unit, with the abstract universalism of its view of happiness which is taken to have an existence divorced from the concrete individuals who are singularly capable of experiencing it.

Ritchie maintains that Utilitarianism is not without its merits, but it took the doctrine of evolution, particularly natural selection, to correct its errors and vindicate its truth. While Bentham and Austin did much to divorce jurisprudence and ethics from vague appeals to natural law, on the constructive side their ethical theories were too closely allied to hedonism and therefore needed to be separated from it by being re-interpreted in the light of evolutionary theory, and their jurisprudence needed to be permeated with an evolutionary and historical spirit (Ritchie 1998c: 127). Societies are engaged in a struggle for existence in relation to nature and other societies, and that which furthers them in the struggle is good, that which hinders bad. The development of reason and the broadening of horizons from primitive virtues lead to good qualities being recognized in wider spheres. A society whose welfare determines what is right may expand and change its character.

In Ritchie's view, the good of a community provides us with the only criterion of what an individual ought to do, and is itself identical with the good of the individual – there is mutual dependence or inclusiveness. This good is not static and constant because what the community is changes over time, and hence the standard of our moral judgement progresses. As the range of persons we take into account when we think of the common good broadens, changes are effected in our moral judgements. There are variations in moral judgements because societies are variable in character, and conflicts of duties and of moral judgements are possible in complex societies because each individual belongs to many overlapping communities. Natural selection becomes transformed, Ritchie maintains, into rational selection among self-reflective and intelligent human beings. It is therefore feasible and desirable that some social organisms may cease to serve a useful purpose and become superseded by others of a higher type into which individuals become absorbed.

Natural selection, or the struggle for existence, occurs at an altogether higher level among humans than among other gregarious animals. The struggle between social groups altogether complicates and mitigates the struggle between individuals within a particular group. Animals tend to belong only to one social organism or group, a herd, school or flock, for instance, whereas humans belong to multiple social organisms, many of them overlapping; an observation that is often ignored among writers on social evolution who equate the nation, class or humanity with the social organism. Many of the organisms may be in competition with each other for membership, and give rise to competing obligations and loyalties. We must therefore be extremely cautious in applying biological analogies such as natural selection to social organisms. It is most typically manifest not in the odd war between states, but in economic competition among individuals in the same line of business, and between commercially trading nations. There is for Ritchie, however, a very important respect in which the ideas of the social organism and natural selection are invaluable in ethical and political thinking. They put utilitarianism on a scientific footing, rescuing it from the more obvious objections of intuitionism, while at the same time protecting ethics and politics from the arbitrary and subjective standards of intuitionists (Ritchie 1997: 80). He is critical of Alfred Russel Wallace, for instance, because he posits a spiritual force independent of nature in order to counter utilitarian ethics. From an intuitionist standpoint Wallace claims that there is an innate sense of right and wrong quite distinct from experiences of utility (Ritchie 1917: 104). The advantage of utilitarianism, Ritchie insists, is that it emphasizes the importance of taking consequences into consideration before pronouncing something right or wrong. It recognizes that rules need to be revised, but not in the moment of their application – 'the battlefield is not the place for examining bayonets, though it certainly does test them (Ritchie 1891a: 171). Ritchie does not believe that natural selection can serve to explain the ultimate nature of right and wrong, but it can explain the content of our ethical judgements.

This is what Ritchie calls a transition from Individualist Utilitarianism to Evolutionist Utilitarianism, by which he means a Copernican change of perspective from the eighteenth century view that society was instituted to secure the protection of pre-existing natural rights to the modern view influenced by advances in scientific thinking that 'Natural Rights' are those fundamental rights that *ought* to be recognized by a society, and judged wholly from the point of view of society. Social cohesiveness requires any society to adhere to certain ground rules or conditions which inform the actions of their individual members: 'In order to hold together, every society formally, or informally, agrees to observe, or, let us say, finds itself compelled to observe, these conditions of common life, and thereby creates rights and duties for its members' (Ritchie 1891a: 39). Ritchie has in mind the evolutionary theories of W. K. Clifford and Leslie Stephen who modified utilitarian principles by moving from an individualistic to a collectivist conception of the good. They moved away from the Benthamist individualistic utilitarianism of a balance of pleasures and pain, in which the common good was conceived as an aggregate of individual pleasures, to the idea of the well-being of society as a worthy ethical end (Ritchie 1917: 106).

Idealism while rejecting hedonism could acknowledge that a modified utilitarianism was not incompatible with the idea of self-realization, that is, the realization of a social self in contributing to the common good (Ritchie 1891a: 116). Ritchie takes Sidgwick's broad based utilitarianism, for example, to be compatible with Green's ethics which equates self-realization with the common good.

Sidgwick argues, however, that he cannot conceive of an argument that could succeed in proving that the good of an individual had to be sacrificed for the good of a group or community without at the same time conceding that a similar obligation is owed to the whole of humanity. Here, Ritchie suggests, Henry Sidgwick seems to be accepting as indisputable Bentham's claim that every individual constitutes an equal unit in our moral judgements, but that such a philosophical dogma has never been manifest as the practical maxim of any considerable number of human beings. Such a criterion could only be feasible in the context of some ideal of a world state, federation or truly universal church, which Sidgwick expressly rejects (Ritchie 1998d: 538). The principle to be applied to human actions is to what extent they contribute to the greater well-being of that portion of mankind that we can feasibly encompass in our considerations? In other words, will society be healthier as a result of a particular act? (Ritchie 1891a: 107). Sidgwick's utilitarianism was, in Ritchie's view, a sleeker and tamer version than Benthamism, and not only contained elements of the common good compatible with Green, but also sought, in an almost Hegelian fashion, to discern the rational in the real, to the extent that he claimed that the practical conclusions of utilitarian ethics will differ little from the actual code of morality that prevails (Ritchie 1998d: 225; cf. Taylor 1992: 220).

In the form of seeing 'natural rights' as that which is socially useful or advantageous it is not an appeal to the abstract conceptions of intuitionism, but one which can be tested with reference to experience, and with reference to the evolution of institutions, not an absolute immutable and imprescriptible criterion, but one which develops over time. Here Ritchie sees himself in conformity with Green, whom he contends had much more in common with Bentham and J. S. Mill than with intuitionism in using the common good, which was closely tied to self-realization, as the criterion of natural rights, or what rights a society ought to afford its citizens (Ritchie 1998e: 549).

In Ritchie's view, the common good which acts as the criterion of appropriate conduct changes from age to age and depends upon what actions and virtues contribute to the realization of the well-being of society. In other words, for New Radicals such as Ritchie, some elements of Benthamism could be retained, particularly its critical spirit of questioning existing institutions and proposing radical reconstructions (Ritchie 1891a: 80). However, Ritchie argues that when people appeal to justice against society what they are really doing is claiming that a higher form of society should replace the lower, and it would be better if they were honest about it rather than appeal to abstract justice and natural rights (Ritchie 1894: 106–7).

Ritchie's argument about the social recognition of 'natural rights' judged in relation not only to current members of society, but also for future generations and even for humanity as a whole requires societies in which there is an advanced respect for 'human rights' to consider the consequences of their violation elsewhere. An idealist system of ethics implies equality, the recognition of others as moral agents capable of freedom of choice and rational development. The equality of human beings as such consists in their potential participation in a common society. If we are not able to think of humanity as a potential society, then we are not able to conceive of all humans as equal moral entities.

Ritchie, like Bosanquet, believes that the thin universalism of an international moral community can only arise out of the thick moral particularism embedded in actual communities much closer to home. The more positive elements of patriotism must be built upon in order to promote close international ties, eventually leading to the attainment of a world federation. It was to be a long process with the differences between levels of civilization presenting one of the main obstacles. Ritchie believed that we had not yet reached the stage where the citizen could be submerged in the man. Citizens' rights were still more tangible and historically embedded than the rights of man.

Idealism and Slavery

How, then, would the idealist theory of 'Natural Rights' deal with the issue of slavery? Thomas Carlyle who played a significant part in introducing German ideas into Britain, and in encouraging British Idealists to read Kant and Hegel (Caird 1892: 230–7), was one of the nineteenth century's leading authors, and a 'potent force' in cultural and intellectual circles in Britain and America (Hook 1998: 144). In a mocking tone Carlyle berates the do-gooders of Exeter Hall, a meeting place on the Strand in London for Christian and Philanthropic causes, for getting their way in slave emancipation. Carlyle portrays the blacks in the West Indies as lazy, indolent, and stupid, up to their ears in pumpkins, needing to work only half an hour a day to satisfy their needs, and refusing to harvest the sugar cane, while poor whites in Britain and England live in social deprivation. Carlyle demanded that they be compelled to work under a system similar to serfdom, *Adscripti glebae*, where each is obliged to work a few days a week for the lord, or plantation owner (Carlyle 1866: 376). Alternatively, the blacks, or niggers as he pejoratively calls them, who in terms of wisdom are at the bottom of society, next to the horse (Carlyle 1866: 310), will through their idleness 'inevitably *rot*, and become putrescent; and I say deliberately, the very devil is in *it*' (Carlyle 1866: 243). He is disdainful of the 'rights of negroes', and maintains that the fruits of the West Indies would be nothing if it were not for the enterprise of Europeans (Carlyle 1866: 372–4). Carlyle, however, is not typical of the Idealists, who on the whole abhorred slavery, and any relations between individuals that did not acknowledge their natural equality and inherent dignity. Edward Caird, in an appreciation of Carlyle's genius, condemns these views as an aberration, and an 'astonishing blunder' (Caird 1892: 263). The reason, Caird suggests, was because at heart Carlyle was an individualist with little understanding of the organic unity of social life.

Nevertheless, the recognition theory of rights would appear to exclude the slave from having any such rights. Green does not accept this. As we saw, rights belong to the moral person who has a capacity for conceiving of a good that is common, and of acting in such a way as to attain it. These rights or powers are not dependent on the state, but upon social relations, and slaves, in so far as they have social relations, both with other slaves and with the families who own them, exhibit this capacity for conceiving a common good and for acting upon it:

The law cannot prevent him [the slave] from acting and being treated, within certain limits, as a member of a society of persons freely seeking a common good. Now that capability of living in a certain limited community with a certain limited number of human beings, which the slave cannot be prevented from exhibiting, is in principle a capability of living in community with any other human beings, supposing the necessary training to be allowed; and as every such capability constitutes a right, we are entitled to say that the slave has a right to citizenship, to a recognized equality of freedom with any and every one with whom he has to do, and that in refusing him not only his citizenship but the means of training his capability of citizenship, the state is violating a right founded on that common human consciousness which is evinced both by the language which the slave speaks, and by the actual social relations subsisting between him and others (Green 1917: §140, p. 145).

The important point is this: in so far as membership of any community is in principle membership of all communities each person has a right to be treated as a free person by all other persons, and not to be subjected by force unless it is to prevent force.

It would appear, then, that recognition is not necessary for the possession of a right. This, of course, is a contentious issue because it would appear to undermine the whole theory. Recognition, in addition to being explicit, may be implied or tacit, and may be embedded in the logic of a situation. The fact that a slave lives with others, including the slave master as part of a limited community in which a common good may be perceived, and that the use of language implies self-consciousness, and that the slave is capable of purposive activity, that is, comprehending instructions and carrying them out, means that the slave owner is acting in contradiction in denying the slave recognition of his rights. On the one hand, to give an instruction to a slave entails believing that he or she is a purposive creature capable of comprehending it and acting upon it in a way that no non-human creature can. On the other hand, the slave is treated like an instrument or tool by the slave master, who in doing so is implicitly denying the purposive capacity that marks out his or her humanity. Such a contradiction is present, however hazily, to both the master and slave. The logic of the situation, then, implies recognition that the slave has rights like any other person (see Tyler 1997: 185–8).

Rights, considered 'natural' now, may not always have been so. Consistent with Hegelian principles the Idealists were historicist, but not relativists. Truth is relational in so far as it depends upon its historical context, but there is an overarching metaphysics of the development of freedom and rationality by which one set of values may be judged against another. Thus, for example, Ritchie, like Hegel, acknowledges that slavery may once have served a useful purpose. As many of their predecessors acknowledge, at the very least it prevented the wholesale slaughter of captives. In Ritchie's view there must have been a time when slavery contributed to the progress of mankind, and was not contrary to what then may have been considered natural rights. Slavery permitted the leisure of some to develop arts, sciences, and the very ideas that have now contributed to its abolition. But the historical justification for an institution is no justification for its revival nor continuance when it is no longer 'socially beneficial, or when the purpose it once served can be otherwise provided for' (Ritchie 1903: 104).

IDEALS BEYOND THE STATE

Is the ethical community upon which rights depend for their recognition continuous with the state? Contrary to received opinion, none of the British Idealists saw the ethical community necessarily terminating at state borders. Green, for example, maintains that on the same principle that a state is violating natural rights in maintaining slavery, it does the same when it uses force against members of other communities, except in self defence (Green 1919: §140, p. 145). Associations beyond the state were both advantageous and desirable, but not yet fully realized. For Ritchie, anything that promoted the establishment of a political federation and held out the possibility of a durable peace must be welcomed (Ritchie 1998*f*: 495). The British Idealists would not want to deny that there is a basis for obligation in international relations, and that this obligation must rest upon the existence of a wider community. Where they differ amongst themselves is not over the question of the possibility of a world community, but over the question of the extent to which it already exists. Even Hegel believed that the shared religious and cultural heritage of states in close proximity gave rise to customary behaviour and agreements, some of which were articulated in international law and which served to constrain states in their relations with each other (Hegel 1991*b*: §339).

Green and the British Hegelians in general were more forceful than Hegel in maintaining that the organization of sovereign states would be superseded by a gradual extension of the community within which a common will prevailed. Even in the most primitive communities, Green suggests, there is a consciousness of a good and of participators in it. Reason and the consciousness of the unfulfilled potential of a common rationality lead us to acknowledge wider and wider circles of people who have claims upon us and who are capable of participating in the common good. He contends that 'It is not the sense of duty to a neighbour, but the practical answer to the question Who is my neighbour? that has varied' (Green 1899: §207). Furthermore, it is not the idea of a cosmopolitan humanity that needs to be explained, but the retreat from it by sectional interests and privileged classes who are prepared to lend their weight to any counter-theory that furthers their exclusive ends (Green 1899: §209). Watson contends that an appeal to 'Natural Rights' can only be justified as an appeal to what is socially beneficial, not what is immediately convenient to one's own fellow citizens, but in relation to 'the whole of mankind' (Watson 1919: 230). There is no international moral tradition comparable with that sustained within a state, but states' relations are nevertheless 'mitigated by humane conventions and usages' (Bosanquet 1915:149; also see, 135, 137, and 150; Bosanquet 1917: 288, 192, 295, and 297).

The existence of these conventions and usages functioning as and constituting a code of morality is emphasized much more prominently by Caird, Sorley, MacKenzie, MacCunn, Jones, Watson, A. C. Bradley, and Haldane. They place great store in the fact that constant interaction of nations, especially in the context of the common heritage of Europeans, has given rise to a common morality. Morality, they maintain, does not require or rest upon legal enforcement, and the discharge of one's moral duty does not depend upon legal sanction. There is much in morality that falls outside of the scope of law, such as compassion, decency, and humaneness, the duties attaching to which do not depend upon enforced obedience (see, for example, Bradley, A. C., 1916: 46–77; Watson 1919: 254–5; and Boucher 1994).

This point of view among British Idealists is expressed in the classic statement of Lord Haldane in his 'Higher Nationality: A Study in Law and Ethics' (Haldane 1928: 49–93). He argues that in addition to law there is a broader body of guidance quite different in character and distinctive in sanction. It is *Sittlichkeit*, defined as 'the system of habitual or customary conduct, ethical rather than legal, which embraces all those obligations of the citizen which it is "bad form" or "not the thing" to disregard' (Haldane 1928: 68). It is highly esteemed and those who disregard it suffer the social sanction of disapproval or of being slighted. It is not the ethics of conscience as such. Its standard is the example of respected decent people in their relations with members of the community to which they belong. Haldane suggests that 'it is this instinctive sense of obligation that is the chief foundation of society' (Haldane 1928: 69).

It is wrong to suggest as many critics have, such as L. T. Hobhouse and J. A. Hobson, that the British followers of Hegel acknowledged no obligations outside of the state (Hobson 1909: 248–260, 1916: 307–8, 1915*a*: 113–8, 1915*b*: 178–9, 1988: 166–7; and Hobhouse 1972: 270). They differed in the extent to which they acknowledged the actual achievement of a wider international community, but agreed both in its desirability and the possibility of its extension. The crucial question now is how is international society to be extended?

The answer that the British Idealists gave attempts to reconcile the duties of men and citizens. Contrary to the view of most natural law and natural rights thinkers morality and the higher ideals of humanity do not pre-exist in a realm outside of the state awaiting apprehension and application. Like modern international relations scholars the British Idealists believed that a contrived legal framework could not force the rules of morality on an unreceptive world. A common sympathy may be assisted by a legal framework, but the sympathy itself is a prerequisite of its success. This, of course, is widely acknowledged in current international relations theory. J. E. S. Fawcett, for example, argues that: 'Law cannot of itself create order, but emerges only where there is a minimum degree of order, which it may, however, serve to rationalise and extend' (Fawcett 1992: 195; cf. Bosanquet 1917: 315; and MacKenzie 1918: 78).

It is our participation in a moral community that gives rise to, and constitutes the partial realization of, our conception of the good life and of the highest ideals of civilization. The standards that we project on humanity are those that are provided and sustained by our national moral communities. There is no suggestion that one ideal is as good as another. The purpose of the state is to enhance human freedom, and it achieves it by providing and sustaining the conditions for self-realization, and ensuring that all participate in the common good. The good cannot be small-minded, sectional, harmful or demeaning to anyone with the capacity for a good life. This proviso covers the whole of humanity. The path that each state travels may be different, but all aspire to emulate what they admire most in the representatives of civilization that they hold in the highest esteem. For the British Idealist, to be a Patriot and a humanitarian are not incompatible. We make our contribution to humanity through the state by being a good citizen and ensuring the genuine commitment of the state to its purpose, and in doing so we contribute what is best in the state to the cosmopolitan ideal. The patriotism of the good citizen serves to diminish and extinguish sectional interest and privilege, which are the causes of external and internal antagonism. Bosanquet suggests that the road to peace 'is to do right at home, and banish sinister interests and class privileges from the commonwealth' (Bosanquet 1917: 309; cf. Caird 1917: 110). Among these cosmopolitan ideals freedom is not a gift that can be bestowed upon one people by another. The best that one can hope for is that the nation helps to create the conditions that enable another people through its own efforts to attain freedom. There can be no doubt that this is not the reiterative universalism about which Michael Walzer speaks (Walzer 1994). The moral principle employed was essentially one of maternalism, that is, the guiding of a 'primitive' people to the age of reason at which point it could untie itself from its mother's apron strings. For most this entailed a commitment to what they believed was the right kind imperialism to which even vehement critics of Cecil Rhodes' social imperialism, such as Hobhouse and Hobson could also subscribe.

CONCLUSION

Whereas Bentham and Marx want to deny the efficacy of the very idea of natural rights, Tocqueville emphasizes the importance of a shared moral community in the development of compassion and mutual understanding which gives rise to rights. The Idealists are not denying natural rights as such, but natural rights as traditionally conceived. Natural rights understood as those rights which are socially recognized and necessary for the continuance and flourishing of society are fundamental. As long as so-called 'Natural Rights' include social recognition in their definition, and the common good as part of their justification, they are a socially useful concept. They emphasize the historical dimension in the emergence of fundamental rights, but continue to employ a strong foundationalism in embedding the rights in a conception of universal reason, and self-realization.

Whereas each society is unique and develops traditions appropriate to its way of life, Ritchie maintains that the life of any society must entail the sustaining of certain conditions by conferring rights and duties on its members. Such rights may be essential to social life, and without society as we know it would be inconceivable. Such rights are justified in that they contribute to the common good. While they are not the arbitrary creations of the state, they must nevertheless have social recognition (Bosanquet 1923: 66). Green thought that rights depended upon recognition, but nevertheless acknowledged that there was a difference between a legal right and a right that ought to be acknowledged in law

(Green 1919: §§136–41). For Bosanquet, however, that social recognition had to be by the state. Rights are attached to what Bradley called 'stations', and these positions, such as father, employer, employee etc., are recognized by the state. While rights require a moral community to sustain them, the British Idealists without exception believe that an international moral community is both possible and desirable, but differ in the degree to which they consider it already manifest. In general, they believe that the cause of humanity is furthered by putting one's own house in order, and this requires ensuring that the institutions and relations of the state are imbued with morality. Advanced nations have a moral responsibility in assisting the less advantaged to attain the ideals of civilization, and for many this entailed an attachment to a limited form of imperialism.

9

The Human Rights Culture and Its Discontents

> ... "human rights" ... are too often but code expressions of a modernity that itself recognizes no theoretic basis but general will or positivism (Schall 1991–2: 1000).

> ... both the *existence* and the *content* of rights will always be a matter of choice (Freedon 1991: 62).

INTRODUCTION

In this chapter I want to suggest that even though natural rights and human rights are often associated, in so far as it is claimed that we have them independently of governments and by the mere fact that we are human, they are in fact quite different. There are some recent scholars who hang on tenaciously to the link between the two, and who even throw in their common association with natural law for good measure, because they think that the concept of human rights is incoherent and lacks moral force without the foundations that underpinned the natural law and natural rights traditions. I want to argue that while natural rights and human rights are quite different, even though they may have similar objectives or policy goals, they are nevertheless related in that they are part of the same historical process by which the one develops into the other.

Most modern conceptions of human rights, legal, political, and philosophical, I suggest, rest on some version of constitutive theory in ethics. The shift from 'Natural' to 'Human' is not without significance. It reflects an unease about whether nature, or any derivative term for the world as it is, is capable of generating any normative principles. The term human rights shifts the focus from the source of the rights on to those who possess them. The basis of such rights is left uncomfortably vague (Weinreb 1992: 280). Ronald Dworkin, for example, commenting upon a commonly acknowledged human right, suggests that it has now become such an obvious and generally accepted truth that governments must treat their citizens as equal, that it would be almost sacrilege to deny it (Dworkin 2000: 128). There is a tendency in this respect to think about what it means to have a human right; what human rights we have: and what policy goals are implied in the assumption that we have them. The presupposition is that we have them, and this presupposition provides the background commitment to giving answers to the other questions.

In other words the deeper philosophical questions about what human rights are and how we come to have them, that is, the questions of foundations, are avoided.

I have suggested that there was not a sudden leap from the foundationalism of natural rights to the anti-foundationalism of much modern human rights thinking, and that this transition finds its clearest articulation in the little noticed work on natural rights done by the British Idealists who are often criticized for denying the rights of the individual by prioritizing the absolutism of the State.

Despite the denial of natural rights in their traditional form, namely as resting upon some conception of human nature, universal principles, or as having some religious foundation, the Idealists suggested that the term was better used in the sense that there are certain rights that are absolutely imperative for the social relations of a community at any one time, and that these rights, despite the fact that they are conventional and justified on the principle of their contribution to the common good, could with justification be described as 'natural'. The Idealists, nevertheless, ultimately relied upon a metaphysic and a conception of the person that was difficult to reconcile with the conventionalism posited in their accounts of natural rights. Many modern philosophers have retained the conventionalism, or communitarianism, sometimes called constitutive theory, and jettisoned the metaphysics. The Idealists, then, stand in an intermediary position between natural rights and the modern human rights culture, and have contributed significantly to modern ideas on the moral community and how conceptions of human rights have to be conceived in terms different from the natural rights tradition.

The Human Rights Culture

The language of human rights is now the *lingua franca* of the international order and invoked on a wide variety of issues ranging from religious toleration and economic development, to regime change and humanitarian intervention. Jeremy Waldron contends that 'there is now scarcely a nation on earth which is not sensitive to or embarrassed by the charge that it is guilty of rights-violations' (Waldron 1987: 155). Richard Rorty, following Eduardo Rabbossi, has suggested that we live in a human rights culture, and Michael Ignatieff claims that 'there is now a single human rights culture in the world' (Rorty 1993: 115). Mervyn Frost in the field of international relations theory argues that there are agreed sets of norms to which the international community subscribes, and one such set relates to human rights. We know that these norms are operating when governments feel it necessary to justify their actions when they violate them, or violate them clandestinely. In this respect they serve to constrain the behaviour of states (Frost 2002). The presumption is, then, that we have human rights, and among them are the right to life, the idea of basic equality, and freedom of belief.

The twentieth century has seen a proliferation of the rights that we have gradually come to term human rights, so many, in fact, that many complain of the trivialization of the concept which combines a wish-list of unattainable aspirations with fundamental protections without which the concept of 'human' itself is degraded. There is no doubt that the human rights culture and vocabulary of inalienable rights form part of the current landscape of moral, political, and legal discourse. The widespread acknowledgement and endorsement or ratification of many of the formal documents give rise to the view that there appears to be a world-wide consensus on human rights (Fields 2002: 42). When probed more deeply this consensus proves to be the idea that people have human rights, and not an agreement about what human rights we have, or indeed where they come from. There are three generations of rights with quite specific injunctions and aspirations in the realms of political, social, economic, and cultural spheres, and those termed solidarity rights, such as those to development (UN declaration 1986) and peace (UN declaration 1984). The danger, as Maurice Cranston has pointed out, is that the fundamental rights to life and liberty are devalued by claiming much lesser rights such as to two weeks paid holiday a year (Cranston 1967 and 1973).

There was certainly some momentum building up for the international protection of individual rights between the two world wars, and as we have seen the idea of natural rights remained part of the political vocabulary in the latter part of the nineteenth and early part of the twentieth century. Of considerable importance in keeping the idea alive was the work of the Russian émigré Andre Nicolayevitch Mandelstam and his associates, including the Greek Antoine Frangulis. As a result, for example, in 1929 the commission of the International Law Institute adopted a Declaration of the Rights of Man (Burgers 1992).

It was H. G. Wells and his associates, including J. B. Priestley and A. A. Milne, who revived the idea of natural rights in the public consciousness, suggesting that since birth is an accidental occurrence, as a matter of justice, everyone ought to have access to food, shelter, clothing, education, and information, and also enjoy freedom of discussion as a minimum to the realization of one's potential. In addition, each individual should enjoy security of person and property. Wells initiated discussions in the *Daily Herald* and a drafting committee for a 'Declaration of Rights'. The committee included Norman Angell, the recipient of the 1933 Nobel Peace Prize, and Viscount Sankey, a former Lord Chancellor, whose name the final document bore, namely, the 'Sankey Declaration' (Burgers 1992). In an immensely successful Penguin Special, *The Rights of Man: or What are we Fighting For?* translated into thirty languages and serialized in newspapers throughout the world, Wells launched devastating attacks on Stalin and Hitler, maintaining that only a reassertion of individual rights, protected by international law rather than diplomacy, could act as a safeguard against totalitarianism (see Robertson 2000: 20–4). The preservation of human rights officially became a war aim in 1942.

The Roosevelts were immensely moved by Wells' arguments and it was the Americans who were responsible for giving human rights such a prominent place in the UN Charter. This prominence could not have been achieved, however, if it were not for the momentum building up throughout the war for an international bill of rights. The San Francisco Conference formulated the UN Charter that was signed on 26 June 1945, almost two months before the end of the Second World War, but it was not the horrors revealed about the concentration camps that gave impetus to the inclusion of the protection rights in the Charter. Indeed, before the revelations, it had already been decided that such international protections of individuals were imperative (Burgers 1992). The Universal Declaration, as Eleanor Roosevelt made clear, was not meant to be a treaty or international agreement, and placed no legal obligations on states. It was the Convention on the Prevention and Punishment of Genocide, which came into force in 1951, which was to have that status. Nevertheless, although not a binding legal instrument, the Universal Declaration has come to be understood as embodying human rights obligations. The first World Conference on human rights held in Tehran in 1968, for example, proclaimed that the Universal Declaration expressed a common understanding of the peoples of the world about the inalienable and inviolable rights of all of humanity and the obligation of the international community to uphold them. The Declaration along with the International Covenant on Economic, Social and Cultural Rights, and the International Covenant on Civil and Political Rights, both of which were adopted in 1966, and came into force in 1976, constitute what is often known as the International Bill of Rights.

The human rights culture, or movement, is relatively new and arose post 1945. The emphasis upon minority rights that characterized the preoccupation of the League of Nations in the inter-war years was considered a failure, and had been cynically exploited by the Nazis in their demands at Munich to promote its racist policies. The solution of the United States for racial harmony was the assimilation of the melting pot, and not the affirmation of separate group identities (Krasner 1999: 110–11).

The United States was fundamentally opposed to the inclusion of minority rights in both the Charter of the United Nations and the Universal Declaration of Human Rights (Donnelly 1989: 21). The human rights regime that succeeded it almost immediately went into abeyance with the advent of the Cold War. While on the formal front advances were made in formulating conventions, the political will to put them into practice was conspicuously absent. The role of non-governmental organizations such as Amnesty International and Human Rights Watch served to keep human rights issues on the agenda much more than the representatives of western governments, even those such as Australia and Britain which purported to be following ethical foreign policies.

A. H. Robertson and J. G. Merrills explicitly affirm the contingency of human rights when they argue that ratifying human rights treaties is unavoidably political, and entails endorsing a specific set of political values. They argue that 'Ratifying a human rights treaty is therefore no more than a moral gesture. It is recognition of the special status of certain ideals, with the political expectations which that creates' (Robertson and Merrills 1996: 335). Human rights, they contend, are the outcome of bargaining and political assessment.

Immediately at the inception of the contemporary human rights culture political controversy brought into question the integrity of the motives of those who professed moral indignation at the atrocities committed against their own peoples and foreign nationals by the Germans and Japanese. This culture emerged out of the widespread revulsion against the systematic inhumanity practised by states upon sections of their own people, or by the representatives of states upon the citizens of other states. The impetus arose from the criminalization of individuals acting on behalf of their governments perpetrating war crimes and, or, crimes against humanity committed in the context of war. The fact that the same standards were not applied in the cases of alleged Nazi and Japanese war criminals immediately undermined the professed indignation and moral outrage of the Allies. Political expediency and endemic racism led to the Japanese atrocities being treated differently. It was expedient to allow the Emperor to continue his reign, and implicitly racist the same standards of civilized behaviour not to expect of the Asian hordes as of Europeans.

Almost thirty years after the Universal Declaration of Human Rights, the International Covenant on Civil and Political Rights came into force (1976), with little super power support. The USA, for example, did not ratify the Covenant until 1992, and states such as Singapore, Malaysia, and Indonesia still have not done so, while Cuba and Pakistan signed only in 2008. The all important accompanying Optional Protocol which gave individuals the right to complain of human rights violations to the Human Rights Committee attracted very few signatories. Even signing this Protocol did not signify a willingness to co-operate with the Human Rights Committee nor implement its decisions.

The human rights culture is one to which states subscribe, not without considerable pressure from governmental and non-governmental agents alike. It is based on the principle of opting-in, and until such time the various conventions are explicitly adopted by governments their citizens are effectively excluded from having such rights. The philosophical questions about the foundation of human rights tend to be avoided in order to reach the destination of universal, inalienable rights for all. Even the devoutly religious can see the pragmatic value in this approach. The French Catholic philosopher and theologian Jacques Maritain, who was a member of the Commission of Human Rights responsible for the Universal Declaration, for example, advised that the basis of human rights could be put to one side in the interests of determining what rights there are (Maritain 1949: 9–17). Suspending the search for foundations is a common feature of the modern human rights culture even among liberals. Michael Ignatieff, for instance, maintains that foundational claims in human rights discourse, such as appeals to innate human dignity, natural and intrinsic self-worth, or that humans are sacred, are divisive and detract from what may unite the broader community of supporters of human rights. He argues that it is much better to 'forego these kinds of foundational arguments altogether and seek to build support for Human Rights on the basis of what such rights actually *do* for human beings' (Ignatieff 2001: 54).

The culture is developmental in form and new treaties proclaiming or defining fundamental rights are constantly being added. In 2006, for instance, two important UN conventions were adopted: the 'International Convention on the Rights of

Persons with Disabilities' and the 'International Convention for the Protection of All Persons from Enforced Disappearance'. The latter is a rather belated formalized prohibition in response to the epidemic of abductions and killings during the mid 1970s in Chile, Guatemala, and Argentina (Lutz and Sikkink 2000: 634).

It is, of course, testimony to the inadequacy of the United Nations to deliver an effective human rights culture that regional arrangements emerged and even provided alternative routes to the redress of grievances in Europe, America, and Africa, but these, too, require governmental acceptance, without which their citizens simply do not have the rights. The most effective of the regional arrangements, the European Convention on Human Rights, established by the Council of Europe, and which had the effective enforcement mechanisms of the Commission and European Court at Strasbourg, streamlined into a two stage judicial process, covers only signatories. The preamble to the convention does not even feign universalism. It is quite explicit that like minded western European states sharing a common heritage involving 'political traditions, ideals, freedoms, and the rule of law' have agreed upon certain standards that must be maintained by those states who wish to subscribe to them (see Milne 1986: 3). Since 2000 it is permissible to bring violations of the rights contained in the European Convention before national courts in Britain under the terms of the Human Rights Act.

The first article of the Convention charges 'Contracting Parties' to secure the stated rights and freedoms to everyone within their jurisdiction. It does, however, have the treaty power to compel compliance with its rulings, which often means compelling a change in domestic law, unless a state formally 'derogates' from the Convention in preference to accepting an unpalatable ruling. The human rights promulgated in the European Convention are not even universal within their European context because of the political sensitivities of different states. Freedom of speech, therefore, means different things in different countries when filtered through the principle of 'the margin of appreciation'.

The 'Cairo Declaration on Human Rights in Islam, 1990' is heavily culturally biased, and much more explicitly foundational than any of its counterparts. It affirms the unity of the human race in its submission to God and descent from Adam, privileging Islam as the religion of 'unspoiled nature'. All of the rights and freedoms it specifies are subject to Islamic Shari'ah law, and it is from it that questions of definition and further clarification must be sought (Brownlie and Goodwin-Gill 2006: articles 24 and 25, p. 1065). The 2004 League of Arab States' Arab Charter on Human Rights, less explicit in deference to Islam and to Shari'ah, reaffirms the principles of the documents that comprise the International Bill of Rights, while 'having regard for the Cairo Declaration' it emphasizes the right to resist foreign occupation, and endorses the death penalty for the most serious of crimes, even for minors if national laws allow. While prohibiting torture it says nothing of cruel or unusual punishments (see Brownlie and Goodwin-Gill 2006: 1070–84).

The American Convention on Human Rights has a Commission in Washington DC and a Court in Costa Rica, but its credibility is undermined by the fact that even though the USA is a signatory to the treaty it refuses to accept the jurisdiction of the Commission or the Court. The African Charter on Human and People's Rights' although laudable because of its emphasis on third generation rights and the obligations of individuals to their communities, is nevertheless the treaty of the Organization of African Unity which includes among its number some of the most notorious and brutal violators of human rights.

The United Nations Declaration on Human Rights was itself aspirational and provided for no enforcement apparatus. It suggests that the ideals it puts forward should be attained by education and 'progressive measures'. Humanitarian Law to some extent clouds the issue because intervention, which was absolutely ruled out by Article 2(7) of the UN Charter, was a possibility, albeit still remote, under Chapter VII providing for collective action in extreme cases of human rights abuses which threatened world peace and security. The 'Friendly Declaration' of October 1970, however, reaffirmed that no state or alliance of states had a right to intervene directly or indirectly in the internal or external affairs of another sovereign state.

There is a nascent principle of humanitarian intervention emerging over the last twenty years, but only for the most serious crimes against humanity, and then only on a very selective basis. The fear is, of course, that humanitarian intervention will be used as a pretext for military invasion. It was, indeed, one of the reasons given by George W. Bush for invading Iraq, and condemned by Human Rights Watch as unjustifiable in its 2004 *World Report*. Nato's humanitarian intervention in Kosovo, which was not sanctioned by the United Nations and was by no means universally accepted, was almost immediately undermined as an international principle when Indonesian troops were allowed to slaughter the East Timorese until such time as the Jakarta authorities invited the humanitarian forces, led by the Australians, into its sovereign territory. Despite the endorsement of the Heads of State and Government at the 2005 UN summit of the International Commission on Intervention and State Sovereignty to divest humanitarian intervention of its military connotations by reconceptualizing it as 'a responsibility to protect', there is still a conspicuous absence of will to step in and protect the people of Darfur from systematic rape and killing.

Peter Baehr quite rightly points out that 'There is a big difference between universalism in standard-setting and universalism in implementation' (Baehr 1999: 11). As Geoffrey Robertson remarks, 'There is no "universality" about this human rights system' (Robertson 2000: 53). What needs to be emphasized as clearly as possible is that human rights of the first generation are subject in varying degrees to regional recognition and enforcement. The so-called second and third generations of human rights are much less subject to judicial supervision, and the various bodies established to monitor them are really committees of scrutiny which report on progress in response to periodic reviews by states which have signed-up to the various conventions. This is clearly illustrated by the two Covenants approved by the General Assembly of the United Nations on 16th December, 1966. Both the International Covenant on Economic, Social, and Cultural Rights and the Covenant on Civil and Political Rights begin with a common guarantee that all peoples have the right to self-determination. Articles 2 to 5 in each Covenant set out the general obligations of the signatories which are quite different in character. In relation to civil and political rights the contracting parties immediately assume the obligations, whereas with the Covenant on Economic, Social, and Cultural Rights the parties are obliged to take steps to the maximum of their resources to bring about the realization of the rights recognized in the Covenant (Robertson and Merrills 1996: 275). It is, then, a promotional convention. The rights in the two charters are formulated differently. In the first individuals are typically said to have a right to, or shall not be subject to etc., while in the second the articles typically take the form of the states acknowledging certain rights, or undertaking to ensure progress towards their attainment.

The governmental reviews for progress on economic, social, and cultural rights are usually either late or never materialize at all. As far as universal jurisdiction is concerned it is only certain categories of abuse that are subject to it. In particular crimes against humanity, which attribute individual responsibility to agents of governments, *de facto* powers, or political organizations which systematically and as a matter of policy engage in acts of genocide, torture, murder, or gross degradation of minority groups. Annual human rights reports by non-governmental organizations such as Amnesty International and Human Rights Watch continue to catalogue serial violations of human rights despite the proliferation of regional conventions and protection. Amnesty's reports for 2005 found systematic abuse in Africa, the Americas, Asia, the Middle East, and North Africa, despite committing themselves to respect and protect of human rights. Europe, too, fell far short of its obligations, especially on the principle of asylum. Issues of illegal immigration and security were used to flout due process, putting at risk of further violations those who had already suffered and fled abuse. It concluded that, 'Asylum-seekers, migrants and minorities remained among those continuing to face racism and discrimination across the region' (Clapham 2007: 56).

With the undermining of the UN Commission on Human Rights, which increased its governmental representation from 18 to 32 to 53, by states seeking election not to promote, but to prevent, close scrutiny of their records – in 2001 Congo, Kenya, Libya, Saudi Arabia, Syria, and Vietnam were elected – it was replaced in 2006 by the new Human Rights Council, which is attempting to escape the charge of selectivity by conducting universal periodic reviews of all member states on the record of their compliance with their human rights obligations. It is too early to say whether the new arrangements will lead to the United Nations more emphatically condemning violators.

One may view with cynicism the commitment of states to pursue and bring to justice those who have violated human rights. The ruling of the British Law Lords in March 1999 against Augusto Pinochet, however, gave heart to supporters of universal justice, and is only one of many reminders of the fragile relation in which hundreds of millions of people world-wide stand to their governments, upon which they are dependent for the protection of their rights, but which nevertheless systematically violate them. In ruling that Pinochet is not immune from prosecution and could be extradited to Spain for violating the 1984 'Convention against Torture and Other Cruel, Inhuman or Degrading Treatment or Punishment', the issue of where national sovereignty ends and where international law begins came sharply into focus. The ruling acknowledged the authority of a Spanish court to indict Pinochet for human rights violations, including the torture and murder of his own citizens.

The Law Lords ruled that Pinochet could not be tried for crimes committed before 1988, the year that Britain signed the UN Torture Convention incorporating such crimes committed anywhere in the world into British law. Under its terms Pinchoet could be tried in Britain or extradited to Spain. Despite the limitation the ruling was greeted in some quarters of the Spanish press as opening the door to universal justice and the establishment of an international penal court. It does, however, highlight the fact that subscription to international conventions is a prerequisite to being deemed to fall under their jurisdiction. A more unequivocal prosecution under the Torture Convention was that of Faryadi Zardad, the leader of the Afghan rebels, in London in 2005. He was found guilty of taking and torturing hostages and sentenced to 20 years imprisonment. These 'humanitarian rights' are so fundamental that exceptions and qualifications, including weighing one against another, cannot be permitted. While the political will to pursue perpetrators of such crimes is not all that it should be, the principle that they can be punished by any state wherever the crimes may have been committed has become well established.

It is of course fashionable to subscribe to the rhetoric in principle in the United Nations, but state interest, whether economic or strategic, often undermines the commitment to human rights. Geoffrey Robertson has suggested that diplomacy is the exact antithesis to a serious commitment to human rights. Diplomacy notoriously trades off human rights violations against other interests, and allows international criminals to escape justice. The massacre in Tiananmen Square, for example, while condemned world wide, was after a respectable interlude, quietly forgotten in the interests of stronger economic links with China, and even its record on Tibet did not prejudice the decision to allow China to stage the 2008 Olympic Games.

It is evident that the momentum towards global justice has been in the face of strong opposition affirming the principle of state sovereignty. Despite the fact that there are examples of international criminal justice, such as in the European Court on Human Rights, the Inter-American Court, and the Privy Council in Britain, as well as the International Criminal Court established in 2002, it remains true that major powers are often reluctant to compromise their sovereignty by submitting to external legislation. The United States, for example, refuses to ratify the treaty establishing the International Criminal Court in the Hague because it believes that its citizens may be indicted for politically motivated reasons. For the United States human rights violations take place in other countries, and the fact that the Constitution incorporates one of the first great bills of rights has led to an identification of what were initially natural rights with civil rights. It is interesting that the movement to empower blacks in America fought not for human or natural rights, but civil rights, even though Martin Luther King preached that these rights were the entitlement of blacks by virtue of their embodiment in the law of God which stands above nations. The country that potentially has the most to contribute to international justice in enforcing human rights will it seems do so on the condition that other countries are the violators (Robertson 2000: 67).

We will see when examining the legal view of human rights that although there is a residue of the natural law and natural rights traditions there is a convergence on the view that the human rights culture, or movement, is one of consensus and agreement, and that the framework of human rights is constituted by convention and customary law to which states subscribe, out of which something like a nascent universal jurisdiction is emerging.

Among those who view human rights politically, there are many who would deny that they have a foundational character, or indeed deny the relevance of such considerations when it comes to acting politically in their name. Jack Donnelly and Mervin Frost, for example, reject the search for philosophical foundations to human rights, and instead, in Donnelly's case tries to describe the way that human rights work or function in contemporary social relations (Donnelly 1989 and 1999). There is no appeal to a universal human nature, but instead an attempt to analyse social practices in which the concept of a human right figures prominently. Similarly, Mervin Frost suggests that there is an international consensus on human rights. He calls them settled norms, and their existence can be identified by the fact that states, when they violate them, feel the need to justify their actions, and this in itself is a moderating and constraining force, and alternatively if they violate human rights they find it necessary to do so clandestinely. Thus in their systematic violation these international norms still have a bearing on the behaviour of states. Given that there is an almost universal consensus that human beings have human rights, even if there is no consensus upon what these rights are, no states want to be publicly condemned as a violator (Frost 1996 and 2002).

It is often the case that natural law is associated with the discharge of duties and obligations, whereas natural rights give much more emphasis to individual protections. Neither one-sided view, as we have seen, captures the multiple nuances that have come to characterize the concepts. In recent discussions of human rights popular and political belief has begun to swing against such principles as inalienable, imprescriptible, and inviolable, as increasingly human rights are being invoked to protect prisoners and suspected terrorists against possible serious and sometimes trivial violations of their rights. In Great Britain, for example, there is discussion about supplementing the European Convention of Human Rights, incorporated into British law, with a statement of responsibilities. While responsibilities may have been somewhat eclipsed in discussions of human rights, they were never forgotten. In the UN Declaration it is repeatedly emphasized that humans are social beings, and in article 29 it is explicitly avowed that obligations are attached to community membership: 'Everyone has duties to the community in which alone the free and full development of his personality is possible' (Brownlie and Goodwin-Gill 2006: 28). The African Charter, reacting to the belief that existing documents are too individualistic in emphasis, wished to redress the imbalance by being more emphatic about the rights of peoples as collectives, and about individual responsibilities. The African Charter on Human and Peoples' Rights (1981) is a highly politically charged anti-colonialist statement vowing to eradicate any vestiges of it in foreign bases, discrimination, language, and religion. In its preamble it states that, 'the enjoyment of rights and freedoms also implies the performance of duties on the part of everyone' (Brownlie and Goodwin-Gill 2006: 1008). Apart from being charged with duties to the community and to the state, and to African culture and African Unity in general, the individual is given the specific responsibility, 'To preserve the harmonious development of the family and to work for the cohesion and respect of the family; to respect his parents at all times, to maintain them in case of need' (Brownlie and Goodwin-Gill 2006: 1013).

Natural Law and Natural Rights Today

There is little in contemporary philosophy that makes the connection between natural law and natural rights, except perhaps for rhetorical effect (Weinreb 1992: 279). A notable exception is John Finnis' spirited defence in suggesting that the main elements of natural law can be expressed in the vocabulary of rights (Finnis 1980: 198–230). There is certainly a residue of the traditional ideas of natural law and natural rights that co-exist with the modern. We saw in Chapter Four how despite the so-called secularization of the tradition, it was God who was predominantly invoked as the source of moral obligation. Among contemporary moral philosophers Elizabeth Anscombe most strongly reflects this view. She argues that without a continued belief in God as the divine lawgiver then the term obligation becomes merely metaphorical. If you take God out of the equation of moral obligation it is like saying that criminality continues to exist in the absence of criminal law (Anscombe 1997).

In addition, Jose Manuel de Aguilar, having witnessed the disastrous consequences of positivist international law in the devastation of Europe, contends that if the international order wishes to orient itself by means of sound norms and principles of justice, it is imperative that it returns to the teachings of Vitoria (Aguilar 1946: 221). Leszek Kolakowski maintains that there is little difference between the modern idea of human rights and traditional natural law theory. He argues that 'the notion of immutable rights of individuals goes back to the Christian belief in the autonomous status and irreplaceable value of the human personality' (Kolakowski 1990: 214).

Modern natural law tolerates a wide variety of views, and different positions on such questions as the absoluteness of its tenets, but in general such diverse thinkers as Martha Nussbaum, Pope John Paul II, Noam Chomsky, Bernard Williams, Joseph Boyle, and Michael J. Perry have this in common: that the fundamental principles of morality that should inform legislation are, for one reason or another, objective, discoverable by reason, and related to human nature (see Perry 1998: 68 and Boyle 1992: 4). Modern natural law theorists, while elaborating and applying ideas rooted in Aquinas, are cognizant of the fact that it is not merely an inheritance but a developing doctrine (Boyle 1992: 7).

Some writers on human rights contend that without a religious element or theological foundation to the doctrine sanctifying human dignity then human rights for the protection of the person have very little purchase. In other words, their efficacy relies on their relation to natural law (Perry 1998: 11–41 and Stackhouse 1999: 16). Perry, for example, argues that to posit the inherent dignity of every individual person is inextricably religious, and cannot credibly rest on any other foundation, let alone on a foundationless conception of human rights. This enables him to take the major documents that comprise the so-called 'International Bill of Rights' – The Universal Declaration of Human Rights (1948); the International Covenant on Civil and Political Rights (1976); and, the International Covenant on Economic, Social, and Cultural Rights (1976) – and highlight the fact that they all begin with the presupposition of human dignity, a claim that is unintelligible to Perry if divorced from a religious foundation (Perry 1998: 11–12). The claim is, then, that natural law, natural rights, and human rights have in common an inherently religious foundation without which their moral efficacy is severely undermined.

Perry cannot understand how Dworkin can claim that we may still think of humans as sacred without invoking a religious perspective. Instead we may do so out of deep philosophical convictions. Something is sacred for Dworkin because it inspires awe in us and we value it, rather than in the strong sense that because something is sacred it inspires awe in us. To suggest that human rights is necessarily a religious doctrine is not to recommend any particular religious beliefs to anyone (Perry 1998: chapt. 1).

Jeffrie Murphy insists that it is, for him, 'very difficult – perhaps impossible – to embrace religious convictions', but he nonetheless claims that 'the liberal theory of rights requires a doctrine of human dignity, preciousness and sacredness that cannot be utterly detached from a belief in God or at least from a world view that would properly be called religious in some metaphysically profound sense' (cited by Perry 1998: 87). Harries argues that both the American and French Declarations have religious elements, and that all talk about 'human rights presupposes the recognition of the dignity and worth of the human person' (Harries 1991: 1). He argues that God has created us in his own image, and 'respects the worth and dignity of what he has created' (Harries 1991: 3), and such is that value to Him that God himself became a human person so that humans may share in His divine nature. Harries argues that:

From the United Nations Charter in 1945 to the latest instrument of the ILO people of the most diverse backgrounds have agreed on a long series of laws and rights. This agreement and the discussion that produced it presupposes capacity for moral, and not just legal, discourse that belongs to human beings as such: that is *natural*' (Harries 1991: 6).

From a Christian point of view, 'These rights are *natural*; that is, they belong to all human beings qua human beings and they can be recognized as such by everyone whatever their religious convictions (Harries 1991: 6).

Indeed, the discussions surrounding the establishment of the Nuremberg Tribunal most immediately highlight the tension. After the Second World War the allies were faced with the dilemma of how to punish those war criminals who claimed to be obeying the laws and orders of the governments and commanders they served. Various international treaties were invoked to establish the idea of crimes against humanity. Such arguments as were presented often implicitly invoked the idea of a natural law, and derivative human rights inhering in individuals, which stand above any particular state's power and therefore should act as a restraint upon, and as a standard by which to judge, their conduct. More recently Martin Luther King in his campaign for civil rights in America, the Solidarity Movements in Poland, the liberation theology of Roman Catholic priest in Central America, and Pope John Paul II, in emphasising the dignity of man, have all appealed to notions of the natural law or a higher law to condemn the actions of those whom they believe to be acting inhumanely and unjustly. King, for example, exhorted his fellow Americans to emulate the spiritual dissenters of the revolutions and like them, 'giving our ultimate allegiance to the empire of justice, we must be that colony of dissenters seeking to imbue our nation with the ideals of a higher and nobler order' (King 1967: 157–8).

Natural law persists today in discussions of human rights in order to counter what is perceived to be an incipient relativism that serves to undermine the dignity of the person and makes his or her fundamental rights contingent upon recognition and enforcement by governments. Such writers as Walter Lipmann and Alexander Solzhenitsyn reject any suggestions that universal moral principles reflect national or ideological considerations (Schall 1991–2: 997). James Schall contends that the modern conception of rights has become so relativistic that we need to return to the foundationalism of natural law and the Law of Nations which is the conclusion from its first principles. The Law of Nations, he contends, is based on reason, disclosing what every society has in common, and is raised above the contingent and acts as a standard by which civil laws and the actions of states may be judged. He argues that, 'the relation of Natural Law to *ius gentium* is designed to guarantee that no civil society can escape from the judgment of itself, both by others and by its own citizens' (Schall 1991–2: 1028).

There is, of course, internal variety among those who espouse modern natural law, ranging from a firm commitment in all circumstances to the absoluteness and immutability of its principles, to an acknowledgement of the necessity to inject a certain degree of pragmatism when principles come into conflict. John Finnis, for example, espouses the incommensurability thesis, and contends that fundamental moral principles cannot be weighed against each other, and sacrificed on the basis of cost/benefit analysis. Those principles, what R. G. Collingwood would call absolute presuppositons, are what we use to make comparisons in terms of moral action, and are not themselves comparable in terms of a consequentialist analysis because they are our standards of comparison (Finnis 1992: 143–52). In so far as God has made his moral absolutes accessible to us through reason and faith we are in cooperation with Him. Knowledge of God's providence is beyond our comprehension, and to demur from a moral absolute is to be inconsistent with faith in Divine providence (Finnis 1991: chapt. 1).

The modern obsession with rights has led to a revival of interest in the natural rights tradition, and a preoccupation among theorists with the importance of human rights attaching to the individual independently of society. Many who would not subscribe to the religious foundationalism of natural law and its derivative rights posit the idea of fundamental moral rights that serve the same function as the classic natural rights doctrines, that is, posit a set of rights and protections inherent in the individual independent of governments, and irrespective of whether they are recognized, upheld, and protected.

Robert Nozick, as we saw, gives one of the strongest reiterations of this individualist conception of rights: 'Individuals have rights, and there are things no person or group may do to them (without violating their rights)' (Nozick 1974: 5). There are some writers who suggest that human rights and natural rights are basically the same. Immediately after the Second World War the highly respected international lawyer Hersch Lauterpacht argued that natural law, natural rights, and human rights were almost indistinguishable, having a common ancestry, and that any attempt to sever an international bill of rights from its religiously grounded ancestors would rob it of its moral force (Lauterpacht 1945: 9).

Undoubtedly there are many theorists who want to retain the character and function of natural rights, and for the same reasons as those who originally propounded them, that is, as protections against the arbitrary decisions of governments. Theorists want to retain the independence of natural rights from anything that governments may say or do by insisting upon the primacy of individual autonomy and agency, or by grounding human rights in some conception of humanity such as shared fundamental universal moral characteristics, like human interests or capabilities, the realization of which constitutes being minimally human (Buchanan 2003; Nickel 1987; Nussbaum 2000; Sen 1999; and Shue 1996). Buchanan, for example, in the course of formulating a moral theory of international law, contends that 'Human Rights, as the name implies, are ascribed to all human beings simply by virtue of their humanity or personhood, regardless of whatever other characteristics differentiate them from one another and regardless of where they live' (Buchanan 2003: 121–2).

Peter Jones, as we saw, argued that the contemporary doctrine of human rights is a direct descendant from liberal theories of natural rights (Jones 1991: 223). Alan Gewirth makes the very strong claim that 'We may assume, as true by definition, that Human Rights are rights that all persons have simply insofar as they are human' (Gewirth 1982: 41). For Gewirth, human rights are claim rights necessary for protecting the conditions of fulfilling the needs of human agency. Because humans have the prospect of being purposive agents the claim rights to which they are entitled are necessary to maintain freedom and well-being. The aim of human rights is to ensure that the individual is able to be self-controlling, and self-developing, and to interact with others on the basis of mutual respect and cooperation. Human rights, then, maintain rational autonomy (Gewirth 1982: 5–20). It follows for him that 'agents and institutions are absolutely prohibited from degrading persons, treating them as if they had no rights or dignity' (Gewirth 1984: 108). Similarly, Joel Feinberg maintains that human rights are 'independent of *any* institutional rules, legal or nonlegal' (Feinberg 1980: 85, n. 27). The thrust of this conception of human rights is that rights are valid moral claims or entitlements. As Rex Martin suggests, the word moral in this context seems to be doing much of the work that 'natural' used to do (Martin 2003: 180).

Contrary to these views, there is more of a lacuna than most writers want to acknowledge between the modern human rights culture and the natural rights tradition that is often assumed to underpin it. Indeed, this gap is acknowledged by James Griffin when he contends that for the most part it is argued that natural rights are derived from natural law, but it is 'altogether harder to say from what "human rights" are supposed to be derived' (Griffin 2008: 9).

Human Rights Dialects

Numerous conventions have proliferated since the promulgation of the United Nations Declaration on Human Rights, in 1948, which followed the systematic and brutal policies of extermination perpetrated in Hitler's Germany and Stalin's Russia. The trials of Nazi war criminals for crimes against humanity put onto a quasi-legal footing the long-standing moral claim that individuals have rights by the mere fact of being human, which are independent of any government, whose principal obligation to humanity is to protect and respect them. Until this time international lawyers argued that the acts of state could not be attributed to the crimes of any individual person. The traditional notion of sovereignty provided the principle. Sovereign states acknowledged no superior and therefore accepted no external judgements. Officials carrying out their authoritative duties on behalf of the state could not be indicted as criminals, unless domestic laws covered such cases. International law related to the rights and duties of states in their relations with each other. Morally speaking, of course this argument has little effect. Everyone is capable of passing moral judgements on the acts of politicians, and the idea of legal sovereignty no longer exempts states from external judgement.

The Nuremberg trials were decisive in translating moral condemnation into formal principles of international law. The International Military Tribunal had jurisdiction over crimes of peace (that is the waging of aggressive war, war crimes), and crimes against humanity. While the idea of a war crime was well established by this time, the idea of crimes against peace and against humanity was not very well understood. The judgement of the Nuremberg Tribunal distinguishes between aggressive and defensive war, rather than unjust and just wars, and goes to some lengths to emphasize that in respect of crimes against peace (*jus ad bellum*) the signatories to the Pact of Paris, or the Kellog-Briand Pact, which included Germany, Italy, and Japan, had renounced war as an instrument of policy. War crimes, the Tribunal argued, were already well established in international law and irrespective of whether parties to the Second World War were signatories to the Hague Convention of 1907 and the Geneva Convention of 1929, they were bound by their terms because they merely clarified and were declaratory of the rules already generally accepted (Steiner and Alston 1996: 102–9).

The most important legacy of Nuremberg was in recognizing the idea of crimes against humanity. It gave formal recognition to the idea that there could be a crime committed against persons not just in a national context, but in the context of humanity as a whole in which the whole of mankind had an interest and the right to bring offenders to justice. In defining crimes against humanity the London Charter for the Nuremberg trials made it clear that the perpetrators of such crimes as murder, extermination, racial and political persecution, enslavement, and enforced deportation were to be made answerable 'whether or not they were committed in violation of the domestic law of the country where perpetrated' (cited in Goldstone 1996: 2).

Crimes against humanity were, however, limited to those committed after 1939 and in the context of war (Steiner and Alston 1996: 108–9). Nuremberg's jurisdiction was limited in that the crimes against humanity it was empowered to try had to be in the context of war crimes and crimes against peace, which meant that persecution of communists or Jews in Nazi Germany before the War were not part of its brief. As Justice Richard Goldstone remarks: 'Thus, while the inclusion of crimes against humanity within the Nuremberg Charter constituted a significant development in humanitarian law, it did not signify the triumph of individual human rights over state sovereignty' (Goldstone 1996: 3).

This indicates that the modern language of human rights has various dialects that are not immediately intelligible to each other. On the one hand there is a reluctance to let go of the idea of moral rights existing independently of governments, and on the other hand those who believe that such rights are not rights at all because they lack legal recognition and the political will of governments to enforce them. They are not incompatible views. As Thomas Pogge suggests, those who subscribe to the existence of moral human rights readily accept that law greatly facilitates their realization. Those who believe that human rights are rights proper only when codified, readily accept that what is being codified are moral claims that have become widely recognized as pressing and imperative (Pogge 2002).

To contend that moral rights are independent of governments and legal systems, we do not have to believe that they have their foundation in the natural law and natural rights traditions. As we saw, Idealists such as Green while stressing the conventional character of natural rights/human rights could acknowledge that they were independent of government recognition (but not of social recognition). More recently Mervyn Frost illustrates the point. In his view, as human beings we participate in two nearly global practices. Firstly, I have citizenship rights that I claim as a member of a state within the global practice of sovereign states. In addition, I participate in global civil society, in which I consider myself to have equal human rights, such as freedom of speech, of movement, contract, assembly, and the right to life, personal security, and to own property. It may well be that the state in which I enjoy citizenship rights protects these human rights that I consider myself to have, and it is an expectation of citizenship that it would do so. They are nevertheless moral rights independent of governments, without which I would have a completely different self-conception and identity. In this sense the rights are constitutive of me (Frost 2002). 'These rights', Amartya Sen contends, 'are not derived from citizenship of any country, or membership of any nation, but are taken as the entitlement of every human being' (cited in Frost 2002: 5).

On the other hand, to suggest that human rights are not properly rights is not to deny that there are fundamental rights, or to deny that they are acknowledgements of deeply rooted moral claims. This was a position that Bosanquet maintained. In this second category Rex Martin in his *A System of Rights* equates human rights with civil rights, making them both dependent upon government recognition and enforcement. The great human rights documents, he argues, are not primarily addressed to individuals, although individuals are the beneficiaries, but principally to governments of states. In so far as this is the case any account of human rights cannot ignore governmental practices of recognition and maintenance in characterizing them. Even rights *to* freedom from torture and injury claimed *against* individuals are also at once addressed to governments who are expected to protect and maintain these rights. Martin does, nevertheless, acknowledge that without recognition they may be valid moral claims, but not rights. It was the blatant disregard of the so-called 'natural rights' of whole categories of German peoples by first depriving them of their citizenship rights that gave rise to one of the most powerful critiques of the twentieth century of the idea of natural rights as protections against inhumane and inhuman treatment.

HANNAH ARENDT AND FUNDAMENTAL RIGHTS

In one of the most compelling discussions of natural/human rights to have been written since the Second World War, Hannah Arendt demonstrated the fragility of human rights when faced with the systematic withdrawal of citizenship rights: 'Denationalisation became a powerful weapon of totalitarian politics, and the constitutional inability of European nation-states to guarantee Human Rights to those who had lost guaranteed rights, made it possible for the persecuting governments to impose their standard of values even upon opponents' (Arendt 1973: 269). Using a different vocabulary, but equally critical of traditional conceptions of natural rights as the British Idealists had been, Arendt does not want to deny that there are fundamental rights. They are fundamental to a community, and guaranteed as the rights of citizens, and not as abstract universal rights that cannot be claimed by anyone, and which states lack the political will to enforce.

Arendt rejects natural law as the foundation of the notion of crimes against humanity on the grounds that it is obsolete in positing a fixed human nature and thus falls foul of the metaphysics of substance. Like Han-Georg Gadamer she relies upon Heidegger's insight that *Dasein* is the only being for which the question of its existence is meaningful. It is what Heidegger calls our factuality, that is, our abandonment by the drama of the past into a world as it is. We are thrust into the midst of an on-going performance. Instead of the language of human nature Arendt prefers that of the 'human condition'. She contends that 'the human condition is not the same as human nature' (Arendt 1958: 10). The Human Condition refers to the context in which life is bestowed upon human beings. Arendt argues that 'Whatever touches or enters into a sustained relationship with human life immediately assumes the character of a condition of human existence. This is why men, no matter what they do, are always conditioned beings' (Arendt 1958: 9). The circumstances constrain but do not determine our choices (Benhabib 2006: 21). We are the makers of the world. What are universal are not human rights or human nature, nor even human reason, but plurality, in which we are all the same, yet uniquely different. Plurality is part of the structure of life; we have no choice in the matter, but how this plurality is manifest is not easily predictable (Lang and Williams 2005: 11).

Arendt is dismissive of natural law as a foundation of universal rights because of what she witnessed during the Nazi era. Because of the unsettled surface of juridical and institutional attempts at universalization she was extremely sceptical of the efficacy of natural or human rights, and of the prospects for an international criminal court with powers to bring individuals to account. She refused to believe in the possibilities that were nascent in her time. Instead, having witnessed the consequences of denaturalization of citizens, and the degradation they faced as a consequence, she tenaciously believed that the rights of citizenship provided a much greater safeguard against crimes against humanity.

Arendt identifies three components in the latter part of the nineteenth and for over half of the twentieth centuries that served to diminish a common sense of humanity. They are anti-semitism, imperialism, and totalitarianism. The political, economic, and legal equality of Jews did not imply social equality. Only exceptional Jewish individuals were granted such privilege. They were the '*parvenu*' expected to rise above their Jewishness and act differently from other Jews, or 'pariah'. The '*parvenu*' felt different from other men in the street because he was a Jew, and different from other Jewish nationals because he was not an 'ordinary' Jew. When the issue of Jewish identity within the state was political, to be Jewish could be deemed a crime, but because of the ambiguous social situation they occupied it became a vice, a character flaw. Judaism could be escaped by conversion to Christianity, but Jewishness could not be abjured. As long as Judaism was considered a crime it could be constrained by laws. As a vice it had to be eliminated (Arendt 1973: 87).

The imperialism of the nineteenth century gave rise to the emergency explanation of racism to rationalize the confrontation between Europeans who were appalled to be associated with the same species as Africans. Racism arises in conjunction with imperialism, and is employed as the political device to promote it. The liberal idea of equality is undermined by the making of racial distinctions. Race justified the domination of one people over another, while bureaucracy facilitated the process. Bureaucracy siphons off power from the many into the hands of the few, subverting democratic ideals of human equality, and destroying the notion of a common humanity. The combination of racism and bureaucracy in imperialism eradicates notions of a common humanity, and of universal human rights.

In her book *The Origins of Totalitarianism*, Arendt demonstrates the extent to which totalitarianism poses a threat to human rights, not only in its own disregard for universal inalienable rights, but also because it disposes the recipients, the host countries, of dispossessed peoples to look upon them, not as human, but as something else not deserving of such rights. Human rights become cut loose from political identity, and to be denied citizenship is to be denied human rights. There is no natural equality, Arendt argues, we attain equality through membership of groups on the basis of mutual decisions to endow ourselves with, and protect equal rights (Johnson 2001: 25).

Post First World War Europe saw the emergence of minorities in Eastern and Southern Europe. The movement of stateless people to Central and Western Europe introduced a new element of disintegration into European politics. The consequence was that 'Denationalisation became a powerful weapon of totalitarian politics, and the constitutional inability of European nation-states to guarantee human rights to those who had lost nationally guaranteed rights, made it possible for the persecuting governments to impose their standard of values even upon opponents' (Arendt 1973: 269). Minority treaties placed restrictions and obligations upon states to recognize the special status of minority groups within their borders, and thus essentially ended aspirations of enforced assimilation. Minorities were only half-stateless in that they had a place in some political body, even if they needed additional secondary rights such as speaking one's own language, and enjoying a distinct cultural heritage. While these may not have been seriously protected by the dominant culture, more elementary rights like those to work and reside were not threatened.

The more serious problem has been statelessness. Between the two world wars almost every country in Europe introduced some legislation of denationalization which would enable it to get rid of vast sections of its citizenship at opportune times. Many did not invoke the powers, but many did. Arendt contends that:

No paradox of contemporary politics is filled with more poignant irony than the discrepancy between the efforts of the well-meaning idealists who stubbornly insist on regrading as 'inalienable' those human rights, which are enjoyed only by citizens of the most prosperous and civilised countries, and the situation of the rightless themselves. Their situation has deteriorated just as stubbornly, until the internment camp – prior to the Second World War the exception rather than the rule for the stateless – has become the routine solution for the problem of domicile of the "displaced persons" (Arendt 1973: 279).

Arendt argues that as a result of hundreds of thousands of stateless people arriving in foreign nation states the only right that was of any true significance of the Rights of Man in international relations, the right of asylum, was under threat. While Arendt was sceptical of its continuance it has nevertheless become an important aspect of the work of the United Nations, and is embodied in British law as a result of incorporating the European Convention on Human Rights, but is, nevertheless, the first right to be under threat as security tightens and the fear of international terrorism increases.

Arendt contended that the reliance of universal rights upon governments became evident very soon after the early declarations of rights. The Rights of Man were pronounced as inalienable and irreducible to other rights and laws, nor were they derived from them. They rested upon Man's authority. No law was needed to protect them, because all law ultimately was said to derive from them.

Man was sovereign in matters of law just as the people were sovereign in matters of government. This sovereignty was claimed in the name of man, and it appeared natural that the 'inalienable' rights of man would find their guarantee in the right of the people to sovereign self-government. Human rights and national emancipation, the rights of people to sovereign self-government, became inextricably linked. The Rights of Man were proclaimed as inalienable because they did not depend upon governments while at the same time as soon as human beings lacked a government and needed to invoke their minimum human rights, there was no institution to uphold or enforce them. Arendt contends that 'The Rights of Man, supposedly inalienable, proved to be unenforceable – even in countries whose constitutions were based upon them – whenever people appeared who were no longer citizens of any sovereign state' (Arendt 1973: 293). Her point is that the Rights of Man were established during the American and French Revolutions. Even though the idea of natural universal rights is much older, their practical realization occurs in the context of two national struggles. Despite this, these rights were still proclaimed as natural, inalienable, and universal, even though they rely upon the internal jurisdiction of states for their enforcement, are almost exclusively related to citizens, and are therefore exclusive and conditional in so far as they belong only to those who are legally citizens of states. If the Rights of Man have a concrete existence they would belong to every one unconditionally by the mere fact of being human (see Cotter 2005: 97).

People interviewed in the refugee camps established as a result of the expulsion of the Albanians from Kosovo in 1999 were under no illusion that the deprivation of their national rights was correlative with the loss of their human rights. They felt that they were no longer recognized as persons, merely dependants to be clothed and fed. As Arendt argued, there is an awareness among refugees and displaced persons that the one inevitably leads to the other and this is why they develop a 'violent group consciousness' forcefully claiming rights as Poles, Jews or Germans, and not merely as humans.

No amount of physical protection, provision of food by governmental or voluntary agencies, and freedom of expression alters the fact that they are fundamentally rightless: 'The prolongation of their lives is due to charity and not to right, for no law exists which could force the nations to feed them; their freedom of movement, if they have it at all, gives them no right to residence which even the jailed criminal enjoys as a matter of course; and their freedom of opinion is a fool's freedom, for nothing they think matters anyhow' (Arendt 1973: 296).

Arendt is conscious of the extent to which human rights depend upon being first and foremost a citizen enjoying the rights of citizenship. To be deprived of those also effectively stripped you of human rights. Between the two world wars, Arendt argues, denationalization became a powerful weapon in the hands of totalitarian regimes. The Nazis, for instance, paved the way in their Nuremberg Laws, which distinguished between citizens of the Reich, and nationals, or second class citizens who had no political rights, which led eventually by decree to the deprivation of all nationals of 'alien blood' of their nationality.

The fact that European nation-states were constitutionally unable to guarantee the human rights of those people who had been deprived of states' rights meant that the persecutors were effectively able to impose their own scale of values on their opponents. Those whom the persecutors described as scum were received and treated as scum everywhere. No one wants displaced persons, or persons without states. The fact that they became described after the Second World War as displaced persons was a refusal to accept that they were stateless. Arendt argues that 'Non recognition of statelessness always means repatriation, i.e., deportation to a country of origin, which either refuses to recognise the prospective repatriate as a citizen, or, on the contrary, urgently wants him back for punishment' (Arendt 1973: 279). It quickly became evident that the practical substitute for the lack of a homeland was not political asylum, but an internment camp from which refugees could be deported again. They are people without identities. This is illustrated by the extent to which the Serbian expulsion of Albanians from Kosovo, and the confiscation of the identity documents of many of them is cause for considerable consternation. They were citizens stripped of national rights and Nato was unable to guarantee or protect their human rights.

Our experience of human rights, their dependence upon national rights, Arendt argues, confirms Burke's argument that they are nothing but abstractions, and that it is our traditional inheritance of rights, embedded in our long-standing social and political practices, that are of more significance. When faced with man in his abstract nakedness, Arendt argues, the world found nothing sacred. To be regarded merely as human is to be regarded as nothing more than a savage, and the fear is that you may quickly come to be regarded as a beast. This is why people cling on so tenaciously to their nationality when deprived of it and the rights it afforded them because this national inheritance is testimony to their membership of the civilized world.

Arendt wants to insist upon our right to have rights (Arendt 1973: 290). As Benhabib maintains, what this means is the prohibiting of states from denaturalizing individuals by withdrawing state protections and citizenship rights (Benhabib 2006: 25). It is for Arendt an unconditional right, but quite distinct from universal human rights or the Rights of Man. As Bonnie Honig contends, the right to have rights is a double-edged sword: it at once reproaches, in different degrees, every particular order of rights, while demanding that everyone should belong to such an order. This double-edged gesture is required because we depend upon rights because we are sceptical of being treated with dignity and respect by the political communities to which we belong, while at the same time being dependent for those rights on those very same political communities (Honig 2006: 106–7). Whatever advances have been made in constructing an international juridical system of rights it is nevertheless still the case, as Benhabib argues, that, 'the state remains the distributor and guarantor of Human Rights. The individual who is stateless, in our times as much as in Arendt's, becomes a non-person, a body that can be moved around by armies and police, customs officers and refugee agencies' (Benhabib 2006: 175).

In discussing the trial of Adolph Eichmann, Arendt argues that the general picture of anti-semitism formed the backdrop, but that this only served to obscure the fact that only Eichmann was on trial for his life, and to confuse his trial with that of the Nazi system clouds the issue of individual responsibility. Arendt argues that 'the physical extermination of the Jewish people, was a crime against humanity, perpetrated upon the body of the Jewish people, and that only the choice of victims, not the nature of the crime, could be derived from the long history of Jew-hatred and anti-Semitism' (Arendt 1977: 269). For Arendt, however, the Nazi reasoned and rationalized murder of whole populations portended a new set of frightening and horrific possibilities. In other words the Nazi atrocities were not the last chapter in anti-semitism, but the first chapter in modern totalitarianism. Bruno Bettelheim argues that despite the questions of the legality of the trial, because of the kidnap of Eichmann, 'It brought the world face to face with those dangers of totalitarianism that it seems all too willing to avoid examining' (Bettelheim 1963: 33).

In Arendt's view the category of 'crimes against humanity' was invented to describe a new act, the act of genocide against a people by the mere fact that it exists on this earth as a particular type of people (Benhabib 2000: 79). The study of Eichmann shows that the gross violations of human rights that totalitarian regimes are capable of perpetrating do not depend upon mad psychotic lunatics, but upon people like Eichmann, who many psychiatrists pronounced perfectly normal in his affections and attachments to people, and who in his vanity, detachment from reality, and stupidity was swept along in the tide of the machinery of the final solution, implementing his orders with dutiful enthusiasm. It is a warning that human rights are fragile, and that states with far greater potential for centralization of power and communications constitute an ever present threat.

Arendt's description of evil as banal, based upon her observations of Eichmann at his trial, is nevertheless a generalization based upon one instance. We have to be careful that we do not take one facet of the holocaust and take it for the whole. Eichmann is indeed emblematic of the holocaust, but he should not be taken to be representative of the kind of people who were its perpetrators. Those who committed the crimes were of many different characters ranging from Eichmann himself to Ivan the Terrible and Dr. Mengele. The pathological brutes and sadists, the so called monsters, give us nothing to distinguish the holocaust from the countless atrocities throughout history, but reflection upon the character of Eichmann may add depth to our understanding of essential parts, if not the essence of the holocaust. For Arendt, describing Eichmann as banal was not intended to diminish the evil of the holocaust. Its banality was in some ways even more frightening than her earlier sense of its radicalness (Gaita 2002: 153–4). The example of Eichmann demonstrated the consequences of what happens when thinking fails to inform the behaviour of a person and a culture (Johnson 2001: 48).

COLLINGWOOD AND RORTY

R. G. Collingwood and Richard Rorty both recognize the dependence of rights upon community and solidarity, and the imperative for extending the moral community if rights are to become truly universal. One might reasonably claim that both Collingwood and Rorty are addressing the issue of what are the constituents of the civilizing process, and they both agree that a principal feature is that of reducing or eliminating force from our relations with others. They differ in the mechanism by which this may be accomplished. The interesting contrast between Collingwood and Rorty is that Collingwood lays much more emphasis upon the power of rational thinking in overcoming the barriers to acknowledging others as human, while at the same time placing emotion at the centre of his theory.

We saw in T. H. Green that the crucial factor in recognizing that others have rights is to widen the terms of reference of those we regard as our neighbours. The means by which this extension takes place may rest upon a combination of developing and acknowledging emotional ties with those we once regarded as 'them', somehow different from, and lesser than 'us'. The idea expressed perhaps in the sentiment of the French President with the fall of the Berlin Wall; Mitterand declared in his New Year's Eve message of 1989/90, 'Europe is returning home to its history and geography'. It was in fact a Europe, Eastern Europe, that had never been fully recognized as part of our moral community, an East altogether more exotic, barbaric, and cruder than the West (Judt 1996).

What does it take to go beyond the idea of 'we Europeans' and to acknowledge a common humanity? Hannah Arendt showed how the Prime Minister of Israel, Ben Gurion, and the court in Jerusalem missed an important opportunity to emphasize that what was done to the Jews in the name of humanity, that is ridding it of a cancerous parasite, was not just a crime against the Jewish people, but an affront to humanity in general. The whole rationale of Nazi propaganda was to depict the Jews as less than human, who could be stripped of citizenship rights, and who would not fully qualify as human, and could have no human rights. As vermin they did not even have the honorary rights, to use Ritchie's term, of domestic animals, which we have made honorary humans as members of our family and communities.

What Rorty wants to show is that the process of incorporating 'them' into our notions of 'we' requires much more than rational argument. It requires an emotional outreach, an extension of our sympathies, an activation of our sentiments of pity, compassion, and revulsion. For him this may be achieved by immersing ourselves in, saturating our emotions with, sad and sentimental stories, so that those who have been denied the apparel of humanity are recognized, or acknowledged, to have the same moral capacities as us.

This may be an apt characterization of what Las Casas was doing in his exchanges with Sepúlveda, and in his accounts of the actions of the Spanish in the Indies. His is not a philosophical argument designed to counter the claim that the American Indians are natural slaves in the Aristotelian sense. Instead, he gives a graphic account of the brutality and depravity of the Spanish. The Indians are depicted as gentle, caring, sensitive, and creative, the finest qualities of humanity, and it is the Spanish and not they who have fallen below the level of humanity. It is a technique designed to evoke sympathy, compassion, revulsion, and horror.

The concept of recognition is integral to the idea of extending the moral community. It is a concept that shoulders a heavy burden in modern political theory and has become the cornerstone of discussions relating to individual, cultural, sexual, and state authenticity (see Boucher 2000). Recognition is about having a voice, and having that voice heard; an authentic voice that expresses a self-reflective sense of the self, an identity in relation to others, rather than an identity that others impose. To misrecognize someone, that is to impose an identity on someone, is a form of oppression (Taylor 1992).

R. G. Collingwood made an important, but little acknowledged contribution to our understanding of this process of widening the moral community through recognition. He posits two forms of recognition. There is a recognition of others within one's own community which entails a recognition of their capacity to choose freely, reflecting their possession of rational consciousness. Beyond this, there is recognition of others outside of one's own community, and the necessity of not falling into the temptation of imposing our own criteria of value upon them. To acknowledge that a person is capable of entering society is in itself a recognition of that person's attainment of the capacity rationally to choose; of an equal possession of 'that degree of freedom which the decision to join that society demands' (Collingwood 1992: 21.6). The possession of self-respect is equated with the consciousness of each person of his or her freedom (Collingwood 1992: 13.18 and 37.11). The politics of recognition is all about attributing equal value and affording equal respect to others, while at the same time acknowledging their differences. What is being acknowledged and recognized is the capacity for choice, not the equal worth of the choices themselves. To inhabit the same community individuals are equal in that they equally possess membership (Collingwood 1992: 21.61).

The emphasis upon freedom and the capacity to choose has implications for social justice and morality. A civilized society is one in which force is gradually being replaced by cooperation, and decisions are made by agreement and compromise rather than confrontation. Force gives way to rational discussion. Force, of course, denies the capacity of choice and restricts human freedom. There are three dimensions, or constituents, to this civilizing process which are directly related to the expansion of the moral community. The dimensions of civility are first, the elimination of force in our relations with each other within the body politic; second, the elimination of unintelligent exploitation in our relations with nature, what would be called today sustainable development; and, third, the elimination of force in relations between and among bodies politic, and between one people and another. The civilizing process is one that relies on recognition both in relation to other persons and to nature.

The first constituent in the process requires us to act civilly in relation to our compatriots. It prohibits us from actions that diminish the self-respect of the individual by diminishing his or her consciousness of freedom by undermining the capacity for choice. To do so is to exercise force, and put at risk the person being overcome by passion or desire. The term force includes both mental and physical acts of coercion. He does not, then, distinguish between force and coercion because he wishes to highlight the fact that violence may be inflicted by the state, community or individual upon other persons without physical force. It puts on par both psychological and physical damage.

With regard to relations among members of the same community or body politic institutional arrangements may be put in place, refined, and adjusted to promote the necessary recognition that gives rise to self and mutual respect, regardless of ethnic or cultural differences. Economic inequalities cannot be ignored because the economically advantaged stand in a relation of force in comparison with the disadvantaged who are rarely in a position to resist. The presence of ethnic minorities within the body politic brings into focus the additional consideration of to what extent the civilizing process within the community should be extended to relations between it and members of other communities. This third constituent, the second being our relation to nature, has historically been a difficult one because it involves asking the question whether civility entails treating the members of other communities civilly. The answer depends upon how that community responds to a prior question, are foreigners human? If we do not regard the foreigner as fully human, as we have seen a not unusual attitude throughout history, then they become for us part of the natural world and eligible for systematic exploitation. Even those who enjoy a relatively high degree of civilization look upon foreigners with disdain, and treat them with the utmost incivility. This, as we have seen, goes as far as maiming or murdering them, often with impunity, despite having a conviction that fellow human beings deserve to be treated civilly, 'all that is lacking is a conviction that strangers are human beings' (Collingwood 1992: 35.67).

The question, 'are "foreigners" human', is one that persists throughout human history, and the failure to answer affirmatively has led to the most horrific acts of inhumanity. Richard Rorty has identified this question as the key to understanding the brutal attitude of Nazis towards Jews, of white racists towards blacks, male misogynists towards women, and Serbs towards Muslims in Bosnia and Kosovo. It is in refusing to acknowledge others as fully human that we are able to act inhumanely towards them.

Acknowledging that 'others' are the same as us, that they have human rights, is contingent upon expanding the moral community, to see an ever increasing circle of people as one's neighbours. The lack of a human essence, and our capacity for endless re-description implies that there is no necessity to feel obliged to others in respect of their needs and interests. Nor are we constrained from acting in ways that violate an essential human nature, therefore nothing is naturally inhuman (Rorty 1989: 189). Our obligations are generated by particular loyalties, our sense of solidarity with others of our kind. Community, and the expansion of the moral community, are an achievement, and not a given (Festenstein in Festenstein and Thompson, eds. 2001: 11).

Rorty's denial of anything like human essences, or human nature, or foundations of any kind makes it impossible to invoke any notion of transhistorical principles at times when human institutions and traditional notions of decency and behaviour are collapsing, as in the case of Auschwitz and more recently the conflict between Serbs and Muslims in Bosnia. At such times we want to appeal to some notion of human solidarity and declare that because these people, the Muslims and Jews, are like us it is inhuman to be committing such crimes against them. Rorty wants to argue in the final chapter of *Contingency, Irony, and Solidarity* that the notion of we or us is crucial in understanding the idea of moral obligation.

The idea of a fellow comrade, a co-national, a Catholic, all invoke strong senses of being one of us. Rorty says quite emphatically: 'I want to deny that "one of us human beings" (as opposed to animals, vegetables, and machines) can have the same sort of force as the previous examples. I claim that the force of "us" is, typically, contrastive in the sense that it contrasts with "they" which is also made up of human beings – the wrong sort of human beings' (Rorty 1989: 190). To rescue Jews from the horrors of Auschwitz on the grounds that they were fellow human beings would be, Rorty contends, a poor explanation of a generous action. Those Danes and Italians who rescued Jews at the risk of their own lives would surely, if questioned, have said because they were my neighbours, or fellow Milanese, fellow Zealanders, or members of the same profession, rather than fellow human beings.

Rorty's claim that few rescuers would have cited a common humanity as the motive for acting righteously is, of course, testable. There are in fact many accounts by rescuers of why they harboured or saved Jews. Many do appeal to a common humanity and in research into the motivations of rescuers it has been suggested that predominantly some universal principle of humanity is being appealed to (see Geras 1995). Many of the rescuers felt somewhat alienated from their own communities, and may because of this have sought a reference point outside. It may also be that they were moved by more immediate considerations and rationalized their actions in terms of universal principles.

In his Amnesty lecture Rorty argues that inhuman treatment or the refusal to treat people equally is justified by the perpetrators in treating the victims as non-human or pseudo human. Firstly, the victim can be portrayed as an animal, as opposed to human. This is how the Nazis portrayed Jews. In fact they portrayed them as vermin. Secondly, humans can be portrayed as children as opposed to adults and therefore denied their claim to equal treatment, Blacks, for instance, being referred to as boy. A third form of exclusion is to use man as the generic term for men and women. Rorty suggests that in Catherine MacKinnon's view for most men a woman is not synonymous with being human.

Rorty does offer us a sense in which there is moral progress, and that is by achieving greater human solidarity. Its attraction to us is not because it accords with a universal human nature, but because of our experience of moral communities, with friends, neighbours, members of the same church, or fellow nationals. We extend these sentiments to more and more people, by extending the notion of one of us. As Geras argues, 'moral sentiment in this is more important than moral rationality or principle' (Geras in Festenstein and Thompson (eds) 2001: 168).

The contingency of the human condition and the human capacity to create its own future is affirmed by both Collingwood and Rorty. They denied the prescriptive and descriptive versions of natural law and natural rights, and subscribed instead to a version of the immanent criterion of fundamental rights posited by Hegel and the British Idealists. It is an implausible fiction to view character as a static entity; it is constantly in the process of being formed, and developed. Both give considerable emphasis to the self-making capacity of the human personality. Collingwood contends, for example, that 'The self is really in constant flux, a process of creating itself and its world' (Collingwood 1923: 20a).

Philosophers have tried to find some essential ingredient that defines human nature in order to avoid arbitrary exclusions, but, Rorty argues: 'We have come to see that the only lesson of either history or anthropology is our extraordinary malleability. We are coming to think of ourselves as the flexible, protean, self-shaping, animal rather than as the rational animal or the cruel animal.' (Rorty 1993: 115). For Rorty our ideas and beliefs are simply contingent and ungroundable. He describes himself as a bourgeois liberal ironist. A liberal is someone who believes that 'cruelty is the worse thing we can do' (Rorty 1989: xv). The ironist being sufficiently historicist and nominalist is aware of the contingency of his, or her, own fundamental beliefs. A liberal ironist would count among these ungroundable fundamental beliefs the desire that human suffering be reduced and that humiliation perpetrated by human beings upon one another cease. In other words, the liberal ironist does not ground his, or her, beliefs on such a foundation as a universal human nature.

The only distinct trait that Rorty finds in the human species is language, used either to make things better or worse, rendering Humanity just as malleable as Life (Rorty 2001: 172, 174–5). As Rorty says, 'There is no *neutral*, noncircular way to defend the liberal's claim that cruelty is the worst thing... We cannot look back behind the processes of socialization which convinced us twentieth-century liberals of the validity of this claim and appeal to something which is more "real" or less ephemeral than the historical contingencies which brought those processes into existence' (Rorty 1989: 197–8).

In demonstrating the contingency of things and beliefs Rorty shows how the search for foundations is an impossible enterprise. In his book *Philosophy and the Mirror of Nature* Rorty calls those who search for unifying universal theories systematic philosophers, and those who are critical of our current vocabularies and deny that philosophy is the search for truth are designated edifying philosophers. In *Contingency, Irony and Solidarity* Rorty argues these are the sort of philosophers who attempt to dissolve rather than solve inherited problems (Rorty 1989: 20). Truth is not a property of the world, but is instead a property of language which is a human creation (Rorty 1989: 6). Furthermore, truth is not a matter of correspondence to an independent reality but instead what came to be believed as a result of 'free and open encounters' (Rorty 1989: 68). Rorty relies upon Wittgenstein and Donald Davidson to show that language itself has no foundations but is a product of time and chance. In other words it is contingent.

Liberal societies, Rorty argues, are not held together by philosophical beliefs. They hold together because they have common vocabularies and common hopes. The vocabulary plays on hopes by telling stories about desired futures to be generated by the sacrifices of the present (Rorty 1989: 86). As human beings we are capable of powerful re-descriptions, of imagining new paradigms and languages deliberately to improve the condition of humankind. Acceptance of the contingency of language renders us in the position of an ironist. In the ideal liberal society intellectuals would be ironists, people whose fundamental values and attachments, that is, their final vocabularies, present particular problems. They are never completely able to take themselves seriously, because of their awareness that the terms in which they describe themselves are constantly susceptible to change. They are aware of the fragility and contingency of their final vocabularies, of their very selves. They realize, for example, that anything, desirable or undesirable, can be re-described, and that there are no neutral criteria to inform a choice between final vocabularies (Rorty 1989: 73–4). For the ironist, this realization is liberating.

The non-intellectuals would, however, accept their liberal vocabulary along with its stories and dreams, but nevertheless still be commonsensically nominalist and historicist. In other words they would acknowledge their own contingency without having any serious doubts about the particular contingency they have happened to become. Non-ironists tend to distrust the powers of re-description, and are disturbed by the claim that their final vocabularies are contingent. Rorty contends that the sure way to cause anyone lasting pain is to humiliate them by making the things that they hold most dear 'look futile, obsolete, and powerless' (Rorty 1989: 89).

The liberal ironist is redeemed, however, in eschewing cruelty, and would therefore desist from publicly offering humiliating re-descriptions of fellow citizens. The fundamental premise of Rorty's theory is that belief without philosophical foundations is capable of guiding action. Furthermore, that belief may still be worth dying for even when its adherents are aware that it is nothing more than the result of historical contingencies (Rorty 1989: 189). Rorty maintains that 'It is pictures rather than propositions, metaphors rather than statements, which determine most of our philosophic commitments' (Rorty 1980: 12).

Our human rights culture is one such recent shape that human nature has taken. What Rorty wants to argue is that 'nothing relevant to moral choice separates human beings from animals except historically contingent facts of the world, cultural facts.' (Rorty 1993: 116). The realization that we shape our own future, and that we can transform ourselves into whatever we are courageous enough to imagine, substitutes for Kant's question 'what is man?' the quite different question of what sort of world can we make in the future. In other words we are dispensing with the search for foundations in ethics and epistemology. In rejecting the search for foundations we can move away from an emphasis upon rational argument and acknowledge that what makes us different from the animals is not the fact that they feel and we know, but instead the fact that we feel for each other to a much greater extent than they do (Rorty 1993: 122).

To include others in the moral community that we regard our own is possible only by broadening our emotional experience. This is done not by rational argument but by playing on our sympathies through exposure to great literature and other artistic endeavours that manipulate the sentiments. The aim of focusing on sentiment in this way is to extend the boundaries of who we are prepared to regard as one of us. Rational argument did not persuade the Serbs that the Muslims deserve equal respect as humans, nor many men that intelligent women, or Nazis that intelligent Jews, deserve equal status as humans. Feelings of solidarity with others who we include among 'us' emerge in circumstances.

Liberal societies for both Collingwood and Rorty value civility, and abhor violence and cruelty. Collingwood explains this with reference to a theory of mind that explains the development of rational consciousness. It is not a necessary development in that it is contingent. It could have been other than it is. Civility, associated with the highest level of rational consciousness, requires that the recognition of a civil demeanour in others entails treating them civilly. In conceding that foreigners are human, civility requires treating them civilly. To the extent that we ourselves are civilized with reference to our own rules and moral standards, people from outside our community have a right to have those standards extended to them (Collingwood 1992: 35.63).

Collingwood would agree with Rorty in disparaging the belief among many liberal philosophers that rational argument is the route to moral progress. Only a utilitarian society prides itself upon its rationality, but it is deluding itself in thinking that it has overcome superstition and irrational sentiments (Collingwood 2005a: 206–21). Rorty's emphasis is upon the solidarity of community as the essential requirement of acknowledging human rights and of regarding 'them' as encompassed by the idea of 'us'. In privileging sentimentality, almost to the exclusion of rationality, there is a capriciousness in the process that is difficult to condone, for just as tales of emotional depth and sentiment may broaden our moral community, tales of depravity, cruelty, torture, and disgust may narrow it, and may lead us to exclude 'others' whose actions we do not regard as fully human.

What is needed is a sense of community that takes rationality and sentimentality as part and parcel of what social sinews enable a society to cohere. In this respect we may look to Collingwood as a catalyst to the theory of extending the moral community in the way that acknowledges the imperative need to recognize the roles of emotion, but which is nevertheless integrally related to rational consciousness (Boucher 2000*b*). Self-knowledge of one's emotions is integral to sociality and civility. To suppress or deny one's emotions, that is, to prevent them from being expressed, results in corruption of consciousness, a form of delusion that tarnishes and taints social relations (Collingwood 1938: 282–5). Collingwood goes further than Rorty in maintaining that an emotional attachment to, or sympathy for, strangers is not in itself enough to regard them as human or to treat them civilly. After all, we can have sympathy for and feel sentimental about the suffering of animals, but this in itself is not an invitation to include them in our moral community. Collingwood argues that:

The social consciousness on my part towards a foreigner, which brings him from my point of view within the circle of human beings and converts him from something I exploit or even, if so disposed, murder with a clear conscience into something which in proportion as I am a civilized man I have to treat civilly, and see to it that others shall treat civilly, is an entirely different thing from an affectionate or expansive emotion, what is called 'liking' him or 'being fond of' him (Collingwood 1992: 35.73).

Liking someone whom one does not regard as one of us, and not fully human, is perfectly compatible with treating that person uncivilly. Disliking someone, however, whom one regards as a fellow human being is not compatible with treating that person uncivilly. Collingwood is not suggesting that social cooperation rest solely on a foundation of human reason (Collingwood 1992: 36.73). His account of our emerging propensity to associate is similar to that of Kant's characterization of the state of nature as unsocial sociability. Our capacity to need others while at the same time being hostile towards them; to cooperate while wanting to dominate; to comply and at the same time to compete; to be confrontational and conciliatory are all part of the 'tangled skein' of what we carry with us at the level of will. Our confused, contradictory, and ambivalent feelings, appetites, passions, and desires need not, however, alarm us because within limits we can choose between these contradictory tendencies. 'We can now use our will instead of being blown about by the veering wind of emotion' (Collingwood 1992: 36.83). It is by means of some form of common action that we develop our social consciousness and recognize foreigners not as other, but as one of us. Frequently this common action which facilitates our being accustomed to treat strangers with civility is commercial activity, that is, trading relations.

Rorty favourably cites Annette Baier who contends that Hume's notion of corrected sympathy is preferable to Kant's idea of a law discerning reason. In this respect trust replaces obligation as the fundamental moral notion. The extension of the moral or human rights community then becomes not a question of a progressive widening of the moral law, but instead a progress in sentiments. The question then becomes not that of the rational egoist who asks 'Why should I be moral', but instead 'Why should I care about a stranger, a person who is no kin to me, a person whose habits I find disgusting?' This replaces the traditional answer to the question, that the only morally relevant factor is recognition of each as members of humanity.

This begs the question of whether such species membership constitutes a strong enough tie to generate trust, the sort of trust that is associated with more concrete relationships like family and kinship. Rorty argues that the better answer is one that relies on 'sad and sentimental stories'. He states quite clearly in *Contingency, Irony and Solidarity* 'that detailed descriptions of particular varieties of pain and humiliation (in e.g. novels or ethnographies), rather than philosophical or religious treatises, were the modern intellectual's principal contributions to moral progress' (Rorty 1989: 192). Feelings of solidarity with others arise in the context of which similarities and dissimilarities strike us as important at any historical time. Which are important is a matter of contingency. He claims that his position is not incompatible with extending as far as possible the terms of reference of 'we' to those whom we have historically regarded as 'they'.

Rorty then agrees with Rabossi that it is futile to look for the foundations of the modern human rights culture in the theorists of human rights. It is a post Second World War development, precipitated by the holocaust. He argues that the superiority of human rights need not rest upon a theory of universal human attributes. Human rights need only cohere with our beliefs.

Rorty concurs with Dewey's contention that all inquiry is an exercise in practical problem solving, and with C.S. Peirce's view that all beliefs are action guiding. The best argument for moving beyond human rights foundationalism is that we need to get on with the business of manipulating sentiments. It is a matter of the pragmatist principle of efficiency (Rorty 1995: 122). The human rights culture in which we live 'owes nothing to increased moral knowledge and everything to hearing sad and sentimental stories' (Rorty 1995: 118–9).

For Rorty consolidating and expanding our human rights culture entails imaginatively identifying with the lives of others. This is not a process of applying universal and timeless principles, but of extending the particular sympathies and motives we have already come to possess historically. Extending the moral community entails:

First, we must promote sentimental education in order to acquaint different people with each other so that the temptation to think of others different from themselves as quasi-human is diminished.

Second, we must rid ourselves of condescension in philosophy, that is, the propensity to think of others without moral truth as bad people, and substitute for this tendency the realization that those who violate human rights are deprived of both security in their own conditions of life, and the sympathy engendered by sentimental education.

Third, we must learn to trust that sentimentality provides a strong enough bond to ensure that our human rights culture coheres.

What this means, then, from the position of anti-foundationalism and anti-essentialism, is that expanding our sense of we to those whom we have previously thought of as they, while employing the vocabulary of human solidarity, is to sever it from its philosophical presuppositions (Rorty 1989: 192). In this respect the right way to think about the slogan inextricably attached to such doctrines as natural rights, that we have rights by virtue of being human, as a reminder constantly to strive to increase the number of people we come to think of as we. Read the wrong way, however, the slogan that we have rights by virtue of our common humanity may mistakenly be taken as a philosophical foundation for democratic politics (Rorty 1989: 196; cf. Geras 1995: 76). Geras sums up Rorty's position succinctly: 'From a radically communitarian and apparantly anti-universalist premises, then, we get human solidarity – and in an outlook which Rorty is also happy on occasion to call 'humanist' [Rorty 1989: 113, fn. 13, 116] and to connect most recently, with the culture of human rights' (Geras 1995: 76).

How deep does Rorty's 'solidarity' go, and how wide is the community that he envisages encompassed under 'we'? There are cultures that for the liberal ironist are beyond the pale, and which only with extreme difficulty and a renunciation of principles could be encompassed by our sense of we. Some cultures are an abomination. They cause too much pain to be tolerated. They must be resisted and perhaps deserve to be eradicated (Rorty 1993: 3). Expanding or contracting our circle of obligation is not a conflict between loyalty to one's comrades, compatriots, family or friends on the one hand, and justice towards others who do not fall within our moral community. It is, in Rorty's view, a conflict of loyalties. For Kantians, justice is related to reason, and loyalty to sentiments. It is then for Rorty a matter of expanding our loyalty to others by extending our sentimental range.

The rhetoric of universal moral obligations inhering in the species serves no useful purpose, and should be replaced by the idea of fostering a community of trust between ourselves and others. This entails being more ethnocentric rather than universalist. It entails showing how we in the West look as a result of abolishing slavery, educating women, separating church and state, and of treating certain distinctions between people as arbitrary rather than morally significant or relevant. It suggests to other peoples that they too may like the results if they try all of these things. Getting rid of the rationalism of the Enlightenment permits the West to address the non-West in the manner of one who has an instructive story to tell, 'rather than in the role of someone purporting to be making better use of a universal human capacity' (Rorty 2001: 223–37).

What does this mean in practical terms, for example, in redistributing the wealth of the West to poorer parts of the world? For Thomas Pogge freedom from poverty is a moral human right 'whose validity is independent of any and all government bodies' (Pogge 2007: 13). For him moral human rights are quite distinct from legal human rights, and 'even all governments together cannot legislate such rights out of existence' (Pogge 2007: 13). For him needs imply must. That we all need basic necessities for human life is evidence of the claim that we have a human right to them (Pogge 2007: 14).

For Peter Singer neither personal relations nor geography are morally relevant considerations if we believe that we ought to prevent others from suffering harm if we can. On the basis of an argument depending upon marginal utility Singer argues that transferring resources to the poor means that we have to reject conspicuous consumption on luxury items. From a constitutive or communitarian perspective, Amartya Sen thinks that such consumption has grown as rapidly as global warming or the depletion of the ozone layer (Sen 1998: 6). Singer requires us to deprive ourselves of the exchange value of a proportion of our income in order to become more virtuous people. We would also, however, deprive ourselves of our identity, given that it is shaped in the context of embedded communities. The very core of who we are would considerably be transformed as the values of Western society underwent radical change.

Rorty, who is proud of his socially constituted bourgeois liberal identity, with all the refinements that it entails, views with incredulity demands such as those of Singer. The key question for Rorty is not the metaphysical one of 'what are we', or 'what is man', but the political question of 'who are we?' The purpose of this primordial question in philosophy is to forge a moral identity by identifying and demarcating a group of human beings who appear to be better suited for some particular chosen purpose than other human beings. Those deemed to be better suited for the purpose constitute a self-conscious moral community capable of demonstrating mutual trust, and a willingness to offer reciprocal assistance. In Rorty's view, 'To ask who we are becomes a way of asking what future we should try, cooperatively, to build' (Rorty 1996: 8). Moral universalists, such as Singer and Brian Barry, conflate the metaphysical and political questions by supposing that shared human traits, such as a common human nature, testify to a common purpose. On this basis they think it suffices to demonstrate why humanity should compose itself into a cosmopolis or universal moral community.

A commitment to universal distributive justice is premised on assuming that our moral community and humanity are co-extensive, and that the purpose is to re-distribute the earth's resources so that all children have available to them the life chances of every other. Putting aside the desirability of the project, Rorty maintains that it is not feasible. The size of the world's population and the comparatively diminishing resources make it impossible. In Rorty's view, there is no viable scheme that allows the people of the affluent part of the world to redistribute their wealth in such a way to create optimistic prospects for children in developing countries without, at the same time, seriously diminishing or eradicating the prospects of their own children and communities. A politically feasible project to redistribute wealth depends upon adequate resources being available so that after redistribution 'the rich will still be able to recognize themselves – will still think their lives worth living' (Rorty 1996: 15). It is useful to distinguish between two types of objection to moral universalism. The first is normative and consists in claiming that it entails morally unacceptable conclusions. The second is conceptual and objects to moral universalism on the grounds that it lacks a key feature or features of a moral theory (Caney 2005: 31). Rorty denies that his theory is normative in that he claims not to be recommending anything. By implication, however, he does want to say that helping the world's poor is unacceptable if it is at the expense of damaging the prospects of one's own children. When weighed against each other he is essentially claiming that the preservation of one's identity is preferable to undermining one's own self-recognition by redistribution. The theory is also conceptual in that he assumes that moral universalism entails regarding the whole of humanity included in the same moral community as ourselves, and that this entails not only a willingness to help those in need, but also the ability to do so; ought implies can. In Rorty's view it is a naive belief that 'depends on our ability to believe that we can avoid economic triage' (Rorty 1996: 15).

His normative claim seems to be based on cultural identity. The claim is that our identity is partly constituted by conspicuous consumption which is essential to it. In order to protect this identity we are morally justified in excluding eighty per cent of humanity from our 'moral community' on the grounds that we think them not particularly suitable for the purpose we have set ourselves. That the lifestyle we have come to enjoy is part of our culture, as Barry so forcefully contends, 'cannot possibly do duty as a justification for anything...' (Barry 2001: 258).

Rorty's argument offers us an all or nothing alternative based on a feasibility criterion. It depends upon the dubious assumption that in order to include the people of underdeveloped countries as part of our own moral community it would be inconceivable to have to resort to economic triage. Rorty fails to see, however, that economic triage is just as much a feature within a particular community as it would have to be among communities comprising a single whole. In a world of scarce resources economic triage is unavoidable. In a medical context, for example, we rank people in relation to their life chances, with those most ill or severely injured having low priority (Walzer 1994: 25). Any public system of health care does this all the time. While everyone may have a right to equal consideration, limited resources dictate that the criteria against which they are judged are ultimately economic. There is a trade-off between people's pain and lives according to a set of priorities constrained by resources. The egalitarian principle of equal consideration does not entail equal outcomes. A privately funded system of health care rests upon the ability to pay, and may entail minimal provision for those who are unable. If the private model is superimposed globally then Rorty's nightmare scenario of losing our identity is avoided. Within the constraints of an affordable budget, we are committed to no more than providing a minimum level of resource to prevent extreme suffering. This operates on the principle of a threshold, rather than an egalitarian, criterion of international social justice. So, for example, to bring the 2.8 billion people living below the World Bank's $2 per day poverty line above that level would require $300 billion dollars annually, or 1.2 per cent of the aggregate annual gross national incomes of the more affluent economies (Pogge 2002: 7).

In the absence of a crystal ball predicting future technological advances, Rorty's tactic is to present the extreme case in order to achieve maximum impact, as he did, for example, in discussing human rights and solidarity in his Amnesty lecture (Rorty 1993). He portrays a situation in which large scale redistribution from the rich to the poor would so fundamentally alter the wealthy West, including its democratic and socio-political institutions, that it would become unrecognizable, and would in any case be futile, like a person sharing one loaf of bread with a hundred starving people, ensuring that everyone dies including himself or herself. It is to some extent a reiteration of Hardin's lifeboat ethics (Hardin 1974). The implication of Rorty's argument is the 1 billion richest people in the world are no longer able to view the poorer 5 billion as part of their moral universe, that is, unable to view them as part of the same moral community, and therefore have no obligations towards them.

Following Peirce's notion that beliefs must be indicative of future action, Rorty makes the strong claim that if we want to include the people of the developing world within our moral community, and it is not feasible to extend assistance to those in need, then the moral gesture is vacuous. This is an argument against egalitarian projects of international distributive justice. Indeed, it is not even a question of justice unless we count those in need of aid among those included in the answer to the question 'who are we?' (also see Boucher 2006*b*).

Does the extension of the moral community necessarily entail eliminating difference? Can we have universal principles and at the same time respect diversity? Rorty's answer is that we should not have to apologize for being committed to liberal bourgeois values, especially the deeply embedded idea that we liberals think that inflicting physical harm is one of the worse things that can be done to a person. The extension of these liberal values would be a good thing for liberals and for the rest of the world. The sad and sentimental stories of great literature and poetry are the vehicles of such dissemination, but it is unclear to what extent, if at all, Rorty's theory is culturally sensitive, or indeed feasible if at the expense of maintaining our own lifestyles and sense of self, we disregard the cries of the poor, down-trodden, and victims of systematic violence elsewhere in the world.

Collingwood is most famous for his work in the philosophy of history, but the main purpose of all his investigations is self-knowledge of the mind. In understanding human endeavour historically, and this includes anthropologically, we learn not to impose our own preconceptions on others, but also learn something about ourselves, that we may have suppressed or which persists as survivals in our culture without apparent purpose. What we gain by such historical sensitivity is a better understanding of ourselves and of our own society. The utilitarian values that have so thoroughly permeated modern society have inured us to demand of everything that it be viewed in terms of means and ends relations, and justified in terms of usefulness. The irrational and the emotional are suppressed in the interest of the rational. Understanding other peoples whose practices are unfamiliar and strange to us enables us to understand those practices which persist in our own culture, which may serve the same purpose of resolving emotional tensions, but which do not conform to the utilitarian demands for justification.

How do such injunctions avoid the charge of relativism without positing something like a universal human nature, or an objective reason or rationality? Those very things that Rorty suggests have been tried and tested, and ultimately found wanting in the history of philosophy. Like Rorty, Collingwood wants to argue that judgements can be made internal to a civilization or culture, and the whole of the *New Leviathan* is concerned to show that the European mind has developed, without necessity, into a hierarchy of forms of practical and theoretical reason indicative of the value we put on freedom of choice. The less capricious the choice the greater the freedom achieved. The institutional arrangements of each community within European civilization have a role to play in the recognition of the attainment of such freedom. Any attempts to suppress the exercise of free will are retrograde steps in the development of European consciousness towards freedom. In other words, acts of barbarity, by which Collingwood means the deliberate attempt to stifle freedom of thought, and the exercise of free will, fall far short of the ideals of European civilization and may justifiably be condemned, as he himself condemned the Nazi threat, and certainly would have condemned the more recent atrocities in Bosnia, Kosovo, and Darfur. Collingwood is not suggesting that European, or any other civilization, is homogeneous. Each may contain different civilizations that differ in kind, but this does not mean that they are incompatible. In so far as they share what Wittgenstein calls family resemblances, they constitute a single European civilization.

Collingwood's contention is that European civilization has certain ideals, and that in fact there may be many failures to live up to them, which do not nevertheless negate the ideals. All of those associated issues relating to the development of consciousness, such as the elimination of force from our social relations; closing the gap between the rich and poor; and protection of minorities from the tyranny of the majority, we call first, second, and third generations of human rights, roughly corresponding to the three ideals of the French Revolution, liberty, equality, and fraternity. Rorty's theory of human rights is essentially addressed to this European culture within which, to put it in Collingwood's terms, there has been a revolt against civilization, the return of barbarism intent on reintroducing force into the equation of human relations.

I have been discussing a situation in which the people who violate human rights themselves subscribe to the culture of human rights. They disagree over who should be acknowledged human. A quite different scenario arises in non-western communities or civilizations in which what is in dispute is not who is human, but the very idea of human rights itself. How are we to respond to those non-western civilizations who reject the ideals and assumptions of individualism and autonomy that are the foundation of the western human rights culture?

In comparing different civilizations or cultures Collingwood argues that we should not take barbarism and civilization to be opposite ends of a continuum in relation to which we ask to what degree a particular civilization is civilized. This conception is the result of nineteenth-century historical monism and has been superseded by twentieth-century historical pluralism, which accepts that at various times different peoples have adopted different ideals of civilization and instituted their own processes to achieve them. All of the civilizations that we currently seek to understand, whether past or contemporary, are different in kind, having realized, or attempted to realize, their own ideals, and it is therefore futile to characterize them as embodiments of one single ideal. Each society has its own standards of civilization, and believes itself to be civilized in so far as it lives up to those standards. In so far as other societies do not conform to the standards they are viewed as barbarous. On this view, each society aspires to live a different type of civilized life, and the question to be asked is no longer to what degree a society is civilized on a single scale, but in what way can it be taken to be civilized.

This characterization may imply historical or cultural relativism in that it appears to deny a single ideal of civilized life, and instead appears to affirm that there are many different ideals. If the way each society behaves is understood by that society to be civilized, then there is no ideal character to the meaning of the term 'civilized'. It has merely a factual content which is potentially different for each society. This robs the verb to civilize of any meaning because there can be no civilizing process unless it implies that 'the process has direction and the act purpose, and these imply a distinction between fact and ideal' (Collingwood 1992: 488–490).

Collingwood argues that his position does not entail relativism because he is not substituting social facts for social ideals. What he contends is that social facts, or civilizations, are not bereft of ideals, and are instead pursuing different ideals. These different ideals, in a sense, have something in common. Even though they are diverse, 'the plurality of civilizations does not exclude a sense in which civilization is one' (Collingwood 1992: 490).

Collingwood argues that each civilization is both a fact and an ideal. What exactly does Collingwood mean by this? It is fact and actually exists in the sense that it will have attained a certain degree and kind of civilization that it conceived to be desirable. By the very fact that each civilization promotes the civilizing process, the degree and kind of civilization achieved will have been deemed worth pursuing. In other words, each civilization as a social fact, currently existing, is the attainment of an ideal. Its future depends upon the ideal continuing to be thought a desirable attainment. In this respect, each civilization is both fact and ideal, but in so far as it is an attainment of a certain degree and kind, it implies a further ideal that is yet to be realized. The ideal is the idea that in a particular civilization, fact and ideal, there are still degrees of civilization to be attained. Ideals that are pursued and achieved by individuals are social facts, that is, ideals of the first order. Second-order ideals are those that are recognized but not yet realized. Every individual recognizes shortcomings in his or her own conduct, and in the conduct of others, and to that extent is conscious of shortcomings in his or her civilization. It is possible for these second-order ideals to vary considerably from one civilisation to another, but less so than first-order ideals.

Second-order ideals differ from first-order ideals and vary from person to person, as well as from society to society. It would be ludicrous to expect everyone to agree even within the same civilization on what acts are civilized and what are barbarous on specific occasions. There is, nevertheless, a third ideal of civilization, which lacks the level of particularity of the other two. Here, it has to be admitted that Collingwood's attempted resolution of the problem of relativism is not as clear as it should be. This third-order ideal, he says, is the 'ideal of universal civility' which stands in a logical rather than a temporal connection with second-order ideals. It is the ideal that is constantly referred to in Christian literature, but which is not unique to it.

What exactly is Collingwood trying to get at here? In saying that the third-order ideal is logically the source of first- and second-order ideals he does not mean that it is reached before them. Like de Tocqueville and Eleanor Roosevelt, he believes that civility begins in one's own back yard and extends to a wider and wider community which gradually becomes ever more inclusive, but without eradicating differences. To be civil on determinate occasions, and to attain certain ideals of civility, and in addition recognize those that are not yet realized is, in Collingwood's view, logically to presuppose the third-order ideal of civility. Acting civilly on certain kinds of occasion is indicative of what Spinoza would call a 'mode of being'. Acting civilly towards others, then, implies that that mode of being is fulfilled not only on some occasions and in relation to some people, but in an unqualified way. This third-order ideal is what all civilizations have in common, the ideal of acting civilly in an unqualified manner (Collingwood 1992: 494).

He is not talking of a developing consensus among cultures or civilizations, but merely a logical connection to this universal. Its content is something similar to that which Walzer would call thin universalism. In other words, the very idea of a society living together collectively implies the existence of cooperation, an element of trust, keeping one's word, and desisting from force as far as possible. How these are manifest in different societies is largely contingent. It is also the case, of course, that since Collingwood's day it could reasonably be argued, as Jeremy Waldron does, that we now live in a cosmopolitan world in which it makes very little sense to individuate cultures as somehow being uniquely distinctive and free from wider cultural influences (Waldron 1995: 79–92).

CONCLUSION

We have seen in this chapter how the human rights culture comprises many different components, including survivals of the natural law and natural rights traditions. Foundationalism has, however, largely been rejected, or at least the question of the source of human rights is frequently bracketed in order to begin from the assumption that it is now a well-established fact that we have them, and to ask instead what rights we have, and what it means to have them. Arendt, who tends to conflate the descriptive and prescriptive versions of natural rights, warns of the extent to which they are illusory protections against states who deprive you of your citizenship rights, and instead of placing rights outside of the political community, wants firmly to equate them with citizenship rights. It is the right to have rights, that is, the rights of a citizen to which we need tenaciously to adhere. Totalitarian regimes are guilty of depriving whole sections of their populations of their citizenship rights, and creating refugees, and displaced persons with no citizenship rights, and treated by their reluctant hosts with the same contempt as they were treated by their persecutors.

Since Arendt wrote we have seen systematic attempts to eradicate whole populations or significant sections of them in Cambodia, Bosnia, East Timor, Rwanda, Kosovo, and Darfur, to mention only a few. In response, Richard Rorty has maintained that over two thousand years of rational argument has not persuaded human beings to respect one another's rights, because this would first entail acknowledging that those whose rights we violate are in all relevant respects the same as us, namely human. He identifies the mechanism of extending the moral community so that those we regard as 'them' may come to be regarded as 'us', as playing upon the sympathies of those who are potential human rights violators. He does not, however, think that human society is sufficiently solidarist to sustain a principle of redistributivist justice, because redistribution would so radically diminish our quality of life in the West, that we would no longer retain nor recognize our identities. His either or alternative fails to acknowledge the extent to which economic triage goes all the way down, at the international and local levels, and that it is a matter of degree rather than of egalitarianism how much may be designated for retribution. Both Collingwood and Rorty believe in the contingency of our natures, and the self-creative capacity of our characters. Collingwood, however, believed that the extension of the moral community to encompass all within universal principles entailed both rational and emotional responses to our relations with our fellow citizens, between citizens and nature, and between citizens of different polities, which entailed ceasing to see them as aspects of nature ripe for exploitation. The route to such expansion, as we saw, differs from Tocqueville's equality of conditions to Rorty's sad and sentimental stories. Collingwood's position did not wholly reject either of these positions, but may instead be seen to incorporate them. Equality of conditions is necessary for achieving self-respect and for affording respect to others. While being fully mindful of the emotional aspects of our psyche, and understanding completely the extent to which an emphasis upon reason and rationality has a tendency to suppress them, he nevertheless could not discount the rational basis to our recognition of others as human and therefore worthy of our respect, irrespective of our feelings towards them. Furthermore, despite being an historicist Collingwood sought to reject any implications of relativism, and like Walzer and Taylor did not see particularism and difference to be incompatible with the existence of universal principles.

10

Modern Constitutive Theories of Human Rights

> Human Rights norms have constitutive effect because good Human Rights performance is one crucial signal to others to identify a member of the community of liberal states (Sikkink 1998: 520).
>
> Rights do not exist in nature. They are products of social relations and of changing historical circumstances and balance of forces, so that the claim for rights is always in terms of some rights rather than others (Weeks 1995: 119).
>
> ... "human rights" ... are too often but code expressions of a modernity that itself recognizes no theoretic basis but general will or positivism (Schall 1991–2: 1000).

I have already shown in the previous chapter how something like a communitarian or constitutive understanding of human rights has emerged as a reaction against the perceived inadequacy of foundationalist theories to offer plausible protections against those who would deprive citizens of their citizenship rights, and even withdraw, or fail to acknowledge, the humanity of certain categories of humans. Let me now illustrate this move towards constitutive theory, or conventionalism in the construction of human rights, by taking a wider range of examples from both international relations theorists and political theorists of international relations. In the next chapter, I will show how the fundamental human and humanitarian rights have emerged and been understood in legal theory and practice.

The propensity, then, is to take the human rights culture as it is and ask, not about foundations but what human rights there ought to be, and in Rex Martin's terms, exactly what does it mean to have a human right? (Martin 1993: 73–97). Ignatieff puts the question slightly differently: 'if human rights are a set of beliefs, what does it mean to believe in it?' (Ignatieff 2001: 53). What I want to suggest is that modern constitutive theory, the type of theorizing that British Idealists engaged in, but without the metaphysics, as the philosophical basis of the modern human rights culture is better grounded and provides better justification for adherence to principles of universal human rights than theories which construct aspirational ideals from outside of the practices they seek to regulate. As we saw in relation to the Idealists there is nothing inherently conservative in their theory of rights because incorporated in it is a vision or ideal of what society ought to be.

I want to suggest that in contrast with the features of natural rights a great deal of current discussion about human rights is conducted in roughly the terms set out by the British Idealists. Natural rights, as we saw, have the following features: First, the language is individualistic, prioritizing the individual over the community or society. Second, the doctrine is rationalist, relying upon the exercise of reason, independent of experience, for the discovery of rights. Third, the doctrine was noted for its radicalism.

The British Idealists and modern proponents of human rights share quite different assumptions from the traditional natural rights theorists. First there is a widespread assumption that the rights we have, moral or legal, depend upon a moral community, and that we do not have them independently of that community. The extent to which that community already extends beyond traditional national borders is disputed, just as it was by Idealists. On the one hand Green and Jones thought it extensive in its scope with moral ties extending far beyond state borders, whereas Bosanquet and Bradley, while not denying the possibility and desirability of such an extension, thought such a moral community was not yet sustained outside the state. Second, it is widely believed that the rights we have, moral or legal, are constitutive of the self. We may have them independently of governments, but we do not have them independently of society. We are what we are because of the rights our communities extend to us, whether that community is a global society, or a more localized polity. Third, the rights we have are historical and contingent in character, rather than 'natural'.

These features are evident, I think, in the discussions that surrounded the composition of the United Nations Declaration on Human Rights. When Eleanor Roosevelt, one of the prime movers behind the United Nations Declaration of Human Rights, rhetorically asked where after all do human rights begin, and answered that it is in small places, close to home, she was immediately shifting the ground for human rights away from the more traditional conceptions. Neither God nor Man was being invoked as the measure. She implies that our respect for others, and our propensity to treat them civilly, begin with a common sympathy which arises in the first instance from common proximity and familiarity, but which eventually extends as we come to regard more and more people as being like ourselves, until eventually the whole of humanity is encompassed in one moral community with common fundamental rights (see Glendon 2001).

While I have suggested that the British Idealists most adequately articulated the theory of rights formation that bridges the gap between traditional conceptions of natural rights and modern conceptions of human rights, I have not suggested that the conception was wholly new, indeed such thinkers as Burke and de Tocqueville point the way.

The modern conception of human rights, and the declarations and agreements in which they are embedded, is an achievement rather than a given. It is acknowledged that the fundamental ideas upon which the concept are built is Western in origin, and for some this is an insurmountable limitation, and for others, in order to appeal to a global constituency, those origins needed to be divested. The Christian foundations that upheld both the natural law and natural rights traditions have for the most part been jettisoned in favour of a variety of ideas that convey the role of human artifice in the creation of our moral world and the values that we have come to accept as those of civilization. Kymlicka, for example, believes that the 'construction' of a system of human rights under the auspices of the UN was 'one of the great moral achievements of the twentieth-century' which 'protected members of minority groups as individuals' (Kymlicka 2007: 30). He wants, not to dismantle the system, but to supplement it with liberal multicultural rights.

Attempts to get around the difficulty of finding firm foundations for human rights have centred upon various forms of conventionalism or constructivism, some of which are explicitly indebted to the Hegelian tradition out of which the British Idealists emerged and others which rely upon constitutive theories which are neo-Hegelian and communitarian in their leanings. In the first group are such normative theorists of international relations as R. J. Vincent, Terry Nardin, Mervyn Frost, and Chris Brown, and the philosophers Alan Milne and Charles Taylor. In the latter group we find such international relations theorists as Janna Thompson, Andrew Linklater, Friedrich Kratochwil, Alexander Wendt, Emanuel Adler, Stephen Krasner, and Peter Sutch. Among the philosophers are Michael Walzer, David Miller, Rex Martin, Gerry Gaus, John Charvet, Jeremy Waldron, and Richard Rorty, and even the later Rawls's. In other words, there is an attempt to get away from the suggestion that human rights are possessed by humans by the mere fact of being human, or that they in any way predate political society because they have some Divine or natural origin.

Instead, it is suggested that with human progress standards of behaviour among individuals have become more civilized, and that these civilized standards become extended to broader and broader communities. There is the sense of overlapping communities where standards employed within one become extended into others by a process of recognizing others to be the same as us. By this I mean that certain standards of civility within classes or communities become more generalized as a result of recognizing others. This effectively means that guarantees of the rights of citizens are taken to be the prerequisite for human rights, and not human rights the prerequisite for guaranteeing the rights of citizenship.

INTERNATIONAL RELATIONS THEORY

That international order must be premised on some conception of international justice, which includes respect for human rights, is widely accepted among international relations theorists. They do not rely upon foundational arguments based on an omnipotent Creator, nor on a universal human nature as the source of such conceptions, but instead the practical and pragmatic idea of consensus or moral constructivism. That is not to say that the grounds do not shift during the course of the same argument, and ultimately most want to bracket the philosophical issues of foundations, that is answering the question where do human rights come from, and ask instead what human rights we have and how they work in the contemporary world. Ken Booth is quite explicit about this. He is sceptical of the search for eternal foundations as the basis of human rights which demand meeting rigorous requirements. He prefers the metaphor of anchoring human rights to practices and beliefs that may not be eternal, but which at present provide the best language we have for securing human emancipation (Booth 1999: 65). For him, anchorage implies 'a resting point in a dynamic process', and allows room for 'immanent critique', that is, the recognition of better possibilities (Booth 1999: 43).

He wants to argue that we should have human rights not because we are human, but to make us human. I take this to mean that there is social recognition of what it now means to live a life consistent with moral ideals that are the product, not of rationalist thinking, but of centuries of social practices in which a conception of human dignity has become gradually refined and accepted. The sort of thing de Tocqueville meant when he talked about the refinement of manners. Indeed, Booth is quite explicit that human rights are socially made over time and in human history which is always potentially open-ended (Booth 1999: 34 and 51–2).

Jack Donnelly in his seminal study of human rights tries to describe the way that human rights work or function in contemporary social relations (Donnelly 1989, 1999). There is an attempt to analyse social practices in which the concept of human rights figures prominently. However, he wants the best of both worlds. He claims that human rights are universal both in the sense that we all have them as a consequence of our nature, and that they are held against all other persons and institutions. What is more, they are inalienable (Donnelly 1999: 80). On the other hand he wants to maintain that human rights are the result of a social choice arising from a certain vision of moral human flourishing which has in fact resulted in a particular 'construction' of right and wrong (Donnelly 1989: 1 and 16, 1999: 100). He maintains that they are in fact 'a distinctive, historically unusual set of social values and practices' and that the 'international normative consensus on human rights clearly has deepened in the last few years' (Donnelly 1999: 81 and 89). In other words, he offers parallel accounts that are not compatible with each other. Michael Freeman focuses on Donnelly's latter account and takes him to be basing human rights on consensus in order to avoid the difficult philosophical issues surrounding theories of human nature. In doing so, Freeman contends, Donnelly is assuming a consensus that is far from consensual, and presenting not a moral basis to human rights, but simply one that is factual, namely that this is what people have come to agree (Freeman 2002: 64).

Krasner contends that the focus on individual human rights is a phenomenon of the twentieth century, and such rights are recognized in agreements that usually take the form of conventions in which rulers of states undertake to act, or desist from acting, in certain ways in relation to the ruled under their jurisdiction (Krasner 1999: 109). The conventions, he argues, are voluntary and have never violated the principle of legal sovereignty 'which stipulates that juridically independent territorial entities have the right to free choice' (Krasner 1999: 118). Among the motivations he attributes to signatories, a deeply held moral conviction is conspicuously absent. The motivations are to constrain future governments; to conform to the script of modernity; and in the case of the Soviet Union, to elicit support from third countries (Krasner 1999: 121).

Hedley Bull contends that 'Order' itself is considered a good, or norm, worth promoting and preserving because of its beneficial consequences; the achievement of Order may be facilitated by incorporating justice and human rights into the scale of international values, but without a consensus on these norms the international Order itself may be put in jeopardy. In other words Order, to use Dworkin's words, may trump justice and rights on the scale of values, and militate against humanitarian intervention in the absence of consensus. This is clearly acknowledged by Ignatieff, and is implicit in the work of all commissions of reconciliation which seek to restore order without necessarily administering justice to the victims or to their families.

Bull recognizes that the international society of which he speaks is not solidarist enough at present to overcome the tension between state sovereignty and non-intervention on the one hand, and the principle of humanitarian intervention on the other. There is an extreme reluctance at the international level even to entertain the possibility of conceding a right of humanitarian intervention to states, and little agreement on what human rights actually are (Bull 1979: 155–9 and Dunne 1998: 152–5). The extension of the moral community, in the sense of its becoming more solidarist and being able to act in unity to promote justice and protect human rights, is a matter for him of attaining consensus, and the basis of a gradual and progressive negotiation of terms of reference.

It was John Vincent who placed human rights firmly on the international relations theory agenda in 1986 with the publication of his book *Human Rights and international Relations*. His account is not without ambiguity because he wants to combine the pragmatist principle of running with what works, with a conception of human rights that performs the same function as natural law and natural rights, that is putting certain fundamental rights beyond the reach of governments by claiming that everyone needs basic subsistence, the right to which, although not based on a universal conception of human nature, ought to be non-negotiable. He is implicitly conceding what Jeremy Waldron was later to maintain, that if basic rights are to carry the moral purchase that we generally want them to have, they have to be grounded in a theory that functions something like that of Locke which derives its obligatory character from God as the source of natural law. Neither Waldron nor Vincent, however, are prepared to go down that route.

Vincent wanted to place human rights at the centre of world politics because he contends that they are those rights that everyone should have by virtue of being human, and that they thus perform the same function as traditional theories of natural law, that is, putting certain claims about how people should be treated beyond the arbitrary whims of tyrants. He is aware, however, that he is constrained by realistic considerations of what is possible (Vincent 1986: 111).

He is clear that human rights are a Western conception, and that the bid for their ascendancy is ideological. The universal human rights culture is a project which is global in aspiration, but Vincent does not want to base this project on anything as unsustainable as a theory of basic needs. He does, nevertheless, think that the project should have as its bottom line the guarantee of the right to basic subsistence, not because he wants to contend that this right is prior to other basic rights, such as those to liberty and security, but because on pragmatic grounds he believes that international cooperation to aid the deprived is more worthy, and less ideologically divisive, than other human rights projects (Vincent 1986: 2).

Vincent rejects the traditional foundationalist grounds for justifying human rights, and instead puts forward a version of the social recognition theory. He does not clearly distinguish what it means to have a human right from the justification of that right, but it is clear that he is grappling with both issues. In the first place he contends that a right is a justifiable claim, but that the claim itself does not gain status as a right without social recognition. This clearly deviates from the natural law and natural rights traditions where a right is right irrespective of whether anyone knows it or claims it. For Vincent, 'social acceptance of the right is of great importance' (Vincent 1986: 9), and is part of what it means to have a right. Although he conflates justification with social recognition, the former can be separated in principle from the latter. He acknowledges that a human right may be justified by a range of reasons including appeal to custom, regional and international law, but also at a higher level, that of 'what ought to prevail' (Vincent 1986: 11). In this respect Vincent connects human rights with the spirit of natural law and natural rights. From the perspective of 1986 Vincent was able to discern modest signs of a 'solidarist' international moral community emerging at the institutional level in which human rights claims were able increasing to be observed. Among the reasons are that there is a growing number of states committing themselves to upholding human rights in domestic politics, and that the principle that domestic courts may indict foreign nationals for crimes committed outside their domestic jurisdiction has become increasingly accepted, especially in relation to torture. Humanitarian intervention, in order to be both legitimate and potentially successful requires, in his view, a much more robust solidarist community which requires substantive agreement on the values that should inform intervention. A human rights regime as firmly established as this would presuppose something like what Suarez called *ius gentium intra se*, that is the area of the Law of Nations that describes what all nations in their domestic law have in common, having grown to the point where differences among states had become negligible. Again in the theory of international relations John Vincent has identified three levels at which rights operate internationally: the individual, the state, and non-state organizations. It is the state, however, which dominates in terms of being the repository of rights and the location of obligation. Individuals and non-state organizations are not free-floaters inhabiting a plane above communities and states. Individuals derive their identities from being members of communities which are themselves subsumed under the auspices of states. Citizenship is part of what it means to be human because there is no global polis. This is why the plight of refugees is taken so seriously. The loss of citizenship rights in one state, whether by fleeing its borders, or by being stripped of them by governments, is accompanied by no guarantee that other states will accept such 'displaced persons' and re-institute them into humanity (Vincent 1992: 261; cf. Arendt 1973).

Based on these criteria, as we have seen, and as we will see in the next chapter, significant advances have been made in a relatively short period of time. While there is a continuing reluctance in the international community to designate gross violations of human rights as acts of genocide in such places as Darfur, the Congo and East Timor, there is certainly a growing expectation that there is a responsibility to intervene, and a growing acceptance of the principle of humanitarian intervention.

Developing this solidarist theme, Rorty and the English School in international relations, Mervyn Frost and Chris Brown, for example, employ a demythologized or secular Hegelianism in order to establish the point that in order for rights to function certain conditions have to pertain which together comprise an ethical community. What is presupposed in the general liberal account of the individual is that human nature is universal. Constitutive theory, on the other hand thinks human nature circumstantial. It seems to me that the basic point of what Frost is getting at is this: irrespective of the reasons we may give for saying that morality cannot be grounded in any firm foundations, or that the realities of power and politics militate against the appropriateness of moral considerations in the behaviour of states, it is nevertheless the case that there are shared moral assumptions that are explicitly appealed to, and we do have moral expectations not only of ourselves and other individuals but also of politicians and states. Such shared values have to be accounted for rather than explained away. While the foundations of ethical reasoning may not be of the type for which philosophy once hoped, in other words there may be plenty of reason to be sceptical about the foundations of ethics, this does not provide conclusive argument for desisting from talking about ethics altogether. Reasoning about ethics can take place on the basis of identifying shared premises.

Brown, for instance, suggests that: 'Human beings live in different kinds of groups and these different types of group create different kinds of individuals' (Brown 1994: 168). Human nature is a product of the different social formations in which people find themselves. The role of politics in this formative process is much more pronounced in constitutive theory than in liberalism. A political structure is part of the social fabric that shapes individuals. Thus republicanism as a political structure provides the conditions constitutive of republicans.

In order to avoid the charge of conservativism, constitutive theory needs to show how development and change can be incorporated into the theory without presupposing an ahistorical pre-social individual as the reference point. What Frost and Brown retain of Hegelianism is the idea that the self is constituted by the relationships in which it stands to the family, civil society, and the state. In other words the self is nothing outside of the social relationships that have served to form it. Similarly, the settled norms, what Hegel called *Sittlichkeit*, or customary morality, both implicit and explicit, in the relations among states can for Frost be explained in terms of constitutive theory in a way that alternative background theories such as the contractarian rights based theories, or utilitarianism, fail to do because of their inability to reconcile norms of sovereignty with human rights norms, both of which are integral to modern international relations. The privileging of human rights over sovereignty in cosmopolitan theories simply does not square with the discourse or norms of the modern state system. Constitutive Hegelianism does not acknowledge a conflict between human rights and state sovereignty because both are part of and arise from the social practice of international relations (Frost 1996; Brown 1999; and Sutch 2001).

These normative issues can only arise in a domain of discourse in which they have meaning and are recognized as important problems. To those who do not belong to the domain of discourse, or do not subscribe to it, the issues do not arise. A constitutive theory does not start with the premise that individuals are rights holders independently of the state, and that the state is somehow, often by means of contract, the instrument to protect those rights. Frost simply brackets the problems of induction in relation to determining what human rights we are said to have by the mere fact of being human. Cultural diversity makes it impossible to compile a list inductively. A second approach is that human rights may be revealed to us by reason. But what if my right reason reveals different natural human rights from your right reason? This 'second intractable problem, then, may be stated thus: the search for the foundation of rights in "right reason" quickly leads theorists to the domain of "high philosophy" (a domain once known as "metaphysics") in which what has to be confronted are questions about rationality, epistemology and ontology' (Frost 2002: 38). Instead, individuals are seen to be constituted by the relationships, social and political, into which they enter and the rights they possess are the products of these institutions (Frost 1996: 138–9; cf. Brown 1992: 173).

Like Hegel, and for that matter Francis Fukuyama (Fukuyama 1993), Frost stresses the importance of the role of recognition in the development of individuality. Individuals recognize and value each other in the context of social practices which serve to constitute the individuality of the person. Frost tries to show how selves are constituted through a hierarchy of social institutions including the family, civil society and the state. Frost contends that the two global practices are constitutive of our identity, and that they are foundational authoritative practices in that 'we would judge exclusion from them to be damaging to our sense of ourselves as fully fledged ethical beings' (Frost 2002: 45). Civil society, in Frost's view, is a society in which each recognizes others as rights holders. It is conceptually wrongheaded to think of ourselves as rights holders outside of an authoritative practice, and the idea that there are natural rights, understood as inhering in the individual by virtue of the fact that that person is human, is illusory: 'The activity of rights holding only makes sense within a social formation within which rights holding is a recognized form. Just as the idea of playing a trump card only makes sense within the context of a specific card game' (Frost 2002: 57).

If we hold such rights as participants in global civil society, it goes without saying that to claim them does not require living in a functioning state. Nor is it necessarily a legal claim that we are making when we claim a human right, because legal claims necessarily entail functioning legal systems within which they are made. Those who claim they have human rights also claim that everyone else has these same rights, and therefore to afford these rights to those who as yet are not participants is a necessary corollary. What Frost is implicitly doing is trying to reconcile the rights of citizens with universal rights in which everyone may be said to participate. The global practice of a society of democratic states has distinctive rights attached to it, and these are citizenship rights: 'The idea of the citizen as a rights holder is fundamental to our understanding of the practice of the modern democratic state. No sense could be made of a democratic state without some concept of the democratic rights of citizens' (Frost 2002: 63). Frost argues that our participation in the society of democratic and democratizing states, necessarily entail citizenship rights, and one of these rights, may be termed the right to have rights. That is, the right to have your rights as a civilian in the global civil society, protected by the state in which you are a citizen (Frost 2002: 106). These citizenship rights are always held within the context of a legal system.

In identifying the settled body of norms in international relations Frost argues that there are three main characteristics to bear in mind. First, a norm is settled when it is generally regarded that to be in breach of it needs special justification. This is not to say that states necessarily obey the norm. Non-interference, for example, is a basic norm subscribed to in international law, but numerous states disregard it from time to time. To point out that the norm is persistently transgressed does not suggest that it is not a settled norm. Only if those states which periodically transgress the norm consistently fail to give any justification would it show that the norm is not recognized. As Lutz and Sikkik contend, the justification of norm breaking may itself be norm affirming, especially if it includes an explanation of why it was not possible to act in the expected way in these particular circumstances (Lutz and Sikkink 2000: 656). Second, a norm can generally be considered settled when breaches of it are undertaken clandestinely. The United States has notoriously done so in Cambodia, Loas, Chile, Nicaragua, and Columbia. Third, he says, 'it must be remembered in the case of each settled norm that it is the concept of that norm which is regarded as settled within the modern state domain of discourse, and not any particular conception of the concept.' Non-intervention, for example, may be widely accepted as a concept, but how it is interpreted may differ considerably (Frost 1996: 105–6).

Brown contends that constitutive theory can share with many cosmopolitans a commitment to human rights. These human rights, they claim, have to be realized in a state. It needs to be emphasized that the source of these rights is seen to be the various communities which give them expression. In other words the individual doesn't possess them independently of the community, nor because there is a commitment to a universal human nature in virtue of which human rights are anchored. This is expressed well among the 'Constructivists' in international relations by Yosef Lapid and Friedrich Kratochwil who maintain that: 'identities are emergent and constructed (rather than fixed and natural), contested and polymorphic (rather than unitary and singular), and interactive and process-like (rather than static and essence-like)' (Lapid and Kratochwil, 1996: 8). Emanuel Adler's cognitive evolution similarly rests upon a developmental view of human identity which gives due deference to history and historicity. The emphasis is upon the manner in which social facts become established in the social world in order to identify the ways in which they exert influence, and constitute collective understandings. Cognitive evolution postulates a process of international learning, which means the adoption by policymakers of different conceptions of reality are as they intruded into the political environment by individuals and social actors. The political importance of novel conceptions of reality is not that they are true, but that they are intersubjectively shared across institutions and peoples. Adler argues that fifty years ago there was no political mileage in arms control, sustainable development, and universal human rights. Now these values are very much to the fore. 'Human Rights,' for example, 'have become a central factor in the interests of democratic nations because they increasingly define their social identities' (Adler 2005: 106–7).

PHILOSOPHICAL PERSPECTIVES

What has proved contentious is not that humans have rights, but that rights inhering in the individual could be the starting point of a theory of political morality. The riposte has been that rights are only intelligible when set against a suitable background theory of political and social morality such as utilitarianism (Waldron 1984: 1).

Jeremy Waldron argues that at the rhetorical level the shift from natural rights to human rights betrays a loss of faith in the possibility of justifying rights with reference to truths about human nature. The term human rights now signifies the scope of the claims rather than hints at anything that might justify them (Waldron 1987: 63). Increasing scepticism about objective values and principles in moral philosophy has not terminated moral argument or justification. Moral justification may no longer be characterized by the search for ultimate truths irresistible to rational beings, but it is concerned to determine the shared foundations, sympathies, and considerations that underpin claims about taking rights seriously (Waldron 1987: 165). In answer to the question 'where do human rights come from', or more prosaically, 'what is their ontological status,' he agrees with theorists such as Benhabib in rejecting natural law, but he is not as ready as her to reject positive law. When one moves beyond the command and sanctions theory of law associated with Hobbes and Austin, we have to acknowledge that law may also contain customs and practices that grow out of and constitute the social order and which express our mutual sense that relations with each other are constrained by norms, most of which may be unenforceable (Waldron 2006: 93). Lord Haldane, as we saw in Chapter Eight, suggested that the norms that govern the relations among the 'higher' nations, especially those among Britain and her former colonies are of this character. Such norms are so highly esteemed that those who disregard them suffer the social sanction of disapproval or of being slighted (what Benhabib and Ignatieff may refer to as naming and shaming). It is not the ethics of conscience as such. This is to some extent what Hart was getting at when he maintained that 'secondary rules', resembling customary practices, form the basis of a juridical system of enacted rules, and not, as was usually asserted, the reverse (Hart 1994).

Waldron, like the Scottish Enlightenment theorists, gives a great deal of emphasis to commercial society as a source of the emergence of normative customs, i.e., the *lex mercatoria*. His point is that 'the mundane growth of repeated contact between humans and different human groups can lay the foundation for the emergence of cosmopolitan norms, in a way that does not necessarily presuppose a formal juridical apparatus' (Waldron 2006: 94).

The communitarian positions of Michael Walzer and Charles Taylor acknowledge both the possibility and desirability of reaching a consensus on universal principles, while at the same time maintaining that they necessarily emanate from and rest upon different cultures and traditions. In other words, the thick morality of a community is the background sustaining a thin universalism. Walzer suggests that the thin morality we claim to be universally valid among human beings by the very fact that they are human, and among different states as the instruments through which they act on the world stage is a projection of the thick morality that pertains in civilized communities. The thin universalism about which Walzer talks is the result of an historical process which has given rise to a moral minimum, far less specific than the norms that Frost detects, but settled norms nevertheless. When we act in ways which support this reiterative universalism, such as protesting in the name of justice against the human rights violations perpetrated by corrupt governments, we are affirming a '(partial) communality' which does not extend to a full endorsement of the values of another culture, but merely to this thin shared communality (Walzer 1992: 17).

This minimum international morality amounts to the principles of self-determination (non-intervention), non-aggression, and pluralism (the accommodation of tribalism within borders). Walzer's fundamental point is that the international community regards infringements of territorial and political sovereignty as self-evidently wrong. Sovereign integrity is ensured by the internationally accepted right of non-intervention which is equivalent to the moral right of the individual to self-determination. Any infringements would therefore require extra-ordinary circumstances and special justifications. Given that the rationale of a state in his view is the protection of individual rights, particularly human rights, only gross infringements on a significant scale, for example genocide, would justify intervention if there are 'reasonable expectations of success' (Walzer 1994: 107). In such circumstances a state falls significantly below what the idea of statehood requires, and breaches the trust endowed upon it by its citizens in some form of social contract. Walzer concedes, however, that it is not always clear when a community is self-determining and thus entitled to claim the right of non-intervention.

Walzer argues that the type of morality embedded in our societies and social practices, what he calls maximal morality, precedes universal minimal morality, which is in fact abstracted from the former (Walzer 1994: 13). This is because he wants to maintain an emphasis upon difference while at the same time giving credence to a thin universalism. Walzer has suggested that there is a minimal code of universal morality constituting cross-cultural requirements of justice, such as the expectation not to be deceived, treated with gross cruelty or murdered (Walzer 1992: 22). He suggests that there is an international society which is grounded, not on a natural or hypothetical contract in a Rawlsian orginal position, but on norms that have become commonly acknowledged by leaders of states and their citizens.

Charles Taylor has taken up Rawls's idea of an unforced overlapping consensus and applied it to the idea of human rights. In order for there to be such a consensus there would have to be agreement on fundamental norms of behaviour, while at the same time acknowledging that the norms may be valued for very different and incompatible reasons from our own which are anchored in quite different background views of theology, metaphysics, and human nature. In exploring this question Taylor makes a threefold distinction between 'norms, legal forms, and background justifications' (Taylor 1999: 143). When objections are made against the Western rights tradition by, for example, Lee Kwan Yew in Singapore or Fidel Castro in Cuba, one or all levels could be implicated in the attack; norms, legal systems, and justifications.

The norms have to be enforceable on governments, have some philosophical justification and actually be enforced, that is, be articulated in the context of legal institutions. We cannot assume from the outset that a consensus formulated in terms of rights, or some other universal value such as human dignity or well-being is possible. What we need is not necessarily consensus on universal values, but on norms of conduct which outlaw such things as genocide, slavery, and torture.

Indeed, norms play an important role in the international system, and what may be described as the international community is regulated by such norms, some of which are embedded in treaties and formalized in law. Lutz and Sikkink suggest that norms have an oughtness that ordinary rules do not, because they set standards of appropriate and proper behaviour. We recognize norm-breaking behaviour because it generates disapproval or stigma. There is evidence to suggest that a cascading effect takes place in the acceptance and implementation of norms, not so much through actual changes in behaviour, but instead through discursive norm-affirming events, that is, verbal and written statements affirming the norm (Sikkink 1998: 518 and Lutz and Sikkink 2000: 655).

In Taylor's view, the idea of certain norms of conduct related to subjective rights has given rise to legal systems which incorporate bills and charters of rights, whose underlying justification is the view of human nature implied. Human rights in the West have been tied to the development of humanism which emphasizes the exalted status of humans in the cosmos and stresses the importance of human autonomy and agency. Human rights and democracy are inextricably linked as co-requirements of human dignity. Human rights to some extent stand apart from the rest of our moral values and may even be in conflict with them. Alternatively, reform Buddhism in Thailand with its emphasis upon non-violence, comes from quite a different place but seems to ground many of the same norms and leads to similar conclusions in relation to democratic development and human rights. They are linked and grounded differently from how they are linked in the

West. Reform Buddhism is committed to people-centred development which is ecologically sensitive. In other words, we may have a reiterative universalism in which basic norms of conduct coincide, but at the level of justification there may be considerable incomprehension at what is sustaining support for them.

Agreement at the level of norms of conduct is a useful first step, Taylor maintains, but unless there is mutual respect for what sustains them the agreement is liable to be fragile. This is because the agreement can never be complete, and the different sustaining background ideas may, when it comes to implementing norms, have different practical effects on, for example, the ordering of such norms, and the attitudes we express. The place of indignation, anger, punishment, and righteous condemnation is different with Thai Reform Buddhism and Western Humanism. This may involve coming to some compromise version of the interpretation of norms that requires mutual respect and understanding if they are to be acceptable to both sides. Secondly, disagreements may lead to a breakdown in the consensus which may need to be renegotiated, which is impossible without mutual respect. We in the West have to reconcile ourselves with the fact that the route that we took which led to human rights is not the route that other societies will take.

One of the most significant barriers to achieving mutual understanding and overlapping consensus is the fact that most Westerners view the current human rights culture that we embrace as the outcome of the falling away of the barbarity of our ancestors – the adoption, for example, of a more humane attitude towards punishment and cruelty. This is what Tocqueville referred to as the softening of manners. The tendency is to think that the path to convergence is for a similar process to take place among those of whose practices we disapprove. They, like us, should cast off their traditional and religious heritage. Taylor argues, in typical Collingwoodian terms, that 'Only if we in the West can recapture a more adequate view of our own history, can we learn to understand better the spiritual ideas that have interwoven in our development and hence be prepared to understand sympathetically the spiritual paths of others towards the converging goal. Contrary to what many people think, world convergence will not come through a loss or denial of traditions all around, but rather by creative re-immersions of different groups, each in their own spiritual heritage, traveling different routes to the same goal (Taylor 1999: 144).

What is missing in Taylor's account is the broader context. Consensus about which Taylor speaks does not take place in isolation of international consensus on a whole range of other values, which may in their different spheres be equally fundamental, and which may at present be seen to complement or even conflict with the norms of conduct we call human rights. The norms of sovereignty are almost wholly accepted and firmly embodied in the whole legal, normative, and institutional ethos of the United Nations and in the conduct of states towards each other, to the extent that humanitarian intervention is nearly completely outlawed unless civil society has broken down and the government no longer appears to be in control. Similarly, international trade is based on trust and the notion of obligations.

Taylor maintains that it should be possible to gain an overlapping consensus on norms of conduct while at the same time having to accept that each culture would have its own way of justifying them in relation to its 'profound background conception' (Taylor 1999: 124). The very language of human rights with its individualistic connotations and concomitant legal framework is objectionable to many non-Western states. The question then becomes what variety in legal and philosophical traditions is possible as background to agreed and enforceable norms? It is not possible to be indifferent to these background conditions. It is all very well achieving a consensus on norms, but we must assume a developmental consensus in which the process is never complete. Variations over the implementation of norms in practice, and the different priority of ranking given to such norms, will vary because of the background theories. Negotiation and compromise require mutual understanding for the positions from which the negotiators come. Secondly, the resolution of particular disagreements requires mutual respect. To be disdainful or hostile to the fundamental beliefs is in itself a barrier to working out solutions to practical consensus. What Taylor is suggesting, then, is that bare consensus must develop into what Gadamer calls a fusion of horizons. It is not always the case, of course, that convergence comes first, and mutual understanding and respect follow. In some cases convergence may depend upon prior attainment of mutual understanding. Rex Martin makes a helpful suggestion by drawing upon Dworkin's notion of pre-interpretative and interpretative phases of principled judicial decision-making (Martin and Reidy (eds.) 2006a and Martin 2006b). Considerable agreement is usually associated with the former. Lawyers and judges may agree to a considerable extent on the sources of law, and on what counts as law in their shared jurisdiction. When it comes to interpretation, however, we can expect them to arrive at different conclusions as they invoke their different historical backgrounds and deeply held convictions. If we think of the pre-interpretative stage as broad agreement on a limited and thin list of fundamental human rights we may use the principles of basic human interests, acknowledgements of diversity and distinctive values, and the basic requirement of reciprocity to arrive at a thicker interpretation of the list of human rights that may differ from one location to another depending upon comprehensive doctrines, and even parochial values (Martin 2006b: 207).

The arguments that I have been discussing have broadly been characterized as communitarian, and they have been concerned with the questions of self-knowledge and understanding of others through historically sensitive perspectives. They are not disinterested historical undertakings, but have the explicit purpose of facilitating the expansion of the moral community in order to become more and more inclusive of those we regard as other.

THE MODERN RECOGNITION THEORY OF RIGHTS

Modern variants of communitarianism, widely conceived, identify the source of rights in the community, and make their exercise dependent upon the solidarity of that moral community. Such rights are socially recognized practices. Modern recognition theories of human rights are the most directly related to the theories of the British Idealists in so far as T. H. Green, for example, provides direct inspiration for those who maintain that what it means to have a right is that it is recognized by the relevant community, and that it is justified with reference to its contribution to the common good. In direct contrast with those modern political theorists who want to argue that a right is a valid moral claim independent of social recognition, there are many, such as Ewing (1987), Sumner (1987), Freeden (1990a, 1990b, and 1991), Martin (1993 and 2003), Gaus (1995 and 2005), Sutch (2001), Darby (2003 and 2004), and even in a modified form, Raz (1984), Dworkin (1978), and Rawls's (1999), who contend that rights cannot fulfill their moral and practical functions unless they have wide social acknowledgement and acceptance.

Gaus argues, for example, that rights serve to distribute authority within society, and therefore create various authority relations, so that in many disputes that may arise the person with the right may make an authoritative pronouncement, against which there is no legitimate recourse. Ownership of a piece of land, for instance, gives the right, or distributes the authority, to the owner to deny someone who has designs on it from using it to graze his or her sheep. For both practical and moral reasons rights require authoritative recognition (Gaus 1995: 202). Practically, if they are to avoid disputes by apportioning authority, they must elicit wide agreement, and morally they are necessary to avoid moral dogmatism. Social recognition may be deployed in a relatively narrow sense relating to social or governmental authorities (Martin 1993: 83), or more broadly to mean the conferring of social standing requisite to possessing a right (Darby 2004: 21). This thesis is sometimes called rights externalism (Gaus (2005: 8), however, uses the term to denote rights objectivism), or a social practice conception of rights, which is contrasted with rights internalism in which something inhering in the person qualifies him or her for possessing moral rights independently of whether the rights are recognized, as espoused, for example, by Melden (1980), Feinberg (1980), and Wellman (1995).

Recognition, of course, may imply that in order to be recognized something must already exist. Hence it is absurd to suggest that a right is only a right when it is recognized. As we saw in Chapter Eight this was the flaw that W. D. Ross saw in T. H. Green's argument. It is not, however, the sense in which Green and his successors, including Darby, used the term. As already indicated Green's exemplar of recognition appears to be the process by which a chairperson of a meeting recognizes a speaker. The chair actually confers a status upon someone by giving him or her the floor (Gaus 2005: 6).

On this understanding, then, it is clearly the case that Arendt, Collingwood, and Rorty are rights externalists whose rights holders require the conferral of a certain status – in Arendt's case, for example, nationality or citizenship – for the enjoyment of fundamental rights. Modern theorists who may loosely be called rights recognition proponents want to emphasize the social dimension of rights, as being valuable both for the individual and society, and entailing assumptions and considerations beyond the postulates of a rational calculator, maximizing his or her own interests pursuant to self-conceived ends. To posit such rational enlightenment encourages overly formal and abstract discussions of human rights (Freeden 1990*b*: 492). The capacities of individuals are considered to be both developmental and social, and human rights the vehicles by which self-fulfillment is facilitated, and which require both individual and social responsibility. Michael Freeden identifies David Ritchie as an important figure in the development of rights theories because of his refusal to oppose rights and utility. He made the justification of a right dependent on the welfare of the community, and tied the idea to a developmental view of human nature in which human happiness and health were related in a much wider conception of human nature than that which informed traditional natural rights arguments (Freeden 1990*a*: 56–7).

Rex Martin's theory of human rights sets out to demonstrate the contingency of their recognition and promotion. We have already seen that Pogge distinguishes between moral rights and legal rights, but this is not a distinction to which Martin subscribes. So-called moral rights, he maintains, lack the required features of rights. They are instead moral claims, perhaps perfectly valid moral claims, and he is prepared to call them 'human rights norms' (Martin 1993: 89, 2003: 193, fn. 19), but they are nevertheless independent of human rights in the absence of any legal system to enforce them, until they attain formal recognition of some kind, and are maintained by governments. All rights, Martin argues, have one thing is common, that they in some way benefit the right-holder. For rights to attain the status of rights there must be a process or apparatus instituted to identify, or to articulate, from among a myriad of claims, those that may be supposed to be in everyone's interest (Martin 2003: 175). In this respect he ties civil rights to a suitably justified set of democratic institutions. The rights and the institutions are mutually supportive (also see Griffin 2008: 254).

For Martin, human rights are equated with civil rights, particularly fundamental civil rights, sometimes called fundamental constitutional rights (Martin 2003: 173). These fundamental civil rights will have proved themselves durable, by being enacted by the requisite authority, and affirmed and supported over time by various checks and balances such as judicial review.

Martin denies the principal contention of the natural rights based theories, and of those theorists who distinguish between moral and legal human rights. Martin denies that we are capable of possessing human rights prior to and independently of legal systems. Martin argues that we cannot understand what it is to have a human right unless we accommodate the practices of recognition, promotion, and maintenance of such rights. Human rights are more than valid moral claims or norms. A valid moral claim may be distinguished into two distinct features: it is at once a justifiable claim *to* something, and in addition, it is attached to particular individuals and a claim *against* someone. In what respects are human rights more than valid moral claims? Martin contends that arguments justifying human rights must resonate with the actual moral beliefs and practices of a community. He is not suggesting for a moment that people have only the duties that they believe themselves to have. Any duties assigned to them, however, have to be consistent and compatible with, or at least derivable from, the critical moral principles that permeate the overall system of existing societal moral beliefs. It makes little sense to talk of duties of which people could not become reflectively aware. What this means is that in addition to being a morally valid claim a human right must also be reflectively available, that is, it must be recognized as such.

Such a right is nothing more than nominal, and provides no normative direction for persons. It does not function as a right, without the will to promote and protect it. Human rights have the appropriate moral backing, but they have something else in addition: 'A human right is defective, not as a morally valid claim but as a right, in the absence of appropriate practices of recognition and maintenance. The absolute difference between morally valid claims and human rights, then, is that rights do, and claims do not, include such practices within their concept' (Martin 1993: 85).

In subjecting the idea of human rights to philosophical analysis Martin maintains that there are certain factors that are constitutive of them. The principal addressees of all the great human rights documents are not individuals as such, although they are the beneficiaries, but governments of states (Martin 2003: 184). Jack Donnelly concurs in maintaining that 'the modern state has emerged as both the principal threat to the enjoyment of rights and the essential institution for their effective implementation and enforcement' (Donnelly 1999: 85). It follows, for Martin, that any consideration of human rights ignores at its peril the practices of governmental recognition and maintenance in characterizing them. Governments, as the addressees of such rights as freedom from torture, are expected to protect and maintain such rights. A human right, on this account, is a morally valid claim, recognized by governments in being given the backing of law. Human rights are equated with legal or civil rights, but it is not suggested that all civil rights are also human rights. There may be many civil rights that lack the necessary moral backing, and in this respect they would also fail to qualify as valid moral claims.

In what does the universality of a human right consist? In so far as they are claims to something human rights are universal, but because they are addressed to specific agencies or representatives of government, and not to all persons, they cease to be universal. The addressees of claims are not primarily individuals as such, that is, all of humanity, but typically representatives or agents of organized societies, and principally this means governments. The language of human rights presupposes that individuals live in organized societies in which the goods claimed as a right are conceived and enjoyed. Even those who claim that their rights are being violated and demand to have them protected and maintained live in some organized society, and are for the most part making their claim against representatives or officials of that society. Martin concludes that: 'These important points, though little noted, set a powerful constraint on the sense in which Human Rights can be regarded as universalism' (Martin 1993: 91).

Martin presents us with an ideal characterization of an organized society with the capacity to convert morally valid claims into human rights by means of recognizing and maintaining them with the backing of law. Such a view which claims philosophically to disclose what is historically embedded in the notion of a human right does, however, as I have suggested elsewhere, present us with some difficulties (Boucher 1998: 382–3). It is precisely in circumstances where there is a systematic refusal to acknowledge valid moral claims, or a breakdown of the capacity to do so, that we are most likely to want to talk about violations of human rights. In cases where civil society has broken down into a form of barbarism, and respect for human life or bodily integrity is not equally afforded to all, we may in Martin's terms talk of the denial of valid moral claims providing that the perpetrators could in principle become reflectively aware of their obligations, but we could not justifiably use the much stronger condemnatory language of human rights violations. It may well be the case that the only validity that human rights is capable of having is through recognition and maintenance, but it is an entirely different claim to suggest that this is part of what we mean by a human right. The appeal to human rights becomes most audible when the will or capacity to sustain them does not exist, or is ceasing to exist. When rape and genocide is systematically practised during civil wars, and when agencies fail to represent the whole society, or are unwilling or incapable of maintaining the rule of law in the protection of people's rights we would have to conclude that these victims of violence no longer have human rights, but it is precisely during such crises that they are most frequently invoked.

Rawls's as a Constitutive Theorist

In their different ways the thin universals of Michael Walzer, David Miller, John Rawls's, and even Richard Rorty arise out of and are embedded in the thick particulars of specific cultures possessing a moral integrity and status of their own. Rawls's, Charles Taylor, Amy Gutmann, and Michael Ignatieff agree that a human rights regime ought to be compatible with value pluralism and therefore cannot be anchored to any one version of foundationalism. Gutmann is more insistent than the other three that human rights need not deny all foundations. As Gutmann suggests, if we believe that human rights are important instruments for the protection of human beings against oppression, cruelty, and degradation, that is all we need to believe in order to defend them (Gutmann 2001: xi). This, of course, is a rather weak foundation in comparison with traditional justifications, and amounts to little more than Rorty's contention that because we happen to think that liberalism is a good thing that is sufficient justification for wanting others to do so. For Gutmann, to some extent echoing the spirit of Taylor's argument, it is preferable for pragmatic and moral reasons that human rights rely on a variety of foundational arguments. In other words, 'an overlapping consensus is more compatible with moral pluralism' (Gutmann 2001: xix).

It is my contention that the later Rawls's embraces a version of the recognition theory of rights which at the same time rejects subjectivism in the form of realism in international relations, and intuitionism in the form of natural law. It does not, however, address modern-day theories that premise human rights on universal moral attributes, or capabilities, on the grounds that such theories in some way rest on comprehensive doctrines, and therefore militate reasonable pluralism (see Buchanan 2006: 154–5). For Rawls's 'The Law of Peoples', of which respect for human rights is an integral constituent, is not arbitrary; it is not the reaction to a felt need, but has an underlying manifold of reasonableness (Boucher 2006a). Nor is it so abstract that it fails to connect with the interests of the society of peoples it regulates. Rawls's does not want to deny the validity of the emphasis upon interests found in the Realist tradition in international relations. He contends that peoples must have interests – otherwise they would be either inert or passive, or likely to be swayed by unreasonable and sometimes blind passions and impulses. The interests which move peoples (and which distinguish them from states) are reasonable interests guided by and congruent with a fair equality and due respect for all peoples. Rawls's account of human rights is latent within the self-understanding of liberal democratic peoples, but sufficiently restricted as to be acceptable to decent hierarchical non-liberal peoples (Reidy 2006: 185).

In *The Law of Peoples* Rawls's acknowledges that realism is the predominant manner of conceiving international relations. He clearly rejects the realist view of international relations that is predominantly associated with state-centric models. Liberal and decent peoples, he contends, 'are not moved solely by their prudential or rational...interests, the so-called reasons of state' (Rawls's 1999: 27). Against realism he argues that it is not always reasonable to be rational. In opposition to Realists who believe with Thucydides that human nature is everywhere and always the same and that international relations is an ongoing struggle for wealth and power, Rawls's chooses to avoid the term state because of its association with the Westphalian model of sovereign rights, and instead makes 'peoples' the subject of his international law, or 'Law of Peoples' (Rawls's 1999: 28 and 46). Unlike states, 'liberal' peoples limit their rational self-interest to what is reasonable (Rawls's 1999: 28). The Law of Peoples sharply restricts peoples' rights to independence and self-determination, eliminating the propensity for the subjugation of other peoples (Rawls's 1999: 38). This constitutes an explicit attack on sovereignty. Rawls's wants to limit it both in its external and internal dimensions.

For Rawls's, peoples, unlike states, do not possess sovereignty as traditionally conceived in the body of positive international law. They lack the right of war in pursuit of state policy and the right to autonomy within their own borders: 'We must reformulate the powers of sovereignty in the light of a reasonable Law of Peoples and deny to states the traditional rights to war and to unrestricted internal autonomy' (Rawls's 1999: 26–7). This means that Rawls's, in line with Kant and Walzer, wants to restrict the right of forcible intervention for all but a few extreme cases. Exceptions may include outlaw, or rogue, states that constitute a significant threat to the Society of Peoples, or where grave violations of human rights are being perpetrated. Furthermore, peoples have a duty to assist other peoples, especially in those cases where adverse conditions inhibit the attainment of a just or a decent political regime (Rawls's 1999: 37). Rawls's, then, self-consciously departs from the Westphalian model of international relations by acknowledging that sovereignty is constrained by having to respect basic human rights, and by prohibiting aggressive war. Whether it is a significant departure is a matter of contention.

Rawls's also rejects natural law and natural rights as the basis of human rights. For Rawls's, Christian natural law is a 'reasonable comprehensive doctrine', and like other such doctrines it is not precluded by, but is nevertheless rejected as foundational to, the Law of Peoples (Rawls's 1999: 107). The term 'law of peoples', Rawls's suggests, relying upon John Vincent (Vincent 1986: 27), derives from the idea of *ius gentium*. The phrase, '*ius gentium intra se*' indicates what all laws have in common. Rawls's use of the term 'law of peoples' does not, however, have the same meaning. Rawls's uses the term 'Law of Peoples' to refer to those principles that regulate mutual political relations among peoples, not among individuals or states as such, as was traditionally the case with natural law and Law of Nations theorists (Rawls 1999: 3, fn. 1).

He argues that the similarity between his Law of Peoples and natural law resides in the fact that they both hold out the possibility of universal peace among nations, conditional upon nations conforming to the principles of natural law or the Law of Peoples. The two concepts are, nevertheless, conceived very differently. Rawls's characterization of natural law, and its relation to other law, such as eternal, and revealed law, or scripture, is essentially Thomist: 'The Natural Law is thought to be part of the law of God that can be known through the natural powers of reason by our study of the structure of the world. As God has supreme authority over all creation, this law is binding for all humankind as members of one community. Thus understood the Natural Law is distinct from the eternal law, which lies in God's reason and guides God's activity in creating and sustaining the world' (Rawls's 1999: 104). Such a characterization grossly over-simplifies what was an immensely complex set of issues, especially that, as we saw in chapter three, of the relationship between the natural law and the Law of Nations.

The method for discovering the content of the law of nature was a matter of contention. Grotius, as we saw, posited the *a priori* and *a posteriori*. *A priori* reasoning demonstrates that something is in conformity with, or fails to conform to a reasonable and social nature. *A posteriori* reasoning deals in probabilities by taking common agreement or practices, among at least the civilized peoples, and infers from this conformity that something is consistent with the law of nature.

Rawls's explicitly distances himself from modern cosmopolitans, but by implication also theorists who put individuals at the centre of their conception of international law and justice. Cosmopolitans, he claims, in contrast with his own position, are ultimately concerned with individual well-being and not the justice of societies (Rawls's 1999: 99). In addition, Rawls's specifically singles out those versions of cosmopolitanism that ground principles of international justice, including human rights, on arguments such as 'human beings are moral persons and have equal worth in the eyes of God; or that they have certain moral and intellectual powers that entitle them to these rights' (Rawls's 1999: 68; also see Caney 2002: 99).

The Law of Peoples that regulates the Society of Peoples takes peoples as the actors, just as individuals are actors in domestic society. The society of peoples comprises both liberal and 'decent' peoples. Liberal peoples have three basic features. Their interests are served by a reasonably just constitutional democratic government, they cohere as a society in sharing common sympathies, and they have a moral nature (Rawls's 1999: 23). On the principle of toleration liberals have to acknowledge that there are decent societies capable of subscribing to and upholding various international principles such as human rights, but whose societies are hierarchical and not democratic.

Individuals and peoples have duties of civility, which are moral and not legal, within domestic societies, and also in the society of peoples where it is a requirement to give public reasons 'appropriate to the Society of Peoples for their actions' (Rawls's 1999: 58; cf. Rawls's 1993: 217–8). The habitual honouring of the terms of a just Law of Peoples, exhibiting an evident and mutually recognized intention to comply, generates mutual trust and confidence. They come to see these norms as mutually advantageous, and in time adopt them as ideals of conduct. This process of moral learning is integral to the success of the Law of Peoples, and includes a proper sense of pride in the historical achievements of one's forebears (Rawls's 1999: 44).

The rights of sovereignty that peoples enjoy derive from the Law of Peoples and result from their common agreement in 'suitable circumstances' (Rawls's 1999: 27). There is the realization that between the immutable miseries of the human condition such as pestilence, plague and epidemics on the one hand, and unfathomable irresistible causes such as fate and the will of God, the civil social life is the creation of human beings and can be modified to respond to new contingencies (Rawls's 1999: 46). Like Vico, Burke, and Dilthey, Rawls's realizes that whereas the natural world may be a mystery to everyone save its creator, we are the authors of our social world and we are everywhere at home in it because we are capable of changing it and ourselves through manipulating institutional arrangements by means of reasonable agreements.

The later Rawls's, because of his emphasis upon a political liberal conception of justice, has increasingly been allied to a communitarian or particularist position in which the elements of universalism derive from the principles which regulate communities or peoples. Peter Sutch, in viewing Rawls's from a communitarian point of view, is able to maintain that talk about basic rights in Rawls's is only possible because 'there is a vague consensus about the need for and purpose of such rights' (Sutch 2001: 187). Peter Jones, too, recognizes the contingency of basic human rights in Rawls's theory, but for him it is a matter of regret. Jones bemoans the fact that Rawls's is offering a political conception of human rights which for Jones lacks the moral force of the traditional conception of natural rights. Jones accuses Rawls's of offering a 'parsimonious' conception of human rights which posits a set of standards that peoples, and not persons, have good reasons to adopt in their relations with one another. The conception is impoverished, in Jones' view, because traditional conceptions of fundamental rights 'have generally been conceived as rights possessed by human beings as such and as rights that must therefore be respected in all the various contexts and circumstances in which human beings find themselves' (Jones 1996: 189).

It is indeed such foundational comprehensive theories of human rights that modern human rights theorists have found unsustainable, not by rejecting the idea of fundamental rights, but as the Idealists long ago argued, by grounding them in a theory that requires social recognition as part of their definition, and a conception of their contribution to the common good as their justification. Hence, as Allen Buchanan remarks, Rawls's does not ground his doctrine of human rights in a conception of a minimum human good, nor in any fundamentally moral human characteristics that all humans share (Buchanan 2006: 150). He also accuses Rawls's of not going far enough in so far as it is not clear whether Rawls's 'duty to assist' burdened peoples, unable to raise themselves up to the level of decent peoples, is an imperfect obligation to act charitably, or whether it is a duty of justice (Buchanan 2000: 697–721).

It is no longer sustainable to accuse Rawls's, as communitarians such as Sandel did, of viewing the person as unencumbered or pre-social. To include Rawls's among the company of constitutive communitarians is by no means eccentric. Sibyl A. Schwarzenbach goes as far as to suggest that the early Rawls's of *A Theory of Justice* employs much of the structure of Hegel's political theory while jettisoning the metaphysics (Schwarzenbach 1991: 541). For Rawls's theory personality depends upon both the formation and pursuit of a conception of the good, and in being embedded in the political culture of liberal democracy, or at least a well ordered hierarchical society that respects human rights, which are 'a special class of urgent rights' (Rawls's 1999: 79). In order to avoid the charge of parochialism human rights cannot be justified by comprehensive doctrines or by a conception of the good, but they must, of course, be compatible with them.

Human rights figure prominently in Rawls's *Law of Peoples*. Rawls's enumerates eight principles upon which his Law of Peoples rests. The sixth is that: 'Peoples are to honour human rights' (Rawls's 1999: 37). One may say that the other seven principles of the Law of Peoples are to a large degree dependent on this principle of honouring human rights in so far as they imply the rights of individuals who are subsumed under the category of peoples to enjoy liberties and prevent being acted upon in unwelcome ways. For example, the first principle requires each People to be free and independent, and to respect the freedom and independence of other Peoples. This, for example, is a stricture against colonialism and the suppression of one people by another. The fourth principle posits a duty of non-intervention; the fifth a right to self-defence; the seventh to observe the constraints of *jus in bello*; and the eighth, to assist peoples living in such unfavourable conditions that they are unable to sustain a decent political and social regime. These are what Rawls's calls 'burdened' peoples. All of these principles which comprise the Law of Peoples, and which are already widely recognized in international law, imply fundamental rights which, if Peoples renege on their duties, may be seriously violated.

Human rights fulfill three roles: they are the necessary conditions of the decency of a society's institutions and legal system; upholding them rebuffs any question of justifying foreign intervention in a people's domestic affairs, such as trade sanctions or military force; and, they circumscribe reasonable pluralism among peoples (Rawls's 1999: 80). Their justification is not solely that they are consistent with the current practices and morality of states, that is, conventional, but also they have a normative dimension. First, the liberties and non-injuries that they privilege are fundamental or urgent rights necessary to guard against the most grave of injuries. Second, the liberties, or ways of acting, and non-injuries, or ways of being treated, are necessary for social cooperation (Martin 2006b: 194–5). In other words, such a conception of human rights is premised upon an underlying notion of human interests that includes minimum conditions for freedom of choice and social cooperation.

Rawls's makes it clear that a restricted list of those that appear in the UN Declaration (articles 3–18), and some derivative from them (such as the convention on genocide 1948, and apartheid, 1973) is subject to consensus among decent peoples, liberal and non-liberal. In other words, they are not parochial or peculiarly liberal, nor do they depend upon any comprehensive doctrine, or philosophical theory of human nature. Human rights are those rights that have come to be recognized as essential for social cooperation, and for promoting the common good. In fact they are universal, subscribed to by decent peoples all over the world and ought to be by those who are not. Human rights are extremely important in the theory because they constrain the sovereignty of governments in what they may do to their own peoples (Rawls's 1999: 27, 42, 79–81). The violation of human rights is the only justification in addition to self-defence for military intervention once diplomatic and economic sanctions have proved unsuccessful (Rawls's 1999: 38, 81, and 93, fn. 6). They are also universal in that not only decent peoples, both liberal and non-liberal, but also outlaw peoples are bound by them.

Responsibility for ensuring the operation of human rights is placed firmly in the hands of governments. They are rights relating to basic needs such as the right to life, and to the means of subsistence and security, including the protection of ethnic minorities against genocide and ethnic cleansing, and to freedom from slavery. In addition, he advocates basic political rights such as liberty of conscience, equality before the law, and the right to personal property (Rawls's 1999: 65 and 79). Rawls's list of human rights has been criticized for its 'extreme narrowness' (Macleod 2006: 138), and for being rather 'sparse and minimalist' (Hinsch and Markus 2006: 123). The point, of course, is that Rawls's is specifying a minimum that should be acceptable to both liberal and decent peoples. Liberal societies, may and do, go beyond these rights in their internal arrangements because their values differ from decent but non-liberal peoples, but these are the minimum that we could expect decent peoples to embrace (see Martin 2006b: 194–5).

Allen Buchanan wants to go much further than Rawls's in this respect because he believes that Rawls's minimalist approach on human rights unintentionally allows for gross inequalities in status, gender and wealth within both liberal and non-liberal, but decent, societies. What concerns me here is the character of his argument and how it too embraces features of the type of understanding that the Idealists exemplify. Here again it is important to distinguish between what it means to have a human right, and the justification of human rights as such. We have already seen that Buchanan, contends that human rights are ascribed to all individuals by virtue of their humanity, regardless of whatever other characteristics may differentiate them from each other (Buchanan 2003: 121–2). The justification for such rights is that they secure certain basic human needs that provide for a 'decent human life' (Buchanan 2003: 128), without which personhood would be inconceivable.

Buchanan's answer to the former question, that is, what does it mean to have a human right, is not without ambiguity. In fact, it relies to a large degree upon social recognition and agreements among states. In other words, the moral claim being formulated on the basis of basic needs is being converted into a human right by means of recognition. Buchanan wants to show that there is a 'widely shared conception of human rights', what he calls 'the nascent global culture of human rights' that with some philosophical refinement can serve as the foundation of a 'justice-based moral theory of international law' (Buchanan 2003: 118 and 131). The emergent culture, Buchanan argues, constitutes a new cultural tradition, and reflects the fact that a variety of cultural communities increasingly embrace respect for human rights (Buchanan 2003: 153). What does this amount to? Well, something like an increasing recognition of some moral claims as human rights. As Buchanan contends: 'there does seem to be a movement toward wider consensus that some rights are Human Rights and that this consensus has both been facilitated by international legal institutions and has contributed to their improvement' (Buchanan 2003: 155). This is a far cry from the imprescriptible self-evidence of the rights about which natural rights theorists spoke. It starts from where we are now, that is, a recognition that human beings have human rights, and he wants to suggest that those rights may be justified in relation to basic human needs. Buchanan's human rights are rights which fulfill basic human needs. David Lumsdaine has provided a wealth of documentation to demonstrate that norms about foreign aid, far from emanating from universal principles, are in many respects a projection on top of the international sphere of the modern welfare state and its domestic anti-poverty norms (Lumsdaine 1993).

While Rawls's relies a good deal on John Vincent's account of human rights and International Relations, the basic rights upon which all ideologies (or comprehensive doctrines) may converge, namely subsistence rights, are covered to some degree in Rawls's duty to assist, but do not take centre stage as they do for Vincent, and as Buchanan laments, it is unclear whether the duty to assist relates to a right, or whether it is a duty of charity. One of the important figures in anchoring international economic and social issues to the language of human rights was Henry Shue. In defining the idea of a basic right Shue contends that there is a minimum requirement to which all human beings may reasonably lay claim to the rest of humanity. There are two components to the claim. The first is security rights, which necessarily excludes others from committing murder, torture, rape, and serious assault. The second component relates to the right to minimal economic security in the form of the basic necessities of clothing, medical treatment, shelter and unpolluted air, and water (Shue 1996: 19–33; first published

1983). The obligation to ensure basic subsistence would appear to be, however, of a different kind from that of personal security. We may all, for example, desist from torturing our fellow human beings, but whether we all have the capacity to provide for the subsistence of those who are starving is not so clear.

Rawls's did not extend his principles of justice to the international sphere until the publication of *The Law of Peoples* in 1999, and then only to a limited extent, and in response to those of his admirers who believed that his notion of a basic structure was equally as applicable to the international context as it was to the domestic. Rawls's denies the relevance of the arbitrariness of resource distribution to international justice. A country's fortunes, he contends, are due more to its political culture and the virtues of its people than to natural resources. Indeed, the discovery of natural resources may have bad as well as good effects (Rawls's 1999: 117; see Boucher 2006*b*: 176–91).

Charles Beitz and Thomas Pogge, however, were inspired to extend Rawls's principles of justice to the international sphere. They advocate a form of cosmopolitanism that is not premised on the idea of a universal political community. States, in their view, are interdependent. The complex interdependence of states entails a myriad of relations among them, many of which have moral significance. In circumstances where the effect may be beneficial or detrimental some form of regulation and cooperation is required. Where the action of each may impact upon others it is imperative, as Kant recognized, that just institutions be established. Beitz maintains that the Rawlsian difference principle is applicable to the international sphere. This principle requires that society's socio-economic order should maximize benefits to those individuals in the lowest socio-economic position. Beitz suggests that the extensive global system of trade, and complex interdependence, widely accepted among international relations analysts, constitute a world-wide co-operative scheme in which every country is implicated (Beitz 1979: 149).

For Rawls's, despite the degree of complex interdependence, there was not a sufficient degree of cooperation to constitute a common co-operative that qualifies for considerations of distributive justice comparable with bounded communities. The absence of a global society in which there is no co-operative surplus means that there is no requirement to find principles of distribution. Although Rawls's concedes that there is a case for the just distribution of basic liberties, and agrees with the aims of neo-Rawlsian internationalists, such as Beitz (1979) and Pogge (1994), in their advocacy of liberal institutions, securing human rights and providing for basic needs in accordance with what he calls a 'duty of assistance', he rejects the principles presented for redistributive justice (Rawls's 1999: 116).

The bottom line is that Rawls's believes that his 'Difference Principle' applies only to bounded communities, or to a people. Between peoples the non-egalitarian principle of mutual aid applies (Hinsch 2001: 62). How, then, do they differ? The duty to assist is a value based norm, which requires a publicly recognized criterion by which to translate it into specific claims. The need may be for certain goods, such as food or shelter, in order to achieve a specific value, like health or protection, which from a moral point of view is of high priority if the person is not able to secure them for herself or himself. Not to respond positively to such claims is a moral wrong because of the high importance they have for the life of the person. The Difference Principle is unlike the duty to assist in that it is designed to benefit the least well off people within a society, irrespective of claims of need or publicly recognized want. The redistribution is effected purely on the grounds of equality in order to alleviate the consequences of inequalities of income or wealth. The principle presupposes equal claims, and only mutual advantage, where everyone, including those relatively less well off, benefit from the uneven distribution, may justify economic inequalities (Hinsch 2001: 64).

Furthermore, the duty to assist is a threshold principle whereas the Difference principle is a maximizing norm. Publicly recognized need is not of course absolute, but relational. To be deprived of something that your society regards as basic, and morally good, is to have a claim of need and imposes duties of assistance. There is no question of maximizing equality and it is not an egalitarian principle.

CONCLUSION

What is being suggested, then, is that modern constitutive theory is widely acknowledged and used to account for the emergence of the human rights culture, and how we have the human rights we have, by developing arguments that are familiar to us from discussing the British Idealists, but which nevertheless reject the metaphysical foundations that characterized their ethical and political thinking. None wish to suggest that the human rights that we have come to value are arbitrary, nor capricious. All want to suggest that there are certain rights so fundamental that social relations as we know them would be inconceivable without such rights. In other words, we have good reasons for valuing the rights we value, and they may be justified from a variety of starting points, which may not all have the same reasons for valuing them. The suggestion, then, that there is something like an overlapping consensus which at the level of fundamental principles or rights constitutes a thin universalism able to sustain such basic principles as the keeping of promises, respect for life, abhorrence of torture and human trafficking, and much more. It is disputed, however, whether the thin morality constitutes a substantive enough cohesiveness to produce the degree of solidarity required for international distributive justice.

11

Human Rights and the Juridical Revolution

Whereas it is essential, if man is not to be compelled to have recourse, as a last resort, to rebellion against tyranny and oppression, that human rights should be protected by the rule of law ...

(Paragraph three of the preamble to the Universal Declaration of Human Rights (UDHR), adopted by the United Nations General Assembly on December 10, 1948).

Custom is not a special department or area of public international law: it is international law (Brownlie 1998: 18).

Both the establishment of the Nuremberg Tribunals and the ad hoc Tribunals for the Former Yugoslavia and Rwanda were of major, perhaps even monumental importance for the establishment of the rule of law in the international community (Meron 1998: 198).

INTRODUCTION

Hanna Arendt's scepticism about the ability of governments to respond to human rights violations by the imposition of a juridical system of laws and institutions designed to defend human beings against the atrocities of totalitarianism betray the extent to which she was not sensitive, despite her favourable view of Burke, to the process by which flickerings of humanity expressed in cries of outrage, manifest in so called soft law (which does not have the status of formal treaties), the potential for the emergence of norms out of practice – low in attainment and high in their aspirational ideals – are nevertheless the elements out of which the modern human rights culture grew. Her view of the human condition, that is the process by which universal human rights emerge, was not therefore consistent with those of Tocqueville, the British Idealists, and indeed Eleanor Roosevelt. Waldron puts it nicely when he contends that: 'The successful coming into being of human rights law was not a fore-ordained conclusion; but Arendt missed the point that if it were to come into being, this is what its earliest stages would look like, and that its coming-into-being would involve not the thunderous imposition of positive law from on high but the accretion and gradual crystallization of materials such as these' (Waldron 2006: 96).

Michel Villey contrasts classical natural rights theories with modern theories of individual rights, which he contends are too subjectivist. He is sceptical of the more or less worthy catalogue of aspirations that masquerade in the guise of human rights, such as the right to work, to leisure, to health and culture. The modern attempt to establish a system of jurisprudence on individual rights is misguided. The supposed absolute rights are, in his view, utopian fictions. They are arbitrary rights because they are based on subjective whims which undermine our conception of justice, equating it with subjective preferences. He maintains that modern rights theories assert conflicting rights and are sterile because they cannot form the basis of a coherent jurisprudence. Juridical thought has to establish just relationships between people and between people and property. This entails determining what is objectively right, and not the assertion of absolute rights. This for him entails returning to the classical tradition of Aristotle and Aquinas (Tierney 1988: 8–9). The legal and political practices which emphasize the conventional and contingent character of human rights cannot, however, be dismissed or ignored in the name of moral purity.

Acts of piracy were the first to fall under universal jurisdiction as states disregarded nationality in bringing perpetrators to justice in their own courts (Steiner and Alston 1996: 98). The juridical approach to human rights is not free of a residue of natural law and natural rights. Like the traditions from which this residue or 'survival' remains there is a heavily religious element that feels fundamental metaphysical questions cannot be bracketed and ignored. Lauterpacht, for example, argues that the rights of man must be enacted in the legal codes of each state: 'the law of nature as it has done in the past, supply much of the spiritual basis and much of political inspiration of that elevation of the rights of man to a legal plane superior to the will of sovereign states. Nothing short of the spiritual basis will be sufficient authority to lend permanent support to an innovation so significant and so far reaching' (Lauterpacht 1945: 52).

There has been, in Michael Ignatieff's words, a 'juridical revolution' in the international protection of individuals' (Ignatieff 2001: 5). This juridical revolution provides for the recognition, promotion, and protection of human rights. In other words, an important aspect of the modern human rights culture is the emphasis to which human rights are not only deemed moral claims, but also, and necessarily, legal claims enforceable in courts or tribunals of law, both domestic and international. It is the substitution of justice for revenge. The immensity of the change has not gone unnoticed by Anne-Marie Slaughter who believes that the twenty-first century will witness an acceleration of the trend to confer rights and responsibilities directly on individuals, as has already occurred in the field of international criminal law (Slaughter 2003: 42–3). Seyla Benhabib detects in this juridical revolution a move from international to cosmopolitan justice, where the latter signifies the elevation of the individual to the subject of a nascent international public law that binds and constrains the will of sovereign nations (Benhabib 2006: 16).

I suggested in Chapter Nine that we now operate on the assumption, or absolute presupposition, that we have human rights, that they are settled norms (Frost 1996: 111), the existence of which needs no or little justifications, but the content of which is a matter of contention, and this assumption provides the background commitment to giving answers to other questions. The fundamental philosophical questions about what human rights are and how we come to have them, that is, the question of foundations are bracketed. For Dworkin, to believe in natural or human rights is evidently to take 'the protection of certain individual choices as fundamental' (Dworkin 1978: 177).

If we assume that we have human rights, the issue then becomes how best to protect and promote them. Is law, for example, the best instrument for the universal promotion and protection of human and humanitarian rights? Many argue that international law lacks the principal requirement of law, a legislature to enact it and a sovereign authority to enforce it. Both Hobbes and Hegel subscribed to such a view, but neither underestimated the role of custom, honour and good form, in mitigating outright anarchy or hostility in the international realm. Others, such as T. E. Holland, recognize the special character of international law, as the 'vanishing point of Jurisprudence; since it lacks any arbiter of disputed questions, save public opinion ...' (Holland 1880: 261). It is important, however, not to confuse the issue of whether international law is law with the issue of the effectiveness and enforcement of international law (Malanczuk 1997: 5). H. L. A. Hart refutes the idea that international law fails to be law because it does not rely on a system of orders or commands backed by threats. Hart maintains that law does not merely rest on the threat of coercion, but also creates obligations and relies upon a person's or state's sense of duty (Hart 1994: 208–31). Even Hans Kelson, the legal positivist, accepts Austin's definition of law as requiring a coercive element, but sees in the international arena decentralized sanctions depending on each state to implement them. International law is formulated by those states and not by sovereign command (Kerr 2004: 7).

As we saw, during the early modern period the individual stood at the centre of natural law and the Law of Nations, related to others in a universal moral community. We find in the writings of Vattel the consolidation of a trend that had already begun in such writers as Pufendorf, that is, the giving of primacy to the state in the Law of Nations. Individuals, at the international level, were represented by states which were the subjects of the Law of Nations or international law. Under the older conception of the Law of Nations there were certainly justifications for humanitarian intervention, as an obligation rather than a right, to protect individuals against gross violations of the natural law.

In modern international law, however, the idea of the protection of human rights by collective international action is a novel and revolutionary idea. In 1880 Thomas Erskine Holland, Chichele professor of international law and diplomacy at Oxford University, was able to distinguish international from ordinary law by contending that the former 'is unsupported by the State...[and] differs from ordinary morality in being a rule for States and not for individuals (Holland 1880: 261). Juristic persons, or normal persons, in international law were States that possessed full external sovereignty, and were acknowledged members of the 'family of nations'. To be defective in either was to be an 'abnormal international person' (Holland 1880: 267). A 100 years ago L. Oppenheim, the principal authority on international law in Britain, maintained that 'the rights of man' do not and cannot enjoy the protection of international law. International law was concerned solely with relations between states and could not confer rights on individuals. Such protections were a matter for domestic law (Robertson and Merrills 1996: 1–2). The state was seen to have primary responsibility, for example, for violations of the laws of war. Individual responsibility was restricted to the trying for war crimes of military personnel in your custody (Olonisakin 1997: 822). Although international law has grown to encompass not only relations among states, but also relations with international organizations, and with persons, both natural and juridical, it is nevertheless the case that 'the international legal system is still *primarily* geared towards the international community of states, represented by governments' (Malanczuk 1997: 2).

CUSTOM AS A SOURCE OF HUMAN RIGHTS AND HUMANITARIAN LAW

Steiner and Alston contend that custom is referred to as the original and most ancient source of international law, and custom, of course, is not legislated (Steiner and Alston 1996: 27). The theologians of the Salamanca School, and after them Suarez, insisted that the Law of Nations, although related to the natural law, was not directly derived from it, and as a consequence, it requires the consent of mankind, not that of each assembled, but the common consent as evidenced from customary conduct. As de Soto contended: 'in order to constitute the law of nations...the common consent of men is sufficient and that it be introduced by custom as very fitting for the Natural Law' (cited in Aguilar 1946: 199). Writing in 1941, R. G. Collingwood contended in *The New Levithian* (Collingwood 1992: 219–20) that to assume that international law requires a legislative body and sovereign authority betrays a profound ignorance of European history and amounts to the deliberate sabotage of international law. International law in modern Europe is the offspring of the customary law of an ancient international nonsocial community which resembles the law as it is described in Icelandic sagas. Authorities could be found who knew what it was, and would pronounce on its content when called upon to do so, but there was no person, or group of persons professionally called upon to enforce it. Most people for the most part obeyed it, and it was not regarded as good form to disregard it. Collective action by those obedient to law against those who were not was the only effective way of enforcing it (Collingwood 1992: 28.76–28.79).

This assumes that law comes into being as the living embodiment of the activities of a community, even if its social sinews, or its solidarity as Richard Rorty and Hedley Bull would call it, is relatively weak. In other words the rules embedded in social practices need to be articulated discursively rather than 'made'. In the Icelandic sagas, for example that of Njal, the law is seen to have an objective existence. In the tenth century Icelandic settlers would meet in quarter session to administer the law, but there is no suggestion that they would legislate or change the law. *Njal's Saga* is in two parts, the Pagan and the Christian, and there is continuity between the laws. Christians could conform to the laws of the Pagan era because they claimed that they had their origin in God's natural law (Njal 1956: 211–21).

International law is declaratory of what is already immanent in the international community. Natural rights and human rights, on this view, are developmental and evolutionary, and not immutable and absolute. A near contemporary of Collingwood's and a fellow idealist denied the rationalist reasoning behind the very idea of natural rights. Even the so-called rights of man pronounced by the French Revolutionaries were nothing other than the common-law rights of Englishmen. In Oakeshott's famous inaugural lecture, 'Political Education', he is not criticizing natural rights as such, but merely our manner of conceiving them as premeditated principles determining the end to be pursued in politics. They are, he argues, abstracted from political activity, and not independently acquired prior to it (Oakeshott 1991: 51). Such rights are not the result of establishing first principles from a *tabula rasa*. Even the Magna Charta was not the *establishment* of newly declared rights of Englishmen, but instead the formal recognition of those that were already customarily enjoyed. For Oakeshott, this entails a particular conception of freedom, not one that is subordinate to power, and won as a concession from it, but instead viewed as an original ingredient in social life, which does not have to be dreamed or invented from the contemplation of an 'idea', because freedom is already in some respects embedded and enjoyed as a social practice, if by only the few in the form of privileges and exemptions. Such freedoms are not expressions of an abstract idea; they are the concrete exemplifications capable of being appropriated for extension. 'It is "liberties" of this sort', Oakeshott argues, 'which appear, for example, in *Magna Charta*. *Magna Charta* is a "charter of liberties". But it is not a Bill of Rights. It is a *record of specific liberties* already enjoyed, *not a statement of claims requiring authorization by a supreme power*' (Oakeshott 2004: 239–40).

The suggestion is, then, that rights recognized and acknowledged as fundamental to the social, moral, and political fabric of a society, already to some extent structure and define, or are at least immanent in, that society in the form of customary, but not always fully articulated, rules. Customary law is best exemplified in the English common law tradition, and it is worth looking at some of its features in order better to understand the customary character of the most important of our human and humanitarian rights in international law.[1] Indeed, their authority is deemed to be derived from their customary character, and not from the dictates of right reason, or logical deduction from universal natural attributes. Classical common law theories were partially initiated in response to the centralization of power in the hands of those who desired to make law on the basis of their own diagnoses of the demands of justice in accordance with their determination of

---

[1] I am indebted to Richard Mullender for suggesting the parallel and for directing me to some useful references.

the common good (Hayek 1960: 163). The common law was not made by king or parliament, but expressed in the work of legislators and judges. Blackstone characterizes the common law as immemorial custom. It is comprised of maxims and customs, manners of thinking, settled practices, established attitudes, and historical conceptions embedded in the spirit or memory of a people (Blackstone 1767: vol. 1, 17). To establish the existence of a common law requires demonstrating that it is the custom to observe it, and that its continuing use has endowed it with obligatory power, evidenced by public recognition of, and participation in, the enduring practice. Its legitimacy, or what Blackstone calls its 'weight and authority' (Blackstone 1767: vol. 1, 67; cf. vol. 68), derives from the longevity of usage, during which time there is not evidence to the contrary. Practice over time gives validity to a rule. Law is not viewed as external and imposed from above, but instead is the expression of the life of a people who understand and cherish it as their law, giving coherence and meaning to their lives.

For Gerald J. Postema, the legality or legitimacy of the law, that is its authority, is inextricably bound with its reasonableness and historical appropriateness (Postema 1986: 5). By historical appropriateness he does not mean a historically objective criterion, but instead the traditional character of the law, its continuing use within what Oakeshott calls a tradition of behaviour. States, like individuals, Postema contends, participate in discursive, practically oriented normative activities in the context of and interdependent material and deliberative social environment, in which customary norms are yielded, nurtured, and sustained (Postema 2007: 306). Principal among the features of common law are the ideas of identity in difference, and continuity in change. The law is not static, it does not appear full grown like Athena from the head of Zeus. It is in a continuous process of change and adjustment. It is not characterized by an essentialist core. There may be nothing in it that is identical with the Saxon law, but it is nevertheless the same law. It is not that the components are identical, it is because they maintain an identity in change, a continuity with the past. It is the identity of which we speak when we talk of the Argo being the same ship when it returned after setting out on the long quest for the Golden Fleece, even though it 'had successive Amendments, and scarce came back with any of its former Materials' (Matthew Hale cited in Postema 1986: 6). It is what F. H. Bradley calls our ordinary notion of identity, illustrated by both Bradley and Oakeshott in the example of Sir John Cutler's silk stockings. They were over time so continuously darned with wool that no particle of silk remained, and it became a matter of contention whether they were the same or completely new stockings. The identity of a thing depends on the view one takes of it in maintaining a continuous character (Bradley 1930: 63 and Oakeshott 1983: 114n). It is not the origin but an enduring living practice and a shared conviction that gives something its continuing validity.

Acceptance of the common law is based upon a sense of its reasonableness. Common law jurisdiction frequently invokes the idea of the reasonable person, and the associated notion of reasonableness, and by implication relying upon a sense of community and the standards embedded in it, especially in negligence, criminal and administrative law (Mullender 2005: 681). This does not mean that it is measured against an independent criterion of rationality, but instead understood to have emerged from a process of reasoning 'fashioned by the exercise of the special, professional intellectual skills of Common Lawyers over time refining and co-ordinating the social habits of a people into a coherent body of rules' (Postema 1986: 7). Coke uses the concept of 'artificial reason' to encapsulate the idea of the distilled wisdom of ages expressed through the judgements of the courts. It is not the result of philosophical reflection, but of the accumulation and refinement of experience (Pocock 1974: 35). Common law, in general terms, may be said to be the repository of the collective wisdom of the traditional practices of a people, where their present authority is evidence, without searching for historical origins which are irrelevant, for the rationality and reasonableness of the law. The assumption is, then, that wisdom accumulates more smoothly than error, which may or may not be the case (Schauer 2007: 33).

Among the sources of international law identified in Article 38 (1) of the Statute of the International Court of Justice, the judicial arm of the United Nations, provided for in the Charter, are: (b) 'international custom, as evidence of a general practice accepted as law', and (c) 'the general principles of law recognized by civilized nations'. Just as classic common law theory is informed by a consensus model of society in which a preponderant proportion of the law's addressees share certain basic values (Mullender 2006: 6), customary international law, especially relating to humanitarian rights, assume an international consensus (among civilized peoples), a degree of solidarity, in relation to a fundamental code of ethics, what Walzer may call a thin universalism, that abjures torture, genocide, and violent discrimination on grounds of race, gender or creed. Common lawyers themselves frequently invoked the Law of Nations, in so far as they saw it based on reason and the natural law, as a source of the common law. In cases where judges claimed that the Law of Nations was part of the common law, they could treat Acts, such as the Diplomatic Privileges Act of 1708 as merely declaratory of rights that already exist (Lobban 2007: 265).

The Legal Exemplification

The modern human rights culture is very much based upon the principle of the rule of law, and assumes no necessary philosophical foundations. In the view of many international human rights lawyers legal discussions of human rights begin where philosophical discussions end. Contrast Peter R. Baehr's position with that of Hersch Lauterpacht, for example. Lauterpacht contended that natural law, natural rights, and human rights were, as we saw, more or less the same, having a common ancestry, and that any attempt to sever an international bill of rights from its religiously grounded ancestors would deprive it of its moral force (Lauterpacht 1945: 9). Lauterpacht is here denying the formal existence of law by making it subordinate to, or dependent upon, something else, namely morality and religion. Baehr contends that 'human rights are internationally agreed values, standards or rules regulating the conduct of states towards their own citizens and towards non-citizens' (Baehr 1999:1). They are self-imposed rules, or international standards that are not absolute. They may come into conflict with each other and have to be weighed against each other in any relevant practical situation.

Baehr's position is widely shared among international jurist, and he has been placed among what Marie-Bénédicte Dembour terms 'deliberative scholars' who believe that human rights are the result of consensus and agreement (Dembour 2006: 232). The point is, however, those who engage in such deliberations and agreement do not begin with a *tabula rasa*. Human rights practices and values are already immanent in and inform the international community, and it is these values that press for recognition in deliberation and agreement. It is equally the case that the same may be said of 'discourse scholars', among whom Dembour counts herself, who give human rights reality by talking about them. She denies, for example, that rights exist irrespective of social recognition, and that every human being has them on account of being human. She acknowledges that they have become a fact in that they are invoked in politics, law, and common discourse. She is quite emphatic, however, that 'I do not believe that they would continue to exist were we to cease to talk about them' (Dembour 2006: 235). The international lawyer Owen M. Fiss argues that human rights are not derived from a common understanding of human nature, nor are they deduced philosophically from first principles. They are instead the articulation of aspirations immanent in a culture, a statement of what that society wants to become, and which provides a standard by which to judge what is (Fiss 1999: 273–4).

Stanley Fish makes the telling point that law is not philosophy, and to take law from the environment in which it works and judge it by extraneous philosophical principles may expose doctrinal inconsistencies, but at the same time exhibit an ignorance of its pragmatic nature. It is the doctrinal inconsistencies that enable law to work, to be accommodated to situations it did not anticipate, and to be incorporated in to stories that are more compelling than those previously told (Fish 1999: 193 and 201). A. H. Robertson and J. G. Merrills explicitly affirm the contingency of human rights when they argue that ratifying such a treaty is unavoidably political, and entails endorsing a specific set of political values. They argue that 'Ratifying a human rights treaty is therefore no more than a moral gesture. It is recognition of the special status of certain ideals, with the political expectations which that creates' (Robertson and Merrills 1996: 335). Human rights, they contend, are the outcome of bargaining and political assessment.

Here I want draw the legal landscape that has been called the juridical revolution in human rights, and to demonstrate how through conventional and customary law the body of human rights valued in the human rights culture has come to be developed.

The source and content of the Law of Nations was always a matter of contention, and arguments rested upon various combinations of customary law, the settled practices of nations, and fundamental principles derived from natural law. It is important to distinguish between the source of law in the sense of identifying the circumstances that gave rise to it, Hart's material or historical sense (Hart 1994: 246–7), and the source of law in the formal or legal sense in which criteria have to be met in order for a rule to be accepted as valid and legally binding. The criteria distinguish between law as it stands (*de lege lata*), and law as it might be (*de lege ferenda*). In other words, 'source' has a technical meaning in law referring to the process by which it can be identified as authoritative (Malanczuk 1997: 35).

One of the principal sources of international human rights and humanitarian law is custom, based upon the principle that general and consistent state practice, that is not in some sense qualified by statements that deny the existence of a rule, exhibits a sense of legal obligation (*opininio juris*), not withstanding the logical absurdity of legal obligation arising before a custom has matured into customary international law. Customary international law is the principal source of the major advances in human rights and humanitarian justice in the twentieth and twenty-first centuries. The architects of the Nuremberg and Tokyo tribunals constituted by the victorious allies, the International Criminal Tribunals for the former Yugoslavia and Rwanda, and the International Criminal Court established by the United Nations all rely heavily upon customary international law for the basis of their jurisdiction. Customary international law arises in essence as a result of the actual practices of states in their relations, developing the notion of civilized conduct appropriate to a moral community of states and individuals. The Supreme Court of the United States of America, for example, in ruling on the question of the legality of seizing coastal fishing vessels, their cargo and crew as prizes of war (The Paquete Habana case 1900), argued in its majority opinion that by virtue of ancient usage among civilized nations such conduct was prohibited. Cognizant of the fact that this doctrine had been widely contested Mr Justice Gray maintained that 'It is therefore worth the while to trace the history of the rule, from the earliest accessible sources, through the increasing recognition of it with occasional setbacks, to what we may now justly consider as its final establishment in our own country and generally throughout the civilized world' (reprinted in Steiner and Alston 1996: 61).

In 1980 the United States Court of Appeal ruled that on examination of the sources of international customary law, the usage of nations, judicial opinions and the Law of Nations, that official torture is prohibited. The implication being that the United States courts had the jurisdiction to enforce customary norms involving foreign citizens resident in the United States regarding crimes of torture committed in another country: 'the torturer has become – like the pirate and the slave trader before him – *hostis humani generic* (an enemy of all mankind)' (*Filartiga v. Pena-Irala* in Steiner and Alston 1996: 787). The customary basis of human rights and humanitarian law, while drawing upon some elements of the determination of the Law of Nations, is nevertheless anti-rationalist, shunning abstract principles for practice based precepts. As Jane Stromseth maintains: 'when the non-intervention norm and the developing norm to protect victims of atrocities pull in different directions, as they sometimes will, the resulting tension is best resolved in practice rather than in a doctrinal formulation abstractly in advance' (Stromseth 2003: 271).

International lawyers generally agree that changes in international law may come about as a result of changes in state practice, on condition that the changes are unequivocally stated and have been widely accepted by an overwhelming majority of states. Human rights do not easily lend themselves to formulation in customary law. It is not simply a matter of observing states in their relations with other states, or of states in relation to individuals. The main emphasis must be placed upon official statements and acts of state. This entails following the methodology of the International Court of Justice in its judgement on Nicaragua (1986), comprehending the relevant practice and *opinio juris*. This entails verifying the extent to which states present their actions and practices as conforming with the rule of law, or whether they simply deny the charges levelled against them. Even systematic and gross violations do not militate against assuming the existence of a customary rule if the responsible state seeks to act clandestinely instead of justifying its actions with reference to legal reasoning (Tomuschat 2003: 34). The observance of a widespread practice among states, is mere usage, or international comity, if there are no signs of acting out of a sense of legal obligation (Malanczuk 1997: 2).

This, of course, is the understanding we encountered in the Idealists. It is neither an appeal to natural law, nor to legal positivism, but instead the recognition that moral rights, or moral claims, that is, the aspiration for what ought to be, and which are immanent in society, precede their legal recognition. In one of the most widely read books on the international protection of human rights the authors suggest that 'only when the process of law making has taken place can any "new human right" move from the realm of aspiration' (Robertson and Merrills 1996: 296). This is not to deny that the aspiration may have moral force, and it is moral force that drives the recognition of international customary law. As Christian Tomuschat maintains: 'Custom, closely intertwined with considerations of morality, has always played a leading role in international humanitarian law' (Tomuschat 2003: 249).

Law, of course, wishes to have formal existence, that is, it seeks to be autonomous and independent of, and not subordinate to, morality and interpretation. In no area of law is it as imperative that what is legally valid coincides with what is morally right, and in which political interpretation plays such a significant role. But if the law were to coincide in all respects with morality then law would be superfluous (Fish 1999: 167), and if it were seen to be subordinate to politics it would lose all credibility. That is partially why the law which the ad hoc tribunals for the former Yugoslavia and Rwanda, and the International Criminal Court had to be seen as untarnished by 'western morality', and reflective of universal principles, and in addition have an objective existence free of political influence. The formal conventions of human rights have the status of treaties in international law, and achieve validity by conforming to a recognizable process of agreement and ratification. They have nevertheless persistently been criticized for their insensitivity to Asian values, and to presuppose a notion of individuality, that is of rights as morally or legally valid claims or prohibitions, derived from liberal ideology. The codification of customary law of the standards and obligations that states in their practices and pronouncements were already deemed to be obligated would give formal recognition to internationally and universally accepted standards.

This may appear to be a conservative and essentially non-progressive view of human rights, rooted in the status quo, and unable to develop beyond what is already accepted. Such pessimism is unwarranted. Just as the common law of England is constantly in flux, and articulated by the skilful interpretation and mediation of interlocutor lawyers skilled in the art of persuasion whose purpose is to construct a story into which his or her interpretation of what the law intimates 'fits' better than that of another, so the business of international law, particularly international humanitarian law resembles this model. In no area of law is legal formalism that is the view that the law has a literal meaning free of interpretation, less appropriate.

In the development of war crimes and crimes against humanity in codifying the terms of reference of the ad hoc tribunals and the International Criminal Court, there was not a simple attempt to achieve identity between what was codified, and what was deemed to be practice constitutive of obligation, but also a clarification and extension of those obligations in the process of which the definition of genocide was refined to encompass the systematic destruction of the whole or part of an ethic group, not only by violent extermination, but also by systematic rape as an instrument of policy.

Customary humanitarian law resembles common law in that it exhibits a degree of openness, as evidenced by judicial receptiveness to criticisms of existing doctrine, and is reflexive when the ideals that inform it are put into the service of pressing for, giving guidance to, and justifying the reconfiguration of doctrine (Mullender 2005: 687). Steven J. Burton's description of law as rhetorical (cited by Fish 1999: 196), although formulated in relation to 'local law', has a great deal of force in relation to the formulation of international customary and conventional human and humanitarian rights law. He argues that the local law of a society projects an image of social relations as they may aspire to be, and indicates a public commitment to bring it into being. Ignatieff is suggesting something similar when he maintains that the principal function of human rights language is to highlight the gap between what we say and what we do (Ignatieff 1999: 323).Their function is therefore aspirational, and their application precipitous of attaining the aspiration. Each application and formulation, Burton contends, in some respect brings that imagined world into being. Rhetorical jurisprudence does not ask perennial questions, just as R. G. Collingwood's philosopher or historian does not (Collingwood 1970: 53–76), but instead investigates the context of conventions in which to achieve persuasive uptake (Austin 1975), that is, it looks for the reasons that work. The law, in Stanley's Fish's terms, is 'something we believe in because it answers to, even as it is the creation of, our desires' (Fish 1999: 203).

The Importance of Customary Law

Why is customary law important in determining states' human rights obligations? There are certain things that people do to each other in the name of the state that are so morally repugnant that we could characterize them as peremptory norms of *jus cogens*. This is to suggest that they are principles accessible to all rational human beings, or at the very least recognized by all civilized states. This, of course, is the strategy of natural law, natural rights, and Law of Nations thinkers who want to invoke universal moral truths. It would, for example, go against the vast body of evidence to suggest that all civilized peoples abhor torture and sexual discrimination. To invoke a customary norm has a certain advantage over this type of strategy. The emergence of a customary norm does not require the consent of all states, and when it comes into existence, it may be made to constrain all states. This is not to ignore the fact that general and consistent state practice consistent with the emergent norm and *opinio juris* in conformity with international law, is required to establish its obligatory force (see Tasioulas 2007: 308).

Despite the many treatises and conventions that now exist by agreement, a large number of states have not signed-up to them all. They are therefore not bound by the treaty obligations, nor do they have a right to invoke them against the signatories. It is therefore a matter of importance to determine their obligations and rights under customary law. For example, there are many cases that specify the customary character of the prohibition of deporting people from occupied areas, for purposes of enforced labour, enslavement, or extermination. Even if states are not subscribers to conventional international agreements that proscribe such activities, then they are nevertheless in breach of customary law. These humane standards of warfare had previously been established by the laws and customs of war, which were later codified by the Hague Conventions of 1899 and 1907. They testify to the effort of the civilized participating nations to diminish the evils of war by limiting the power of the invading occupiers, placing the inhabitants of the occupied territories 'under the protection and rules of principles of law of nations as they result from usage established among the civilized peoples from the laws of humanity and the dictates of public conscience' (Meron 1998: 151).

Customary law was particularly important in the establishment of the International Criminal Tribunal for the former Yugoslavia. The drafters of the Statute establishing the Tribunal wished to avoid the criticisms leveled at the Nuremberg and Tokyo tribunals, that persons were on trial for crimes formulated after the fact, and thus violated one of the most fundamental tenets of law, the principle of '*nullem crimen sine lege, nulla poena sine lege* (no act is criminal unless it is laid down in law and no act can be punished unless punishment is prescribed in law)' (Kerr 2004: 60). More importantly, the Security Council did not have criminal law making powers, and even if it did, those powers could not extend to making criminal laws retroactive (Tomuschat 2003: 250). The Secretary General of the UN was at pains to emphasize that the Tribunal applies principles of international humanitarian law that are 'beyond any doubt part of customary law so that the problem of adherence of some but not all States to specific conventions does not arise' (Kerr 2004: 61).

The establishment of the International Criminal Tribunal for the former Yugoslavia, in accordance with Chapter VII of the UN Charter constituted for Geoffrey Robertson 'a seismic shift from diplomacy to legality in the conduct of world affairs (Robertson 2000: 194). The moral and political, if not legal, success of the tribunals for the former Yugoslavia and Rwanda gave momentum to the movement for the establishment of an International Criminal Court, the establishment of which 'constitutes a benchmark in the progressive development of international human rights' (Schabas 2004: ix).

The customary character of a norm is most obviously significant because it binds states who are not signatories to instruments in which the customary norm may be restated (Meron 1989: 3). Articles 43 and 60 of The Vienna Convention on the Law of Treaties is particularly significant in this respect. Obligations that exist independently of a treaty in which they are restated are in no way impaired if a state subsequently has reservations about that treaty. The suspension of a treaty because of the violation of an essential provision by the other party by right of article 60 highlights the importance of the distinction between conventional and customary law (Meron 1989: 7). The International Court of Justice reinforces the importance of the distinction in its ruling on the Convention of Genocide. The court maintained that objections to the convention had to be consistent with the convention's aims. Genocide so shocks the conscience of mankind that it contravenes moral law. According to the advisory opinion, 28 May (1951, ICJ Rep. 15) the principles of the Convention are declaratory of customary law. There are further implications of the distinction between conventional and customary law for the Geneva Conventions. The universal acceptance of the customary norms, in contrast with human rights instruments, bind states which are not parties to the human rights instrument in which the norm is reiterated (Meron 1989: 79–80).

There are, of course, difficult cases, which are bound to be disputed, in which a state's refusal to sign a treaty, constitutes for it a clear signification that it is not bound by any of its terms. This is where the reality of the power of the state intrudes. When the United States fails to sign-up, the political and moral significance is very different from, say, Tunisia's failure to do so. The human rights culture, as I suggested in Chapter Nine, is one into which states opt-in, often with considerable pressure from governmental and non-governmental organizations. As Jon Holbrook contends, international treaties are regarded as binding only upon those states that ratify them, and therefore even if every state in the world signed the Kyoto Protocol except the United States, few would maintain that the United States was bound by its provisions (Holbrook 2002: 143). This, however, is open to dispute. Robertson and Merrills argue that as conventions become widely accepted, the absence of this or that state will become of less importance because the 'obligations can become binding on all States by virtue of customary international law' (Robertson and Merrills 1996: 327).

Another important implication of customary law is that conventions which codify or establish human rights or humanitarian norms do not exclude those customary norms it does not mention from retaining their moral legal force. For example, the so-called Martens clause (named after the Russian diplomat who drafted it) in the preamble to the Hague Conventions makes it clear that the provisions are incomplete, but guarantees in the absence of a more complete code of the laws of war that 'the inhabitants and the belligerents remain under the protection and the rule of the principles of the law of nations, as they result from the usages established among civilised peoples, from the laws of humanity, and the dictates of public conscience' (cited in Schabas 2003: 2 and Tomuschat 2003: 248). The drafters of the 1998 Rome Statute of the International Criminal Court were sensitive to the issues of customary law. To a certain extent the Statute codifies customary international law, and instead of using modern terminology such as gross violations of human rights, adopts the vocabulary of crimes against humanity and war crimes. In anticipation of critics who argue that the Statute does not go far enough, article 10 inserts the disclaimer that nothing in the Statute should be interpreted as prejudicing or limiting current or 'developing rules of international law for purposes other than this statute' (Schabas 2004: Appendix I, The Rome Statute, Article 10). If customary law is deemed to go beyond the provisions of the statute in, for example, prohibiting certain weapons not listed in Article 8, or if customary law overtakes the provisions, in say raising the minimum age of military recruitment from age fifteen, Article 10 provides no comfort for those who would demur from existing or developing customary international law not provided for in the Statute (Schabas 2004: 28).

HISTORICISM AND HUMAN RIGHTS

An example of a new norm supplanting, or partially supplanting an old can be illustrated with reference to humanitarian intervention. There is a nascent principle of humanitarian intervention that has developed over the last decade or so, but only for the most serious crimes against humanity, and then only on a very selective basis. With the increasing level of humanitarian intervention during the 1990s in the form of the no fly zones in Iraq; the UN sanctioned securing of humanitarian relief zones in Somalia; the UN authorized use of force, specifically air power, to secure unimpeded delivery of humanitarian supplies in Bosnia, acted upon by NATO in 1995; and the March 1999 bombing campaign by NATO against Serbia and Montenegro to force the Yugoslav government to allow a military presence in Kosovo, the principle of humanitarian intervention was gradually becoming accepted. The NATO action was significant in a number of ways. It was unique in that no other regional security organization had before used force to pre-empt serious breaches of international criminal law, nor employed force outside of the territories of its member states. It overruled state sovereignty in favour of upholding international human rights by humanitarian intervention (Walther 1999: 1002).

In April, 1999, although the UN had not authorized the NATO action, Secretary General Kofi Annan recognized the emergence of an international norm 'against the violent repression of minorities that will and must take precedence over concerns of State sovereignty' (Holbrook 2002: 138). Both in relation to Kosovo and the no fly zones in Iraq the British government implicitly rejected its former view of the mid 1980s that no right of humanitarian intervention existed. Defence

Secretaries George Robertson in 1999, and Geoffrey Hoon in 2000 affirmed that there was a clear justification in international law outside of the UN framework that recognized the right to intervene in order to avert overwhelming catastrophes (Holbrook 2002: 140). The exact specification of the norm is yet to crystallize, but this is simply testimony to the process of the emergence and development of customary law. There is an element of normative consensus for intervention in exceptional circumstances, and the degree of consensus is seen to emerge from recent state practice, and colours how one delimits the character of such a norm (Stromseth 2003: 247–8).

My point is this: even though there is a perceptible residue of natural law and natural rights in the modern human rights movement or culture it does not predominantly assume that human rights are absolute, imprescriptible, and inalienable. It does not assume that the universal rights of which it talks are independent of the human will, out there awaiting discovery by the exercise of rational or right reason. It therefore stands outside of the declaratory tradition. To a large extent it espouses the ideals of liberal internationalism. It assumes instead a convergence and agreement upon values that then need to canvas wider and wider support in the process of being accepted as 'universal'. Its emphasis is upon conventional and customary law, as opposed to right reason.

NUREMBERG AND THE HUMAN RIGHTS TRIBUNALS

The language of human rights has increasingly come to the fore in the twentieth century as the reference point by which to judge the adequacy of existing regimes in the international system. The idea that we are first and foremost human beings, and only secondly citizens is the foundation upon which human rights talk builds. The tribunals in Nuremberg and at The Hague and Arusha were of immense significance because they affirmed and developed international humanitarian law, and confirmed its customary character, and thus made an historic contribution to the international rule of law. In addition, they reaffirmed the moral importance of attaching criminal responsibility to individuals for the crimes they commit against humanity (Meron 1998: 201–3).

A significant feature of attempts to apply the rule of law to the international sphere is that it has been the aspiration of liberal democracies projecting what they take to be civilized norms onto the wider world, and in the process of which attempting to extend the moral community in which more and more peoples may be regarded as neighbours.

The success of Nuremberg has led to a convenient silence about, or even a forgetfulness of, previous failures to bring war criminals to trial. Had not the attempt failed to hold the Ottomans responsible for the Massacre of Armenians in 1915 the Constantinople War Crimes Trials 'would have been remembered as comparable only to Nuremberg and Tokyo' (Bass 2000: 106). Many of the features so inextricably linked to Nuremberg, such as individual criminal responsibility, the importance of the rule of law and due process, as well as the very notion of crimes against humanity, were all present in the arguments surrounding the case for prosecuting the Ottomans (Bass 2000: 114–5). Bass argues that during the planning stages of Nuremberg, while the failures of Leipzig and even of Napoleon's exile to St. Helena were raised, no one mentioned Constantinople, not even when trying to establish a precedent for crimes against humanity, even though that very term was used by the allies as early at 1915 (Bass 2000: 144).

The significance of the ad hoc tribunals is that they reinforce and reinvigorate the importance of customary law in the development of international humanitarian law. In its ruling on the Tadic Appeal on jurisdiction the International Criminal Tribunal for the former Yugoslavia crystallized and clarified an important principle. In refusing to designate the war in Yugoslavia international in character it made an immense normative contribution to humanitarian law because it affirmed that violations of international humanitarian law perpetrated in internal wars are nevertheless international crimes under customary law (Meron 1998: 202 and 263). The Tribunal affirmed that it is now a settled norm of customary international law that international armed conflict is not a prerequisite for crimes against humanity, and that there may be no connection with conflict at all. The Statute of the Tribunal for the former Yugoslavia (Article 5) did specify internal and international conflict as the context of crimes against humanity, and in doing so the Security Council defined the crimes more narrowly than necessary. The Rwanda Statute (Article 3) dispelled the ambiguity and made no reference to armed conflict, giving weight to the view that crimes against humanity, such as genocide, may take place in peacetime (Meron 1998: 267).

The important differences between the Nuremberg and ad hoc tribunals need to be emphasized. Nuremberg and Tokyo were the result of agreement by the allies, and included no independent judges, and did not wholly rely upon conventional and customary international law, and were open to the charge of victors' justice. The tribunals in The Hague and Arusha were established by the UN Security Council and its terms of reference were almost wholly based upon customary international law in order to avoid the criticism that a non-legislative body was in fact making humanitarian law. The context of the latter two tribunals is a much greater codification of human rights law and they have to be sensitive to the international norms embodied in such documents as the International Covenant on Civil and Political Rights (Fenrick 1999: 769).

With the limited success of the two ad hoc tribunals came pressure to make permanent a court able to try serious humanitarian crimes. However, if Richard Goldstein's criterion is to be adopted, namely that the real contribution of the ad hoc tribunals in the long run will depend upon their contribution to the establishment of an international criminal court, then they have to be deemed a success (Goldstone 1997a: 106). The ad hoc tribunals demonstrated that that they could overcome in practice the lack of serious precedents, and conflicts between legal systems. They also proved invaluable in inducting people into the international community who simultaneously agitated for the establishment of a permanent criminal court (Glasius 2006: 13).

In 1998 120 nations voted in Rome in favour of the draft charter to create the International Criminal Court. Twenty-one abstained and seven opposed. The opposition, however, included United States, China, India, and Israel, on the grounds that they did not want external interference in their internal affairs. The United States, for example, thought that there were unacceptable implications for US peacekeeping efforts. It may inhibit the United States from participating in multinational peacekeeping operations, because it would expose its troops to politicized prosecutions (Zwanenberg 1999: 126). Russia also opposed the Court. International law accepts the right of peaceful protest, and affirms the proportionality principle, that is, reasonable force may be used to break up demonstrations for public order violations. The use of excessive force in crowd dispersal is condemned. Under the Rome Statute commanders who order their soldiers to fire upon peaceful demonstrators may be subject to criminal proceedings for crimes against humanity. This, indeed may be the motivation behind China's refusal to ratify the statute. While other states who opposed the Criminal Court were content with failing to ratify the treaty and withdraw from negotiations, the United States is the only one actively to have opposed it. The United States has in fact secured numerous bilateral agreements with states, on threat of withdrawing some benefit or privilege, establishing immunity for their citizens against arrest and trial. The first of which was Romania, which ratified the International Criminal Court in April, 2002, and entered into a non-surrender agreement with the United States in August, 2002. President Bush 'unsigned' the treaty that Clinton had signed (but did not intend to ratify), and Congress passed in May 2002 the 'American Service-members Protection Act' which authorizes the President to take any measures necessary to release certain American personnel 'who is being detained or imprisoned by, on behalf of, or at the request of the International Criminal Court' (cited in Glasius 2006: 18).

On 11 March 2003 eighteen judges were sworn in at The Hague in the world's first permanent war crimes and crimes against humanity court. Even though it is unlikely that the court will free itself from charges of political manipulation, it moves beyond the unsatisfactory situation where a political body, the United Nations Security Council, decided where the enforcement of humanitarian law was activated. In Richard Goldstone's words, 'It should be enforced wherever it is violated' (Goldstone 1997: 108). The Court is, however, the result of compromise on the issue of sovereignty. The Preamble to the Statute makes it clear that the Court is complementary to national criminal jurisdiction. Without a strong emphasis upon the principle of 'complementarity' throughout the formative process, the International Criminal Court would have had little support. It acknowledges that the primary responsibility for investigating and prosecuting international crimes is in the hands of national authorities. Only when national prosecutors or courts fail to act does the International Criminal Court intervene. If a national court decides on solid grounds that it will not prosecute then the International Criminal Court has no jurisdiction. As Marten Zwanenburg maintains: 'The national sphere is given precedence over the international, unless the national sphere is not up to the task' (Zwanenburg 1999: 130). There is certainly a retreat from the position established by the International Criminal Tribunal for the former Yugoslavia in the Tadic appeal against jurisdiction.

CONCLUSION

It has been argued that the juridical revolution, particularly the developments in the protection of human rights and humanitarian norms, has largely been based upon the principle of customary law, state practice, and the statements of classic jurists who have in some sense articulated the principles in terms of which states and individuals in the international sphere, broadly defined, have to conduct themselves. I have not suggested that all international law is customary, only that the fundamental rights, what are best described as humanitarian rights, have their source in customary law, and that the terms of reference for the ad hoc tribunals for the former Yugoslavia and Rwanda, as well as the Rome Treaty for the International Criminal Court are declaratory of principles and practices which their authors take to be already well established and obligatory. In other words, they are rights, duties, and obligations that have the social recognition of the international community, and they are justified on the grounds that they contribute to the common good of global society. That is not to say that the activities of states are always consistent with these global norms. The point is that states consistently confirm them in public rhetoric, and in public actions, and if they deviate from these norms they either do so clandestinely, or they attempt to justify their acts in some way. The United States, for example, publicly and consistently condemns torture as a means of extracting information or confessions from detainees, and in the face of condemnation for using water boarding as a method of interrogation at Guantanamo Bay, it denies that it is a form of torture. And, in addition, it engages in third-party torture by clandestinely practicing extraordinary rendition, and refuses to confirm it.

The formulations of the principles in international agreement and conventions, particularly in relation to the ad hoc tribunals initiated by the UN and the crimes specified in the terms of reference of the International Criminal Court have been declaratory of customary law. The process has not been the rationalist method of right reason deriving principles from natural law, nor of establishing indubitable data about human nature from which natural rights are deduced, but instead from the careful and considered understanding of how practices have arisen, how they have been understood by classic writers on international law, and contributed to what may be deemed the customary law of human and humanitarian rights. In essence, the tribunals of the second half of the twentieth century and the establishment of the International Criminal Court in the twenty-first century have served to establish what may be deemed a crime against humanity. First, it is one of an enumeration of acts, including murder; extermination; enslavement; deportation or forceable transfer of a population; imprisonment or other severe deprivation of physical liberty; torture; rape, including sexual slavery, enforced sterilization, and other sexual violence of comparable gravity; persecutions of any identifiable group on political, racial, ethnic, gender, and religious grounds; and other inhumane acts. It also includes the enforced disappearance of persons and the crime of apartheid. Second the crime has to be committed as part of a widespread or systematic attack which is pursuant or in furtherance of a state or organizational policy. And, third, the policy must be directed against a civilian population cognizant of the fact. There is no requirement that violations have to be in the context of an armed conflict (Fenrick 1999: 779).

The International Criminal Court represents one of the most significant achievements for a universal moral order, against the principle of inviolable sovereignty, ever to have been attained, despite the fact that 'complementarity' was the price of acceptance. While it remains to be seen how unconstrained it will be in it activities, it was a considerable achievement that signatories accepted the principle of the independent authority of the prosecutor to initiate his or her own cases. As we will see in the next chapter, the Statute of the International Criminal Court marks a milestone in the degree to which human rights and humanitarian rights under international law have become more sensitive to gender issues. Recognition of customary law by codifying it in statutes or treatises need not be inherently conservative, nor *de facto* supportive of the status quo. Recognizing any customary norm entails interpreting it in the light of current expectations and practices, and in articulating its content generally accepted prohibitions, such as that on genocide, may be extended. Genocide is quite obviously an evaluative/descriptive concept. That genocide is to be abhorred, that is, its evaluative element, few would want to dispute, but what actually constitutes genocide, that is, its descriptive element, is open to discursive negotiation and interpretation. It is at this level that the articulation of customary norms may far outstrip what is customary. In having to think about what in practice may result in an act of genocide, scenarios have to be faced that may previously have been considered 'too hard' to resolve. The ad hoc tribunals and the International Criminal Court, while retaining the evaluative connotation of the term genocide, have extended its descriptive content to include gender specific acts, such as that of systematic rape.

12

Women and Human Rights

> The laws of war have been written by men and for that reason it is not surprising that gender-related offences have not been dealt with adequately or appropriately in international conventions. (Goldstone 1997*b*: 3)
>
> ... a good case can be made that the development of women's rights is the most important development in the history of human rights. (Talbot 2005: 89)

INTRODUCTION

The 2008 Amnesty International Report on Human Rights complained that there was no global leadership to eradicate gender violence. It maintained that in almost all regions of the world women suffer from high degrees of sexual violence. Rape with impunity persists in Darfur, but even in USA among rape victims in marginalized poor and indigenous communities federal and tribal authorities fail to deliver either justice or protection. The report calls upon leaders to give more attention 'to making rights real for women and girls' (Amnesty International 2008: 14).

The ancient heritage of natural law and natural rights, if they included women at all, assumed their interests to be represented by their male superiors. Indeed, property ownership, to which so many of the rights were attached, was not within the reasonable grasp of a woman whose status was in almost all respects defined in relation to that of a man. The conditions for full membership in the club of rights holders were at best partially met, making women more or less associate members. Natural rights, both in the objective and subjective senses, far from being universal were in fact special rights, and predominantly the preserve of property-holding male citizens. Women simply lacked the full capacity, as they still do in vast portions of the world, to be rights bearers on a par with their male counterparts.

In relation to human rights the idea that was dominant up until recently in law, political theory, and ordinary opinion was that they are gender neutral. This assumption has been forcefully challenged, and there is a continuing debate amongst feminists over the issue of whether women have been excluded from human rights because they have been heavily gendered towards men's fears. Rights, many feminists suggest, are protections from the dangers that arise from activities in which men engage (Brown et al. 2002: 128). The emphasis in international law upon the right to life, for example, does not acknowledge the gender specific violations of rights that women endure, such as sexual abuse and rape in detention and in war. Indeed, in the most war torn areas of the world we hear reports on a daily basis of horrific, degrading, dehumanizing sexual violence committed on girls and women, even by UN peacekeepers whose role it is ostensibly to protect them.

The question is, are universal rights adequate to protect women, or do women's rights need to be specified separately from men's, emphasizing gender specific forms of violence, and relations between the sexes, which require a reconfiguration of the relation in which women stand to violence, the state, and the economy (Pettman 1996: 209). The place of women in the Law of Nations, and in the modern human rights regime, has tended to be obscured by emphasizing the 'big' issues, such as genocide, and humanitarian intervention. Women, however, are central to such issues, in that the violations of human rights associated with humanitarian abuses are perpetrated against them in ways that are often gender specific. In addition, women play a significant role in globalization, yet their contribution is little noticed. They are, like commodities, exported and imported for fulfilling traditional gendered roles. Millions of women have migrated from poorer countries to work as maids, nannies, carers of the elderly, and sometimes as sex workers in countries that are economically advantaged (Marks and Clapham 2005: 411). The irony is that many successful western women have succeeded in competition with men only by transferring the caring or their children, or of elderly parents, and of tending to the house, to women from the third world. In the modern human rights regime considerable strides have been taken in the juridical equality of women, but in practice and politically they remain dominated by patriarchal structures, and even the law itself unwittingly reflects these structures.

HISTORICAL PERSPECTIVES

The classic writers in the natural law and natural rights traditions were not completely insensitive to the violations of women's rights, but the status of women was almost invariably inferior to that of men. White females have fared little better than non-whites in the ways that universal rights have been deemed to be inappropriate for exercise by women, particularly in the ways that they have been deemed at the disposal of their masters as an extension to their property. Plato is often heralded as an exception to ancient misogyny in that he subscribes to the equality of men and women in the Guardian class, and theoretically they can aspire to be, although unlikely, philosopher kings. There is no indication, however, that in the economic class that their status would be anything other than subservient to men. Plato's universalism, although ostensibly favourable to the predicament of women, applies criteria that deny difference, and judge women in terms of male constructed attributes, which they are deemed to possess, in general, to a lesser degree than men. In other words, there is an in-built inequality programmed into the supposed equality of universalism. On the other hand, Aristotle acknowledges difference, but instead of celebrating the differences as equal but different expressions of humanity, he places them in a hierarchy in which women are deemed incapable of the higher pleasures such as contemplation. Their place is firmly in the household.

Generally in the history of natural law and natural rights there was no question of women being fully human, they either lacked, or possessed to a different degree, those attributes that were essential for a fully functioning rational life. Their role was subordinate to that of men, and men, as a matter of entitlement under natural law and natural right, ruled over women in the household. The universality of rights derivative from natural law, and possessed by the mere fact of being human in natural rights theories, were nevertheless exclusionary when it came to issues of women. Women lack the essential attributes for full individuality, and it is assumed that they flourish within the context of the household (see, for example, Coole 1993: 19–34).

Women, although inferior to men, both legally and rationally, were nevertheless bearers of rights. The social contract tradition, and its modern revival, has long assumed a state of nature in which there is natural equality, and in which no one has natural authority over any other without consent. The state of nature, and the idea of a social contract, that provides for the transition to political society, has been inseparable from the idea of natural and inalienable rights, but not until recently has it been asked where are women in this story that continues to resonate in modern times. Carole Pateman contends that the social contract tradition depends upon a prior sexual contract that deprives women of many of their rights, and establishes men's patriarchal right over them, leaving men free to dominate them both in the public and private spheres. It is a story of freedom and domination in which women are dominated by men whose civil rights depend upon patriarchal power (Pateman 1988: 2). Far from these rights being universal, then, they are special rights which men possess to the exclusion, and detriment of women (Pateman 1998: 213–31). In many poorer traditional cultures patriarchal structures are a matter of life and death, with women victims of rape, for example, whether within the family or by men outside, the victims of honour killings for the shame they have brought on the family. We are familiar, of course, with the political crime of disappearances in South America and elsewhere, but the disappearance of women in traditional patriarchal societies such as India and China is vast in comparison. Amartya Sen has concluded that by his calculation over 100 million women were 'missing' in Asia and North Africa, attributable to the excessive difference between male and female mortality rates (Sen 1990 and 2003).

All the major commentators, Pateman contends, have tended to ignore the fact that the state of nature is sexually differentiated, and that the sexual difference is used to support the claim that difference in rationality follows. The patriarchal construction of masculinity and femininity endows men, but not women, with the attributes and capacities necessary for entering into contractual agreements, most fundamentally, ownership of property in one's body. Only men are truly individuals (Pateman 1988: 5–6). Lacking individuality women are deemed incapable of entering into the social contract, that is, of entering into political society on an equal basis with men, but paradoxically, they are deemed capable of entering into the marriage contract, as owners of property in themselves, in which they subordinate themselves to men. There is little denying the overt and covert strategies to which theorists of natural law and natural rights have adopted to exclude women from universal rights on a par with those of men. Let me illustrate the strategies by which such exclusions are achieved by taking an example from the descriptive and prescriptive strands of natural right theory. Pufendorf, like Hobbes, posits the natural equality of men and women in the state of nature, but only in terms of right (Pufendorf 1717: Bk. VI, chpt. I, §ix), but unlike Hobbes believes matrimony to be a condition consistent with nature, and the most natural of human relations willed by God to propagate the species. Thomas Hobbes is quite clear that in a state of nature both women and men are naturally equal. In terms of the exercise of authority, women exercise powers and rights over their children, partly on the grounds that only they know for sure who the father is.

On the prescriptive side of natural law, Pufendorf agrees that there is a natural equality in a state of nature. Both agree from the different starting points, the one from an amoral and the other from a moral state of nature, that violence, in Hobbes' case in need of no justification, in the other as an instance of just war, may lead to mastery and obedience. Without consent, however, the relationship is unsatisfactory. Without consent the woman would be a mere slave, for both Hobbes and Pufendorf. For Hobbes, in the state of nature, consent even under duress makes her a servant, and everything she has, including children belong to the master. For him marriage is a civil condition, defined by law, and entered into by consent. Families exist is Hobbes's state of nature, and women may for purposes of protecting themselves and their children make compacts subjecting themselves to men. A compact of equality would be unstable without a superior to enforce it (Coole 1993: 61–2).

For Pufendorf marriage is a natural relationship found in the state of nature and willed by God for the more efficient propagation of the species, based on 'mutual good-will'. Nevertheless, for both writers, what is given up in marriage is the woman's natural equality, and her liberty to act in the public sphere. Men, too, give up a great deal in agreeing to obey Leviathan, but they remain in name freemen on an equal footing with others. The difference between men and women, as Carole Pateman notes, is that 'No woman is a free subject. All are "servants" of a peculiar kind in civil society, namely, "wives"' (Pateman 1988: 50). It is also the case, however, that all men become masters of a peculiar kind. In marrying their captives, for example, 'Men lay aside the severe authority of masters, for a more gentle and agreeable sway' (Pufendorf 1717: Bk. VI, chpt. I, §ix). While Pufendorf acknowledges all sorts of 'irregular' unions, they are on the whole 'repugnant to the Law of Nature' (Pufendorf 1717: Bk. VI, chpt. I, §xv), and not in his view consistent with nature, nor with the characters of men and women.

Grotius, for example, believes marriage to be the most natural of associations arising from consent, in which the authority of the male and female are unequal because, 'the Husband is the Head of the Wife in all conjugal and family affairs; for the Wife becomes a Part of the Husband's Family, and it is but reasonable, that the Husband should have Rule and Disposal of His own House' (Grotius 2005: Bk. II, chpt. v, §viii). It is natural, in Pufendorf's view, that the man initiates the contract, he admits the woman into his household, chooses their place of residence, has ownership of their children, and can expect his wife not to 'ramble abroad, lodge apart, or deny him reasonable favours...' (Pufendorf 1717: Bk. VI, chpt. I, §x).

If it were not for the purpose of procreation, Pufendorf contends, men would have no need of women. For intellectual pursuits and serious conversation boys, who have not yet tasted the passion of love, and old men, who have passed beyond it, prefer the company of their own sex. Women, then, although naturally equal in rights, and therefore having to consent to being ruled by the master of the house as her husband, is naturally inferior in the philosophical arts, being 'able to afford little assistance in deep speculations and in studious enquiries' (Pufendorf 1717: Bk. VI, chpt. I, §xxiv). She compensates for her inadequacies with the sweetness of her favours and the responsibilities she shoulders in the home. Pufendorf contends that 'The duty of a husband is to love, support, govern and protect his wife; of a wife to love and honour her husband, and to be a helpmate to him, not only in bearing and raising children, but also in taking upon herself some of the concerns of the household' (Pufendorf 1991: Bk. II, chpt. 2, §10).

Turning to the critics of the natural law and natural rights traditions, Rousseau is perhaps the most notorious and most explicit in strictly differentiating men and women in terms of their capacities, and hence in terms of the education they must receive. In doing so he insists that we must follow nature in determining the different characters of each, but at the same time he wants to modify what is 'natural' in order to make women more intriguing and attractive to men. For Rousseau, women and men complement each other. Like Pufendorf, Rousseau believes that a woman must be a helpmate of a man, and her education must be appropriate for such a role. Like Aristotle, then, Rousseau rejects the universalism of Plato, and acknowledges difference, and denies equality. In a perceptive criticism of Plato, Rousseau contends that 'Having got rid of the family there is not place for women in his system of government, so he is forced to turn them into men' (Rousseau 1911: 326). Acknowledging the differences is to concede that 'woman is worth more as a woman and less as a man' (Rousseau 1911: 327). While their characters, or capacities, complement each other, the sexes are not equal.

Those things that women and men have in common are characteristics of the species. It is her sex that differentiates a woman from a man, and without which she would be a man (Rousseau 1911: 321). It is in the nature of man to be strong and active, and in that of woman to be weak and passive. Women are made for men's delight, to please and be subject to them. The passions of women are boundless, but restrained by modesty. It is the ability of women to arouse in men passions in excess of their ability to satisfy them, and it is this that makes the apparently stronger party dependent on the weak, having to endeavour to please her in order to persuade her to submit to his superior strength.

Dependence is something, however, that Rousseau abhors, and it is something that his political philosophy aims to avoid. The social contract, for example, is designed to make men dependent on the whole, that is, the sovereign, of which they are constitutive parts. Even his philosophy of international relations is designed to ensure that states do not become dependent on each other by making each isolationist and almost self-sufficient (see Boucher 2003a: 235–52 and Boucher 1998: 289–307). For a man to become dependent on a woman, then, one may infer, is a sign of weakness. While Rousseau warns of the dangers to freedom of dependence of men on the economic or arbitrary powers of other men, he has no compunction about cultivating the dependency of women on men in providing for their subsistence, choosing their religion, and standing in judgement of their virtue (cf. Coole 1993: 85).

Compensating for her inferior strength, cunning is among a woman's natural attributes, which Rousseau believes education should develop, and without which women would not be helpmates to, but slaves of, men (Rousseau 1911: 334). Nevertheless, the advantage that Rousseau attributes to women is soon taken away. In order that men may be certain of their children, women must not only be faithful, but also have the reputation of being faithful. Women are therefore much more socially constrained than men, having to be scrupulous about their appearance and manners, for fear of losing their reputation. To suggest that there is an equality and similarity of duties between the sexes are merely empty words (Rousseau 1911: 325). Women are more dependent upon men, than men are upon women, because 'Nature herself has decreed that woman, both for herself and her children, should be at the mercy of man's judgment' (Rousseau 1911: 329).

For Rousseau, as it was for Pufendorf, women are inferior both in the speculative and physical sciences because they are incapable of works of genius that require 'wide generalization', and because of their limited range of observation, capacity for attentiveness and accuracy in discerning the physical laws of nature (Rousseau 1911: 350).

We saw how Mary Wollstonecraft from the position of devotional literature extended the arguments of Joseph Priestley and Richard Price to include women as possessors of natural rights on the grounds of equal capacity for reason, irrespective of sex. She was not alone in the latter part of the eighteenth century. Olympe de Gouges, Catherine Macauley, and Mary Hayes all pointed to the contradictions in celebrating the rights of man while excluding half of the population from their domain (Garrett 2006: 203). De Gouges, for example, was guillotined for her impudence for neglecting the virtues of her sex and aspiring to become a statesman (Dembour 2006: 188).

Even the great declarations of natural rights during the eighteenth century give little comfort to women. The American Declaration of Independence asserted the equality of all men in nature and before the law, independently of the creation of any human law. It is implied in the 1789 French Declaration, and made explicit in the Declaration of 1793. The Declarations of Rights of some of the state constitutions explicitly affirm the principle of equality, for example, that of Connecticut in 1818, and even some of the more stalwart slave holding states, such as Mississippi in 1817, and Alabama in 1819, affirmed the equality of rights (Ritchie 1903: 244–5).

It was, however, an equality of adult male voters, and all other categories of person were 'virtually' represented by the full-rights holders. Not even among the French Revolutionaries was it deemed desirable or appropriate to admit women to full political rights. Indeed, calls to do so were met with condemnation and a reaffirmation of the view that the rightful place of women is the home. Louis Marie Prudhomme (1752–1832), the founder of the much respected radical newspaper, *Revolutions of Paris*, was so disturbed by the agitation of women to share in political power that he sought to remind them, and men, that women have only private virtues, ill suited to the rough and tumble of politics. The only vocation and duty of a woman was to keep her mother company, to ease the worries of her spouse, and raise children (Prudhomme in Hunt ed. 1996: 131).

Condorcet was one of the few exceptions to take the Declaration of the Rights of Man and Citizen seriously in drawing out its full implications. Not only did he advocate the granting of rights to Jews and Protestants, but also campaigned for the abolition of the slave-trade and of slavery itself. He was far more progressive than any other leading spokesman of the Revolution in insisting that women should not be denied political rights. His newspaper article caused a sensation, but its impact was nevertheless short-lived because of entrenched and sustained opposition. Condorcet forcefully argues that violations and loss of natural rights have rendered some people ignorant that they ever had them. There is no excuse, however, for legislators and philosophers who ignore and perpetuate this injustice. They have violated the principle of equality in excluding half of humanity from participation in the formations of laws. It is an act of tyranny mitigated only if it could be proved that the grounds upon which men enjoy such rights are not also shared by women. Men have these rights because they are sentient beings, capable of apprehending and reasoning about moral ideas, capacities which women also possess in abundance (Condorcet in Hunt ed. 1996: 119–20).

Women, such as Etta Palm D'Aelders (1743-n.d.) and Olympe de Gouges (1748–1793), argued forcefully for equality of rights, imploring the beneficiaries of the century of enlightenment not to endorse and consecrate the abuses of power that characterized the preceding century of ignorance (D'Aelders in Hunt ed. 1996: 123). De Gouges moved the debate about the relation between the sexes firmly away from an emphasis on comparative virtues to a demand for equal rights under law (Garrett 2006: 220). De Gouges produced *The Declaration of the Rights of Women*, a pamphlet written in September 1791, in which she called upon women in the postscript 'to wake up; the tocsin of reason sounds throughout the universe; recognise your rights' (De Gouges in Hunt ed. 1996: 126). The overt political acts of women, and the establishment of radical women's clubs, led to a political backlash. De Gouges, for example, was denounced as an unnatural woman and a counter revolutionary. Her name was invoked in Chaumette's (1763–1793) denunciation of women's political activism.

It was in the context of the abolition of slavery, however, that women first organized to retrieve and claim their natural rights. A free-born black woman, Maria Stewart, was the first American woman to speak out publicly on civil and women's rights in 1832. The religious foundations of her argument are evident in invoking the bible to emphasize the moral responsibilities of women as mothers. In 1833 the American Anti-Slavery Society was formed in Philadelphia, including blacks and whites. Like the rational dissenters they combined non-conformist Christianity with the principles of the enlightenment, using scripture and claiming natural rights. Angelina Grimkè, for example, the daughter of a slave owning family in the south, joined the movement with her sister Sarah, and argued that 'the present arrangements of society...are a violation of human rights, a rank usurpation of power, a violent seizure and confiscation of what is sacredly and inalienably hers' (cited in Rowbotham 1992: 46). The fourteenth and fifteenth amendments (1870) to the Constitution notionally gave black men citizenship and voting rights in what was termed by the Abolitionists 'the Negroes' hour', but excluded black women and left a bitter legacy in the movement. Sojouner Truth, born a slave as Isabella Bormfree, contended that affording 'coloured' men rights would simply make them masters over 'coloured' women, making the situation as bad as it was before. She later came to support the amendments in the interests of black unity (Rowbotham 1992: 49).

This emphasizes the point that natural right violations, based on a foundationalist absolute presupposition that God is omnipotent, are very different from a right possessed under the human rights regime. For Idealists who rejected the rationalism of natural rights, but who nevertheless adhered to a metaphysics that gave foundations to their view of fundamental rights, an historicist, but not relativist answer would have to be given, and related to the level of consciousness attained in particular historical epochs. British Idealists in general were advocates of women's rights and have been acknowledged as making a significant contribution to the emancipation of women, and to the development of social welfare policies in which women have a significant presence (see Anderson 1991: 685–93; Sawer 2003: 143–86; and Offer 1999: 467–88). The idealists were advocates of equal access to education, and were politically active in ensuring that avenues of opportunity were opened to women at the universities. T. H. Green, for example, became the first Secretary, in 1878, of the Association for Promoting the Higher Education of Women in Oxford, and had much to do with the establishment of Somerville Hall, where women who had to travel some distance to attend the lectures of the Association could stay (Nicholson, introduction to Green 1997: xvii). Edward Caird fought for over twenty-five years at Glasgow University to extend its education to women. Between 1868 and 1877, when lectures were offered on a more systematic basis, Caird and three other young lecturers, much to the chagrin of many Senate members, offered short courses to women. He was persistent in his efforts to overcome the opposition of Senate to the opening up of the University to women, and worked closely with the Association for the Higher Education of Women, which developed into Queen Margaret College in 1883, and in 1892, the year before Caird left Glasgow for Balliol, it became incorporated into the University (Jones and Muirhead 1921: 96–101).

Women, if they were to attain self-realization, had to be able to develop their capacities unhindered by sex or social background. Equality of opportunity in education would 'bring together boys and girls of different social circumstances, and unite them in that freemasonary of a common education which was the strongest of all ties' (Green 1997: 324). Ethical development, or self-realization, transcends all social distinctions, and is the vocation of every individual, attained through full-active citizenship, that must as a consequence be open to all equally (Anderson 1991: 692). As a member of a social community able to conceive of a common good there should be no impediments placed in her way. Green contends that 'it is impossible for one whose mind is open to the claims of others to ignore the wrong of treating a woman as the servant of his pleasures at the cost of her own degradation' (Green 1899: §267, p. 325). Whereas such wrongs are habitually perpetrated, they are nevertheless committed with pangs of conscience which in earlier times, such as in Ancient Greece with a very different structure of society from the present, the pangs would have been precluded. Green argues that:

The sensibility could only arise in sequence upon that change in the actual structure of society through which the human person, as such, without distinction of sex, became the subject of rights. That change was itself... the embodiment of a demand which forms the basis of our moral nature – the demand on the part of the individual for a good which shall be at once his own and the good of others (Green 1899: §267, pp. 325–6).

This, of course, follows from the general Idealist metaphysics, articulated by Green, but loosely subscribed to by most of the Idealists. There could be no permanent innate inscribed superiority of the husband and father over the wife and child. Patriarchy was not for them a legitimate basis for social authority, and was in conflict with their inclusive conception of citizenship which did not discriminate on grounds of nationality, race, gender or class. Respect for persons entailed that all are afforded the same rights which constitutes a negative equality before the law, but in addition, women must also be granted the positive equality of improvements in the material and social conditions of their lives so that it becomes a real possibility for them to pursue a career, should they so choose (Green 1899: §267, p. 326; also see Tyler 1997: 238). All hindrances to self-realization had to be removed, and equality of opportunity afforded to everyone. Without a more robust system of women's rights, and great educational opportunities, rectifying gender inequalities social harmony and political stability were impossible to sustain (Leighton 2004: 305).

As in all matters of social policy Idealists did not advocate the application of an *a priori* formula. The test of extending the involvement of the state in securing rights for individuals who were excluded in some way should always be that of whether such intervention enhanced or diminished individual freedom. They supported a national postal service despite the fact that it restricted the rights of individuals to engage in the provision of private postal services, on the grounds that it enhanced everyone's capacity effectively to communicate with others throughout the world. As in everything else, their view of 'natural rights' for women was developmental, and historicist, against the background of a universal reason gradually revelatory of the development of freedom in the world.

The extension of rights to women is integral to the more general process of conceiving of a wider and wider range of persons to which the common good is believed to be common (Green 1899: §206, p. 245). In so far as women are regarded outside of the moral community, that is, as appendages to the household, as they were in Greece and Rome, 'the sacredness and the persons of women' are denied (Green 1899: §267, p. 326).

David Ritchie, illustrative of the historicist turn of mind, argues that the assertion of equal rights is contingent on historical circumstances. Not all those who claim equal rights, he argues, maintain the equal right to vote. It is absurd to think of an equal right to vote prior to and independent of law. Constitutions may be thought to provide liberty, peace, and security, and not to exist for the sake of allowing certain persons to vote. 'On whom the suffrage should be conferred is a matter not to be settled *a priori*, but by reference to the particular circumstances of the country' (Ritchie 1903: 255). In general the Idealists were active in agitating for the extension of the franchise to women (Carter 2003: 72–3), but in Green's and Ritchie's view, the equality of the sexes implies much more than equality of political rights and duties, and of the right to vote. For the more intelligent supporters of female suffrage the franchise is predominately a useful symbol of social equality. The more logical advocates recognize that the economic independence of women is 'necessary for the real social equality of the woman with the man' (Ritchie 1903: 261).

Green's views on the emancipation of women were indeed radical, especially by Victorian standards. While Idealists are summarily accused of subsuming the individual in ever expanding social wholes, such as the family, the state, and the Absolute, none wished to deny individual personality. The point is that personality and moral growth could not flourish without social relations, not that it should be totally crushed by them. If women were to be more than domestic slaves at the sexual mercy of their husbands, and if husbands were to be more morally upstanding and faithful, then domestic equality had to be achieved, in which both were equal in status, possess rights, but not exactly the same rights, and in which the woman can achieve economic independence. To this end, coveture, a fundamental principle of English law, was an anachronism. It posited that husband and wife constitute one person, and that the interests of the wife were virtually represented by the husband. In acknowledgement of the equal moral capacity of both parties to marriage Green endorsed the sentiments behind the Married Women's Property Acts of 1870 and 1882, which potentially afforded women a degree of independence (Leighton 2004: 307).

Women should have the same rights as men to divorce on grounds of adultery, which should not be a protracted process. His rationale was that an unwilling union undermined the moral purpose of the matrimonial condition. He did not, however, advocate that adultery should be a criminal offence on the grounds that the rights to which marriage gives rise, and the moral purpose for which the rights are intended, would be undermined by too strong an element of enforcement by the state. While the rights of the woman and child would be protected, a man whose passion was neutralized by the fear of punishment by the state would contribute little to family life and the moral development of the individuals within it (Green 1899: §244, p. 240). Even after the liberalization of the divorce laws in England by the Acts of 1857, 1858, and 1878, the initiation of the process by a woman was fraught with impediments. She had to prove that her husband was an adulterer in combination with incest, bigamy or extreme violence (Leighton 2004: 205).

Green reluctantly took a stance against Josephine E. Butler, who openly opposed the Liberal candidate, John Delamore Lewis, in the 1874 Oxford by-election for his support of the Contagious Diseases Act, on the grounds that the Act promoted the State provision and regulation of prostitution, which allowed for the enforced isolation, testing and treatment of prostitutes in garrison towns. Green, without wishing to endorse the Acts, took exception to what he thought a gross misrepresentation of the legislation. His analysis got to the heart of the problem. The military system itself enticed men from the margins of society, bound them for long periods, often in virtual idleness, and without opportunities for marriage. It was not therefore the fault of the prostitute that garrison towns were in moral decay. The social conditions that caused women to become 'victims of the bad passions of men' had to be eradicated (Green 1997: 224).

Green's radicalness should not, however, be exaggerated. In many respects he has affinities with Wollstonecraft. His is a deeply religious view, but without the natural rights foundations that underpinned her theory. Women should be provided with choices by educating them and developing their rational faculties, to enable them to become economically independent, should they so wish. It was the dependency of women on men, and the virtual enslavement that it entailed to which they both objected. For both Green and Wollstonecraft, the status of the woman in relation to the husband would change, but for the most part her gender role would remain the same. At the opening of the Wyggeston Girls School in Leicester, Green reassured his audience that in seeking to provide greater educational advantages to women he did not seek to make them more like men, but instead better equipped and suited to fulfil those functions already allotted them. The added advantage was that women would acquire the resources for better earning their own living, but a condition in which women had to earn a living was to be avoided. A sure sign of the advancement of civilization is the extent to which women are not subservient to the pleasure of men, 'but their habitual associates' (Green 1997: 327). Such views were echoed by R. B. Haldane, a strong advocate of women's education and of extending the franchise. He maintained that 'I never believed that women would become warriors, nor commanders-in-chief, nor that men would take to nursing children on any large scale' (cited in Carter 2003: 75).

More recent Idealists, Michael Oakeshott and R. G. Collingwood, present us with versions of the recognition thesis of fundamental rights in relation to women. The rights of women, that are formally recognized in legislation, are not the result of rationalistic abstract reasoning derived from first principles, but instead an acknowledgement of moral claims that are pressing to be heard, or of anomalies that call out for rectification. Oakeshott argues that if abstract rational principles were to be applied to the design of the most suitable garment for a woman to wear while riding a bicycle in Victorian England, the likely answer would be shorts. However, to the designers of Victorian 'rational dress' such an answer would have been inconceivable. What the designers actually came up with was bloomers. The designers nevertheless believed themselves to have acted rationally in escaping the very considerations that in fact constrained the answer that it was appropriate and possible to give. The real question they asked, and to which bloomers was the answer, was what item of clothing combines within itself the qualities of being well equipped to ride a bicycle, while at the same time being a suitable form of attire for a young English woman in 1880 to wear, given the cultural context (Oakeshott 1991: 115–6). Similarly, it was not abstract principles based on universal equality that persuaded Englishmen in Parliament to extend women the vote, but that they were unable any longer to resist the undoubted extent to which women had already assumed the responsibilities commensurate with full citizenship. In other words, rights including fundamental rights are contextual, and recognition of pressing claims is the pursuit of intimations already inherent in the practices of a society. Oakeshott contends that 'the only cogent reason to be advanced for the technical "enfranchisement" of women was that in all or most other important respects they had already been enfranchised. Arguments drawn from abstract Natural Right, from "justice," or from some general concept of feminine personality, must be regarded as either irrelevant, or as unfortunately disguised forms of the one valid argument; namely, that there was an incoherence in the arrangements of the society which pressed convincingly for remedy' (Oakeshott 1991: 57).

THE CODIFICATION OF WOMEN'S RIGHTS

While feminists were slow to demand a voice and a place in international relations issues the focus upon difference gave impetus to a much more internationally oriented outlook. Women were, of course, afforded formal equality with men in article 1 of the 'Universal Declaration of Human Rights' (1948), which was reaffirmed in subsequent conventions on economic and political rights, racial discrimination, and apartheid. Women's rights have been specifically affirmed in the UN Declaration on the 'Elimination of Discrimination against Women' (1967) and conventions on the political rights of women (1952), marriage (1962), and the nationality of married women (1957).

Such formal recognition of women as rights holders at the international level was given impetus by the establishment in 1947 of the Commission on the Status of Women; and by the United Nations' Decade for Women (1976–1985) following International Women's year (1975) with its conference in Mexico City. The conference internationalized women's issues and created a powerful transnational pressure group, with regular world meetings. A new convention on the elimination of discrimination against women was voted on by the UN General Assembly in December, 1979, with 130 votes in favour and ten abstentions, and has subsequently been adopted by over ninety countries, and came into effect in 1981 (Haslegrave 1988; Light and Halliday 1994). This convention included placing an obligation on states to implement proper measures, including legislation, to hinder all forms of trafficking in women, and exploitation for purposes of prostitution. With the enlargement of Europe and greater freedom of movement trafficking and sexual exploitation have become more prevalent, and linked to organized crime. In 2000 the UN issued a protocol, the Protocol to Prevent, Suppress and Punish Trafficking in Persons, Especially Women and Children. States were called upon to incorporate such prohibitions in their criminal law, and to co-operate with international enforcement agencies.

While the prevention of sex and slave trafficking is of the highest priority, the remedy may be unintentionally discriminatory against women. The tendency of campaigns to portray women in the postcolonial world as vulnerable victims, the prey of ruthless exploiters, has led to blanket responses that restrict legitimate freedom of movement for women. The government of Burma, for example, reacted to a Humans Rights Watch report on the trafficking of women and girls to the Thai sex industry by imposing a blanket ban on all women between the ages of sixteen and twenty-five from travelling without being accompanied by a legal guardian. The Nepalese government refused to issue employment licenses to women to work abroad without the consent of a spouse or male guardian, while Bangladesh, in 1998, prohibited women from going abroad to work as domestic workers (Phillips 2007: 123). Paternalistic protectionism, then, was motivated by the familiar stereotypes that anti sex-trafficking campaigners generated.

The World Conference on Human Rights of 1993 resulted in the 'Vienna Declaration and Programme of Action' which emphasized the responsibilities of all states to 'encourage respect for human rights and fundamental freedoms for all, without distinction as to race, sex, language or religion' (Brownlie and Goodwin-Gill 2006: 138). Such commitment to equality and non-discrimination are similarly reflected in the various regional conventions on human rights.

The formal international recognition of women's fundamental rights is something quite different from recognition in practice or as a key factor in formulating policy. John Vincent has argued that human rights conventions are difficult to ground and largely lack teeth, requiring the agreement of states for their enforcement (Vincent 1986: ch. 2).

CULTURE AND HUMAN RIGHTS

Many states simply do not agree to accept those aspects of the conventions they do not like. In the case of women's human rights they often come into conflict with the so-called third generation rights. Hilary Charlesworth and Christine Chinkin maintain that while gender equality can be achieved by limiting religious and cultural rights, politically religious and cultural freedoms are accorded a much higher status both nationally and internationally (Charlesworth and Chinkin 2000: 239). The individual rights of women may often be 'trumped' by and undermined by the rights of various cultural and religious groups. In many of the poorer countries of the world the laws of marriage and divorce are usually religiously based and considerably weighted in favour of the male. The convention that has by far the most reservations expressed against it is that on the 'Elimination of All Forms of Discrimination Against Women'. Many states object to the whole or part of the clause affirming the equality of women and men in marriage and divorce, arguing that it contravenes Islamic Shari'a, as controlled by various religious communities within the state, or within Israel Jewish Family Law (Okin 2005: 92–5). Sexuality and reproduction in particular are closely regulated by most cultures, and almost invariably entail the subordination of women by men. Women within such cultural groups, however, may not be as enthusiastic about the injunctions as the men who contribute much to their formulation (Okin 1999).

A growing amount of literature points to the inimical effects of multiculturalism within states, especially upon women, in that multicultural policies shore up the power bases of cultural groupings, typically of old men, and perpetuate inequalities, especially in relation to women. Feminists have warned that there is a tendency for discourses about culture to offer the opportunity to the more powerful to impose their own meaning on practices by codifying what are normally contested and fluid and demand a conformity that serves their own interests. Such conclusions lead to a considerable scepticism about culture and what the term is deployed to do (Phillips 2007: 18). Okin, for example, is accused of essentializing culture, and hence setting-up an artificial dualism between feminism and multiculturalism (Benhabib 2002: 102). Both Tariq Modood and Anne Phillips acknowledge and endorse the rising tide of anti-essentialist critiques of culture, but do not wish to follow such criticisms to their logical conclusion, that is, if cultures are characterized more by their fluidity than by their homogeneity, and if they are easily permeable, what is there left for multiculturalism to do? Both want to resist a too indecent haste towards transnational cosmopolitanism. Modood and Phillips want to retain the idea that culture constitutes and gives meaning, at least partially, to lived experience, and that a greater emphasis upon the multi as opposed to the culture points the way to a society that acknowledges differences, including those of faith, without the exoticization of cultures. Indeed, one of the central points of Phillips' book is that there is a need to challenge the exoticization of other cultures. The danger, she argues, is to exaggerate the differences among cultures, and to portray others as animated by considerations and impulses mysteriously alien. In other words, to use Anne Phillips' terms, what is required is a multiculturalism without culture, and one which protects and promotes the enjoyment of rights, including those of women (Modood 2007 and Phillips 2007).

When it comes to homosexuality the clash between universal rights and culture is even more pronounced. As Alan Sinfield has argued, 'intervening in the sex/gender systems of other countries necessarily involves disputing, not only the laws or the abuses, but the mores of those cultures' (Sinfield 2005: 152). Indeed, whereas most countries deny that they engage in the violation of human rights, many openly condemn gays and lesbians in the most virulent of terms, as do, for example, Robert Mugabe of Zimbabwe and Nujoma of Namibia.

The onward and upward view of progress in the universal acceptance of human rights has been severely shaken (Patterson 1995: 132–3). Feminist analyses of international relations increasingly reveal that human rights and international law are essentially gendered. Human rights, it is claimed, are androcentric (Peterson and Parisi 1998: 132). Studies of cases brought before the European Court of Human Rights, for example, have concluded that the decisions of the Court are insensitive to the experience of women (Palmer 2002: 114). It is not enough, Eva Brems argues, to apply liberal principles of equality. The 'add women and stir' approach has serious consequences because it merely requires equality of treatment, irrespective of differences (Brems 1997: 138). Playing the cultural card in courts has often proved inimical to women, because it almost invariably entails an attempt to legitimate the unacceptable behaviour of males in relation to women on the grounds that it is 'normal'. When courts become involved in legitimating and recognizing particular cultural associations, they have a tendency to ossify cultures and make them less susceptible to internal criticism and reform. Such legal boundaries once constructed are much more difficult to scale than the cultural (Sunder 2001: 503).

CASUALTIES OF WAR

Women have more often than not been the first causalities of war from the rape of the Sabine women in ancient Rome to reports of rape camps in the recent Bosnian war between Serbs and Muslims. In Ancient Greece, for example, where it was common for heads of households to take female slaves for sexual gratification, women were frequently regarded as possessions that in war constituted just another form of booty to be awarded as prizes for military success. In the opening chapter of Homer's *Iliad* two women are depicted at once as the prizes of war, and the causes of conflict among men. Agamemnon, the king and Achillês, the prince of the Achaians, after success in battle against Thebê, were awarded the prize of Chryseïs and Briseïs, respectively. Chryseïs was the daughter of the priest Chrysês who implored the people of Achaian to call upon Agamemnon to release his daughter for a generous ransom, or incur the displeasure of Apollo Farshooter, son of Zeus. Agamemnon refused on the grounds that if he were to give up Chryseïs he would be the only one without a prize of war. His refusal brought the deadly shafts of Apollo raining down on the camp leaving in its wake death and destruction. After being berated by Achillês, Agamemnon angrily and reluctantly gives up the woman to whom he looked forward working his loom and lying in his bed in Argos, warning that he would now take Briseïs instead. The seizure of Briseïs by Agamemnon's envoys is depicted both as an insult, a loss of face and pride, and as a personal emotional loss to Achillês of his beautiful prize from the spoils of war. Neither of the captives has a voice, nor are they thought of as anything other than rewards for battle to be enjoyed as gifts bestowed upon them by the people (Homer n.d., bk. I, pp. 1–20).

The laws of war have prohibited rape for centuries on pain of execution. The military codes of Richard II (1385) and Henry V (1419) forbade rape on punishment of death, and more recently the United States Leiber instructions (1863) designate rape a capital crime. Rape committed on the initiative of individual soldiers has frequently been prosecuted in national courts.

Some of the classic writers, however, reluctantly condoned conduct which would in all probability result in acts of rape as a spoil of war. Vitoria asks the question whether it is justifiable in war to permit the sacking of a city by one's own soldiers, in order to strike terror into the enemy or to motivate your troops, or even to set fire to the city when there are good reasons for doing so. To accept such reasons, Vitoria claims, is to license the barbarians among the soldiery to commit all kinds of atrocities, including murder, torture, pillage of churches, and the rape of virgins and women. To destroy a Christian city must always be unjust, except in cases of extreme and grave necessity. If necessity demands the destruction of a city, then it is not unlawful to do so, even if it is probable that crimes of the kind enumerated will be perpetrated. While officers have to issue the orders to plunder or burn a city, and soldiers have no authority to do so on their own initiative, commanders also have a responsibility to issue orders forbidding excesses. While Vitoria is not condemning rape outright as a spoil of war, he is nevertheless acknowledging that it is wrong and must be forbidden (Vitoria 1991: 323, §§52–3).

Gentili defended the natural rights of women much more rigorously. He warned rulers who allowed their troops to rape women in occupied territories that the violation of the honour of women is an injustice subject to universal jurisdiction. Rapists would have to be held account to their victims for their wrongs, and if no magistrate in a nation were able to do so, account would have to be rendered to God, and to the rest of the world through sovereigns committed to observe honourable causes of war and uphold God's common law of nature and nations (Gentili 1933: 257[421]). Gentili maintains, 'Surely if it is not lawful to kill women and children, it is still less lawful to inflict upon them loss of modesty; for this is a greater wrong. And although one is not really disgraced who suffers violation unwillingly, yet she seems to be, which amounts to the same thing' (Gentili 1933: 258 [423–4]). This inflection is indicative of the underlying attitude to women. It is her sexual being that is more important than her life. To rape a married woman is to violate the property of her husband, and bring apparent disgrace on the family, and to rape a virgin is to damage the potential goods of a prospective husband.

Grotius and Vattel were less forceful than Gentili, but more emphatic in denouncing rape in the context of war than Vitoria. Grotius did not endorse the argument that everything that belongs to the enemy in war is at the disposal of the victor. Rape, he argued, in the view of the better nations, is related neither to security nor punishment, and is just as much of a crime in war as it is in peace (Grotius 2005: bk. III, ch. IV, Pt XIX (1)). Under natural law, and as a matter of natural right, women had a right not to be violated, and violators of their rights would, in this world or the next, be held to account. They would ultimately have to answer to God. Vattel contends that it is acknowledged among nations, even those with the merest of civilization, that it is a maxim of justice and humanity that those who offer no resistance in war, even though they are classified as enemies, such as women, children, and the sick, have a right not to be maltreated nor have any violence committed against them. Vattel is circumspect in the way that he expresses himself. He maintains that officers lament the excesses of out-of-control soldiers. They brutally violate the chastity of women, and even massacre women, children, and men. He observes that officers 'exert their utmost efforts to put a stop to them; and a prudent and humane general even punishes them whenever he can' (Vattel 1834: Bk. III, chpt. viii, §145). This is rather a half-hearted condemnation, and places no obligation on the part of officers either to stop such violations, nor to punish the perpetrators of them. Indeed, he goes on to place the onus on women, arguing that if they are to be spared such violations, they must ensure that they 'confine themselves to the occupations peculiar to their own sex, and not meddle with those of men, by taking up arms' (Vattel 1834: Bk. III, chpt. viii, §145).

Grotius confirms the customary status of such prohibition by reviewing the practice and pronouncements of the most civilized states, including Roman and Hebrew law. He maintains that the prohibition on rape should be 'observed among Christians, not only as Part of military Discipline, but as Part of the Law of Nations, *viz.* that whosoever ravishes a Woman, tho' in Time of War, deserves to be punished in every Country' (Grotius 2005: bk. III, ch. IV, Pt XIX (2)).

The instances of recognition of the rights of women in war revolve around issues of modesty and virginity, and assume that violations of either are incidental to rather than an integral part of the process of war. The point is that individual soldiers are liable for the crimes they commit during war and are subject to military discipline, or criminal discipline. There is no suggestion that the crime may be more that incidental to war, and may in fact be indicative of humanitarian violations, or even genocide.

Rape was not mentioned in the Nuremberg Charter, nor were there any prosecutions for rape at Nuremberg. In Tokyo rape was prosecuted as a war crime and individuals held responsible for the actions of their subordinates in failing to prevent such violations of human rights happening (Meron 1998: 206).

Rape as an Act of Genocide

One of the most notorious cases, in recent times, of rape being used as an instrument of policy in war is the occupation of Bangladesh by Pakistan when the female body became the arena in which cultural disputes were rehearsed. Prior to the independence of Bangladesh (formerly East Pakistan) in 1971 women symbolized political dissent, wearing Bengali dress and bindis, and singing the banned songs of the Bengali Hindu poet Tagore, in the protests against the threatened Islamization of Bengali society. Women, without a particular feminist agenda, were highly visible in projecting a strong sense of cultural identity, and symbolized dissent in their wearing of traditional Bengali red and yellow saris. Dina M. Siddiqi maintains that the involvement of women took on particular significance because they were taken to symbolize the geographical space of the nation and its property, and were perceived to be the repositories and transmitters of cultural and traditional values, manifest in their reproductive capacities (Siddiqi 1998: 206–7).

In the suppression of Bengali discontent it was women who disproportionately suffered the political backlash of the Pakistani army during the nine month occupation. An estimated 30,000 Bengali women were raped by Pakistani troops as part of a systematic policy to redeem their culture and purify the tainted blood of the dissident society (Kabeer 1991: 122). The victims were captured, incarcerated, raped, and held in custody until pregnant beyond the point where the foetus could be safely aborted. It was a political act designed to demonstrate the retention of power by the Pakistani army over Bengali territory and an attack on the honour of the people, particularly in the possession of its women (Siddiqi 1998: 209). After independence the position of the victims was ambivalent. On the one hand hailed as war heroines, or *birangona* by the Mujab led government of Bangladesh, but on the other symbolic of shame and cultural pollution.

Ethnicity has been the predominant category in terms of which to characterize the conflict in Bosnia, yet victims of the conflict may not always, or primarily, see their identities as Muslims, Serbs or Croats above that of, say, their identity as women. As Catherine MacKinnon maintains, women's human rights are systematically violated in ways that men's rarely are. To see Serbian aggression as an ethnic conflict, or civil war, among equal aggressors masks the extent to which rape and misogyny were central to the strategy of genocide in this conflict. Most human rights conventions empower states to act against states, not individuals to act on their own behalf or on behalf of others. Similarly, states and not individuals are identified as the violators. MacKinnon argues that no state effectively protects women's human rights within their borders, and none is prepared to set standards internationally for bringing to account the violators of women's human rights (MacKinnon 1993: 83–109).

The law is a male preserve and sees and treats women the way that men see and treat women. MacKinnon contends that 'Substantively, the way the male point of view frames an experience is the way it is framed by state policy' (MacKinnon 1982: 544). There has been a much greater recognition in recent years of the extent to which rape is used as a military tactic. According to two human rights and humanitarian monitoring organizations, 'Human Rights Watch' and 'Women for Women' what differentiates the Serbian perpetration of rape from rapes committed on all sides in war is that they use it as an instrument of policy. Considerable evidence has been gathered to demonstrate that, particularly in the case of Bosnia-Hercegovinia, rape was used as a method of ethnic cleansing with the intention of humiliating, shaming, degrading, and terrifying the whole ethnic group (Meron 1998: 205). Ralph Reagan of 'Human Rights Watch' has argued that 'Rape is a deliberate weapon of policy in Kosovo as it was in Bosnia' (Guardian April 14, 1999). United Nations estimates suggest that 20,000 women were raped in Bosnia as part of a systematic policy by the Serbian Army. Young Albanian women fleeing into Albania and Macedonia from Kosovo reported Serbian rape camps in the 1999 conflict.

Despite the fact that the Hague Tribunal set up in 1993 to punish crimes committed in the former Yugoslavia was very much a smokescreen to disguise the embarrassment of the UN's initial reticence to enter the Balkans, the two ad hoc tribunals have contributed significantly to the much greater recognition in recent years of the extent to which rape is used as a military tactic. The policy is one which is meant to humiliate and degrade the enemy. Power was asserted against the Albanians by picking off young women and impregnating them with a Serbian child. It is a way of destroying a person who in these communities not only has to live with the horrific memories, but also the social stigma and shame associated with rape for both the victim and her family. Furthermore, it is a form of identity politics in which the victim's identity is assaulted and subverted when the result is the birth of a Serbian child.

The significance of the two ad hoc Tribunals for the former Yugoslavia and Rwanda is that rape and sexual assaults came to be part of their jurisdiction. The former chief prosecutor, Justice Goldstone, commented that the evidence of systematic rape in both the former Yugoslavia and Rwanda was overwhelming, and while such violations have undoubtedly characterized many other conflicts, they have never before been considered war crimes. He argues that it is testimony to the fact that men were the drafters of the instruments upon which the jurisdiction of the Tribunals is based that there is hardly any reference to rape at all. He goes on to argue that 'We in the Hague, Kigali and Arusha regard it as an important part of our mission to refine and consolidate the place of these offences in international humanitarian law and to prosecute their commission in the former Yugoslavia and Rwanda sensitively and appropriately' (Goldstone 1996: 9). Similarly, the United Nations International War Crimes Tribunal sent representatives to Albania and Macedonia in 1999 to collect evidence of allegations of rape and massacre from Kosovan refugees.

Such violations are, however, in the context of war or civil war and to address them to some extent avoids the endemic and widespread serial violation of women in the daily ordinary, and not extraordinary, course of everyday life. In Susan Brownmiller's extensive study of the legal and social remedies for rape in a wide range of traditional cultures she concluded that in almost all women were no more than chattels (Brownmiller 1975: 7). Amnesty International concluded that women suffer human rights violations disproportionately to minority groups both in time of war and as a result of traditional practices endorsed by culture (Peterson and Parisi 1998: 132). Millions of young girls are forced into marriage before the age of twelve; between 80 and 100 million African women have undergone genital mutilation in order to suppress sexuality; the trade in child prostitution is increasing at alarming rates with girls being sold from Cambodia to Vietnam, or from Nepal to India; religious fundamentalism has in many parts of the world reduced to a negligible degree the visibility of women, the most extreme of which in recent times was in Afghanistan under the Taliban, but even in Pakistan it is punishable by stoning for a married woman to look at an unrelated man. In many poor societies males have priority of access to food, education, and even life itself (Ashworth 1999: 264). It is common in many traditions that women are portrayed as less important than men. As Nussbaum suggests, they are seen as 'less deserving of basic life support or of fundamental rights that are strongly correlated with quality of life, such as the right to work and the right to political participation' (Nussbaum 1999: 29).

ONTOLOGY OF HUMAN RIGHTS

Traditional inequalities may become so embedded and seem so natural or right that women themselves endorse their second-class status. The inequalities are such, Nussbaum contends, that there is an urgent need for 'moral standtaking'. In order to do this effectively there has been a convergence of opinion on a comparative model that measures capabilities and asks the question what are the people of a country actually able to do and to be? This is what Darendorf referred to as 'life chances'. Such an approach necessarily raises issues of cultural universalism because in asking questions about how people function, we cannot avoid abstracting certain components that we believe to be at the core of human life and ignore others that are not. In this respect we cannot avoid having some idea of what human functions are most worthy of 'the care and attention of public planning the world over' (Nussbaum 1999: 34).

Against anti-universalists who emphasize the importance of difference, Nussbaum argues that a culture is not a museum piece that must be preserved at all costs: 'There would appear, indeed, to be something condescending in preserving for contemplation a way of life that causes real pain to real people' (Nussbaum 1999: 37). In answering various forms of anti-universalist arguments Nussbaum suggests that we can identify a core of central human capabilities without which we may no longer regard the person as human. Intuitively, she argues, there are certain human functions that are central to human life, in the absence of which human life itself may be deemed to be absent. Furthermore, that there is a distinctly human, as opposed to animal, way of performing these functions (Nussbaum 2000: 71–2). The commitment to protecting and promoting everyone's capabilities is based upon the Kantian principle of treating everyone as an end, or what Buchanan called the Moral Equality Principle which boils down to the equal consideration of persons (Buchanan 2003: 138 and 145).

The method Nussbaum recommends is not anti-historicist nor *a priori*. It entails a cross-cultural enquiry that can always be contested and modified. Because it is evaluative from the start it projects a conception of the good. The central human functional capabilities include: life, that is freedom from premature death; adequate food and shelter for bodily integrity, including reproduction; bodily integrity entailing freedom of movement and protection against violence and marital rape; the use of ones senses, imagination and thought, that is the unimpeded ability to feel, think, and reason; emotional integrity, that is making emotional ties of one's choice; practical reason in which one can formulate one's own conception of the good, engage in critical reflection and plan its attainment; affiliation, entailing freedom of association and social interaction, and being treated as of equal worth to others; being able to express concern about and live with other species; the opportunity to play and enjoy recreational activities; and, control over one's environment, both political, that is participation, and material, including ownership of property, and equal employment rights. Nussbaum's goal is the same as that of Amartya Sen, that the 'central goal of public planning should be the *capabilities* of citizens to perform various important functions' (Nussbaum 1999: 42).

The purpose of politics is to get as many people as possible, able to exercise their interrelated capability functions enumerated in the list. It is capabilities and not functions that must be the political goal, because if it were merely functions choice would be eliminated. A person who has normal opportunities for sexual satisfaction may choose to be celibate, and that is fine. But it is not fine to practice female genital mutilation which deprives the female of the choice of sexual functioning, and the opportunity of celibacy too. In Nussbaum's view, universal values do not entail a choice between the embedded life of a community and the autonomy of individualism, 'Universal values build their own communities, communities of resourcefulness, friendship, and agency, embedded in the local scene but linked in complex ways to groups of women in other parts of the world. For these women the new community was a lot better than the one they had inhabited before' (Nussbaum 1999: 49).

Nussbaum argues that there is a close relation between a list of basic human rights and the list of human capabilities she identifies. 'A human right', in her view, 'unlike many other rights people may have, derive not from a person's particular situation of privilege power or skill but, instead, just from the fact of being human'. She goes on to contend that 'Human rights are, in effect, justified claims to such basic capabilities or opportunities' (Nussbaum 1999: 87). She argues that human beings should not be violated and that human rights should have a very high degree of priority even if they interfere with traditionalist religious discourse and practice on the ground. There are simply things that we do not allow people to do to others (Nussbaum 1999: 102). Many of the restrictions upon women denying them rights do not infringe the basic right of freedom of worship. The rights to divorce, to contraception, and to adoption, for example, do not require anyone to do these things against their religious principles, but instead provides people with the capacity to choose. Nussbaum contends that 'We should not accept the idea that denying any fundamental right of any individual is a legitimate prerogative of a religious group' (Nussbaum 1999: 107).

The social contract tradition upon which many natural rights theories depended, while important in formulating protections for the individual, and in emphasizing dignity and reciprocity, nevertheless rested on a suspect picture of social relations. The tendency has been to view the basic structure of society as the outcome of a contract among individuals who are roughly equal in power and ability. The emphasis upon equality and independence may implicitly encourage the stigmatizing of those who do not conform to the stereotype and who may in various ways have disabilities and be dependent on others. What is required is a conception of the person that acknowledges human frailty and vulnerability and the fact that we are all needy and disabled in varying ways (Nussbaum 2004: 341). The capabilities approach, Nussbaum argues, demands a great deal of people. It requires sustained sympathy and benevolence over time. Unlike many classic theorists who tend to think that the moral sentiments or emotions are fixed, Nussbaum concurs with Rousseau that they may be cultivated through education. She argues that a just society depends for its stability upon its ability to impart the right attitudes and sentiments to people in that they may be consistent with substantial changes in distributive justice. Compassion may be cultivated by criticizing and undermining pernicious attitudes such as racial intolerance and misogyny, that once characterized the public culture of many societies, and which are now much less acceptable (Nussbaum 2006: 408–15).

Seyla Benhabib also finds inspiration in Kant for her version of cosmopolitanism. She agrees with Hanna Arendt and Karl Jaspers that natural law cannot be the foundation of human rights because human nature is developmental. The human condition is, then, a changing one and the human rights regime is one that evolved over time exhibiting a transition from international justice to cosmopolitan justice, evident in the shift from the state to the individual as the subject of international law. The ontological status of human rights, or cosmopolitan norms, in a post-metaphysical world is that they are 'morally constructive'. They are generative of 'a universe of meanings, values, and social relations that had not existed before by changing the normative constituents and evaluative principles of the world of "objective spirit", to use Hegelian language' (Benhabib 2006: 72). We have here a version of the recognition theory of rights in which the acknowledgement and naming of morally unacceptable actions give them a new normative status moving them into a universe that now incorporates a new 'moral fact'. In naming 'genocide' as the ultimate crime against humanity, for example, we enter a new normative universe (Benhabib 2006: 72).

This has entailed a move away from Westphalian sovereignty in which the state had ultimate authority over everyone in its domain, and could do anything to them with impunity, to cosmopolitan justice in which international law has eroded state sovereignty by making states accountable for the use and abuse of power, and by placing at its centre individual human beings who are political agents (Benhabib 2006: 13–44). The evolution of cosmopolitan justice and the vast waves of immigration have brought about a disjuncture between 'the entitlements of social rights and benefits' and 'shared collective identity and political membership'. The result is the disaggregation of citizenship and the contestation of 'the boundaries of the demos' (Benhabib 2006: 45–7). In order to cope with these transformations Benhabib commandeers into service the concepts of 'democratic iteration' and 'jurisgenerative politics'. Adapting Derrida's notion of 'reiteration' which suggests that each iteration adds something to and changes meaning, but cannot be said to deviate from an original meaning, Benhabib suggests that in relation to documents such as laws and 'other institutional norms' reiteration may be assumed to make reference to antecedents considered authoritative. She argues that, 'Democratic iterations are linguistic, legal, cultural, and political repetitions-in-transformation, invocations that also are revocations. They not only change established understandings but also transform what passes as the valid or established view of an authoritative precedent' (Benhabib 2006: 48).

The interesting point from our perspective is what Benhabib has to say about the way in which the disjuncture between law as power and law as meaning is overcome by the politics of 'jurisgenerative processes'. A democratic people that subscribes to guiding norms and principles engages in acts of reiteration by reappropriation and reinterpretation, and in doing so is at once the subject and author of the laws. This process rejects both the idea of natural rights and of legal positivism. The former assumes principles that are the foundation of democratic politics and which are not susceptible to acts of transformation by the collective popular will, while the latter equates democratic legitimacy with faithfulness by a sovereign legislator to the proper procedures for generating legal norms. Benhabib maintains that 'jurisgenerative politics is a model that permits us to think of creative interventions that mediate between universal norms and the will of democratic majorities' (Benhabib 2006: 49). In such processes citizenship is reconfigured as new considerations are accommodated, as for example in the recent French example of 'L'Affaire du Foulard' (the Scarf Affair).

Unlike the enacted legislation, cosmopolitan norms do not depend for their validity upon jurisgenerative and democratic iterations. They are nevertheless mediated by such processes into the particular contingencies of each polity. In the case of the French ban on the wearing of religious symbols in schools, pursuant to its strict policy of the separation of the state and church, the threshold of justification of formerly exclusionary practices is raised much higher by cosmopolitan norms which act as a break even upon democratic majorities. Benhabib contends that the authority of such cosmopolitan norms derives from the '*the power of democractic forces within global civil society*' [italics in the original] (Benhabib 2006: 71).

The process by which human rights have been extended to women has been characterized by William J. Talbot in terms reminiscent of Tocqueville, the Idealists, Rorty and the recognition theorists. He maintains that moral training is not so much a matter of applying principles, but instead, developing a moral sensitivity. The process is one of extending one's own moral community to be inclusive of others. The means by which this occurs is, for Talbot, 'empathetic understanding' (Talbot 2005: 65). This entails extending the range of 'who counts morally, extending the concept of *us* to include *them*' (Talbot 2005: 79). This is what Dilthey described as understanding the I in the thou. Anne Phillips, too, acknowledges the historical contingency of such principles as equality, 'New circumstances enabled new ways of thinking, and a notion that seemed bizarre at one point in time – that all humans are born equal – came to be regarded as relatively commonplace during another' (Phillips 2007: 35).

CONCLUSION

The significance of the 1993 Vienna World Conference on Human Rights was that there was a general acknowledgement that many gender-specific issues simply did not figure in the human rights agenda, and that this was partly because of the artificial division of the social world into public and private spheres. Governments throughout the world acknowledged that women as well as men were entitled to enjoy fundamental rights (Kapur 2006: 105). The irony is, however, that one of the landmark decisions in the United States affirming the right to abortion did so on the grounds of privacy. Justice Blackmun, in *Row v. Wade*, argued that a woman's right to terminate her pregnancy was derived from her Constitutional right to privacy. For many feminists this has unacceptable implications. Elizabeth Fox Genovese, for example, argues that it is difficult to reconcile the right to abortion on the grounds of privacy at a time when the women's movement has made a sustained attempt to break-down the traditional public/private dichotomy (see Wellman 1999: 85).

While since the Vienna Conference, which generated the Declaration on the Elimination of Violence Against Women, a great deal has been done by both intergovernmental and non-governmental agencies and organizations to highlight the plight of women in traditionally patriarchal societies, a growing number of feminist writers question the adequacy of human rights, or rights-based language, to provide a moral framework for responding to the plight of women in the world. While not wishing to reject the value of rights altogether, some feminists wish to contextualize them. They suggest that the claim that all human beings have fundamental rights was advanced by early liberals for a specific reason. It was a radical and revolutionary idea which posited a natural equality as the basis for equal political and legal rights. Such rights were protections against what early modern liberals feared most, arbitrary government. It is the language of individualism and self-regarding interests, a plea for autonomy and self-determination, at the expense of submerging the virtues characteristic of community. As Fiona Robinson argues, 'The individualism inherent in liberalism – the belief that the ideal human condition is one in which each individual is surrounded by an "invisible fence" separating and protecting each individual from the interference of others – emphasises autonomy over attachment, and non-interference over responsiveness' (Robinson 1998: 62).

Following Annette Baier, Robinson argues that while the idea of negative liberty is a useful notion for asserting claims to non-interference, it is woefully inadequate as a basis for morality. There is a need, she argues, to clarify the difference between first generation rights of the negative liberty type and the economic and cultural rights of the second and third generation. While citing Charles Taylor, she actually draws upon an argument presented many years ago by W. David Ross. He makes a distinction between the Right and the Good (Ross 1930). A right is a rule of some sort, a prohibition or permission; what R. G. Collingwood calls a regular principle (Collingwood 1992: 113). Robinson suggests that the Good designates a substantive moral goal, whereas as a right is significant in its instrumentality in achieving that goal. The concept of a right, in her view, cannot tell us why someone should have food or shelter. The so called economic and cultural rights are in fact substantive judgements about what constitutes the good life, 'which require much more than a statement of right to give them moral legitimacy' (Robinson 1998: 65). A rights based ethics is seen to be too narrow, and at the very least needs to be supplemented, if not replaced, by concepts of care, responsibility and trust, as opposed to rights and obligations, and mutual advantage, reciprocity, and a fairness conception of justice.

Juridically, and formally the recognition of women's rights, or human rights that are specifically gendered, has made significant progress, the highlight of which is the Statute for an International Criminal Court which for the first time places among the most serious crimes in international law acts of sexual and gender violence, including forced pregnancy (Glasius 2006: 76 and 92). It was the experience of women's rights groups with victims testifying to the tribunal for the former Yugoslavia, and the conviction for genocide by systematic rape and sexual violence in the Akayesu case before the Rwanda tribunal, that inspired them to press heavily for the recognition of such crimes in the Statute for the ICC (Glasius 2006: 79). This formal legality in relation to the most serious violations of human rights gives hope to victims of systematic sexual crimes of policy in times of war, or civil strife, but in other circumstances such force fields as culture, and despite the vast edifice of human rights law, mediate and militate basic rights, where even in cases of rape blame and dishonour are attributed to the woman, and where death is often the consequence of being born female. Indeed, Ratna Kapur questions the ability of law to deliver universal justice 'given that subjects are not equally situated' (Kapur 2006: 103).

Conclusion

> It is remarkable that an oft-heard plea is that human rights should be less 'politicized'. This makes no sense. Human Rights *are* political: they articulate the relationship between individuals and groups within a community and their relationship with others, particularly those with power and authority (Clapham 2007: 161).

> Human rights are not western values—indeed, western governments have shown as much disdain for them as any other. They are global values and, as such, the likelihood of their success is entwined with the leadership of the UN (Amnesty International 2008: 13).

> We must ask whether any of us would care much about rights if they were articulated only in universalist documents like the Universal Declaration, and whether, in fact, our attachments to these universals depends critically on our prior attachment to rights that are national, rooted in the traditions of a flag, a constitution, a set of founders, and a set of national narratives, religious and secular, that give point and meaning to rights (Ignatieff 2005: 25–6).

It has been contended throughout that the modern human rights culture owes its existence and intellectual heritage to Western ideas about ethical constraints on both individual and collective relations. The process for most of the formative history of the culture has been one of what Waltzer calls covering law universalism. The high moral ground was occupied by the west, or at least the west thought so, and its standards set the criteria of expectation in relations with the less, and non-civilized worlds.

I have argued that natural law and natural rights are constellations of ideas and presuppositions that exhibit far greater similarities than most commentators want to admit. I particularly reject the view that natural rights constituted a secularization of natural law ideas by showing that most of the significant thinkers in the field, in their various ways, believed that reason leads you to the discovery of your obligations, while God provides the ground, or at least adds significant force, for discharging them. Furthermore, I have maintained that natural rights and human rights are far less closely related than is often asserted because natural rights, in my view, never cast adrift the religious foundationalism, whereas human rights, for the most part, have jettisoned the Christian metaphysics upon which both natural law and natural rights depended. The conceptual importance of the British Idealists cannot be underestimated. They play a critical role in the process of transition from natural rights to human rights. The British Idealists at once dispensed with the rationalist element in natural rights, while retaining the religious in their doctrine of Divine immanence. For them, rights develop over time within the context of a divinely unfolding rationality. Human rights theories, on the whole, abjure the divine and present us with foundationless universal constraints on the actions of individuals, both domestically and internationally, and within and between states. Finally, one of the principal contentions has been that these purportedly universal rights and duties almost invariably turn out to be conditional, and upon close scrutiny end up being 'special' rights and privileges as my examples of multicultural encounters, slavery and racism, and women's rights demonstrate.

In contemporary understanding of human rights it is undeniable that there is a considerable degree of international convergence on the idea that there are agreed human rights norms, and that their efficacy does not depend upon common agreements about their foundation. There is shared commitment that if human life and its flourishing is valued above all else, then special protections, and modes of assistance to promote the ideas in theory and in practice, are required. The motivations for such commitments are often challenged, and indeed a good deal of hypocrisy demonstrably accompanies those world leaders who at once subscribe to and violate the principles of human rights. Universal rights always were, and remain, conditional and all sorts of pretexts may be invoked to suspend their application, from the promotion of better trading relations, which made world leaders quickly forget Tiananmen Square, to the desire for order over justice, in which justice is traded for truth.

Where may one look for the limits of ethics in international relations?

I have suggested that natural law, natural rights, and human rights are conditional. Even today large groups of people consider some groups of human beings, usually those they are in conflict with, and not necessarily of different ethnic origin, as sub-human, and therefore not capable of having their human rights violated. Over most of the globe women are regarded as occupying a subordinate place in relation to men, and therefore not eligible for the enjoyment of the full range of human rights. In India and China, for example, among many communities, girls are not even afforded the right upon which every other right is premised, namely the right to life. Newly born girls are valued far less, or not at all, in comparison with newly born boys. Amnesty International's, 2008 report calls upon world leaders to give more attention to making the formal rights that women have achieved into a practical reality. One commentator has recently concluded that, 'The gap between formal rights and the actual status of disadvantaged groups has not decreased as a result of the legalization process' (Kapur 2006: 102).

Secondly, universal ethical constraints are not merely moral. They are also political, and politically negotiated, and dependent on the political will of states to ensure their effective implementation. One of the reasons why the ad hoc tribunals of the former Yugoslavia and Rwanda were not as successful as they might have been is because they depended upon the good will of NATO, the United Nations, and of individual governments, not only for adequate funding, but also in the apprehension of those charged with war crimes and crimes against humanity.

In addition, human rights have often cynically been invoked to pursue political goals, and have been accused of being the instrument of Western, and particularly United States, hegemony.

The perception of Western or US hegemony is exacerbated by the perceived politically motivated prosecutions of the International Criminal Court. All four cases proceeding to date are from Africa, and the court is in danger of alienating the continent and precipitating African non-cooperation. In addition, the process of prosecution is extremely slow, indeed Milosevic died in custody before his trial at the tribunal for the former Yugoslavia was concluded. In 2005, the International Criminal Court issued an arrest warrant for Joseph Kony, the leader of the Lord's Resistance Army in Uganda. The warrant has not yet been enforced, nor has a peace deal been negotiated. Despite Sudan failing to acknowledge the International Criminal Court, the United Nations Security Council resolution 1593 in March 2005 gave the court a mandate to act. It was over two years before arrest warrants were issued for government minister Ahmed Haroun who allegedly organized the Janjaweed militia in Darfur, and that Ali Kushayb, a leader of the Janjaweed, ordered murder, torture, and mass rape in the villages of western Darfur. Sudan has refused to give them up to the court.

In July 2008, Mr Moreno-Ocampo, the chief prosecutor, told the Security Council that Sudan was not co-operating and that he had 'compelling evidence' identifying 'those most responsible for crimes against civilians'. The Security Council warned Sudan to comply in July 2008. Because of the independence of the International Criminal Court the chief prosecutor does not have to balance issues of justice against those of *realpolitik*, and is able to take bold human rights initiatives such as seeking the arrest of President Omar al-Bashir of Sudan, the first serving head of state to face charges of genocide.

Politically, however, it now makes a peaceful settlement to bring the conflict in Darfur to an end very unlikely and may undermine UN peacekeeping attempts in the region. The difference between the indictments of Slobodan Milosevic from Bosnia and Charles Taylor from Liberia in comparison with that of Omar al-Bashir of Sudan is that they necessitated special decisions by the United Nations, and the west supported regime change, while in Sudan the chief prosecutor has initiated the warrant. A panel of three judges will now consider the warrant request for Mr Bashir, and if issued Sudan will have to arrest its own president. Under Article 89 of the court's statute Bashir may be arrested in any of the 106 states that have signed up to the treaty.

The high profile call for an arrest warrant to be issued has led to criticism of Moreno-Ocampo for political posturing, and trying to give the International Criminal Court a greater visibility in order to disguise its singular lack of success. It has not yet successfully initiated any trials. The one that was scheduled for June 2008 was set aside by the Trial Chamber for irregularities in the collection and use of evidence. Much to the embarrassment of the Court the prisoner was released. In other words, issues of justice are not merely abstract. Political considerations have hampered the work of both ad hoc tribunals, and threaten the effectiveness of the International Criminal Court.

Fourthly, rights are not always trumps, and other values may take priority, in post conflict situations. At a time when people demand justice for the gross violation of their rights, political considerations are the priority that often determine that order, rather than rights or justice prevail.

We have seen throughout this book that universal principles almost invariably turn out to be conditional, and that in practice universal rights are converted into 'special' rights. For much of the history that this book covers, it was the special rights of Western white males. We saw in the cases of multicultural encounters, racism and slavery, and women that whole groups of people were often deemed to fail to meet the threshold conditions of being fully human, and therefore capable of enjoying universal rights to a much lesser degree, while at the same time being deemed to have the full range of obligations.

Despite advances in the formal legal equality of all human beings in the proliferation of declarations, charters and agreements violations of such rights persist to a horrifying and alarming extent. Law cannot of itself deliver human equality and respect, nor prevent heinous acts of gratuitous or systematic violence. Law is the expression of a culture, and this human rights culture that is so widely acknowledged depends upon more than legal formalism. The voice of law in the conversation of human rights always threatens to dominate because it is the most authoritative voice, and its pronouncements, although less so in the international arena, nevertheless, stipulate 'what something is or is not and how a situation or event is to be understood' (Finley 1989: 888). Success through the United Nations in formalizing law and highlighting the inadequacy of national legislation in the areas of domestic violence, rape, and child abuse, for example, has encouraged the view that law is the exclusive idiom in which to articulate issues of social justice and emancipation in the pursuit of women's human rights, serving to marginalize the potential benefits of other vocabularies of emancipation. Campaigns to enact law have nevertheless been highly successful in highlighting particular issues, but their success in bringing about social change must be measured against the powerful constraints of material and cultural contexts (Kapur 2006: 106 and 111).

We have seen that the modern human rights culture comprises many strands that invoke or echo natural law, natural rights, and human rights discourses, and in these discourses the voices of law, ethics, philosophy, and politics, with their differently nuanced idioms, all make claims to be heard. The human rights culture may be characterized as an historical population of idioms, for which different principles of appraisal may apply, but for which ultimately the eradication of man's inhumanity to man, and woman is the guiding light. What does this mean?

If we think of each of these idioms as fibres in the thread of human rights, the place of each in supporting the strength of the whole may better be conceived. As Wittgenstein perceptively contended, 'the strength of the thread does not reside in the fact that some one fibre runs through its whole length, but in the overlapping of many fibres' (Wittgenstein 1973: 32, §65). The diversity of grounds that sustain the edifice of human rights is not necessarily a negative feature of the culture or regime. The project has always been to establish the mechanisms by which the moral community on which such a culture depends becomes wider and wider, and the strengthening of the thread in order to encompass the whole of humanity depends upon the extent to which the fibres that do not emanate from the west contribute. This is a point that we saw Charles Taylor and Michael Walzer make in their different ways, and which Ignatieff makes at the start of this chapter, but it is also what was implied in Tocqueville's remarks on the development of manners, and elaborated by numerous thinkers since, including Eleanor Roosevelt.

Because rights have become the international *lingua franca* we must not delude ourselves into thinking that they are independent of culture and somehow stand outside of it in judgement. Rights may already too often have been exposed as the emperor's new cloths. Alongside what we may describe as the culture of justice and rights, that entails the juridical examination of alleged war crimes and crimes against humanity, has grown up a culture of impunity. In liberal culture, as Dworkin tells us, rights are trumps, and internationally human rights are the highest trumps in the deck. Nevertheless, the universal principle of justice has relentlessly been trumped by Truth. Amnesties have routinely been granted for human rights violations by governments seeking to effect peaceful transitions in South America and South Africa. International law does not explicitly prohibit national amnesty laws. Indeed, the United Nations itself has supported amnesties in El Salvador, South Africa, Cambodia, and Haiti (Freeman 2006: 59).

Victims and their families are denied justice and purportedly placated by the 'Truth' in the interests of political stability. In other words, individual rights are subordinated to the common good. The purpose of such tribunals is not to adjudicate, but to confront the facts of systematic rights violations in order to effect a reconciliation. There have been such commissions most famously in South Africa and Chile, but also in Uganda, Guatemala, El Salvador, Indonesia, Chad, and Argentina.

International jurisdiction for humanitarian violations highlight a tension between justice and order, and the issue of whether the former has to be sacrificed for the latter. Rulers in preparing their countries for democracies try as best they can to secure immunities, and if the prospect is remote they hang on tenaciously to power. The granting of amnesties is a contentious issue among advocates of humanitarian rights. The word is derived from the Greek 'amnestia' meaning forgetfulness or oblivion (Cassese 1998: 3). Amnesties were granted in such societies in transition as Haiti and Argentina, while truth and reconciliation commissions, some with the powers of granting amnesty, were established in Guatemala, Chile, El Salvador, and South Africa. Despite the high profile establishment of the ad hoc tribunals for the former Yugoslavia and Rwanda, and the International Criminal Court, a culture of impunity has emerged. The need to re-establish or maintain order may outweigh questions of justice in relation to the violation of rights. When immunities are granted it is often in exchange for participation in an investigative tribunal of some kind authorized to determine the facts relating to human rights abuses in order to placate the victims and their families, and in order to facilitate peace and reconciliation. The question then becomes one of order *or* justice. This is the question of peace versus justice. Those guilty of crimes may be the very same people with the knowledge and skills needed to rebuild a country. This very quickly became evident in Iraq.

The need for reconciliation is not a new phenomenon; it has often outweighed considerations of rights and justice. The English Civil War, for example, was horrific in its brutality. King Charles II had Cromwell's body exhumed and displayed at the public execution site at Marble Arch. He prosecuted a limited number of the regicides, executing only ten of the forty-nine named (and the two executioners who were anonymous), but granted amnesties to all others in his act of indemnity of 1660. It was said to be a case of forgive and forget, which the Loyalists severely resented. It was, they argued, a case of the Roundheads being forgiven and the Royalists forgotten.

We tend to think of natural law, natural rights, and human rights in absolutist and universalist terms, but such rigidity, it may be argued, is inapplicable to societies that do not fit the model of settled societies in which the rule of law is a valued and treasured principle. When gross violations of human rights have been perpetrated, the society in which they occurred is at best in the process of becoming settled, and in a period of transitional justice. The rule of law even in settled societies is not an uncontested concept, but its relation to the past unjust regime in a transitional society is even more of a difficulty (Teitel 2000: chapter 1).

One may view the ad hoc tribunals for the former Yugoslavia and for Rwanda, as well as the Rome statute for an International Criminal Court as the legacy of Nuremberg. In other words, they may betray a willingness on the part of many states, to lower the priority of sovereignty in the interest of universal justice. The emblematic nature of Nuremberg in which war criminals were individually held to account for their actions has led us to equate justice with criminal trials. Nuremberg has, however, been the exception rather than the rule in states in the process of transitional justice. In such states – South Africa, Argentina, Uruguay, Chile, and Indonesia – the preference is for domestic rather than international approaches to justice, truth telling, and reconciliation rather than criminal prosecution (Abbott 1999: 373). In such states the threat of a military backlash or the destabilization of the ruling regime precipitates political expediency. Justice is traded for peace and security.

In such places as the southern cone of Latin America the legacy of Nuremberg may well have prolonged authoritarian dictatorships and even exacerbated brutal and tense political situations. Those who resorted to crimes against humanity, such as systematic torture, rape, and murder, do not readily let go of power when the spectre of international justice looms large. It has been suggested, for example, that Mugabe was so embroiled in the culture of violence and rights abuse that his henchmen would not allow him to concede the 2008 election in Zimbabwe for fear of reprisals. Indeed, the call by the chief prosecutor of the International Criminal Court for a warrant to arrest the president of Sudan, Omar al-Bashir, has given rise to fears of a government backlash, and a withdrawal of all but essential UN personnel for fear of governmental reprisals.

The one hundred or so revolutionary and regional wars since 1945 are testimony not to universal justice, but instead to universal non-accountability for war crimes and genocide. For example, the killing of almost 2 million people between 1975 and 1979 by Pol Pot and his Khmer Rouge in Cambodia was universally condemned, yet he acted with impunity (Ball 1999: 5). On his death in 1998 there had been no indictments under Cambodian criminal law, nor under international criminal law. Huen Sen, the Cambodian leader, chose the course of amnesty, in order to avoid civil war, which he granted to Khieu Samphan who defected from the Khmer Rouge. Sen argued that they must forget the past in order to rebuild the country and reach national reconciliation, peace, and stability.

Upon being granted amnesty two other Khmer Rouge leaders gave themselves up to the civilian authorities after Pol Pot's death. Hun Sen welcomed them, in his own words, 'with bouquets of flowers, not with prisons and handcuffs' (Ball 1999: 1). In March 1999, Hun Sen, with characteristic unpredictability, declared that the Khmer Rouge leaders would face charges of genocide under a 1994 Cambodian law in Cambodian courts (Ball 1999: 120).

In Argentina, Uruguay, and Chile, the political will to prosecute the violators of human rights was weak or non-existent because of fear of the military, divided peoples, and a commitment to future oriented policies of reconciliation, stability, and instituting democracy and the rule of law (Freeman 2006: 59). In Uruguay the military made a peaceful transition to democracy dependent on complete impunity. This was backed by President Sanuinetti, but was opposed by human rights groups. The issue was put to a referendum and 57 per cent of voters favoured amnesty (Freeman 2006: 58).

It has been suggested that it is extremely doubtful whether truth and reconciliation commissions could validly grant amnesties for genocide under international law. *Jus cogens* would preclude amnesty. Customary international law precludes genocide and imposes obligations to bring the perpetrators to justice, an obligation which cannot be derogated by international agreement (Cassese 1998: 5).

The granting of an immunity by the Chilean parliament to General Pinochet was challenged by the Spanish courts which sought to extradite him from Britain for the crimes for which he had responsibility in Chile, such as rape, unlawful detention, and torture against Spanish citizens. The Pinochet case raised the important issue, not of diplomatic immunity of former heads of states, but instead whether immunities granted by governments to former heads were to be recognized internationally. In fact, the democratically elected government of Chile requested the release and return of Pinochet. As Richard Falk has suggested, 'The encounter can be understood as between the implementation of universal standards and the encouragement and maintenance of past and future peaceful transitions to democracy' (Falk 2001: 128). The House of Lords accepted the Spanish case, but its full impact was not manifest because Pinochet was deemed unfit to plead in such a trial. The ruling effectively meant that sovereign immunity does not extend to action taken by a leader who violates the legal and ethical principles of universal justice established and confirmed by civilized societies since

1899. The judgement, at least, forms the potential basis for justice without borders (Ball 1999: 232).

Nevertheless many perpetrators of lesser crimes against humanity than genocide have been granted amnesty. Apartheid was itself declared a crime against humanity by the international community. Cross-border raids organized by the South African Security Forces almost certainly violated humanitarian rights. Should an international court override a national government that believes a truth commission would more effectively heal the wounds of apartheid than criminal justice which would exacerbate violence? The South African Truth and Reconciliation Commission ruled in a response to a challenge by the widow of Stephen Biko that it had the power to extend amnesty to individuals even in cases of crimes against humanity on the justification that there was an imperative need to discover the truth about a shameful past, and effect as rapid a transition as possible to a new society. In other words she was to be denied justice in the interests of reconciliation (Hesse and Post 1999: 14).

The 'Promotion of National Unity and Reconciliation Act 34' of 1995 gave to victims a voice, and made provisions for reparations and rehabilitation. Indemnity was offered for human rights violations when such violations were politically motivated, full disclosure made, and that the violation was proportionate with the political goal sought. Reconciliation did not merely substitute order for justice, because the aim was to link reconciliation with issues of social justice. This entailed acknowledging the illegitimacy of the apartheid regime and rectifying its economically and socially distorted racial legacy. At its centre was the establishment of equality before the law, which itself entailed a radical reformation of the criminal justice system. The system itself could not be at the centre of transition, when it was part of the problem transition was meant to solve (Asmal, 2000: 12). The South African Constitutional Court ruled in 1996 that a Truth Commission was appropriate for a nation freeing itself from a regime of terror and undergoing a transition to democracy (Cassese 1998: 3). In the view of Richard Goldstone, the incontrovertible evidence amassed of gross abuses of human rights during the apartheid era made any credible denial impossible (Goldstone 2000: 70).

There are alternative ways, then, to criminal tribunals in which accountability for international crimes has been expressed. What many of the victims, or families of the victims, want is a formal public acknowledgement of what has happened to them. One way in which such guilt has been acknowledged is through the offering of formal apologies. President Aylwin of Chile offered an apology on behalf of the state for the crimes of the Pinochet regime. The Roman Catholic Church in Argentina, at the insistence of the Pope, asked for forgiveness of its involvement in the 'dirty war' during the military dictatorship between 1976 and 1983. A great deal of discussion persists on the issue of the degree to which governments can accept responsibility for the actions of previous governments, and how far back should this responsibility reach. Should the British government apologize on behalf of the Gladstone Government for British imperialism, or later governments for the slaughter of aboriginals in Australia? Should John Howard, the former prime minister of Australia, have apologized to the aboriginals for the policies of successive governments in depriving them of basic rights? His successor, Kevin Rudd, offered a formal apology. Should George Bush junior apologize for the Kennedy, Johnson, and Nixon administrations for American policies in Vietnam and Cambodia? The Japanese government has been pressed on numerous occasions to apologize for the treatment of British prisoners of war, and for enslaving Koreans and citizens of other Asian countries as comfort girls. If responsibility is acknowledged should reparations be paid? The Japanese government belatedly apologized for forcing almost two hundred thousand women into prostitution, and set up a private fund for reparation. The largest financial reparations were paid by Germany, 100 billion deutschemarks, for the crimes committed between 1933 and 1945. In some instances a symbolic gesture may be more effective than a formal apology, as for example, when Chancellor Willy Brandt knelt before the Jewish memorial for Jewish war victims in 1970.

Truth and reconciliation is premised upon a wider conception of justice than criminal responsibility. There is the restoration of human dignity by violators of human rights who confess their role and ask for forgiveness, and in so doing may deter others from committing such crimes. Social justice may be achieved by requiring those who perversely benefited from the corrupt regime to share their ill-gotten gains in acts of redistribution. Rehabilitation of both victims and perpetrators of crimes may in themselves be part of restorative justice. Such tribunals may serve to exonerate those who have been wrongly accused of crimes, or who were in the past vilified as terrorists, but who in the act of atonement are transformed into liberators. From this perspective properly constituted truth and reconciliation commissions may be viewed not as sacrificing justice for truth, but providing a different means by which justice is attained. Justice, then, in a transitional state need not be measured by the number of prosecutions, and we may begin to think instead of reparations and restorative rather than punitive justice (Asmal 2000: 13 and 15).

There is no doubt that the human rights culture and vocabulary of inalienable rights form part of the current landscape of moral, political, and legal discourse. The widespread acknowledgement and endorsement or ratification of many of the formal documents give rise to the view that there appears to be a worldwide consensus on human rights (Fields 2002: 42). When probed more deeply this consensus proves to be to the idea that people have human rights, and not to an agreement about what human rights we have. The three generations of rights with their quite specific injunctions and aspirations in the realm of the political, social, economic, and cultural, and those termed solidarity rights, such as those to development (UN declaration 1986), and peace (UN declaration 1984), are in danger of failing to be deeply rooted in the actual conditions that they are designed to eradicate. The danger is that the fundamental rights to life and liberty are devalued by claiming much lesser rights such as to two weeks paid holiday a year.

One may view with cynicism the commitment of states to pursue and bring to justice those who have violated human rights. It is of course fashionable to subscribe to the rhetoric in principle in the United Nations, but state interest, whether economic or strategic often subsumes the commitment to human rights. Geoffrey Robertson has suggested that diplomacy is the exact antithesis to a serious commitment to human rights. Diplomacy notoriously trades off human rights violations against other interests, and allows international criminals to escape justice. The massacre in Tianamen Square, for example, while widely condemned world wide, was after a respectable interlude, quietly forgotten in the interests of stronger economic links with China. It is evident that the momentum towards global justice has been in the face of strong opposition affirming the principle of state sovereignty. Despite the fact that there are examples of international criminal justice, such as in the European Court on Human Rights, the Inter-American Court, and the Privy Council in Britain, as well as the International Criminal Court established in 2002, it remains true that major powers are often reluctant to compromise their sovereignty by submitting to external legislation. The United States, for example, refuses to ratify the treaty establishing the International Criminal Court in Hague because it believes that its citizens may be indicted for politically motivated reasons. For the United States, human rights violations take place in other countries, and the fact that the Constitution incorporates one of the first great bills of rights has led to an identification of what were initially natural rights with civil rights. American exceptionalism has proved to be a significant barrier to the universal applicability of ethics in international relations.

We saw when examining the legal view of human rights that although there is a residue of the natural law and natural rights traditions there is a convergence on the view that the human rights culture, or movement is one of consensus and agreement, and that the framework of human rights is constituted by convention and customary law to which states subscribe, out of which something like a nascent universal jurisdiction is emerging. Among those who view human rights politically, there are many who would deny that they have a foundational character, or indeed deny the relevance of such considerations when it comes to acting politically in their name.

While there have been considerable advancements in the development of international law, monitoring and the establishment of judicial bodies to deal with human rights violations, no body of rules or laws can be effective without the political will to implement and enforce them. Unless there is a spirit of adherence to the principles of human rights, and to the mechanisms to enforce their observance, there is a danger of the human rights culture resting on a facade of rhetoric. Tony Evans has described this as a disjuncture between the theory and practice of human rights (Evans 1998: 1). The Declaration of 1948, he claims, has had little impact on the lives of those who stand most in need of protection. Public embarrassment with the publicity given to human rights violations by such bodies as Amnesty International still seems to be one of the main constraints on governments disinclined to respect the human rights of their citizens. Despite the Declaration of Universal Human Rights being at the centre of the United Nations achievements, and despite widespread subscription to human rights conventions the catalogue of organized ruthless violations grows longer every day, mostly without investigation and almost never with intervention by other states. Why do such crimes go unpunished?

There are many aspects to the answer. The United Nations is not an organization comprised of the peoples of the world. Its members are governments. A significant number of these governments are neither representative of their people, nor do they attempt to promote the common good. Indeed they are prepared to wage war against their own people if it furthers their interests. The most recent example is the ruthless disregard for democracy by Robert Mugabe in Zimbabwe by falsifying election results and violently intimidating opposition supporters. Of those governments that are broadly democratic not enough of them act in a determined way to further the cause of human rights at the United Nations or elsewhere in order to expose and embarrass the violators. The problem is compounded by the fact that many governments best placed to put moral pressure on violators are prepared to overlook infringements in the interests of economic co-operation and advantage (Ekins 1992: 65).

The one world super-power that could occupy the high moral ground often places itself outside of the human rights regime and exhibits with arrogance the doctrine of American exceptionalism. What characterizes this exceptionalism is a remarkable record of leadership in universal human rights coupled with a resistance to complying with human rights standards domestically, and to aligning US foreign policy to them abroad. Ignatieff identifies three facets to American exceptionalism. First, America signs up to international conventions and agreements, and then exempts itself from their provisions by formal reservation, a refusal to ratify, or simply by non-compliance. What this means in practice is that those UN instruments and standards from which United States has exempted itself have no legal standing in American courts. Secondly, the United States employs double standards in judging itself and its allies by more permissive criteria than those it applies to its enemies. What this means is that the United States at once criticizes other states for ignoring reports produced by UN rights bodies, while dismissing those critical of its own domestic rights performances. This is particularly the case with capital punishment, especially in relation to the execution of juveniles (Ignatieff 2005: 7). And, third, the United States denies the jurisdiction of international law within its own domestic law, on the grounds that the land of Jefferson and Lincoln 'has nothing to learn about rights from any other country' (Ignatieff 2005: 8).

From the political perspective, Chomsky, for example, relentlessly exposes the double standards applied by the USA and its allies. He argues that the rhetoric of the 1993 Vienna Conference was nothing but a sham. At the same time the universality of human rights was being reaffirmed, France and Britain were selling arms to Indonesian and Rwandan mass murderers, while the USA flouted article 14 of the Universal Declaration which guarantees rights of asylum, by returning Haitian refugees who the United States claimed were fleeing poverty rather than the rampant terror of Duvalier. While the civil and political rights are largely rhetorical except when used selectively as a weapon against other states, the economic, cultural, and social, and community rights and rights to development, the so-called second and third generation of rights are treated with contempt by the United States. Jeanne Kirkpatrick, the former UN Ambassador, described them as 'a letter to Santa Klaus' (Chomsky 1999: 21).

Many critics claim that the moral universalism that is claimed as the foundation of human rights is little more than a pretext safeguarding other interests. Opponents of NATO's intervention in Yugoslavia in 1999 maintain that once again it exposed the operation of dual standards. The intervention was not itself sanctioned by the United Nations, even though the bombing of Belgrade was justified on the grounds of human rights, yet no such action was taken against the much stronger state of Russia in its assaults on Chechnyan rebels. Only Yugoslav leaders and not Albanian rebels or NATO were indicted for war crimes.

In the same month as past violations were highlighted in the Pinochet case, violations in contemporary Yugoslavia were cited as just cause for NATO air strikes on Kosovo to protect the ethnic Albanians from Slobodan Milosevic's policy of ethnic cleansing. Such military operations, however, serve to bring into sharp relief how rare such humanitarian interventions are, and critics and allies of the policy may with justification ask why not intervene to prevent the persecution of pro-democracy supporters in China, Chinese oppression in Burma, and the slaughter of 800,000 people in Rwanda in 1994. Such inconsistencies engender cynical interpretations of humanitarian interventions. The first Gulf war, for example, was justified on the grounds that citizens of Kuwait had their territorial sovereignty violated and were in danger of having their human rights disregarded by Saddam Hussain who in his persecution of the Kurds demonstrated that he was no respecter of human rights. The second Gulf war has similarly been viewed with incredulity. The claim that one of its aims was humanitarian to prevent a ruthless dictator inflicting further human rights violation in Iraq. The American and British action was widely interpreted as having economic rather than humanitarian motivations.

Similarly, the cynical view of the motivation to bomb the Federal Republic of Yugoslavia to prevent the expulsion of Albanians from Kosovo relates to issues that extend beyond humanitarian concerns. The destabilization of the region, along with the historical memory of the place of the Balkans in the wars of the twentieth century, raise strategic issues. Kosovo is two hours by plane from London and something like eighteen hours from Cambodia and East Timor.

The discontents with the human rights culture are various. Politically it is by no means universally accepted by governments that human rights are a good thing, but few would deny what may be called the fundamental humanitarian rights such as the right to life and freedom from torture, even if only to save international embarrassment, but on such issues as free speech, freedom of movement, freedom of worship, or a variety of social and political rights, that consensus would evaporate, and perhaps this is why there was such impetus to establish the American, European, and African regional declarations of rights.

When one looks at those who criticize what is described as the Western conception of the individual, and the ascription of rights to individuals, such as freedom of speech, in the face of other values, perhaps more highly valued by non-Western societies, such as order, deference, and stability, it is often the leaders of what Western states would regard as traditional and hierarchical regimes. The West was accused of cultural imperialism and of promoting a conception of human rights detrimental to Asian economic development. Asian leaders resisted any idea of the erosion of sovereignty and any move to legitimate intervention on so called humanitarian grounds (Evans 1998: 18). This was the argument put forward by Mahathir of Malaysia, Lee Kuan Yew of Singapore, and Suharto of Indonesia at the 1993 Vienna Conference. Even after the fall of Suharto it was with extreme reluctance that the Indonesian authorities allowed the humanitarian force led by Australia to prevent further atrocities in East Timor.

The invocation of cultural relativism, which usually means traditionalism, too often translates into special pleading for the retention of certain privileges, whether class or gender based (Booth 1999: 40). The caste systems in India and Japan, for example, are not easily reconciled with the idea of universal human rights based on the principle of equal human dignity. The plea of cultural relativism to justify such practices as foot binding and female circumcision was used to secure a great deal of political capital by the USA at the Vienna Convention whose representatives protested that they would not allow the universality of human rights to be undermined. Indeed, the formal documents that emerged at least in principle betray a much greater consensus on the universalism of human rights than ever before. Paragraph 5 of the Vienna declaration and Programme of Action states that 'All human rights are universal, indivisible and interdependent and interrelated.... [I]t is the duty of States, regardless of their political, economic and cultural systems, to promote and protect all human rights and fundamental freedoms'. Paragraph 10 makes it clear that states may not invoke the lack of development, as they had done in the 1970s and 1980s in mitigation of their lack of implementation (see Donnelly 1999: 89).

No plea of cultural relativism, and those who make them of course are more often than not claiming the absoluteness of their own cultural practices backed with religious sanction, can undermine the actual universality of those aspects of the human rights culture that transcend all cultural barriers. Crimes against humanity which demand humanitarian intervention and universal jurisdiction are quite distinct from the political rights claimed to be subordinate to collective goals. We are still, however, a very long way from thinking in terms of a right to humanitarian intervention, and states remain firmly at the centre of the recognition, promotion, and maintenance of human rights for their own citizens and foreign nationals within their own borders. Ignatieff recognizes that human rights are not above politics, and that to imagine a globalized world that somehow supersedes state sovereignty is not only utopian but dangerous. It is necessary to acknowledge the extent to which state sovereignty creates and sustains the international order within which national constitutional regimes provide the best for guaranteeing human rights (Ignatief 2001: 35). It is nevertheless the case that while states may take care of business at home, few are prepared to take more than symbolic action against human rights violations short of genocide in other states, and even then with considerable reluctance.

Much of the discontent about human rights, however, centres on the charge of hypocrisy and cynicism; the disjuncture between its rhetoric and its practice.

These criticisms range from the principle that human rights are a good thing, but governments disingenuously subscribe to them and systematically violate them, to the idea that they are an advanced form of imperialism, a hegemonic ideology by means of which the West dominates the rest of the world. In between we have liberal criticisms suggesting that human rights need to be supplemented with special or cultural rights, or indeed that human rights are not only culturally but also gender blind. In other words, human rights are indeed special rights attached largely to men at the expense of women.

From a politico-legal point of view many experts in international law expose the cynicism with which politicians and the United Nations itself have more often than not sought to gain political capital rather than genuinely promote the cause of human rights by agreeing to support various conventions and covenants, in the expectation that they could never be enforced. It is to the credit of Justice Goldstone and his successors that they vociferously complained that the legislation embodied in the ad hoc Tribunals for the former Yugoslavia and Rwanda was undermined by the lack of political will on the part of governments in apprehending the indicted suspects who often continued, as Milosevic did until October 2000, to hold prominent positions of power. They also did more than any other tribunal or covenant to establish as a crime against humanity the systematic use of rape to further military and political ends.

Some international legal experts are sceptical of taking the power of enforcing human rights out of the hands of sovereign governments that are elected and accountable for their actions. By implication the belief is that the apparatus and instruments of human rights are open to political abuse, and that international bodies are further removed from democratic control than domestic courts. John Laughland maintains that the assumption that international law and its institutions rest upon a universal morality, and therefore require international bodies with universal jurisdiction, does not necessarily follow. He points to the example of the 1948 'Convention on the Prevention and Punishment of Genocide' which placed responsibility upon signatory countries to prosecute those accused of genocide in their own courts (Laughland 2002).

The International Criminal Tribunal for the former Yugoslavia universally rescinded this provision when it ruled that it and not national courts had jurisdiction over persons accused of genocide in the former Yugoslavia (Laughland 2002: 42). Furthermore the political character of human rights is exposed by the fact that the universal norms are flexible and manipulated by the more powerful nations. For example, aerial bombardment of military and civilian targets is outlawed under the Hague Conventions of 1899 and 1907, in anticipation of future developments in technology, but the widespread use of such military tactics has led to its convenient suppression in texts on humanitarian law. It does not figure at all, for example, in the 1998 Rome Treaty (Laughland 2002: 44). Indeed, with the aerial bombardment of the former Yugoslavia by NATO, and of Iraq by the allied forces in the name of upholding human rights, there appears to be a complete reversal. Similarly, there seems to have been a dilution of the principle established at Nuremberg outlawing crimes against peace. The denial of the right to wage war was reiterated time and time again in post-war documents. Peaceful coexistence and the rejection of aggressive war form the basis of the international order. The 1998 Rome Treaty on the establishment of the International Criminal Court defers discussion of how crimes against peace are to be adjudicated, and the statute that established the International Criminal Tribunal for the former Yugoslavia is silent on crimes of aggression or crimes against peace. When asked to rule on the legality of NATO's aerial bombardment of Belgrade the Tribunal's Prosecutor solicited a report that concluded that whereas there may be a case to answer the International Criminal Tribunal lacked the jurisdiction to adjudicate in such matters. Its establishment was opposed by the Yugoslav government, partly on the grounds that it should have been established by the General Assembly of the United Nations, and not the Security Council, and that its jurisdiction was another case of victors' justice. Milosevic asserted, for example, that the Tribunal was political and not judicial, and that it is no more than a tool of NATO policy and consequently anti-Serb (Kerr 2004: 174). The fact that it is a body set up by the Security Council of the United Nations and funded by Western Governments, many of them NATO members conscious of their role in establishing the Tribunal and of supporting its daily activities, detracts from the appearance of impartiality (Laughland 2002: 53). It was viewed by Serbs as selective and politically biased justice. It had a political purpose, the restoration and maintenance of peace in the former Yugoslavia. Why here and not elsewhere? Furthermore, although Goldstone, the first of the prosecutors maintained that it was not politically biased, the vast majority of the early indictees were Serbian, and only one Bosnian Muslim, up to March 1996 (Kerr 2004: 180).

Laughland contends that human rights activists are rather naïve in believing that by virtue of sitting at an international level with individuals from other countries appointees from various countries take on a higher moral significance. The power they exercise 'is itself political and must, as such, be subjected to the usual checks and balances which we generally associate with the liberal order' (Laughland 2002: 50). The presupposition that Laughland's argument rests upon is that the state is essential to the operation of law, both domestically and internationally, and that the international apparatus for human rights is politically manipulated. He contends that, it is necessary to be aware of the political way in which allegedly universal norms are applied. Without any mechanisms of accountability, these attempts to replace domestic with international jurisdiction can only lead to greater arbitrary rule and to the further erosion of the rule of law (Laughland 2002: 55).

With the growing hegemony of the United States and its allies in NATO it is unlikely that countries such as India, Turkey, Vietnam, and Tanzania could intervene for humanitarian reasons, as they previously have, because they lack the political presence or power in the current environment. It is not that humanitarian intervention can no longer be abused, but rather that it can only be abused by powerful states, evidence of which is manifest in the interventions of NATO powers during the 1990s and 2000s. Holbrook argues that those states that claim that a right to humanitarian intervention has been established over the last decade disregard the principle that international legal norms can only be established when there is a clear consensus (Holbrook 2002: 142–3). The implication of such a view is that unilateral deviations from international norms may themselves set precedents that are binding on less powerful states.

The idea of a universal natural law was subject to the charge that it was the universalization of the Christian-centric view of the world, and hence a form of cultural domination demanding that not only the Europeans but also the Americans were subject to it and obliged to follow its precepts, at the risk that if they did not comply they would give just cause for war with all that it entailed in the loss of rights to property, seizure of land, and the right of reparations on the part of the injured party. This is essentially a foundational charge which is reflected in modern criticism of human rights which claim that they are Eurocentric betraying a bias towards individuals, as opposed to non-Western cultures which have a more collective and communitarian conception of what constitutes human identity, or that they reflect particular interests.

Particularly in the area of humanitarian intervention political factors seem to explain the significant increase during the 1990s and into the twenty first century. Before 1991, the year in which the United Nations sanctioned force to expel Iraq from Kuwait, the Soviet Union acted as a significant constraint on the United States by pursuing a foreign policy that was antagonistic towards the west. By 2003, not even the United Nations, with a considerably weakened Russia, could prevent America and her allies entering Iraq on the justification first that it constituted a threat to world peace, and second that Saddam Hussain systematically violated the human rights of his people.

A development of the criticism of human rights reflecting Western conceptions of the individual, and the charge of cultural imperialism is the introduction of the issues of power and politics into a debate largely conducted in the languages of law and philosophy, with the former focusing upon the legislative protections and judicial processes of redress, and the latter examining the source and justifications of human rights claims. When politics and power are introduced into the discussion they are conceived in conventional and standard forms relating to issues of sovereignty and non-intervention either in the context of power politics or the idea of a world community (Evans 1998: 3). From a Gramscian perspective, however, the human rights culture looks very different when related to the idea of hegemony, that is, the attempt by one culture to become dominant. In the Realist tradition of international politics hegemony is understood to be achieved and maintained by power and coercion. Gramsci, however, recognized the need for the hegemon to achieve legitimacy for its exercise of power and claims to intellectual and moral leadership. Hegemony, he argues, is sustained in two ways. First, by influencing external behaviour with a series of rewards and punishments. And, secondly, moulding opinions, values, and personal beliefs in conformity with prevailing interests. The hegemon consolidates and perpetuates its dominance by achieving a widely accepted moral and social language, which reaches its epitome when it attains the status of common sense. In other words, the dominant power socializes lesser powers into a common acceptance of an order in which their subordinate and superordinate relationship is legitimized, creating the impression that it is based upon will and not force, right rather than might. It has been contended that America has developed and exploited the idea of human rights in the furtherance of its hegemonic world aspirations to convince its own people that post-war reconstruction was not merely a philanthropic gesture, but a matter of securing world freedom, the freedom embedded in its own traditions and constitution. To get a wide acceptance of human rights furthers American hegemonic aspirations, enabling them to exercise influence over wider areas of the globe and to gain access to global markets. Wide acceptance of the human rights culture also provides the pretext for intervention when countries need to be brought into line. Bourdieu and Wacquant (1999) maintain that hegemonic or the imperial process of global asymmetry, should lead us to abandon the euphemism of an 'international community', which implies dialogue and mutual respect among equals, in favour of the stark reality of Western powers using international organizations as instruments for advancing geopolitical interests. In diffusing multicultural values as concomitants of human rights and liberal democracy the cunning of imperialist reason permeates the globe.

As we saw, the human rights culture, or movement, is relatively new and arose post 1945. The emphasis upon minority rights that characterized the interwar year was considered a failure, and had been cynically exploited by the Nazis in its demands at Munich to promote its racist policies. The solution of the United States for racial harmony was the assimilation of the melting pot, and not the affirmation of separate group identities (Krasner 1999: 110–11). The United States was fundamentally opposed to the inclusion of minority rights in both the Charter of the United Nations and the Universal Declaration of Human Rights (Donnelly 1989: 21). The human rights regime that succeeded it almost immediately went into abeyance with the advent of the Cold War.

There is a wide range of criticism of the human rights culture. There is an acknowledgement that the whole project is western orientated and liberal based upon the idea of the possession of individual rights which nevertheless require for their exercise and protection an ethical community within which to operate. Alistair MacIntyre rejects the idea of natural and human rights out of hand. There are no such rights attaching to every one equally by the mere fact that they are human. In most cultures, he suggests, the concept of possessing a right simply did not exist until the late medieval and early modern period. Without the conceptual apparatus even if there were human rights no one could have been cognizant of them. He suggests that all attempts to establish such rights have failed, and belief in them is equivalent to believing in witches and unicorns (MacIntyre 1981: 67ff). As currently constituted, the human rights culture, or regime, is not universally welcomed. Makau Matua, for example, is extremely pessimistic about its prospects of success because it is currently widely perceived as an alien ideology. He maintains that, 'In order ultimately to prevail, the human rights movement must be moored in the cultures of all peoples' (Matua 2002: 14).

Rights are the result of a well functioning ethical community, and are incapable of being abstracted and superimposed upon an oppressive world as the solution for prejudice, hatred, and arbitrary justice (Brown 1999: 120). In other words what matters in establishing the rule of law is a legal culture, and a moral community to sustain it. No matter how effective international tribunals such as that at the Hague may be in bringing to account those who have committed crimes against humanity, they cannot establish the rule of law in Bosnia, Yugoslavia or Rwanda. A legal culture is a local achievement (Hesse and Post 1999: 18).

What, then, is the way forward? Do we follow the Kantian route in setting good examples for the rest of the world to emulate? Rawls's certainly found inspiration there in formulating a minimal set of universal rights to which both liberal and non-liberal, but decent peoples, could subscribe. Rawls's list of human rights was considered too minimalist, but as Rex Martin remarked, liberal peoples would go much further and set examples to which decent peoples may aspire. Kant's peaceful confederation of republics in their relations with each other would renounce and eliminate force, and provide exemplars that others aspire to attain. The confederation of perpetual peace in its relations with belligerent, or what Rawls's called outlaw states, would resort to force in compelling them to come into line. Liberal democracies are frequently setting conditions for the respect of minority rights if benefits are to be conferred on potential state partners in trade and defense alliances. In general, international organizations, in Kymlicka's view, promote liberal multiculturalism which subscribe to the values of freedom, equality, and democracy, but with little success, except where coercive measures are taken. The nearest institutional arrangements that we have to Kant's model is one which champions Human and minority rights internal to its members, and which sets stringent criteria relating to the respect for rights to those who wish to have trading dealings with it, or aspire to membership.

There is little enthusiasm, for example, among the reforming elements in post-communist and post-colonial states. The recognition of cultural diversity, liberal multiculturalists assume, enhances freedom, strengthens human rights, diminishes hierarchies of inequality, and more deeply roots the principles of democracy (Kymlicka 2007: 18–9).

Kymlicka points to the successful policy of the European Union of including respect for minority rights as one of its accession criteria and also as a condition of the receipt of EU development aid by developing countries (Kymlicka 2007: 37–8). While the accession criteria are clear, and for the most part, rigorously applied, once an applicant becomes a member of the European Union, however, there is very little that can be done to force that member to adhere to human rights principles that are not covered by EU law. The Fundamental Rights Agency, created in 2007, has such a narrow mandate that it is not able to hold member states accountable (Amnesty International 2008: 7).

Demanding respect for minority rights and for human rights has a price. The European Union assumes that the enjoyment of membership is premised upon a government which respects human rights, democratic participation, and a functioning judiciary relatively free from corruption. Even when these political criteria are met the economy of a putative member must undergo a process of convergence to comply with the strict European criteria. The process is essentially one of homogenization and assimilation. On the one had the EU is saying if you want the benefits of joining the EU you have to respect difference, while at the same time saying you must become more like us, that is, liberal democracies with social market economies, in which there is respect for the liberal principles of equality, tolerance, freedom of speech and movement.

Article 49 of the Treaty of the European Union states that respect for the principles of the EU is a prerequisite for applying. It does not attempt to define Europe, and this is because Europe is still essentially contested. If, for example, Europe is viewed as a peninsular of Asia, then Turkey, geographically, is clearly part of it. It is rarely questioned whether Cyprus should be included in Europe, but geographically it is much closer to the Middle East and North Africa. As Neill Nugent suggests, 'The "what is Europe?" question becomes even more complex and contestable when other criteria are added, such as common culture, shared values and common historical experience' (Nugent 2004*b*: 273). The problems that currently beset European identity and citizenship are bound to be exacerbated by the enlargement of the Union. It is possible that the EU will expand into both Asia and Africa raising its population to over a billion people, and its membership to forty two countries. The key determinant on the Copenhagen criteria would be the achievement of 'stability of institutions guaranteeing democracy, the rule of law, human rights and respect for and protection of minorities, and the existence of a functioning market economy'. They would also need to adhere 'to the aims of political, economic and monetary union'. A fourth criterion that related to the EU itself is the capacity of the EU to absorb and accommodate new member states.

The enlargement of the EU, having to accommodate a greater diversity of peoples, from states such as Poland and the Czech Republic, to the micro-states of Cyprus and Malta, has the potential for the multiplication of cultural clashes and diversity of interests (Bellamy and Warleigh 2001: 11). But, as Klaus von Beyme has suggested, it is hard to love a market, and despite the rhetoric of citizenship, Europe is first and foremost a market (von Beyme 2001: 73). The Maastricht Treaty is heavily focused on provisions for the market, and the negotiations for EU enlargement, while requiring aspirants to meet the political criteria of Copenhagen, gave much more emphasis to those states meeting the economic criteria, and to ensuring a functioning market economy. As Kymlicka himself admits, the EU is less than vigorous in applying respect for minority rights criteria when it has other imperatives for admitting accession counties (Kymlicka 2007: 41). The same is true of the other political criteria where respect for human rights, democracy, and a functioning judiciary, including the rule of law, are not stringently applied (see Boucher 2005).

We should not, however, be discouraged. Kant took the long-view and envisaged a time-frame of centuries before ethical principles would subordinate all others in relations among states. The modern human rights culture is relatively new, and has incorporated much that is old in its ethical vision, and its construction of a legal framework that aims, as Grotius did, to subject states to the rule of law. The ad hoc tribunals and the International Criminal Court provide glimmerings of success, and coupled with the political will of international organizations may yet lead the way to global justice. The European Union, despite its many faults, may have positive benefits in creating the wider solidarist community upon which a human rights culture depends. In relation to Turkey's application to join the EU it has made it clear that not only will it have to meet the political and economic criteria, but it will also have to bring about a resolution to the problem of Cyprus and reintegrate the Greek and Turkish communities. In the case of Bosnia it appears that the allure of membership in a privileged economic club overcomes the objections it had to apprehending and handing over to international justice those who have been indicted for genocide and war crimes. On the news of the capture of Radovan Karadzic, one of the most wanted war criminals in the world, the European Commission President welcomed the news as a sign of the new Serbian government's determination to cooperate with the International Criminal Tribunal for the former Yugoslavia, and added that it was of crucial importance for Serbia's European aspirations. Mr Radovan Karadzic and the Bosnian Serb military leader Ratko Mladic were indicted in 1995 for alleged war crimes committed during the war of 1992–1995. Karadzic's arrest after nearly thirteen years marks a major breakthrough for international justice, but the political motivation of the Serbian government and the political will of the European Union should not be overplayed. It is premature to announce with confidence, as Serge Brammertz, head prosecutor for International Criminal Tribunal for the former Yugoslavia has done, that the arrest 'clearly demonstrates that nobody is beyond the reach of the law and that sooner or later all fugitives will be brought to justice'. It is nevertheless a significant milestone on the way.

American exceptionalism remains a source of moral disquiet. The reaction by America to the threat of terrorism – extraordinary rendition, the use of waterboarding, the detention of suspects in Guantanamo Bay, mental and physical abuse of prisoners in Iraq – has detracted from its potential leadership role in championing the human rights of equality and freedom around the world. The special arrangements for placing detainees of Guantanamo Bay outside of American domestic jurisdiction, overruled by the Supreme Court in allowing appeals to it, and the lamentably low rate of conversion from incarceration to concrete charges and convictions, has undermined the credibility of international justice. The failure to convict Salim Ahmed Hamden, Osama bin Laden's driver, of conspiracy to murder, and to find him guilty of the lesser and newly manufactured war crime of providing material support for terrorism, has a hint of desperation about it. The conviction has done nothing to allay criticisms of human rights abuses at Guantanamo Bay. Much of Hamden's trial was conducted in secret and the prosecution built its case on evidence extracted during forty interrogations, some undertaken by the CIA. Of over 700 detainees only about 60 are likely to reach trial.

After over 2,500 years of trying to subordinate the actions of individuals, peoples, and states to ethical constraints in their relations with each other, what are the limits of ethics in international relations? In so far as any rule can never merely be applied to a circumstance that fits the criteria for its application without the mediation of human judgement and thought, the efficacy of such rules can only be as robust as the integrity of the character and processes that apply them. Whether they are up to the task, it is too soon to tell!

Bibliography

Abbott, Kenneth W. (1999), 'International Relations Theory, International Law, and the Regime Governing Atrocities in Internal Conflicts', *The American Journal of International Law*, vol. 93, pp. 361–79.
Abel, Lionel (1963), 'The Aesthetics of Evil', *Partisan Review*, vol. xxx, pp. 211–30.
Adler, Emanuel (2005), *Communitarian International Relations: The Epistemic Foundations of International Relations*, London, Routledge.
Aguilar, Jose Manuel De (1946), 'The Law of Nations and the Salamanca School of Theology', *Thomist: A Speculative Quarterly Review*, vol. 9, pp. 186–221.
Amnesty International (2008), *Amnesty International Report, 2008.*
Anderson, Olive (1991), 'The Feminism of T. H. Green: A Late-Victorian Success Story?', *History of Political Thought*, vol. XII, pp. 671–93.
Annan, Kofi A. (1998), 'Peacekeeping, Military Intervention and National Sovereignty in Internal Armed Conflict' in *Hard Choices: Moral Dilemmas in Humanitarian Interventions*, Jonathan Moore, ed., Lanham, Maryland, Rowman and Littlefield, pp. 55–70.
Anscombe, Elizabeth (1997), 'Modern Moral Philosophy' in *Virtue Ethics*, Roger Crisp and Michael Slote, eds., Oxford, Oxford University Press, pp. 26–44.
Aquinas, St. Thomas (1974), *Selected Political Writings*, A. P. D'Entréves, ed., Oxford, Blackwell.
—— (1988), *Aquinas: On Law, Morality, and Politics*, William P. Baumgarth and Richard J. Regan, eds., Indianapolis, Hackett.
Arendt, Hannah (1958), *The Human Condition*, Chicago, University of Chicago Press.
—— (1973), *The Origins of Totalitarianism*, third edition, New York, Harcourt, Brace and World.
—— (1977), *Eichmann in Jerusalem: A Report on the Banality of Evil*, revised edition, Harmondsworth, Penguin.
Aristotle (1973), *Ethics*, trans. J. A. K. Thomson, Harmondsworth, Penguin.
—— (1984), *The Athenian Constitution*, trans. P. J. Rhodes, Harmondsworth, Penguin.
—— (1988), *Politics*, Cambridge, Cambridge University Press.
Armitage, David (2000), 'Edmund Burke and the Reason of State', *Journal of the History of Ideas*, vol. 61, pp. 617–34.
Arneil, Barbara (1992), 'John Locke, Natural Law and Colonialism', *History of Political Thought*, vol. XIII, pp. 587–603.
Arnold, E. Vernon (1911), *Roman Stoicism*, Cambridge, Cambridge University Press.
Arnold, Thomas (1831*a*), 'The Labourers of England', *Englishman's Register*, No. 5, 4 June, pp. 143–7.
—— (1831*b*), 'The Labourers of England', *Englishman's Register*, No. 6, 11 June, pp. 155–9.
Aron, Raymond (1967), 'What Is a Theory of International Relations', *Journal of International Affairs*, vol. xxi, pp. 185–206.
Ashley, Maurice (1971), *Charles II: The Man and the Statesman*, London, The History Book Club.
Ashworth, Georgina (1999), 'The Silencing of Women' in *Human Rights in Global Politics*, Tim Dunne and Nick Wheeler, eds., Cambridge, Cambridge University Press, pp. 259–76.

Asmal, Kader (2000), 'Truth, Reconciliation and Justice: The South African Experience in Perspective', *The Modern Law Review*, vol. 63, pp. 1–24.
Astell, Mary (1996), *Political Writings*, Patricia Springborg, ed., Cambridge, Cambridge University Press.
Augustine, St. (1974), *The Essential Augustine*, Vernon J. Bourke, ed., Indianapolis, Hackett.
—— (1984), *Concerning the City of God against the Pagans*, trans. Henry Bettenson and introduced by John O'Meara, Harmondsworth, Penguin.
—— (1998), *The City of God against the Pagans*, ed. and trans. R. W. Dyson, Cambridge, Cambridge University Press.
Aurelius, Marcus (1908), *The Meditations of the Emperor Marcus Aurelius Antoninus*, trans. George Long, London, Collins.
Austin, J. L. (1975), *How to Do Things with Words*, second edition, Harvard, Harvard University Press.
Ayala, Balthazar, [1582] (1912), *On the Law of War and on Duties Connected with War and on Military Discipline*, trans. John Pawley Bate, Washington, D.C., The Carnegie Foundation.
Ayer, A. J. (1992), *Hume* in *The British Empiricists* by John Dunn, J. O. Urmson and A. J. Ayer, Oxford, Oxford University Press.
Baehr, Peter R. (1999), *Human Rights: Universality in Practice*, Basingstoke, Macmillan.
Baier, Annette (1988), 'Hume's Account of Social Artifice – Its Origins and Originality', *Ethics*, vol. 98, pp. 757–78.
Bain, William (2003), *Between Anarchy and Society: Trusteeship and the Obligations of Power*, Oxford, Oxford University Press.
Ball, Howard (1999), *Prosecuting War Crimes and Genocide: The Twentieth Century Experience*, Lawrence, Kansas University Press.
Banner, Stuart (2005*a*), 'Why *Terra Nullius*? Anthropology and Property Law in Early Australia', *Law and History Review*, vol. 23, pp. 95–132.
—— (2005*b*), *How the Indians Lost Their Land: Law and Power on the Frontier*, London, Belknap.
Barker, Ernest (1934), 'Introduction' to Otto Gierke, *Natural Law and the Theory of Society 1500–1800*, Cambridge, Cambridge University Press, 1934.
—— (1956), ed. and trans., *Alexander to Constantine*, Oxford, Clarendon Press.
Barnes, Jonathan (1982), 'The Just War' in Norman Kretzmann, Antony Kenny, Jan Pinborg, eds., *The Cambridge History of Later Medieval Philosophy: From the Rediscovery of Aristotle to the Disintegration of Scholasticism 1100–1600*, Cambridge, Cambridge University Press, pp. 771–84.
—— (1991), 'Partial Wholes' in *Ethics, Politics and Human Nature*, Ellen Frankel Paul, Fred D. Miller, Jr., and Jeffrey Paul, eds., Oxford, Blackwell, pp. 1–23.
Barry, Brian (1991*a*), 'Humanity and Justice in Global Perspective' in Brian Barry, *Liberty and Justice: Essays in Political Theory*, vol. 2, Oxford, Clarendon Press, pp. 182–210.
—— (1991*b*), 'Justice as Reciprocity' in Brian Barry, *Liberty and Justice: Essays in Political Theory*, vol. 2, Oxford, Clarendon Press, pp. 211–41.
—— (2001), *Culture and Equality*, Cambridge, Polity.
Bartlett, Richard H., ed. (1993), *The Mabo Decision*, Sydney, Butterworths.
Bass, Gary Jonathan (2000), *Stay the Hand of Vengeance: The Politics of War Crimes Tribunals*, Princeton, Princeton University Press.
Bauer, Joanne R. and Bell, Daniel A., eds. (1999), *The East Asian Challenge for Human Rights*, Cambridge, Cambridge University Press.

Beattie, James (1770), *An Essay on the Nature and Immutability of Truth: In Opposition to Sophistry and Scepticism*, Edinburgh, Kincaid and Bell.

Beitz, Charles (1979), *Political Theory and International Relations*, Princeton, Princeton University Press.

—— (1994), 'Cosmopolitan Liberalism and the States System' in *Political Restructuring in Europe*, Chris Brown, ed., London, Routledge, pp. 123–36.

—— (2001), 'Does Global Inequality Matter' in *Global Justice*, Thomas W. Pogge, ed., Oxford, Blackwell, pp. 106–22.

Bell, Daniel (1963), 'The Alphabet of Justice: Reflections on *Eichmann in Jerusalem*', *Partisan Review*, vol. xxx, pp. 417–29.

Bellamy, R. and J. F. Warleigh-Lack (2001), 'Introduction: The Puzzle of EU Citizenship' in *Citizenship and Governance in the European Union*, Bellamy and Warleigh, eds., London and New York, Continuum Press, pp. 3–18.

Belli, Pierino [1563] (1936a), *A Treatise on Military Matters and Warfare in Eleven Parts*, trans. Herbert C. Nutting, Oxford, Clarendon Press.

Benedict XVI, POPE (2007), 'Apostolic Journey of His Holiness Benedict XVI to Brazil on the Occasion of the Fifth General Conference of the Bishops of Latin America and the Caribbean: Address of his Holiness Benedict XVI', Rome, Liberia Editrice Vaticana, http://www.vatican.va/holy_father/benedict_xvi/speeches/2007/may/documents/hf_ben-xvi_spe_20070513_conference-aparecida_en.html

Benhabib, Seyla (2000), 'Arendt's *Eichmann in Jerusalem*' in *The Cambridge Companion to Hannah Arendt*, Dana Villa, ed., Cambridge, Cambridge University Press, pp. 65–85.

—— (2002), *The Claims of Culture: Equality and Diversity in the Global Era*, Princeton, New Jersey, Princeton University Press.

—— (2006), *Another Cosmopolitanism*, with Jeremy Waldron, Bonnie Honig and Will Kymlicka, Oxford, Oxford University Press.

Bennett, Mary Montgomerie (1930), *The Australian Aboriginal as a Human Being*, London, Alston Rivers.

Bentham, Jeremy (1988), *A Fragment on Government*, introduced by Ross Harrison, Cambridge, Cambridge University Press.

Ben-Yehuda, Nachman (1992), *Political Assassinations by Jews: A Rhetorical Device for Justice*, New York, SUNY Press.

Berki, R. N. (1977), *The History of Political Thought*, London, Dent.

Bettelheim, Brunno (1963), 'Eichmann: the System of Victims', *The New Republic*, no. 184, 15th June, pp. 23–33.

Beyme, Klaus Von (2001), 'Citizenship and the European Union' in *Between European Citizenship: National Legacies and Postnational Projects*, Klaus Eder and Bernhard Giesen, eds., Oxford, Oxford University Press, pp. 61–85.

Black, Antony (1992), *Political Thought in Europe 1250–1450*, Cambridge, Cambridge University Press.

Blackstone, William (1765–69), *Commentaries On the Laws of England*, Oxford, Oxford University Press.

Booth, K. (1999), 'Three Tyrannies' in *Human Rights in Global Politics*, Tim Dunne and Nick Wheeler, eds., Cambridge, Cambridge University Press, pp. 31–70.

Borch, Merete (2001), 'Rethinking the Origins of *Terra Nullius*', *Australian Historical Studies*, vol. 117, pp. 222–39.

Bosanquet, Bernard (1915), 'Patriotism in the Perfect State' in Eleanor Sidgwick *et al.*, *The International Crisis in Its Ethical and Psychological Aspects*, London, Humphrey Milford and Oxford University Press, pp. 132–54.

Bosanquet, Bernard (1917), *Social and International Ideals*, London, Macmillan, New York, Krauss Reprint 1968.
—— (1918), *Some Suggestions in Ethics*, London, Macmillan.
—— (1923), *The Philosophical Theory of the State*, fourth edition, London, Macmillan.
Boucher, David (1985), *Texts in Context: Revisisionist Methods for Studying the History of Ideas*, Dordtrecht, Martinus Nijhott.
—— (1991), 'The Character of the History of the Philosophy of International Relations and the Case of Edmund Burke', *Review of International Studies*, vol. 17, pp. 128–48.
—— (1994), 'British Idealism, the State and International Relations', *Journal of the History of Ideas*, 55, pp. 671–94.
—— ed. (1997), *The British Idealists*, Cambridge, Cambridge University Press.
—— (1998), *Political Theories of International Relations: From Thucydides to the Present*, Oxford, Oxford University Press.
—— (2000*a*), 'Hegel and Marx on International Relations', Tony Burns and Ian Fraser, eds., London, Palgrave, pp. 217–39.
—— (2000*b*), 'Tocqueville, Collingwood, History and Extending the Moral Community', *British Journal of Politics and International Relations*, vol. 2, 326–51.
—— (2001*a*), 'British Idealism and the Human Rights Culture', *History of European Ideas*, vol. 27, pp. 61–78.
—— (2001*b*), 'Resurrecting Pufendorf and Capturing the Westphalian Moment', *Review of International Studies*, vol. 27, pp. 557–77.
—— (2003*a*), 'Rousseau' in *Political Thinkers from Socrates to the Present*, David Boucher and Paul Ketty eds., Oxford, Oxford University Press, pp. 235–52.
—— (2003*b*), 'Burke' in *Political Thinkers from Socrates to the Present*, David Boucher and Paul Ketty eds., Oxford, Oxford University Press, pp. 363–82.
—— (2005), 'The Rule of Law and the Modern European State: Michael Oakeshott and European Enlargement', *European Journal of Political Theory*, vol. 4, pp. 89–107.
—— (2006*a*), 'Uniting What Right Permits with What Interest Prescribes: Rawl's Law of Peoples in Context' in *Rawls's Law of Peoples: A Realistic Utopia*, Rex Martin and David A. Reidy, eds., Oxford, Blackwell, pp. 19–37.
—— (2006*b*), 'Thin Universalism and Distributive Justice' in *Principles and Political Order*, Bruce Haddock, Peri Roberts, and Peter Sutch, eds., London, Routledge, pp. 176–91.
—— and Vincent, Andrew (2000), *British Idealism and Political Theory*, Edinburgh, Edinburgh University Press.
Bourdieu, Pierre and Wacquant, Loïc (1999), 'On the Cunning of Imperialist Reason', *Theory, Culture and Society*, vol. 16, pp. 41–58.
Bourke, Vernon (1974), 'Is Thomas Aquinas a Natural Law Ethicist', *The Monist*, vol. 58, pp. 52–66. Reprinted in John Dunn and Ian Harris, eds., *Aquinas I*, London, Elgar, 1997, pp. 486–500.
Boyle, Joseph (1992), 'Natural Law and the Ethics of Traditions' in *Natural Law Theory*, Robert P. George, ed., Oxford, Clarendon Press, pp. 3–30.
Bradley, A. C. (1916) 'International Morality' in *The International Crisis in Its Ethical and Psychological Aspects*, *The International Crisis: The Theory of the State* by Louise Creighton *et al.*, London, Milford and Oxford University Press, pp. 46–59.
Bradley, F. H. (1894) 'The Limits of International and National Self-Sacrifice', *International Journal of Ethics*, vol. 5, No. 1, pp. 17–28.
—— (1927) *Ethical Studies*, second edition, Oxford, Clarendon Press.
—— (1930), *Appearance and Reality*, ninth impression (corrected), Oxford, Clarendon Press.

Brems, Eva (1997), 'Enemies or Allies: Feminism and Cultural Relativism as Dissident Voices in Human Rights Discourse', *Human Rights Quarterly*, vol. 19, pp. 136–64.

Broome, Richard (2002), *Aboriginal Australians: Black Responses to White Dominance 1788–1994*, third edition, St. Leonards, Allen and Unwin Australia.

Brown, Chris (1992), *International Relations Theory: New Normative Approaches*, Hemel Hempstead, Harvester.

—— (1994), 'The Ethics of Political Restructuring in Europe' in *Political Restructuring in Europe*, C. Brown, ed., London, Routledge, pp. 163–86.

—— (1998), 'Human Rights' in *The Globalization of World Politics: An Introduction to International Relations*, John Baylis and Steve Smith, eds., Oxford, Oxford University Press, pp. 469–82.

—— (1999), 'Universal Human Rights. A Critique' in *Human Rights in Global Politics*, Tim Dunne and Nicholas J. Wheeler, eds., Cambridge, Cambridge University Press, pp. 103–27.

—— (2001), *Sovereignty, Rights and Justice: International Political Theory Today*, Cambridge, Polity.

—— Nardin, Terry, and Rengger, Nicholas, eds. (2002), *International Relations in Political Thought*, Cambridge, Cambridge University Press.

Brownlie, Ian (1998), *The Rule of Law in International Affairs*, Dordtrecht, Martinus Nijhoff.

—— and Goodwin-Gill, Guy, eds. (2006), *Basic Documents on Human Rights*, fifth edition, Oxford, Oxford University Press.

Brownmiller, Susan (1975), *Against Our Will*, New York, Bantam.

Buchanan, Allen (2000), 'Rawls's Law of Peoples: Rules for a Vanished Westphalian World', *Ethics*, vol. 110, pp. 697–721.

—— (2003), *Justice, Legitimacy, and Self-Determination: Moral Foundations of International Law*, Oxford, Oxford University Press.

—— (2006), 'Taking the Human Out of Human Rights' in *Rawls's Law of Peoples: A Realistic Utopia*, Rex Martin and David A. Reidy, eds., Oxford, Blackwell, pp. 150–68.

Buckle, Stephen (1991), *Natural Law and the Theory of Property: Grotius to Hume*, Oxford, Clarendon Press.

Bull, Hedley (1991), 'Martin Wight and the Theory of International Relations', in Martin Wight, *International Theory: The Three Traditions*, Eabriele Wight and Brian Porter, eds., London and Leicester, Leicester University Press, pp. ix–xxiii.

—— (1977), *The Anarchical Society: A Study of Order in World Politics*, New York, Columbia University Press.

—— (1979), 'The Universality of Human Rights', *Millennium: Journal of International Studies*, vol. 8, pp. 155–9.

Burgers, Jan Herman (1992), 'The Road to San Francisco: The Revival of the Human Rights Idea in the Twentieth Century', *Human Rights Quarterly*, vol. 14, pp. 447–77.

Burke, Edmund (1907), *Works*, 6 vols., London, Henry Froude for Oxford University Press.

—— (1987), *Speeches on the Impeachment of Warren Hastings*, Delhi, Discovery Publishing House, 2 vols.

—— (1999*a*), *Select Works of Edmund Burke*, Indianapolis, Liberty Fund, 4 vols.

—— [1780] (1999*b*), 'Sketch of the Negro Code' in *Selected Works of Edmund Burke*: vol. 4, *Miscellaneous Writings*, Francis Canavan, ed., Indianapolis, Liberty Fund, pp. 253–89.

Burlamaqui, Jean Jacques [1747] (1819), *The Principles of Natural Law*, trans. Thomas Nugent, Dublin, Dublin University Press.

Butler, Peter F. (1978), 'Legitimacy in a States-System: Vattel's Law of Nations' in *The Reason of States: A Study in International Political Theory*, Michael Donelan, ed., London, Allen and Unwin, pp. 45–63.

Bynkershoek, Cornelius Van (1930), *Quaestionum Juris Publici Libri Duo*, Oxford, Clarendon Press.

Caird, Edward (1892), 'The Genius of Carlyle' in Edward Caird, *Essays on Literature and Philosophy*, Glasgow, Maclehose, pp. 230–67.

—— (1917), 'The Nation as an Ethical Ideal' in *Lay Sermons Delivered in Balliol College*, Glasgow, Maclehose, pp. 97–122.

Cameron, David (1973), *The Social Thought of Rousseau and Burke: A Comparative Study*, London, Weidenfeld and Nicolson for The London School of Economics.

Campbell, Tom (2001), *Justice*, second edition, London, Macmillan.

Caney, Simon (2002), 'Cosmopolitanism and the Law of Peoples', *The Journal of Political Philosophy*, vol. 10, pp. 95–123.

—— (2005), *Justice Beyond Borders*, Oxford, Oxford University Press.

Carlyle, R. W. and Carlyle, A. J. (1970), *A History of Medieval Political Theory in the West*, sixth impression, Edinburgh, Blackwood.

Carlyle, Thomas (1866), 'Occasional Discourse on the Nigger Question' in *The Old Guard* (New York), vol. 4, issue 4, pp. 239–45; issue 5, pp. 308–11; and issue 6, pp. 372–7.

Carter, Matt (2003), *T. H. Green and the Development of Ethical Socialism*, Exeter, Imprint Academic.

Cassese, Antonio (1998), 'Reflections on International Criminal Justice', *The Modern Law Review*, vol. 61, pp. 1–10.

Cassirer, Ernst (1989), *The Question of Jean-Jacques Rousseau*, second edition, trans. Peter Gay, New Haven, Yale University Press.

Castiglione, Dario (1994), 'History, Reason and Experience: Hume's Arguments against Contract Theories' in *The Social Contract from Hobbes to Rawls*, David Boucher and Paul Kelly, eds., London, Routledge, pp. 95–114.

Caton, Hiram (1988), *The Politics of Progress*, Florida, University of Florida Press.

Chadwick, Henry (1986), *Augustine*, Oxford, Oxford University Press.

Chapman, John W. (1956) *Rousseau—Totalitarian or Liberal?* New York, Columbia University Press.

Charlesworth, Hilary and Chinkin, Christine (2000), *The Boundaries of International Law: A Feminist Analysis*, Manchester, Manchester University Press.

Chinkin, Christine (1998), 'International Law and Human Rights' in *Human Rights Fifty Years On: A Reappraisal*, Tony Evans, ed., Manchester, Manchester University Press, pp. 105–29.

Chomsky, Noam (1999), *The Umbrella of U. S. Power: The Universal Declaration of Human Rights and the Contradictions of US Policy*, New York, Seven Stories Press.

Christopher, Paul (1994), *The Ethics of War and Peace*, Englewood Cliffs, New Jersey, Prentice Hall.

Chroust, Anton-Hermann (1942), 'The "Jus Gentium" in the Philosophy of Law of St. Thomas Aquinas', *Notre Dame Lawyer*, vol. XVII, pp. 22–8. Reprinted in John Dunn and Ian Harris, eds., *Aquinas I*, London, Elgar, 1997, pp. 80–6.

—— (1974), 'The Philosophy of Law of St. Thomas Aquinas: His Fundamental Ideas and Some Historical Precursors', *American Journal of Jurisprudence*, vol. 19, pp. 1–38. Reprinted in John Dunn and Ian Harris, eds., *Aquinas I*, London, Elgar, 1997, pp. 501–39.

Cicero (1986), *On the Commonwealth*, G. H. Sabine and S. B. Smith (trans.), London, Collier Macmillan.

Cicero (1991), *On Duties*, M. T. Griffin and F. M. Atkins, eds., Cambridge, Cambridge University Press.
—— (1999), *On the Commonwealth and On the Laws*, James E. G. Zetzel, ed., Cambridge, Cambridge University Press.
Claeys, Gregory (1989), *Thomas Paine: Social and Political Thought*, Boston, Unwin Hyman.
Clapham, Andrew (2007), *Human Rights: A Very Short Introduction*, Oxford, Oxford University Press.
Clinebell, John Howard and Thomson, Jim (1977–78), 'Sovereignty and Self-Determination: The Rights of Native Americans Under International Law', *Buffalo Law Review*, vol. 27, pp. 669–714.
Coleman, Janet (2000), *A History of Political Thought from Ancient Greece to Early Christianity*, Oxford, Blackwell.
Collingwood, R. G. (1921), '*Lectures on Moral Philosophy for M-T 1921*', unpublished manuscript, DEP 4, Bodleian Library, Oxford.
—— (1923), '*Action*', unpublished manuscript, DEP 3, Bodleian Library, Oxford.
—— (1938), *The Principles of Art*, Oxford, Clarendon Press.
—— (1970), *An Autobiography*, Oxford, Oxford University Press.
—— (1992), *The New Leviathan: or Man, Society, Civilization and Barbarism*, new edition, David Boucher, ed., Oxford, Oxford University Press.
—— (1993), *The Idea of History*, revised edition, Jan van der Dussen, ed., Oxford, Clarendon Press.
—— (2005*a*), *The Philosophy of Enchantment: Studies in Folktale, Cultural Criticism, and Anthropology*, David Boucher, Wendy James, and Philip Smallwood, eds., Oxford, Clarendon Press.
—— (2005*b*), *An Essay on Philosophical Method*, revised edition, James Connelly and G. D'Oro, eds., Oxford, Oxford University Press.
Collini, Stefan (1979), *Liberalism and Sociology: L. T. Hobhouse and Political Argument in England 1880–1914*, Cambridge, Cambridge University Press.
Connolly, William E. (1983), *The Terms of Political Discourse*, second edition, Oxford, Robertson.
Connor, Michael (2005), *The Invention of Terra Nullius: Historical and Legal Fictions on the Foundation of Australia*, Sydney, Macleay Press.
Cook, Mercer (1936), 'Jean Jacques Rousseau and the Negro', *The Journal of Negro History*, vol. 21, pp. 294–303.
Coole, Diana (1993), *Women in Political Theory*, Hemel Hempstead, Harvester Wheatsheaf.
Cortes, Hernan (2001), *Letters from Mexico*, translated, edited with a new introduction by Anthony Pagden, with an introductory essay by J. H. Elliot, New Haven, Yale University Press.
Cotter, Bridget (2005), 'Arendt and "The Right to Have Rights"' in *Hannah Arendt and International Relations*, Anthony F. Lang Jr. and John Williams, eds., London, Palgrave, pp. 95–112.
Cox, Richard H. (1960), *Locke on Peace and War*, Oxford, Clarendon Press.
Cranston, Maurice (1967), 'Are Human Rights, Real and Supposed' in *Political Theory and the Rights of Man*, D. D. Raphael, ed., Bloomington, Indiana, Indiana University Press, pp. 43–53.
—— (1973), *What Are Human Rights*, New York, Taplinger Publishing Company.
Creede, Constance (1992), 'Epictetus' in *Great Thinkers of the Western World*, Ian P. McGreal, ed., New York, Harper-Collins, pp. 48–50.

Darby, Derrick (2003), 'Grounding Rights in Social Practices', *Res Publica*, vol. 9, pp. 1–18.
—— (2004), 'Rights Externalism', *Philosophy and Phenomenological Research*, vol. LXVIII, pp. 620–34.
D'Entrevès, A. P. (1972), *Natural Law*, revised edition, London, Hutchinson.
Deane, Herbert A. (1963), *The Political and Social Ideas of St. Augustine*, New York, Columbia University Press.
De Las Casas, Bartolome (2004), *A Short Account of the Destruction of the Indies*, London, Penguin.
Dembour, Marie-Bénédicte (2006), *Who Believes in Human Rights? Reflections on the European Convention*, Cambridge, Cambridge University Press.
den Boer, Pim (1995), *The History of the Idea of Europe*, London, Routledge and The Open University.
De Vaca, Alvar Numez Cabeza (2007), *The Shipwrecked Men*, London, Penguin Classics.
Dietz, Mary (2000), 'Arendt and the Holocaust' in *The Cambridge Companion to Hannah Arendt*, Dana Villa, ed., Cambridge, Cambridge University Press, pp. 86–109.
Diggins, John P. (1976), 'Slavery, Race, and Equality: Jefferson and the Pathos of the Enlightenment', *American Quarterly*, vol. 28, pp. 206–28.
Dimova-Cookson, Maria (2000), 'T. H. Green and Justifying Human Rights', *Collingwood and British Idealism Studies*, vol. 7, pp. 97–115.
Donelan, Michael (1990), *Elements of International Political Theory*, Oxford, Clarendon Press.
Donisthorpe, Wordsworth (1981), 'The Limits of Liberty' (1891) in Thomas Mackay, ed., *A Plea for Liberty*, Indianapolis, Liberty Fund, pp. 79–134.
Donnelly, Jack (1989), *Universal Human Rights in Theory and Practice*, Ithaca, New York, Cornell University Press.
—— (1999), 'The Social Construction of International Human Rights' in *Human Rights in Global Politics*, T. Dunne and N. Wheeler, eds., Cambridge, Cambridge University Press, pp. 71–102.
Draper, G. I. A. D. (1990), 'Grotius' Place in the Development of Legal Ideas About War' in *Hugo Grotius and International Relations*, Hedley Bull, Benedict Kingsbury, and Adam Roberts, eds., Oxford, Clarendon Press, pp. 177–208.
Dunbabin, J. (1982), 'The Reception and Interpretation of Aristotle's *Politics*' in Norman Kretzmann, Antony Kenny, Jan Pinborg, eds., *The Cambridge History of Later Medieval Philosophy: From the Rediscovery of Aristotle to the Disintegration of Scholasticism 1100–1600*, Cambridge, Cambridge University Press, pp. 723–37.
Dunn, John (1969), *The Political Thought of John Locke*, Cambridge, Cambridge University Press.
—— (1984), *Locke*, Oxford, Oxford University Press.
Dunne, Tim (1998), *Inventing International Society*, London, Macmillan.
—— and Wheeler, Nicholas J. (1999), *Human Rights in Global Politics*, Cambridge, Cambridge University Press.
Dworkin, Ronald (1978), *Taking Rights Seriously*, London, Duckworth.
—— (2000), *The Theory and Practice of Equality*, Cambridge, Massachusetts, Harvard University Press.
Edelstein, Ludwig (1966), *The Meaning of Stoicism*, Published for Oberlin College by Harvard University Press, Cambridge, Massachusetts.
Eide, Asbjørn (1998), 'The Historical Significance of the Universal Declaration', *Human Rights: 50th Anniversary of the Universal Declaration, International Social Science Journal*, vol. 158, pp. 475–97.

Eikema, Hommes and Hendrik Van (1983), 'Grotius on Natural and International Law', *Netherlands International Law Review*, vol. XXX, pp. 61–71.
Ekins, Paul (1992), *A New World Order: Grassroots Movements for Global Change*, London, Routledge.
Evans, Tony, ed. (1998), *Human Rights Fifty Years On: A Reappraisal*, Manchester, Manchester University Press.
Ewing, R. E. (1987), *Liberty, Community and Justice*, Totowa, New Jersey, Rowman and Littlefield.
Falk, Richard (2001), 'Accountability for War Crimes and the Legacy of Nuremberg' in *War Crimes and Collective Wrongdoing: A Reader*, Aleksandar Jokic, ed., Oxford, Blackwell, pp. 113–38.
Fawcett, J. E. S. (1992), 'The Development of International Law' in *International Relations in the Twentieth Century*, Marc Williams, ed., London, Macmillan, pp. 185–94.
Feinberg, Joel (1980), *Rights, Justice and the Bounds of Liberty*, Princeton, Princeton University Press.
Fennessy, R. R. (1963), *Burke, Paine and the Rights of Man*, The Hague, Martinus Nijhoff.
Fenrick, William J. (1999), 'Should Crimes against Humanity Replace War Crimes?', *The Columbia Journal of Transnational Law*, vol. 37, pp. 767–86.
Fenwick, Charles (1913), 'The Authority of Vattel', part I, *American Political Science Review*, vol. 7, pp. 375–92.
—— (1914), 'The Authority of Vattel', part II, *American Political Science Review*, vol. 7, pp. 395–410.
Ferguson, Adam (1966), *An Essay on the History of Civil Society 1767*, edited with an introduction by Duncan Forbes, Edinburgh, Edinburgh University Press.
Festenstein, Matthew, and Thompson, Simon (2001), *Richard Rorty: Critical Dialogues*, Cambridge, Polity.
Fields, A. Beldon (2002), *Rethinking Human Rights for the New Millenium*, London, Palgrave.
Finley, L. (1989), 'Breaking Women's Silence in Law: The Dilemma of the Gendered Nature of Legal Reasoning in Law', *Notre Dame Law Review*, vol. 64, pp. 886–910.
Finnis, John (1980), *Natural Law and Natural Rights*, Oxford, Clarendon Press.
—— (1991), *Moral Absolutes: Tradition, Revision, and Truth*, Washington D.C., Catholic University of America Press.
—— (1992), 'Natural Law and Legal Reasoning' in Robert P. George, ed., *Natural Law Theory: Contemporary Essays*, Oxford, Clarendon Press, pp. 134–57.
—— (1998), *Aquinas*, Oxford, Oxford University Press.
Fish, Stanley (1999), 'The Law Wishes to Have a Formal Existence' in *The Stanley Fish Reader*, H. Aram Vesser, ed., Oxford, Blackwell, pp. 165–206.
Fiss, Owen M. (1999), 'Human Rights as Social Ideals' in *Human Rights in Political Transitions: Gettysburg to Bosnia*, Carla Hesse and Robert Post, eds. New York, Zone Books, pp. 263–76.
Fletcher, F. T. H. (1933), 'Montesquieu's Influence on Anti-Slavery Opinion in England' *The Journal of Negro History*, vol. 18, pp. 414–25.
Flew, A. (1982), 'Could there be Universal Natural Rights', *The Journal of Libertarian Studies*, [online], vol. 6, No. 3, pp. 277–89.
Forbes, Duncan (1975), *Hume's Philosophical Politics*, Cambridge, Cambridge University Press.
Francis, Mark (2007), *Herbert Spencer and the Invention of Modern Life*, Stocksfield, Acumen.

Frankena W. K. (1955), 'Natural and Inalienable Rights', *The Philosophical Review*, [online], vol. 64, No. 2, pp. 212–32.
Freeden, Michael (1980), *Edmund Burke and the Critique of Political Radicalism*, Chicago, University of Chicago Press.
—— (1990*a*), 'Human Rights and Welfare: A Communitarian View', *Ethics*, vol. 100, pp. 489–502.
—— (1990*b*), 'Rights, Needs and Community: The Emergence of British Welfare Thought' in R. E. Goodin and A. Ware, eds., *Needs and Welfare*, London, Sage, pp. 54–72.
—— (1991), *Rights*, Minneapolis, University of Minnesota Press.
—— (2002), *Human Rights: An Interdisciplinary Approach*, Cambridge, Polity.
—— (2006), 'Putting Law in Its Place: An Interdisciplinary Evaluation of National Amnesty Laws' in *The Legalization of Human Rights*, Saladin Meckled-Garcia and Başak Çali, eds., London, Routledge, pp. 49–64.
Frost, Alan (1980–81), 'New South Wales as *Terra Nullius*: The British Denial of Aboriginal Land Rights', *Historical Studies*, vol. 19, pp. 513–23.
Frost, Mervyn (1996), *Ethics and International Relations: A Constitutive Theory*, Cambridge, Cambridge University Press.
—— (2002), *Constituting Human Rights: Global Civil Society and the Society of Democratic States*, London, Routledge.
Fukuyama, Francis (1993), *The End of History and the Last Man*, new edition, London, Penguin.
Gaita, Raimond (2002), *A Common Humanity: Thinking about Love and Truth and Justice*, second edition, London, Routledge.
Gallie, W. B. (1979), *Philosophers of Peace and War*, Cambridge, Cambridge University Press.
Garrett, Aaron (2004), 'Hume's "Original Difference": Race, Natural Character and the Human Sciences', *Eighteenth-Century Thought*, vol. 2, pp. 127–52.
—— (2006), 'Human Nature', *The Cambridge History of Eighteenth-Century Philosophy*, Knud Haakonssen, ed., Cambridge, Cambridge University Press, pp. 160–233.
Gaus, Gerald F. (1995), *Justificatory Liberalism*, Oxford, Oxford University Press.
—— (2005), 'Green's Rights Recognition Thesis and Moral Internalism', *British Journal of Politics and International Relations*, vol. 7, pp. 5–17.
—— (2006), 'The Rights Recognition Thesis: Defending and Extending Green', *T. H. Green: Ethics, Metaphysics, and Political Philosophy*, Maria Dimova-Cookson and W. J. Mander, eds., Oxford, Clarendon Press, pp. 209–35.
Gauthier, David (1969), *The Logic of Leviathan*, Oxford, Clarendon Press.
—— (1986), *Morals by Agreement*, Oxford, Clarendon Press.
—— (1998), 'David Hume, Contractarian' in *Social Justice from Hume to Walzer*, David Boucher and Paul Kelly, eds., London, Routledge, pp. 17–44.
—— and Sugden, Robert, eds. (1993), *Rationality, Justice and the Social Contract: Themes from 'Morals by Agreement'*, London, Harvester Wheatsheaf.
Gentili, Alberico [1661] (1921), *The Two Books of the Pleas of a Spanish Advocate of Alberico Gentili, Jurisconsult*, New York, Oxford University Press. Carnegie Endowment for International Peace.
—— (1933), *De Iure Belli Libre Tres*, translation of the edition of 1612 by John C. Rolfe, and introduced by Coleman Phillipson, Oxford, Clarendon Press.
George, Henry (1884), *Progress and Poverty*, London, Kegan Paul, Trench & Co.
Geras, Norman (1995), *Solidarity and the Conversation of Humankind*, London, Verso.

Gewirth, Alan (1982), *Human Rights: Essays on Justifications and Applications*, Chicago, University of Chicago Press.
—— (1984), 'Are There Any Absolute Rights' in *Theories of Rights*, Jeremy Waldron, ed., Oxford, Oxford University Press, pp. 91–109.
—— (1998), *Self-fulfillment*, Princeton, New Jersey, Princeton University Press.
Gilligan, Carole (1982), *In a Different Voice: Psychological Theory and Women's Development*, Cambridge, Massachusetts, Harvard University Press.
Glasius, Marlies (2006), *The International Criminal Court: A Global Civil Society Achievement*, London, Routledge.
Glausser, Wayne (1990), 'Three Approaches to Locke and the Slave Trade', *Journal of the History of Ideas*, vol. 51, pp. 199–216.
Glendon, Mary Ann (2001), *A World Made New: Eleanor Roosevelt and the Universal Declaration of Human Rights*, New York, Random House Trade.
Goldstone, Richard J. (1996), 'Prosecuting War Criminals', The David Davies Memorial Institute of International Studies, Cardiff, Occasional Paper No. 10, pp. 1–21.
—— (1997a), 'War Crimes a Question of Will', *The World Today*, April, 1997, pp. 106–8.
—— (1997b), 'Conference Luncheon Address', *Transnational Law and Contemporary Problems*, vol. 7, pp. 1–13.
—— (2000), *For Humanity: Reflections of a War Crimes Investigator*, New Haven and London, Yale University Press.
Gough, J. W. (1957), *The Social Contract*, Oxford, Clarendon Press.
Gramsci, Antonio (1971), *Selections from the Prison Notebooks*, Q. Hoare and G. Howell, eds., London, Lawrence and Wishart.
Green, L. C. and Dickason, Olive P. (1993), *The Law of Nations and the New World*, Edmonton, University of Alberta Press.
Green, Otis H. (1940), 'A Note on Spanish Humanism: Sepúlveda and His Translation of Aristotle's *Politics*', *Hispanic Review*, vol. VIII, pp. 339–42.
Green, T. H. (1899), *Prolegomena to Ethics*, fourth edition, Oxford, Clarendon Press.
—— (1917), *Lectures on the Principles of Political Obligation*, London, Longmans Green.
—— (1997), *Collected Works of T. H. Green: Additional Writings*, Peter Nicholson, ed., Bristol, Thoemmes Press.
Greengarten, I. M. (1981), *Thomas Hill Green and the Development of Liberal-Democratic Thought*, Toronto, University of Toronto Press.
Greenleaf, W. H. (1964), 'The Thomassian Tradition and the Theory of Absolute Monarchy', *English Historical Review*, LXXIX, 747–60. Reprinted in John Dunn and Ian Harris, eds., *Aquinas I*, London, Elgar, 1997, pp. 379–92.
Griffin, James (2008), *On Human Rights*, Oxford, Oxford University Press.
Griswold, Charles L. (1992), 'Rights and Wrongs: Jefferson, Slavery, and Philosophical Quandaries' in *A Culture of Rights: The Bill of Rights in Philosophy, Politics, and Law 1791–1991*, Cambridge, Cambridge University Press, pp. 144–214.
Grotius, Hugo (2004), *The Free Sea*, trans. Richard Hakluyt, with an Introduction by David Armitage, Indianapolis, Liberty Fund.
—— (2005), *The Rights of War and Peace* (1625), trans. Jean Barbeyrac, three books, edited with an introduction by Richard Tuck, Indianapolis, Liberty Fund.
Gutmann, Amy (2001), 'Introduction' in *Human Rights as Political and Idolatry*, Amy Gutmann, ed., by Michael Ignatieff, Princeton, Princeton University Press, pp. vii–xxviii.
Haakonssen, Knud (1985), 'Hugo Grotius and the History of Political Thought', *Political Theory*, vol. 13, pp. 239–65.

Haakonssen, Knud (1996), *Natural Law and Moral Philosophy from Grotius to the Scottish Enlightenment*, Cambridge, Cambridge University Press.
Haddock, Bruce (1994), 'Hegel's Critique of the Theory of Social Contract' in *The Social Contract from Hobbes to Rawls*, David Boucher and Paul Kelly, eds., London, Routledge, pp. 147–63.
Haldane, R. B. (1928), 'Higher Nationality: A Study in Law and Ethics' reprinted in *Selected Addresses and Essays*, London, Murray, pp. 49–3. The essay was written in 1913.
Hampshire-Monk, Iain (2005), 'Edmund Burke's Changing Justification for Intervention', *The Historical Journal*, vol. 48, pp. 65–100.
Hanke, Lewis (1949), *The Spanish Struggle for Justice in the Conquest of America*, Philadelphia, University of Pennsylvania Press.
—— (1959), *Aristotle and the American Indians: A Study in Race Prejudice in the Modern World*, Bloomington, Indiana University Press.
—— (1974), *All Mankind Is One: A Study of the Disputation between Bartolome de Las Casas and Juan Ginés de Sepúlveda on the Religious and Intellectual Capacity of the American Indians*, DeKalb, Illinois, University of Illinois Press.
Hannaford, Ivan (1996), *Race: The History of an Idea in the West*, Washington, D.C., Woodrow Wilson Centre Press.
Hardin, G (1974), 'Lifeboat Ethics: The Case against Helping the Poor', *Psychology Today*, vol. 8, pp. 38–43.
Harle, Vilho (2000), *The Enemy with a Thousand Faces: The Tradition of the Other in Western Political Thought and History*, Westport, Connecticut, Praeger.
Harries, Richard (1991), 'Human Rights in Theological Perspective' in *Human Rights for the 1990s: Legal, Political and Ethical Issues*, Robert Blackburn and John Taylor, eds., London, Mansell, pp. 1–13.
Hart, H. L. A. (1984), 'Are There Any Natural Rights?' in *Theories of Rights*, Jeremy Waldron, ed., Oxford, Oxford University Press, pp. 77–90.
—— (1994), *The Concept of Law*, second edition, Oxford, Clarendon Press.
—— (1999), 'Human Rights' in *The New Fontana Dictionary of Modern Thought*, Allan Bullock and Stephen Trombley, eds., New York, Harper Collins, p. 405.
Hartigan, Richard Shelly (1973), 'Francesco Vitoria and Civilian Immunity', *Political Theory*, vol. 1, pp. 79–91.
Haselgrave, Marianne (1988), 'Women's Rights: The Road to the Millenium' in Peter Davies, ed., *Human Rights*, London, Routledge, pp. 21–30.
Hayek, F. A. (1960), *The Constitution of Liberty*, Chicago, Chicago University Press.
Headley, John M. (2008), *The Europeanization of the World: On the Origins of Human Rights and Democracy*, Princeton, Princeton University Press.
Hegel, G. W. F. (1964), *Political Writings*, trans. T. M. Knox and introduced by Z. A. Pelczynski, Oxford, Clarendon Press.
—— (1971), *Philosophy of Mind*, trans. William Wallace and A. V. Miller, Oxford, Clarendon Press.
—— (1975), *Natural Law: The Scientific Ways of Testing Natural Law, Its Place in Moral Philosophy, and Its Relation to the Positive Sciences of Law*, trans. T. M. Knox and introduced by H. B. Acton, Pennsylvania, University of Pennsylvania Press.
—— (1977), *Phenomenology of Spirit*, A. V. Miller, trans., with an analysis of the text and foreword by J. N. Findlay, Oxford, Oxford University Press.
—— (1991a), *The Encyclopaedia of Logic*, trans. T. F. Geraets, W. A. Suchting, and H. S. Harris, Indianapolis, Hackett.

——(1991b), *Elements of the Philosophy of Right*, trans. H. B. Nisbet and ed. Allen W. Wood, Cambridge, Cambridge University Press.
Henkin, Louis (1992), 'The Role of Law and Its Limitations' in *International Relations in the Twentieth Century*, Marc Williams, ed., London, Macmillan, pp. 185–94.
Herbert, Auberon (1978), *The Rights and Wrong of Compulsion by the State* (1885). Reprinted in *The Rights and Wrong of Compulsion by the State and Other Essays*, Indianapolis, Liberty Fund.
Hesse, Carla and Post, Robert, eds., (1999), *Human Rights in Political Transitions: Gettysburg to Bosnia*, New York, Zone Books.
Hickford, Mark (2006), '"Decidedly the Most Interesting Savages on the Globre": An Approach to the Intellectual History of Māori property Rights, 1837–53', *History of Political Thought*, vol. xxvii, pp. 122–67.
Hinsch, Wilfred (2001), 'Global Distributive Justice' in *Global Justice*, Thomas Pogge, ed., Oxford, Blackwell, pp. 55–75.
—— and Markus, S. (2006), 'Human Rights as Moral Claim Rights' in *Rawls's Law of Peoples, a Realistic Utopia?*, Rex Martin and David Reidy, eds., Oxford, Blackwell, pp. 117–33.
Hitchens, Christopher (2007), *Thomas Jefferson: Author of America*, London, Harper Collins.
Hobbes, Thomas (1841), *Philosophical Rudiments Concerning Government*, in *English Works*, vol. II, W. Molesworth, ed., London, Bohn.
——(1991), *Leviathan*, Richard Tuck, ed., Cambridge, Cambridge University Press.
——(1994), *The Elements of Law: Human Nature and De Corpore Politico*, J. C. A. Gaskin, ed., Oxford, Oxford University Press.
Hobhouse, L. T. (1951: first published 1918), *The Metaphysical Theory of the State: A Criticism*, London, Macmillan.
——(1972: first published 1904), *Democracy and Reaction*, Peter Clarke, ed., London, Harvester. This edition includes Hobhouse's introduction to the second edition of 1909.
Hobhouse, Leonard (1898), 'The Ethical Basis of Collectivism', *International Journal of Ethics*, vol. VII, pp. 137–56.
——(1899), 'The Foreign Policy of Collectivism', *Economic Review*, vol. IX (Christian Social Union), pp. 197–220.
Hobsbawm, E. J. (1987), *The Age of Empire: 1875–1914*, London, Weidenfield and Nicolson.
Hobson, J. A. (1901), 'Socialistic Imperialism', *International Journal of Ethics*, vol. 12 pp. 44–58.
——(1909), *The Crisis of Liberalism*, London, King.
——(1915a), *Democracy after the War*, London, Allen and Unwin.
——(1915b), *Towards International Government*, London, Allen and Unwin.
——(1916), 'The War and British Liberties', *The Nation*, June 10, pp. 307–8.
——(1988), *Imperialism: A Study*, edited with an introduction by J. Townshend, third edition, London, Unwin Hyman.
Holbrook, Jon (2002), 'Humanitarian Intervention and the Recasting of International Law' in *Rethinking Human Rights*, David Chandler, ed., London, Palgrave, pp. 136–54.
Holland, T. E. (1880), *The Elements of Jurisprudence*, Oxford, Claredon Press.
Hollis, Martin (1996), 'Honour Among Thieves' in *Reason in Action: Essays in the Philosophy of Social Science* by Martin Hollis, Cambridge, Cambridge University Press, pp. 103–30.
Holmes, Robert L. (1989), *On War and Morality*, Princeton, Princeton University Press.
Homer (1970), *Iliad*, trans. W. H. D. Rouse, London, Heron Books.
——(2003), *The Odyssey*, trans. E. V. Rieu, revised by D. C. H. Rieu, London, Penguin.

Honig, Bonnie (2006), 'Another Cosmopolitanism? Law and Politics in the New Europe' in Seyla Benhabib, with Jeremy Waldron, Bonnie Honig and Will Kymlicka, *Another Cosmopolitanism*, Oxford, Oxford University Press, pp. 102–27.
Hook, Andrew (1998), *From Goosecreek to Gandercleugh: Studies in Scottish-American Literary and Cultural History*, East Lothian, Tuckwell Press.
Housley, Norman (2006), *Contesting the Crusades*, Oxford, Blackwell.
Hume, David (1964), *The Philosophical Works of David Hume*, T. H. Green and T. H. Grose, eds., 4 vols, London Aalen.
—— (1987), *Essays, Moral, Political, and Literary*, Eugene F. Miller, ed., revised edition, Indianapolis, Liberty.
—— (1992), *A Treatise of Human Nature*, L. A. Selby-Bigge, ed., second edition revised by P. H. Nidditch, Oxford, Oxford University Press.
—— (1994), *Political Essays*, Knud Haakonssen, ed., Cambridge, Cambridge University Press.
—— (2004), *Enquires Concerning Human Understanding and Concerning the Principles of Morals*, Indianapolis, Liberty Fund.
Humm, Maggie (1989), *The Dictionary of Feminist Theory*, Hemel Hempstead, Harvester Wheatsheaf.
Hunt, Lynn, ed., and trans. (1996), *The French Revolution and Human Rights: A Brief Documentary History*, New York, St Martin's.
Hutson, James H. (1992), 'A Bill of Rights and the American Revolutionary Experience', in *A Culture of Rights: The Bill of Rights in Philosophy, Politics and Law, 1791–1991*, Michael J. Lacey and Knud Haakonssen, eds., Cambridge, Cambridge University Press, pp. 62–97.
Huxley, T. H. (1890a), 'On the Natural Inequality of Men', *The Nineteenth Century*, vol. clv, January, pp. 1–23.
—— (1890b), 'Natural Rights and Political Rights' *The Nineteenth Century*, vol. clvl, February, pp. 173–95.
—— (1989), *Evolution and Ethics: T. H. Huxley's Evolution and Ethics with New Essays on Its Victorian Sociobiological Context*, J. Paradis and G. C. Williams, eds., Princeton, Princeton University Press
Ignatieff, Michael (1999), 'Human Rights' in *Human Rights in Political Transitions: Gettysburg to Bosnia*, Carla Hesse and Robert Post, eds., New York, Zone Books, pp. 313–24.
—— (2001), *Human Rights as Politics and Idolatry*, Amy Gutmann, ed., with commentary by K. Antony Appiah, David Hollinger, Thomas W. Laqeur, Diane F. Orentlicher, Princeton, Princeton University Press.
—— (2005), 'Introduction: American Exceptionalism and Human Rights' in *American Exceptionalism and Human Rights*, Michael Ignatieff, ed., Princeton, Princeton University Press, pp. 1–26.
Immerwahr, John (1992), 'Hume's Revised Racism', *Journal of the History of Ideas*, vol. 53, pp. 481–6.
Inwood, Brad and Gerson, Lloyd P. (1988), *Hellenistic Philosophy*, Indianapolis, Hackett.
Ireland, Ralph R. (1951), 'Auguste Comte's View of Slavery', *The Journal of Negro Education*, vol. 20, pp. 558–61.
Isaac, Benjamin (2004), *The Invention of Racism in Classical Antiquity*, Princeton, Princeton University Press.
Jahn, Beate (2000), *The Cultural Construction of International Relations: The Invention of the State of Nature*, London, Palgrave.
Jefferson, Thomas (1964), *Notes on the State of Virginia*, New York, Harper Torchback.

Jennings, J. Y. (1981), 'What Is International Law and How Do We Tell When We See It?', *Annuare Suisse de Droit International*, vol. 37, pp. 59–88.
Jennings, Jeremy (1994), 'Rousseau, Social Contract and Modern Leviathan' in *The Social Contract from Hobbes to Rawls*, David Boucher and Paul Kelly, eds., London, Routledge, pp. 115–31.
Johnson, James Turner (1981), *Just War Tradition and the Restraint of War*, Princeton, Princeton University Press.
Johnson, Patricia Altenberd (2001), *On Arendt*, Belmont, California, Wadsworth.
Johnson, Paul (1984), *A History of Christianity*, Harmondsworth, Pelican Books.
Jones, Henry (1914–15), 'Why We Are Fighting', *Hibbert Journal*, XIII, pp. 50–67.
—— (1916), 'Morality in Relation to the War' in *Ethical and Religious Problems of the War*, London, Lindsay, pp. 21–45.
—— (1918), Jones, 'Form the League of Peace Now: An Appeal to My Fellow Citizens', London, League of Nations Union.
—— (1919), *The Principles of Citizenship*, London, Macmillan.
—— (1997), 'The Social Organism' in *The British Idealists*, D. Boucher, ed., Cambridge, Cambridge University Press, pp. 3–29.
—— and Muirhead, John Henry (1921), *The Life and Philosophy of Edward Caird*, Glasgow, Maclehose.
Jones, Peter (1991), 'Human Rights' in *The Blackwell Encyclopaedia of Political Thought*, David Miller, Janet Coleman, William Connelly and Alan Ryan, eds., Oxford, Blackwell, pp. 222–5.
—— (1996), 'International Human Rights: Philosophical or Political?' in *National Rights, International Obligations*, Simon Caney et al., eds., Boulder, Colorado, Westview, pp. 183–204.
Jordan, Winthrop (1968), *White over Black: American Attitudes towards the Negro, 1550–1812*, Chapel Hill, University of North Carolina Press.
Joyce, J. A. (1978), *The New Politics of Human Rights*, London, Macmillan.
Judt, Tony (1996), *A Grand Illusion: An Essay on Europe*, New York, Hill and Wang.
Kabeer, Naila (1991), *Gender, Production and Well-Being: rethinking the household economy*, Brighton, Institute of Development Studies.
—— (1998), 'Money Can't Buy Me Love'? *Re-evaluating Gender, Credit and Empowerment in Bangladesh*, Institute of Development Studies Discussion Paper, No. 363.
Kant, Immanuel (1991), *Political Writings*, Hans Reiss, ed., second edition, Cambridge, Cambridge University Press.
—— (1997*a*), 'On the Different Races on Man', *Race and the Enlightenment: A Reader*, Emmanuel Chukwudi Eze, ed., Oxford, Blackwell, pp. 38–49.
—— (1997*b*), 'On National Characteristics, So Far As They Depend upon the Distinct Feeling of the Beautiful and Sublime', *Race and the Enlightenment: A Reader*, Emmanuel Chukwudi Eze, ed., Oxford, Blackwell, pp. 49–57.
Kapur, Ratner (2006), 'Revisioning the Role of Law in Women's Human Rights Struggles' in *The Legalization of Human Rights: Multidisciplinary Perspectives on Human Rights and Human Rights Law*, Saladin Meckled-García and Bažak Çali, eds., London, Routledge, pp. 101–16.
Keene, Edward (2002), *Beyond the Anarchical Society: Grotius, Colonialism and Order in World Politics*, Cambridge, Cambridge University Press.
—— (2005), *International Political Thought: A Historical Introduction*, Cambridge, Polity.
Kelly, J. M. (1992), *A Short History of Western Legal Theory*, Oxford, Oxford University Press.

Kerr, Rachel (2000), 'International Judicial Intervention: The International Criminal Tribunal for the Former Yugoslavia', *International Relations*, vol. 15, pp. 17–26.
—— (2004), *The International Criminal Tribunal for the Former Yugoslavia: An Exercise in Law, Politics and Diplomacy*, Oxford, Oxford University Press.
King, Martin Luther (1967), *Where Do We Go from Here: Chaos or Community*, New York, Harper Row.
Kirk, Russell (1987) *Edmund Burke: A Genius Reconsidered*, New Rochelle, Open Court Publishing.
Knowles, Dudley (2001), *Political Philosophy*, London, Routledge.
Knutsen, Torbjörn (1992), *A History of International Relations Theory*, Manchester, Manchester University Press.
Koebner, Richard and Schmidt, Helmut Dan (1964), *Imperialism: The Story and Significance of a Political Word 1840–1960*, Cambridge, Cambridge University Press.
Koh, Harold Hongju (2006), 'The New Global Slave Trade' in *Displacement, Asylum, Migration*, Kate E Tunstall, ed., Oxford, Oxford University Press, pp. 232–55.
Kolakowski, Leszek (1990), *Modernity on Endless Trial*, Chicago, University of Chicago Press.
Krasner, Stephen D. (1999), *Sovereignty: Organized Hypocrisy*, Princeton, Princeton University Press.
Kretzman, Norman, Kenny, Anthony, Pinborg, Jan, eds., Stump, Eleonore, associate ed. (1982), *The Cambridge History of Later Medieval Philosophy*, Cambridge University Press.
Kymlicka, Will (1998), 'Human Rights and Ethnocultural Justice', John Rees Memorial Lecture, Swansea, University of Wales.
—— (2006), 'Liberal Nationalism and Cosmopolitan Justice' in Seyla Benhabib (2006), *Another Cosmopolitanism*, with commentaries by Jeremy Waldron, Bonnie Honig, and Will Kymlicka, Oxford, Oxford University Press, pp. 128–44.
—— (2007), *Multicultural Odysseys: Navigating the New International Politics of Diversity*, Oxford, Oxford University Press
Lang, Anthony F. Jr. and Williams, John, eds. (2005), *Hannah Arendt and International Relations*, London, Palgrave.
Lapid, Josef and Kratochwil, Friedrich, eds. (1996), *The Return of Culture and Identity*, Boulder, Colorado, Lynne Rienner.
Laughland, John (2002), 'Human Rights and the Rule of Law: Achieving Universal Justice' in *Rethinking Human Rights*, David Chandler, ed., London, Palgrave, pp. 38–56.
Lauterpacht, Hersh (1945), *An International Bill of the Rights of Man*, New York, Columbia University Press.
Lebovics, Herman (1986), 'The Uses of America in Locke's Second Treatise of Government', *Journal of the History of Ideas*, vol. 47, pp. 567–81.
Leighton, Denys P. (2004), *The Greenian Movement: T. H. Green, Religion and Political Argument in Victorian Britain*, Exeter, Imprint Academic.
Leon-Portilla, Miguel (1992), *The Broken Spears: The Aztec Account of the Conquest of Mexico*, Boston, Beacon Press.
Lester, Geoffrey S. (1984), *Inuit Territorial Rights in the Canadian Northwest Territories*, Canada, Published by Tungavik Federation of Nunavut.
Light, Margot and Halliday, Fred (1994), 'Gender and International Relations' in A. J. R. Groom and Margot Light, eds., *Contemporary International Relations: A Guide to Theory*, London, Pinter, pp. 45–55.
Lindqvist, Sven (2007), *Terra Nullius: A Journey Through No One's Land*, trans. Sarah Death, London, Granta Books.

Linklater, Andrew (1990), *Men and Citizens in the Theory of International Relations*, second edition, London, Macmillan.
Lisska, J. Antony (1996), *Aquinas's Theory of Natural Law: An Analytic Reconstruction*, Oxford, Clarendon Press.
Livingstone, Donald (1989), 'Hume's Criticism of Natural Rights: Taking Virtues Seriously', *The World and I*, Issue 3.
Lloyd, Thomas D. A. (1995), *Locke*, London, Routledge, 1995.
Lobban, Michael (2007), 'Common Law Reasoning and the Law of Nations' in *The Nature of Customary Law: Legal, Historical and Philosophical Perspectives*, Amanda Perreau-Saussine and James Bernard Murphy, eds., Cambridge, Cambridge University Press, pp. 256–78.
Locke, John (1988), *Two Treatises of Government*, Peter Laslett, ed., Cambridge, Cambridge University Press.
Lorimer, James (1883), *The Institutes of the Law of Nations: A Treatise of the Jural Relations of Separate Political Communities*, vol. 1, Edinburgh, William Blackwood and Sons.
Lumsdaine, David Halloram (1993), *Moral Vision: The Foreign Aid Regime, 1949–1989*, Princeton, Princeton University Press.
Luscombe, D. E. (1982a), 'Natural Morality and Natural Law' in N. Kretzmann, Antony Kenny, J. Pinborg, eds., *The Cambridge History of Later Medieval Philosophy: From the Rediscovery of Aristotle to the Disintegration of Scholasticism 1100–1600*, Cambridge, Cambridge University Press, pp. 705–19.
—— (1982b), 'The State of Nature and the Origin of the State', N. Kretzmann, Antony Kenny, J. Pinborg, eds., *The Cambridge History of Later Medieval Philosophy: From the Rediscovery of Aristotle to the Disintegration of Scholasticism 1100–1600*, Cambridge, Cambridge University Press, pp. 757–70.
Lutz, Ellen L. and Sikkink, Kathryn (2000), 'International Human Rights Law and Practice in Latin America', *International Organization*, vol. 54, pp. 633–59.
MacCallum, Gerald Jnr. (1967), 'Negative and Positive Freedom', *Philosophical Review*, vol. 76, pp. 312–34.
MacCunn, John (1899) 'Cosmopolitan Duties', *International Journal of Ethics*, vol. 9, no. 2, pp. 152–68.
MacDonald, Margaret (1970), 'Natural Rights' in *Human Rights*, A. I. Meldon, ed., Belmont, California, Wadsworth, pp. 40–60.
MacIntyre, Alasdair (1967), *A Short History of Ethics*, London, Routledge and Kegan Paul.
—— (1981), *After Virtue: A Study in Moral Theory*, London, Duckworth.
MacKenzie, J. S. (1918), *Outlines of Social Philosophy*, London, George Allen and Unwin.
MacKinnon, Catherine (1982), 'Feminism, Marxism and Method and the State: An Agenda for Theory', *Signs*, vol. 7, pp. 515–44.
—— (1987), *Feminism Unmodified: Discourses on Life and Law*, Cambridge, Massachusetts, Harvard University Press.
—— (1989), *Towards a Feminist Theory of the State*, Cambridge, Massachusetts, Harvard University Press.
—— (1993), 'Crimes of War, Crimes of Peace' in *On Human Rights: The Oxford Amnesty Lectures, 1993*, Stephen Shute and Susan Hurley, eds., New York, Harper Collins, pp. 83–109.
MacKinnon, D. M. (1966), 'Natural Law' in *Diplomatic Investigations: Essays in the Theory of International Politics*, Herbert Butterfield, ed., London, Allen and Unwin, pp. 74–88.

Macleod, Alistair M. (2006), 'Rawls's Narrow Doctrine of Human Rights' in *Rawls's Law of Peoples: A Realistic Utopia*, Rex Martin and David A. Reidy, eds., Oxford, Blackwell, pp. 134–49.
Maddock, Kenneth (1983), *Your Land Is Our Land: Aboriginal Land Rights*, Ringwood, Victoria, Penguin Books.
Malanczuk, Peter (1997), *Akehurst's Modern Introduction to International Law*, London, Routledge.
Maritain, Jacques (1949), 'Introduction' in UNESCO, ed., *Human Rights: Comments and Interpretation*, Westport, Connecticut, Greenwood Press.
Marks, Susan and Clapham, Andrew (2005), *International Human Rights Lexicon*, Oxford, Oxford University Press.
Markus, R. A. (1983), 'St. Augustine's Views on the "Just War", The Church and War, *Studies in Church History*, vol. 20, 1–13. Reprinted in John Dunn and Ian Harris, *Augustine*, II, Cheltenham, Elgar, 1997.
Martin, Rex (1986), 'Green on Natural Rights in Hobbes, Spinoza and Locke' in *The Philosophy of T. H. Green*, Andrew Vincent, ed., Aldershot, Gower Publishing, pp. 104–26.
—— (1993), *A System of Rights*, Oxford, Clarendon Press.
—— (2003), 'Rights and Human Rights' in *Multiculturalism, Identity and Rights*, Bruce Haddock and Peter Sutch, eds., London, Routledge, pp. 176–95.
—— and Reidy, David A., eds. (2006*a*), *Rawls's Law of Peoples: A Realistic Utopia*, Oxford, Blackwell.
—— (2006*b*), 'Rawls on Human Rights: Liberal or Universal?' in *Principles and Political Order*, Bruce Haddock, Peri Roberts and Peter Sutch, eds., London, Routledge, pp. 192–207.
Marx, Karl (1978), 'On the Jewish Question' in *The Marx-Engels Reader*, second edition, Robert C. Tucker, ed., New York, Norton, pp. 26–52.
Mather, Janet (2004), 'The Citizenry: Legitimacy and Democracy' in *European Union Enlargement*, Neill Nugent, ed., London, Palgrave, pp. 103–17.
Matua, Makau (2002), *Human Rights: A Political and Cultural Critique*, Philadelphia, University of Pennsylvania Press.
McCrystal, John Williams (1992), 'A Lady's Calling: Mary Astell's Notion of Women', *Political Theory Newsletter*, pp. 156–70.
McGrade, A. S. (1982), 'Rights, Natural Rights, and The Philosophy of Law' in N. Kretzmann, Antony Kenny, J. Pinborg, *The Cambridge History of Later Medieval Philosophy: From the Rediscovery of Aristotle to the Disintegration of Scholasticism 1100–1600*, Cambridge, Cambridge University Press.
McIlwain, C. H. (1932), *The Growth of Political Thought in the West*, New York, Macmillan.
Melden, A. I. (1970), *Human Rights*, Belmont, California, Wadsworth.
—— (1980), *Rights and Persons*, Berkeley, University of California Press.
Meron, Theodor (1989), *Human Rights and Humanitarian Norms as Customary Law*, Oxford, Clarendon Press.
—— (1998), *War Crimes Law Comes of Age: Essays*, Oxford, Clarendon Press.
Mills, Charles W. (1997), *The Racial Contract*, Ithaca, Cornell University Press.
Milne, A. J. M. (1962), *The Social Philosophy of English Idealism*, London, Allen and Unwin.
—— (1986), *Human Rights and Human Diversity: An Essay in the Philosophy of Human Rights*, London, Palgrave Macmillan.
Mitsis, Phillip (1992), 'Natural Law and Natural Right in Post-Aristotelian Philosophy: The Stoics and Their Critics', *Aufstieg und Niedergang der Romischen We*, pp. 4813–50.

Modood, Tariq (2007), *Multiculturalism*, Cambridge, Polity.
Montesquieu, Charles-Louis De Secondat (1989), *The Spirit of the Laws*, Cambridge, Cambridge University Press.
Moore, S. (1991), 'Rousseau on Alienation and the Rights of Man', *History of Political Thought*, vol. XII, pp 73–86.
Morton, Eric (2002), 'Race and Racism in the Works of David Hume', *Journal of African Philosophy*, vol. 1, pp. 1–19.
Muirhead, J. H. (1900), 'What Imperialism Means', in *The British Idealists*, ed. David Boucher, Cambridge, Cambridge University Press, pp. 237–52.
—— ed. (1935), *Bosanquet and His Friends*, London, George Allen and Unwin.
Mullender, Richard (2005), 'The Reasonable Person, The Pursuit of Justice, and Negligence Law', *Modern Law Review*, vol. 68, pp. 681–95.
—— (2006), 'Negligence Law's Addressees and the Concept of Community', unpublished paper.
Nelson, Brian, Roberts, David, and Viet, Walter, eds., (1992), *The Idea of Europe: Problems of National and Transnational Identity*, ed., New York, Berg.
Nichols, Robert Lee (2005), 'Realizing the Social Contract: The Case of Colonialism and Indigenous Peoples', *Contemporary Political Theory*, vol. 4, pp. 42–62.
Nickel, James (1987), *Making Sense of Human Rights*, Berkeley, University of California Press.
Nielsen, Kai (1959), 'An Examination of the Thomistic Theory of Natural Moral Law', *Natural Law Forum*, vol. 4, pp. 44–71. Reprinted in John Dunn and Ian Harris, eds., *Aquinas I*, London, Elgar, 1997, pp. 254–81.
Njal's Saga (1956), edited and translated by Carl F. Bayerschmidt and Lee M. Hollander, Lond, Allen and Unwin.
Norman, Richard (1976), *Hegel's Phenomenology: A Philosophical Introduction*, London, Chatto and Windus for University of Sussex Press.
Nozick, Robert (1974), *Anarchy State and Utopia*, Oxford, Basil Blackwell.
Nugent, Neill (2004a) 'The EU and the 10 + 2 Enlargement Round: Opportunities and Challenges' in *European Union Enlargement*, Neill Nugent, ed., London, Palgrave, pp. 34–55.
—— (2004b), 'Conclusions' in *European Union Enlargement*, Neill Nugent, ed., London, Palgrave, pp. 266–73.
Nussbaum, Arthur (1953), *A Concise History of the Law of Nations*, New York, Macmillan.
Nussbaum, Martha C. (1999), *Sex and Social Justice*, Oxford, Oxford University Press.
—— (2000), *Women and Human Development*, Cambridge, Cambridge University Press.
—— (2004), *Hiding From Humanity: Disgust, Shame, and the Law*, Princeton, Princeton University Press.
—— (2006), *Frontiers of Justice: Disability, Nationality, Species Membership*, Cambridge, Massachusetts, Harvard University Press.
O'Hagan, Timothy (2003), *Rousseau*, London, Routledge.
O'Neill, Onora (1996), *Towards Justice and Virtue: A Constructive Account of Practical Reasoning*, Cambridge, Cambridge University Press.
Oakeshott, Michael (1933), *Experience and its Modes*, Cambridge, Cambridge University Press.
—— (1975a), *Hobbes on Civil Association*, Oxford, Blackwell.
—— (1975b), *On Human Conduct*, Oxford, Clarendon Press.
—— (1983), *On History and other Essays*, Oxford, Blackwell.

Oakeshott, Michael (1991), *Rationalism in Politics and Other Essays*, new and expanded edition, Timothy Fuller, ed., Indianapolis, Liberty.
—— (2004), *What Is History and Other Essays*, Exeter, Imprint Academic.
—— (2006), *Lectures in the History of Political Thought*, Exeter, Imprint Academic.
O'Brien, Conor Cruise (1969), 'Introduction' to Edmund Burke, *Reflections*, Harmondsworth, Penguin.
Ockham, William Of (1992), *A Short Discourse of Tyrannical Government*, edited by A. S. McGrade and translated by John Kilcullen, Cambridge, Cambridge University Press.
Offer, John (1999), 'Idealist Thought, Social Policy and the Rediscovery of Informal Care', *British Journal of Sociology*, vol. 50, pp. 467–88.
Okin, Susan Moller (1999), 'Is Multiculturalism Bad for Women' in *Is Multiculturalism Bad for Women: Susan Moller Okin with Respondents*, Joshua Cohen, Matthew Howard and Martha Nussbaum, eds., Princeton, Princeton University Press, pp. 9–24.
—— (2005), 'Women's Human Rights in the Late Twentieth Century: One Step Forward and Two Steps Back' in *Sex Rights*, Nicholas Bamforth, ed., Oxford, Oxford University Press, pp. 83–118.
Olonisakin, Funmi (1997), 'An International War Crimes Tribunal for Africa: Problems and Prospects', *African Journal of International and Comparative Law*, vol. 9, pp. 822–35.
Onuf, Nicholas Greenwood (1998), *The Republican Legacy in International Thought*, Cambridge, Cambridge University Press.
Oppenheim, Lassa (1955), *International Law: A Treatise*, 1905, revised eighth edition, *Peace*, vol. 1, prepared by Sir Hersch Lauterpacht, London, Longmans Green and Co.
Otter, Sandra Den (1996), *British Idealism and Social Explanation*, Oxford, Clarendon Press.
Pagden, Anthony (1982), *The Fall of Natural Man: The American Indian and the Origins of Comparative Ethnology*, Cambridge, Cambridge University Press.
—— (1987), 'Dispossessing the Barbarian: The Language of Spanish Thomism and the Debate Over the Property Rights of the American Indians' in *The Languages of Political Theory in Early-Modern Europe*, Anthony Pagden, ed., Cambridge, Cambridge University Press, pp. 79–98.
—— (1990), *Spanish Imperialism and the Political Imagination: Studies in European and Spanish-American Social and Political Theory*, New Haven, Yale University Press.
—— (1993), *European Encounters with the New World: From Renaissance to Romanticism*, New Haven and London, Yale University Press.
Paine, Thomas (1987), *The Thomas Paine Reader*, Michael Foot and Isaac Kramnick, eds., Harmondsworth, Penguin.
—— (1989), *Political Writings*, Bruce Kuklick, ed., Cambridge, Cambridge University Press.
Paley, William (1799), *The Principles of Moral Philosophy*, twelfth edition corrected by the author, London, Faulder.
Palmer, Stephanie (2002), 'Feminism and the Promise of Human Rights: Possibilities and Paradoxes' in *Visible Women: Essays on Feminist Legal Theory and Political Philosophy*, Susan James and Stephanie Palmer, eds., Oxford, Hart, pp. 91–115.
Pangle, Thomas L. (1991), 'Montesquieu, Michel De', in *The Blackwell Encyclopaedia of Political Thought*, David Miller, Janet Coleman, William Connelly, and Alan Ryan, eds., Oxford, Blackwell, pp. 344–7.
Parkinson, Frank (1977), *The Philosophy of International Relations*, Beverly Hills, Sage.
Parry, John H. (1981), *The Age of Reconnaissance: Discovery, Exploration and Settlement 1450–1650*, Berkeley, University of California Press.
—— (1990), *The Spanish Seaborne Empire*, Berkeley, University of California Press.

Pateman, Carole (1988), *The Sexual Contract*, Cambridge, Polity.
—— (1998), 'Democracy, Freedom and Special Rights', in *Social Justice from Hume to Walzer*, David Boucher and Paul Kelly, eds., London, Routledge, pp. 215–31.
—— (2003), 'Wollstonecraft', in *Political Thinkers from Socrates to the Present*, David Boucher and Paul Kelly, eds., Oxford, Oxford University Press, pp. 270–87.
—— and Mills, Charles (2007), *Contract and Domination*, Cambridge, Polity Press.
Patterson, Orlando (1995), 'Freedom, Slavery and the Modern Conception of Rights' in Olwen Hufton, ed., *Historical change and Human Rights*, New York, Basic Books, pp. 131–78.
Perry, Michael J. (1998), *The Idea of Human Rights: Four Inquiries*, Oxford, Oxford University Press.
Peterson, V. Spike and Parisi, Laura (1998), 'Are Women Human? It's not an Academic Question' in *Human Rights Fifty Years on: A Reappraisal*, Tony Evans, ed., Manchester, Manchester University Press, pp. 132–60.
Pettman, Jan (1996), *Worlding Women: Feminist International Politics*, London, Routledge.
Phillips, Anne (2007), *Multiculturalism without Culture*, Princeton, Princeton University Press.
Phillipson, Coleman (1911), *The International Law and Custom of Ancient Greece and Rome*, London, Macmillan.
—— (1915), 'Franciscus A Victoria (1480–46) International Law and War', *Journal of the Society of Comparative Legislation*, New Ser., vol. 15, No. 2, pp. 175–97.
—— (1968), 'Albericus Gentili' in *Great Jurists of the World*, John MacDonell and Edward Manson, eds., reprint 1914, New York, Kelley, pp. 109–143.
Philp, Mark (1989), *Paine*, Oxford, Oxford University Press.
Pink, Thomas (2004), 'Moral Obligation' in *Modern Moral Philosophy*, Anthony O'Hear, ed., Cambridge University Press, pp. 159–86.
—— (2005), 'Natural Law and the Theory of Moral Obligation' in *Moral Philosophy on the Threshold of Modernity*, Jill Kraye and Risto Saarinen. eds., Dordrecht, Springer, pp. 31–50.
Plato (1934), *Laws*, trans. A. E. Taylor, London, Dent.
—— (1987), *Protagoras*, Harmondsworth, Penguin.
Pocock, J. G. A. (1974), *The Ancient Constitution and the Common Law*, Bath, Cedric Chivers for the Library Association.
—— (1987), 'Introduction' to *Reflections on the Revolution in France*, Indianapolis, Hackett, pp. vii–xlviii.
—— (2001), 'The Treaty Between Histories' in *Histories, Power and Loss: Uses of the past – A New Zealand Commentary'*, Andrew Sharp and Pane McHuge, eds., Wellington: New Zealand, Bridger Williams Books, pp. 75–95.
Pogge, Thomas (1994), 'Cosmopolitanism and Sovereignty' in *Political Restructuring in Europe*, Chris Brown, ed., London, Routledge, pp. 89–122.
—— ed., (2001), *Global Justice*, Oxford, Blackwell.
—— (2002), *World Poverty and Human Rights*, Cambridge, Polity.
—— (2007), 'Severe Poverty as a Human Rights Violation' in *Freedom from Poverty as a Human Right*, Thomas Pogge, ed., Oxford, Oxford University Press, pp. 11–54.
Popkin, Richard H. (1977), 'Hume's Racism', *Philosophical Forum*, vol. 9, pp. 211–26.
—— (1992), *The Third Force in Seventeenth-Century Thought*, Leiden, Brill.
—— (1993), 'The Philosophical Bases of Modern Racism', in *The High Road to Pyrrhonism*, Indianapolis, Hackett, pp. 79–102.

Porter, Jean (2007), 'Custom, Ordinance and Natural Rights in Gratian's *Decretum*' in *The Nature of Customary Law: Legal, Historical and Philosophical Perspectives*, Amanda Perreau-Saussine and James Bernard Murphy, eds., Cambridge, Cambridge University Press, pp. 79–100.

Postema, Gerald J. (1986), *Bentham and the Common Law Tradition*, Oxford, Oxford University Press.

——— (2007), 'Custom in International Law' in *The Nature of Customary Law: Legal, Historical and Philosophical Perspectives*, Amanda Perreau-Saussine and James Bernard Murphy, eds., Cambridge, Cambridge University Press, pp. 279–306.

Price, Richard (1991), *Political Writings*, D. O. Thomas, ed., Cambridge, Cambridge University Press.

Priestley, Joseph (1993), *Political Writings*, Peter Miller, ed., Cambridge, Cambridge University Press.

Pufendorf, Samuel Von (1717), *The Law of Nature and Nations*, trans. Basil Kennet, London, R. Sare, *et al.*

——— (1931), *Elementorum Jurisprudentiae Universalis Libri Duo*, Oxford, Clarendon Press, vol. II, translation.

——— (1991), *On the Duty of Man and Citizen*, trans. and ed. J. Tully, Cambridge, Cambridge University Press.

——— [1687] (2002), *Of the Nature and Qualifications of Religion in Reference to Civil Society*, trans. Jodocus Crull, edited with an introduction by Simone Zurbuchen, Indianapolis, Liberty Fund.

Quirk, Robert E. (1954), 'Some Notes on a Controversial Controversy: Juan Ginés de Sepúlveda and Natural Servitude', *The Hispanic American Historical Review*, vol. 34, pp. 357–64.

Rachel, Samuel, [1676] (1916), *Dissertations on The Law of Nature and of Nations*, trans. John Pawley Bate, with an introduction by Ludwig von Bar, Washington, D.C., Carnegie Institution.

Radin, Max (1950), 'Natural Law and Natural Rights', *Yale Law Journal*, vol. 59, pp. 214–37.

Rajan, Rajeswari Sunder (2005), 'Women's Human Rights in the Third World' in *Sex Rights*, Nicholas Bamforth, ed., Oxford, Oxford University Press, pp. 119–36.

Ramsey, Paul (1961), *War and the Christian Conscience*, Durham, North Carolina, Duke University Press.

——— (1992), 'The Just War According to St. Augustine' in *Just War Theory*, Jean Bethke Elshtain, ed., Oxford, Backwell, pp. 8–22.

Rawls, John (1972), *A Theory of Justice*, Oxford, Oxford University Press.

——— (1993), *Political Liberalism*, New York, Columbia University Press.

——— (1999), *The Law of Peoples*, Cambridge, Massachusetts, Harvard University Press.

Raz, Joseph (1984), *Morality and Freedom*, Oxford, Oxford University Press.

Reidy, David A. (2006), 'Political Authority of Human Rights' in *Rawls's Law of Peoples: A Realistic Utopia*, Rex Martin and David A. Reidy, eds., Oxford, Blackwell, pp. 169–88.

Remec, Peter Pavel (1960), *The Position of the Individual in International Law According to Grotius and Vattel*, The Hague, Nijhoff.

Reynolds, Henry (1992), *The Law of the Land*, Ringwood, Penguin Books Australia.

——— (1999), *Why Weren't We Told? A Personal Search for the Truth about Our History*, Ringwood, Penguin Books Australia.

——— (2004), 'Terra Nullius Reborn' in *Whitewash: On Keith Windshuttle's Fabrication of Aboriginal History*, Robert Manne, ed., Melbourne, Black.

Richter, Melvin (1996), *The Politics of Conscience: T. H. Green and His Age*, Bristol, Thoemmes Press.
Riedel, Manfred (1971), *Between Tradition and Revolution: The Hegelian Transformation of Political Philosophy*, Cambridge, Cambridge University Press.
Riley-Smith, J. (1980), 'Crusading as an Act of Love', *History*, vol. 65, pp. 177–92.
—— (1984), 'The First Crusade and the Persecution of the Jews', *Studies in Church History*, vol. 21, pp. 51–72.
—— (1987), *The Crusades: A Short History*, Athlone Press.
Risse, Thomas, Ropp, Stephen C. and Kathryn Sikkink, eds. (1999), *The Power of Human Rights: International Norms and Domestic Change*, Cambridge, Cambridge University Press.
Rist, J. M. (1977), *Stoic Philosophy*, Cambridge, Cambridge University Press.
Ritchie, David (1891*a*), *Principles of State Interference*, London, Swan Sonnenschein.
—— (1891*b*), 'On the Conception of Sovereignty', *Annals of the American Academy of Political and Social Science*, vol. 3, pp. 385–411.
—— (1894), *Natural Rights*, London, Swan Sonnenschein.
—— (1900–1901), 'War and Peace', *International Journal of Ethics*, vol. XI. pp. 137–58.
—— (1903*a*), *Natural Rights*, second edition, London, Swan Sonnenschein.
—— (1903*b*), *Natural Rights: A Criticism of Some Political and Ethical Conceptions*, second edition, London, George Allen.
—— (1917), *Darwinism and Politics*, fourth edition, London, Swan Sonnenschien.
—— (1997), 'Ethical Democracy: Evolution and Democracy', with annotations, in *The British Idealists*, David Boucher, ed., Cambridge, Cambridge University Press, pp. 60–93. It is also reprinted in vol. 6 of Ritchie's *Collected Works, Miscellaneous Writings: Articles and Discussion, Book Reviews and Critical Notices, Letters*, Peter Nicholson, ed., Bristol, Thoemmes Press.
—— (1998*a*), Review of Burgess, *Political Science and Comparative Constitutional Law*, in *Miscellaneous Writings: Articles and Discussion, Book reviews and Critical Notices Letters*, Peter Nicholson, ed., Bristol, Thoemmes Press, pp. 439–42.
—— (1998*b*), Review of *Knowing and Being* by John Veitch, in *Miscellaneous Writings*, Peter Nicholson, ed., Bristol, Thoemmes Press, pp. 574–79.
—— (1998*c*),'Is Human Law the Basis of Morality, or Morality of Human Law' in *Miscellaneous Writings*, Peter Nicholson, ed., Bristol, Thoemmes Press, pp. 124–9.
—— (1998*d*), Review of *The Elements of Politics*, in *Miscellaneous Writings*, Peter Nicholson, ed., Bristol, Thoemmes Press, pp. 254–7.
—— (1998*e*), Review of James Bonar, *Philosophy and Political Economy in Some of their Historical Relations*, in *Miscellaneous Writings*, Peter Nicholson, ed., Bristol, Thoemmes Press, pp. 541–55.
—— (1998*f*), 'Moral Problems of the War – in reply to Mr. J. M. Robertson', *Miscellaneous Writings*, Peter Nicholson, ed., Bristol, Thoemmes Press, pp. 493–505.
Robertson, A. H. and Merrills, J. G. (1996), *Human Rights in the World*, Manchester, University of Manchester Press.
Robertson, Geoffrey (2000), *Crimes against Humanity: The Struggle for Global Justice*, London, Penguin. Includes additional material. First published by Allen Lane 1999.
Robinson, Fiona (1998), 'The limits of a rights-based approach to international ethics' in Tony Evans, ed., *Human Rights Fifty Years On: A Reappraisal*, Manchester, Manchester University Press, pp. 58–76.
Rorty, Richard (1980), *Philosophy and the Mirror of Nature*, Oxford, Blackwells.
—— (1989), *Contingency, Irony and Solidarity*, Cambridge, Cambridge University Press.

Rorty, Richard (1993), 'Human Rights, Rationality, and Sentimentality' in *On Human Rights*, Stephen Shute and Susan Hurley, eds., New York, Basic Books, pp. 111–34.
—— (1996), 'Who Are We: Moral Universalism and Economic Triage', *Diogenes* (173), vol. 44, pp. 5–15.
—— (2001), 'Justice as a Larger Loyalty' in Matthew Festenstein and Simon Thompson, eds., *Richard Rorty: Critical Dialogues*, Cambridge, Polity, pp. 223–37.
Ross, W. D. (1930), *The Right and the Good*, Oxford, Clarendon Press.
Rousseau, Jean-Jacques (1911), *Émile*, trans. Barbara Foxley, London, Everyman.
—— (1987), *The Basic Political Writings*, Donald A. Cress, ed., intro. Peter Gay, Indianapolis, Hackett (includes *Discourse on the Sciences and Arts*; *Discourse on the Origin of Inequality*; *Discourse on Political Economy*; *On the Social Contract*).
—— (1988), *Rousseau's Political Writings*, Alan Ritter and Julia Conaway Bondanella, eds., New York, Norton (includes *Discourse on the Origin and Foundations of Inequality Among Men*, *Discourse on Political Economy* and *On Social Contract or Principles of Right*. It also includes reactions to and commentaries on Rousseau).
—— (1991), *Rousseau on International Relations*, Stanley Hoffmann and David P. Fidler, eds., Oxford, Clarendon Press (includes the Geneva Manuscript of *The Social Contract*; *Constitutional Project for Corsica*; *Considerations on the Government of Poland*; *The State of War*).
—— (1994), *The Collected Writings of Rousseau*, vols. 2 and 4, Roger D. Masters and Christopher Kelly, eds., Hanover and London, University Press of New England.
Rowbotham, Sheila (1992), 'The Abolition of Slavery and Women's Emancipation' in Sheila Rowbotha, *Women in Movement: Feminism and Social Action*, London, Routledge, pp. 44–53.
Ruddy, Francis Stephen (1975), *International Law in the Enlightenment: The Background of Emmerich de Vattel's Le Droit des Gens*, Dobbs Ferry, New York, Oceana Publications.
Russell, F. H. (1975), *The Just War in the Middle Ages*, Cambridge, Cambridge University Press.
Samuel, Herbert (1902), *Liberalism: An Attempt to State the Principles of Contemporary Liberalism*, London, Grant Richards.
Sawer, Marian (2003), *The Ethical State? Social Liberalism in Australia*, Melbourne, Melbourne University Press.
Schabas, William A. (2004), *An Introduction to the International Criminal Court*, Cambridge, Cambridge University Press, 2nd edition.
Schall, James V. (1991–92), 'Natural Law and the Law of Nations: Some Theoretical Considerations', *Fordham International Law Journal*, 15, pp. 997–1030.
Schama, Simon (2005), *Rough Crossings: Britain, the Slaves and the American Revolution*, London, BBC Books.
Schauer, Frederick (2007), 'Pitfalls in the Interpretation of Customary Law' in *The Nature of Customary Law: Legal, Historical and Philosophical Perspectives*, Amanda Perreau-Saussine and James Bernard Murphy, eds., Cambridge, Cambridge University Press, pp. 256–78.
Schlaifer, Robert (1936), 'Greek Theories of Slavery from Homer to Aristotle', *Harvard Studies in Classical Philology*, vol. 47, pp. 165–204.
Schofield, Malcolm (1991), *The Stoic Idea of the City*, Cambridge, Cambridge University Press.
Schwarz, Wolfgang (1962–3), 'Kant's Philosophy of Law and International Peace', *Philosophy and Phenomenological Research*, vol. 23, pp. 71–80.

Schwarzenbach, S. A. (1991) 'Rawls, Hegel and Communitarianism', *Political Theory*, vol. 19.
Sellars, J., (2007), 'Stoic Cosmopolitanism and Zeno's *Republic*', *History of Political Thought*, vol. XXVIII, pp. 1–29.
Sen, Amartya (1990), 'More Than a Hundred Women Are Missing', *New York Review of Books*, 20 December, pp. 61–7.
—— (1998), *Reason before Identity*, The Romanes Lecture for 1998, Oxford, Oxford University Press.
—— (1999), *Development and Freedom*, New York, Knopf.
—— (2003), 'Missing Women – Revisited', *British Medical Journal*, 327, 6 December, 1297–8.
Seneca (1995), *Moral and Political Writings*, John M. Cooper and J. F. Procopé, eds., Cambridge, Cambridge University Press.
Sepúlveda, Juan Ginés De (1973), *Apology for the Book on the Just Causes of War: Dedicated to the Most Learned and Distinguished President, Antonio Ramirez, Bishop of Segovia*, trans. Lewis D. Epstein, unpublished, Bowdoin College, USA.
Sharples, R. W. (1996), *Stoics, Epicureans and Sceptics*, London, Routledge.
Sheehan, Michael (1996), *The Balance of Power – History and Theory*, London, Routledge.
Shue, Henry (1996), *Basic Rights*, Princeton, Princeton University Press.
Siddiqi, Dina M. (1998), 'Taslimma Nasreen and Others: The Contest Over Gender in Bangladesh' in *Women and Muslim Societies: Diversity within Unity*, Herbert L. Bodman and Nayereh Tohidi, eds., Colorado and London, Lynne Rienner Publishers, pp. 205–28.
Sikkink, Kathryn (1998), 'International Relations Theory, and Human Rights', *PS: Political Science and Politics*, vol. 31, pp. 516–32.
Sinfield, Alan (2005), 'Rape and Rights: *Measure for Measure* and the Limits of Cultural Imperialism' in *Sex Rights*, Nicholas Bamforth, ed., Oxford, Oxford University Press, pp. 140–58.
Singer, Peter (1971), 'Famine, affluence and morality', *Philosophy and Public Affairs*, vol. 1, pp. 229–43.
—— (1999), 'The Singer Solution to World Poverty', *The New York Times*, September 5.
—— (2002), *One World: The Ethics of Globalization*, Melbourne, Text Publishing.
Skinner, Quentin (1978), *The Foundations of Modern Political Thought*, Cambridge, Cambridge University Press, vols. 1 and 2.
—— (2001), 'The Rise of, Challenge to and Prospects for a Collingwoodian Approach to the History of Political Thought' in *The History of Political Thought in National Context*, Dario Castiglione and Iain Hampshire-Monk, eds., Cambridge, Cambridge University Press, pp. 175–88.
Slaughter, Anne-Marie (2003), 'Leading Through Law', *Wilsonian Quarterly*, vol. 27, pp. 37–44.
Smith, Adam (1982), *An Inquiry into the Nature and Causes of the Wealth of Nations*: vols. 1 and 2 (The Glasgow Edition of the Works & Correspondence of Adam Smith), Indianapolis, Liberty Fund.
Smith, Stephen B. (1989), *Hegel's Critique of Liberalism*, Chicago and London, University of Chicago Press.
Sophocles (1994), *Oedipus the King in Antigone, Oedipus the King, Electra*, Harmondsworth, Penguin.
Sorley, W. R. (1916), 'The State and Morality' in *The International Crisis: The Theory of the State* by Louise Creighton *et al.*, London, Milford and Oxford University Press. pp. 25–55.

Spencer, Herbert [1893] (1978), *The Principles of Ethics*, Indianapolis, Liberty.
—— [1884] (1982), *The Man versus the State: With Six Essays on Government, Society and Freedom*, Indianapolis, Liberty Press.
St. Paul (1926), *The Letters of St. Paul to Seven Churches and Three Friends, with the Letter to the Hebrews*, trans. Arthur S. Way, London, Macmillan.
Stackhouse, M. (1999), 'Human Rights and Public Theology: The Basic Validation of Human Rights' in *Religion and Human Rights: Conflicting Claims*, C. Gustafson and P. Juviler, eds., Armonk, New York, Sharpe, pp. 12–30.
Stanlis, Peter J. (1953), 'Edmund Burke and the Law of Nations', *The American Journal of International Law*, vol. 47, pp. 397–413.
—— (2003), *Edmund Burke and the Natural Law*, with a new introduction by V. Bradley Lewis, New Brunswick, Transaction Publishers.
Stein, Peter (1988), 'Roman Law' in *The Cambridge History of Medieval Political Thought c. 350–c.1450*, J. H. Burns, ed., Cambridge, Cambridge University Press, pp. 42–7.
Steiner, Henry J. and Alston, Philip (1996), *International Human Rights in Context: Law Politics Morals*, Oxford, Clarendon Press.
Steiner, Hillel (1996), 'Territorial Justice' in *National Rights, International Obligations*, Simon Caney, David George, and Peter Jones, eds., Boulder, Colorado, Westview Press, pp. 139–48.
Story, Joseph (1833), *Commentaries on the Constitution of the United States with a Preliminary Review of the Constitutional History of the Colonies and States before the Adoption of the Constitution*, Boston, Hilliard, Gray and Company.
Strauss, Leo (1952), *Persecution and the Art of Writing*, Glencoe, Illinois, The Free Press.
—— (1965), *Natural Right and History*, Chicago, Chicago University Press.
Stromseth, Jane (2003), 'Rethinking Humanitarian Intervention: The Case for Change' in *Humanitarian Intervention: Ethical, Legal and Political Dilemmas*, J. L. Holzgrefe and Robert O. Keohane, eds., Cambridge, Cambridge University Press, pp. 232–72.
Suarez, Francisco (1944), *Selections from Three Works,* translation of the 1621 edition by Gwladys L. Williams, Ammi Brown and John Waldron, Washington, Carnegie Classics.
Sumner, L. W. (1987), *The Moral Foundation of Rights*, Oxford, Clarendon Press.
Sunder, Madhavi (2001), 'Cultural Dissent', *Stanford Law Review*, No. 545, December, pp. 495–567.
Sutch, Peter, *Ethics Justice and International Relations: Constructing an International Community*, Routledge, 2001.
Sweet, William (1997) *Idealism and Rights: The Social Ontology of Human Rights in the Political Thought of Bernard Bosanquet*, Lanham, USA, University of America Press.
Swift, Adam (2001), *Political Philosophy*, Cambridge, Polity.
Sypher, Wylie (1939), 'Hutcheson and the "Classical" Theory of Slavery', *The Journal of Negro History*, vol. 24, pp. 263–80.
Talbot, William J. (2005), *Which Rights Should Be Universal*, Oxford, Oxford University Press.
Tasioulas, John (2007), 'Customary International Law and the Quest for Global Justice' in *The Nature of Customary Law: Legal, Historical and Philosophical Perspectives*, Amanda Perreau-Saussine and James Bernard Murphy, eds., Cambridge, Cambridge University Press, pp. 307–35.
Taylor, Charles (1988), 'The Hermeneutics of Conflict' in *Meaning and Context*, James Tully, ed., Cambridge, Cambridge University Press, pp. 218–28.
—— (1992), *Multiculturalism and the Politics of Recognition*, Princeton, Princeton University Press.

—— (1999), 'Conditions of an Unforced Consensus on Human Rights' in *The East Asian Challenge for Human Rights*, Joanne Bauer and Daniel Bell, eds., Cambridge, Cambridge University Press, pp. 123–44.
—— (2007), *A Secular Age*, Cambridge, Massachusetts, The Belnap Press of Harvard University.
Taylor, M. W. (1993), *Men versus the State: Herbert Spencer and Late Victorian Individualism*, Oxford, Clarendon Press.
Teitel, Ruti G. (2000), *Transitional Justice*, New York, Oxford University Press.
Textor, Johann Wolfgang [1680] (1916), *Synopsis of the Law of Nations*, trans. John Pawley Bate, with an introduction by Ludwig von Bar, Washington, D.C., Carnegie Institution.
Thomas, D. A. (1995), *Locke on Government*, London, Routledge
Thompson, Janna (1992), *Justice and World Order*, London, Routledge.
Thompson, Kenneth (1994), *Fathers of International Thought: The Legacy of Political Theory*, Baton Rouge, Louisiana State University Press.
Tierney, Brian (1984), 'Tuck on Rights: Some Medieval Problems', *History of Political Thought*, vol. IV, pp. 429–42.
—— (1988), 'Villey, Ockham, and the Origin of Individual Rights' in *The Weightier Matters of Law. A Tribute to Harold J. Berman*, T. Witte, and F. S. Alexander, eds., Atlanta, Scholars Press, pp. 1–31.
—— (1989), 'Origins of Natural Rights Language: Texts and Contexts, 1150–1250', *History of Political Thought*, vol. X, pp. 615–46.
—— (1991), 'Aristotle and the American Indians – Again', *Critical Studies*, vol. 12, pp. 295–322.
—— (1997), *The Idea of Natural Rights*, Grand Rapids, Michigan, Eerdmans.
—— (2001), 'Permissive Natural Law and Property: Gratian to Kant', *Journal of the History of Ideas*, vol. 62, pp. 381–99.
—— (2004), 'The Idea of Natural Rights-Origins and Persistence', *North Western Journal of International Human Rights*, vol. 4, pp. 1–12.
—— (2007), 'Vitoria and Suarez on Ius Gentium, Natural Law, and Custom' in *The Nature of Customary Law: Legal, Historical and Philosophical Perspectives*, Amanda Perreau-Saussine and James Bernard Murphy, eds., Cambridge, Cambridge University Press, pp. 101–24.
Timothy, R. S. (1973), *The Tenets of Stoicism: Assembled and Systematised from the Works of L. Annaeus Seneca*, Amsterdam, Hakkert.
Tocqueville, Alexis De (1976), *Democracy in America*, New York, Knopf, 2 vols.
Tolan, J. V. (2002), *Saracens: Islam in the Medieval European Imagination*, New York, Columbia University Press.
Tomuschat, Christian (2003), *Human Rights: Between Idealism and Realism*, Oxford, Oxford University Press.
Tooke, Joanne D. (1965), *The Just War in Aquinas and Grotius*, London, S.P.C.K.
Tuck, Richard (1979), *Natural Rights Theories: Their Origin and Development*, Cambridge, Cambridge University Press.
—— (1987), 'The "modern" theory of natural law' in *The Languages of Political Theory in Early-Modern Europe*, Antony Pagden, ed., Cambridge, Cambridge University Press, pp. 99–122.
—— (1993), 'Grotius and Selden' in *The Cambridge History of Political Thought*, ed. J. H. Burns with the assistance of Mark Goldie, Cambridge, Cambridge University Press, pp. 499–529.

Tuck, Richard (1999), *The Rights of War and Peace: Political Thought and International Order from Grotius to Kant*, Oxford, Oxford University Press.
Tully, James (1999), 'Aboriginal Property and Western Theory: Recovering a Middle Ground', *Social Philosophy and Policy*, vol. 11, pp. 153–80.
Tyler, Colin (1997), *Thomas Hill Green (1836–1882) and the Philosophical Foundations of Politics*, Lewiston, Edward Mellen.
Vattel, Emerich de (1834), *The Law of Nations or the Principles of the Law of Nature: Applied to the Conduct and Affairs of Nations and of Sovereigns*, translation of the 1758 edition by Joseph Chitty, London, Sweet, Stevens, Maxwell and Milliken.
—— (2008), 'Essay on the Foundation of Natural Law and on the First Principle of the Obligation Men Find Themselves Under to Observe Laws' in *The Law of Nations*, ed. Béla Kapossy and Richard Whatmore, Indianapolis, Liberty Fund, pp. 747–71.
Vincent, John (1986), *Human Rights and International Relations*, Cambridge, Cambridge University Press.
—— (1992), 'The Idea of Rights in International Ethics' in *Traditions of International Ethics*, Terry Nardin and David R. Mapel, eds., Cambridge, Cambridge University Press, pp. 250–69.
Vitoria, Francisco De (1991), *Political Writings*, Anthony Pagden and Jeremy Lawrence, eds., Cambridge, Cambridge University Press.
Walbank, F. W. (1992), *The Hellenistic World*, London, Fontana.
Waldron, Jeremy, ed. (1984), *Theories of Rights*, Oxford, Oxford University Press.
—— ed. (1987), *Nonsense Upon Stilts: Bentham, Burke and Marx on the Rights of Man*, London, Methuen University Paperbacks.
—— (1992), 'The Irrelevance of Moral Objectivity' in *Natural Law Theory: Contemporary Essays*, Robert P. George, ed., Oxford, Clarendon Press, pp. 158–87.
—— (1995), 'Minority Cultures and the Cosmopolitan Alternative' in *The Rights of Minority Cultures*, Will Kymlicka, ed., Oxford, Oxford University Press, pp. 79–92.
—— (2002), *God, Locke, and Equality: Christian Foundation in Locke's Political Thought*, Cambridge, Cambridge University Press.
—— (2006), 'Cosmopolitan Norms' in Seyla Benhabib, with Jeremy Waldron, Bonnie Honig, and Will Kymlicka, *Another Cosmopolitanism*, Oxford, Oxford University Press, pp. 83–101.
Walker, R. B. J. (1992), *Inside/Outside: International Relations as Political Theory*, Cambridge, Cambridge University Press.
Walther, Steven T. (1999), 'The Globalization of the Rule of Law and Human Rights', *Futures*, vol. 31, pp. 993–1003.
Waltz, Kenneth N. (1979), *Theory of International Politics*, New York, McGraw-Hill, 1979.
Walzer, Michael (1983), *Spheres of Justice*, Oxford, Basil Blackwell.
—— (1990), 'Nation and Universe' in *Tanner Lectures on Human Values*, G. B. Petersen, ed., Salt Lake City, University of Utah Press, pp. 509–56.
—— (1992), *Just and Unjust Wars*, second edition, New York, Basic Books.
—— (1994), *Thick and Thin*, Notre Dame, Indiana, University of Notre Dame Press.
—— (1995a), 'Response' in *Pluralism Justice and Equality*, David Miller and Michael Walzer, eds., Oxford, Oxford University Press, pp. 280–97.
—— (1995b), 'The Concept of Civil Society' in *Toward A Global Civil Society*, Michael Walzer, ed., Oxford and New York, Berghahm Books, pp. 7–28.
—— (1997), *On Toleration*, New Haven and London, Yale University Press.
—— and Dworkin, Ronald (1983), '*Spheres of Justice*, an Exchange', *New York Review of Books*, 21 July, pp. 43–6.

Watson, Gerard (1971), 'The Natural Law and Stoicism' in *The Problems of Stoicism*, A. A. Long, ed., London, Athlone Press, pp. 216–38.
Watson, John (1919), *The State in War and Peace*, Glasgow, Maclehose.
Weeks, Jeffrey (1995), *Invented Moralities*, Cambridge, Polity Press.
Weinreb, Lloyd W. (1992), 'Natural Law and Rights' in *Natural Law Theory: Contemporary Essays* (1991), Robert P. George, ed., Oxford, Clarendon Press, pp. 278–305.
Weinstein, D. (1990), 'Equal Freedom, Rights and Utility in Spencer's Moral Philosophy', *History of Political Thought*, vol. XI, pp. 119–42.
Wellman, Carl (1995), *Real Rights*, Oxford, Oxford University Press.
—— (1999), *The Proliferation of Rights*, Boulder, Colorado, Westview Press.
Wells, H. G. (1940), *The Rights of Man or What Are We Fighting For?*, London, Penguin.
Welsh, Jennifer (1995), *Edmund Burke and International Relations: The Commonwealth of Europe and the Crusade against the French Revolution*, New York, St. Martin's Press.
Werner, John M. (1972), 'David Hume and America', *Journal of the History of Ideas*, vol. 33, pp. 439–56.
White, Stephen K. (1994), *Edmund Burke: Modernity, Politics and Aesthetics*, Thousand Oakes, California, Sage.
Wight, Martin (1991), *International Theory: The Three Traditions*, G. Wight and B. Porter, eds., Leicester University Press.
—— (2005), *Four Seminal Thinkers in International Theory*, Oxford, Oxford University Press.
Wilde, Lawrence (1994), 'Marx against the Social Contract' in *The Social Contract from Hobbes to Rawls*, David Boucher and Paul Kelly, eds., London, Routledge, pp. 164–74.
Williams, Howard (1992), *International Relations as Political Theory*, Milton Keynes, Open University Press.
Wilson, Anna (1989), 'Mary Wollstonecraft and the Search for the Radical Woman', *Genders*, vol. 6, pp. 88–101.
Wittgenstein, Ludwig (1973), *Philosophical Investigations*, Oxford, Blackwell.
Wolff, Christian [1764] (1934), *The Law of Nations Treated According to Scientific Method in Which the Natural Law of Nations Is Carefully Distinguished from That Which Is Voluntary, Stipulative and Customary*, trans. Joseph H. Drake, with an introduction by O. Nippold, Oxford, Claendon Press.
Wolff, Jonathan (1991), *Robert Nozick: Property Justice and the Minimum State*, Cambridge, Polity Press.
Wolin, Sheldon S. (2001), *Tocqueville between Two Worlds: The Making of a Political and Theoretical Life*, Princeton, Princeton University Press.
Wollstonecraft, Mary (1988, first published, 1792), *A Vindication of the Rights of Woman*, second edition, Carol H. Poston, ed., New York, Norton.
—— (1989, first published 1790), *Vindication of the Rights of Man, Works*, vol. 5, London, William Pickering, pp. 1–69.
Zack, Naomi (1999), 'Philosophy and Racial Paradigms', *The Journal of Value Inquiry*, vol. 33, pp. 299–317.
Zouche, Richard, [1650] (1911), *An Exposition of Fecial Law and Procedure, or of Law between Nations, and Questions Concerning the Same: Wherein Are Set Forth Matters Regarding Peace and War between Different Princes or Peoples, Derived from the Most Eminent Historical Jurists*, trans. L. L. Brierly, T. E. Holland, ed., Washington, DC, Carnegie Institution.

Zuckert, Michael P. (1989), ' "Bringing Philosophy Down from the Heavens": Natural Right in the Roman Law', *Review of Politics*, vol. li, pp. 70–85.
Zunz, Olivier, and Kahan, Alan S., eds. (2002), *The Tocqueville Reader: A Life in Letters and Politics*, Oxford, Blackwell.
Zwanenburg, Marten (1999), 'The Statute for an International Criminal Court and the United States: Peacekeepers under Fire?', *European Journal of International Law*, vol. 10, pp. 124–43.

Index

The letter n refers to a footnote

abduction 250
Abelard, Peter 48
Aboriginal peoples *see* Australia: Aboriginals
abortion 354
Addison, Joseph 159
Adler, Emanuel 293–4
aerial bombardment 371
Africa
  European Trusteeship 124
  families in 255
  and International Criminal Court 359
  and slavery 196
  see also Rwanda; Darfur; Somalia; South Africa; Sudan
African Charter on Human and People's Rights 251, 254–5
agriculture 121, 122, 123
Aguilar, Jose Manuel de 255
al-Bashir, Omar 359, 362
Alanus 97
Alcatraz island (United States) 138
Alexander the Great 25–6
Ambrose, St 45
  on government 47
  and Jews 62
  and just war 58
  and property 57
Ambrosiaster 57
America *see* New World; United States
American Anti-Slavery Society 338
American Convention on Human Rights 250–1
American Declaration of Independence 336–7
American Independence: Hume and 172
American Indians 102, 104
  and agriculture 123
  and Alcatraz island 138
  barbaric practices of 106, 109–10, 112
  and *encomienda* system 191–2
  and humanitarian intervention 109, 114
  and just war 110
  and nationhood 135–7
  and property 108, 129, 133, 178–9
  and slavery 25, 188, 189, 190–4, 198, 201
  and women 197
amnesties 361–2, 363

Amnesty International 1 (quoted), 247–8, 252, 349–50, 357 (quoted)
  International Report on Human Rights 331
Angell, Norman 247
animals
  and morality 171
  and natural law 75, 143, 171, 175
  treatment of 196–7
Annan, Kofi 324
Anscombe, Elizabeth 255
anti-Semitism 65–6, 262, 266
Antiphon 20, 21, 22
apartheid 364
Aquinas, St Thomas
  and civil law 52
  and customary law 55
  and human law 52
  and human virtue 50–1
  and just war 60–2
  and justice 51–2, 55
  and natural law 43–4, 49–56
  and property 57–8
  and reason 50, 54
  and slavery 50
'Arab Charter on Human Rights' 250
Arendt, Hannah 261–7, 282–3, 299, 311
Argentina 364
aristocracy 222
Aristotle
  Athenian Constitution 25
  and morality 22
  Rhetoric 23
  and slavery 14, 15, 24–5, 188–9, 191
Armitage, David 181
Arnold, Thomas 121–2
Aron, Raymond 5
Arusha tribunal 326
Association for Promoting the Higher Education of Women 338, 339
asylum: Europe 252, 264
Athualpa 118
Augustine, St
  City of God, The 46–7
  on government 47
  and heresy 63
  and human nature 43, 44
  and just war 58, 59

Augustine, St (*cont.*)
  on justice 47–8
  and natural law 45
  on original sin 47, 48
  and slavery 46
  and Stoics 28 n2, 47
Australia
  Aboriginals 102, 124, 134, 138, 140, 198, 364–5
  'discovery' 118–19, 120
  Mabo judgement 137
authority: and rights 299
Ayala, Balthazar 71, 74, 80, 108, 112, 116, 189, 194
Ayer, A. J. 169
Aztecs 103–4

Baehr, Peter 251, 317–18
Baier, Annette 172, 274
Bangladesh 343, 348
Banner, Stuart 120
Barbeyrac, Jean 75–6
Barry, Brian 278
Beattie, James 202, 210–11
Beitz, Charles 309
belief 73 *see also* religion
Bellarmine, Robert 72
Belli, Pierino 108, 194
Ben-Gurion, David 267
Benedict XVI, Pope 101–2
Benhabib, Seyla 266, 312, 352–3
Bentham, Jeremy 5, 88, 217, 218, 219–21
Berlin Conference (1884–1885) 124
Bettelheim, Bruno 266
Beyme, Klaus von 375
Bible: natural law in 45
Biel, Gabriel 72
blacks: and slavery 14–15
Blackstone, William 316
Bonaparte, Napoleon 213
Booth, Ken 288
Borch, Marete 125
Bosanquet, Bernard 243, 261, 286
Bosnia 348, 376
Bourdieu, Pierre 373
Bourke, Vernon J. 49
Boyle, Joseph 255
Bradley, F. H. 7, 286, 316
Brandt, Willy 365
Brems, Eva 345
Britain
  and European Convention of Human Rights 254
  India and 207
  and slave trade, abolition of 187, 207
British Constitution 160, 181–2

British Idealists 3
  and citizenship 242–3
  and communitarianism 299
  and human rights 13, 246, 285–6
  and moral community 219
  and natural rights 217–18, 223–4, 226–43, 357–8
  and social policy 339
  and women's rights 338–9
Brown, Chris 6, 8, 291, 293
Brownlie, Ian 311 (quoted)
Brownmiller, Susan 349
Buchanan, Allen 258, 306, 307–8
Buckle, Stephen 93
Buddhism, reform 296–7
Buffon, George-Louis Leclerc, Comte de 197
Bulkley, John 123
Bull, Hedley 7, 8, 289
Burke, Edmund 15, 156, 167 (quoted)
  and Christianity 183
  and colonies 206–8
  and French Revolution 159
  and God 183
  and natural rights 167–9, 180–6, 221
  and Paine, Thomas 163
  and race 203
  and slavery 15, 207–8
  and Wollstonecraft, Mary 160
Burlamaqui, Jean Jacques 78, 91
Burma 343
Burton, Stephen J. 321
Bush, George W. 63 n1, 251
Butler, Josephine E. 341
Bynkershoek, Cornelius van 86–7, 107

Cabbot, John 117
Caird, Edward 239, 338–9
'Cairo Declaration on Human Rights in Islam' 250
Callicles 21
Cambodia 363
Cameron, David 184
Campbell, Tom 1 (quoted), 146, 147
Canada: and Iroquois independence 136
cannibals 106, 110, 111, 112
canon law 48, 54
capabilities 351
Carlyle, R. W. and A. J. 39, 40, 41
Carlyle, Thomas 239
Carneades 26, 30–1
Carr, E. H. 7
Cassirer, Ernest 175
caste system 369
Cayuga Indians 136
Charles II, King 362
Charles V, Emperor 191, 192
Charlesworth, Hilary 344

children 30
Chile 363, 364
China 253, 366
Chinkin, Christine 344
choice, freedom of 280
Chomsky, Noam 255, 367–8
Christendom 63–4
Christians
 and humanitarian intervention 114
 and just war 58–61
 and natural law 42, 44–57, 107
 and New World 70, 101–2
 and property 57
 and rights 44, 140
 and slavery 15, 45–6, 191, 194, 195
 and Stoicism 45
Chrysippus 28, 30
church law *see* canon law
Cicero 20, 32–6
 and duty 90
 on fellowship 34–5
 and law of nature 33
 on natural law 36
 and philanthropy 42
 and reason 33
 on tyrants 35
 on war 35–6
cities, cosmic 32
citizenship
 British Idealists and 242–3
 displaced people 264, 265, 266, 290
 former slaves 338
 French colonies 213
 Greece 22, 23
 and human rights 293
 rights of 261, 282–3
 Roman 32
 and slaves 240
civil law 52, 54, 55
civil liberty 157
civil rights 164–5, 301
civil wars: St Augustine on 59
civility 273, 274, 287
civilization
 Collingwood and 280–2
 Greece 24
 and rights 11, 103
 and slavery 202, 210–11
Clapham, Andrew 357 (quoted)
class: Tocqueville on 222–3
Collingwood, R. G. 6, 7–8, 257
 and fundamental rights 299
 and international law 314
 and moral community 267, 268–9, 271, 273, 274, 279–82, 283
communitarianism 298
Comte, Isadore Auguste 15

Condorcet, Marquis de 202, 337
Connelly, William 6
Connor, Michael 125
conquistadors, Spanish 103–4, 106, 107, 108–9, 110, 111–12, 115, 118, 121, 268
'Constructivists' 6, 293
conventions: human rights 343
 'Convention against Torture and Other Cruel, Inhuman or Degrading Treatment or Punishment' 253
 Convention on the Prevention and Punishment of Genocide (1948) 323, 370
Cook, James 119, 120
Cortés, Hernán 103–4, 179
cosmopolitanism 304
Covenant on Civil and Political Rights 251–2
coveture 340
Cranston, Maurice 247
crimes 54, 146 266, 323, 329, 348–50, 363, 370
 against humanity 252, 260, 262, 266, 328–9 *see also* genocide
 against peace 259, 260
cruelty: and liberalism 271–2, 279
crusades 61, 63, 64, 65, 66–7
cultural identity 278
cultural relativism 369
culture 344–5, 350–1
customary law 314–24
 and human rights 16 *see also* thesmos
 and Indian question 105
 and Law of Nations 86
 St Thomas Aquinas and 55
Cynics 26
Cyprus 375

D'Aelders, Etta Palm 337
Darfur 251, 332, 359
de Gouges, Olympe *see* Gouges, Olympe de
decision-making, principled judicial 298
Declaration of the Rights of Man 229, 247, 337
Declaration of the Rights of Women (Gouges) 337
Decretists 97
Dembour, Marie-Bénédicte 318
Democritus 21, 22
denationalization 264, 265
D'Entrèves, P. 39
Descartes, Rene 159
Difference Principle (Rawls) 309–10
dike: Homer and 20
Dilthey, Wilhelm 7, 354
Diogenes Laertius 30
diplomacy: and human rights violations 253
displaced persons 249–50, 263–5, 290 *see also* asylum

divorce 341
'Doctrine of Recognition' (United States) 134
dominium 188
Donisthorpe, Wordsworth 229, 232
Donnelly, Jack 254, 288, 301
duty 14
Dworkin, Ronald 245, 256, 313

East India Company 207
East Timor 251, 369
Edelstein, Ludwig 30
Edict of Thessalonica (380) 58
Eichmann, Adolf 266–7
'Elimination of All Forms of Discrimination Against Women' 344
Elizabeth II, Queen 101
emotions 274
empiricism 224–5
encomienda system: American Indians 191–2
Enlightenment, The
  and property 122
  and slavery 15–16
Epicureans 26–7
equality
  and health care 278
  Jews and 262
  Tocqueville on 223
  and women 16
Erasmus, Desiderius 56
Europe
  and asylum 252
  and humanity 267–8
  and New World 9–14, 101–29
European Convention on Human Rights 250
European Court of Human Rights 345
European state 69–70
European Union: minority rights 374–5, 376
Europeanization 2–3
Evans, Tony 366
exceptionalism: United States 367, 376–7
exclusion: Aboriginal peoples 102

faith communities: medieval period 63–7
Falk, Richard 363
families: Africa 255
fate: Chrysippus and 28
Fawcett, J. E. S. 242
Feinberg, Joel 259
feminism: Pope Benedict XVI on 101 *see also* women: and rights
Filmer, Sir John 200
Finnis, John 51, 255, 257–8
Fish, Stanley 318, 321
Fiss, Owen M. 318
Flew, Anthony 151
Florentinus 41
Fontenell, Bernard le Bovier de 159

Fordyce, James 161
foreigners: humanity of 268–9, 273
formalism 225
foundationalism 282
Fox, Charles James 208
France
  Constitution 155–6
  Rights of Man 154–8
  slave trade 212–13
  see also French Revolution; Huguenots
Frangulis, Antoine 247
Franklin, Benjamin 202
freedom 230, 243, 315 *see also* liberty
Freedon, Michael 245 (quoted), 300
Freeman, Michael 288
French Revolution 159, 203, 337
Frost, Mervyn 6, 246, 254, 260–1, 291–3
fundamental rights: Arendt and 261–7
Fundamental Rights Agency 374–5

Gaius 39–40, 56, 188
Galen 29
Gaus, Gerald E. 299
Gauthier, David 141 (quoted), 148, 165, 166, 171 n1
gender violence 331, 332
genocide 266, 323, 329, 348–50, 363, 370
Genovese, Elizabeth Fox 354
Gentili, Alberico 9
  and humanitarian intervention 106, 107, 109
  and just war 108–9, 110, 112, 114
  and Law of Nations 80, 81–2, 87–8, 92
  and natural law 74, 80
  and rape 346–7
  and slavery 190–1, 195
  and *terra nullius* 116
  and travel, right to 111
George, Henry 226
George, Jim 6
Geras, Norman 271, 276
Germany
  citizenship rights 261
  war reparations 365
  see also Nazis; Nuremburg Tribunal
Gerson, Jean 97
Gewirth, Alan 258–9
Glasgow University 338–9
Glaucon 21
globalization 101, 139
God
  and animals 196–7
  belief in 73, 77, 142, 158
  Burke and 183
  and law 45, 52–3, 72, 93, 94
  and obligation 74–7, 255
  and reason 257–8

Index 413

and rights 157
  Stoics and 29
  and war 59
  see also religion
Goldstone, Justice Richard 260, 327, 331
  (quoted), 349, 364
Gorgias 21
Gouges, Olympe de 336, 337–8
government
  Hume on 169
  Paine on 164, 165
  St Ambrose on 47
  St Augustine on 47
governments: and human rights 301, 367–9
Gramsci, Antonio 372–3
Gratian: *Decretum* 45, 48, 60, 74
Greeks
  and morality 21–2
  and natural law 19–20, 22–6
Green, T. H. 217 (quoted)
  and morality 286
  and rights; modern recognition theory of 299; natural 227–8, 230, 239–40, 241, 243–4; women's 338, 339–42
Gregory of Rimini 72
Griffin, James 73, 259
Grimkè, Angelina 338
Grotius, Hugo 69 (quoted)
  and just war theory 111, 112
  and marriage 335
  and natural law 71, 73, 74, 75, 82–3, 88, 92–4, 152, 181
  and natural rights 98–9
  and New World 9–10
  and punishment for injury 109
  and rape 347
  and slavery 199–200
  and *terra nullius* 117–18, 119
Guantanamo Bay 376–7
Gulf Wars 368
Gutmann, Amy 302

Haakonssen, Knud 12, 95, 96
Hague Conventions 322; Martens clause 323–4
Hague tribunal 326
Haiti *see* Saint Dominique
Haldane, Richard Burden 242, 341–2
Hamilton, Alexander 155
Hampsher-Monk, Ian 183
Haroun, Ahmed 359
Harries, Richard 256
Hart, H. L. A. 142, 294–5, 313
Hastings, Warren 181–2
Headley, John M. 2, 142
Hegel, Georg Wilhelm Friedrich 180, 218, 224–5, 241, 291–2, 313

hegemony 359, 372–3
Heidegger, Martin 262
Hellenism 25, 26
Henry VI, Emperor 66
Herbert, Auberon 226, 230
heretics 63
Hippias 21, 22
Hobbes, Thomas
  and equality 334
  and Gauthier, David 148
  and God 3
  and human rights 174, 313
  and Law of Nations 83
  and morality 2
  and natural law 143, 166
  and natural rights 12–13, 97
  and slavery 15, 198–9, 202
  and *terra nullius* 118
Hobhouse, Leonard 219, 242
Hobson, John 219, 242
Holbrook, Jon 323, 372
Holland, Thomas Erskine 313
Hollis, Martin 180, 313
holocaust 267
Homer 19, 20, 345–6
homosexuality 345
Honig, Bonnie 266
Hooker, Robert 72
Hoon, Geoffrey 325
Hostiensis 67
Hrabanus Maurus 188
Huguccio 97–8
Huguenots 151
human dignity: and human rights 256, 257
human law 52, 54–5
human nature
  Burke and 185
  Grotius on 75–6
  Seneca and 37
  St Augustine and 43
  Wollstonecraft on 162
human rights 1, 2–3, 11–12, 16–17, 138–9
  and capabilities 351–2
  and consensus 296, 297–8
  and culture 344–5, 360
  culture of 245–83, 275, 280, 372–4
  dialects of 259–61
  and human dignity 256, 257
  modern constitutive theories of 285–310
  and natural rights 141–2, 245, 317
  and 'others' 268–2
  philosophical perspectives of 294–8
  and religion 351–2
  and social recognition 290
  universal 289–90
  violations of 16–17
  and women 331–55

Human Rights Act 250
Human Rights Council (United Nations) 252
Human Rights Watch 247–8, 252, 343, 349
human sacrifice 106, 110, 115
humanism 296
humanitarian intervention 106, 109–16, 251, 290, 291, 324–5
Hume, David
  and American Independence 172
  and contractarianism 148
  and natural rights 167–73
  and polygenesis 208–9, 211
  and race 197
  and slavery 14–15, 202, 210, 211–12
husbandry *see* agriculture
Hussain, Saddam 368, 372
Hutcheson, Francis 15, 16
Hutson, James 155
Huxley, T. H. 229, 231

Iceland *see* sagas, Icelandic
Idealism 13, 229, 232–9
Idealists *see* British Idealists
ideals 281–2
identities: and international relations 293–4
Ignatieff, Michael 246, 249, 285, 302, 312, 321, 357 (quoted), 367, 369–70
Incas *see* Athualpa
India: Burke and 207
Indians, American *see* American Indians
individuality 146, 292, 293
Innocent III, Pope 64
Innocent IV, Pope 191
International Bill of Rights 248, 256
International Commission on Intervention and State Sovereignty 251
'International Convention for the Protection of All Persons from Enforced Disappearance' 250
'International Convention on the Rights of Persons with Disabilities' 249–50
International Court of Justice 317; Nicaragua judgement (1986) 320
International Covenant on Civil and Political Rights 249
International Covenant on Economic, Social and Cultural Rights 251–2
International Criminal Court 16, 253–4, 324, 327, 328–9, 355, 359
International Criminal Tribunal (former Yugoslavia) 322–3, 326, 371
International Labour Organization 139
international relations 4–7, 287–98, 293, 303
International Women's Year (1975) 343
intervention *see* humanitarian intervention
Iraq 251, 324, 372
Iroquois Indians 136

Isadore of Seville: *Etymologies* 48
Islam 63, 64, 65 *see also* 'Cairo Declaration on Human Rights in Islam'; Muslims
Isocrates 26

Jahn, Beate 6
Japan: war reparations 364–5
Jefferson, Thomas
  and polygenesis 208–9
  and slavery 15–16, 197–8, 202, 209, 210
Jews
  and equality 262
  and holocaust 267–8
  and humanity 270–1
  medieval period 44, 62, 63
  persecution of 65–6
  see also anti-Semitism
jihads: Islam 65
Jines, Henry 228
John Paul II, Pope 255
Johnson v. M'Intosh ruling(1823) 117, 119–20, 123, 126, 129
Johnson, James Turner 80
Jones, Peter 12, 141–2, 258, 286, 305–6
juridical revolutions 312
jurisgeneration 353
Jurists, Roman 39–41, 56, 78, 93, 142–3, 178
jus sacrum 38
just war theory 38–9, 57–62, 106, 107–9, 111
justice
  Aristotle and 23
  Cicero and 33, 36
  Epicureans and 27
  global 253
  and human rights abuses 361–6
  Hume on 172
  and natural law 36
  Romans and 39
  Spencer, Herbert and 144–5
  St Augustine on 47–8
  St Thomas Aquinas and 51–2, 55
  universal distributive 277–8
Justinian, Emperor 39; *Institutes* 39, 40, 41

Kant, Immanuel 197, 225, 376
Kapur, Rata 355
Karadzic, Radovan 17, 376
Keene, Edward 6, 7
Kelson, Hans 313
Kersaint, Armand Guy 213
Khmer Rouge 363
King, Martin Luther 254, 257, 366
kings 25–6, 74, 151, 362 *see also* rulers; sovereigns
Knowles, James 226
Knutsen, Torbjorn L. 8
Kolakowski, Leszek 255

Kony, Joseph 359
Kosovo 251, 264, 265, 349, 368
Krasner, Stephen D. 1, 8, 135, 288–9
Kratochwil, Friedrich 293
Kushayb, Ali 359
Kymlicka, Will 2–3, 138–40, 287, 374, 375

labour, manual 30
Lactanius 45, 58
land *see* property; *terra nullius*
language: Rorty on 271–2
Lapid, Yosef 293
Las Casas, Bartolomé de 9, 108, 114–15, 189, 192, 193–4, 195–6, 268
Lathrop, John 123
Laughland, John 370–1
Lauterpacht, Hersh 11, 141, 258, 312, 317
law 360
    canon 48, 54
    common 315–31
    customary 315–24
    Divine 54, 73
    Eternal 46, 52–3
    human 52, 54–5
    international 313–15, 317–28
    Mosaic 45
    natural *see* natural law
    Roman 39, 40, 98
    volitional 94
    see also Criminal Court; Human Rights Act; International Court of Justice; Married Women's Property Acts; Nuremburg Laws
Law Lords: ruling on Augusto Pinochet 252–3
Law of Equal Freedom 230
Law of Nations (*ius gentium*) 9, 10–11, 55–6, 194–5, 313
    and Aboriginal peoples 103
    Cicero on 33
    Connor on 125
    Gaius on 39–40
    and natural law 44, 78–98, 100
    necessary and voluntary 84, 89–91
    Rachel on 125
    Schall on 257
    and settler contract 126
    Suarez on 125
    and travel 107, 111
    Vattel and 84, 180–1
    Wolff and 72, 84
law of nature 19, 22
    Chrysippius and 28
    Huxley on 231
    local 321
    Romans and 32, 33, 39

'Law of Peoples, The': Rawls and 303, 304, 305, 306
League of Nations: and Six Nations Iroquois Confederacy 136
League of Nations 'Slavery Convention' (1927) 213
Leon-Portilla, Miguel 103
Lewis, John Delamore 341
liberalism: and cruelty 271–2, 279
Liberation Theology 101–2
liberty
    Burke and 184–5
    civil 157
    negative 355
    Party of Individual Liberty 230
    Rousseau and 179
    see also freedom
life, right to 358
Linklater, Andrew 6
Lipmann, Walter 257
Locke, John 5
    and American Indians 10, 128
    and natural rights 52–4, 113, 178
    and private property 9, 13, 119, 127–9
    and slavery 15, 200–2
    and *terra nullius* 118, 121
Long, Edward 198
Lugard, Lord 124
Lumsdaine, David 308
Luther, Martin 66
Lutz, Ellen L. 293, 296
Lycurgus 22

Maastricht Treaty 375
Mabo judgement (Australia) 137
McGrade, A. S. 73
Machiavelli, Niccolò 2
MacIntyre, Alistair 373–4
MacKinnon, Catherine 271, 348
MacKinnon, D. M. 150–1
Magna Carta 315
Major, John (Scottish philosopher) 191
Mandelstam. Andre Nicolayevich 247
Maori people 123
Marcanianus 41
Marcus Aurelius Antoninus, Emperor 32, 37–8
Maritain, Jacques 249
Markward of Anweiler 66
marriage: and equality 334
Married Women's Property Acts 340–1
Marshall, Chief Justice John 119–20, 129, 131, 135, 136–7
Martens, Georg Friedrich 86–7
Martin, Rex 259, 261, 285, 298, 300–2, 374
Marx, Karl 167, 218
Matua, Makau 374

Meron, Theodor 11–12, 311 (quoted)
Merrills, J. G. 248, 318, 320, 323
Mills, Charles 102
Milosevic, Slobodan 359, 370, 371
minorities *see* rights: minorities
Mitterand, François 267
Modood, Tariq 140, 344
Montecuhzoma (Montezuma) 104
Montesquieu, Charles-Louis de Secondat, Baron de 204–6
More, Sir Thomas: *Utopia* 116
moral community
  Collingwood on 267, 268–9, 271, 273, 274, 279–82, 283
  Rorty on 267, 268, 271–6, 277–9, 283, 291
moral duties: Hume on 171–2
Moral Equality Principle 351
moral obligation 73–8, 90–1, 270
moral realism 1–2
moral rights *see* rights: moral
morality 20, 353–4, 355
  British Idealists and 241–2
  and communities 295–6
  Gauthier and 148–9
  Greeks and 21–2
  and law 320
  see also Moral Equality Principle; Universal Moral Order
Moreau, Jacob N. 178
Moreno-Ocampo, Luis 359
Mornay, Philippe de 151
Mosaic law 45
Moser, Johann Jakob 86–7
Moses 22
Mugabe, Robert 362, 367
Muhammad 65
multiculturalism 16, 140, 344–5
Murphy, Jeffrie 256
Muslims 16, 44, 63, 64–5

nationality 265
NATO 251, 324, 368
natural law 2, 3, 70–87
  and American Indians 104–5
  Ayala on 92
  Christian 42, 43–68
  Classical 19–42; Romans 40–1; Cicero 33–6; Seneca 36–7, 42
  and Eternal Law 46
  and justice 36
  and Law of Nations 33–6, 78–98
  and Law of Peoples 304
  medieval period 44
  in New Testament 45
  and rights 11–12; natural 95–9, 102–40, 255–9, 357–8
  and *terra nullius* 116

  St Thomas Aquinas and 43–4, 49, 52–4
  universal 372
  Vitoria on 91–2
natural rights 2, 3, 11–13, 286
  critics of 167–86; Bentham, Jeremy 217, 218, 219–20; Burke, Edmund 180–6, 221; Hegel, Georg Wilhelm Friedrich 224–5; Hume, David 169–73; Marx, Karl 217, 218, 221; Rousseau, Jean Jacques 167–9, 173–80
  descriptive and prescriptive 141–65
  and human rights 141–2, 245, 317
  and Idealism 232–9
  and natural law 95–9, 102–40, 255–9, 357–8
  and slavery 198–9
  Stoics and 42
  Tocqueville and 222–3
nature, law of *see* law of nature
Nazis: and Jews 266, 268, 271
'Negro Code' (Burke) 207–8
Nepal 343
New World 9–14, 70
New Zealand 123, 134
Nicaragua 320
Njal's Saga 315
noble savage, idea of 175, 203 n1 *see also* American Indians
norms
  conduct 297–8
  human rights 296, 352
  international relations 293, 294–5
  manipulation 370–1
  sovereignty 297
Nozick, Robert 141, 146–8, 165, 166, 258
Nugent, Neill 375
Numa 22
Nuremburg Laws 265
Nuremburg Tribunal 257, 259–60, 325–8, 347, 362
Nussbaum, Arthur 73, 77, 143
Nussbaum, Martha 255, 350–2

Oakeshott, Michael 69 (quoted)
  and 'European', idea of 2
  and history 6, 7
  and law 21, 39
  and natural rights 217, 228–9, 315
  and women's rights 342
  obligations 89–90; moral 73–8
O'Brien, M. D. 226
Observateur Hollandais, L' (tract) 178
Ockham, William of 72, 96, 97
Ogé, Vincent 213
O'Neill, Onora 147
Onuf, Nicholas 6
Oppenheim, L. 313–14

order
    and human rights 289
    political 30–1
Organization of African Unity 251
original sin 47, 48, 174
Overton, Richard 144
Oviedo y Valdes, Gonzalo Fernández de 191
Oxford, University of 338, 339

pacifism: and Christianity 59, 62
Pagden, Anthony 103
Paine, Thomas
    Age of Reason 158
    and Burke, Edmund 163
    and French Revolution 159
    and God 156, 157–8
    and natural rights 142
    Rights of Man, The 163–4
    and slavery 209
Paley, William 196–7, 202
Panaetius of Rhodes 31–2
Paquete Habana case (United States) 319
Parkinson, Fred 4
particularism 218
Party of Individual Liberty 230
Pateman, Carole 102, 333–4 *see also* settler contract
Paul, St 45, 189
Paul III, Pope 102
Paz, Matías de 190
Peace of Utrecht (1713) 180
Peace of Westphalia (1648) 6, 9, 180
Penn, William 129
Perry, Michael J. 255, 256
Personal Rights and Self-Help Association 230
philanthropy: Stoics and 42
Phillips, Anne 344–5, 354
Phillipson, Coleman 79
Philp, Mark 157
Pinochet, Augusto 252–3, 363–4
pity: Rousseau on 174
Plato 21, 22, 332–3; *Republic* 23
plurality 262
Plutarch: on Alexander the Great 25–6
Pogge, Thomas 142, 260, 276–7, 309
Pol Pot 363
polygenesis 208–9
popes 96
    Benedict XVI 101–2
    Innocent III 64, 66
    Innocent IV 191
    John Paul II 255
    Paul III 102
    Urban II 63, 64
Popkin, Richard H. 210, 211

Postema, Gerald J. 316
poverty 276–9
Price, Richard 156–7
Priestley, Joseph 156, 157
Primrose League 229 n2
prisoners: United States 16
'Promotion of National Unity and Reconciliation Act 34' (1995) 364
property 9–10, 331
    and Aboriginal peoples 102
    and American Indians 106–9
    Bynkershoeck and 107
    Hume and 173
    and just war 57–62
    and natural law 70–1
    Nozick on 148
    Rousseau and 175–6, 178–9
    and slavery 14–17, 198–9
    see also Married Women's Property Acts; *terra nullius*
prostitution 341, 365 *see also* sex trafficking
Protagoras 21
protectionism: women 343
Prudhomme, Louis Marie 337
Puerto Rico: slave trade 196
Pufendorf, Samuel von
    and equality 334–5
    and international relations 9
    and '*ius*' 99
    and just war 112–13
    and Law of Nations 83
    and law of nature 94–5
    and natural law 71, 73, 75, 76–7, 95
    and natural rights 12, 98
    and slavery 187 (quoted), 200
    and sovereignty 180

Quakers: and slave trade 196
queens *see* Elizabeth II, Queen
Quirk, Robert 192

race: and rights 11
Rachel, Samuel 67, 69 (quoted), 71, 75, 77, 83–4, 88–9, 100, 125, 150
racism
    origins of 24
    and slavery 187–215
    see also anti-Semitism
Radical Dissenters 156, 157, 159
Ramsey, James 187
rape 331
    as genocide 348–50
    and war 332, 345–6, 355
Rational Dissenters 166
rationality, principle of 28, 273–4
Rawls, John 302–10, 374
Reagan, Ralph 349

reason
    Burke and 184
    Cicero and 33
    Descartes and 159
    Hume and 170–1
    Montesquieu and 205
    and natural law 75–6, 77–8
    and rights 3, 292
    St Thomas Aquinas and 50, 54
    Stoics and 29, 30
    Wollstonecraft and 160, 161
reasoning: *a priori* and *a posteriori* 304
reconciliation 362
refugees *see* asylum; displaced persons
'reiteration' 353
religion
    Aztecs and 103
    Burke on 182–3
    and ethnic diversity 140
    and law 22
    and rights 155–8, 256, 351–2
    see also Christianity; Islam; symbols, religious
Remec, Peter Pavel 94 n3
reparations, war 364–5
Ricardus 97
right
    idea of 96
    subjective 98–9
Right and Good (Ross) 355
rights 14, 67, 68, 96
    civil 164–5, 301
    declarations of *see* Declaration of the Rights of Man; *Declaration of the Rights of Women*
    externalism of 299
    fundamental 261–7 *see also* Fundamental Rights Agency
    internalism of 299
    to life 358
    minorities 135, 138, 139, 374–5, 376
    modern recognition theory of 298–302
    moral 231–2, 260, 261, 300
    property 9–10, 24
    right to 266
    slaves and 24
    special 331, 333, 358, 360, 370
    St Thomas Aquinas and 51
    universal 137–8
    women and 331–55, 358
    see also equality; human rights; natural rights
Rights of Man 154–8, 221, 264
Riley-Smith, J. 66
Ritchie, David
    and rights theories 300, 399; equal 339; natural 226, 228, 229–31, 240, 241, 243
    and slavery 15

Robertson, A. H. 248, 318, 320, 323
Robertson, Geoffrey 251, 253, 366
Robertson, George 325
Robinson, Fiona 354–5
Roman law 39, 40, 98
Romania 327
Romans
    and Stoicism 32
    and just war 38–9
    see also Jurists, Roman
Rome, Treaty of *see* Treaty of Rome
Roosevelt, Eleanor 286
Rorty, Richard
    and fundamental rights 299
    and human rights culture 246
    and liberalism 302
    and moral community 267, 268, 271–6, 277–9, 283, 291
Ross, W. David 355
Rousseau, Jean Jacques
    and equality 335–6
    and Hobbes, Thomas 174
    and natural rights 167–9, 173–80
    on pity 174
    and slavery 15, 202–3
    and war 203
    and women 161
Row v. Wade (United States) 354
Rudd, Kevin 140
Rufinus 45, 48–9, 97
rulers 104, 135 *see also* kings; sovereigns
Russell, F. H. 59
Rwanda 323, 349, 370
Rwanda Statute 326

sagas, Icelandic 314–15
sages, Stoic 29
Saint Dominique (later Haiti): slavery 212–13
Salamanca School 188, 314–24
Sankey, John, Viscount 247
Saracens 44, 64
Scarf Affair, the (France) 353
Schall, James 245 (quoted), 257, 285 (quoted)
Schofield, Malcolm 32
Schwarzenbach, Sibyl A. 306
Scipio Africanus minor 31–2
sea, freedom of the 71
self-determination 295
self-preservation: Rousseau on 173–4
Sen, Amartya 261, 276–7, 333
Sen, Huen 363
Seneca 33, 36–7, 42
sentimentality: and human rights 275, 276
Sepúlveda, Juan Ginés de 9, 108, 109–10, 189, 191–2, 193

Serbia 348, 349, 376
settler contract 120–9
Sévigné, Madame de 222–3
sex crimes *see* rape
sex trafficking 343
Shue, Henry 308–9
Siddiqi, Dina M. 348
Sikkink, Kathryn 285 (quoted), 293, 296
Sinfield, Alan 345
Singer, Peter 277
Six Nations Iroquois Confederacy 136
Skinner, Quentin 6
Slaughter, Anne-Marie 312
slave trade 187, 195–213
slavery
    Aristotle and 24–5
    Australian Aboriginals and 198
    black 198, 206
    Carlyle and 239
    Enlightenment attitudes to 15–16
    Green and 239–40
    modern 214
    and property 14–17
    and racism 187–215
    Ritchie and 240
    Roman Jurists and 41
    Rousseau and 179–80
    Seneca and 37
    St Thomas Aquinas and 50
    Stoics and 30
    women and 338
'Slavery Convention' (League of Nations) 213
slaves
    revolts 209, 213
    treatment 207–8
Smith, Adam 135
social contracts 134, 169, 336, 352
society: Church Fathers' understanding of 49, 50
Solzhenitsyn, Alexander 257
Somalia 324
Sophocles 19 (quoted); *Oedipus the King* 22–3
Soto, Domingo de 72
South Africa 364
sovereigns: moral obligations of 90–1 *see also* Elizabeth II, Queen; kings; rulers
sovereignty
    and Aboriginals 129
    challenges to 8–9, 366
    and global justice 253
    and peoples 303
    and *terra nullius* doctrine 132–5
Spanish Empire 180, 188, 189 *see also* conquistadors, Spanish
speech, freedom of 250
Spencer, Herbert 144–5, 226, 229, 230
Stanlis, Peter J. 181

states: European 69
Stein, Peter 78
Stewart, Maria 338
Stoics 22, 26–39, 42, 45, 47
Story, Joseph 133
Strauss, Leo 4, 95, 203
Stromseth, Jan 319
Suarez, Francisco 9, 72–3, 80–1, 92, 98, 99, 109, 110–11, 116, 125
Sudan 359
Sutch, Peter 305
symbols, religious 353
Sypher, Wylie 201

Talbot, William J. 331 (quoted), 353–4
taxation: Nozick and 146
Taylor, Charles 73, 295, 296, 297–8, 302
terra nullius, doctrine of 10, 105, 116–20, 129–32
    and settler contract 125–9, 132
    and sovereignty 132–5
terrorists 254, 365, 376–7
Textor, Johann Wolfgang 71–2, 73, 77–8, 84, 105
themis: Homer and 20
thesmos: Homer and 20–1
Thrasymachus 21
Tiananmen Square massacre (Beijing) 253, 366
Tierney, Brian 12, 67, 95, 96, 115, 143
Tilley, Michael 55
Tocqueville, Alexis de 222–3
Tomuschat, Christian 320
torture 250, 253, 319, 327
totalitarianism 263, 266
travel, right to 107, 111
Treaty of Rome (1998) 371
Treaty of the European Union (Article 49) 375
treaty of Waitangi 134
tribunals 325–8, 358, 361, 362, 364, 370, 371
Truth, Sojourner 338
truth and reconciliation commissions 363–5
Tuck, Richard 95, 97, 119
Tully, James 102
Turkey 375, 376
tyrants: Cicero on 35

Ulpian 39, 40–1, 56
unbelievers: St. Thomas Aquinas and 61
United Nations 140, 297, 343, 366–7
United Nations Charter on Human Rights 247–8, 251
United Nations Commission on Human Rights *see* United Nations Human Rights Council
United Nations' Decade for Women 343

United Nations Declaration on Human Rights 254, 286
United Nations Human Rights Council 252
United Nations Security Council 327
United Nations Torture Convention 253
United States
  'Doctrine of Recognition' 134
  and exceptionalism 367, 376–7
  and hegemony 359, 372–3
  and human rights 247–8, 253–4, 366, 373
  and International Criminal Court 327
  Johnson v. M'Intosh ruling(1823) 117, 119–20, 123, 126, 129
  and norms 293
  and Paquete Habana case 319
  and prisoners 16
  and Rights of Man 155
  and torture 319, 327
  and treaties 323
  see also American Indians
United States Court of Appeal 135–6, 319
United States v. Consolidated Wounded Knee Cases 137
Universal Declaration of Human Rights 248, 259, 311, 342, 366–7
Universal Moral Order 8–9
universalism 218, 251, 296
Urban II, Pope 63, 64
Uruguay 363
utilitarianism 148
Utrecht, Peace of *see* Peace of Utrecht

values: European 2
Vásquez, Gabriel 72
Vattel, Emerich
  Burke and 183
  and humanitarian intervention 114, 115–16
  and Law of Nations 84–5, 89–91, 180–1, 313
  and rape 347
  and settler contract 122–3, 126
  and slavery 195
  and *terra nullius* 10, 118–19
victims: treatment of 271
Vienna Convention on the Law of Treaties 323
Vienna World Conference on Human Rights (1993) 343, 354, 367, 369
Villasante, Antonio de 192–3
Villey, Michel 95, 96, 311–12
Vincent, John 154, 289–90, 343
virtue
  St Thomas Aquinas and 50–1
  Stoics and 29–30
Vitoria, Francisco de
  and American Indians 9, 104, 105, 190–1

  and humanitarian intervention 106, 109
  and *ius* 98
  and Law of Nations 79–80
  and natural law 91–2, 107
  and slavery 189
  and *terra nullius* 116
  and war 346
volitional law 94
Voltaire: and slavery 202
vote, right to 338, 339

Wacquant, Loïc 373
Waitangi, treaty of *see* treaty of Waitangi
Waldron, Jeremy 1 (quoted), 154, 246, 282, 289, 294, 295, 311
Walker, R. J. B. 6, 8
Wallace, Alfred Russel 231
Waltz, Kenneth N. 4
Walzer, Michael 21, 295–6
war
  Cicero on 35–6
  civil 59
  foreign 59
  Greece 24
  Hobbes and 176
  just 38–9, 57–62, 106, 107–9, 111
  Rousseau and 176–7
  and Voluntary Law of Nations 90–1
  women and 345–50
  see also crusades; jihad
war crimes 249, 257, 259–60, 321, 347 *see also* Nuremburg Tribunal
Watson, Gerard 32, 45
Watson, John 241
Weeks, Jeffrey 285 (quoted)
Weinstein, D. 145
Wells, H. G. 247
Welsh, Jennifer 181
Wendt, Alexander 6
Westphalia, Peace of *see* Peace of Westphalia
White, Charles 198
Wight, Martin 4, 5, 7
William of Conches 48
Williams, Bernard 255
Wilson, Anna 161
Winthrop, John 116
wisdom
  Stoics and 30
  divine: Homer and 20
Wittgenstein, Ludwig 360
Wolff, Christian
  and humanitarian intervention 114, 115
  and Law of Nations 84, 85–6, 87, 89
  and natural law 72, 99, 113
  and property rights 126, 128–9, 134–5
Wollstonecraft, Mary 157, 159–63, 336, 341

Index

women
    Australian Aboriginal 138
    American Indian 197
    Descartes and 159
    and education 161, 338–9, 341
    and equality 16
    and protectionism 343
    and race 11
    and rights 358, 331–55
    and slavery 208, 213–14, 338
    status of 196
    Stoics and 30
    and war 345–50
    see also feminism; International Women's Year

'Women for Women' (monitoring organization) 349

xenophobia: medieval period 64 *see also* anti-Semitism

Yugoslavia, former 17, 322–3, 324, 326, 348–9, 359, 368, 370, 371, 376

Zardad, Faryadi 253
Zeno 27–8, 29, 30
Zoroastrianism 65
Zouche, Richard 88
Zuckert, Michael P. 41
Zwanenburg, Martin 327